11138301

KT-550-134

DISCARD

B.C.H.E. – LIBRARY

00021656

ISLAMIC SPIRITUALITY
Foundations

World Spirituality

An Encyclopedic History of the Religious Quest

1. Asian Archaic Spirituality
2. European Archaic Spirituality
3. African and Oceanic Spirituality
4. South and Meso-American Native Spirituality
5. North American Indian Spirituality
6. Early Hindu and Jain Spirituality
7. Post-Classical Hindu and Sikh Spirituality
8. Buddhist Spirituality: Indian, Siri Lankan, Southeast Asian
9. Buddhist Spirituality: Chinese, Tibetan, Japanese, Korean
10. Taoist Spirituality
11. Confucian Spirituality
12. Ancient Near Eastern Spirituality: Zoroastrian, Sumerian, Assyro-Babylonian, Hittite
13. Jewish Spirituality: From the Bible to the Middle Ages
14. Jewish Spirituality: From the Sixteenth-Century Revival to the Present
15. Classical Mediterranean Spirituality: Egyptian, Greek, Roman
16. Christian Spirituality: Origins to the Twelfth Century
17. Christian Spirituality: High Middle Ages and Reformation
18. Christian Spirituality: Post-Reformation and Modern
19. Islamic Spirituality: Foundations
20. Islamic Spirituality: Manifestations
21. Modern Esoteric Movements
22. Spirituality and the Secular Quest
23. Encounter of Spiritualities: Past to Present
24. Encounter of Spiritualities: Present to Future
25. Dictionary of World Spirituality

Board of Editors and Advisors

EWERT COUSINS, *General Editor*

A. H. ARMSTRONG
Dalhousie University

R. BALASUBRAMANIAN
University of Madras

BETTINA BÄUMER
Alice Boner Foundation, Varanasi

THOMAS BERRY
Fordham University

JOSEPH EPES BROWN
University of Montana

JOHN CARMAN
Harvard University

JOSEPH DAN
Hebrew University

LOUIS DUPRÉ
Yale University

MIRCEA ELIADE
University of Chicago

ANTOINE FAIVRE
Sorbonne

LANGDON GILKEY
University of Chicago

GARY GOSSEN
State University of New York, Albany

ARTHUR GREEN
University of Pennsylvania

JAMES HEISIG
Nanzan Institute for Religion and Culture, Nagoya

THORKILD JACOBSEN
Harvard University

STEVEN T. KATZ
Cornell University

JEAN LECLERCQ
Gregorian University

MIGUEL LEÓN-PORTILLA
National University of Mexico

CHARLES LONG
University of North Carolina

BERNARD MCGINN
University of Chicago

FARHANG MEHR
Boston University

JOHN MEYENDORFF
Fordham University

BITHIKA MUKERJI
Banaras Hindu University

SEYYED HOSSEIN NASR
George Washington University

JACOB NEEDLEMAN
San Francisco State University

HEIKO OBERMAN
University of Tübingen

ALBERT OUTLER
Southern Methodist University

RAIMUNDO PANIKKAR
University of California, Santa Barbara

JAROSLAV PELIKAN
Yale University

JILL RAITT
University of Missouri

DON SALIERS
Emory University

ANNEMARIE SCHIMMEL
Harvard University

KARAN SINGH
New Delhi

VIBHUTI NARAIN SINGH
Varanasi

KRISHNA SIVARAMAN
McMaster University

HUSTON SMITH
Syracuse University

DOUGLAS STEERE
Haverford College

YOSHINORI TAKEUCHI
University of Kyoto

WEI-MING TU
Harvard University

JAN VAN BRAGT
Nanzan Institute for Religion and Culture, Nagoya

FRANK WHALING
University of Edinburgh

Volume 19 of
World Spirituality:
An Encyclopedic History
of the Religious Quest

ISLAMIC SPIRITUALITY

Foundations

Edited by
Seyyed Hossein Nasr

ROUTLEDGE & KEGAN PAUL
LONDON

BATH COLLEGE
OF
HIGHER EDUCATION
NEWTON PARK
LIBRARY
DISCARD
CLASS No. 297.4 NAS.
ACC No. 11138301

First published in Great Britain in 1987 by
Routledge & Kegan Paul Ltd.
11 New Fetter Lane, London EC4P 4EE

World Spirituality, Volume 19
Diane Apostolos-Cappadona, Art Editor

Printed in the United States of America

Copyright © 1987 by The Crossroad Publishing Company

No part of this book may be reproduced in
any form without permission from the publisher,
except for the quotation of brief passages
in criticism.

British Library Cataloguing in Publication Data

Islamic spirituality: foundations.–
(World spirituality; v. 19)
1. Islam 2. Spirituality
I. Nasr, Seyyed Hossein II. Series
297'.4 BP163

ISBN 0-7102-1097-3

بسم الله الرحمن الرحيم

In the Name of God, Most Merciful, Most Compassionate

قُلِ الرُّوحُ مِنْ أَمْرِ رَبِّي

Say, the Spirit is from the Command of my Lord

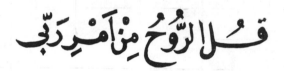

Contents

Preface to the Series

THE PRESENT VOLUME is part of a series entitled World Spirituality: An Encyclopedic History of the Religious Quest, which seeks to present the spiritual wisdom of the human race in its historical unfolding. Although each of the volumes can be read on its own terms, taken together they provide a comprehensive picture of the spiritual strivings of the human community as a whole—from prehistoric times, through the great religions, to the meeting of traditions at the present.

Drawing upon the highest level of scholarship around the world, the series gathers together and presents in a single collection the richness of the spiritual heritage of the human race. It is designed to reflect the autonomy of each tradition in its historical development, but at the same time to present the entire story of the human spiritual quest. The first five volumes deal with the spiritualities of archaic peoples in Asia, Europe, Africa, Oceania, and North and South America. Most of these have ceased to exist as living traditions, although some perdure among tribal peoples throughout the world. However, the archaic level of spirituality survives within the later traditions as a foundational stratum, preserved in ritual and myth. Individual volumes or combinations of volumes are devoted to the major traditions: Hindu, Buddhist, Taoist, Confucian, Jewish, Christian, and Islamic. Included within the series are the Jain, Sikh, and Zoroastrian traditions. In order to complete the story, the series includes traditions that have not survived but have exercised important influence on living traditions—such as Egyptian, Sumerian, classical Greek and Roman. A volume is devoted to modern esoteric movements and another to modern secular movements.

Having presented the history of the various traditions, the series devotes two volumes to the meeting of spiritualities. The first surveys the meeting of spiritualities from the past to the present, exploring common themes that

A longer version of this preface may be found in Christian Spirituality: Origins to the Twelfth Century, *the first published volume in the series.*

can provide the basis for a positive encounter, for example, symbols, rituals, techniques. Finally, the series closes with a dictionary of world spirituality.

Each volume is edited by a specialist or a team of specialists who have gathered a number of contributors to write articles in their fields of specialization. As in this volume, the articles are not brief entries but substantial studies of an area of spirituality within a given tradition. An effort has been made to choose editors and contributors who have a cultural and religious grounding within the tradition studied and at the same time possess the scholarly objectivity to present the material to a larger forum of readers. For several years some five hundred scholars around the world have been working on the project.

In the planning of the project, no attempt was made to arrive at a common definition of spirituality that would be accepted by all in precisely the same way. The term "spirituality," or an equivalent, is not found in a number of the traditions. Yet from the outset, there was a consensus among the editors about what was in general intended by the term. It was left to each tradition to clarify its own understanding of this meaning and to the editors to express this in the introduction to their volumes. As a working hypothesis, the following description was used to launch the project:

> The series focuses on that inner dimension of the person called by certain traditions "the spirit." This spiritual core is the deepest center of the person. It is here that the person is open to the transcendent dimension; it is here that the person experiences ultimate reality. The series explores the discovery of this core, the dynamics of its development, and its journey to the ultimate goal. It deals with prayer, spiritual direction, the various maps of the spiritual journey, and the methods of advancement in the spiritual ascent.

By presenting the ancient spiritual wisdom in an academic perspective, the series can fulfill a number of needs. It can provide readers with a spiritual inventory of the richness of their own traditions, informing them at the same time of the richness of other traditions. It can give structure and order, meaning and direction to the vast amount of information with which we are often overwhelmed in the computer age. By drawing the material into the focus of world spirituality, it can provide a perspective for understanding one's place in the larger process. For it may well be that the meeting of spiritual paths—the assimilation not only of one's own spiritual heritage but of that of the human community as a whole—is the distinctive spiritual journey of our time.

EWERT COUSINS

Introduction

THE SPIRIT MANIFESTS ITSELF in every religious universe where the echoes of the Divine Word are still audible, but the manner in which the manifestations of the Spirit take place differs from one religion to another. In Islam, the Spirit breathes through all that reveals the One and leads to the One, for Islam's ultimate purpose is to reveal the Unity of the Divine Principle and to integrate the world of multiplicity in the light of that Unity. Spirituality in Islam is inseparable from the awareness of the One, of Allah, and a life lived according to His Will. The principle of Unity (*al-tawḥīd*) lies at the heart of the Islamic message and determines Islamic spirituality in all its multifarious dimensions and forms. Spirituality *is tawḥīd* and the degree of spiritual attainment achieved by any human being is none other than the degree of his or her realization of *tawḥīd*. For the Word manifested Itself in what came to be the Islamic universe in order to declare the glory of the One and to lead human beings to the realization of the One.

The central theophany of Islam, the Quran, is the source *par excellence* of all Islamic spirituality. It is the Word manifested in human language. Through it, knowledge of the One and the paths leading to Him were made accessible in that part of the cosmos which was destined to become the abode of Islam. Likewise, the soul and inner Substance of the Prophet are the complementary source of Islamic spirituality—hidden outwardly but living as presence and as transforming grace within the hearts of those who tread the path of realization. Moreover, it can be said that both the created order and man himself are also marked by the imprint of Divine Unity and must be taken into consideration in any study of Islamic spirituality. According to the Quran, God has manifested His signs upon the "horizons" or the macrocosmic world and also within the soul of man, for He has "breathed into man" His own Spirit (*nafakhtu fīhi min rūḥī* (XXXVIII, 72).[1] To be fully human is to stand on the vertical axis of existence and to seek *tawḥīd,* to see the reflection of the One in all that makes up the manifold order from the angelic to the mineral.

Related to Islamic spirituality are all the doctrines that speak of the One, all the artistic forms that reflect the principle of Unity, and all human actions that issue from the inner man as a theomorphic being. To live by the Will of God Who is One and to obey His Laws is the alpha of the spiritual life. Its omega is to surrender one's will completely to Him and to sacrifice one's existence before the One Who alone can be said ultimately to be. Between the two stand various levels of correct and ever more interiorized action, and above the plane of action stand the love of God and finally knowledge of Him, the knowledge that is summarized in the testimony (*Shahādah*) of Islam *Lā ilāha illa' Llāh* (There is no divinity but God, but Allah, the One). All that one needs to know and can know is already contained in this testimony. To accept it along with the second *Shahādah*, *Muḥammad*^{un} *rasūl Allāh* (Muḥammad is God's Messenger) is to become a Muslim. To realize its full meaning is to reach the highest degree of spirituality, to act perfectly according to His Will, to love only the Beloved, and to know all that can be known. It is to gain sanctity and attain the crown of spiritual poverty. It is to become a friend of God, *walī Allāh*, the term that Muslims use for saint.

In a profound sense, Islamic spirituality is nothing other than the realization of *tawḥīd*. Its study is nothing other than tracing the impact in depth of *tawḥīd* upon the life, actions, art, and thought of that segment of the human race which makes up the Islamic people or *ummah*. One might, however, ask how this definition differs from that of Islam as a whole. The answer lies in the dimension of depth or inwardness which distinguishes Islamic spirituality from the Islamic religion as a whole. Islam embraces all of human life, both the outward and the inward. Any comprehensive work on Islam would have to consider both aspects, the socio-political and economic dimension as well as the inner dimension. But a work devoted to Islamic spirituality must concern itself primarily with what leads to inwardness and the world of the Spirit. It must deal with the outward elements of the religion to the extent that they serve as vehicles for the life of the Spirit without in any way losing sight of the great significance of the outward dimension, which is indispensable for the inner life.

The Term "Spirituality" in Islamic Languages

Since the term "spirituality" as used in the English language has obviously strong Christian connotations, some may raise the question: What does spirituality mean in the context of the Islamic tradition itself? The answer to such a question could best be found by turning to the term "spirituality" in the major Islamic languages such as Arabic, Persian, and Turkish. In these and most other languages in which the ethos of Islam and its spirituality have found expression, the terms used for "spirituality" are *rūḥāniyyah* (Arabic), *ma'nawiyyat* (Persian), or their derivatives. An analysis of these terms alone is sufficient to provide a key for understanding the meaning of spirituality in its Islamic context. Both terms are of Arabic origin, drawn from the language of the Quran and the Islamic Revelation. The first is derived from the word *rūḥ,* meaning spirit, concerning which the Quran instructs the Prophet[2] to say, when he was asked about the nature of spirit, "The Spirit is from the command of my Lord" (XVII, 85). The second derives from the word *ma'nā,* literally "meaning," which connotes inwardness, "real" as opposed to "apparent," and also "spirit" as this term is understood traditionally—that is, pertaining to a higher level of reality than both the material and the psychic and being directly related to the Divine Reality Itself.

In summary, these terms refer to that which is related to the world of the Spirit, is in Divine Proximity, possesses inwardness and interiority, and is identified with the real—and therefore also, from the Islamic point of view—permanent, and abiding rather than the transient and passing. Taken together, these meanings reveal aspects of Islamic spirituality as it is understood by traditional Islam and from the Islamic point of view, which is the perspective of this work.

There is also another dimension to the meaning of "spirituality," as used in Islamic languages. When this term is employed, there is always evoked a sense of the presence of the *barakah,* or that grace which flows in the vein of the universe and within the life of man to the extent that he dedicates himself to God. There is, in addition, the sense of moral perfection and beauty of the soul as far as human beings are concerned. There is also a "presence" which brings about recollection of God and the paradisal world when ideas, sounds, and words and, in general, objects and works of art are involved. In all these cases, the term "spirituality" evokes in the Muslim mind a proximity to God and the world of the Spirit.

The term always possesses a positive connotation, never being either anti-intellectual or antinomian. If there is anything that can be opposed to it, in the Islamic context, it is that interpretation of Islam which would limit itself only to the outward forms without consideration of the inner reality and the spirit that resides within these forms. Otherwise, the spiritual is never opposed to the formal. Rather, it always makes use of the formal, which it interiorizes. Also, the spiritual cannot be simply equated with the esoteric as opposed to the exoteric. Although the spiritual is more closely related to the esoteric dimension (*al-bāṭin*) of Islam than to any other aspect of the religion, it is also very much concerned with the exoteric acts and the Divine Law as well as theology, philosophy, the arts, and the sciences created by Islam and its civilization. But its concern with the exoteric is always with the aim of making possible the journey from the outward to the abode of inwardness.

The essence of Islamic spirituality, then, is the realization of Unity, as expressed in the Quran, on the basis of the prophetic model and with the aid of the Prophet. The goal of this spirituality is to become embellished by the Divine Qualities through attainment of those virtues which were possessed in their perfection by the Prophet and with the aid of methods and the grace which issue from him and the Quranic Revelation. The spiritual life is based at once upon the reverential fear of God and obedience to His Will, love of God to which the Quran refers in the verse, "He loves them and they love Him" (V, 54), and knowledge of God which is the ultimate goal of creation. Islamic spirituality is a love always colored and conditioned by knowledge and based on an obedience already practiced and contained in living according to the Divine Law, which embodies God's concrete will for Muslims.

This spirituality has rejuvenated Islamic society over the ages and produced countless men and women of saintly nature who have fulfilled the goal of human existence and brought joy to other human beings. It has caused the flowering of some of the world's greatest art, ranging from gardening to music, and made possible the appearance of some of the most outstanding philosophers and scientists whom the world has known. It has also carried out a discourse with other religions when circumstances have demanded. It has always remained at the heart of Islam and is the key for a deeper understanding of Islam in its many aspects.

Design of the Islamic Volumes

There are two volumes devoted to Islamic spirituality in the series World Spirituality: An Encyclopedic History of the Religious Quest. Their purpose, in contrast to studies on the Islamic religion itself, is to bring out the spiritual aspect of Islam, as described above. Much has been written in European languages on nearly every aspect of Islam, mostly from an outsider's point of view and some from either within the Islamic tradition or sympathetic to it. Yet Islamic spirituality has rarely been treated as a distinct category in either type of work, so that the present volumes may, in a sense, be considered as the first major collection of essays in English on this crucial subject. This lack of precedent has posed many problems and challenges not only in the conception of the work but also in its execution.

This first volume is designed to present the foundations of Islamic spirituality, treating in the first section its roots in the Quran, the Prophet, his life and sayings, the Islamic rites of prayer, fasting, pilgrimage, and *jihād.* The second section presents the basic traditions of Islam: Sunnism, Twelve-Imam Shīʿism, and Ismāʿīlism, along with a study of female spirituality in Islam. The third section is devoted to Sufism: its nature, origin, early development, and spiritual practices, as well as the Sufi science of the soul. The fourth section deals with knowledge of reality: the Islamic doctrines of God, angels, the cosmos and natural order, man, and eschatology.

The second volume will present Islamic spirituality in its manifestations in history and culture as it has developed throughout a vast area of the globe in the form of Sufi orders, in the arts and literature, from architecture to poetry, and in philosophy and the sciences. Throughout the two volumes the goal will be to show how the essence and manifestations of Islamic spirituality are concerned with the principle of Divine Unity.

As treated in the first part of this volume, the roots and definitive sources of Islamic spirituality are, of course, the Word of God as revealed in the Quran and the nature and inner Substance of the Prophet, who received the Word and made it known to mankind. The significance of these principal sources can be understood only if one turns to the inner aspect of the Quranic and Prophetic realities and does not limit oneself to the external meaning of the words of the Quran or merely the historical events in the life of the Prophet. Of great importance, therefore, have been the esoteric commentaries on the Quran in the spiritual life of the Islamic community and of the individual Muslim. Likewise, in addition to the spiritual significance of the Prophet, one must consider his sayings and traditions, *Ḥadīth* and *Sunnah,* which have crystallized this spirituality in specific words, norms, and deeds that have been emulated over the centuries by all Muslims, especially those in quest of the spiritual life.

The roots of Islamic spirituality are also found in the Islamic rites that constitute the pillars of the faith: the rites of daily prayers, fasting, and pilgrimage as well as the paying of religious tax, and that exertion upon the path of God, or *jihād,* which is usually mistranslated as "holy war." The description of these rites in their external forms and the legal conditions pertaining to them belong to general works on Islam and need not be treated in detail in a study devoted to spirituality. But because these rites are the means by which man approaches God, they are of the utmost importance in Islamic spirituality. They are like the descent of the inward and the spiritual toward the outward and material worlds in order to enable man to return to the inward and reach the world of the Spirit. That is why so many classical works on Islamic spirituality have major sections devoted to what they call secrets of worship, *asrār al-ʿibādāt,* that is, the inner meaning of the Islamic rites.

The second part of this volume deals with the major segments of the Islamic community: Sunnism and Shīʿism. This division does not destroy the unity of Islam, since both issue from the same source. They are united in their acceptance of Divine Unity, prophecy, and eschatology, as well as reverence for the text of the Quran. But they emphasize different aspects of Islamic spirituality and have their own doctrinal and practical formulation concerning the theological, philosophical, and social teachings of Islam. Moreover, each possesses a profound piety which, although Islamic, possesses what can be called its own particular spiritual perfume. In order to bring out the full flavor of the spiritual life in each of these schools, this volume has considered them from the point of view of those who live and practice their distinctive piety. At the same time, it has provided a scholarly understanding of the theological and historical differences that have distinguished them from each other over the ages, as well as a description of the different ways in which each has emphasized an aspect of Islamic piety and has reflected a particular dimension of the inner nature of the Prophet himself. Although separate articles are devoted to Sunnism and Shīʿism, most of the volume, including the articles on Sufism and on doctrine, has been written predominately from the Sunni point of view, so that Sunni spirituality is not confined merely to the article specifically on Sunnism.

Included in this part is an article on female spirituality. In the context of today's world, it is of the utmost importance to make it clear that it is possible for a woman to follow the spiritual life in Islam. It is also important to bring to light the characteristics of such a life and to observe how Islamic female spirituality has manifested itself over the ages. This subject is especially timely in view of the interest in female spirituality in the West along with considerable misunderstanding about the teaching of Islam concerning women. To do full justice to this subject, it must be treated by a Muslim woman who has herself lived the spiritual life and who can at the same time express something of its features to a Western audience in English. There exists in Islam a type of spirituality with a distinct feminine color. This needs to be made known in a language that does justice to it by beginning from within and remaining faithful to its nature and norm.

Part 3 deals with Sufism, the most accessible source of the inner dimension of Islam. Some aspects of this inner dimension, or *al-bāṭin,* also manifest themselves in both Twelve-Imam and Ismaʿīlī Shīʿism. Sufism, which is found predominantly in Sunnism, also exists, however, within Shīʿism, independently of the partly esoteric nature of Shīʿism as a whole. In order to grasp the essence of Islamic spirituality, one must know Sufism in its nature, for this nature itself derives from the substance of the Prophet and the inner teachings of the Quran. One must see Sufism as rooted in the Islamic Revelation in order to appreciate its flowering into a vast tree during later centuries. It is also essential to delve into the Sufi disciplines of meditation, contemplation, and invocation. These practices are, in a sense, none other than the Islamic rites in their inner dimension. But they have developed to such an extent as distinct practices that they need to be considered on their own.

Sufism also possesses a science for the cure of the ailments of the soul, for untying the knots that entangle the soul and prevent it from becoming wed to the Spirit. This science, which is a spiritual alchemy, is a veritable "psychotherapy," far superior to modern psychotherapy, for the latter claims to cure the soul without possessing any power belonging to a world standing above that of the soul. Therefore, it often drags the soul to lower psychic regions. The Sufi master, on the contrary, helps to cure the soul of the disciple by means of the Spirit, which stands above the soul and which alone is able to pacify and at the same time excite the soul, to illuminate it and bring about the ecstasy that is the result of spiritual union.

The final section of this volume deals with doctrinal knowledge. Since in Islam the intellect (*al-ʿaql*) and the Spirit (*al-ruḥ*) are closely related, the acquiring of knowledge itself has always been seen as a religious activity. In fact, supreme knowledge is identified with the highest spiritual realization, and Islamic spirituality as a whole possesses a sapiential and gnostic character. That is why the Islamic doctrines on the nature of Reality or the knowledge of Reality constitute a basic element of Islamic spirituality. At the apex of this knowledge stands, of course, knowledge of God. The raison d'être of Islamic revelation is to make known the doctrine of the Divine Nature in all its depth and amplitude, to reveal the knowledge of God as both absolute and infinite, transcendent and immanent, beyond all description yet possessing Names and Qualities by which man is asked to call upon Him and to pray to Him. The knowledge of God is the goal of all Islamic injunctions and the purpose of creation, according to the famous *ḥadīth,* "I was a hidden treasure; I wanted to be known; therefore I created the world so that I would be known." This knowledge is, therefore, also the goal of the spiritual life and both the basis and the fruit of Islamic spirituality.

Knowledge of reality in the metaphysical sense comprises also that of the angels, who are often mentioned in the Quran. The angelic orders in their dazzling depth and breadth, as described in traditional sources, are related to the ritual aspect of religion and to daily piety as well as to eschatology, cosmology, and psychology understood in its traditional sense. From its expression in daily piety to its manifestation in philosophy, Islamic spirituality is intertwined with the function and presence of angels. Angelology is a key to the understanding of the Islamic universe.

No sacred scripture emphasizes more than the Quran the participation of the cosmos in God's Revelation. Through the Quranic Revelation, the cosmos is in a sense re-sacralized and returned to its primordial spiritual status. Meditation on the phenomena of nature is considered a religious duty in the Quran. On the basis of its injunctions and the very spirit of Islam, throughout the centuries Muslims have continued to draw spiritual sustenance from virgin nature. It is not possible to understand Islamic spirituality fully without comprehending the spiritual significance of nature in both the Quran and subsequent schools of Islamic thought. The sun and the moon are not only astronomical bodies but also cosmic realities that participate in the Islamic universe and which, in the Quran, God Himself takes as witnesses.

Islam contains a doctrine of man that complements its doctrine of God in His absoluteness and oneness. It presents a message based on God as He is in Himself—on His absoluteness and infinitude—and not on a particular manifestation. In his role as a theomorphic being, man is at once "nothing" before the Divine Majesty and the vice-gerent of God who by his theomorphic nature reflects God's Names and Qualities in this world. All human beings have the possibility of realizing the fullness of human nature, or *insān*, and of becoming the perfect or universal man (*al-insān al-kāmil*), although in actuality such a possibility is realized only by the prophets and great saints. The "universal man," the perfect example of which was the Prophet, serves as the model for the spiritual life.

The last chapters of the Quran emphasize above all else the eschatological realities in a powerful language that has left its permanent imprint on the minds and hearts of all Muslims. The everyday life of traditional Muslims is intertwined with the reality of death. In accordance with the texts of the Quran, masters of Islamic spirituality over the ages have emphasized the importance of remembering death at all times and of realizing the ephemeral nature of life in this world. There is a vast corpus of literature in various Islamic languages on eschatology: on both the end of the world and the posthumous states that the individual soul must traverse after death. This type of writing ranges from popular works of pious literature to philosophical and gnostic texts of the greatest intellectual and spiritual significance.

The above themes constitute the foundations of Islamic spirituality, to which this volume is devoted. These foundations have been and remain an ever-present reality, like the Ka'bah itself, for all generations of Muslims from East to West. From these foundations have issued the manifestations of Islamic spirituality in diverse regions throughout history, which will be the subject of the next volume.

Traditional Islamic Scholarship

Before we describe the individual articles in this volume, it is wise to examine the nature of scholarship within the Islamic tradition. It is essential to remember that Islamic spirituality, as well as the Islamic scholarly tradition, is still very much alive. We are not dealing with an archaic civilization that has already passed into the pages of history and is resuscitated only through Western scholarly efforts. To bring out the significance of this spirituality, it is necessary to remain faithful to its norms and also its own traditional scholarship. However, it is imperative to remember that this tradition has not undergone the same changes related to the spread of humanism, rationalism, empiricism, historicism, and positivism which, since the Renaissance, have deeply affected Western scholarship in all domains including religion itself. The vast majority of Muslims simply do not have the same attitude toward their Sacred Scripture or the *Ḥadīth* as those in the West who follow the methods of what has become known as higher criticism. Nor can the Muslims be accused of shortcomings if they have not followed the prevalent, modern Western world view but have remained faithful to their own tradition. Islamic spirituality is a living reality and must be presented as such rather than as a cadaver dissected according to a world view that is alien to it. This is the necessary condition for a study that seeks to be authentic. And yet Islamic spirituality must be presented to the Western world in a language that is comprehensible to that world.

These are the considerations that have determined the choice of the contributors to the Islamic volumes. The editor sought to invite scholars and spiritual authorities who could express various facets of Islamic spirituality in a manner that would be Islamically authentic and at the same time intelligible to a Western audience. It was necessary to invite scholars who were immersed in traditional Islamic scholarship with its emphasis on the oral as well as the written tradition, along with scholars well versed in Western methodologies yet sympathetic to Islamic spirituality. It was essential to include writings of men and women who have themselves lived and experienced this spirituality as well as those well acquainted with the written primary and secondary sources and with Western as well as Islamic methods of scholarship.

In certain essays, the reader may encounter a manner of looking upon traditional sources, the question of authority, authenticity, and transmission different from what current Western scholarship upholds. This is due not to a lack of scholarship but to the presence of another scholarly tradition—and, most of all, the presence of a living spiritual tradition whose authenticity and legitimacy cannot be simply determined by nineteenth-century European methods of historical criticism.

What are the characteristics of traditional Islamic scholarship? Islam developed its own indigenous modes of scholarship at the same time that it assimilated certain aspects of the linguistic, literary, scientific, and philosophical traditions of the Greco-Alexandrian and Persian worlds as well as those of other cultures it encountered throughout its history. In addition, through the centuries Islam cultivated and refined spiritual techniques based on Prophetic practice and elaborated by later masters. It amassed a body of spiritual wisdom that was often expressed in complex literary forms with an elaborate symbolic language and supported by architectonic philosophical structures. There is, in fact, not one form of traditional scholarship in Islam but many, which throughout its history have been integrated into various patterns and which have developed their own methodologies while maintaining a spiritual and intellectual cohesion. These have every right to be acknowledged as authentic modes of scholarship and means of attainment of knowledge. It is true that for a variety of reasons Islam has not assimilated the techniques and attitudes of Western historical criticism to the same extent as Jewish and Christian scholarship. The Islamic volumes in this series reflect this reality and the existing state of Islamic scholarship: rooted in its own spiritual experience with its accumulated spiritual wisdom, reflected upon through its classical scholarly traditions, and employing Western methods of scholarship to the degree that these methods do not distort the authenticity of the Islamic tradition.

The reader must accept the right of other religious universes to live and function according to their own ethos and principles in order to gain some authentic insights into those universes rather than viewing them simply through the perspective of current Western modes of thinking. The reader, then, should not be surprised if articles on the Quran do not raise the kinds of questions that Western scholars since the nineteenth century have raised about the Bible. Nor should the reader expect to find references to all quotations from the *Ḥadīth* or sayings of spiritual teachers. The articles in this and the subsequent volume reflect a predominantly oral tradition, where exact references to written sources have not been established in certain instances, nor are they expected, as would be the case in a more textually grounded ethos.

The Authors and Their Contributions

In the light of these considerations, the editor invited a diverse group of scholars and spiritual authorities to contribute to these volumes. Some of the authors are well-known scholars, and some younger ones of promise. Some are spiritual authorities, and others Western—and in one case Japanese—

scholars who have penetrated deeply into Islamic spirituality and through both empathy and knowledge are in a position to speak about it in an authentic manner. Moreover, the Muslim scholars are drawn from the length and breadth of the Islamic world and are known for both their knowledge and their deep attachment to the Islamic tradition. It is hoped that in this fashion the richness of Islamic spirituality has been presented in such a way as to preserve its authentic nature and reflect the diversity of schools and approaches while expressing the message in a language that is comprehensible to the Western reader.

Several of the essays written by Muslim scholars have been edited by us in order to conform to the norms of the series. In all such cases we have sought to preserve the tenor of the original work while adjusting it to the guidelines established for all the volumes of the series. Our editing has, however, avoided any attempt to bring about uniformity. Since each essay is written by a scholar immersed in the subject and reflects a particular spiritual evaluation of the material, we have allowed the individual characteristics of each essay to stand even at the expense of a lack of uniformity of presentation. Likewise, the translations of the Quran have not been made uniform and are either by the author of the article or from the Arberry or Pickthall translations. This lack of uniformity is amply compensated for by the unity which dominates the work and which results from the inner unity of Islamic spirituality itself.

Part 1 of the present volume, "The Roots of Islamic Tradition and Spirituality," begins with several essays on the Quran. The first essay, by Seyyed Hossein Nasr, discusses the way the Quran was revealed and assembled, its names and their significance, its language and some of its themes. It explores the important role the Quran plays in the lives of Muslims and the way it serves as the source of all Islamic teachings. The article focuses on the inner meaning of the Sacred Text and the way in which the spiritual teachings of Islam are present in the inner dimension of the Quran. Allahbakhsh K. Brohi also deals with the significance of the Quran in the life of Islam but treats the subject more as a Muslim meditating on its verses and chapters. His essay is an existential witness to the spiritual significance of the Book and a vivid example of how a pious Muslim draws sustenance from it and is nourished by its message. Abdurrahman Habil turns to a more scholarly and historical treatment of the esoteric commentaries on the Quran, showing their central importance for all aspects of spiritual life within the Islamic world. Beginning with the second/eighth-century commentary of Imam Jaʿfar al-Ṣādiq, he deals with various periods in the history of Quranic interpretation, including both Sufi and Shīʿite commentaries.

This part includes an exceptional essay by Frithjof Schuon on the spiritual significance of the Substance of the Prophet. Speaking as a spiritual authority, Schuon deals with a subject that has not been treated in such an explicit manner even in traditional Islamic sources. He brings out the significance of that invisible yet very real presence of the inner being of the Prophet in all Islamic spirituality. Ja'far Qasimi then turns to the life, or *Sīrah,* of the Prophet. He gives a detailed account of the life of the founder of Islam based completely on traditional sources, as these sources have been understood and accepted by Muslims all over the world. His goal is not historical criticism in the Western sense of the term, but his work is based on solid traditional scholarship. Rather, he seeks to make known the life of the Prophet as it affects the religious and spiritual life of Muslims. In a complementary chapter, S. H. Nasr discusses the significance of the *Ḥadīth* literature, that is, the body of the sayings of the Prophet as sifted and studied by the traditional scholars who over a millennium ago assembled the canonical collections that were accepted by the Sunnis and were also assembled separately by authoritative Shī'ite sources. Although he devotes some space to a response to Western criticism of the authenticity of the *Ḥadīth,* the author seeks to bring out the role of the *Ḥadīth* in the spiritual life. In a similar vein, he discusses the actions of the Prophet (*Sunnah*) in the light of their importance to spiritual practice.

Syed Ali Ashraf turns to the study of the meaning of the Islamic rites: the canonical prayers, fasting, pilgrimage, the religious tax, and *jihād,* or holy effort or exertion. He demonstrates how the rites performed by all Muslims also possess an inward meaning, which, however, is discovered only by those who follow the path of inwardness. A. K. Brohi concludes this part by delving more deeply into the rite of prayer. Basing himself mostly on the opening chapter of the Quran, the *Sūrat al-fātiḥah,* Brohi shows how and why the Quran commands men and women to pray and how prayer transforms and interiorizes them.

Part 2, "Aspects of the Islamic Tradition," begins with the article of Abdur-Rahman Ibrahim Doi on Sunnism. The author delineates the principles of Sunni belief and the differences between Sunnism and Shī'ism, provides a brief history of the various caliphates throughout Islamic history, and treats practices and virtues emphasized in Sunnism. In his discussion of Twelve-Imam Shī'ism, Syed Husain M. Jafri points to the Shī'ite principles of belief and the differences between Shī'ism and Sunnism. He discusses extensively the role of the Imam and the significance of the lives of some of the Imams in the history of Shī'ism and treats specific features of Shī'ite piety and practices. Azim Nanji deals with the early development of Ismā'īlism, the foundation of the Fāṭimid dynasty, the later proliferation of Ismāʿīlism into the Nizārīs and Mustaʿlīs, the growth of the Yemeni form of Ismāʿīlism, and finally the spread of Ismāʿīlism in India. He also deals with some of the major figures of Ismāʿīlī thought and the central themes with which they were concerned.

Finally, in this section Saadia Khawar Khan Chishti, a Pakistani woman who is both a scholar and a follower of the Islamic spiritual path, deals with female spirituality in Islam. She treats these themes both historically, as embodied in the wives of the Prophet and the early women saints, and as it can be practiced today. She deals with the spiritual life as it concerns women and the spiritual significance of the life of women as ordered by the *Sharīʿah* or Divine Law. Although her treatment of feminine spirituality is very different from the discussion of women's issues in the West today, it stands in the mainstream of traditional Islamic life. The author herself is at the center of the religious life of her country and very active in the question of the role of women in the present-day life of Pakistan.

Part 3, "Sufism," begins with an essay on the nature and origin of Sufism written from within the Sufi tradition by Abu Bakr Siraj Ed-Din. Basing himself entirely on the Quran, the author demonstrates the completely Islamic origin of Sufism and shows why Sufism could not but be the response of the Muslim soul at its deepest level to the call of the Quran. Victor Danner likewise emphasizes the Islamic origin of Sufism in his essay on its early development. He demonstrates the necessity of the rise of the Sufi circles and orders and provides a history of early Sufism seen from within. He also treats the tension between Sufism and the exoteric dimension of the religion, which necessitated the synthesis of al-Ghazzālī in the fifth/eleventh century. Jean-Louis Michon turns to the specific question of spiritual practices, again emphasizing the origin of these practices in the Quran and the *Sunnah*. He analyzes the major Sufi practices, such as the chanting of poems in praise of the Prophet, litanies, and invocations. Mohammad Ajmal concludes this section with a study of the Sufi science of the soul. Basing himself chiefly on the fourteenth/twentieth-century Indian Sufi authority Mawlana Thanvi, the author analyzes the Sufi science of the soul and compares it with schools of Western psychotherapy.

Part 4, "Knowledge of Reality," concludes the volume by treating knowledge of divine, cosmic, and human reality. In his essay on God, S. H. Nasr points to the centrality of the doctrine of God as the One in all aspects of Islam and the knowledge of the One as the supreme goal of Islamic spirituality. The author also elaborates the Quranic doctrine of the transcendence and immanence of God and of the Divine Names. Sachiko Murata turns to the Islamic doctrine of angels, drawing from the Quran and *Ḥadīth* as well as later traditional sources. She discusses the meaning of angels, their hierarchy, and their role in religious life and in the life of the cosmos. She treats also the function of the angels as instruments of illumination and their significance in the spiritual life, as attested by Gabriel's role in guiding the Prophet in his Nocturnal Ascension to the Throne of God. In his essay on the cosmos and the natural order, S. H. Nasr highlights the cosmic dimension of the Quranic Revelation. Nature is a cosmic book revealing the "signs" of God, and the Quran emphasizes the spiritual relation that exists between man and nature. The author explores Islamic cosmology, its relation to the Quran, and its significance for the spiritual life. In his essay on the Islamic doctrine of man, Charles le Gai Eaton explains the importance of the rapport between man and the cosmos. As the "caliph of God" (*khalīfat Allāh*) on earth, man is the custodian of the natural environment and the bridge between heaven and earth. Eaton discusses the responsibilities of man toward God, himself, society, and the cosmic order. Finally, William C. Chittick turns to the complex question of eschatology, beginning with the references to eschatology in the Quran and *Ḥadīth*. He deals with traditional accounts of death and the afterlife, the metaphysical discussion of eschatology, the lesser and the greater resurrection, and the significance of eschatology for the spiritual life.

The diversity of themes and approaches in this volume reflects the reality of its subject matter as well as the world to which it is addressed. By seeking to treat the major aspects of Islamic spirituality with authenticity and sympathy in a language comprehensible to a Western audience, we hope not only to make Islamic spirituality better known but also to serve the cause of spirituality itself in the deepest sense possible. To know an authentic spirituality in depth is to know spirituality as such, especially if the spirituality in question is of the universality, diversity, power, and living presence of that of Islam.

In conclusion, we wish to thank all the contributors from both the Orient and the Occident, who have made this and the subsequent volume possible despite great distances and difficulties of communication. We also wish to thank especially Katherine O'Brien, who has assisted us with both the editing and the selection of illustrations. Our thanks are also due to Sarolyn Joseph, who has helped in typing the manuscript, and to S. V. R. Nasr, who has assisted in the preparation of the glossary and bibliography. Finally, we express our gratitude to Ewert Cousins for his continuous help, to William Chittick for his assistance in correcting the proofs and making many valuable suggestions, and to Carrie Rodomar for her help in the latter stage of the editing process. May the collaboration of all involved in this work make possible a better understanding of Islamic spirituality in a world so much in need of the message of the Spirit that bloweth where it listeth.

Wa mā tawfīqī illā bi'Llāh
Our success comes only through God.

Seyyed Hossein Nasr

Notes

1. In accordance with the Islamic perspective and the wish of the authors of this work, the word "man" in English is used as corresponding to the Arabic *insān,* or human, and possesses no "sexist" connotations.

2. In traditional Islamic sources, the name of the Prophet is always followed by the formula *ṣalla 'Llāhu 'alayhī wa sallam*—that is, "blessings and peace be upon him." The names of the other prophets—and in Shī'ism also the Imams—are followed by *'alayhī-'s-salām,* that is, "peace be upon him." Since this work is written in English for a predominantly non-Muslim audience, the traditional formulas are not included. Moreover, throughout the two Islamic volumes in this series, whenever the term "Prophet" is used with a capital *P,* it refers to the Prophet of Islam. As for the Quran, in Arabic it is usually called the Noble or Glorious Quran (*al-Karīm, al-Majīd*), the term "Holy Quran" being a modern Muslim usage derived from the term "Holy Bible." In the case of the sacred book of Islam also, for the same reasons as above, only the term "Quran" will be used.

List of Transliterations

Arabic characters

ء	ʼ	ك	k
ب	b	ل	l
ت	t	م	m
ث	th	ن	n
ج	j	ه	h
ح	ḥ	و	w
خ	kh	ي	y
د	d	ة	ah; at (construct state)
ذ	dh	ال	(article) al- and ʼl- even before the anteropalatals)
ر	r		
ز	z		
س	s		
ش	sh		
ص	ṣ		
ض	ḍ		
ط	ṭ		
ظ	ẓ		
ع	ʻ		
غ	gh		
ف	f		
ق	q		

long vowels

اى	ā
و	ū
ي	ī

short vowels

ـَ	a
ـُ	u
ـِ	i

diphthongs

ـَو	aw
ـَي	ay
ـِيّ	iyy (final form ī)
ـُوّ	uww (final form ū)

Persian letters added to the Arabic alphabet

پ	p
چ	ch
ژ	zh
گ	g

Part One

THE ROOTS OF THE ISLAMIC TRADITION AND SPIRITUALITY

1

The Quran as the Foundation of Islamic Spirituality

SEYYED HOSSEIN NASR

IF THE SOUL OF THE PROPHET is the fountainhead of Islamic spirituality, the Quran is like that lightning which having struck the human receptacle caused this fountainhead to gush forth or like the water descending from heaven which made streams to flow from this fountainhead. The Quran is the origin and source of all that is Islamic, including, of course, spirituality and the Muḥammadan grace (*al-barakat al-muḥammadiyyah*); and the whole of the spiritual path that emanates from the very Substance of the Prophet owes its existence to the descent of the Word of God upon the virgin soul of His Messenger. If there had not been a Night of Power (*laylat al-qadr*), when the Quran descended from the Divine Empyrean to the human plane, there would have been no Night of Ascension (*laylat al-mi'rāj*), when the Prophet ascended from the earth to the Divine Throne, an ascension that is the model of all spiritual realization in Islam.

The Nature of the Quran

The Quran is the verbatim revelation of the Word of God, revealed in Arabic through the archangel Gabriel to the Prophet during the twenty-three-year period of his prophetic mission. The first verses were revealed when the Prophet was meditating in the cave of Ḥirā' on the Mountain of Light (*jabal al-nūr*) near Mecca, and the last shortly before his death. The verses were memorized by many of the companions and gradually set to writing by such companions as 'Alī and Zayd. Finally, during the time of 'Uthmān, the third caliph, the definitive text based on these early copies and the confirmation of those who had heard the verses from the mouth of the Prophet was copied and sent to the four corners of the Islamic world. The text of the Quran is thus not based on long periods of compilation and interpretation by human agents.[1] Rather, the Quran is the actual Word of God as revealed to His Messenger and is like Christ for Christians, who is himself the Word of God brought into the world through the Virgin Mary. She, therefore, plays a role analogous to that of the soul of the Prophet; both are pure, immaculate, and virginal before the Divine Word.[2] Consequently, not only the meaning of the Quran but also its form—and, in fact, all that relates to it—is of a sacred character. The written words as calligraphy, the sounds of the recited text, the very physical presence of the Book, as well as, of course, the message contained therein, are sacred and spiritually important.

To understand the spiritual significance of the Quran, it is essential to remember that the Quran was a sonoral revelation. The first words of the Sacred Text revealed by Gabriel surrounded the Prophet like an ocean of sound as the archangel himself filled the whole of the sky. The sound of the Quran penetrates the Muslim's body and soul even before it appeals to his mind. The sacred quality of the psalmody of the Quran can cause spiritual rapture even in a person who knows no Arabic. In a mysterious way, this sacred quality is transmitted across the barrier of human language and is felt by those hundreds of millions of non-Arab Muslims, whether they be Persian, Turkish, African, Indian, or Malay, whose hearts palpitate in the love of God and whose eyes are moistened by the tears of joy upon simply hearing the Quran chanted. It can be said that the Muslim lives in a space defined by the sound of the Quran and that the sonoral character of the Quranic revelation remains central to the spiritual life of Islam.[3]

It must, furthermore, be remembered that the soul of the Muslim is composed of Quranic formulas and quotations which the faithful recite in the language of the Quran whatever might be their mother tongue. The Muslim begins every action with *bismi'Llāh al-Raḥmān al-Raḥīm* ("in the Name of God Most Merciful, Most Compassionate"), ends every action with *al-ḥamdᵘ li'Llāh* ("praise be to God"), resigns himself to what has passed by placing it in God's hand with the statement *māshā' Allāh* ("what God has willed") and, in planning all future action, realizes that the future is determined by God's Will by asserting *inshā' Allāh* ("if God wills"). The attitudes embedded in these and many other Quranic formulas determine the framework of the spiritual life for the Muslim. Through them he places his action in God's hand and the past and future in the care of His Will and Providence.[4] The power of these phrases over the soul and mind of Muslims depends upon the spiritual presence inherent in the sacred sound of these and other verses of the Sacred Text as well as their meaning. It is the sound of the Quran which the newly born child first hears as the *Shahādah* is chanted into his or her ears. The Quran is thus the very first sound that welcomes the Muslim to the first stages of his journey in this world. And it is the Quran that is chanted at the moment of death and accompanies the soul in its posthumous journey to the Divine Presence. The chanted Quran is the prototype of all sacred sound. It is the divine music that reminds man of his original abode and at the same time accompanies him in his dangerous journey of return to that abode; for the Quran, although chanted in this world, reverberates through all the cosmic levels to the Divine Presence from which it has issued.

Presence of the Quran

The language of the Quran is the crystallization of the Divine Word in human language, which seems to be shattered by the "weight" of the revelation from on high.[5] The supreme miracle of Islam is, in fact, considered to be the eloquence (*balāghah*) of the Quran, which is for the Muslim the prototype of language. This eloquence, much debated and discussed by Muslim scholars over the ages,[6] does not reside so much in the ordering of the words into powerful poetic utterance as in the degree of the inspiration as a result of which every sentence, every word, and every letter scintillate with a spiritual presence and are like light congealed in tangible form.

This presence is to be found in the written as well as the sonoral Quran. The art of writing the text of the Quran is the sacred art of Islam *par excellence.* The art of calligraphy, which is so central to Islamic civilization, is inseparable from the Quran; for it was for the purpose of writing the Sacred Text that this art was developed, the earlier styles such as Kufic being nearly completely and solely identified with the writing of the Quran.[7] Moreover, the art of illumination, which came into its own and reached its peak of perfection in the Il-khānid and Mamlūk periods, is the visualization of the spiritual inspiration related to the writing and recitation of the text of the Word of God. To understand the reverence that Muslims show toward the Quran, it is necessary to take cognizance of the spiritual presence in the calligraphy of the words as well as in the sounds that surround and penetrate man when the text is chanted. It is this presence that every faithful Muslim feels instinctively. As a result, he finds comfort and protection even in the physical book itself and carries the Sacred Text with him wherever and whenever possible. The sage finds the same protection in carrying the quintessence of the Quran, which is God's Name, in his heart. According to a *ḥadīth,* "He who protects the Name of God in his heart, God protects him in the world."

The Quran possesses a mysterious presence, which might be called "magical," in addition to the Book's being the source of Islamic doctrine, ethics, and sacred history. It is this "magic" that is untranslatable and can only be experienced in the language of the revelation, while the doctrinal content, ethical injunctions, or accounts of the prophets and peoples of old can be rendered into other tongues. This "magic" is inseparable from the spiritual presence of the sonoral revelation, which captures the soul of man as a net cast into the sea in order to return the soul from the domain of multiplicity to Unity.

> The Quran is, like the world, at the same time one and multiple. The world is multiplicity which disperses and divides; the Quran is a multiplicity which draws together and draws to Unity. The multiplicity of the holy Book—the diversity of its words, sentences, pictures and stories—fills the soul and thus absorbs it and imperceptibly transposes it into the climate of serenity and immutability by a sort of divine "cunning". . . . The Quran is like a picture of everything the human brain can think and feel, and it is by this means that God exhausts human disquiet, infusing into the believer silence, serenity and peace.[8]

The Quran is a "world," but one that leads man to Unity and prevents the soul from being scattered and dispersed.[9]

The Names of the Quran

The sacred Book of Islam has many names, of which *al-Qur'ān,* meaning "recitation," is the best known. If this name refers to the essentially auditory and sonoral nature of the Text as that which is read and recited,[10] some of the other well-known names of the Book refer to the fact that it contains all Islamic doctrine and, in fact, the root of all knowledge. The Quran is thus also known as *al-Furqān,* literally, "the discernment," that is, that which enables man to distinguish between truth and falsehood, good and evil. The Book is known also as *al-Hudā,* the Guide, since it contains the knowledge that the Muslim must possess in order to remain upon the straight path (*al-Ṣirāṭ al-mustaqīm*) and become aware of God's Will as it concerns him. Moreover, the Quran is the *Umm al-kitāb,* the Mother of Books, since it is the prototype of all "books," of all that can be known, the archetype of all things, and since the roots of all knowledge are contained in the eternal Quran.

All the doctrine and all the knowledge in the Quran are summarized in the *Shahādah, Lā ilāha illa'Llāh* ("there is no divinity but God"), the supreme metaphysical formula stating the Oneness of the Divine Principle and the reliance of all existence and all qualities upon the One. In a sense, the whole of the Quran is one long litany with the refrain of *Lā ilāha illa'Llāh* and a commentary upon the truth of Unity (*al-tawḥīd*) contained therein. Not only the metaphysical, cosmological, and eschatological doctrines of the Quran but also the ethical precepts that run throughout the Text are so many ways of asserting the Oneness of God, the reliance of all things upon Him, and the way to live according to His Will.

Another name of the Quran is *dhikr Allāh,* the remembrance of God. The Quran is itself the reminder of God's Truth and Presence, and to recite it is to remember God. Not only is the first chapter of the Book, the *Sūrat al-Fātiḥah,* the central part of the daily prayers; but also the quintessential prayer of the heart, or *dhikr,* finds its roots in the Quran and may be said to be the essence of its message. The Quran therefore contains both the doctrine and the method of Islamic spirituality, the doctrine being contained in its quintessential form in the *Shahādah* and the method in the invocation of the Name of God or *dhikr.* The Quran, the grand theophany of Islam, is both *Lā ilāha illa'Llāh* and *dhikr Allāh.* It comes from Allah and provides the means and the methods of returning to Him.

The Quran and Sacred History

The Sacred Book of Islam is replete with episodes of sacred history. It speaks of people and prophets of old, of battles, rebellions, love and death, of God's forgiveness and punishment. But the Quran, and with it Islam, is singularly indifferent to the merely historical significance of this sacred history. The Quran is not a book of history and is even less concerned with history than is the Bible. The sacred history recounted in the Quran is in reality the epic of the life of the soul. The forces of good and evil mentioned in its pages are to be found within ourselves, and even the prophets are the objective and external counterparts and complements of the inner Intellect, which illuminates the heart and mind of man.[11] To recite the pages of the Quran is to become aware of the history of one's own being, the forces of one's own soul, and the conditions of the journey of life at the end of which stand death and Divine Judgment. It is to see the Will of God in shaping man's destiny and man's own role in weaving the substance that constitutes our being once the journey of life terminates and suddenly we find ourselves before the blinding reality of God's Presence.

The Quran as the Source of Islamic Thought and Law

Not only the supreme doctrine of Unity but all Islamic doctrine originates in the Quran or the *Ḥadīth,* which is the inspired commentary upon it. All schools of theology and philosophy, all schools of law and political theory, all branches of Islam whether Sunni or Shīʿite base their teachings upon the tenets of the Quran. Whether they agree or differ on the question of determinism and free will, the primacy of faith or action, or the relation of God's Mercy to His Justice, they all derive their teachings from the verses of the Quran, which is like an ocean into which all streams of Islamic thought flow and from which they ultimately originate. There is no claim to Islamicity without a Quranic basis.

Likewise, the practices of Muslims as ordained by the *Sharīʿah* have their origin in the Quran. Although the foundations of the *Sharīʿah* must also be sought in the *Ḥadīth* and the elaboration of the Law depends, furthermore, upon consensus (*ijmāʿ*) and analogical reasoning (*qiyāṣ*), in principle all of the *Sharīʿah* is already contained in the Quran. The other sources are only means of elaborating and making explicit what is already contained in the Sacred Text. As for ethical attitudes related to the practice of the Sacred Law, they too are to be found in the Quran, which determines for Muslims all ethical norms and all moral principles. What the Quran teaches constitutes morality, not what human reason determines on the basis of its own judgments.

The Quran as the Source of the Spiritual Path and Art

The Quran is the source of not only the Law but also the Way or the *Ṭarīqah*. The spiritual life of Islam as it was to crystallize later in the Sufi orders goes back to the Prophet, who is the source of the spiritual virtues found in the Muslim soul. But the soul of the Prophet was itself illuminated by the Light of God as revealed in the Quran, so that quite justly one must consider the Quranic revelation as the origin of Sufism.[12] It is not accidental that over the ages the Sufis have been the foremost expositors and commentators upon the Quran and that some of the greatest works of Sufism such as the *Mathnawī* of Jalāl al-Dīn Rūmī are in reality commentaries upon the Sacred Text. Only the Sufis have, in fact, been able to cast aside the veil of this celestial bride, which is the Quran, in order to reveal some of her beauty, which it hides from the eyes of those who are strangers to her.

Even Islamic art, which may be called "the second Revelation" of Islam, is rooted in the Quran, not in its outward form or as a result of applying explicit instructions contained in the Text but in its inner reality.[13] Without the Quran there would have been no Islamic art. The rhythm created in the soul of the Muslim, his predilection for "abstract" expressions of the truth, the constant awareness of the archetypal world as the source of all earthly forms, and the consciousness of the fragility of the world and the permanence of the Spirit have been brought into being by the Quran in the mind and soul of those men and women who have created the works of Islamic art. Islamic art is the crystallization of the inner reality of the Quran and the imprint of this reality on the soul of the Prophet and, through him, on the soul of Muslims.

The chapters that follow demonstrate clearly the role of the Quran in Islamic spirituality. From the study of this Sacred Book there have come into being numerous sciences, while the souls of men and women have been molded by the repetition of its phrases and the carrying out of its injunctions. Like the original revelation of the Word which filled the totality of space, the Quran has created a whole cosmos within which the Muslim lives and dies. But the Quran is also that net cast by the One to pull men and women lost in the labyrinth of multiplicity back to the Divine Origin. To live in the world of the Quran and according to its injunctions is to be guaranteed a life of spiritual felicity and a death that leads to the abode of peace. In the Islamic universe there is no spirituality possible without the aid of the Book, which teaches man all that he can know or that can be known and which leads man to the goal for which he was created.

Notes

1. As viewed by Muslims, what is called higher criticism in the West does not at all apply to the text of the Quran. Elaborate sciences concerning conditions in which the verses were revealed (*sha'n al-nuzūl*), how the Quran was compiled, how the verses were enumerated, as well as the science and art of the recitation of the Quran, have been developed by Muslim scholars over the centuries. We cannot, however, deal with them here since our goal is to outline the spiritual function and significance of the Quran. But these traditional sciences provide all the answers to questions posed by modern Western orientalists about the structure and text of the Quran, except, of course, those questions that issue from the rejection of the Divine Origin of the Quran and its reduction to a work by the Prophet. Once the revealed nature of the Quran is rejected, then problems arise. But these are problems of orientalists that arise not from scholarship but from a certain theological and philosophical position that is usually hidden under the guise of rationality and objective scholarship. For Muslims, there has never been the need to address these "problems" because Muslims accept the revealed nature of the Quran, in the light of which these problems simply cease to exist.

2. The comparison of the Quran to Christ and the Virgin to the soul of the Prophet is a most profound one that was first studied by F. Schuon and later by W. C. Smith and certain other Western scholars. See Schuon, *The Transcendent Unity of Religions*, trans. P. Townsend (Wheaton, IL: Theosophical Publishing House, 1984).

3. See E. McClain, *Meditations through the Quran: Tonal Images in an Oral Culture*

(York Beach, ME: Nicolas Hays, 1981); see also S. H. Nasr, *Islamic Art and Spirituality* (Albany, NY: State University of New York Press, 1987) chap. 3.

4. On these and other Quranic statements of which the Muslim soul is composed as a mosaic, see Schuon, *Understanding Islam,* trans. D. M. Matheson (London: Allen & Unwin, 1979) 66–68.

5. "It is as though the poverty-stricken coagulation which is the language of mortal man were under the formidable pressure of the Heavenly Word broken into a thousand fragments" (Schuon, *Understanding Islam,* 44).

6. See, e.g., al-Baqillānī's *I'jāz al-Qur'ān,* studied by G. von Grunebaum, *A Tenth-Century Document of Arabic Literary Theory and Criticism: The Sections on Poetry of al-Baqillānī's I'jāz al-Qur'ān* (Chicago: University of Chicago Press, 1950).

7. See M. Lings, *The Quranic Art of Calligraphy and Illumination* (London: Festival of the World of Islam, 1976); and A. M. Schimmel, *Calligraphy and Islamic Culture* (New York: New York University Press, 1984).

8. Schuon, *Understanding Islam,* 50.

9. "Just as the world is an immeasurable carpet in which everything is repeated in a rhythm of continual change, or where everything remains similar within the framework of the law of differentiation, so too the Quran—and with it the whole of Islam—is a carpet or fabric, in which the center is everywhere repeated in an infinitely varied way and in which the diversity is no more than a development of the Unity" (Schuon, *Understanding Islam,* 58).

10. The very first verse of the Quran that was revealed begins with the verb *iqra',* recite! The command concerns the whole of the Book, which is meant to be recited and heard as well as read in the ordinary sense of the term.

11. Certain Sufis have, in fact, identified the prophets mentioned in the Quran with degrees of man's inner being, speaking of the "Abraham of thy being," "Moses of thy being," etc. See H. Corbin, *En Islam iranien* (Paris: Gallimard, 1971–72) vol. 3, chap. 4.

12. This fact, long denied by orientalists, has finally become accepted by a number of well-known Western Islamicists from L. Massignon to A. M. Schimmel. See chapter 12 of this volume, by Abu Bakr Siraj ad-Din, "The Nature and Origin of Sufism"; and Mir Valiuddin, *The Quranic Sufism* (Delhi: Motilal Banarsidass, 1959).

13. See T. Burckhardt, *The Art of Islam* (London: Festival of the World of Islam, 1976) 8–9.

2

The Spiritual Significance of the Quran

Allahbakhsh K. Brohi

Spirituality and Human Growth

In considering the approach that the Quran makes to spirituality, one has to be clear about what the term "spirituality" in the context of present discourse implies. Spirituality means many things to many minds and is undeniably a term that is used in varying contexts with different shades of meanings. Many have used this term to designate a special mark of spiritual disposition, and others have employed it to mark off a higher and final development of life itself. In the way the present writer understands it, it will be appropriate to say that anyone who reflects God or the Holy Spirit as the vital, determining norm or principle of his or her life could validly be called "spiritual." Understood in this sense, the whole of the Quran seems to highlight the importance of the operation of this norm or principle over the life of the believer, if he is going to be saved and admitted to the company of the elect. Negatively, the word "spirituality" is not to be confused with spiritualism, a term that is rather incorrectly used for what is really spiritism, that is, the phenomenon of communicating through media with the departed spirits on the other side of the river of life.

By and large, every religion, including of course Islam, ultimately deals with the supreme issue of what may be called spiritualization of man's consciousness. The biological base of life in a human being is the same as in any subhuman animal species such as dogs or cats—at least insofar as the primary instincts of preservation of self and preservation of the species to which the animal belongs are concerned. Religion fosters consciousness, which, functionally regarded, aims at inducing the believer to transcend his animal nature, or reach or acquire what—for want of a better expression—

may be called a higher kind of life, a life that is, as the Quran puts it: *khayrun wa abqā,* better and eternal.

In life there is such a thing as biological growth of the individual organism. But this growth is primarily physical in character; that is, it comes to prevail automatically by the unfolding of some latent forces inherent in life. It is basically a kind of growth that consists merely of the addition or accretion of more to the same. A plant grows in this sense when it puts on more leaves, more twigs, or thicker leaves and thicker twigs. It registers a sort of quantitative growth in bulk, and this virtually implies an accretion of the more to the same structure and original content of plant life. There is no transcendance of plant life reflected in such a growth. There is no going beyond the basic matrix of life, which throughout remains the same. This may be likened to a sort of horizontal growth of an organism in the context of the symbolism of the cross, where the vertical coordinate denotes the possibility of a movement upward. The vertical dimension reveals the possibility that the whole horizontal base of the organism is capable of being considered in a new dimension and being led to a new domain. In the case of plant life and using the symbolism of the growth of plants, one could say that it is only when the green plant, which was fed upon filthy manure, bears fruit, a flower, or a blossom that the plant's life grows into a higher dimension.

This growth in the world of the beyond, or in a higher direction, is capable of being achieved at the human level by a conscious effort to make certain choices that are available to man. These choices within the matrix of a religious consciousness enable its votaries to opt for the higher or uphill or difficult path. The making of these choices takes life on its upward path to God. The answer to the questions of how and why these choices have to be made is found at the heart of religion. No wonder then that the Quran calls itself by yet another but a well-known name, *al-Furqān* (literally, "the discernment"), for the good reason that here the revelation is geared to the master purpose of showing the difference between good and evil, so that correct choices can be made. It also deals with the morphology of awareness in terms of which these choices have to be made. For every choice there is an appropriate occasion, as for any period or epoch or phase of life there is an appropriate destiny, which is described traditionally as *li-kulli ajalin kitāb* (all that is decreed is written). If these choices are not made at the appropriate time as commanded under the mandate of heaven, man will be placed in the serious difficulty of having to put forward a greater effort to negotiate the course of his future development—to say nothing of the suffering that would be involved in the threatened consequences stemming from false choices. The Quran deals at great length with this aspect

1. Illuminated frontispiece of the Quran, Y.Y. 913 f.4a, 1491.

of human action and emphasizes that when lapses occur the Mercy of God, Who is forgiver of sins and Whose grace knows no limit, takes notice of man's repentance and forgives his sins. Indeed, God's Mercy surrounds everything, man included, and yet man is called upon to perform his part of begging for forgiveness, which literally means doing *tawbah.* This repentance or *tawbah* consists in striving to return to the point where the deviation took place when the false choice was made and restarting the labor of recovering the path that is straight—the path that in fact the Quran calls "the straight path" (*al-ṣirāṭ al-mustaqīm*).

The Quran refers characteristically to two paths that are available to man to choose from and stresses the desirability of choosing the higher, the more difficult path. In the words of the Quran:

> Thinketh he that none hath power over him?
> And he saith: I have destroyed vast wealth:
> Thinketh he that none beholdeth him?
> Did We not assign unto him two eyes
> And a tongue and two lips,
> And guide him to the parting of the mountain ways?
> But he hath not attempted the Ascent—
> Ah, what will convey unto thee what the Ascent is!—
> (It is) to free a slave,
> And to feed in the day of hunger
> An orphan near of kin,
> Or some poor wretch in misery,
> And to be of those who believe and exhort one another to
> perseverance and exhort one another to pity. (XC, 5–17)

The Human Predicament

The Quran has set forth the predicament of man resulting from his fall from grace, which is allegorically represented in his having been ejected from the paradisal state in consequence of his disobedience to the Divine Command not to approach "this Tree." In the words of the Quran, "And We said: Adam dwell thou and thy wife in the Garden and eat thereof easefully where you desire; but draw not nigh this Tree lest you be evildoers" (II, 35). The unending conflict engendered by the disobedience of Satan in not bowing before Adam and his malicious resolve to mislead man by making evil appear as good to man has been stated in the Quran at several places. For instance, the Quran states:

> And when We said to the angels, "Bow yourselves to Adam"; so they bowed themselves, save Iblis; he said, "Shall I bow myself unto one Thou hast created of clay?"

> He said, "What thinkest Thou? This whom Thou hast honoured above me—if Thou deferrest me to the Day of Resurrection I shall assuredly master his seed, save a few."
> Said He, "Depart! Those of them that follow thee—surely Gehenna shall be your recompense, an ample recompense!
> And startle whomsoever of them thou canst with thy voice; and rally against them thy horsemen and thy foot, and share with them in their wealth and their children, and promise them!" But Satan promises them naught, except delusion.
> "Surely over My servants thou shalt have no authority." Thy Lord suffices as a guardian. (XVII, 61–65)

In this contest between man and Satan, who is his avowed enemy, the man who is righteous is not alone. It is clear from the verses quoted above that, although God has permitted Satan to carry out his attempt to mislead man, it is He who in the last resort has supreme power over Satan to help man. He has sent prophets to man who have brought guidance to him. Thus, in effect, only those who neglect God's guidance come within the reach and grip of Satanic influence. But those who live in full consciousness of God's supreme Presence and His ubiquitous law are protected against Satanic designs and machinations. The righteous are supported and, indeed, it is said in the Quran that the earth is inherited by the righteous. The evil, of course, is backed by a "slinking prompter," but then he can be defeated by seeking refuge with the Lord. Satan has been described as the avowed enemy of man, and the prophets have been called warners and guides because their historical function has been to warn man against serious consequences of his disobedience to God's commands. They have attempted to guide man, despite the designs of Satan, to make correct choices in order to be able to fulfill the Law and to be able to earn the reward of higher life.

From what has been said so far, it is clear that man is here to submit at the altar of the Higher Presence, and the very Law by which his own development takes place is precisely in accord with the Divine Nature. It is in this very perspective that he is called by the Quran to seek his salvation:

> So set thy face to the religion, a man of pure faith—God's original upon which He originated mankind. There is no changing God's creation. That is the right religion; but most men know it not. (XXX, 30)

All spiritual development for man signifies his effort to grow in the mold in which by his own nature he has been invited to grow. There are other verses to show the way nature bows before God:

> Have they not regarded all things that God has created casting their shadows to the right and to the left, bowing themselves before God in all lowliness?

> To God bows everything in the heavens, and every creature crawling on the earth, and the angels. They have not waxed proud; they fear their Lord above them, and they do what they are commanded. (XVI, 48–50)

The Love of God

Man too is here to serve his Lord. There are many pathways that the traditional religious teaching of mankind appears to recommend for securing its true growth or self-realization and for attaining to higher levels of spiritual attainment. Among these paths, the love of God would appear to be highlighted by the universal religious tradition of mankind as the best means for spiritual realization and self-development.

One of the Names of God mentioned in the Quran is *al-Wadūd*, that is, one who loves:

> And ask forgiveness of your Lord, then turn to him. Surely your Lord is merciful, loving and kind. (XI, 90)

Similarly the Quran stresses the same fact:

> Surely He it is Who creates first and reproduces. And He is the forgiving and loving. (LXXXV, 13–14)

Or in another place:

> Every one of them shall come to Him upon the Day of Resurrection, all alone. Surely, those who believe and do good deeds of Righteousness—unto them the All-Merciful shall assign love. (XIX, 96)

The Quranic view of God is that He is indescribable and that there is nothing like unto Him and, furthermore, that no matter what one says about Him, He is completely beyond it. Therefore, it is difficult at first to understand how one could love that which one has not seen and cannot imagine. For all love presupposes the vision or sight of the beloved and the attraction that is cast by his presence upon human sensibility. It would appear that the Quranic view about steps to be taken to show one's love for God is, in the first instance, to obey unconditionally what the Prophet says, not only because obedience to the Prophet is obedience to God but essentially because, to use the words of the Quran (where the Prophet is made to say), "If you love God, then obey me, then God will *love you* and forgive your sins" (III, 31). There are, in several verses in the Quran, references to God loving those who do good to others (II, 195; III, 133, 147). Furthermore, God loves those who are patient (III, 145) and the *muttaqīn*, that is, those who control themselves and do not allow false inducement to abjure the path prescribed by God for them to follow (III, 55; IX, 4). God

2. The Opening of Sura VII of the Quran, Arabic MS OR. 1401, ff. 116v–117r, 14th century, Egyptian.

also loves those who trust in Him (III, 158) and those who are just (V, 42). All these references show that in the last prophetic dispensation love is pre-eminently reflected by deed, which takes the form of obedience to the Lord as this may be exhibited by the quality of higher virtue. It is to be noticed that love is not here treated as merely a function of the act of making a declaration of love. The test of the love of God is obedience to the Prophet and obedience to what is prescribed in the Divine Word. Islam, therefore, consists essentially in conscious submission to the Law of God and that which is commanded by His Prophet. There is also emphasis in the Quran on *dhikr Allāh* (the remembrance of God), saying prayers, and countenancing other such modes of activity in which man, by participating in the Divine Presence, cultivates within himself a disposition to render service for God. After all, the Jinn and mankind, as the Quran says, have been created only to serve Him.

To Please God

The whole purpose of these teachings in the Quran is to educate men concerning how to please God. For it is by pleasing Him that one secures within oneself a state of being at rest. It is in that state (*al-nafs al-muṭma'innah*) that man returns to the Lord well pleased and well pleasing:

> No indeed! When the earth is ground to powder, and thy Lord comes, and the angels rank on rank, and Gehenna is brought out, upon that day man will remember; and how shall the Reminder be for him?
>
> He shall say, "O would that I had forwarded for my life!" Upon that day none shall chastise as He chastises, none shall bind as He binds. "O soul at peace, return unto thy Lord, well-pleased, well-pleasing! Enter thou among My servants! Enter thou My Paradise!" (LXXXIX, 20–28)

What man does in this life is therefore reaped by him in what the Quran calls the *ākhirah,* that is, in the phase of life that is to come or the hereafter. And according to the Quran, it is life in the hereafter that is real life, but it is a reality that can also be experienced in this life. The whole of the Quran is full of admonitions to the believers to treat this life seriously, for they will all be questioned and their accounts will be audited rigorously but impartially. This world has not been created in vain. There is a serious purpose for which this universe and men have been created. If men are to give a worthwhile account of the way in which they have spent their lives, they must allow the commandments of God to become the decisive norms for regulating their conduct, and they must accept the values that have been stressed in the Quran as the decisive norms for determining the great divide between good and evil. It is this life which, according to the Quran, is spiritual, for it eventually leads to the realization of the highest state of being of which man is capable. No wonder it has been said, "By their fruits shall you find them out." And it is what men do consciously to serve the Lord that counts more than anything else. For indeed the commitment of one who is a Muslim according to the Quran is to stand for advancing God's Law and that of His Prophet:

> Indeed, my prayer, my sacrifice, my life, and my death are for God, Who hath no compare; this I have been commanded to accept and submit to and this I do and I am the first of the Muslims. (VI, 162)

Meeting the Lord

In the final analysis the most important fact of life is man's meeting with his Lord; if that be so, would not this prospect of accounting enable him to live and act in such a manner that his life would reflect the divinely ordained injunctions? But those who are unmindful of this ultimate meeting with the Lord can afford to be negligent of the Divine Commandment. Indeed, the Quran refers to this aspect of life over and over again by pointing out that those who are defying the Divine Law do so because they do not believe that they shall meet their Maker. The whole discipline enjoined by Islam, whether it be ritual prayer, almsgiving, fasting, or pilgrimage, is ultimately a form of struggle with the lower self or the animal self with which man is endowed by nature. This self is called *al-nafs al-ammārah,* a self that according to the Quran inclines him toward evil. But the guidance that has been brought to him on the basis of superior knowledge, with which prophets are blessed by reason of their learning at the high station of wisdom to which they have been called by destiny, enables man to reach the state of *al-nafs al-lawwāmah,* the quarreling self, a self that enters a caveat each time the lower self in man inclines him toward evil. By the frequent choices he makes while siding with the deliverance of *al-nafs al-lawwāmah,* he breaks down the resistance of the animal impulses within him and secures their sublimation in attaining to a state that is being called *al-nafs al-muṭma'innah,* the self at rest where agitation and travail have ceased (see LXXXIX, 28). He thus enters a higher state of being of which little can be conveyed by mere words. In some of the utterances of those who are wayfarers on the path of God some idea can be gained of the high watermarks of excellence they have reached.

The Quran and the Problems of Life

The foregoing thoughts on the Quran and spirituality may be understood somewhat more meaningfully if one casts a glance upon the fundamental distinction between answers to the perennial problem of life that are provided by the philosophic method of enquiry (as this is currently understood) concerning man and his destiny and answers that are provided by the way that is based upon the revealed Word of God, which has reached mankind through the prophets of universal religion. The Quran affirms eloquently this grand tradition of the revealed Word of God from Adam down to Muḥammad and indeed makes the Prophet of God say that he has come to verify and affirm all the preexisting religious revelations that have been brought to mankind by earlier prophets. The essential difference between the view of modern philosophy about man and his destiny and that of religion is that the philosophical view is based on reason when it works upon and elaborates the data furnished to it by man's senses and his sensibility. Religion, however, calls upon man to surrender, but not at the altar of reason nor again at the altar of what may be called natural duties—much less at the altar of the cravings of the animal self. Islam, which is a "natural religion" in a more fundamental sense than "the natural theology" prevalent in the modern world, confirms the validity of reason but without surrendering it to the senses. Rather, Islam admits the competence of human reason to comprehend the meaning of the revealed Word of God. It declares that human reason is capable of development and that the more it is developed in the service of understanding religious truths, the more it will accept religious imperatives as a matter of course. Indeed, Islam claims that man has to be educated to adhere to the cardinal claims of his own mental makeup, his spiritual yearnings. He is not to take a position against the demands that his nature makes upon them. The nature of man has been patterned by God on *fiṭrat Allāh,* that is—if the expression be permitted—on "God's own nature," and the religious dispensation that the Quran calls *al-dīn al-qayyim,* the right religion, does not intend to alter that human nature. The following Quranic verse has already been reproduced the way Arthur J. Arberry has translated it; however, since it is somewhat untranslatable, here is another attempt, that of Mohammed M. Pickthall, at articulating this great truth:

> So set thy purpose (O Muhammad) for religion as a man by nature upright—the nature (framed) of Allah, in which He hath created man. There is no altering (the laws of) Allah's creation. That is the right religion, but most men know not. (XXX, 30)

Any religion that claims to be true must present as an indelible mark the claim that its teachings are in accord with human nature. It is true that the prophets of universal religion demanded from their people faith in whatever teachings they had brought. The only mistake that arose in the history

3. Ornamental title-page of a Quran in seven volumes, written and illustrated for Rukn ad-Din Baybars, afterwards Sultan Baybars II, Arabic MS Add. 22406, f. 1b, Ad 1304, Egyptian.

of religion in relation to their teachings was that unthinking people felt that this demand of having faith entailed an immediate understanding of religious injunctions or a direct and instantaneous realization of the truth that the prophets had brought. This, however, was not the demand. All that was solicited was belief in what was revealed, the awareness that the truth of the Word of God would come if the belief was genuine and was followed by righteous conduct. When Adam was being created, the angels had said that "when created he will spill blood and spread mischief in the land," to which God had replied "I know what you do not know" (II, 30). What God knew was that, with a divinely implanted source of knowledge in the soul of man (suggested by the words "I have breathed My spirit into Adam," XV, 29), man would be able to acquire knowledge to see the value of righteous conduct and would refrain from being disobedient to God's commands. God taught the names of all things to Adam and educated him to name things that angels could not name. This process of acquiring knowledge about the nature of things invested man with cognitive ability to discriminate between right and wrong. It enabled man to realize full knowledge of both a unitive and an analytical kind even beyond the knowledge of the angels. Spirituality means, in fact, the attainment of higher levels of being in which this knowledge is fully realized in conformity with man's destiny on earth. Indeed, the fact that man is here on earth to realize that higher state of being has been asserted by the revealed Word of God. That is what the Quran calls *dhālika taqdīr al-'azīz al-'alīm* (that is the ordaining of the All-mighty, the All-knowing).

What is called the *Ṭarīqah* or the esoteric path in the mystical tradition of Islam is not opposed to the *Sharī'ah,* that is, the Divine Law, but its discipline is designed to make human nature accept that Law as a part of its own inner demand. This is possible because God has breathed His Spirit into Adam, as is suggested by the words *nafakhtu fīhi min rūḥī* (I have breathed My spirit into him). Thereby the inner resources of man, after obedience is shown by him to the teaching of universal religion, enable him to have access to progressively higher levels of knowledge while helping him to have an ever-widening vision. The higher one ascends a mountain, the farther one sees, says Ghazzālī. When one takes his stand firmly upon the straight path, soon, very soon, a time comes when what was accepted on faith is discovered to be a truth that can be realized in principle. Thus, a man who witnesses the awakening of his inner resources also witnesses within himself, by a gift of direct awareness, the true meaning of religious truths that he had earlier accepted on premises of faith. It is this process that is capable of securing the spiritual development of man. Spirituality has no other meaning and it has no other content apart from this link that man has with this process of realizing the truth of the revealed Word of God. The process of accepting on faith the religious truth is an essential prerequisite for securing the awakening of inner powers and hidden resources of man in order to be able to witness the higher truths in terms of experience.

After the Quran came to mankind, the age of new revelations came to an end. What began was the age of realization of the age-old truths received through the last revelation, through the Quran whose outer form and inner meaning, content and sound, laws and "presence" are all basic to Islamic spirituality and have acted over the centuries as the fundamental source of all that constitutes spirituality in its Muḥammadan form and in the world created and molded by the Quranic revelation.

3

Traditional Esoteric Commentaries on the Quran

ABDURRAHMAN HABIL

Nature of the Esoteric Commentaries

WHEN QURANIC COMMENTARIES ARE MENTIONED, they are usually associated in our minds with specialized, voluminous works of *tafsīr*, or exegesis, with their comprehensive interpretative framework covering the whole Quran starting from its first verse to the last. For convenient reasons we tend to ignore the fact that almost every work that deals with the religion of Islam involves, directly or indirectly, a certain understanding of the Quran and certain interpretations of particular Quranic verses. This is simply due to the obvious fact that the whole Islamic religion revolves around this Book. Sometimes even an incidental reference to a verse indicates an implicit, particular interpretation of it. This applies especially to Islamic esotericism. After all is said and done, one comes to the conclusion that the whole Islamic esoteric tradition is essentially an esoteric commentary upon the Quran. Quranic esoteric commentaries, therefore, range from works written for the specific purpose of esoteric commentary to comments scattered throughout all types of Islamic esoteric works. Moreover, the first kind—that is, commentaries in the strict sense—should not be taken as only those that cover the whole of the Quran. They include also commentaries upon one single verse and commentaries upon one sura or group of suras, sometimes very short ones. In addition, many of the commentaries that cover the whole of the Quran are only based on a "reading" of the whole Quran for the purpose of commentary, without giving a systematic, verse-by-verse interpretation of the totality of the sacred Book. Many esoteric interpretations still survive in the form of oral tradition coming down from one generation to another, and many are still in manuscript form and have not as yet been subjected to detailed study. The study of esoteric commentaries is an unexplored, varied, and immense field. In the present survey we shall, of necessity, mention only important authors and works known to contemporary scholarship, works that are far from few in number.

Periods of Esoteric Commentaries

Our task is to discuss the major historical manifestations of the esoteric commentary tradition and to offer descriptions of the process of interpretation and the common features in the works involved. To facilitate the discussion, a historical chronology will be followed whenever possible, but certain discernible phenomena will necessarily be considered independently of the historical context. We observe the following periods: (1) the earliest period, in which all the roots of the tradition are to be found; (2) a period coinciding with the time when the early Sufi commentaries were written; (3) the Twelve-Imam Shīʿite period, when the center of Quranic esoteric commentary shifts to Persia; (4) the period of the great classical Sufi commentaries; and (5) the contemporary period. We must also provide an independent account of the Ismāʿīlī commentary heritage, which parallels the periods of the central tradition. We should bear in mind, however, that this historical division, perhaps somewhat arbitrary, is followed only for reasons of convenience and to emphasize the importance of periods of great achievement. All manifestations of the tradition are deeply rooted in the earliest beginnings, and the later periods possess, historically and essentially, a continuous relation with the earlier periods.

The Language of Symbolism

Esoteric commentaries upon the Quran are essentially united through the principle of symbolism, as understood in its full, traditional sense. Indeed, symbolism serves as the key word to all of them, so that they all may also be called "symbolic commentaries." The process of symbolic, esoteric interpretation is called *ta'wīl,* which technically means symbolic, spiritual hermeneutics.[1] Etymologically, however, it means to take something back to its *awwal,* that is, beginning or origin; hence, to take or to follow symbols back to the origin they symbolize. *Ta'wīl* applies to all kinds of symbols, whether in nature, in the world of man, or in the text of the revelation. The Quran itself applies the word *āyāt,* signs or portents, to its own verses as well as to objects and events within the world of nature and the soul of man.

As far as the Quran is concerned, esoteric commentators have usually referred to four types, or layers, of symbolism and, consequently, of *ta'wīl*. First, the Quran, the Word of God, is as a whole the most direct symbol of the spiritual world. It embodies in the form of its letters and sounds "a concrete active spiritual presence"[2] that can lead directly to realization. The effect of the totality of the Quran on this first level of symbolism does not necessarily coincide with particular interpretations of individual Quranic verses found in esoteric commentaries. The ultimate goal of *ta'wīl* at this stage is realization, through interiorization of the Divine Essence of the Quran, and not the writing of commentaries. To be precise, esoteric commentaries, with regard to this first sense, are not *ta'wīl* but its indirect results. They are attempts to express in the language of man the effects of the spiritual, human-Quranic-Divine experience, as it appears narrowly limited and fragmented when transferred to the plane of writing and interpretation of individual verses. After all, not all who read the Quran as a means of realization have necessarily left us commentaries, and we know that many Muslims who do not know Arabic do feel the Divine Presence in the Quran. However, it is mainly from this symbolic characteristic of the Quran as a whole that the inspirational nature of esoteric commentaries emerges. They are the fruit of an immediate spiritual experience that inspired the apparently isolated interpretations of individual Quranic verses, necessarily confined to the limits of language and ordinary logic and the requirements of expositional writing.

The second type of symbolism found in the Quran is its numerous references to many objective symbols found in the outside natural world and within the human being. Here the Quranic symbolism meets and contains the other two major kinds of symbolism mentioned in the beginning, that is, the macrocosmic symbols in the universe and symbols in the microcosmic world of man. The sky, the sun, the moon, the stars, the sea, the birds, the trees, and the heart of man are only a few of the many symbols found in the Quran. These are symbols in the sense that they lead back to the higher realities they symbolize and participate in them independently of any choice or agreement on our part. They are not conventional or literary symbols, but are so natural and objective that they exist whether we wanted them to exist or not, whether we are aware of them or not. Consequently, esoteric commentaries all abound in references to this type of symbol, and their meanings are elucidated through readings of the Quran as well as through direct meditation upon the outside and inside worlds.

The third layer of Quranic symbolism concerns particular Quranic symbols. When, for instance, the prophet Moses is in the sacred valley of *ṭuwā* and is ordered by God to take off his sandals (XX, 12), esoteric commentators usually interpret this as relating to the body and the soul, or attachment to both this world and the next. However, the sandals here are not a natural symbol, since they are man-made and do not exist in the outside world independent of man's actions. Also among the symbols particular to the Quran are "the pen" (*al-Qalam*) and "the tablet" (*al-Lawḥ*), although they are direct allusions to the masculine and feminine principles in the natural world, which are in turn objective, universal symbols of higher cosmic principles. All the levels of the symbolic structure of the Quran are, therefore, intrinsically tied to one another.

Finally, in addition to the totality of the Book as a symbol and its individual words as universal or particular symbols, the symbolism in the very letters of which the words and the whole Book are composed has been unraveled by the esoteric commentators. Here they focus especially on the *muqaṭṭaʿāt,* or *fawātiḥ al-suwar,* the letters of the Arabic alphabet found detached at the beginning of some Quranic suras. It is especially the *alif* (the Arabic equivalent of the letter *a*) that has seized the attention of esoteric commentators, since it is actually the first letter of the alphabet and the first of the "detached letters" of the Quran and appears at the opening of the second sura (The Cow), the longest sura in the Quran. Traditional esoteric commentators see in it a symbol of the One—the Sufficient by Itself that stands independent from all, yet is the Origin of all. Around the symbolic interpretation of *al-muqaṭṭaʿāt* grew the esoteric, traditional science of *al-jafr,* dealing with the numerical symbolism of all the letters of the alphabet, numbers themselves being considered in their symbolic significance.

The elements of this symbolic reading of the Quran are to be found in the Quran itself. It is, indeed, no exaggeration to say that the principles of esoteric, symbolic commentary upon the Quran are embodied in the Quran. This being so, the Quran is, in a sense, the first and, naturally, the best commentary upon itself. The famous exegetical rule that a part of the Quran explains another (*al-Qurʾān yufassir^u baʿḍuh^u baʿḍ^an*) cannot be limited to the exoterical level but applies to the esoteric as well. Space does not permit an elaboration of this point, and only a few Quranic verses can be mentioned (emphasis added):[3]

> And *in the earth* are portents for those whose faith is sure. And (also) *in yourselves.* Can you then not see? And *in the heaven* is your providence and that which you are promised. (LI, 20–22)

> Glory be to Him who created all *the pairs, of that which the earth grows,* and *of themselves,* and *of that which they know not.* (XXXVI, 36)

> God it is who has created seven *heavens,* and of the *earth the like* thereof. (LVI, 12)

There is not a crawling creature in the earth, nor a bird flying on two wings, but they are species (subdivided) *like* you. (VI, 38)

He has made for you *pairs* from among yourselves, and of the cattle also *pairs.* (XLII, 11)

From these few verses the correspondence that the Quran establishes between the various aspects of nature and between nature as a whole, man, and the higher spiritual realities is quite clear. What is below corresponds to other things below; what is below in general corresponds to "higher" realities "above"; and what is "above" is only a symbol of the interior or the *bāṭin.*

Anyone familiar with the synthetic quality of the Arabic language would know upon a reading of the Quran how it makes full use of this advantage. For example, one Arabic term can denote (apparently) different realities, which conveys the message that sensible realities are but reflections of realities belonging to higher (inner) levels of the hierarchy of being. The reader may compare the usage of terms like *al-samā'* (heaven) in II, 22 and LXVII, 16–17; *al-kitāb* (the book) in LVI, 77–79; X, 94; XI, 17 and V, 48; and *Umm al-kitāb* (the mother [origin] of the book) in XLIII, 4 and III, 7.

The *Sunnah* and Esoteric Commentaries

After the Quran, the second source of esoteric commentary is the *Sunnah,* the *Ḥadīth* of the Prophet, with its two main branches–prophetic tradition (*Ḥadīth nabawī*) and sacred tradition (*Ḥadīth qudsī*). As a matter of fact, just as there are esoteric commentaries on the Quran, there are also esoteric commentaries on the *Ḥadīth,* a point that is usually overlooked. These commentaries find in the *Ḥadīth,* in addition to direct interpretations of Quranic verses, the very principles of symbolism found in the Quran and applied in later Quranic commentaries. Some of the works to which we shall refer later as esoteric commentaries upon the Quran, such as the *Mishkāt al-anwār* of al-Ghazzālī, and the *Fuṣūṣ* of Ibn 'Arabī, are in fact commentaries on both the Quran and the *Ḥadīth.*[4] Similarly, Ibn 'Aṭā' Allāh al-Iskandarī's *Laṭā'if al-minan* contains, as we shall see, Quranic interpretations of Abu 'l-'Abbās al-Mursī and also a section devoted to al-Mursī's interpretations of certain *ḥadīths.*[5] After all, the point of departure for all esoteric Quranic commentaries has always been the famous tradition that "the Quran has an outward and inward dimension," a saying attributed to the Prophet with some variations.

It should, however, be added that for Shī'ite Muslims the concept of

Ḥadīth includes, in addition to the traditions of the Prophet, those transmitted from the Imams, and this leads to the third source of Quranic esoteric commentary in its early period. Among the companions of the Prophet, ʿAbd Allāh ibn ʿAbbās, ʿAbd Allāh ibn Masʿūd, and ʿAlī ibn Abī Ṭālib are the foremost as far as *tafsīr* in general is concerned. As for *ta'wīl*, some interpretations of "the detached letters" are attributed to Ibn ʿAbbās, whose importance has already been mentioned.[6] Indeed, many of the commentary traditions attributed to Ibn ʿAbbās, either on his own authority or connected to the Prophet, turn out, upon careful reading, to be highly symbolic.[7] If we consider the fact that a great number of these sayings are included in the exoteric commentaries themselves, especially those concerned with the *tafsīr bi'l-ma'thūr* (interpretation according to traditions), we realize how deeply esotericism penetrates the whole commentary tradition. To Ibn Masʿūd also is often attributed—sometimes on his own authority and sometimes as transmitted from the Prophet—the previously mentioned tradition stating that the Quran has both outward and inward aspects, a tradition whose importance in the history of esoteric commentaries could not be rivaled.[8]

The Transmission of the Science of Commentary and Its Subsequent History

Ibn ʿAbbās is reported to have said: "What I took from the interpretation of the Quran is from ʿAlī ibn Abī Ṭālib," and Ibn Masʿūd states that "ʿAlī ibn Abī Ṭālib has from [the Quran] both the outward and the inward."[9] Two of the three major figures thereby recognize the third as the most knowledgeable in exegesis in general and esoteric hermeneutics in particular. In fact, both the interpretations of "the detached letters" attributed to Ibn ʿAbbās and the outward-inward tradition attributed to Ibn Masʿūd are simultaneously attributed to ʿAlī.[10] Several other sayings by him also reveal the esoteric nature of the Quran and his own esoteric understanding of it.[11]

One of the important chains of transmission from ʿAlī, as far as commentary is concerned, comes down through his son al-Ḥusayn to the latter's son, ʿAlī Zayn al-ʿĀbidīn.[12] Zayn al-ʿĀbidīn's son, Muḥammad al-Bāqir, the fifth Imam, is the transmitter of commentary from his father as well as a prominent spiritual commentator in his own right. His commentary and that of his son, Jaʿfar al-Ṣādiq, the sixth Imam, were collected between the late third/ninth century and the early fourth/tenth century in a book that still survives to the present day as one of the most important Twelve-Imam Shīʿite commentaries.[13] But it was al-Ṣādiq who played the most important role in the whole history of esoteric commentaries upon the Quran in both its Shīʿite and Sufi facets. His influence on later Shīʿite *tafsīrs* and on all aspects of the religious life in Shīʿism needs no demonstration. In regard to Sufism, suffice it here to point out that a commentary of al-Ṣādiq was known to the Sufis at least as early as the time of Dhu'l-Nūn al-Miṣrī (ca. 180/796–245/860), who made an edition of it.[14] Dhu'l-Nūn, in his turn, is considered the "spiritual forebear" of Sahl al-Tustarī (d. 283/896), the author of the oldest continuous Sufi commentary on the Quran.[15] Despite variations in content, the absence in al-Tustarī's work of references to al-Ṣādiq,[16] and the usual differences between Sunnite and Shīʿite works, it has been pointed out that both *tafsīrs* are connected in their principles and methods of commentary.[17]

A second important channel through which al-Ṣādiq's commentary found its way early into Sufi commentaries is another Sufi recension of it made by Ibn ʿAṭā' (al-Baghdādī) (d. 309/921), who included it in a commentary of his own, which was later incorporated into the *Ḥaqā'iq al-tafsīr* (*The Realities of Quranic Interpretation*) of al-Sulamī (d. 412/1021).[18] This work is the second oldest Sufi compilation of *tafsīr* after al-Tustarī's. The authenticity of al-Ṣādiq's *tafsīr* as it appears in Ibn ʿAṭā's edition incorporated by al-Sulamī, or at least the fact that it came from an early Shīʿite source, is confirmed by the existence of another Shīʿite compilation of it made by Muḥammad ibn Ibrāhīm al-Nuʿmānī (d. 328/940). Despite the (understandable) absence, in Ibn ʿAṭā's edition, of the social and political Shīʿite outlook found in that of al-Nuʿmānī and also important variations in regard to content—perhaps only indicating different chains of transmission—comparison of the two editions has indicated that "we are in the presence of one work, having the same aspiration, same style, and same spiritual content," not to mention "sentences which are literally the same."[19] In fact, the influence of al-Ṣādiq's commentary on the Sufis was not limited to exegetical principles, methods, and content; this commentary went beyond the field of *tafsīr* proper in its elaboration of the esoteric science of *al-jafr*, developed at the hands of al-Ṣādiq. This commentary influenced the very content and vocabulary of Sufi doctrine and perhaps even the method of Sufi experience itself.[20] One may safely conclude, however, that the earliest major sources of esoteric commentary upon the Quran are the Sacred Book itself and the tradition of the Prophet and the companions, especially ʿAlī, together with the latter's descendants.[21]

The second period of esoteric commentary upon the Quran may be in its turn divided into three minor periods. The first starts in the third/ninth century with the appearance of the earliest Sufi commentators. We have already seen that the *tafsīr* of al-Tustarī (d. 283/896) is the oldest continuous Sufi commentary upon the Quran in the sense that it was the first Sufi compilation with the aim of presenting orderly interpretations of Quranic (although selected) verses following the traditional division of the Quran into consecutive suras and verses. A contemporary of al-Tustarī is al-Ḥakīm al-Tirmidhī (d. 285/898), who, although he does not appear to be a commentator in the strict sense like al-Tustarī, made a great contribution to the esoteric commentary tradition through his linguistic study of Quranic terms supported by an analysis of spiritual experience. By use of the psychological analysis of the different actions denoted by different technical terms, he established the impossibility of "synonymy" (*al-tarāduf*, or *al-naẓā'ir*) in Arabic and the Quran. If two words or more are said to have the same meaning, al-Tirmidhī draws the actions corresponding to each word, finds them psychologically different, and thus finds each word to be different from the other in its psychological nuances. Since two words cannot have the same meaning, it follows in a subtle manner that each word has different shades of meaning, or different aspects (*wujūh*), related to each other through a basic sense from which they originally derive. These senses are the spiritual states (*aḥwāl*) issuing from a basic action and emanating in a hierarchical order from unity to multiplicity.[22] The tremendous implications of this principle for the concept of the plurality of meanings of the Quranic word, upon which all esoteric commentaries are based, need no further demonstration.

Also living in the late third/ninth century and early fourth/tenth century were three other Sufi figures who were commentators as well. These are the famous al-Junayd (d. 298/910), al-Ḥallāj (d. 309/922) and Ibn 'Aṭā' (d. 309/921). Their interpretations have reached us in the *Ḥaqā'iq al-tafsīr* of Abū 'Abd al-Raḥmān al-Sulamī (d. 412/1021), whose importance in this respect can hardly be overrated. While al-Tustarī's commentary is not purely esoteric, since it includes exoteric interpretations as well, the *Ḥaqā'iq* of al-Sulamī is devoted exclusively to esoteric Quranic interpretations. It is, moreover, a collection selected from the sayings of almost one hundred authorities, a number that reveals the expansion that the tradition had reached by that time as well as its deep-rootedness in early Islamic times. Among those who are quoted by al-Sulamī, in addition to al-Ṣādiq, Dhu'l-Nūn, al-Tustarī, and the three figures just mentioned, are al-Ḥasan al-Baṣrī (d. 110/728), Abū Sa'īd al-Kharrāz (d. 286/899), Abū Bakr al-Wāsiṭī (d. 320/910) and Abū Bakr al-Shiblī (d. 334/945).[23] Although this very valuable work remains unpublished, its items related to al-Ṣādiq have been edited and those related to al-Ḥallāj have been reproduced in available publications.[24]

Just as al-Sulamī intended, his compilation of exclusively esoteric Quranic interpretations marked the independence of esoteric commentaries from the general science of exegesis. From then on, continuous and often voluminous esoteric commentaries were incessantly written, up to the present day. Moreover, although many esoteric commentators were to continue, like al-Tustarī, to deal more or less with exoteric interpretations in their commentaries, the commentaries would always have their own character and would demand to be treated as distinct from exoteric commentaries proper.

A second or middle era within the stage of great Sufi commentaries was inaugurated by the appearance of *Laṭā'if al-ishārāt* (*The Subtle Quranic Allusions*) (finished 434 A.H.) of Abu'l-Qāsim al-Qushayrī (d. 465/1072), which is, after al-Tustarī's and al-Sulamī's, the third oldest work among the existent continuous Sufi commentaries.[25] It is interesting to add that al-Qushayrī is also credited with another great exoteric commentary devoted to linguistic, legal, and historical matters, and recognized as "one of the best" in its own class.[26] The existence of this exoteric work along with its esoteric counterpart by the same author emphasizes the distinctness of each type of commentary. It also stands as clear proof that a true esoteric commentator is also a master of outward exegesis.

The author of the first Persian Sufi commentary upon the Quran, Khwājah 'Abd Allāh al-Anṣārī of Herat (d. 481/1089), was a contemporary of al-Qushayrī. A Ḥanbalite Sufi,[27] he stands as an even clearer proof that genuine esoteric commentary has never meant disrespect to the letter of the Quran but rather the real respect due it. Al-Anṣārī's commentary, however, stopped at the sixty-seventh verse of the thirty-eighth sura and reached us, completed and greatly amplified, only in the *Kashf al-asrār* (*The Uncovering of the Secrets*), the voluminous Persian commentary by his disciple Rashīd al-Dīn Maybudī (d. 520/1126).[28] This second era in the stage of great Sufi commentaries is dominated by two great names. Abū Ḥāmid al-Ghazzālī (d. 505/1111) wrote an immense, forty-volume commentary called *Yāqūt al-ta'wīl* (*The Ruby of Spiritual Hermeneutics*), which seems to have been lost.[29] However, we still have the *Mishkāt al-anwār* (*The Niche of Lights*), alluded to above,[30] in which al-Ghazzālī gives interpretations of two Quranic verses, the Verse of Light (XXIV, 35) and the Verse of Darkness (XXIV, 40), together with the Seventy Thousand Veils *ḥadīth*. We still have also the famous *Iḥyā' 'ulūm al-dīn* (*The Revival of Religious Sciences*), which contains many interpretations of individual verses along with a chapter on interpretation (and recitation) of the Quran,[31] in which the author has summed up the general theory of esoteric commentary as a necessary complement of exoteric interpretations. The second great name is Rūzbihān Baqlī (d. 606/1209), author of *ʿArā'is al-bayān* (*The Brides of Elucidation*).[32] This gnostic commentary, perhaps preceded in its crystallized gnostic outlook only partly by the work of Maybudī, stands at the end of the era that had started with al-Qushayrī and at the beginning of the era of the purely gnostic Sufi commentaries of the seventh and eighth centuries. In addition to Baqlī's own interpretations, this commentary contains many quotations from previous works, especially al-Sulamī's and al-Qushayrī's: it is the fruit of the whole tradition preceding it and the forebear of a chain of purely gnostic commentaries.

The time extending from the late sixth/twelfth century to the first half of the eighth/fourteenth century is marked by the appearance and crystallization of two eminent schools of Sufism, which are, at the same time, two schools of esoteric commentary. These are the Central Asian school of Najm al-Dīn Kubrā and the school of the Andalusian Sufi Ibn ʿArabī. Kubrā (d. 618/1221) left his commentary, *ʿAyn al-ḥayāh* (*The Fountainhead of Life*), unfinished, and it did not go beyond the fifth sura of the Quran. His disciple Najm al-Dīn Rāzī (d. 654/1256) wanted to complete it, but in the same way that Maybudī did for al-Anṣārī's commentary, that is, by embodying it in a new one, entitled *Baḥr al-ḥaqā'iq* (*The Ocean of Realities*), beginning again from the first sura. But Rāzī was prevented by death from going beyond the eighteenth verse of the fifty-first sura. A third member of the school, ʿAlā' al-Dawlah Simnānī (d. 736/1336) completed Rāzī's work, this time to the end. He added an introduction and a new interpretation of his own of the first sura; he started from the fifty-second sura without finishing Rāzī's interpretation of the fifty-first.[33] It is the work of the third, Simnānī, that represents the peak in this school's hermeneutics. Although this work, like its two predecessors, remains unpublished, it is described to us as "interiorization of the sense of the Quranic Revelation to its ultimate esoteric depths."[34]

Many exegetical works of Ibn ʿArabī (d. 638/1240), including a monumental commentary, have not yet been published.[35] However, esoteric interpretations of the Quran penetrate the whole work of Ibn ʿArabī, especially the *Fuṣūṣ al-ḥikam,* alluded to before, which is an indirect commentary on the Quran and the *Ḥadīth.* A close disciple and stepson of Ibn ʿArabī, Ṣadr al-Dīn al-Qūnawī (d. 673/1274), also devoted a whole book to the interpretation of the first, seven-verse sura of the Quran.[36] Another outstanding member and commentator of this school was ʿAbd al-Razzāq al-Kāshānī (d. 730/1330), whose career as a commentator has been eclipsed by the publication, at least three times, of his own commentary under the name of his spiritual forebear, Ibn 'Arabī.[37] The work of al-Kāshānī, a Shī'ite Sufi, is one of the several points where the Shī'ite and Sufi commentary traditions meet each other. It is also an indication that by this time the center of esoteric, gnostic commentary had begun to shift to the Shī'ite world.

Before we leave the Sufi scene for a while, there are still two developments that deserve to be mentioned. Jalāl al-Dīn Rūmī (d. 672/1273) was a friend and close associate of Ṣadr al-Dīn al-Qūnawī and was thus related to the school of Ibn 'Arabī. However, Rūmī remains an independent gnostic of outstanding quality and a unique phenomenon in the whole tradition of esoteric commentaries. His monumental poetical work, the *Mathnawī*,[38] is considered to be in essence "a vast esoteric commentary upon the Quran" in Persian verse.[39] This is confirmed by statements of Rūmī himself, by what we know of his deep knowledge of the Quranic sciences and the commentaries existing in his time, and by the fact that some six thousand verses of the *Mathnawī*—and the *Dīwān*, another work of Rūmī—were found to be "practically direct translations of Quranic verses into Persian poetry."[40] It remains to be pointed out that the Shādhilī order, a Sufi order that flourished in the seventh/thirteenth century, had also made a contribution to the commentary tradition. A very few oral Quranic interpretations of Abu'l-Ḥasan al-Shādhilī, the founder of the order (d. 657/1258), and more interpretations of his successor, Abu'l-'Abbās al-Mursī (d. 686/1287), were preserved by the third Shādhilī shaykh, Ibn 'Aṭā' Allāh al-Iskandarī (d. 709/1309).[41] Judged by their quality, these few, concise interpretations represent yet another major facet of Sufi Quranic commentary in its golden period.

Thus far we have seen esoteric commentaries in their early, formative period and in their second period, marked by the early classical Sufi commentaries. We turn now to a great Shī'ite commentary movement, which is, however, closely connected to the preceding two. Our historical division of the subject is very relative, and the very aspect now under discussion, although crystallized after the middle of the eighth/fourteenth century, the time of the last great Sufi commentaries of al-Kāshānī and Simnānī, finds its roots in a very early stage, that of the Imams and their hermeneutical teachings. In addition to finding its direct roots in the Imams, this Shī'ite movement also benefited from previous Sufi commentaries and from the works of two other figures of the fifth/eleventh and sixth/twelfth centuries. They are Abū 'Alī ibn Sīnā (d. 428/1037) and Shihāb al-Dīn Yaḥyā al-Suhrawardī (d. 587/1191), who precede in time most of the personalities already mentioned and must therefore be discussed before going into Shī'ite commentaries.

The Philosophers and Their Commentaries

The importance of Ibn Sīnā and Suhrawardī in this respect is due to two facts. In general, the philosophy of Ibn Sīnā as interpreted by Suhrawardī, together with the gnostic doctrines of Ibn ʿArabī, was synthesized with Shīʿite theology in the very period of Shīʿite commentaries that is under discussion. This achievement in its turn had its impact upon contemporary Shīʿite commentaries. But, in particular, both Ibn Sīnā and Suhrawardī dealt directly with Quranic interpretation, and it was particularly this tradition of combining philosophy with Quranic interpretation that was carried on in the Shīʿite commentaries of this period.

The fact that there were Islamic philosophers who wrote commentaries upon the Quran shows the importance of the Quran and especially its esoteric understanding as a source of inspiration for Islamic philosophy.[42] It is to this point that the often-repeated question of the relationship between faith and reason in Islamic philosophy is directly connected.[43] Moreover, beyond the faith-and-reason question, the esoteric tendency in Islamic philosophy is best revealed by a study of the Quranic esoteric commentaries written by Islamic philosophers, who in this respect should rather be called "theosophers," or *ḥukamāʾ*. Such commentaries, however, should be judged by their quality and by the significance of their very existence, for they are not huge volumes. This is due to the particular specialty of the authors and to the fact that the process was slow in the beginning and reached its peak only after a few centuries, as we shall later see.

Interpretations of the Quran are found in the works of Islamic philosophers at least as early as the late third/ninth century and the first half of the fourth/tenth century, the time of Abū Naṣr al-Fārābī (d. 339/950), who was a contemporary of al-Tustarī.[44] Ibn Sīnā, who lived in the fourth/tenth and fifth/eleventh centuries, also left us commentaries on at least the short, but highly significant, last three Quranic suras, the celebrated Verse of Light, and a few other Quranic verses.[45] But perhaps the most significant of his writings in this domain is the *Nayrūziyyah* epistle, "on the meaning of the letters of the alphabet at the beginning of some Quranic suras."[46] This last work is based heavily on the tradition of esoteric commentaries upon the Quran in its symbolic treatment of the "detached letters," cultivated a long time before Ibn Sīnā.[47] After Ibn Sīnā we have another attempt to combine philosophy with Quranic interpretation by Shaykh al-ishrāq al-Suhrawardī, more strictly "a theosopher" (*ḥakīm*) than a philosopher in the ordinary sense. He went a step further by seeking support in the Quran for his ideas, quoting Quranic verses in the context of his theosophical discussions.[48] In addition to their significance in themselves, these references to Quranic verses obviously involved hermeneutic interpretations of the Sacred Text.

The theosophy of Suhrawardī and his effort to remove the barriers between the two Islamic traditions of philosophy and Quranic commentary were to find an echo in Shī'ite Persia. The adoption by Shī'ism of his theosophy of "Illumination" and his interpretations of the "esoteric" Ibn Sīnā, together with the Sufi gnostic doctrines of Ibn 'Arabī, were to result in a great intellectual movement represented by a group of *ḥukamā'*, or sages, who were at the same time Quranic commentators.[49]

Shī'ite Commentaries

The historical and doctrinal importance of the esoteric interpretation of the Quran is further emphasized by the fact that the insistence upon the necessity of this interpretation and the question of the authority to which it should be entrusted are two of the main points by which Shī'ism has distinguished itself from Sunni Islam.[50] This is especially the case in the two major branches of Twelve-Imam Shī'ism and Ismā'īlism, which concern us here. The necessity of the existence of an esoteric meaning in the Quran is an idea held by both Shī'ism and Sufism, which exists mostly in the Sunni world. In the final analysis, however, Sufism transcends the Sunni–Shī'ite dichotomy. It is the second point, that is, the necessity of the presence of legitimate authority, which further characterizes Shī'ism and its view of Quranic exegesis.

The interpretation of the Quran for the Shī'ites is essentially the exclusive function of the Imams. They are the successors of the Prophet, to whom the Noble Book was revealed and its full understanding given. This does not mean, however, that a qualified Shī'ite scholar cannot contribute to the field of commentary. Anyone who is qualified, most of all spiritually, may do so. But being "spiritually qualified" is, in fact, another way of saying that the interpreter has gained "inner contact" with the Imams, represented, in the case of Twelve-Imam Shī'ism, by the twelfth and last Imam, the Mahdī.[51] The importance of the *bāṭin* (inward) of the Quran, on the one hand, and the Imams as its interpreters in their other cosmic, initiatic, and social functions, on the other, have bestowed upon Shī'ism an inherent esoteric tone, even in its apparently exoteric dimensions.[52] This trait applies in particular to the Shī'ite exoteric commentaries upon the Quran. A person who reads the apparently exoteric commentaries of al-Ṭūsī and al-Tabarsī, for example, has to grasp their underlying esoteric nature by the very fact of their being Shī'ite and by their heavy reliance upon the sayings of the Imams.[53]

To come back to the Shī'ite theosophers-commentators in the period starting in the eighth/fourteenth century, the first of these figures who should be mentioned is Ḥaydar Āmulī (d. after 794/1392). He wrote a gnostic commentary, in seven large volumes, which is still in manuscript. In it he gave not only verse-by-verse interpretations but also a general theory of the principles and rules of spiritual hermeneutics.[54] A generation later Ṣā'in al-Dīn 'Alī Iṣfahānī (d. 830/1427) composed an epistle, still unpublished, in which he focused on one short Quranic verse, "The hour drew nigh and the moon was rent in twain" (LIV, 1), going deeply in his interiorization of the Quran.[55] But it was at the hands of Ṣadr al-Dīn Shīrāzī (d. 1050/1640), also known as Mullā Ṣadrā, that the synthesis between the three Islamic intellectual currents of Sufi gnosis, philosophy, or theosophy, and Shī'ite theology was ultimately achieved, and was directly reflected in the field of esoteric commentary on the Quran. In the same way that Rūmī was a unique phenomenon among Islamic poets, Mullā Ṣadrā of Shiraz is considered to hold "a unique distinction among Islamic philosophers."[56] The Quran was persistently present in the minds and souls of these two when they composed works of poetry or philosophy. In the case of Mullā Ṣadrā, the influence of the Quran did not stop with direct quotations from the Sacred Text throughout the whole of his writings. It extended to major contributions to the field of direct commentary and made him "a major Quranic commentator in his own right, ranking with the foremost commentators in Islamic history."[57] Mullā Ṣadrā is considered to be "perhaps the greatest Islamic philosopher"; at the same time, "without the direct influence of the Quran his writings would not be conceivable."[58] This is further evidence of the importance of the Quran and its understanding in the intellectual history of Islam.

A contemporary of Mullā Ṣadrā, Sayyid Aḥmad 'Alawī, also wrote in Persian a commentary on different Quranic chapters, which is considered to be one of the outstanding gnostic, theosophical commentaries in the Shī'ite world.[59] Unfortunately it too remains unpublished. Mullā Muḥsin Fayḍ al-Kāshānī (d. ca. 1090/1680), a disciple and stepson of Mullā Ṣadrā, likewise wrote a commentary *bi'l-ma'thūr* (according to traditions), which is mainly based on traditions attributed to the Imams.[60] The traditions have continued in the Twelve-Imam Shī'ite world up to the present time. Before going any further into the modern period, it is necessary to consider briefly another Shī'ite tradition, which had its historical roots in a far earlier era.

We have seen that the Shī'ite view of *tafsīr* is based on the belief in the existence of an interior meaning in the Quran and the Imams as the interpreters of this meaning. When it comes to Ismāʿīlism, there is to be found an even greater emphasis on both principles. It is precisely because of the heavy emphasis on the inward aspect (*bāṭin*) of the Quran—as opposed to its *ẓāhir*, or exoteric, meaning—that the Ismāʿīlīs have also been referred to as the Bāṭiniyyah. This fact in itself is another indication of the important role that interpretation of the Quran has played in Islamic history.

In Ismāʿīlism the Imams are considered to be the exclusive authority on esoteric interpretation (*ta'wīl*), but not exactly in the same sense as in Twelve-Imam Shīʿism. In Ismāʿīlism the Imam is *ṣāḥib al-ta'wīl* (its owner, author, or authority), as compared with the *nāṭiq* (speaker) or *ṣāḥib al-tanzīl* (upon whom the Revelation descended), whose function is to communicate the Revelation to the public and to divulge its exoteric meaning or *tafsīr*. In any case, there are very few Ismāʿīlī commentaries known to us, and none of them contains a complete, or even a continuous, exposition of the inner meaning of the Quran from beginning to end—as one may expect from a movement that is esoteric by definition and has emphasized the esoteric aspect of the Quran so much. We even know that up to the present time the Ismāʿīlīs' favorite commentary has been the one attributed to Ibn ʿArabī, whom they generally consider to have been an Ismāʿīlī.[61] This lack of comprehensive esoteric commentaries on the part of Ismāʿīlīs may be taken by their critics as a refutation of their claim that they insist on an esoteric sense pervading every word of the Quran.

The nature of the movement itself and the historical circumstances surrounding it may, however, account, to a large extent, for the loss or unavailability of Ismāʿīlī commentaries. Moreover, the existence of only partial esoteric commentaries is perhaps in itself an indication that too much emphasis on the esoteric is not a characteristic of every Ismāʿīlī school, with the exception of the movement of Alamut.

At any rate, in this obscure area in the history of Quranic commentary the earliest works having to do with Quranic interpretations that are more or less connected to Ismāʿīlism are *The Epistles of the Ikhwān al-Ṣafā'*, or the Brethren of Purity, which were written around the second half of the fourth/tenth century.[62] Although these encyclopedic epistles do not constitute a commentary in the strict sense, Quranic references and interpretations permeate all of them in the manner characteristic of all Islamic esoteric works. Among the connections found between the Ikhwān and Ismāʿīlism is, precisely, the emphasis of both on the essential notion of *ta'wīl*, cosmic and Quranic alike.[63] From around the same period as these *Epistles* comes a commentary of definitely Ismāʿīlī nature by al-Qāḍī al-Nuʿmān ibn Ḥayyūn al-Maghribī (d. 363/974), who was an eminent *dāʿī* (missionary) as well as a supreme judge in Fāṭimid Egypt. This book on the foundations of spiritual hermeneutics, described by its modern editor as the only work among the Ismā'īlī manuscripts that deals specifically with the Ismā'īlī hermeneutical theory, is not, however, a systematic commentary.[64] It rather focuses on the six *nāṭiqs,* or great prophets, mentioned in the Quran (beginning with Adam), alongside their corresponding Imams and *lawāḥiq* (later followers). Selected Quranic verses are divided into groups, each clustering around one cycle of a *nāṭiq.* This scheme is to be found in the *Fuṣūṣ* of Ibn 'Arabī, an indirect Quranic commentary written more than two centuries later. The other work of continuous commentary attributed to him is highly reputed among the Ismā'īlīs, and, in fact, Ibn 'Arabī is recognized by many members of this movement as one of them. Be that as it may, it should be added that al-Qāḍī al-Nu'mān, in his capacity as judge and jurist, is credited also with another work dealing with the law (the *Sharī'ah*) and the foundations of Islam, the exoteric counterpart of his esoteric commentary.[65] This fact is in itself significant and not unrelated to our previous discussion concerning the role of esoteric exegesis in Ismā'īlism.

Let us return to the Twelve-Imam theosophical commentaries. They have continued uninterrupted to the present day. One of the disciples of Muḥsin Fayḍ al-Kāshānī, Abu'l-Ḥasan Sharīf 'Āmilī Iṣfahānī (d. 1138/1726), started a monumental commentary project with the aim of pointing out the esoteric sense of every Quranic verse with reference to the traditions of the Imams related to each verse. However, what he completed was a large volume of introductions, which is a significant achievement in itself, setting forth the general principles and the rules of Shī'ite hermeneutical methods.[66] During the last and present centuries, one continues to find monumental commentaries, such as those of Sulṭān 'Alī Shāh (d. ca. 1318/1900) and Sayyid Muḥammad Ḥusayn Ṭabāṭabā'ī (1321/1903–1402/1982).[67]

Later Sufi Commentaries

Sufi commentaries in their turn have never ceased to appear. To go back to the seventh/thirteenth century, it is necessary to mention the other Suhrawardī, Abū Ḥafṣ 'Umar (d. 632/1234), among important Sufi commentators.[68] Through the next centuries one encounters the names of Niẓām al-Dīn Nayshābūrī (d. 728/1328),[69] 'Abd al-Raḥmān Jāmī (d. 892/1492),[70] Kamāl al-Dīn Kāshifī (d. 910/1504–5),[71] 'Abd al-Ḥaqq al-Dihlawī (d. 1052/1642),[72] Ismā'īl Ḥaqqī (d. 1127/1715), and Shihāb al-Dīn al-Alūsī (d. 1270–1854).[73] The tradition has continued up to the present century with the *Tafsīr al-Qur'ān* and commentaries upon chapters LIII and CIII of

Shaykh Aḥmad al-ʿAlawī (d. 1352/1934) and, more recently, the *Book of Certainty* by Abu Bakr Siraj Ed-Din.[74]

The Methods and Goals of Esoteric Exegesis

Now that we have analyzed briefly esoteric commentaries on the Quran in their long history, it is perhaps appropriate to consider and reemphasize a few essential points related to their method. In any discussion of this subject, one cannot avoid the well-known question of the exact attitude of esoteric commentaries toward the literal, apparent aspect of the Quran. This question is often raised without true knowledge of the commentaries in question and is indeed irrelevant as far as the true nature of the Quran is concerned. It is particularly reminiscent of the so-called problem of the creation of the Quran, another celebrated question in the history of Islamic thought. Both questions are simply irrelevant to the true nature of the Quran, since they both betray unawareness of the fundamental principle of the hierarchy of reality that is so evident in the Quran itself.[75] However, the real attitude of esoteric commentaries toward the external meaning of the Text becomes clear even from a look at the general plan of many of these commentaries, without going into their content.

Many of the commentaries we have already mentioned contain exoteric, that is, linguistic, historical, moral, and legal interpretations side by side with esoteric ones. This scheme appears as early as the commentary of al-Tustarī, the first known continuous Sufi commentary on the Quran, and as late as the commentary of al-Alūsī in the thirteenth/nineteenth century, as well as between the two in such commentaries as those of Maybudī, Rāzī, Nayshābūrī, and Ḥaqqī. To call these commentaries esoteric is correct with regard to the general tendency of their authors and one aspect of their contents, but with regard to other aspects, these commentaries may be called exoteric. As a matter of fact, some commentators give almost equal space to both kinds of interpretation, as is the case with Nayshābūrī, Ḥaqqī, and al-Alūsī. But even those who exclusively deal with the esoteric side do, of course, recognize the exoteric and many of them emphasize this point in their introductions.

We have also seen the case of the Ḥanbalite Anṣārī, who, we may add here, was persecuted because of his Ḥanbalism, to be sure, not because of his Sufism, and who would therefore be the last person to be suspected of belittling the external meaning and the letter of the Quran. We have seen likewise that al-Qushayrī dealt with esoteric interpretations proper in his

Laṭā'if al-ishārāt, but only after having written an exoteric commentary that is counted among the best by exoteric authorities. Al-Sulamī, who was the first compiler of purely esoteric interpretations, declared in his introduction that he dealt with only the esoteric meaning because exoteric commentaries were already abundantly available.

Another noticeable feature of many esoteric commentaries, which is closely related to the question of their relationship to the external meaning of the text, is that they do not cover all the Quranic verses. Many of the commentaries, starting again from al-Tustarī's, contain only interpretations of selected verses, and it is in this sense that they are called "continuous," not complete or comprehensive. Other examples are the work of al-Sulamī himself and the purely gnostic commentaries of Baqlī and Kāshānī. It may be generally said that the more esoteric a commentary, the fewer Quranic verses it covers. Besides, we have already seen commentaries limited to a few verses and a few suras. Although the tradition that the Quran has both outward and inward aspects has variations that seem to emphasize that "every verse" or "every letter" possesses both aspects, in practice they are understood in their general sense, for no single commentator is expected to reveal the inward meaning of every verse, although some of them have attempted to do so. This might also have to do with the theory of "the variance in the excellence of the Quranic verses" expounded by Abū Ḥāmid al-Ghazzālī.[76] At any rate, Kāshānī states clearly that there are Quranic verses that are not susceptible of *ta'wīl* and should be thus understood only in their literal sense. These are especially the verses that have to do with legal matters. Even when he sometimes "comments" on some of them, he calls this *taṭbīq,* reference to parallels, or correspondents, in the sense of reminding the reader of the general laws of correspondence between the cosmos, man, and the Quran, and not in the sense of introducing something in addition to the external meaning.[77]

Very often the symbolic meaning or meanings of a verse turn out upon careful consideration to be only a development whose roots are contained within the literal meaning itself, so that it becomes difficult to separate the one from the other. We shall select two Quranic verses and see how they are interpreted by the commentators and how their meaning unfolds within the Quran itself. The two verses are the following:

> He (God) has let loose the two seas; they meet one another. Between them is a barrier (*barzakh*), so they encroach not (one upon the other). (LV, 19–20)

The symbolic meaning usually given to "the two seas" by the commentators is "the spirit and the body" or "the next world and this world."[78] Although no type of analysis can substitute for the *dhawq,* or intellectual intuition of the commentators, we shall attempt to follow the meaning of "the two seas" as it develops in the light of other verses and see how the plurality of meaning in the Quran reflects the universal principle of the hierarchy of reality. We shall, to a certain extent, depend upon Quranic allusions (*ishārāt*), which the commentators very often find in the Quran, especially when a certain word is repeated in different verses that are apparently different in context. First, the immediate, literal meaning of "the two seas" is given by the Quran itself in another verse. It is the river with its sweet (*furāt*) water and the ordinary sea with its salty, bitter (*ujāj*) water (XXXV, 12). But another contrast to the salty sea is the rain, described also as *furāt* (LXXVII, 27) and opposed to *ujāj* or bitter water (LVI, 70). The sky, from which the rain descends, has in its turn its stars called *jawārī* (running, or going straight) (LXXXI, 16). Ships in the sea are called *jawārī* (XLII, 32), and both the sun and ships are described as *tajrī* (running) (XXXVI, 38 and II, 164). The *fulk*, the Quranic name of ships, is also etymologically connected to *falak*, the orbit of celestial bodies, where the sun and the moon follow, literally "swimming" (*yasbaḥūn*), as if they were swimming in a sea (XXI, 33). Yet both "the sky" and "heaven" are designated in the Quran by a single word, *al-samā'* (II, 22, LXVII, 16–17). Moreover, the Quran speaks of *majma' al-baḥrayn*, the meeting place of "the two seas," in the famous story of Moses and al-Khiḍr, where this "meeting place" is described as a rock (*ṣakhrah*) (XVIII, 63), which suggests that the barrier between "the two seas" (the *barzakh*) is also an immense vertical one and not only the kind of a barrier that might exist between a river and a sea. This rock is, moreover, called *majma' baynihimā* (XVIII, 61), the meeting place between the two seas, and this Arabic phrase seems indeed to be the only linguistic clue in the whole Quran to *al-Samāwāt wa'l-arḍ wa mā baynahumā*, heaven and earth and what is between them, another often-repeated phrase (e.g., V, 17, 18). However, what we need to realize here is that "the two seas" are, on a fourth level of meaning, heaven and earth or, in other words, the spiritual and the material worlds. A fifth level is further revealed by the other use of the *barzakh* in an eschatological sense, where it stands behind the dead until they are resurrected (XXIII, 100). The first, sweet "sea" is thus the river, the rain, the sky, heaven or the world of the Spirit, and the hereafter. The second, salty "sea" is the sea in the ordinary sense, the earth, the material, bodily world, and this world as opposed to the next. The meaning gradually develops from "below" to "above" to the "inside" of the universe and man as well as from "now" to "later," going through a phenomenon of nature to the four major dimensions of being and of all esoteric doctrines, namely, cosmology, metaphysics, psychology, and eschatology.[79]

We should, however, never forget that the ultimate goal of the spiritual commentators is not just to disclose for their readers the meaning, or meanings, of this or that Quranic verse. Mention was made at the beginning of the Divine Presence inherently embodied in the Book of God, or what has been called its "theurgic power,"[80] with its definite effect on its reciters and hearers, and, with all the more reasons, its spiritual commentators, who more than anyone else partake of its Divine Essence. Being thoroughly prepared by the knowledge of Quranic sciences and previous commentaries, by access to the oral spiritual tradition,[81] and—last but not least—by self-purification, the final aim of the spiritual commentators is "to know" and "to be," that is, to know what the Quran ultimately means as well as to be transmuted by its Divine Power to attain spiritual perfection. In the spiritual hermeneutical process there has been no separation whatsoever between knowing and being, between sacred knowledge and spiritual perfection; "to know has meant ultimately to be transformed by the very process of knowing."[82] Here the effect becomes a cause, and the cause an effect, as knowledge of the Book becomes the direct source of spiritual perfection, and spiritual perfection directly leads to more knowledge. Once the commentators have chosen to commit the fruits of their spiritual hermeneutical experience to writing, it becomes the responsibility of the readers of their commentaries to be constantly aware of their inspirational origin and to attempt to relive the experience of their authors. The real wish of the commentators is to guide the reader, not to entertain him, by disclosing the secret meaning of this or that passage. "God's first wish is to save, not to instruct, and His concern is with wisdom and immortality, not with external knowledge, still less with satisfying human curiosity."[83] After the Books of God this applies to nothing other than their spiritual interpretations.

If one looks for the first and most important source of Islamic spirituality, it is to be found nowhere if not in the spiritual understanding of the Quran. The three dimensions of Islamic spiritual life, that is, the doctrine, the (spiritual) virtues, and the spiritual practices, are all in fact traced back to it.[84] To say that the Quran is the supreme source of Islamic spirituality is only another way of saying that its spiritual comprehension is exactly this source. Without the inspired commentaries upon the Quran, its esoteric reality and far-reaching spiritual potentialities for both spiritual life and knowledge can never be fully perceived. Moreover, it is in the truthfulness of the spiritual understanding of the Quran that the legitimacy of the spiritual life in Islam should be first sought. For it is from the Book that every legitimate aspect, exoteric or esoteric, in Islam derives its first source, and the *Sunnah* of the Prophet, which is the second along the hierarchy of the origins of Islamic life, is essentially a vast commentary upon the Quran.[85]

It is in the same sense that the nature of the Prophet, the ever-living model of Islamic life, was said to have been the nature of the Quran (*kāna khuluquhu al-Qur'ān*).[86]

Notes

1. *Ta'wīl* in this sense is in contrast to *tafsīr*, understood here as the particular process of ordinary or exoteric exegesis. The general science of Quranic exegesis, as well as the totality of a work of Quranic commentary, is still called *tafsīr*, whether an exoteric or an esoteric process is followed. It is in these two last senses that the term *tafsīr* should be understood whenever it is used throughout this chapter, that is, to indicate the general science of exegesis or the works concerned with esoteric commentary, although the process these works use is called *ta'wīl*.

2. Frithjof Schuon, *Understanding Islam*, trans. D. M. Matheson (London: Allen & Unwin, 1963) 48 n.1.

3. Quranic passages are quoted from the Pickthall or the Dawood translation, with some modifications.

4. Abū Ḥāmid al-Ghazzālī, *Mishkāt al-anwār*, ed. Abu'l-'Alā' 'Afīfī (Cairo: al-Dār al-Qawmiyyah, 1964) 39. This work has been translated into English with an introduction by W. H. T. Gairdner as *Al-Ghazzālī's Mishkāt-ul-anwār: The Niche for Lights* (Lahore: M. Ashraf, 1952). Muḥyī al-Dīn Ibn 'Arabī, *Fuṣūṣ al-ḥikam*, ed. A. 'Afīfī (Beirut: Dār al-Kitāb al-'Arabī, 1946). See esp. 98, 159, 215, 222–23.

5. Ibn 'Aṭā' Allāh al-Iskandarī, *Laṭā'if al-minan*, ed. 'Abd al-Ḥalīm Maḥmūd (Cairo: Matba'at al-Ḥisān, 1974) 252–72.

6. See Sahl al-Tustarī, *Tafsīr al-Qur'ān al-'aẓīm* (Cairo: Maṭba'at al-Sa'ādah, 1908), 12; Muḥammad Murtaḍā al-Zabīdī, *Itḥāf al-sādah al-muttaqīn bi sharḥ asrār iḥyā' 'ulūm al-dīn* (10 vols.; Cairo: al-Maṭba'at al-Maymaniyyah, 1893–94) 4:531.

7. See also H. Corbin, *Histoire de la philosophie islamique*, Part I (Paris: Gallimard, 1964) 20–21.

8. Muḥammad Abul Quasem, *The Recitation and Interpretation of the Quran: al-Ghazzālī's Theory* (London and Boston: Kegan Paul International, 1982) 87.

9. Muḥammad Ḥusayn al-Dhahabī, *Al-Tafsīr wa' l-mufassirūn* (2nd ed.; 2 vols.; Cairo: Dār al-Kutub al-Ḥadīthah, 1967) 1:89–90.

10. Al-Tustarī, *Tafsīr*, 12; G. Böwering, *The Mystical Vision of Existence in Classical Islam: The Quranic Hermeneutics of the Ṣūfī Sahl At-Tustarī* (Berlin and New York: de Gruyter, 1980) 140.

11. See Abul Quasem, *Recitation and Interpretation*, 65–66 n. 194, 87, 89.

12. Al-Dhahabī, *Al-Tafsīr*, 1:91

13. Abu'l-Ḥasan 'Alī al-Qummī, *Tafsīr al-Qummī*, ed. Ṭayyib al-Mūsawī al-Jazā'irī (2 vols.; Najaf: Maṭba'at al-Najaf, 1386 A.H.); see esp. 1:5–6, 14, 15.

14. L. Massignon, *Essai sur les origines du lexique technique de la mystique musulmane* (rev. ed.; Paris: J. Vrin, 1968) 201–2.

15. See n. 6 above; Böwering, *Mystical Vision*, 43, 51, 55, 129, 265.

16. To be sure, al-Tustarī quotes the first four Imams; see Böwering, *Mystical Vision*, 67.

17. Böwering, *Mystical Vision*, 141–42.

18. P. Nwyia, *Exégèse coranique et langage mystique* (Beirut: Dar al-Mashriq, 1970) 158; Imām Ǧa'far Ṣādiq, "Tafsīr, recension Sulamī," ed. P. Nwyia, *Mélanges de l'Université Saint-Joseph* 43 (1967) 179–230.

19. Nwyia, *Exégèse coranique*, 159–60.

20. Ibid., 164–207; see also John B. Taylor, "Ja'far al-Ṣādiq, Spiritual Forebear of the Ṣūfīs," *Islamic Culture* 40 (April 1966). There is also a Quranic commentary, limited to the first sura and a part of the second sura, attributed to al-Ḥasan al-'Askārī, the eleventh Imam; see al-Dhahabī, *Al-Tafsīr*, 2:42, 84, 97, 631.

21. See Corbin, *Histoire*, 1:22.

22. Nwyia, *Exégèse coranique*, 117–56.

23. Böwering, *Mystical Vision*, 110–11.

24. See n. 18 above; Massignon, *Essai*, 359–412.

25. Abu'l-Qāsim al-Qushayrī, *Laṭā'if al-ishārāt*, ed. Ibrāhīm Basyūnī (6 vols.; Cairo: Dār al-Kutub al-'Arabī, 1968–71).

26. Jalāl al-Dīn al-Suyūṭī, *Ṭabaqāt al-mufassirīn*, ed. 'Alī Muḥammad 'Umar (Cairo: Maktabat Wahbah, 1976) 74; Shams al-Dīn al-Dāwūdī, *Ṭabaqāt al-mufassirīn*, ed. 'Alī Muḥammad 'Umar (2 vols.; Cairo: Dār al-Kutub, 1972) 1:341, 344.

27. See S. de Laugier de Beaurceuil, *Khwādja Abdullāh Anṣārī, mystique ḥanbalite* (Beirut: Impr. Catholique, 1965) esp. p. 175 n. 3.

28. Rashīd al-Dīn Maybudī, *Kashf al-asrār wa 'uddat al-abrār*, ed. 'A. A. Ḥikmat (10 vols.; Tehran: Intishārāt Dānishgāhī, 1952–60).

29. Abdurrahman Badawi, *Mu'allafāt al-Ghazālī* (Cairo: al-Majlis al-A'lā' li-Ri'āyat al-Funūn wa'l-Ādāb, 1961) 199.

30. See n. 4 above.

31. See n. 8 above.

32. See Massignon, *Essai*, 13, 413–18; Corbin, *Histoire*, 22; al-Dhahabī, *Al-Tafsīr*, 2:390, 632.

33. See H. Corbin, *En Islam iranien*, (4 vols.; Paris: Gallimard, 1971–72) 3:176, 276; al-Dhahabī, *Al-Tafsīr*, 2:395.

34. Corbin, *En Islam iranien*, 3:273; see generally 3:275–355; see also n. 79 below.

35. O. Yahya, *Histoire et classification de l'oeuvre d'Ibn 'Arabī* (2 vols.; Damascus: Institut Français de Damas, 1964) 1:109.

36. Ṣadr al-Dīn al-Qūnawī, *I'jāz al bayān fī ta'wīl umm al-Qur'ān*, ed. 'Abd al-Qādir Aḥmad 'Aṭā', in A. A. 'Aṭā', *Al-Tafsīr al-ṣūfī li'l-Qur'ān* (Cairo: Dār al-Kutub al-Ḥadīthah, 1969).

37. Muḥyī al-Dīn ibn 'Arabī, *Tafsīr al-Shaykh al-Akbar* (Cairo, 1867; Cawnpore, 1883); *Tafsīr al-Qur'ān al-karīm* (Beirut: Dār al-Yaqzat al-'Arabiyyah, 1968). The most recent edition is by Muṣṭafā Ghālib (2 vols.; Beirut: Dār al-Andalus, 1978). See Yahya, *Histoire*, vol. 2, no. 724 (p. 480), no. 732 (p. 483). Selections from al-Kāshānī's commentary are translated into French by M. Valsân in *Etudes Traditionelles* (1963–75 at intervals).

38. Jalā al-Dīn Rūmī, *Mathnawī ma'nawī*, ed. and trans. R. A. Nicholson (8 vols.; Gibb Memorial Series n.s. 4; London: Luzac, 1925–40).

39. S. H. Nasr, *Jalāl al-Dīn Rūmī, Supreme Persian Poet and Sage* (Tehran: Conseil Superieur de la Culture et des Arts, 1974) 27, 40; see also idem, *Rūmī and the Sufi Tradition* (Tehran: RCD Cultural Institute, 1974) 3; idem, *Ideals and Realities of Islam* (London: Allen & Unwin, 1985) 58, 60.

40. Nasr, *Rūmī and the Sufi Tradition*, 3, 19 n. 6.

41. Ibn 'Aṭā' Allāh al-Iskandarī, *Laṭā'if al-minan*, esp. 228–51.

42. See Corbin, *Histoire*, vol. 1, chap. 1, sec. 1; Nasr, *Ideals and Realities*, 61.

43. S. H. Nasr, *Three Muslim Sages: Avicenna, Suhrawardī, Ibn 'Arabī* (Cambridge, MA: Harvard University Press, 1964) 24.

44. Al-Fārābī, *Fuṣūṣ al-ḥikam* (Cairo: Maṭba'at al-Sa'ādah, 1907) 170–75.
45. Ibn Sīnā, *Panj risālah,* ed. Ehsan Yarshater (Tehran: Anjuman-i āthār-i millī, 1953); idem, *Jāmi' al-badā'i'* (Cairo: Maṭba'at al-Sa'ādah, 1917) 27–33; idem, *Tis' rasā'il fi'l-ḥikmah wa'l-ṭabī'iyyāt* (Cairo: Maṭba'at Hindiyyah, 1908) 125–32.
46. Ibn Sīnā, *Tis' rasā'il.*
47. See S. H. Nasr, *An Introduction to Islamic Cosmological Doctrines* (rev. ed.; Boulder, CO: Shambhala, 1978) 209–12; idem, *Three Muslim Sages,* 31, 141 nn. 57, 58. For more on Ibn Sīnā's relation to Islamic esotericism, see Nasr, *Introduction,* 191–96.
48. S. H. Nasr, *Ṣadr al-Dīn Shīrāzī and His Transcendent Theosophy* (Tehran: Imperial Iranian Academy of Philosophy, 1978) 71, 89.
49. Nasr, *Introduction,* 181 n. 6, 183.
50. Nasr, *Ideals and Realities,* 150, 160–62.
51. See Nasr, *Ideals and Realities,* 166.
52. Ibid., 126–27; Nasr, *Sufi Essays* (Albany, NY: State University of New York Press, 1972) 105, 107, 119–20.
53. Abū Ja'far Muḥammad al-Ṭūsī, *Al-Tibyān fī tafsīr al-Qur'ān* (10 vols.; Najaf: al-Maṭba'at al-'Ilmiyyah, 1957–63); Abū 'Alī al-Faḍl al-Ṭabarsī, *Majma' al-bayān fī tafsīr al-Qur'ān* (12 vols.; Beirut: Dār Maktabat al-Ḥayāt, 1961).
54. Corbin, *En Islam iranien,* 3:173–77; 1:27 n. 4.
55. Ibid., 3:234–74.
56. Nasr, *Ṣadr al-Dīn Shīrāzī,* 157, 90.
57. Ibid., 40, 43, 44, 45, 48, 90 (citation, p. 90).
58. Ibid., 157, 71.
59. Corbin, *En Islam iranien,* 3:228 n. 58; idem, *Histoire,* 23; Nasr, *Ideals and Realities,* 60. It should be added that 'Alawī is also connected to Mullā Ṣadrā in that they were both disciples of Mīr Dāmād.
60. Al-Dhahabī, *Al-Tafsīr,* 2:145–85.
61. Nasr, *Sufi Essays,* 100.
62. Ikhwān al-Ṣafā', *Rasā'il Ikhwān al-Ṣafā'* (12 vols.; Beirut: Dār Bayrūt, 1957).
63. Nasr, *Introduction,* 36.
64. Al-Nu'mān b. Ḥayyūn al-Maghribī, *Kitāb asās al-ta'wīl,* ed. Aref Tamer (Beirut: Dār al-Thaqāfah, 1960) 5. For a discussion of al-Qāḍī al-Nu'mān's chapters on the cycles of Adam and Noah, see Corbin, *Face de Dieu, Face de l'homme* (Paris: Flammarion) 108–62.
65. Al-Qāḍī al-Nu'mān, *Da'ā'im al-islām,* ed. Asaf A. A. Fyzee (2 vols.; Cairo: Dār al-Ma'ārif, 1951–60).
66. Corbin, *En Islam iranien,* 1:27 n. 4; idem, *Histoire,* 23; Nasr, *Ideals and Realities,* 60.
67. Sulṭān 'Alī Shāh, *Bayān al-sa'ādah fī maqāmāt al-'ibādah* (quoted in Corbin, *En Islam iranien,* 3:229); 'Allāmah Sayyid Muḥammad Ḥusayn Ṭabāṭabā'ī, *Al-Mīzān fī tafsīr al-Qur'ān* (20 vols.; Beirut: Mu'assasat al-A'lāmī, 1973–74).
68. See al-Dāwūdī, *Ṭabaqāt,* 2:10.
69. Niẓām al-Dīn al-Nayshābūrī, *Gharā'ib al-Qur'ān wa raghā'ib al-Furqān,* ed. Ibrāhīm 'Aṭwah 'Iwaḍ (5 vols.; Cairo: Muṣṭafā al-Bābī al-Ḥalabī, 1962–70).
70. Qāsim al-Qaysī, *Tārīkh al-tafsīr* (Baghdad: al-Majma' al-'ilmī al-'Irāqī, 1966) 80.
71. Nasr, *Sufi Essays,* 26, 115.
72. A. M. Schimmel, *Mystical Dimensions of Islam* (Chapel Hill: University of North Carolina Press, 1975) 363.
73. Ismā'īl Ḥaqqī, *Rūḥ al-bayān fī tafsīr al-Qur'ān* (6 vols.; Cairo: al-Maṭba'at al-Amīrah, 1870); Shihāb al-Dīn al-Alūsī, *Rūḥ al-ma'ānī fī tafsīr al-Qur'ān al-'aẓīm wa'l-*

sab' al-mathānī (Beirut: Dār Iḥyā' al-Turāth al-'Arabī, 1970).

74. M. Lings, *A Sufi Saint of the Twentieth Century, Shaykh Aḥmad al-'Alawī* (2nd ed.; Berkeley: University of California Press, 1971) 230, 231; see also 173–75; Abū Bakr Sirāj Ed-Dīn, *The Book of Certainty* (New York: Samuel Weiser, 1974).

75. See Corbin, *Histoire,* 1:25.

76. Abū Ḥāmid al-Ghazzālī, *The Jewels of the Quran,* trans. M. Abul Quasem (London and Boston: Kegan Paul International, 1983) 64-65.

77. Ibn 'Arabī, *Tafsīr* (1968 ed.) 1:5, 477; see also 441.

78. See, e.g., Ibn 'Arabī, *Tafsīr,* 2:573; Sirāj Ed-Dīn, *Book of Certainty,* 22, 102. See also M. Lings, "The Quranic Symbolism of Water," in *Studies in Comparative Religion* 2 (Summer, 1968) 153–60; al-Tustarī, *Tafsīr,* 95, 97.

79. See Nasr, *Sufi Essays,* 45–47. Commentaries upon the well-known Verse of Light, mentioned several times above, are of the greatest spiritual significance, linked to the whole of the spiritual experience itself; they bring out the same metaphysical, cosmological, and psychological dimensions of the doctrine just outlined, in addition to their strong relation to spiritual practices. See al-Ghazzālī, *Mishkāt al-anwār;* Abdullah Yusuf Ali, *The Meaning of the Glorious Qur'an* (2 vols.; Cairo: Dār al-Kitāb al-Miṣrī, n.d.) 1:920–24 (a summary of al-Ghazzālī's work). See, moreover, F. Schuon, *Dimensions of Islam,* trans. P. N. Townsend (London: Allen & Unwin, 1970) chap. 8 (*An-Nūr*), esp. 108–9; H. Corbin, *The Man of Light in Iranian Sufism,* trans. N. Pearson (Boulder, CO, and London: Shambala, 1978) esp. 106. Chapter 6 of Corbin's book is a study of the (unpublished) commentary of Simnānī (n. 33 above). As shown by Corbin, Simnānī's search for "the seven esoteric meanings of the Quran" gradually leads to the growth of "seven suprasensory, inner organs," each of which is characterized by a certain "colored light." There is perhaps no more eloquent testimony to the unbreakable connection between the method and conclusions of spiritual hermeneutics on the one hand, and the stages and goal of the spiritual experience on the other. See further Corbin, "L'intériorisation du sens en herméneutique soufie iranienne," *Eranos Jahrbuch* 26 (1958) 57–187; the section on Simnānī is also to be found, somewhat revised, in *En Islam iranien,* 3:275–355.

80. Schuon, *Understanding Islam,* 48.

81. Ibid., 46.

82. S. H. Nasr, *Knowledge and the Sacred* (New York: Crossroad, 1981) vii.

83. Schuon, *Understanding Islam,* 45.

84. On the doctrine, the virtues, and the spiritual practices and their relation to the spiritual understanding of the Quran, see Nasr, *Ideals and Realities,* 135–43. See further T. Burckhardt, *An Introduction to Sufi Doctrine,* trans. D. M. Matheson (Lahore: M. Ashraf, 1959) 32–40, 57–142; Nasr, *Sufi Essays,* 35–37; idem, *Three Muslim Sages,* 102–16.

85. Nasr, *Ideals and Realities,* 65.

86. This is the well-known saying attributed to 'Ā'ishah bint Abī Bakr, wife of the Prophet.

4

The Spiritual Significance of the Substance of the Prophet

FRITHJOF SCHUON

The Prophetic Substance: Source of Islamic Spirituality

THE CONCRETE CONTENT—and thus the origin—of Islamic spirituality is the spiritual Substance of the Prophet, this Substance whose modalities such Sufi authorities as al-Qushayrī and Ibn al-ʿArīf have tried to catalog by means of the notion of "stations" (*maqāmāt*). Sufism is the realization of Union, not only by starting from the idea of Unity that is both transcendent and immanent but also, and correlatively, by reintegration into the Muḥammadan Substance that is hidden and yet ever present—and this whether accomplished directly or indirectly or in both manners at once. This means that the mystical "traveler" (*sālik*) may "follow the example of the Prophet" in a way that is either formal or formless, hence indirect or direct. For the *Sunnah* is not just the multitude of precepts; it is also the "Muḥammadan Substance"[1]—of which these precepts are the reflections at various levels—which coincides with the mystery of the "immanent Prophet." The intrinsic qualities are in principle or in themselves independent of outward comportment, whereas the whole reason for the existence of the latter lies in the former, somewhat as, according to the Shaykh al-ʿAlawī,[2] the sufficient reason of the rites is the remembrance of God, which contains all rites in an undifferentiated synthesis.

Man has two kinds of relationship with the Divine Order, one direct and the other indirect. The first encompasses prayer and, more esoterically, intellectual discernment and unitive concentration; the second goes to God through the door of the human Logos, and it comprises the virtues of which the Logos is the personification and model. In question here are not only the elementary virtues, which may be natural to man or which he can draw from himself, but also and above all the supernatural virtues, which on the one hand are graces and on the other require that man transcend himself and even cease to "be" in order to "become." No path exists without reference to a human manifestation of the Logos, just as with all the more reason none exists without a direct relationship with God.

Outwardly, the Prophet is legislator, and he can easily be grasped as such; inwardly, in his Substance, he represents esoterism at every level—whence a duality which is at the source of certain antinomies and which in the last analysis has given rise to the schism between Sunnis and Shī'ites. The legislator points out the way and gives the right example on the formalistic plane of legality and morality, whereas the Muḥammadan Substance—the soul of the Prophet insofar as it is accessible in principle—is a concrete and quasi-sacramental presence that prefigures the state of salvation or of deliverance and that invites one not to legality or to the social virtues but to self-transcendence and transformation—hence to extinction and to a second birth.

The driving idea of Islam is the concept of Unity; it determines not only the doctrine and the organization of society but also the entire life of the individual and in particular his piety, which, moreover, cannot be dissociated from his legal comportment. It is not just a question of accepting the idea of Unity but also of drawing from this idea all the consequences that it implies for man; that is to say, one must accept it "with faith" and "sincerity" in order to benefit from the saving virtue it contains. Thus, in the last analysis the idea of Unity fundamentally implies the mystery of Union, just as, in a related order of ideas, unicity implies as its complement totality. To be able to grasp the geometric point is to be able to grasp all of space; the unicity of the Divine Object demands the totality of the human subject.

Yet despite the clarity of this relationship of cause and effect, Islamic spirituality presents an enigma in that its theoretical and practical expressions often seem to draw away from Islam as such,[3] notwithstanding the efforts of the Sufis to emphasize the legality of their opinions and methods, even those most foreign to the overall perspective of Islam. The entire enigma lies in the fact that there is here a dimension which the Law has not articulated or which it only suggests covertly. This enigma stems from the very person of the Prophet, who privately—if one may say so—practiced an ascesis that he doubtless recommended to some but did not make mandatory, which, moreover, in his own case could not signify the "purgative way" as it did with those who have emulated him. This ascesis—readily confused with Sufism, whereas it may merely be a preparatory trial at the threshold of the mysteries—is far from constituting the Substance itself of the Messenger. Being a spiritual beatitude and thus a state of consciousness, the prophetic Substance remains independent of all formal conditions, even though the formal practices can be rightly considered as paths toward participation in this Substance.

The Prophet and the Spiritual Virtues–Numerical and Spatial Symbolism

The spiritual nature of the Prophet is determined, illumined, and vivified by two poles, which we might designate, quite synthetically, by the terms "truth" and "heart": the truth of God, of the Sovereign Good, and the heart-intellect that mysteriously houses it; transcendence and immanence.

The Muḥammadan Substance comprises all the qualities or the degrees of preeminence which the Sufis term "stations" (*maqāmāt*) and which in principle are innumerable, given that it is always possible to subdivide them and thereby extract new modes from them. But simplicity also has its rights: starting from a given plurality, one can always proceed from synthesis to synthesis toward pure substantiality, which here is none other than the love of God in the widest as well as the deepest meaning of the word. We are then at the source, but lacking differentiated points of reference which could impart to us the internal riches of this love. It is appropriate therefore to halt at a golden mean between synthesis and analysis, and this mean, far from being arbitrary, is offered by traditional symbolism as well as by certain cosmic structures. Paradise contains four rivers that flow from the Throne of Allah, and there are four archangels at the summit of the angelic hierarchy; the Ka'bah has four sides, and space has four cardinal points.[4] But before considering the Muḥammadan Substance in its aspect of quaternity, we must explain the meaning of the numbers that precede it. According to unity, this Substance is the love of God; according to duality, it is the tension between the two poles truth and heart, transcendence and immanence; and according to trinity, this same Substance reveals the mystery of the prophetic quality, which comprises first of all perfect conformity and receptivity with regard to the Lord, then the prophetic Message as "content" of the Prophet and as the quasi-hypostatic link between him and God, and finally the perfect knowledge of Him who gives the Message.

The odd numbers are "retrospective" in the sense that they express an infolding toward Unity, or the Divine Origin, whereas the even numbers are "prospective" in the sense that they express on the contrary a movement in the direction of manifestation, the world, or the universe. In the first *Shahādah* ("There is no divinity but God alone"), which in Arabic comprises four words, the truth of the principle penetrates, so to speak, "prospectively" into the world; in the second *Shahādah* ("Muḥammad is the Messenger of God"), which in Arabic comprises three words, the Prophet is defined "retrospectively" in relation to his Divine Source. The number four in particular (the words of the first *Shahādah: lā ilāha illa'Llāh*) expresses the radiation of the principle with respect to the world and is therefore the number-symbol of radiation. When, correlatively, we consider the source—or the center—of the radiation, we arrive at the symbolism of the number five; and when we take into account the two poles determining the quaternity, namely, the transcendent and the immanent, we come to the symbolism of the number six.

As for the quaternity, which is the mean of our synthesis or analysis—for every number lies between these two poles—its inner significance becomes clear in the light of the symbolism of the cardinal points. The north is negative perfection, which is exclusive and surpasses or transcends; the south is positive perfection, which is inclusive and vivifies and deepens; the east is active perfection, which is dynamic and affirms, realizes and is, if need be, combative; and the west is passive perfection, which is static and peace-giving. We say "perfection" rather than "principle" since we have in view the prophetic nature, which is human.

But let us leave for now these more or less abstract preliminaries and consider concretely the principial aspects of the spiritual Substance of the Prophet, which sums up all the "stations" and, by the same token, all the *Sunnah*—at least as regards its subjective and spiritual motivations. In the soul-intelligence of the Prophet there is, first of all, the quality of serenity; this perfection rises above the turmoil of the contingencies of the world and is linked to the Divine Mystery of transcendence. To be serene is to situate oneself above all pettiness. Serenity is, accordingly, not only an elevation but also an expansion (*inshirāḥ*, "dilation of the breast").[5] In consequence it evokes the boundlessness of heights and the luminosity that fills them and gives them their natural and glorious content. This station, or category of stations, is often represented, in various traditional forms of symbolism, by the eagle soaring above the accidental features of a landscape, in majestic solitude, alone toward the sun. Snow is another image of this station; pure and celestial, it covers the accidental features of a landscape with a white, crystalline blanket, reducing all diversity to the undifferentiation of *materia prima.* This same mystery of elevation, boundlessness, and transcendence finds a religious expression in the call to prayer from the top of the minaret, reducing as it does all earthly agitation and turmoil to a celestial undifferentiation—an undifferentiation that is the opposite of leveling, for the former is qualitative whereas the latter is quantitative. These considerations pertain to the mystery of purity, which is symbolized by the north and thus also by the pole star.[6] And to this order of ideas belong the sacrificial attitudes of abstention, renunciation, poverty, and sobriety; or the virtues of detachment, patience, resignation, and impassibility; or again the conditions of solitude, silence, and emptiness—qualities or stations whose flavor is not one of sadness but of the calm and already celestial joy that is serenity.

Although the "vertical" complement of the north is the south, we prefer to consider first the message of the west, which, being static and pertaining to "passive perfection," prolongs in a certain way the static message of the north. At the same time its quality of mildness, which it shares with the south, distinguishes it from the rigor of both the north and the east.

The message of the west, then, is that of recollection, of contemplation, of peace. Like serenity, recollection implies holy resignation, but in a manner that is gentle and not rigorous, so that immobility here is conditioned not by a void or by the absence of the world with its noise and turmoil but, on the contrary, by a plenitude, namely, the inward and peace-giving presence of the Sovereign Good. Recollection is intimately linked to the sense of the sacred; within the realm of material things, it evokes not the luminous and cold heights of the boundless sky, but rather the sacral and enclosing intimacy of the forest or the sanctuary. It thus evokes that reverential awe—fascinating and immobilizing—which holy places, works of sacred art, and also various manifestations of virgin nature can provoke in the soul. The idea of recollection calls to mind all the symbols of contemplative immobility, all the liturgical signs of adoration: lamps or consecrated candles, bouquets or garlands of flowers—in short, all that stands before God and offers itself to His Presence, which is silence, inwardness, beauty, and peace. It is this atmosphere that is suggested and created in mosques by the prayer niche (*miḥrāb*), the same prayer niche that is the abode of the Virgin Mary, according to the Quran. Mary personifies mystical retreat and prayer, hence the mystery of recollection. All this refers to that holy repose (*iṭmi'nān*, "appeasement of hearts") of which the Quran conveys the echoes.[7]

Recollection, like serenity, is indicated by the word "peace" in the formula eulogistic of the Prophet: "Upon him be blessing and peace" (*'alayhi' ṣ-ṣalāt wa' s-salām*). From the element "blessing" stem the two qualities of which we shall now speak, namely, fervor and certitude. Fervor, in spatial symbolism, is the "horizontal" complement of recollection, certitude being the "vertical" complement of serenity. On the one hand, the east is in a complementary fashion opposed to the west, and on the other hand, the south is opposed to the north. These considerations, although not indispensable, can nevertheless be useful for those receptive to the language of symbolism and analogies.

The quality of fervor seems to be opposed to that of recollection, as action seems opposed to contemplation; nonetheless, without sacramental and actualizing activity, contemplation lacks support, not necessarily at a given moment but as soon as duration makes itself felt. The quality of fervor is, in fact, that disposition of soul which induces us to perform what can be termed "spiritual duty." If this duty is imposed as outward law, it is because it is imposed inwardly and a priori by our own "supranatural nature." In Islam, this immanent law is manifested as the "remembrance of God" (*dhikr Allāh*); now the Quran specifies that it is necessary to remember God "much" (*dhikran kathīran*), and it is this frequency or this assiduousness, together with the sincerity of the act of prayer, that constitutes the quality of fervor. For not only must the sacred act dominate the instant in which it arises; it must dominate duration as well. The perfection of the act requires perseverance as its logical consequence and complement. It is not enough to be a saint "now"; one must be one "always," and that is why the Sufi is the "son of the moment" (*ibn al-waqt*). The comparison between spiritual activity and holy war (*jihād*) will be readily understood: to establish the sacred in a soul by nature exteriorized—dispersed and at the same time lazy—necessarily implies a combat, and one could even say a combat against the dragon, to use an expression belonging to initiatory symbolism. All spirituality requires in consequence the virile virtues of vigilance, initiative, and tenacity. Thus, fervor is a fundamental quality of the Man-Logos, and it can be said that the immensity of the victory of Islam proves the immensity of the strength of soul of the Prophet.

As for the quality of certitude, which takes precedence over that of fervor since it provides the latter with its reason for being, it is the liberating yes to realities that transcend us and to the consequences that they impose upon us. Whether this yes be a gift of heaven or a merit of our own—and the one does not exclude the other, of course—makes no difference psychologically. Certitude of God implies certitude of our own immortality, for to be able to know the Absolute is to be immortal; only the immortal soul is proportionate to this knowledge. Moreover, he who appeals to the Divine Mercy must himself be generous, in accordance with the *ḥadīth* "Who hath no mercy, unto him shall be given no mercy" (*man lam yarḥam lam yurḥam*). This defines the connection between faith in God and charity toward the neighbor, or between hope and generosity, particularly as the acceptance of the Sovereign Good implies or requires the gift of self, hence a kind of generosity toward heaven.

It is true that on the plane of metaphysical intellection the transcendent

Invisible makes itself evident to our mind in such a way that we cannot but accept it. But this impossibility of resisting the truth lies then in our nature, and consequently the gift of self to the Divine Real lies in our very substance. The *a contrario* proof of this is that there are men who, although capable in principle of admitting the highest truth, refuse to admit it, owing to the tendencies of their passionate nature. The sincere yes to that which transcends us always presupposes beauty of soul, just as the capacity of a mirror to reflect light presupposes its purity.

Thus, whether it be a matter of elementary belief, of ardent faith, or of metaphysical knowledge, certitude always goes hand in hand with beauty and goodness of soul. Closely related to faith are trust and therefore hope. To trust in the Divine Mercy without a moment's despair, and yet without temerity—while abstaining from what is contrary to it and accomplishing what is in conformity with it—is a way of saying yes to the Merciful, and no less so to the deiform nature of our immortal soul. It is to say yes at once to God and to immortality. It is in this sense that the Quran tells the believers: "Verily ye have in the Messenger of God a fair example for him who hath hope in God and in the Last Day, and who remembereth God much" (XXXIII, 21), a saying that combines the mystery of certitude with that of fervor. "I am black, but beautiful," says Wisdom in the Song of Songs. She is black because she transcends and thereby negates our all-too-human plane, but she is beautiful because, in revealing herself to us, she reveals the Sovereign Good and thereby its saving Mercy. If the Quran testifies to the supereminent nature (*khuluq ʿaẓīm*) of Muḥammad, it is because, as a Prophet, he realizes the greatest possible receptivity with regard to the highest Reality.

The Significance of Faith

Even in pure intellection the "obscure merit of faith" has its place. With all speculative knowledge there is still a gap between the knower and the known; otherwise the former would be identified with the latter, which indeed is necessarily the case in a certain dimension—that of intellection precisely. But intellection does not encompass the entire being of the subject, or at least it does not encompass it at every moment. Besides, passive union is one thing, whereas active union is another. Therein lies all the difference between a state (*ḥāl*) and a station (*maqām*). At all events, to have certitude is not yet, in every respect, to be that of which one is certain.

Clearly, the value of faith is more than simply moral. Not only is faith good because of the merit entailed by its aspect of obscurity; it is good also and above all because of the certitudes it brings about in souls of good will.

4. The name of Allah inscribed within the name of Muḥammad repeated five times in a pentagonic pattern from the mausoleum of Ulgaiter, Sultaneyyah.

Otherwise expressed, not only does faith imply that its object is hidden from us because our nature comprises a veil; it also implies that we see this object despite the veil, and through it. The element of obscurity remains, since the veil is always there, but at the same time this veil transmits certitude because it is transparent. Thus, if the *Shahādah* signifies a priori that a given quality is unreal since God alone is the Good, it signifies a posteriori that a given quality "is not"—or else it is of God to the extent that it "is"—for to "exist" is a manner of "being." Seen from this perspective, the Divine Beauty manifested through earthly beauties never ceases to be itself, in spite of the limitations of relativity. It is within this context that one must situate that feature of the Muḥammadan Substance which could be called "Solomonian," namely, its spiritual capacity to find concretely in woman all the aspects of the Divine Femininity, from immanent Mercy to the infinitude of universal Possibility. The sensorial experience that produces in the ordinary man an inflation of the ego actualizes in the "deified" man an extinction in the Divine Self.

But the "obscure merit of faith" includes still another and altogether different meaning, which results from the relationship between the subject and the object. On the one hand, the subject—being contingent—has limits that prevent him from knowing in an absolute, hence exhaustive, manner; on the other hand, there appears to be on the part of the object a "desire," as it were, to conceal itself after a certain point, a will not to be known totally, not to be divested of all mystery of aseity or violated and emptied, so to speak, by the knowing subject.[8] The relative subject as such cannot know everything, which amounts to saying that he has no need to know everything, and this is true from the point of view of the adequacy of knowledge itself. This also amounts to saying that the object is by definition inexhaustible and that the more one dissects and systematizes it abusively, the more it will avenge itself by depriving us of its "life," namely, that something which, precisely, is the "gift" of the object to the subject. Total knowledge exists, certainly, for otherwise the very notion of knowledge would lose all its meaning, but it is situated beyond the complementarity between subject and object, in an inexpressible "beyond" whose foundation is the ontological identity of the two terms. For neither the one nor the other can be other than "that which is," and there is but one Being. Total knowledge means that the absolute Knower knows Himself and that there is within us a door that opens onto this knowledge—"within ourselves," yet "beyond ourselves."

In metaphysics there is a principle of "the sufficient point of reference," namely, the awareness of the limit separating sufficient and useful thought from thought that is wrong and useless. It is the former that furnishes us with points of reference enabling us to transcend the indefinite plane of thought as such. For the man insensible to the provisional character of concepts, it is natural to ask thought to provide what it cannot and to reach the conviction that thought is vain and that man can know nothing. But it is not normal for man to take thought as an end in itself.

These reflections may all help to clarify the idea of certitude, but a clearer idea of certitude may also be obtained by calling to mind its contrary, which is doubt. To doubt what is ontologically certain is to want not to be; it is thus a kind of suicide, that of the spirit. To doubt the Divine Mercy is a disgrace as great as to doubt God. Spiritual certitude implies the liberating yes to that which transcends us and which in the last analysis is our own essence—whence the relationship between self-knowledge and the knowledge of God and also between the knowledge of God and workings of Mercy.

The Soul of the Prophet: Sanctity and Art

The qualities, attitudes, or virtues of which we have spoken are rooted in the Logos and consequently pertain also to the "Muḥammadan Substance," which can be defined as a crystallization of the love of God, in a mode that unfolds, like a fan, the fundamental qualities of the soul. According to 'Ā'ishah, the "favorite wife," the soul of the Prophet is similar to the Quran. In order to understand this comparison, one has to know that this Book, parallel to the literal wording and in an underlying fashion, possesses a supraformal "magic," namely, a "soul" extending from the moral qualities to the spiritual mysteries; whence comes the sacramental function of the Text, a function independent of its form and contents.

Although this magic, for a person receptive to it, can be used as a way of approaching the Muḥammadan Substance, there is nevertheless another way of this kind, more readily accessible because far less demanding, and this is the concrete example of holy men in Islamic countries—certainly not hagiography with its stereotyped moralism and its extravagances, but rather the living men who can communicate the perfume of the *barakah muḥammadiyyah* of which they are the vehicles, witnesses, and proofs. For without the qualities of the Prophet, these men would not exist—neither in his time nor, with all the more reason, a millennium and a half later.

Another testimony of this order—and it will come as a surprise to those who fail to see the profound connections between the most diverse traditional phenomena—is of necessity provided by the arts and crafts of the

Muslims, above all architecture and dress, which relate respectively to ambience and man. As with Christian or any other traditional art, the important point to know is not from what source the Muslim peoples drew for the *materia prima* of their art. What is decisive with regard to worth and originality is the way they have used this *materia,* what spirit and what soul they have revealed through this matter, or rather with it as its basis. Islamic art in its most authentic and thus most characteristic realizations in the form of calligraphy, architecture, mosque ornamentation, and dress is the very expression of the soul and the spirit of the Prophet, of his serenity and his recollection before God ever-present.

In summary, and leaving aside all considerations of the mystical character of Muḥammad, we can say with historical accuracy that the Prophet was generous, patient, noble, and profoundly human in the best sense of the word. No doubt there are those who will point out that this is all very well but hardly significant and the least that could be expected of the founder of a religion. Our reply is that, on the contrary, it is something immense if this founder was able to inculcate these qualities into his disciples, both close and distant, if he was able to make of his virtues the roots of a spiritual and social life and to confer upon them a vitality that would carry down through the centuries. Herein lies everything.

What the Prophet Loved

According to a *ḥadīth* as enigmatic as it is famous, "women, perfumes, and prayer" were "made lovable" (*ḥubbiba ilayya*) to the Prophet. Since that is so, we have to admit that these three loves, at first sight disparate, necessarily enter into the Muḥammadan Substance and, consequently, into the spiritual ideal of the Sufis. Every religion necessarily integrates the feminine element—the "eternal feminine" (*das Ewig Weibliche*), if one will—into its system, either directly or indirectly. Christianity in practice deifies the Mother of Christ, despite exoteric reservations, namely, the distinction between latria and hyperdulia. Islam for its part, and beginning with the Prophet, has consecrated femininity on the basis of a metaphysics of deiformity; the secrecy surrounding woman, symbolized in the veil, basically signifies an intention of consecration. In Muslim eyes, woman, beyond her purely biological and social role, incarnates two poles, unitive "extinction" and "generosity." These constitute from the spiritual point of view two means of overcoming the profane mentality, made as it is of outwardness, dispersion, egoism, hardness, and boredom. The nobleness of soul that is or can be gained by this interpretation or utilization of the feminine element, far from being an abstract ideal, is perfectly recognizable in representative Muslims, those still rooted in authentic Islam.[9]

As for the love of perfumes mentioned by the *ḥadīth,* it symbolizes the sense of the sacred and in a general way the sense of ambiences, emanations, and auras. Consequently, it has to do with the "discernment of spirits," not to mention the sense of beauty. According to Islam, "God loves beauty" and He hates uncleanness and noise, as is shown by the atmosphere of freshness, harmony, and equilibrium, in short, of *barakah* to be found in Muslim dwellings that have remained traditional and above all in the mosques—an atmosphere which clearly is also a part of the Muḥammadan Substance.

The *ḥadīth* then mentions prayer, which is none other than "remembrance of God," and this constitutes the fundamental reason for all possible loves, since it is love of the source and of the archetypes. It coincides with the love of God, which is the very essence of the prophetic nature. If prayer is mentioned in the third place, it is by way of conclusion: in speaking of women, Muḥammad is essentially speaking of his inward nature; in speaking of perfumes, he has in mind the world around us, the ambience; and in speaking of prayer, he is giving expression to his love of God.

Regarding the first of the three enunciations in the *ḥadīth,* an additional explanation is called for, and it is fundamental. The apparent moral inconsistency in Islam has its source not only in the antagonism between the public Law, on the one hand, with its concern for equilibrium and harmony, and private ascesis, on the other, intent on detachment and self-transcendence. It has its source also in the personality of the Prophet himself, in what appears at first sight as the divergence between his ascesis and his sexual life. Tradition mentioned, in fact, the virile power of the Prophet as well as his voluntary poverty, his virtually constant hunger, and his regular vigils. This apparent contradiction, which in reality is a positive bipolarity, could not be peculiar to Muḥammad alone—although it characterizes him among the Semitic founders of religions—since it manifests a universal phenomenon and thereby an archetype.

Islam holds in view two aspects of femininity: glorified woman and woman as martyr. It situates two examples outside of Islam, in the past, and two other examples at the beginning of its own history. The martyrs are Āsiyah, the believer-wife of Pharaoh the unbeliever, and Fāṭimah, harshly treated by her father and her husband—and unjustly, from a certain point of view, by the first caliph.[10] The glorious women are Maryam, whom "God hath purified and chosen above all women," and Khadījah, the first wife of the Prophet and his guardian angel, so to speak, as well as "protectress" of the Revelation at the outset of the Prophet's career.

But let us return to the third enunciation of the *ḥadīth,* the love of prayer. A frequently used canonical formula proclaims that "prayer is better than sleep."[11] The Quran enjoins the Prophet to keep vigil part of the night in order to give himself up to prayer, and this reference to the night signifies far more than mere practical advice. More profoundly, it means that knowledge is born in the night of the soul, that is, in the perfect receptivity that is "poverty," "humility," "extinction," or *vacare Deo;* a gift can be given only to a hand that is "below" and opened to what is above. From another perspective, wisdom is a night compared with the profane mentality, just as it is "folly" in the eyes of the world. The same holds true, within the framework of religion, for esoterism, which transcends religious, formal, and psychological limitations. Thus, there is a certain relationship—at once principial and historical—between the Prophet's nights of prayer and esoterism in Islam. This also brings us back to the two caves of the Prophet, that of Mount Ḥirā', where he used to meditate prior to his mission, and the cave of Thawr where during the *hijrah* he taught his companion Abū Bakr the science of the Divine Name. Within the same order of ideas, and preeminently, one should mention the *Laylat al-qadr* and the *Laylat al-mi'rāj,* the Night of the Descent of the Quran and the Night of the Ascension of Muḥammad during the Night Journey.[12]

This vigil that God imposed upon His Messenger has two contents, the recitation of the Revelation and the remembrance of God: "Keep vigil a part of the night, a half thereof or a little less or more thereof, and recite the Quran with care. . . . Invoke the Name of thy Lord and devote thyself with a total devotion" (LXXIII, 1–8). The difference between the two practices—the recitation of the Quran and the invocation of the Divine Name—is the difference between the qualities and the essence, the formal and the non-formal, the outward and the inward, thought and heart. And it is this passage concerning the two nocturnal practices which basically inaugurates the Sufic tradition. It is to be noted that the recitation must be done "with care" (*tartīlā*), whereas the invocation demands that the worshiper "devote himself totally" (*tabtīlā*) to God. The first expression refers to the zeal that satisfies the requirements of the formal place, and the second, to the totality of dedication needed for the realization of the supraformal element, this being the Essence, or the immanent Unity.

The Names of the Prophet

The Prophet of Islam possesses 201 names and titles: the most fundamental, those summarizing all the others, are the two names Muḥammad and

Aḥmad, and next the designations or titles 'Abd, Nabī, Rasūl, and Ḥabīb.

The name Muḥammad designates more particularly the mystery of Revelation, of the Descent (*tanzīl*), hence of the Night of Destiny (*Laylat al-qadr*) during which this Descent took place. The name Aḥmad designates correlatively the mystery of the Ascension (*mi'rāj*), hence of the Night Journey (*Laylat al-mi'rāj*), which transported the Prophet before the Throne of Allah.

The title 'Abd ("Servant") refers to the quality of rigor (*Jalāl*) and expresses the ontological and moral submission of the creature to the Creator, hence "fear"; whereas the title Ḥabīb ("Friend") refers to the quality of gentleness or "beauty" (*Jamāl*) and expresses, in contrast, the participation of the deiform being in its Divine Prototype, hence "intimacy."

The title Rasūl ("Messenger") refers to the quality of activity and expresses the affirmation of the True and the Good; whereas the title Nabī (*ummī*) ("unlettered Prophet") refers to the quality of passivity and expresses receptivity with regard to the heavenly gift.[13] The first function relates to duty, and the second to qualification.

Assimilation of the Prophetic Substance

The initiatory means of assimilating the Muḥammadan Substance[14] is the recitation of the Blessing on the Prophet (*ṣalāt 'ala'n-nabī*), whose constituent terms indicate the different modes or qualities of this Substance. These terms are the following: *'abd, rasūl, ṣalāt,* and *salām;* "servant," "messenger," "blessing," and "peace." Now the disciple, "he who is poor before his Lord" (*al-faqīr ilā rabbihi*), must realize the perfection of the *'abd,* following in the footsteps of the Prophet, by a thorough consciousness of the relation between contingent being and Necessary Being (*Wujūd wājib* or *muṭlaq*), which is *ipso facto* Lord (*Rabb*); correlatively, the perfect and normative man is "messenger," that is to say, "transmitter" of the Divine Message, by his radiation, for a perfectly pure mirror necessarily reflects the light. This precisely is expressed by the terms *ṣalāt* and *salām*—the latter being the purity of the mirror, and the former, the ray of light. Now purity is also a gift of God; it includes all the receptive, stabilizing, preserving, and peace-giving graces. Without it, as the Shaykh al-'Alawī pointed out, the soul could not bear either to receive or to convey the "vertical," illuminative, and transformative graces offered by the Divine Blessing (*ṣalāt*).

Other points of reference for the knowledge of the prophetic nature are to be found in the words of the second testimony of faith: *Muḥammad^{un} rasūl Allāh,* "Muhammad is the Messenger of God." The first word—the name of the Prophet—indicates immanence and, by way of consequence,

Union. The second word connotes the perfection of conformity or of complementarity—one could say piety. And the third—the Name Allah—indicates transcendence and more especially the Muḥammadan knowledge of this mystery.

The Muḥammadan Substance is love of God combined, by the nature of things, with contemplativeness and nobleness of character, also with a sense for outward or practical values, such as the beauty of forms, and cleanliness, or the rules of propriety infused with generosity and dignity. The sense for outward things—although in no wise "vain," for all that—comes, in the final analysis, from the emphasis on "discernment" or from the element "truth." For one who discerns initially between the Absolute and the contingent, between Necessary Being and possible being—and this is the very content of the *Shahādah*—will readily apply analogous discernments in the sphere of contingency. As for the sense of beauty, it is related to the mystery of immanence.

It is from this Substance and its deepest dimensions, as we have said, that Sufism draws its life, with a consistency that sometimes contradicts—or seems to contradict—the general formalism of Islam. Also the *'ulamā'*, who are strangers to Sufism, are all too prone to insist that it is contrary to tradition, in which they are mistaken, though with extenuating circumstances. The Sufi authors for their part affirm the contrary—and sometimes with too much zeal, since esoterism, although formally rooted in the traditional system, constitutes by definition an independent domain, its essence being situated outside all temporal or "horizontal" continuity.

We can liken the particular mode of inspiration and orthodoxy that is esoterism to the rain falling vertically from the sky, whereas the river—the common tradition—flows horizontally in a continuous current. In other words, the tradition springs from a source; it goes back to a given founder of a religion, whereas esoterism refers in addition, and even a priori, to an invisible filiation, one that in the Bible is represented by Melchizedek, Solomon,[15] and Elijah, and which Sufism associates with al-Khiḍr, the mysterious immortal.

Being identified with the Logos itself, the Prophetic Substance coincides with the religion that is celestial, subjacent, primordial, and universal: the *religio perennis* whose sacred Book is the world of nature which encompasses us, and is also our own soul, it being likewise made "in the image of God."[16]

Notes

1. "And in truth thou art of a supereminent nature (*la'ala khuluqin 'azīm*)" (LXVIII, 4); that is of a most exalted character.
2. The great Algerian Sufi master of the present century.
3. Not that we must therefore accept the inadmissible hypothesis of borrowings from Christianity and Hinduism.
4. When a believer is outside the Ka'bah, be it near or far, he prays toward it—hence toward one of its four walls. When he is inside it, he must pray toward each of the cardinal points.
5. "Whomever God desires to guide, He expands his breast for Islam" (VI, 126). "[Moses] said: My Lord, expand my breast" (XX, 25). "Have We (God) not caused thy bosom [O Prophet] to dilate?" (XCIV, 1).
6. By "mystery" we mean a spiritual reality to the extent that it is rooted in the Divine Order.
7. "Those who believe and whose hearts are set at peace in the remembrance of God. Is it not in the remembrance of God that hearts find rest?" (XIII, 28). "O thou soul at peace! Return unto thy Lord, well-pleased, well-pleasing" (LXXXIX, 27–28).
8. This is not without connection with the principle of tithe or sacrifice in general. In order to guarantee fertility, one must not exhaust the divine gift.
9. It is always this Islam that we have in mind and not the so-called revivals, which combine in a monstrous manner Islamic formalism with modernist ideologies and tendencies.
10. It is from this drama of frustration and ingratitude, also surrounding the sons of Fāṭimah and before all her husband, that Shī'ism issues. The antagonism between persons is a function of a providential and inevitable antagonism in perspectives. Exclusivism and ostracism issuing from the exoteric spirit do the rest.
11. The *tathwīb* pronounced at the time of the dawn (*fajr*) prayers. Esoterically, sleep is profane heedlessness and prayer spiritual awaking.
12. An analogous maxim to the *tathwīb* is the following Quranic verse, which also refers to a "better" and a "here below." "In truth, the beyond is better for thee than the here below" (XCIII, 4).
13. These two titles correspond, respectively, in the universal order to the Supreme Pen (*al-Qalam al-A'lā*), which inscribes the cosmic possibilities, and the Guarded Tablet (*al-Lawḥ al-Maḥfūẓ*), upon which the possibilities are written.
14. *Barakat Muḥammad*, "the spiritual aura" of Muḥammad, which is munificent and protecting. The terms *al-nūr al-muḥammadī* and *al-ḥaqīqat al-muḥammadiyyah* refer with different nuances to the Logos itself.
15. He also being "the King of Salem," as his name indicates, but presented in biblical history in his rapport with the exo-esoteric antinomy.
16. In Quranic language the verses of the Quran and the phenomena-symbols of nature are designated by the same word, "signs" (*āyāt*). "We [God] shall show them our signs upon the horizons and within themselves . . ." (XLI, 53). There is an analogy between the macrocosm, the microcosm, and revelation; all three manifest the "signs" of the Sovereign Good.

5

The Life, Traditions, and Sayings of the Prophet

Introduction

As the previous chapter has revealed, the inner Substance of the Prophet is the hidden fountainhead of Islamic spirituality. This inner reality manifests itself in the life (*Sīrah*) of the person considered by Muslims to be the last prophet and the perfect man *par excellence,* and also in his actions (*Sunnah*) and sayings (*aḥādīth*). His beautiful names, which traditionally are said to be 201, are chanted as litanies and recited in certain spiritual exercises.[1] Love for him flows in the veins of all those who aspire to the spiritual life,[2] and emulation of the being called the "good model" (*uswatun ḥasanah*) in the Quran characterizes the whole program of Islamic spiritual life.

If love of God can be said to lie at the center of the spiritual life, it must be asserted that no one can love God unless God loves him, and God loves only the person who loves his Prophet. Since the love of the Prophet is, therefore, a secret key for the unlocking of the gates that open unto the Divine Presence, it is an essential part of Islamic spirituality. His life, as understood traditionally,[3] is read by the devout throughout their earthly journey in a thousand literary forms. His *Sunnah* is not only a basis for the Divine Law but is also the model that all those who aspire to spiritual realization seek to imitate in their lives. The *Ḥadīth,* comprising his sayings, is the supreme commentary upon the Quran and a treasury of wisdom without the help of which one could not progress upon the path of Divine Knowledge. The Prophet is the infallible guide and the source of all spiritual guidance in Islam; and his *Sīrah, Sunnah,* and *Ḥadīth* constitute the ship that carries those who aspire to the spiritual life across the waters of earthly existence to the shore of that land which bathes in the Divine Presence.

I. *The Life of the Prophet*

JA'FAR QASIMI

Historical Background

THE PROPHET MUḤAMMAD WAS A DIRECT DESCENDANT of Ismā'īl (2810 B.C. according to the traditional calendar), whose father, Abraham (Ibrāhīm, 2900 B.C.), was the patriarch of monotheism and the father of both the Jews and the Arabs.[4] The seed of Abraham, who had long been childless, was to be blessed through his two wives. Sarah gave birth to Isaac (Isḥāq in Arabic), and Hagar (Hājar in Arabic) to Ismā'īl—or Ishmael, as he is known in the Bible. Ismā'īl was the elder of the two. His mother was an Egyptian handmaid given to Abraham by Sarah when she was seventy-six years old and he was eighty-five. Bitterness ensued between the two wives and Hagar fled from the wrath of her mistress, Sarah, and besought God's help in her distress. An angel of God appeared to her and said: "Behold, thou art with child and shalt bear a son, and shalt call his name Ishmael; because the Lord hath heard thy affliction" (Gen 16:10–11). Thereupon Hagar returned to Abraham and Sarah and told them about her spiritual experience. In due course, the promised child was born and named Ismā'īl or Ishmael, which means "God shall hear."

When Ismā'īl was thirteen years of age, another miracle took place. Abraham received a divine message to the effect that Sarah too would bear a son, and, fearing lest Ismā'īl should lose favor with God, Abraham prayed: "O that Ishmael might live before Thee!" and God answered his prayer thus: "As for Ishmael, I have heard thee. Behold, I have blessed him . . . and I will make him a great nation" (Gen 17:20–21). Then Isaac was born and was suckled by his own mother. When he was weaned Abraham was advised by Sarah to take Hagar and Ismā'īl elsewhere. He took them to the valley of Becca (Mecca) in Arabia and left them there. Hagar gave expression to grave misgivings at being left alone in a barren valley, but her mind was set at rest when Abraham told her that he was leaving them there by themselves in obedience to a divine command. There followed the miracle of Zamzam, the spring that God caused to well up to quench the thirst of Ismā'īl when he was overcome by thirst and prayed for God's help while Hagar in her distress was passing seven times between the two points of a rock in search of help. "And God heard the voice of the lad; and the angel of God called to Hagar out of heaven and said to her: 'What aileth thee, Hagar? Fear not, for God hath heard the voice of the lad where he is. Arise and lift up the lad and hold him in thy hand, for I will make him a great nation.' And God opened her eyes and she saw a well of water" (Gen 21:17–20). We are further told about Ishmael in the book of Genesis: "And God was with the lad; and he grew and dwelt in the wilderness and became an archer." There is further mention of him in Psalm 84:5–6 as follows: "Blessed is the man whose strength is in Thee; in whose heart are the ways of them who passing through the valley of Bacca make it a well."

Hagar and Ismāʿīl were later visited by Abraham. The father and son built the Kaʿbah together, at the site of the first house of God on earth built, according to the Islamic tradition, by Adam himself. After the completion of the sanctuary, Abraham was commanded by God to institute the rite of pilgrimage to Mecca: "Purify My House for those who go the rounds of it, and who stand beside it and bow and make prostration. And proclaim unto men the pilgrimage, that they may come unto thee on foot and on every lean camel out of every deep ravine" (Quran XXII, 26–27). Hagar's search for help in passing seven times between the two points, later to be known as Ṣafā and Marwah, was commemorated and made part of the rites of the Islamic pilgrimage, the *Ḥajj.* To this day, every pilgrim to Mecca passes seven times between the two points in remembrance of Hagar.

Mecca was not green and fertile like Hebron, and the Quran contains a prayer of Abraham that reflects his intense love and solicitude for the material and spiritual welfare of Ismāʿīl and his progeny in this desolate land: "Verily I have settled a line of mine offspring in a tilthless valley at Thy Holy House. . . . Therefore incline unto them men's hearts, and sustain them with fruits that they may be thankful" (XIV, 37). Thanks to Zamzam, the valley of Becca came now to be inhabited by the tribe of Jurham, whose members were attracted by the spring and settled there with the permission of Hagar. Ismāʿīl grew among these people, spoke the Arabic language, and became a great hunter. It must be added here that it was Ismāʿīl who was offered in sacrifice and ransomed miraculously by a ram prior to the birth of Isaac. Ismāʿīl was until then the only son and, as such, was the sole beloved of his father. That sacrifice continues to be commemorated by the Muslims every year in the month of the *Ḥajj.* No such sacrifice is celebrated in the Jewish tradition.

As already indicated, the Quran makes ample mention of the construction of the Kaʿbah by Abraham and Ismāʿīl. They prayed to God to accept their service: "Our Lord! Accept this service from us. And Thou, only Thou, are the Hearer, the Knower. Our Lord, make us Muslims, bowing to Thy will, and of our progeny a people Muslim, bowing to Thy (will), and show us our ways of worship and turn to us in Mercy" (II, 125–28). They further prayed: "Our Lord! And raise up amongst them a messenger from among them who shall recite to them Thy revelations, and shall teach them the Book and Wisdom and shall purify them. Verily Thou art the Mighty, the Wise" (II, 129).

The Ka'bah brought great honor and comfort to the people of Mecca, who were eventually to be ruled by the Qurayshites, from among the Arab descendants of Abraham. This came about much later. Ismā'īl was succeeded by his eldest son Nabīṭ as the custodian of the Ka'bah. When he died, the Jurhamites took over the custody; but because of their oppressive ways they were driven back to Yemen, from which they had originated. The feat was accomplished by the combined efforts of the Banū Kinānah and Banū Khuzah tribes. However, through the instrumentality of a leader of the latter tribe, the idol Hubal was brought to and set up at the Ka'bah. By and by the number of idols increased and the most sacred center of monotheism came to be infested with idol worship. Assisted by the Banū Kinānah, Quṣayy ibn Kilab became the master and lord of the Meccans. With the advent of idolatry in the Ka'bah, the descendants of Isaac stopped visiting it.

Gradually the entire region suffered a terrible deprivation of the monotheistic tradition and sank into the Age of Ignorance (*al-jāhiliyyah*). People forgot God and succumbed to the temptations of the world and of the lower self. The Arabian peninsula remained in comparative isolation over the centuries. Hardly any impact was left on it by the great events of history, such as the conquest of Babylon by Cyrus and the founding of the Persian Empire, the conquests of Alexander, the foundation of the Roman Empire, the advent of Christianity, the death throes of the ancient Egyptian civilization, the destruction of the temple of Jerusalem, and the founding of the Byzantine Empire and its constant battles with the Persians to the east. Still trade and pilgrimage remained the two chief windows on the world for Arabia.

The Family of the Prophet

The Quraysh, a subdivision of the Banū Kinānah, became the most influential and aristocratic tribe of Arabia. The Quraysh constituted the immediate tribe of the Prophet Muḥammad, for he belonged to the Banū Hāshim, a branch of the Quraysh. Hāshim, the patriarch of the family, was a noble and generous soul who traded widely even as far as Syria and Yemen. His son 'Abd al-Muṭṭalib was the grandfather of the Prophet. To him went the privilege of apportioning the water of Zamzam and he also served as the custodian of the Ka'bah, which was still widely revered despite the taint of idolatry. He treated the pilgrims as God's visitors and guests and urged the Qurayshites to behave as God's neighbors and the people of His house, and he was generous to the pilgrims. In this he was following the example set by his illustrious father Hāshim and uncle Muṭṭalib, whom he surpassed in feeding and watering the pilgrims.

'Abd al-Muṭṭalib's mother was Salmā, who came from Yathrib, an oasis town and one of the first main halts of the summer caravans of the Qurayshites. Yathrib was inhabited by prosperous Jews and controlled by an Arab tribe from South Arabia. The Arabs of Yathrib later branched into the two tribes of Aws and Khazraj under the two sons of Qaylah, one of their ancestors under a matriarchal tradition. Salmā belonged to Khazraj and was the daughter of 'Amr, of the clan of Najjār. She married Hāshim on the condition that she would remain in complete control of her affairs in Yathrib, which she would not leave. She gave birth to a son who was named Shaybah and who remained in Yathrib until the age of fourteen. Hāshim accepted the arrangement and used to stay with Salmā and his son on the way to Syria and on his return. However, Hāshim did not live long, and after an illness during his last journey he died at Gaza in Palestine. Hāshim's younger brother Muṭṭalib visited Salmā and persuaded her to let Shaybah accompany him to Mecca so that he could succeed to the paternal estate and traditional honor as a possible chief of the Quraysh. Muṭṭalib took Shaybah with him on the back of the same camel that he rode. When they entered Mecca, people took Shaybah to be a slave of Muṭṭalib and called him so, namely, 'Abd al-Muṭṭalib, despite the protestations of Muṭṭalib.

'Abd al-Muṭṭalib soon came into his own. He succeeded in securing his rights after a dispute with his uncle Nawfal. In this he received help both from Muṭṭalib, who was his guardian uncle, and his maternal relatives in Yathrib. He had been looked upon as a young man of great promise and he amply justified the hopes raised by that promise. A few years elapsed and then Muṭṭalib died. 'Abd al-Muṭṭalib became the undisputed chieftain of his clan and, as has already been mentioned, he excelled both his father and guardian uncle in feeding and providing water for the pilgrims to the Ka'bah. 'Abd al-Muṭṭalib was blessed with abundance and was also favored with the gift of true visions. It may be recalled that, when the Jurhamites committed excesses and were driven out of Mecca, they sealed and concealed the spring of Zamzam partly as a scorched-earth policy and partly in the hope of returning to Mecca in triumph and rediscovering it. That was not to be.

In contrast, 'Abd Muṭṭalib clung to the Ka'bah and made his permanent seat there. One night he was sleeping in the Hijr at the north corner of the

5. "Arrival of the Prophet in paradise during his nocturnal journey at the door of the gate leading to Eden," Supplement Turc 190, Folio 47v.

holy house when he heard a visitor urging him to "dig sweet clarity." The visitor vanished but returned the following night urging 'Abd al-Muṭṭalib this time to "dig beneficence." Each time the dreamer asked what it was that he was required to dig but received no answer. The same vision recurred the third night and asked 'Abd al-Muṭṭalib to "dig the treasured hoard," and he again asked the visitor to be specific. The fourth night there was a clear command to "dig Zamzam," and there were detailed directions concerning how and where to locate the old and hidden site of Zamzam. With the help of his son Ḥārith and two pickaxes and despite the passive opposition of the onlookers, he succeeded in striking the well's stone covering and eventually in digging out the treasure buried there along with certain other profane objects. Whatever was dug out was distributed by casting lots for each object. Certain objects went to form part of the treasury of the Ka'bah. Some went to 'Abd al-Muṭṭalib himself but the Quraysh in general received nothing.

During the tense moments when the crowd in the Ka'bah was imploring 'Abd al-Muṭṭalib to desist from committing what they considered to be a sacrilege, 'Abd al-Muṭṭalib was depressed by the thought that he had only one son, and that, unlike his cousin Umayyah or for that matter Mughīrah each one of whom was blessed with many sons, he felt very lonely. He felt that if he too had been blessed with many sons nobody would have had the audacity to criticize his well-meant effort to retrieve Zamzam. So with great intensity and earnestness, he prayed to God to bless him with ten sons, making a vow at the time that if his prayer were granted and if all of his sons grew safely to manhood, he would sacrifice one of them to God at the Ka'bah. Although it seemed a remote possibility, God did answer his prayer and blessed him with ten sons with the passage of time. 'Abd Allāh was the youngest. He happened to be the most handsome as well as his dearest son. 'Abd al-Muṭṭalib was a pious man and a man of his word. He cast lots to find out which of his sons he should sacrifice. The lots were cast and to 'Abd al-Muṭṭalib's great horror it was 'Abd Allāh's arrow that came out. But he did not demur and set about to take his vow to its logical conclusion. But the women of the household and their close relatives, particularly those of Fāṭimah, the mother of 'Abd Allāh, his two real brothers, Zubayr and Abū Ṭālib, and five real sisters would not let the venerable chief use the sacrificial knife. They urged him to offer a sacrifice instead, and they offered to part with their entire property as ransom.

'Abd Muṭṭalib was most willing to offer some other sacrifice and he overcame his scruples only after consulting a wise woman in Yathrib. He undertook the journey only to find that she had gone to Khaybar. Eventually he found her and she came out with her answer after consulting her familiar spirits. She advised ʿAbd al-Muṭṭalib to put ʿAbd Allāh and ten camels of the usual bloodwite side by side and cast lots between them. If the result was unfavorable, he was to go on adding more camels and cast lots again until God accepted the camels and spared the favorite son of ʿAbd al-Muṭṭalib. They cast lots again and again, and each time the arrow said that the camels should live and that ʿAbd Allāh should die. When the number of camels reached a hundred, the unfavorable result was reversed. As an exceedingly scrupulous man, ʿAbd al-Muṭṭalib cast the final lot thrice, and having made certain that the camels were acceptable to God as his dear son's ransom, he ordered the camels to be duly sacrificed.

Once ʿAbd Allāh was reprieved, his father determined to find a wife for his son. He chose Āminah, the daughter of Wahb, a grandson of Zuhrah, the brother of Qusayy. Wahb had died and his brother Wuhayb succeeded him as the chief of Zuhrah some years previously. As guardian of Āminah, he approved and accepted the match. He also agreed to give his own daughter Hālah in marriage to ʿAbd al-Muṭṭalib himself. The double wedding was arranged to take place at the same time.

On the appointed day, ʿAbd al-Muṭṭalib took his son by the hand and they set off together for the dwellings of the Banū Zuhrah. On the way, they had to pass the dwellings of the Banū Asad; and it so happened that Qutaylah, the sister of Waraqah, was standing at the entrance of her house, perhaps deliberately, in order to see what could be seen, for everyone in Mecca knew of the great wedding that was about to take place. ʿAbd al-Muṭṭalib was now over seventy years old, but he was still remarkably young for his age in every respect. The slow approach of the two bridegrooms and their natural grace enhanced by the solemnity of the occasion was indeed an impressive sight. But as they drew near, Qutaylah had eyes only for the younger man. ʿAbd Allāh was the Joseph of his times as far as beauty was concerned. Even the oldest men and women of Quraysh could not remember having seen his equal. He was now in his twenty-fifth year in the full flower of his youth. But Qutaylah was struck above all—as she had been on other occasions, but never so much as now—by the radiance which lit his face and which seemed to her to shine from beyond this world. Could it be that ʿAbd Allāh was the expected prophet? Or was he to be the father of the prophet?

They had now just passed her, and overcome by a sudden impulse she said "O ʿAbd Allāh." His father let go his hand as if to tell him to speak to his cousin. ʿAbd Allāh turned back to face her and she asked him where he was going. "With my father," he said simply, not out of reticence but because he felt sure that she must know that he was on his way to his wedding. "Take me here and now as thy wife," she said, "and thou shalt have as many camels as those that were sacrificed in thy stead." "I am with my father," he replied. "I cannot act against his wishes, and I cannot leave him."[5]

The marriages took place according to plan and the two couples stayed some days in the house of Wuhayb. During that time, 'Abd Allāh went to fetch something from his own house, and again he met Qutaylah, the sister of Waraqah. Her eyes searched his face with such earnestness that he stopped beside her expecting her to speak. When she remained silent, he asked her why she did not say to him what she had said to him the day before. She answered him saying: "The light hath left thee that was with thee yesterday. Today thou canst not fulfil the need I had of thee."[6]

The Birth of the Prophet

Within a few months of the marriage 'Abd Allāh had died of an illness. Āminah gave birth to Muḥammad on the 12th of Rabī' al-Awwal in the year of the Elephant, 2 August A.D. 570. It must be remembered that according to tradition, God Himself had given the glad tidings of the birth of Ismā'īl and had promised to bless his seed. Ismā'īl and his mother Hagar had to undergo much suffering. They were subjected to separation from the land of their origin and were compelled to live in the wilderness. Then came the favor of Zamzam, the reconstruction of the Ka'bah, and the emergence of the Arabs. But this people that had descended from Ismā'īl lived in comparative aloofness from the world and had not yet entered the stage of world history. The Arabs possessed the virtues of hospitality and chivalry, of courage and self-sacrifice, of eloquence and love of liberty, of retentive memory and authenticity of genealogy. But also on the negative side there was their forgetfulness of their Divine Origin and mission, their surrender to wild passions, their terrible pride and class-consciousness. Their destiny had not as yet been fulfilled and awaited the birth of the Last Prophet, who was to unify them and make of them a great nation.

The Prophet's birth in Mecca was welcomed by his grandfather, who took him into the Ka'bah, where he gave thanks for the noble birth and named his grandson Muḥammad, the praised one—and, indeed, mankind was to sing his praises throughout the ages. He who experienced the loneliness of an orphan was the recipient of immeasurable love from his grandfather, 'Abd al-Muṭṭalib, as well as from his uncle, Abū Ṭālib. He was suckled by Ḥalīmah of the tribe of Banū Sa'd in the pure surroundings of the desert, the vast and white desert, gentle and rigorous, reflecting the infinitude and transcendence of God and manifesting His infinite nearness and immanence. The boy Muḥammad learned beautiful and clear Arabic there amongst the Banū Sa'd. He learned to appreciate the dignity of labor and the importance of earning one's livelihood by the sweat of one's brow. He worked as a shepherd and had initial lessons in tending flock, a flock that was a symbol of the entire creation. He learned to suffer, to endure, to be self-reliant, to think freely and methodically, to absorb the melody and rhythm of the universe, to see through the veil of relativity, suffering, and transience that which is beautiful, everlasting, and immortal. He experienced the magic of the sunrise, the scented sweetness and coolness of morning breeze, the intense heat of the scorching sun. He sought refuge in solitude and was mysteriously plunged in God. He was deepened, made firm, filled with grace.

Upon leaving the Banū Sa'd and returning to his family, the young Muḥammad became very much attached to his uncle Abū Ṭālib, whom he accompanied on journeys to Syria. It was there that he had his first direct contact with the Christian monk Bahīrah and was given by him the confirmation of his inner stirrings. Here, the inner equilibrium Muḥammad had attained by deep meditation as well as by long periods of solitude was rendered meaningful and comprehensible by the glad tidings of the monk Bahīrah, who at the same time emphasized the need to protect the lad.

With adolescence far behind him, Muḥammad was a most handsome young man of thirty-five when the Ka'bah was once again being rebuilt and a dispute arose over who should replace the black stone. They all agreed to accept the arbitration of Muḥammad, who had by now earned the titles of the True and the Trustworthy. He spread out his mantle on the floor, placed the stone on it, asked the various Qurayshite chiefs to take hold of the ends of the mantle and carry it to the point where the stone was to be restored. Then he lifted up the stone himself and installed it there. Not very long before this, he had subscribed to a charitable scheme for the protection of the unprotected. He was moved by the same spirit of saving life, of promoting harmony without sacrificing the truth.

As a young man, Muḥammad entered into the employment of Khadījah bint Khuwaylid, who, after the death of her father in the battle of Fijar at the age of thirty, had managed his affairs for ten long years on her own. She had been deeply impressed by the honesty, competence, and excellence of character of Muḥammad. Finally, upon his return from a successful journey on her behalf in Syria, she offered herself in marriage to him through her friend Nufaysah. After a certain reluctance, caused chiefly by his lack of means, he agreed to marry her. The Prophet was twenty-five, and Khadījah was forty years of age and had been twice widowed. Nevertheless, the nobles of Mecca coveted her hand because of her beauty, nobility, and wealth. When Muhammad visited her after the acceptance of the proposal, Khadījah addressed him in these words: "Son of mine uncle, I love thee for thy kinship with me, and for that thou art ever in the centre, not being a partisan amongst the people for this or for that; and I love thee for thy trustworthiness and for the beauty of thy character and the truth of thy speech."[7]

Muḥammad began his new life by leaving the house of his uncle Abū Ṭālib and going to the house of Khadījah. On the day of their wedding, he set free Barakah, the female slave he had inherited from his father. Khadījah made a gift of a new slave to him. He was named Zayd and was aged fifteen. Zayd was of noble ancestry, belonging to the great northern tribe of Kalb. His father was named Ḥārithah, and his mother belonged to an equally illustrious tribe of Ṭayy. During a visit to his mother's tribe, Zayd was taken prisoner in a raid by some horsemen of the Banū Qayn, who sold him into slavery at the great fair at ʿUkāẓ. There he was bought by Khadījah's nephew, Ḥākim ibn Ḥizam, who presented him to Khadījah. Zayd managed to send news of himself to his parents through Kalbite pilgrims. When his father and uncle came to reclaim the lad in return for any ransom requested, Zayd was asked to choose whether to return home or to remain with Muḥammad. He chose Muḥammad, who had agreed to set him free for no ransom. The Kalbites were furious with Zayd for having chosen slavery over the freedom he could have had with his father and his family. "It is even so," said Zayd, "for I have seen from this man such things that I could never choose another above him."[8]

The household of Muḥammad and Khadījah attracted many kindred spirits. She understood and respected her husband's ever-increasing inclination for solitude. Gradually he began to consecrate a certain number of nights and days to divine worship. His favorite retreat was a cave in Mount Ḥirā', not very far from the outskirts of Mecca.

Retreat was an age-old practice among certain descendants of Ismāʿīl. It was called *taḥannuth* in Arabic, signifying abstention from sin and devotion to God, a time spent in meditation. *Taḥannuth* also signified an inversion of the soul, a deliberate turning of one's back on the world and its commotion. Muḥammad's inherent sobriety, contemplative nature, and inner equilibrium were evident in his desire for solitude. There was no self-mortification, no excessive fasting, but rather he would take with him provisions and would return for more when these ran out. Occasionally Khadījah joined him. During these few years of periods of retreat, Muḥammad would be greeted by inanimate objects around him such as stones and trees. "Peace be on thee, O Messenger of God" was the usual greeting as recorded by such traditional sources as al-Bukhārī.

6. “The Mirāj of the Prophet,” Persian Miniature.

The traditional retreat was normally made during the month of Ramadān, and it was in this month, in his fortieth year, that an angel in human form appeared to Muḥammad while he was alone in the cave and bade him to recite (*iqra'*). The man who had just been chosen as the Prophet of God answered that he could not, whereupon the angel embraced him in an overwhelming embrace and then released him. This happened thrice and Muḥammad then recited the first verses of the Quran repeating after the angel. It was as if the words were inscribed upon his heart. Overwhelmed by the experience, Muḥammad now Prophet came back home and asked his wife to cover him with a cloth because he was shivering. When he had described to her his experience, she reassured him by affirming his superior qualities of kindness, generosity, and nobility of spirit. She assured him that God would never abandon him. Her words of consolation were in response to the Prophet's apprehensions that under the impact of Divine Revelation either he would lose his reason or life or be confronted with the tremendous responsibility that prophethood was to entail. Khadījah also took the Prophet to a Qurayshite sage who was deeply immersed in the Christian tradition. He confirmed the Divine Nature of the Prophet's experience and predicted the trials and tribulations attendant upon his prophetic mission.

The first verses of the Quran revealed in this manner were:

> Recite: In the Name of thy Lord who created, created Man of a blood-clot. Recite: And thy Lord is the Most Generous, who taught by the Pen, taught Man that he knew not." (XCVI, 1–5)

Following the first Revelation of the first verses the angel Gabriel taught the Prophet to perform the ablutions and the daily prayers in their nascent stage.

The first three years following the first Revelation were devoted to secret preaching. The first followers were Khadījah, the Prophet's wife; 'Alī, the Prophet's cousin, who was then just a young boy; Abū Bakr, a personal friend and a trader by profession; and Zayd ibn Ḥārithah, the freed slave who had preferred the Prophet to his parents. These were followed by Bilāl, the slave from Ethiopia, 'Amr ibn Unaysah, and Khālid ibn Sa'īd ibn 'Āṣ and others. The Prophet was now required to warn his own kith and kin and afterward to preach openly. When he took to the streets, fairs, and nearby tribes, persecution of his person and his followers ensued. This persecution was to take many forms and was to last for the next ten of the Prophet's thirteen years in Mecca. He was personally ridiculed, spat at, stoned, and otherwise accosted during prayer. Two of his daughters were divorced by their husbands as an attempted punitive measure. The Meccans tried to dissuade him by means of worldly temptations from preaching

Islam. They forced his uncle, Abū Ṭālib, to deprive the Prophet of his protection and patronage. He suggested the possibility to his nephew on account of his old age and helplessness, being all alone, and received the well-known answer: "O Uncle, if they place the Sun in my right hand and the Moon in my left hand I will not desist from preaching. I must complete my mission or perish in the process." This firm reply from the profusely weeping nephew moved the uncle, who henceforth never wavered in support for him.

The Prophet and his followers were ostracized and banished to Shi'b Abī Ṭālib, where they subsisted for three long years on the leaves of trees and whatever odd things they could find. The injunction was lifted after three years, but the persecution as such went on relentlessly. Some Muslim families were forced to migrate to Abyssinia, where they sought and secured refuge of the Christian king, the Negus. The Meccans sent emissaries to retrieve the fugitives. Ja'far ibn Abī Ṭālib pleaded the cause of the Muslims and won the day. His speech at the court of the Negus is a classical exposition of the cause of Islam:

> O King, we were a people steeped in ignorance, worshipping idols, eating unsacrificed carrion, committing abominations, and the strong would devour the weak. Thus we were until God sent us a Messenger from out of our midst, one whose lineage we knew, and his veracity and his worthiness of trust and his integrity. He called us unto God, that we should testify to His Oneness and worship Him and renounce what we and our fathers had worshipped in the way of stones and idols; and he commanded us to speak truly, to fulfill our promises, to respect the ties of kinship and the rights of our neighbors, and to refrain from crimes and from bloodshed. So we worship God alone setting naught beside Him, counting as forbidden what He hath forbidden and as licit what He hath allowed. For these reasons have our people turned against us, and have persecuted us to make us forsake our religion and revert from the worship of God to the worship of idols. That is why we have come to thy country, having chosen thee above all others; and we have been happy in thy protection, and it is our hope, O King, that here, with thee, we shall not suffer wrong.[9]

The preaching of Islam by the Prophet and the persecution of his followers by his opponents went on until he was fifty years of age, when he suffered the greatest tragedies of his life in the loss of his wife, Khadījah, and his chief protector and uncle, Abū Ṭālib, in quick succession. The year was called the year of sorrows. His uncle Abū Lahab and the latter's wife were actively hostile to him. The rest of his tribe extended some protection to him, but it did not suffice to save him from the molestation of all and sundry. The Prophet's visit to Taif to teach and preach there brought him much suffering. He was ridiculed and stoned and forced to seek shelter in an orchard whose owners shunned him personally despite some hospitality offered through their slave. That was the most trying day in the Prophet's life, the day that inspired the following prayer:

> O God, to Thee I complain of my weakness, little resource, and loneliness before men. O Most Merciful, Thou art the Lord of the weak, and Thou art my Lord. To whom wilt Thou confide me? To one afar who will misuse me? Or to an enemy to whom Thou hast given power over me? If Thou art not angry with me I care not. Thy favour is more wide for me. I take refuge in the light of Thy countenance by which the dark is illumined, and the things of this world and the next are rightly ordered, lest Thy anger descend upon me or Thy wrath light upon me. It is for Thee to be satisfied until Thou art well pleased. There is no power and no might save in Thee.[10]

Spiritual relief and consolation came in the form of the Prophet's nocturnal Ascension in body and soul (*al-mi'rāj*) to the heavens and finally to the Divine Presence, a miracle incomprehensible to those who hold the modern world view. He was taken from Mecca to Jerusalem, and from there he experienced gradual ascension through the hierarchy of being to the outermost region of the cosmos "the Lote of the Extreme Bounty" and then on to the Divine Proximity as described in sura XVII, 1 of the Quran. In addition to direct contact with previous apostles and prophets, he witnessed paradise and hell and the beatitude and suffering of their respective inhabitants. He saw falsehood in the form of a stone, jealousy as a scorpion, greed as a mouse. He rode Burāq, the white and speedy mythical horse. The angel Gabriel accompanied and guided him but could not keep him company once they reached the proximity of the Divine Presence. The Night of Ascension (*Laylat al-mi'rāj*) was the counterpart of the Night of Power (*Laylat al-qadr*), the night when the Quran was first revealed. The Prophet received many benedictions and spiritual privileges from the Divine Presence. The final stage of this journey to the Divine Proximity is described by a well-known traditional authority, al-Suyūṭī in his *al-La'ālī al-maṣnū'ah* as follows:

The Journey to the Divine Proximity

Now when I was brought on my Night Journey to the (place of the) Throne and drew near to it, a green *rafraf* [narrow piece of silk brocade] was let down to me, a thing too beautiful for me to describe to you, whereat Gabriel advanced and seated me on it. Then he had to withdraw from me, placing his hands over his eyes, fearing lest his sight be destroyed by the scintillating light of the Throne, and he began to weep aloud, uttering *tasbīḥ*, *taḥmīd* and *tathniya* to Allah. By Allah's leave, as a sign of His mercy toward me and the perfection of His favor to me, that *rafraf* floated me into the (presence of the) Lord of the Throne, a thing too stupendous for the tongue to tell of or imagination to picture. My sight was so dazzled by it that I feared blindness. Therefore, I shut my eyes, which was by Allah's good favor. When I thus veiled my sight, Allah shifted my sight (from my eyes) to my heart, so with my heart I began to look at what I had been looking at with my eyes. It was a light so bright in its scintillation that I despair of ever describing to you what I saw of His majesty. Then I besought my Lord to complete His favor to me by granting me the boon of having a steadfast vision of Him with my heart. This my Lord did, giving me that favor, so I gazed at Him with my heart till it was steady and I had a steady vision of Him.

There He was, when the veil had been lifted from Him, seated on His Throne, in His dignity, His might, His glory, His exaltedness, but beyond that it is not permitted me to describe Him to you. Glory be to Him! How majestic is He! How bountiful are His works! How exalted is His position! How brilliant is His light! Then He lowered somewhat for me His dignity and drew me near to Him, which is as He has said in His book, informing you of how He would deal with me and honor me: "One possessed of strength. He stood erect when He was at the highest point of the horizon. Then He drew near and descended, so that He was two bows' lengths off, or even nearer" (LIII, 6–9). This means that when He inclined to me He drew me as near to Him as the distance between the two ends of a bow, nay, rather, nearer than the distance between the crotch of the bow and its curved ends. "Then He revealed to His servant what he revealed" (v. 10), i.e., what matters He had decided to enjoin upon me. "His heart did not falsify what it saw" (v. 11), i.e., my vision of Him with my heart. "Indeed he was seeing one of the greatest signs of his Lord" (v. 18).

Now when He—glory be to Him—lowered His dignity for me He placed one of His hands between my shoulders and I felt the coldness of His fingertips for a while on my heart, whereat I experienced such a sweetness, so pleasant a perfume, so delightful a coolness, such a sense of honor in (being granted this) vision of Him, that all my terrors melted away and my fears departed from me, so my heart became tranquil. Then was I filled with joy, my eyes were refreshed, and such delight and happiness took hold of me that I began to bend and sway to right and left like one overtaken by slumber. Indeed, it seemed to me as though everyone in heaven and earth had died, for I heard no voices of angels, nor during the vision of my Lord did I see any dark bodies. My Lord left me there such time as He willed, then brought me back to my senses, and it was as though I had been asleep and had awakened. My mind returned to me and I was tranquil, realizing where I was and how I was enjoying surpassing favor and being shown manifest preference.

Then my Lord, glorified and praised be He, spoke to me, saying: "O Muḥammad, do you know about what the Highest Council is disputing?" I answered: "O Lord, Thou knowest best about that, as about all things, for Thou art the One who knows the unseen" (cf. V, 109/108). "They are disputing," He said, "about the degrees (*darajāt*) and the excellences. Do you know, O Muḥammad, what the degrees and the excellences are?" "Thou, O Lord," I answered, "knowest better and art more wise." Then He said: "The degrees are concerned with performing one's ablutions at times when that is disagreeable, walking on foot to religious assemblies, watching expectantly for the next hour of prayer when one time of prayer is over. As for the excellences, they consist of feeding the hungry, spreading peace, and performing the *tahajjud* prayer at night when other folk are sleeping." Never have I heard anything sweeter or more pleasant than the melodious sound of His voice.

Such was the sweetness of His melodious voice that it gave me confidence, and so I spoke to Him of my need. I said: "O Lord, Thou didst take Abraham as a friend, Thou didst speak with Moses face to face, Thou didst raise Enoch to a high place, Thou didst give Solomon a kingdom such as none after him might attain, and didst give to David the Psalter. What then is there for me, O Lord?" He replied: "O Muḥammad, I take you as a friend just as I took Abraham as a friend. I am speaking to you just as I spoke face to face with Moses. I am giving you the *Fātiḥa* (sura I) and the closing verses of *al-Baqara* (II, 284–286), both of which are from the treasuries of My Throne and which I have given to no prophet before you. I am sending you as a prophet to the white folk of the earth and the black folk and the red folk, to jinn and to men thereon, though never before you have I sent a prophet to the whole of them. I am appointing the earth, its dry land and its sea, for you and for your community as a place for purification and for worship. I am giving your community the right to booty which I have given as provision to no community before them. I shall aid you with such terrors as will make your enemies flee before you while you are still a month's journey away. I shall send down to you the Master of all Books and the guardian of them, a Quran which We Ourselves have parceled out (XVII, 106/107). I shall exalt your name for you (XCIV, 4), even to the extent of conjoining it with My name, so that none of the regulations of My religion will ever be mentioned without you being mentioned along with Me."

Then after this He communicated to me matters which I am not permitted to tell you, and when He had made His covenant with me and had left me there such time as He willed, He took His seat again upon His Throne. Glory be to Him in His majesty, His dignity, His might. Then I looked, and behold, something passed between us and a veil of light was drawn in front of Him, blazing ardently to a distance that none knows save Allah, and so intense that were it to be rent at any point it would burn up all Allah's creation. Then the green *rafraf* on which I was descended with me, gently rising and falling with me in ʿIlliyun [ʿIlliyun is said to be the highest of all celestial regions] till it brought me back to Gabriel, who took me from it. Then the *rafraf* mounted up till it disappeared from my sight.[11]

After such an overwhelming experience, during which he was declared to be inwardly the synthesis of all previous messengers and was granted assurances of Divine Succour and Glory, the Prophet was naturally reluctant to leave the Divine Presence and to return to the world of relativity and passion. He was, however, promised before his return to earth that he and his followers would experience the ecstasy of ascension in divine worship. That is why the daily prayers are called the *miʿrāj* of the faithful.

Subsequent to the return of the Prophet from the Ascension, the Meccans became all the more baffled and enraged. Their hostility now knew no bounds and the stage was set for the Prophet and his followers to migrate to Yathrib, which afterward acquired the name of Medina, (*Madīnat al-nabī* or *Madīnat al-rasūl*, the City of the Prophet or the City of the Messenger).

7. Torture reserved for the proud. Scene of the visit of the Prophet to hell during his mirāj," Supplement Turc 190, Folio 63v.

Migration to Medina

Gradually and secretly the Muslims left Mecca for Medina. The Prophet was among the last to leave. His companion Abū Bakr had kept two noble she-camels in anticipation of the occasion. The Prophet insisted on paying the price of the one he chose for his personal use. They left Mecca one night and concealed themselves for three nights in the cave of Thawr, where they had a narrow miraculous escape from the close searching by the Meccans, who were in hot pursuit. But as God had willed, the Prophet and his companion Abū Bakr, who henceforth became known as the "Companion of the Cave," eventually reached Yathrib safely.

The Prophet's cousin 'Alī, "the Lion of Allāh," was left behind to sleep in the Prophet's bed on the night of migration and had the most sound sleep of his life despite the danger facing him. Because of his well-known honesty and trustworthiness, he had instructions to return the goods that people had deposited with the Prophet.

The converts to Islam belonging to the tribes of Aws and Khazraj came to be known as the Helpers. They had contacted the Prophet secretly and made two pledges to him at al-'Aqabah to undertake to protect the Prophet as they would their families and children. Islam had penetrated Yathrib and new converts were being methodically educated and trained in the tenets and practices of Islam. The tribes of Aws and Khazraj were able to shed their mutual animosity because of Islam, which prepared the ground for the Prophet to establish himself in Medina. The Prophet had a brief stay at Quba, where he was ultimately joined by 'Alī, and then moved to Medina proper, where he spent some six months as a guest of Abū Ayyūb al-Anṣārī until his mosque and quarters were completed. Among the first orations at Medina was one that included the following teachings:

> Love what God loves. Love God with all your hearts and weary not of the Word of God and its mention. Harden not your hearts from it. Worship God and associate naught with him; fear Him as he ought to be feared; carry out loyally towards God what you say with your mouths. Love one another in the Spirit of God.

On two occasions, the Prophet instituted a formal brotherhood between certain pairs of the migrants and the Helpers, which made the former's financial rehabilitation possible and strengthened the latter spiritually through making sacrifices for the former. The Prophet himself took 'Alī, the Lion of God and the Lion of His Messenger, by the hand and said: "This is my brother." Ḥamzah, his uncle, took Zayd ibn Ḥārithah, the Prophet's freedman, as his brother and heir.

All the Muslims now acknowledged the spiritual as well as the temporal authority of the Prophet, who endeavored to enter into treaty relationships with the Jewish tribes of Medina, Banū Naḍīr, Banū Qurayẓah, and Banū Qaynuqāʿ. This "constitution of Medina" recognized the rights of Jews to practice their religion and to have their property protected and laid down reciprocal obligations in peace and war. It described the signatory groups to the agreement as one community who were to help one another in case of foreign aggression and were themselves to bear the expenses they incurred. Piety and loyalty were to stand in the way of treachery. The wronged were to be helped, and the unjust and the sinners were not to be protected. The constitution of Medina has remained a model for Islamic society throughout Islamic history and contains the universal perspective of Islam, which is capable of coping with all eventualities in both the individual and collective life of man.

After the death of Khadījah in Mecca, the Prophet had married Sawdah and was betrothed to ʿĀ'ishah, the daughter of Abū Bakr. She was then a minor. Among the important events soon after the *hijrah* to Yathrib was the formal declaration of her marriage to the Prophet on her attaining puberty.

The Fast of Ramaḍān and Zakāt

Fasting during Ramaḍān was made obligatory eighteen months after the *hijrah*. *Ṣawm*, or fasting, constitutes the third of the five pillars of Islam after the two attestations—of God's Unity and the prophethood of Muḥammad—and the five daily prayers. Ramaḍān signifies the burning up of impurities through abstention from eating and drinking even lawful food. It creates the sense of love for other human beings and piety among those who fast sincerely. It also inculcates gratitude among the fasters. The Prophet was a great faster, undertaking supererogatory fasts during most of the year in addition to the obligatory fasting during Ramaḍān.

About the same time the fourth pillar of Islam, namely, *zakāt*, which is an obligatory religious tax, was instituted. "And in their wealth, is the right of the needy and of those who are deprived of the means of subsistence" (LI, 19). This Quranic injunction shows that the recipient of charity received it as a matter of right and not as a dole.

The Prophet while in Mecca prayed in the direction of Jerusalem. He was now ordered by God to turn to Mecca. The Divine Injunction came while the Prophet was leading the congregational prayers. Everybody turned toward the Kaʿbah in Mecca with reverence. It evinced immense unity among the Muslims and also absolute obedience to the Prophet. Among new converts there were insincere people who had secret reservations about

Islam and who came to be known as hypocrites (*munāfiqūn*). This group and certain of the Jews who were adversaries of Islam protested against this change. There were other Jews, however, who remained well disposed to the Prophet despite the changing of the *qiblah*. Mukhayriq was one of them. He was a learned rabbi who remained faithful to Judaism. Yet he fought and died for the Muslims in the battle of Uḥud and willed his property to be inherited by the Prophet, who distributed it as alms among the needy in Medina.

Jihād

The *hijrah* marked a new phase in the Prophet's life, making fresh and altogether new demands, which—thanks to his versatility and perfection—were fulfilled. Yathrib contained different elements. It had believers like the migrant Muslims and the Helpers. But there were also the hypocrites and the hostile Jews ready to make alliance with the enemies of Islam in Mecca and elsewhere. Like the human soul standing in need of purification and perfection, Yathrib needed to be purified and perfected and eventually to be converted into Medina, the City of the Prophet. In addition to various spiritual and moral practices, the institution of *jihād* was instrumental in effecting the transformation. *Jihād* signifies primarily striving on all levels; fighting is only one form of that striving. The Prophet is reported to have said after returning from the battlefield: "We have returned from the lesser holy war (*jihād*) to the greater holy war." The greater *jihād* is to be waged against the lower self. Even the fighting on the battlefield had to have noble, spiritual causes and justification. According to Ibn Kathīr, the first Divine Injunction on the lesser *jihād* or *qitāl* is embodied in the chapter on the pilgrimage:[12]

> Leave is given to those who are fought against, because they have been oppressed—and verily to succour them Allāh is potent—those who have been unjustly driven forth from their abodes merely because they say: "Our Lord is Allāh." And were it not for God's repelling of some by means of others, cloisters and churches, synagogues and mosques, wherein the Name of God is mentioned much, would have been pulled down. Surely God shall succour whosoever succoureth Him. Verily, God is strong, mighty. They are those who, if we establish them in the land, establish the Prayer and give the poor-rate and enjoin right and forbid wrong, and unto God is the end of all affairs. (XXII, 39–41)

Quranic passages like II, 251, IV, 75–76, and VIII, 39, read in conjunction with the above passage, make the picture complete. Muslims were required to fight in the way of God against those who fought against them, and they were not to transgress the limit. They were to spare the aged, women, children, people in religious orders, and those fleeing from battle. They were required to be God-fearing and kind under all conditions.

The practice of *jihād* was necessitated by the situation in which the young Muslim community found itself in Medina. The Prophet and his followers in Medina were not left in peace. In the second year after the *hijrah*, the battle of Badr, which was decisive in the life of the new religion, took place. The Muslims were considerably outnumbered, but with divine help they were able to inflict decisive defeat on the Meccan enemy. Abū Jahl, the formidable enemy of Islam, was killed. The victory, which is considered traditionally to have been made possible by direct Divine Intervention, fortified the Islamic community. The Muslims set an excellent example of human treatment of the prisoners of war for later generations to follow.

The Meccans smarted under the defeat and tried to avenge themselves upon the Muslims in the year 3 A.H. by mustering a much larger army of three thousand men. Betrayed by a group of hypocrites in their ranks, the Muslims fought valiantly at first, but they suffered reverses during this second major military encounter with the Meccans, the battle of Uḥud. The companions posted to guard a mountain pass deserted their position in anticipation of imminent victory, in violation of the Prophet's command. Khālid ibn Walīd, still on the Meccan side, took advantage of this disastrous error and routed the Muslims. The Prophet was wounded, and his uncle Ḥamzah was martyred. There were serious casualties on both sides. The Meccans did not, however, complete their rout of the Muslims and went back to Mecca. The Muslims rallied around the Prophet, and a large group of Muslims led by the great warrior, the chivalrous ʿAlī, gave chase to the enemy and set an excellent example of defiance in defeat.

In the year 5 A.H., the Meccans attacked Medina with an unprecedented show of strength and determination with a large contingent of nineteen thousand men. Salman, a man of Persian origin who was one of the first converts to Islam, advised the Prophet to have ditches dug around the city. This successful military strategy gave the name of the Battle of the Ditch (al-Khandaq) to this war. A series of diplomatic moves against the Meccans and abnormal weather conditions contributed to their frustration and ultimate retreat. This victory added considerably to the prestige of the new Islamic community at Medina.

At the end of the year 6 A.H., the Muslims, led by the Prophet, set out for Mecca to make the lesser pilgrimage or *ʿUmrah.* They were not heavily armed for battle and their intentions were peaceful. Nevertheless, their entry into Mecca was barred by the Quraysh. The Prophet sent ʿUthmān ibn ʿAffān as an emissary to Mecca; when he failed to return, the Muslims, sensing acute danger, made allegiance with the Prophet under a tree and promised to fight until death. This vow of allegiance under the tree was later to serve as a prototype for the Sufi rite of initiation. Be that as it may, direct confrontation with the Meccans was averted. The pact of Ḥudaybiyyah was concluded, stipulating the Muslims' immediate return to Medina with permission to have direct access to the sanctuary at Mecca. There was a further humiliating condition to the effect that deserters from Mecca were to be returned to the Meccans, whereas those defeated from Medina could be retained by the Meccans. The treaty was to last for ten years. The Muslims were deeply distressed and depressed. ʿUmar ibn al-Khaṭṭāb was audacious enough to approach the Prophet and give vent to their frustration. The Prophet was adamant, and the truce turned out to be a blessing in disguise, an act of great statesmanship on the part of the Prophet. The Quran described this truce as a clear victory, which it soon proved to be.

In the year 7 A.H., the Muslims subjugated the Jewish settlers of Khaybar after they broke their pact with the Muslims. Until then the Jews, being "People of the Book," were spared expulsion and granted the privilege of paying *jizyah*, a special religious tax, in return for the protection of their property and religion by the state. Subsequently, Christians, Sabaeans, Zoroastrians, and under special circumstances also Hindus were granted the status of "People of the Book." The victory at Khaybar was due chiefly to the consistent and exemplary courage of ʿAlī, the ever-victorious warrior, who had taken part in every battle except that of Tabūk. At that time, he had represented the Prophet at Medina, who had likened him to Aaron with regard to Moses with the difference that Muḥammad, unlike Moses, was the final prophet. In the same year the Prophet sent epistles to the emperors of Persia and Byzantium and to the kings of Abyssinia and the Copts, inviting them to join the fold of Islam.

In the year 8 A.H., the Prophet made the lesser pilgrimage to Mecca peacefully, in accordance with the terms of the agreement of Ḥudaybiyyah. The Muslims rejoiced at the opportunity. Important figures like Khālid ibn Walīd and ʿAmr ibn al-ʿĀṣ embraced Islam. Certain others like Abū Sufyān, the Umayyad and leader of the Quraysh, set about establishing secret rapport with the Muslims without loss of face.

Subsequent to the violation of the treaty of Ḥudaybiyyah by the Meccans, the Prophet set out for Mecca with a sizable army comprising the migrants, the Helpers, and the bedouins. The ruler of Medina was now aware that he had the Meccans, his persecutors and oppressors for twenty years, at his mercy. He entered Mecca triumphantly, granted all his former enemies amnesty, and tried to win them over with magnanimity. The new converts

9. Interior of the Mosque of the Prophet, Medina.

8. The Mosque of the Prophet, Medina.

were to receive special material benefits for quite some time to come. Some of them, however, had mental reservations and were to cause untold misery to the family of the Prophet and his *ummah* in centuries to come. Yet they were accepted with open arms by the Islamic community once they declared their allegiance to the Prophet and accepted Islam.

The Ka'bah was purified of all idols and every vestige of paganism. The heaviest and largest of the idols, Hubal, was demolished by 'Alī. Images inscribed on the walls of the Ka'bah were erased, but icons of the Virgin Mary and Jesus were spared. The Prophet put his hands on them to ensure their protection. Allowance was made for images that were symbols of spiritual realities and not idols. This act of the Prophet also emphasized the universal and all-embracing tolerance of the Islamic perspective toward other religions based on the nature of things, as found in the Quran and *Sunnah.* The easy victory at Mecca was followed by the arduous victory at Ḥunayn. Taif was unsuccessfully besieged, but the people of Taif lost no time in embracing Islam when God changed their hearts soon after.

Contrary to the apprehensions of the Medinese Helpers, the Prophet did not resettle in Mecca but returned to Medina, which became the political and religious center of Arabia. In the year 9 A.H., a difficult and distant march to Tabūk took place, which was a great success. Local Christian and Jewish chiefs made their peace with the Prophet. Dissident and centrifugal forces in Medina were exposed and eventually suppressed or eliminated. Side by side with northern Arabia, territories like Yemen, Oman, and Bahrain, all belonging to the sphere of influence of the Persian Empire, submitted to the rule of Islam.

These areas produced the first Persian converts to Islam after the venerable Salmān al-Fārsī, who together with Uways al-Qaranī of Yemen is among the early saints of Islam. Uways al-Qaranī never saw the Prophet but bore him the most intense love. Bilāl, the muezzin, was the first black to embrace Islam, and Suhayb was of Byzantian origin. These noble representatives of various ethnic groups were the early representatives of the universality and global brotherhood that were to characterize the Islamic *ummah* throughout its later history. Piety and not race or ethnicity came to be the criterion of nobility in Islam. The Islamic collectivity was beginning to live the truth enshrined in the following Quranic verse: "O mankind, Lo! We have created you male and female, and have made you nations and tribes that ye may know one another. Lo! the noblest of you, in the sight of God, is the most God-fearing one. Lo! God is Knower, Aware" (XLIX, 13).

Toward the end of the year 10 A.H., the Prophet undertook the first full-fledged pilgrimage to Mecca in order to teach the rites to tens of thousands of his companions in the journey, so that his example could be followed by coming generations of Muslims. It was destined to be his last or farewell pilgrimage, and the sermon that he delivered on the 9th of Dhu'l-Ḥijjah in the year 10 A.H., toward the end of the ceremonies at 'Arafāt, came to be known as the Farewell Sermon:

The Farewell Sermon

All praise is for Allah. We praise Him; seek His help and pardon; and we turn to Him. We take refuge with Allah from the evils of ourselves and from the evil consequences of our actions. There is none to lead him astray whom Allah guideth aright and there is none to guide him aright whom He misguideth. I bear witness that there is no god but Allah, alone without any partner, and I bear witness that Muḥammad is His slave and His Apostle. I admonish you, O slaves of Allah, to fear Allah and I urge you to be obedient to him and I open the speech with that which is good.

Now to proceed, O people, listen to me; I will deliver a message to you. For I do not know whether I shall ever have an opportunity to meet you after this year in this place.

O people, verily your blood (lives), your properties and your honour are sacred and inviolable to you till you appear before your Lord, like the sacredness of this day of yours, in this city of yours. Verily, you will meet your Lord and He will ask you about your actions. Lo, have I conveyed the message? O Allah, be witness.

So he who bears with himself any trust, should restore it to the person who deposited it with him.

Be aware; no one committing a crime is responsible for it but himself. Neither son is responsible for the crime of his father nor father is responsible for the crime of his son.

Lo, O people, listen to my words and understand them. You must know that a Muslim is the brother of a Muslim and the Muslims are one brotherhood. Nothing belonging to his brother is lawful for a Muslim except what he himself allows. So you should not oppress yourselves. O Allah, have I conveyed the message?

Behold, everything of Ignorance is put down under my two feet. The blood-revenges of the Age of Ignorance are remitted. Verily, the first blood-revenge I cancel is the blood-revenge of Ibn Rabī'ah ibn Ḥārith, who was nursed in the tribe of Sa'd and whom the Hudhayl killed.

The interest of the Age of Ignorance period is abolished. But you will receive your capital-stock. Do not oppress and you will not be oppressed. Allah has decreed that there is no interest. The first interest which I cancel is that of 'Abbās ibn al-Muttalib. Verily it is cancelled entirely.

O people, do fear Allah concerning women. You have taken them with the trust of Allah and you have made their private parts lawful with the word of Allah.

Verily you have received certain rights over your women and your women have certain rights over you. Your right over them is that they should not make anybody, whom you dislike, trample down your beds, and that they should not allow anyone whom you dislike (to enter) into your houses. If they perform such an action, then Allah has permitted you to harass them, keep them separate in their beds and beat them but not severely. If they refrain they must have their sustenance and clothing justly from you.

Behold, receive with kindness the recommendation given about women. For they are middle-aged women (or helpers) with you. They do not possess anything for themselves and you cannot have from them more than that. It they obey you in this way, then you should not treat them unjustly. Lo, have I conveyed? O Allah, be witness.

O people, listen and obey though a mangled Abyssinian slave becomes your ruler who executes the Book of Allah among you.

O people, verily Allah appropriated to everyone his due. No will is valid for an inheritor and a will is not lawful for more than one-third (of the property).

The child belongs to the (legal) bed and for the adulterer there is stoning. He who relates (his genealogy) to other than his father or claims his clientship to other than his master, the curse of Allah, the angels and the people—all these—be upon him. Allah will accept from him neither repentance nor righteousness.

O people, verily Satan is disappointed from being ever worshipped in this land of yours. But he is satisfied to be obeyed in other matters that you think very trifling of your actions. So be cautious of him in your religion.

Verily, I have left behind among you that which if you catch hold of you will never be misled later on—a conspicuous thing, i.e., the Book of Allah and the *sunnah* of His Apostle.

O people, Gabriel came to me, conveyed *salām* from my Lord and said: "Verily Allah, the Mighty and the Great, has forgiven the people of ʿArafāt and the Sanctuary (to forgo) their short comings."

ʿUmar ibn al-Khaṭṭāb stood up and said: "O Apostle of Allah, is it for us only?" He replied: "It is for you and for those who are to come after you till the Day of Resurrection."

And you will be asked about me, then what would you say? They replied: "We bear witness that you have conveyed the message. Discharged (your duty) and admonished."

Then he said, raising his ring-finger towards heaven and pointing it out towards the people: "O Allah, bear witness: O Allah, bear witness: O Allah, bear witness."[13]

Last Days

The Prophet was, to all appearance, in perfect health and attending to state affairs with diligence. He had received deputations from practically all parts of ʿArabia and particularly from the Banū Tamīm, Banū Saʿd, Banū Bakr, Ṭayy, Farwā ibn Musayk al-Murādī, Banū Zubaydah, and Kindah tribes as well as from the kings of Ḥimyar. He kept sending governors, judges, preachers, peacemakers, and collectors of *zakāt* to various regions. He was organizing an expedition to Syria headed by the young Usāmah ibn Zayd ibn Ḥārithah, whose appointment was not liked by some elders among the Muslims. All of a sudden the Prophet fell ill toward the end of

Ṣafar in the year 11 A.H. He suffered from a headache and high fever. The illness lasted for seventeen days, which he spent at 'Ā'ishah's apartment with the consent of his other wives. The illness started when he went to the cemetery Baqī' al-Gharqad in the middle of the night and prayed for the dead. Later on he visited the graves of the martyrs of Uḥud, most prominent of whom was his uncle Ḥamzah. He prayed for the martyrs of eight years ago with great intensity, as if he were taking leave of living beings and journeying with those who were martyred. During this visit, the Quranic verse uppermost in his mind, which he recited probably more than once, was the verse "That is the Last Abode; we appointed it for those who desire not exorbitance in the earth, nor corruption. The ultimate issue is to the Godfearing" (XXVIII, 83).

The Prophet had chosen to join the companion on high and had already turned his back on the world. During this period he addressed his followers from the pulpit when he prayed for the broken-heartedness of the Muslims to be removed. He promised to receive them at the Fountain and warned them that the besetting sin of his *ummah* would be avarice and that they must be on their guard against it. He admonished them to be gracious and forgiving to the early benefactors of Islam, the *Anṣārs* or the Helpers, whose number was on the decrease. He asked Abū Bakr to lead the prayers and in fact made an effort to visit the mosque insofar as it was possible for him. He would be supported by al-Faḍl ibn al-'Abbās, his cousin, and 'Alī, his cousin and son-in-law, the husband of the Prophet's sole surviving and favorite daughter, Fāṭimah. Sayyīdah Fāṭimah was the only person in whom the Prophet confided his approaching death, whereupon she wept. Then he whispered into her ear that she would be the first of the family to join him, which made her smile. Among the last advice given by Mahatma Buddha on his death-bed was the following: "Work out your own salvation, O monks." Likewise, the Prophet admonished his near and dear ones, especially his well-beloved daughter, Fāṭimah, and his aunt Ṣafiyyah in these terms: "Work ye that which shall please the Lord." Among the prayers he made on his deathbed was the following: "O Lord, let my grave be not adopted as an idol. God has cursed the people who have turned the graves of their prophets into objects of worship."

On realizing that there were a few gold coins deposited with his wife 'Ā'ishah, he gave them away in charity, since he did not want to meet his Lord while there were gold coins present in his house. From time to time the Prophet sought relief from the intensity of his fever by having seven skins of water from different wells in Medina poured over him. He was made to sit in a tub in the house of his wife Ḥafṣah bint 'Umar ibn al-Khaṭṭāb for such a bath. He felt better after taking one of these baths and went to the mosque and performed the *ẓuhr* prayers whereafter he took his seat on the pulpit and delivered a long discourse, which included the following statement:

> Verily God the Exalted says: "By the afternoon! Surely Man is in the way of loss, save those who believe, and do righteous deeds, and counsel each other unto the truth, and counsel each other to be steadfast." (CIII)

The Prophet added:

> Verily, the affairs take their course according to the Will of God. Do not let delay in dispensation lead you to despair of demanding Divine Succour. God Almighty, the Great, is not hurried into anything by anyone of you being in a hurry. He who contends with God is overpowered by Him. He who plays false and loose with God is outwitted by Him. If you attain to authority in the near future do not spread mischief on earth and do not sever blood relations.

He then admonished them at length to be constantly and selflessly good to the Helpers. He further said:

> Beware, he who is anxious to rejoin me at the Fountain must hold his tongue and restrain his hand.
>
> O People, verily sins deprive people of blessings and bring about changes in their lot. When people are good their rulers do good to them and when the people are evildoers their rulers oppress them.
>
> There may be amongst you one whom I owe anything. I am after all a human being. So if there is any man whose honour I might have injured, here I am to answer for it. If I have unjustifiably inflicted bodily harm on anyone, I present myself for retribution. If I owe anything to anyone, here is my property and he may help himself to it. Know that the most faithful to me of you is one who having such a claim against me either makes it good or absolves me of it so that I may meet my Lord after I have been absolved of it. Nobody should say: "I fear enmity and rancor of the Messenger of God." I nurse no grudge towards anyone. These things are repugnant to my nature and temperament. I abhor them so.

The Prophet recalled that some people had criticized the appointment of Usāmah as commander of the proposed expedition to Syria. He said:

> O men, dispatch Usāmah's force, for though you criticize his leadership as you criticized the leadership of his father before him; he is just as worthy of the command as his father was.[14]

Usāmah left with his army and went as far as al-Jurf, where he received word from Umm Ayman, the Prophet's childhood nurse, to stay there to see what turn the Prophet's health took.

10. The Dome of the Rock, Jerusalem.

According to the Sunni version, the Prophet praised profusely Abū Bakr for accepting Islam without the least doubt and also for his immense generosity for the cause of Islam. He ordered that all doors opening to the mosque be shut except the one from Abū Bakr's house, a privilege already conferred on 'Alī, according to the Shī'ite version. One morning he is said to have prayed with Abū Bakr as Imam. Once 'Umar mistook orders and led the prayers. This was not approved by the Prophet, who insisted that Abū Bakr alone should lead the prayers. The morning the Prophet prayed behind Abū Bakr, he seemed to have rallied, and the Muslims rejoiced at the recovery that was, however, more apparent than real. Abū Bakr sought and secured the Prophet's permission to visit his wife at al-Sunh outside Medina. 'Alī told the worshipers that the Prophet had recovered and there was no cause for anxiety. Everybody felt relieved.

After the Prophet returned home, however, the picture changed. Before exhaustion rendered the Prophet speechless, his last advice was that the Muslims should be mindful of the daily prayers and of the welfare of those entrusted to them. Among his last acts was to use a green twig as a toothbrush, which 'Ā'ishah softened for him by masticating it. His very last act was an invocation of blessings upon Usāmah, who had rushed to the Prophet's deathbed to pay his final respects. The Prophet had been in intense pain and constantly sought Divine Help to ease the agony of death. His last words were these: "O God, with the supreme communion."[15] He breathed his last on the 12th of Rabī' al-Awwal in the year 11 A.H. with his head resting in the lap of his favorite and noble wife, 'Ā'ishah, in whose house he lived and died and was ultimately buried.

According to the Shī'ite version of the events of the last days of the Prophet, his sudden and serious illness lasted for three days only and he died in the hands of 'Alī as the chief attendant. He was buried by 'Alī, Fāṭimah, and other members of his family in the same house where he lived, while the people of Medina were debating the future of the Islamic *ummah* in the adjacent mosque.

The Prophet breathed his last at the age of sixty-three. The news shook the Muslims. 'Umar was thrown off balance and he reiterated that the Prophet had not died. He threatened to kill anyone holding the opposite view. 'Alī was so overcome by grief that he was unable to stand on his legs. 'Uthmān ibn 'Affān became utterly speechless. Abū Bakr alone was able to retain his poise and sobriety. He kissed the Prophet's forehead and remarked: "Sweet wert thou in life; sweet art thou in death." He then withdrew and addressed the multitude outside the Prophet's chamber. 'Umar would not listen to him, but he proceeded with his address: "Had not God Almighty revealed to the Prophet: 'Verily thou shalt die, and they shall die'?" (XXX, 30).[16] Again: "And Muḥammad is naught but an Apostle. Apostles have died before him. Can it be that if he dies or be killed you would turn back on your heels?" (III, 144). Abū Bakr added, "All praise belongs to Allāh! O people, whoever worshiped Muḥammad, Muḥammad is dead. But for him who worships Allāh, Allāh is living and never dies." He then recited the verse revealed after the battle of Uḥud: "And Muḥammad is naught but a messenger; messengers (the like of whom) have passed away before him. Will it be that when he dies or is slain, you will turn back on your heels? Whosoever turns back does no harm to God and God will reward the grateful" (III, 144). 'Umar was dumbfounded on hearing Abū Bakr speak and fell to the ground on becoming aware of the reality of the Prophet's death. Everybody now tried to hear of the loss with fair patience.

The *Anṣār* assembled in the Hall of Banū Sā'idah to decide the succession. The migrants joined them there, and after an exchange of arguments it was agreed that the Quraysh would be the administrators and that the *Anṣār* would be the ministers or advisors. Abū Bakr proposed the name of 'Umar as the first caliph, but 'Umar firmly took hold of Abū Bakr's hand and hastened to take the oath of fealty. The rest followed him except Sa'd ibn 'Ubādah, a contender from the Helpers, who was removed from the scene. Abū Bakr was elected to be the first caliph. He declared that he was not the best among them and that the weak would be strong while the strong would remain weak in his eyes until he was able to effect justice. Meanwhile, 'Alī, his close relatives, and freedmen of the Prophet took no part in the electoral process. They were engaged in making arrangements for washing, shrouding, and burying the Prophet, who lay in state in 'Ā'ishah's chamber. People filed past the bier after saying the funeral prayers individually and severally. The sacred body was lowered in the grave by 'Alī, Usāmah, and al-Faḍl ibn al-'Abbās. Unbaked bricks were used to build a vault over it, and the rest of the grave was filled with gravel and sand. In this simple manner, the earthly life of the man praised by God and His angels came to an end, and the life of the community founded by him began to flourish on the basis of his example and the message brought by him to spread beyond the confines of Arabia to the farthest lands in the east and west.

Notes

1. For the 201 traditional names of the Prophet, see Sheikh Tosun Bayrak al-Jerrahi al-Halveti, *The Most Beautiful Names* (Putney, VT: Threshold Books, 1985) 143ff. To understand fully the meaning of these names, of which the most famous are perhaps

Muḥammad, Aḥmad, 'Abd Allāh, and Muṣṭāfa, is to gain a glimpse of the contour of the spiritual character of the Prophet.

2. See A. M. Schimmel, *And Muhammad is His Messenger* (Chapel Hill: University of North Carolina Press, 1985).

3. The best traditional account of the life of the Prophet in English is M. Lings, *Muhammad* (London: Allen & Unwin, 1983).

4. The account given here of the life of the Prophet is the traditional one, which alone is of significance as far as Islamic spirituality as it has been lived over the centuries is concerned.

5. Ibn Hishām, *Kitāb sīrat rasūl Allāh,* ed. F. Wüstenfeld (Leipzig: Dieterich, 1900) 1:100.

6. Ibid., 101; taken from Lings, *Muhammad,* 17–18.

7. Lings, *Muhammad,* 35.

8. Ibn Sa'd, *Kitāb al-ṭabaqāt al-kabīr* (Leiden: Brill, 1904–40) 3:28.

9. Lings, *Muhammad,* 83.

10. A. Guillaume, trans., *The Life of Muhammad: A Translation of Ishaq's Sirat Rasul Allah* (London: Oxford University Press, 1955) 193.

11. A. Jeffery, *Islam-Muhammad and His Religion* (Indianapolis: Bobbs-Merril, 1958) 42–46. On the *mi'rāj,* see also S. H. Nasr, *Muhammad, the Man of Allah* (London: Muhammadi Trust, 1982) 14ff.; Schimmel, *Muhammad,* chap. 9.

12. See his *Tafsīr al-qur'ān* (Cairo) 3:225.

13. Maulana M. Ubaidul Akbar, *The Orations of Muhammad* (Lahore: M. Ashraf, 1954) 78–79 (with certain modifications).

14. See A. Guillaume, *Life.*

15. Lings, *Muhammad,* 341.

16. L. Azzam and A. Gouverneur, *The Life of the Prophet Muhammad* (London: Islamic Text Society, 1985) 121.

II. *Sunnah and Ḥadīth*

SEYYED HOSSEIN NASR

The Significance of the *Sunnah* and *Ḥadīth*

THE EMULATION OF THE PROPHET, which lies at the heart of Islamic spirituality and piety, is based upon his *Sunnah,* or traditions and actions. While his inner being or prophetic Substance is the invisible fountainhead of spirituality and his life stands as a portrait whose details the Muslim contemplates throughout his life, the *Sunnah* provides concrete examples and access to that Muḥammadan model which the Quran has commanded the faithful to imitate. Whereas the inner *Sunnah* constitutes those virtues and inner perfections which became echoed during later centuries in works of Sufi ethics, the body of the *Sunnah* as a whole has provided over the ages the guideline for all aspects of the everyday life of Muslims ranging from eating breakfast to ruling over the land. The *Sunnah* is a commentary upon the Quran and the manner by which the Muslims came to learn how the truths of the Sacred Text were lived by the most perfect of God's creation in a life that was human yet completely immersed in the sacred. Through the *Sunnah* every facet of human life has become sacralized, for the Divine Law (*al-Sharīʿah*) itself, which provides the matrix for Islamic life, is based not only on the Quran but also on the *Ḥadīth* and, in a more general sense, the *Sunnah,* which, comprising all of the actions and traditions of the Prophet, in a sense also encompasses the *Ḥadīth.*

There is, however, a difference between the *Sunnah* and the *Ḥadīth* that is often mentioned in traditional Islamic sources. The *Ḥadīth* contains the words of the Prophet, whereas the *Sunnah* includes both his specific words and actions and practices of which he approved among earlier Arab traditions and so allowed to be continued by Muslims. He thereby Islamicized these practices although they were of pre-Islamic origin. The Revelation always takes to some extent the color of the recipient. In the case of the *Sunnah,* although certain aspects were directly derived from, were commentaries upon, and were applications of the teachings of the Quran, other aspects represent the Islamicization of certain Arabic traditions that God had allowed to be integrated into the Islamic universe by permitting the Prophet to accept the continuation of their practice in the light of the new Revelation. The unity of the *Sunnah* as revolving around the Prophet and his traditions and actions as well as response to various situations and circumstances is not, however, in any way compromised by the acceptance of certain older traditions by the Prophet. This very acceptance marked also their integration into the total pattern that he sought to establish as a model for the Islamic life.

The *Sunnah*

The *Sunnah* is central to all aspects of Islamic spirituality, for it is through the emulation of the *Sunnah* of the Prophet that the Muslim is able to gain certain of the virtues which are possessed in their fullness by the Prophet. The Muslim sees the Prophet through his *Sunnah*—how he acted, spoke, walked, ate, judged, loved, and worshiped. The *Sunnah* is, therefore, in a sense the continuation of the life of the Prophet for later generations, complementing the image of his person reflected also in his names, in the description of his physical being, and, of course, in the Muḥammadan *barakah*, which flows through the ever-present power of his names and his *Sunnah*.

The Prophet's Appearance and Names

The perfection inherent in the Prophet as God's most noble and perfect creature could not but manifest itself in his physical features. He was said to possess an exceptionally beautiful countenance, which has been extolled over the ages. His features have been described by several of the companions, such as ʿAlī ibn Abī Ṭālib, his cousin and son-in-law, with whom he was brought up and who knew him so intimately. ʿAlī describes the Prophet in these words:

> He was neither tall and lanky nor short and stocky, but of medium height. His hair was neither crispy curled nor straight but moderately wavy. He was not overweight, and his face was not plump. He had a round face. His complexion was white tinged with reddishness. He had big black eyes with long lashes. His bones were heavy and his shoulders broad. He had soft skin, with fine hair covering the line from midchest to navel. The palms of his hands and the soles of his feet were firmly padded. He walked with a firm gait, as if striding downhill. On his back between his shoulders lay the Seal of Prophethood, for he was the last of the prophets.
>
> He was the most generous of men in feeling, the most truthful in speech, the gentlest in disposition, and the noblest in lineage. At first encounter people were awestruck by him, but on closer acquaintance they would come to love him. One who sought to describe him could only say, "Neither before him nor after him did I ever see the like of him."[1]

The physical beauty of the Prophet, which has been so exquisitely described in Arabic, Persian, and vernacular poetry of the Islamic peoples, possesses a direct spiritual significance. The beauty of his face has been compared to the full moon and his stature to the cypress tree; it has been said that no beauty in the world could ever match the beauty of his countenance. In the Muslim eye, this appreciation of the beauty of the Prophet is directly related to the love for him and constitutes a basic aspect of Islamic spirituality complementing the fear, love, and knowledge of God, the One who is at once transcendent and immanent.

In the same way that *Muḥammadun rasūl Allāh* ("Muḥammad is the Messenger of God) follows *Lā ilāha illa'Llāh*, the names of the Prophet flow from those of God and are a ladder that leads to Him. The Prophet has been even honored by God by having some of the Divine Names such as Ṭa Ha and Nūr also bestowed upon him. The chanting of the litanies of the names of the Prophet is an important practice in Sufism and on a more external level in the everyday activity of many pious Muslims. The Turkish Sufi poet Yunis Emre sang seven centuries ago:

> Please pray for us on Doomsday–
> Thy name is beautiful, thou thyself art beautiful, Muḥammad!
> Thy words are accepted near God, the Lord–
> Thy name is beautiful, thou thyself art beautiful.[2]

Not only is the Prophet called Muḥammad, the most praised one, but he is also Aḥmad, the most praiseworthy of those who praise God. He is Waḥīd, the unique one; Māḥī, the annihilator of darkness and ignorance; and 'Āqib, the last of the prophets. He is Ṭāhir, the pure and clean one; Ṭayyib, he who possesses beauty and fragrance; and Sayyid, prince and master of the universe. He is, of course, Rasūl, messenger, but also Rasūl al-Raḥmah, the messenger of mercy; and Khātim al-rusul, the seal of prophets. He is 'Abd Allāh, the perfect servant of God, but also Ḥabīb Allāh, the beloved of God; and Ṣafī Allāh, the one chosen by God. He is both Nāṣir, the victorious helper of men, and Manṣūr, the one who is made triumphant in this world.

The Prophet is Muḥyī, the vivifier of the dead hearts of men, and Munjī, he who delivers man from sin. He is Nūr, light, as well as Sirāj, the torch that illuminates the path in man's life; Miṣbāḥ, the lamp that contains the light of faith, and Hudā, the guide to God and paradise. He is Dhū quwwah, the possessor of strength; Dhū ḥurmah, possessor of sacred reverence; and Dhū makānah, the possessor of integrity. He is both Amīn, trustworthy, and Ṣadīq, truthful. He is the Miftāḥ, or key to paradise, and Miftāḥ al-raḥmah, the key to God's Mercy. The love of the Prophet is in fact both a sign of the love of God and the gate to that Mercy from which the very substance of the universe was created.

In reciting the names of the Prophet, the Muslim draws closer to the Prophet and participates in some degree in those qualities and virtues which the names reflect. The names of the Prophet are the colors with which the spiritual portrait of the Prophet is engraved in the hearts and souls of the members of his community, facilitating the emulation of his *Sunnah* and providing the channel for that *barakah* which is experienced concretely when his *Sunnah* is lived and emulated in life. In a sense in fact, both the names of the Prophet and the appreciation of his beauty constitute an element of his *Sunnah*, an element that is central to the spiritual life of Islam.

Aspects of the Sunnah

The *Sunnah* comprises the strands of which the fiber of Islamic life is woven. Although not all Muslims live always according to the *Sunnah*—human nature being what it is—the practice of the *Sunnah* has remained always an ideal to be achieved. Moreover, it is an ideal that has been realized to a remarkable degree over the ages and has, in any case, always been of central concern for those who have sought to live a spiritual life according to the "Muḥammadan model."

As already stated, the *Sunnah* itself covers all aspects of human life from praying to dealing with one's family, friends, and the community, carrying out economic transactions, being kind to animals, or running a state. When a Muslim greets another by saying *as-salāmu ʿalayka* ("Peace be upon you"), he is following the prophetic *Sunnah*. When a person tries to treat an orphan with kindness or be respectful of his or her parents and elders or be charitable to the poor, he is following the *Sunnah*. Moreover, when he seeks to be trustworthy and truthful or kind and generous, he is following the *Sunnah*—but this time the inner *Sunnah*, which is central to the spiritual life.

Even minute details of life such as the manner of eating at the table or sitting or entering a house are based on the *Sunnah*, and the pious among Muslims are aware of the *barakah* that emanates from such everyday acts when they are consciously based on the prophetic model. On the higher levels of spiritual realization, the Muḥammadan *barakah* in a sense flows from the being of the person who has lived the inner *Sunnah*, in whose heart lies the constant remembrance of God. That is why in popular parlance it is often said that one can see the reflection of the Light of Muḥammad (*al-nūr al-muḥammadī*) in the countenance of this or that saintly person and to feel the Muḥammadan *barakah* in his presence, movements, and comportment.

From the point of view of spirituality, what is central is the essential or inner *Sunnah,* which is indispensable, whereas the outer *Sunnah* acts as a formal support for it.[3] The essential *Sunnah* concerns most of all the inner virtues of the Prophet and the spiritual perfections that flow from the prophetic Substance discussed earlier in this work. All the external *Sunnah* is a way of leading to those virtues and of enabling the soul to become embellished by them. Although as the final prophet, the Prophet of Islam synthesized the prophetic function and returned man to his state of primordial perfection (*al-fiṭrah*), there are certain central virtues that characterize the inner nature of the Prophet: humility, charity, or nobility, and truthfulness or sincerity. The *Sunnah* reflects on various levels these virtues, and through its emulation the soul of the Muslim becomes gradually imbued with them. In a sense, the practical aspect of Islamic spirituality may be said to consist of the gradual embellishment of the soul with the Muḥammadan virtues. In fact, people of spiritual character in the Islamic world are often said to possess the "Muḥammadan character" (*khū-yi muḥammadī* in Persian), because through the practice of his *Sunnah* they have come to attain some of the virtues possessed in their fullness and perfection by God's Last Prophet.

Sunnah *and* Adab

A key concept in Islamic culture and thought whose understanding is necessary for the comprehension of the various dimensions of Islamic spirituality is *adab,* a word that probably entered Arabic from Pahlavi but is nevertheless a basic Islamic concept. *Adab* means at once courtesy, manners, correct comportment and upbringing, culture and literature. To possess *adab* is to be truly cultured in a manner that embraces not only the mind but also the body and soul. *Adab* means being polite before elders; recognizing the innate hierarchy in human values; knowing when to speak and when to remain silent, how to sit or stand politely, how to eat properly, and how to act correctly in all situations. Although some aspects of *adab,* such as the manner whereby one must be hospitable to guests, are determined by local cultural conditions, there is a deeper aspect of *adab* that concerns the training of the soul and of the body in relation to the soul. This aspect of *adab* is of great importance in the spiritual life, and a certain amount of *adab* is a prerequisite for embarking upon the spiritual path.

Much of Sufism concerns itself with this spiritual aspect of *adab,* and usually each Sufi center possesses elaborate rules for the adepts in their dealing with the master, other disciples, and the world outside. The aim of these rules is to train the soul and bestow upon it the habits necessary for progress upon the spiritual path.[4] *Adab* is especially effective in curbing the passions and bridling the aggressive tendencies of the lower soul and the excesses of its appetites.

Not all the forms and aspects of *adab* are drawn from or based directly upon the *Sunnah*, but much that is basic to *adab* does derive from the *Sunnah*. In a sense, the basic attitudes which the practice of *adab* inculcates in the soul of the Muslim are derived from the *Sunnah*, and in certain areas *adab* and the *Sunnah* coincide. In any case, the *adab*, so visible in traditional Islamic society, is inextricably tied to the *Sunnah* and reflects the prophetic practices and traditions on a particular level that is of great importance both socially and spiritually.

The *Sunnah* of the Prophet is the enactment in human terms of the teachings of Islam as revealed in the Quran, the enactment having been first carried out by the most perfect of God's creatures and the man most able to understand God's commands and to put them into action in concrete situations. To emulate the *Sunnah* is to live Islamically and according to God's will. Moreover, it is to imitate the beloved of God and consequently to be loved by God as the very result of this emulation. The *Sunnah* embraces all domains of human life, but at its heart lies that inner *Sunnah* which is none other than the traces of the spiritual Substance of the Prophet. To live according to this *Sunnah* means to live in constant remembrance of God, to be severe with oneself and generous with those about us, to understand our nothingness before that awesome Majesty that is God and to live in truth and certainty of the saving power of the One who is both Absolute and Infinite. There is no Islamic spirituality possible without the *Sunnah*, for the gate to the higher worlds was opened for the Islamic sector of humanity by the Prophet alone during his nocturnal journey. It is he alone who holds the key to those gates and who alone can guide the Muslim on the path of spiritual realization.[5]

Ḥadīth

The *Ḥadīth* constitutes a part of the *Sunnah*, for it consists of those traditions of the Prophet which are in the form of sayings rather than actions. The word *ḥadīth* itself means "saying," but it is also rendered as "tradition"; the plural is *aḥadīth*. The corpus of the sayings of the Prophet are referred to as *Ḥadīth*, since it constitutes a distinct body of words assembled by later scholars in canonical collections that are of prime importance in all aspects of Islamic thought. Only the Quran is of greater significance and authority.

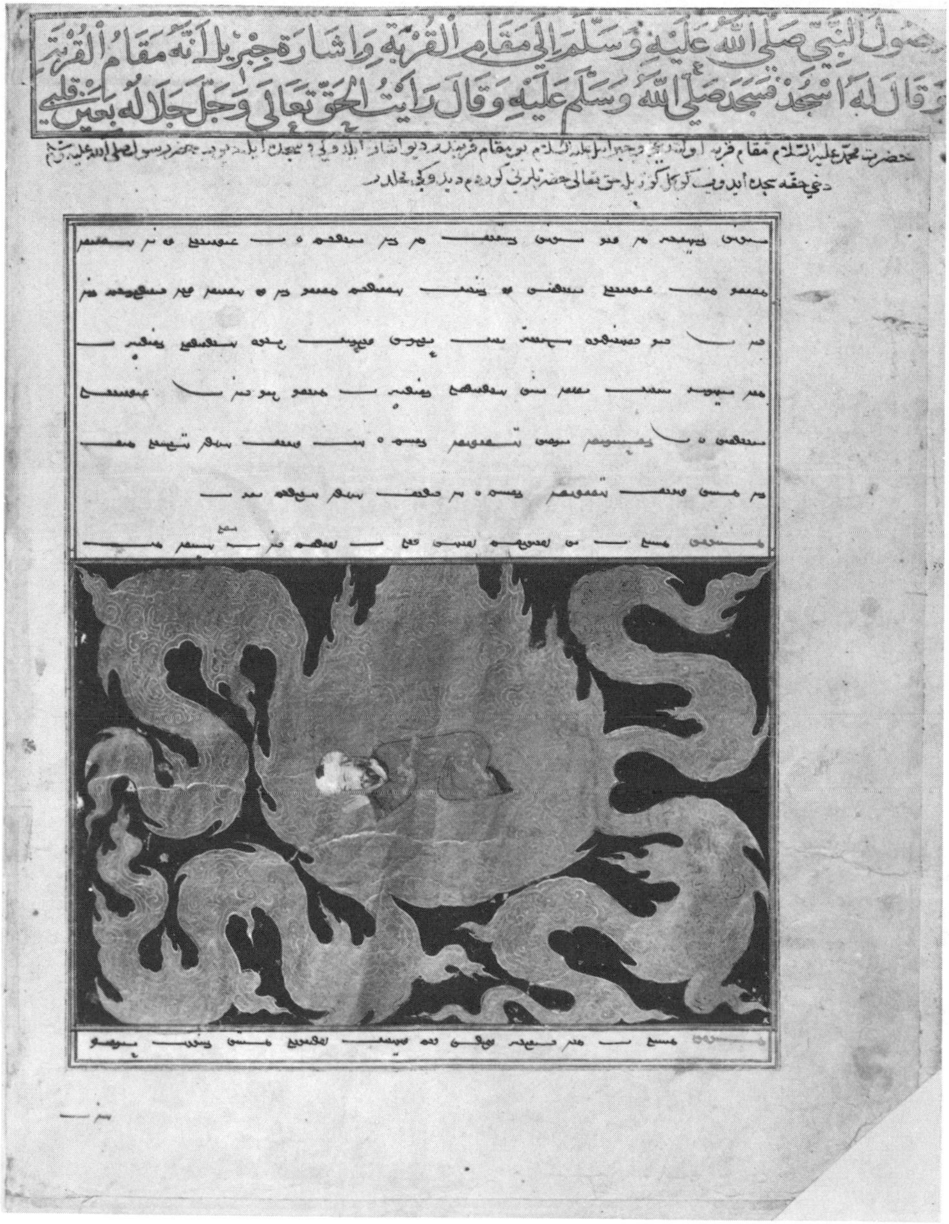

11. “The Prophet praying before the Divine Throne and Receiving from God instructions concerning the daily prayers,” Supplement Turc 190, Folio 34v.

The *Ḥadīth* is, in fact, the first and most important commentary on the Quran. At the same time, it completes the Sacred Text and amplifies and makes explicit many of its verses. The *Ḥadīth* is like the expansion in human language, that of the Prophet, of the Divine Word which is the Quran.

The first two centuries of Islam saw the transmission, application, and first moves toward the codification of the *Ḥadīth.* As the Islamic community spread and the *ummah* became ever more distanced from the lifetime of the Prophet and his immediate companions, the need for compiling, authenticating, and sifting the body of *Ḥadīth* grew, and an ever greater number of religious scholars began to apply themselves to this task. Several sciences were developed in the field of *Ḥadīth* studies, such as *al-dirāyah,* which examines the authenticity of the chain of transmission (*isnād*). This examination includes the ethical character, quality of piety, standing in the community, and trustworthiness of those men and women who were accepted as transmitters of the *ḥadīth*s which came to be accepted by the community. In this process, in which pious women played a major role along with men, both those who transmitted a *ḥadīth* and those who collected and codified the prophetic sayings were God-fearing people. In contrast to many modern Western critics of *Ḥadīth,* for them the fire of hell was a reality, and fabrication of sayings attributed to the Prophet was a grievous sin punishable after death with infernal suffering. The scholars of *Ḥadīth,* or *muḥaddithūn,* were in fact always a small group of religious scholars who were expected to possess great virtue and piety as well as knowledge.

These scholars sifted the vast body of sayings attributed to the Prophet and classified them according to those that were certain, doubtful, and spurious. Gradually this process produced the six major canonical collections which came to be accepted by the Sunni community. These works, usually called *Ṣaḥīḥ* (pl. *Ṣiḥāḥ*), consist of *Jāmiʿ al-ṣaḥīḥ* of Abū ʿAbd Allāh Muḥammad al-Bukhārī, the *Ṣaḥīḥ* of Abu'l-Ḥusayn ʿAsākir al-Dīn Muslim, the *Sunan* of Abū Dā'ūd al-Sijistānī, the *Jāmiʿ* of Abū ʿĪsā Muḥammad al-Tirmidhī, the *Sunan* of Abū ʿAbd al-Raḥmān al-Nasā'ī, and the *Sunan* of Abū ʿAbd Allāh Muḥammad ibn Mājah. There are also other works such as the *Sunan* of al-Dārimī and the *al-Muwaṭṭa'* of Mālik ibn Anas that have also always been highly respected by Sunni Muslims, but none can match the significance of the six works which are usually referred to collectively as *al-Ṣiḥāḥ al-sittah* or the six *Ṣaḥīḥ*s. These works, all compiled in the third/ninth century, received the seal of approval of the *ʿulamā'* and the community in the form of *ijmāʿ*, or consensus. They came to form an indispensable source upon which Sunni Islam has relied for over a millennium for its knowledge of *Ḥadīth,* which along with the Quran constitutes the pillar of the whole religion[6]. There are of course certain *ḥadīths,* especially of an esoteric nature, which continued to be transmitted orally and do not appear in writing until centuries later and then in works of such Sufi masters as al-Ghazzālī and Jalāl al-Dīn Rūmī. But the vast majority of *ḥadīths* upon which the Islamic community has based itself over the centuries in the development of its various sciences ranging from jurisprudence (*fiqh*) to theology (*kalām*) are to be found in these canonical collections.

In Twelve-Imam Shīʿism the collection of *Ḥadīth* includes not only the sayings of the Prophet but also those of the Imams, who bear within themselves the Prophetic Light and represent the prolongation of the function of the Prophet in its nonlegislative aspects. The Shīʿites distinguish between a prophetic saying (*al-ḥadīth al-nabawī*) and the saying of an Imam (*al-ḥadīth al-walawī*). Both these types of *Ḥadīth* were collected and codified by Shīʿite scholars a century after the Sunni canonical collections saw the light of day. The basic Shīʿite works on *Ḥadīth,* which are often referred to as "The Four Books" (*al-kutub al-arbaʿah*), are *al-Kāfī* by Muḥammad ibn Yaʿqūb al-Kulaynī, *Man lā yaḥḍuruhuʾl-faqīh* of Muḥammad ibn Bābūyah al-Qummī, and two works of Muḥammad al-Ṭūsī, *Kitāb al-tahdhīb* and *Kitāb al-istibṣār.* These four works were all compiled in the fourth/tenth and fifth/eleventh centuries and are as essential to all aspects of Shīʿite Islam as the *Ṣiḥāḥ* are to Sunni Islam. The Shīʿite collections played perhaps an even greater role in the development of later Islamic philosophy, when a number of them became the subject of commentaries by some of the outstanding Islamic metaphysicians and philosophers.[7]

Since Islamic studies became a distinct discipline in the West at the beginning of this century, a number of Western scholars—foremost among them I. Goldziher followed by A. J. Wensinck, A. Guillaume, J. Schacht, and others—have tried to apply the critical historical methods developed in the nineteenth century to the collections of *Ḥadīth.* Their work was based on the usually unstated premises that what is not found in written record is a later addition or fabrication, that Islam, being a so-called simple religion of the desert, could not possibly have metaphysical and esoteric doctrines contained in the sayings of its Prophet, and that oral transmission and the whole idea of traditional orthodoxy and its historical continuity are invalid. These Western scholars of Islam came to consider most of the canonically accepted *ḥadīths* to be third/ninth century reflections of the Islamic community upon its religious heritage and therefore not authentic sayings of the Prophet. Later research by scholars such as N. Abbot has modified this criticism by unveiling much earlier documents containing many well-known *ḥadīths.* However, much of Western scholarship still casts a doubtful eye upon the authenticity of *Ḥadīth* in the sense that it has always been understood by traditional Muslims.[8] Muslim scholars have for their part provided answers to orientalists' charges, aware that the authors of the *Ṣiḥāḥ* chose some six thousand *ḥadīths* from among nearly three hundred thousand and declared their authenticity after the most vigorous scholarly examination combined with piety and the protection of tradition, with all that it implies.[9]

This work on Islamic spirituality is not the place to delve into the attacks and responses concerning the *Ḥadīth.* Although there are a number of small Muslim groups in the Indo-Pakistani subcontinent and in the Arab world who want to reinterpret Islam on the basis of the Quran alone, they constitute a marginal phenomenon. They might be taken into consideration in a general study on contemporary Islam, but such movements, as well as Western criticisms of *Ḥadīth,* are not relevant to an understanding of Islamic spirituality. For throughout Islamic history, those who have sought to tread upon the spiritual path have been "nourished" by the *Ḥadīth* and guided by the *barakah* of the Prophet in such a way that they have possessed "an existential" guarantee of the authenticity of the sayings that have guided their lives, the guarantee issuing inwardly from the being who is at the origin of the *Ḥadīth.*

The Scope of Ḥadīth

The *Ḥadīth* literature is a veritable compendium of wisdom and guidance covering every facet of human thought and life. Like the *Sunnah,* it concerns everyday aspects of life such as eating, sleeping, treating one's neighbors, and providing livelihood for oneself and one's family, as well as social, economic, and political affairs concerning society as a whole. It also deals extensively with the rites and ritual aspects of Islamic life as well as the inner life itself. Moreover, being constituted of words rather than actions, as is the case of the *Sunnah,* the *Ḥadīth* also deals extensively with metaphysics, cosmology, cosmogony, the science of the origin and nature of man, and eschatology. It deals also with specifically theological questions such as free will and determinism as well as detailed juridical discussions without which the Divine Law could not have become codified by the great doctors of Law who founded the four Sunni schools of Law (*madhāhib*). The same truth holds true for Shīʿism, where, despite the ever-present authority of the Imam, the Quran and *Ḥadīth* remain the fundamental sources of the Divine Law.

The *Ṣaḥīḥ* of Bukhārī, the most famous of the six Sunni canonical collections, reflects in the titles of its books and sections the scope of the *ḥadīths* that it includes. The work of Bukhārī includes sections devoted to the nature of God and prophecy, creation, ethical questions, rites, acquiring of knowledge, and eschatology. There is hardly an aspect of man's life that is not touched by the light of a *ḥadīth,* and such metaphysical and cosmological questions as the origin of the world, the primacy of the intellect, and man's final end are also included in *ḥadīths* which have served as the source of metaphysical speculation and contemplation over the centuries.

The Shīʿite collections are likewise divided into sections that reflect the wide spectrum of subjects with which the *ḥadīths* deal. There are, however, some differences, although most of the sayings of the Prophet mentioned by the sources traditionally accepted by the Sunnis and Shīʿites are the same. One of the notable differences that has played an important role in the development of Islamic theology and philosophy during later centuries is the emphasis upon the intellect (*al-ʿaql*) in the Shīʿite sources, to such an extent that the *Uṣūl al-kāfī* of Kulaynī, perhaps the most important of the "Four Books" of Shīʿism, devotes a special book to sayings concerned with *al-ʿaql.* There are, of course, also many *ḥadīths* about the virtue and nobility of *al-ʿaql* in Sunni sources, but there is somewhat more emphasis upon this subject in the Shīʿite collections of *Ḥadīth.* Both Sunni and Shīʿite sources, however, deal extensively with questions related directly to knowledge and the spiritual life. There is, in fact, no possibility of understanding Islamic spirituality without comprehending the significance of *Ḥadīth* in all dimensions of the life of Islam, from the most outward to the most central and inward.

Divine Sayings (al-aḥādīth al-qudsiyyah)

There are numerous *ḥadīths* that concern the spiritual life. Within the corpus of *Ḥadīth* there are some in which God speaks in the first person through the mouth of the Prophet, although these sayings are not a part of the Quran. They deal in an especially direct manner with the inner life. These traditions, which are called Divine Sayings (*aḥādīth qudsiyyah*), form, along with certain verses of the Quran, the revealed and prophetic basis of Sufism and are repeated over the ages in numerous works of Sufis.[10] These sayings deal with the inner life, with methods of spiritual practice, with the Mercy of God, and with other themes central to the spiritual life.

In one of these *ḥadīths* God speaks through the mouth of the Prophet:

> I fulfill My servant's expectation of Me, and I am with him when he remembers [or invokes] Me. If he remembers Me in his heart, I remember him in

> My heart; and if he remembers Me in public, I remember him before a public [far] better than that. And if he draws nearer to Me by a handsbreadth, I draw nearer to him by an armslength; and if he draws nearer to Me by an armslength, I draw nearer to him by a fathom; and if he comes to Me walking, I come to him running.[11]

In this *ḥadīth* not only is the central practice of Sufism, the *dhikr*—which is at once remembrance, invocation, and mention of God's Name—emphasized, but also it is pointed out that there is no quantitative reciprocity between man's efforts on the spiritual path and the Divine Response. Whatever steps man takes toward God in complete faith and with all his heart and soul are recompensed in an immeasurable manner far beyond what the acts themselves might warrant if viewed only outwardly.

Yet there is also a reciprocity between man and the Divine Order in the sense that man cannot love God and turn to Him unless God first loves man and turns "His Face" toward him. Man cannot turn toward God unless God also turns toward him. This basic truth is asserted in another famous *ḥadīth qudsī*, "If My servant longs to meet Me, I long to meet him. And if he abhors meeting Me, I abhor meeting him."[12] Also, "My love belongs by right to those who love one another in Me, to those who sit together (in fellowship) in Me, to those who visit one another in Me, and to those who give generously to one another in Me."[13] This saying is also the basis for the Sufi gathering (*majlis*) where men and women sit together to remember and invoke God.

The immeasurable Divine Response issuing from His Mercy to the spiritual efforts of man is emphasized in another *ḥadīth qudsī*, which is perhaps the most famous and often quoted of these sayings in later Islamic sources, especially works of Sufism. This saying, usually called the *ḥadīth* of *nawāfil* (supererogatory works), has several versions, the heart of which is as follows:

> My servant draws near to Me by means of nothing dearer to Me than that which I have established as a duty for him. And my servant continues drawing nearer to Me through supererogatory acts until I love him; and when I love him, I become his ear with which he hears, his eye with which he sees, his hand with which he grasps, and his foot with which he walks. And if he asks Me [for something], I give it to him. If indeed he seeks My help, I help him.[14]

This celebrated *ḥadīth* not only outlines the stages of approaching God but also alludes to the mystery of sanctification and union, for surely he who sees with the eye of God sees God everywhere and he who hears with the ear of God hears the echo of His Name wherever he turns and in whatever sound he experiences.

These sayings always emphasize the lack of equality between God's Mercy and His Justice, according to the verse written on the Throne of God, "Verily My Mercy overcometh My Wrath."[15] In one of these *ḥadīths*, God says, "Whoever does a good deed, to him belong ten like it, and I increase [even this]."[16] Some of these *ḥadīths* also reveal God's desire for man to turn to Him, for God says, "Who entreats Me, that I may answer him? Who asks [something] of Me, that I may give to him? Who asks My forgiveness, that I may forgive?"[17] Only the person of spiritual disposition realizes that the very act of asking God's forgiveness draws the Divine Mercy toward that person and that, as long as man is man, the gate toward the Divine Presence is open and man can draw nigh toward God by asking God's forgiveness. Even the Prophet of God used to invoke *astaghfir Allāh* (I ask forgiveness of God) every day.

The body of Divine Sayings constitutes one of the most sublime works pertaining to the spiritual life. They distill and synthesize the spiritual message of the *Ḥadīth*. Concerned with the whole of life, the *Ḥadīth* also concerns matters that appear to be of a mundane character in the sense of belonging to the domain of everyday life. But even these matters were sanctified by being lived and experienced by the Prophet in accordance with the vocation of Islam to assert, on the one hand, the Unity of God and to integrate, on the other, the whole of life into a sacred mold, leaving nothing outside the domain of the sacred and the religious.

As the Quran asserts, "God and His angels shower blessings upon the Prophet. O ye who believe! Ask blessings on him and salute him with a worthy salutation" (XXXIII, 56). By emulating the *Sunnah* of the Prophet and studying and meditating upon his *Ḥadīth*, man is carried with his help and the attraction of heaven to the Divine Realm and participates in a certain sense in his Nocturnal Ascent (*al-mi'rāj*). God loves the person who loves His Prophet, who is also His beloved. That is why Muslims love the Prophet; and his life, traditions, and sayings provide for the Muslim a lamp which illuminates the path of human existence toward its entelechy, which is God, a path whose ultimate guide is none other than the Prophet himself.

> Between Aḥmad and Aḥad (the One) there stands
> but the letter (m).
> The Universe is immersed in this single letter.
>
> Maḥmūd Shabistarī

Notes

1. Quoted in Sheikh Tosun Bayrak, al-Jerrahi al-Halveti, *The Most Beautiful Names* (Putney, VT: Threshold Books, 1985) 141.

2. Trans. by A. M. Schimmel in her *And Muhammad is His Messenger* (Chapel Hill: University of North Carolina Press, 1985) 105 (modified). See chapter 6 of this volume for the spiritual significance of the names of the Prophet.

3. See F. Schuon, "The Sunnah," in his *Islam and the Perennial Philosophy*, trans. J. P. Hobson (London: World of Islam, 1971) 111–17.

4. There is a whole category of Sufi writings, called *adab al-murīdīn* or *adab-i khānaqāh*, that is concerned with this very subject in which the training of the soul is related to the inculcation of *adab* in the disciples. One of the most famous works of this genre is the *Adab al-murīdīn* of Abū Najīb Suhrawardī.

5. It must be remembered that all Sufi masters derive their right to guide initiatically from the Prophet and represent him within the spiritual community that they guide.

6. On *Ḥadīth* literature see Muḥammad Zubayr Ṣiddiqī, *Ḥadīth Literature* (Calcutta: Calcutta University Press, 1961).

7. The most important of these commentaries is the *Sharḥ uṣūl al-kāfī* of Ṣadr al-Dīn Shīrāzī. See S. H. Nasr, *Ṣadr al-Dīn Shīrāzī and His Transcendent Theosophy* (Tehran: Imperial Iranian Academy of Philosophy, 1978) 47; and H. Corbin, *En Islam iranien* (4 vols.; Paris: Gallimard, 1971–72) 4:63ff. One of Ṣadr al-Dīn's students, Mullā Muḥsin Fayḍ Kāshānī, was an outstanding scholar of *Ḥadīth* besides being a metaphysician and philosopher.

8. One of the scholarly works that reflects the debate of Muslims concerning Western scholarship in the domain of *Ḥadīth* is G. H. A. Juynboll, *The Authenticity of Tradition Literature: Discussions in Modern Egypt* (Leiden: Brill, 1969).

9. See, e.g., S. M. Yusuf, *An Essay on the Sunnah* (Karachi: Institute of Islamic Culture, 1966); and S. H. Nasr, *Ideals and Realities of Islam* (London: Allen & Unwin, 1986) 79ff.

10. On these *ḥadīths*, see W. Graham, *Divine Word and Prophetic Word in Early Islam* (The Hague: Mouton, 1975).

11. Ibid., 127.

12. Ibid., 153.

13. Ibid., 142.

14. Ibid., 173.

15. Ibid., 184.

16. Ibid., 175.

17. Ibid., 177.

6

The Inner Meaning of the Islamic Rites: Prayer, Pilgrimage, Fasting, Jihād

Syed Ali Ashraf

Purification (*ṭahārah*)

As Allāh is both *al-Ẓāhir* (the Outward, the Manifest) and *al-Bāṭin* (the Inward, the Hidden), He has sanctioned for mankind some formal rites to be performed in order for them to draw nearer to Him. This nearness is achieved when the performer tries to realize the inner significance of these rites while maintaining their external form. In order to perform these rites properly, the first necessary element for Muslims is purification (*ṭahārah*), which also has an outward form and an inner meaning. Outwardly, one has to wash one's hands up to the wrist three times, rinse one's mouth with water thrown into it with the right hand, sniff water into the nostrils and throw it out thrice, wash the face thrice, wash first the right and then the left arm up to the elbow thrice, wipe the head with the inner surface of the fingers of both hands, put two forefingers in the two eardrums and wipe the backs of the ears with the thumbs; with the back of the fingers of both the hands jointly one has to wipe the back of the neck, and then wash the right and then the left foot up to the ankles thrice.[1]

This outward form of ablution (*wuḍū'*) turns into a form of prayer of forgiveness and mercy when the person performing the ablution starts praying to God. He prays to God to cleanse him of the sins he has committed with his two hands knowingly or unknowingly, to cleanse him also of the sins committed by his mouth, to fill his nostrils with the sweet scent of paradise, to remove the darkness that has stained his face and to illuminate it with the light of His Wisdom. He entreats God to place the record book of his action in the right hand as it would be done with the righteous people and not in the left hand as it would be done with the sinners. While washing his right foot, he prays to be led upon the straight path, and while washing the left he entreats to be protected from the promptings of the forces of evil, which try to lead man upon the corrupt path, the path of the destruction of all virtues.

Thus, the purification of the outer limbs is accompanied by an inner purification and an intensive prayer for forgiveness, mercy, and guidance. Those who seek the nearness of God always try to remain pure both outwardly and inwardly. The outer form of purification becomes necessary when man serves nature's call or vomits or when he bleeds. The whole body needs purification after the ejaculation of semen or sexual intercourse. As internal purification accompanies this outer ablution, the prophet Muḥammad has said, "He who makes ablution afresh revives and refreshes his faith." He has also said, "Ablution upon ablution is illumination upon illumination." When a person therefore performs ablution, thinking of all the sins committed by him through his different organs, and goes on praying to God as a penitent asking for His forgiveness and mercy, his sins are forgiven and hands and face are illumined. As repentance precedes illumination, ablution precedes formal prayer. Those who want to draw nearer to God always try to regain outward purity as soon as that purity has been broken. They also observe all inner impurities within themselves so as to remove them and become spiritually strengthened. This inner significance gives true meaning to the ritual of outward purification.

Prayer (*al-ṣalāt*)

God says in the Quran, "Preserve prayer and especially the middle prayer" (II, 238). The first prayer refers to regular fixed prayers at fixed times having a fixed form. Commentators of the Quran explain the middle prayer as the afternoon prayer, but Shaykh ʿAbd al-Qādir Jīlānī (Gīlānī), as well as many other Sufis, asserts that this other prayer is the prayer of the *qalb* (heart), which is a spiritual and not a physical organ. It is located, like the physical heart, in the middle of the chest somewhat to the left. The Prophet has said about it, "Verily the *qalb* (heart) of the sons of Adam is between the two fingers of Allāh. He changes it as He wishes." The two fingers signify, according to Shaykh ʿAbd al-Qādir Jīlānī, the two attributes of God signifying His powers of destruction and bounty. Preservation or maintenance of the power of the heart is necessary in order to gain that bounty and save oneself from the wrath of the Almighty.

12. General view of Mecca.

13. Cylindrical Minaret of the Mosque of Moulay Idris, decorated with kufic calligraphy.

14. Jāmi' Mosque, Kuala Lampur.

That this prayer of the heart is the most real prayer and that if a man neglects it his regular formal prayer becomes only an external show are indicated by another statement of the Prophet: "Prayer without the Presence of the Lord in the heart is not prayer at all." Regular formal prayer should be an external manifestation of this internal prayer. Regular prayers are prescribed five times a day: morning (*fajr*), midday (*ẓuhr*), afternoon (*'aṣr*), evening (*maghrib*), and night (*'ishā'*). The timings are as follows: morning prayer is said between dawn and sunrise; midday prayer is between midday and the midpoint between midday and sunset; afternoon prayer is between that midpoint and sunset; evening prayer is between sunset and the time when the darkness of the night covers the twilight; night prayer is between the end of twilight and dawn or, according to some schools, midnight. Internal prayer, or the prayer of the heart, however, has no fixed time. It should, in fact, be continuous and constant. This internal prayer purifies the heart. The Prophet referred to this purification when he said, "There is a piece of flesh inside man's body. When it is purified, the whole body gets purified; when it is impure, the whole body remains impure. That piece is the heart (*qalb*)." The body suffers from impurity when the *qalb* is impure, because then evil thoughts and desires start controlling the mind and guiding the senses. Thus envy, greed, backbiting, love of worldly power, sensual desires, and such other evils try to become the ruling forces dominating the soul. The mind, as a result, begins to indulge in all kinds of unnecessary thoughts at the time of formal prayer; therefore, true prayer is neglected and destroyed. The formal external prayer becomes nothing more than ostentation.

In order that the formal prayer may become what the Prophet meant when he said "Prayer is *mi'rāj* (ascent) for the *mu'min* (faithful)," perfect concentration and constant remembrance of God are necessary. There is no fixed time and place for such a prayer. The whole life of man must become a form of worship. Man must be able to realize the truth of the statement that God has asked each believer to utter in this verse: "Say: O my Lord, my prayers, my sacrifice, my life and my death are for God, the Lord of the worlds who hath no peer" (VI, 162–63). Shaykh 'Abd al-Qādir Jīlānī called this internal prayer the prayer of the path (*ṣalāt al-ṭarīqah*) and described it in the following way: "Its mosque is the *qalb*. Its congregation is the conglomeration of all internal forces in man. It recites with spiritual tongue the Names of God's Unity (*tawḥīd*). Its *imām* is a deep spiritual urge in the heart (*al-shawq fi' l-fu'ād*). Its *qiblah* (direction of prayer) is the Unity of Godhead (*aḥadiyyah*). The *qalb* (heart) and *rūḥ* (spirit) are constantly engaged in this prayer. They neither sleep, nor do they die."[2] When the *qalb* and the *rūḥ* are thus engaged in constant prayer and supplication (*munājāt*), the formal prescribed prayer becomes a true manifestation of internal realization, a contemplation and a secret call exchanged between God and His servant. That is what is meant by God's utterance in the following *ḥadīth qudsī:* "I have divided prayer between Me and My servant into two halves, one being due to Me and the other to My servant; and My servant will receive that for which he asks."[3]

When an individual, therefore, stands before the Lord with bent head and crossed arms, he is a complete slave, helpless and alone. That is why in other rituals it is possible to talk or move, but in prayer one is compelled to annihilate oneself in the presence of the Almighty. He sees the Lord in front of him because the Lord resides in his *qalb.* But if his power of vision is not still so clear, he should pray "as if He sees him." This is what the Prophet meant in his definition of *iḥsān* (spiritual virtue), which is "to adore God as if thou dost see Him, and if thou dost not see Him, He nevertheless sees thee." He therefore should imagine God in front of him because, though he may not see Him or become conscious of His Presence, "He is," as the Prophet has said, "in truth present in the *qiblah* of every one of you." Each individual's consciousness depends on his capability and cultivation. That is why God says, "We will impose on each soul only the obligation of which it is capable" (II, 286; VI, 153; VII, 40).

As the person stands before God, he should "lend his hearing" to what God says in reply to his prayer. In a *ḥadīth qudsī*, the Prophet has narrated what God says when a person recites the *Ṣūrat al-fātiḥah* (the opening chapter of the Quran, which constitutes the principal text of every canonical prayer). The servant says, "In the Name of God the Most Merciful (*al-Raḥmān*), the Most Compassionate (*al-Raḥīm*)," and God says "My servant mentions Me." The servant then says, "Praise be to God, the Master of the Universe," and God says in his turn, "My servant lends Me grace." The servant then says, "The Compassionate, the Merciful," and God replies, "My servant praises Me." The servant says, "The King of the Day of Judgment," and God says, "My servant glorifies Me and submits himself to Me." This first half of this chapter so far cited relates exclusively to God and the servant's invocation of His Attributes. In the next half of the chapter, the servant prays with a complete sense of humility. The servant says, "It is Thee whom we adore, and it is of Thee that we beg for help," and God says, "This is shared between Me and My servant, and My servant will receive that which he asks." When the servant says, "Lead us upon the right path, the path of those to whom Thou hast been most gracious, not of those on whom Thy Wrath has descended, nor of those who have gone astray," God says, "All that comes back to My servant, and My servant will receive that for which he asks." Thus, the second half of this chapter is related exclusively to man. It is because of this mutual participation between God and man in this chapter, which is considered to be the heart of the Quran, that the canonical prayer is regarded as not having been performed if this chapter is not recited.

The form and the substance of what the praying individual utters thereby draw the individual closer to God. The servant bows down (*rukūʿ*) and glorifies the greatness of God. When he straightens up from bowing, he says "God hears those who laud Him." This recitation is a form of announcement to himself and all those who pray behind him, including the angels and jinns, and they reply "Our Lord, praise to Thee." The former statement is, in reality, enunciated by God through the mouth of His adorer. Thus, the intimate God–man relationship is deepened.

When the adorer then prostates himself and says, "Glory be to my Lord, the Greatest of the Great," he is in a state of final annihilation. As *imām* of himself when he prays alone, he leads all the forces in his own being to the stage of complete annihilation (*fanāʾ*). As *imām* of the rest of the congregation, he draws the whole congregation toward the same end. When he again stands up, he repeats the same process in order to draw closer and closer to God. After this repetition the adorer sits in the posture of a humble slave and bears witness to his vision of Unity and his consciousness of the prophethood of the Prophet. Thus he sends his prayers and blessings upon the Prophet and his family and descendants. Since the Prophet is mercy to the entire creation (*raḥmatun liʾl-ʿālamīn*), to send blessings upon him means receiving in return from God blessings and mercy upon the entire creation.

A distinctive character of prayer is that the adorer must keep his vision, both external and internal, concentrated upon his *qiblah*, which is ultimately none but God Himself. He is forbidden to turn aside because turning prevents the adorer from the contemplation of the Most Beloved.

Contemplation leads to and increases realization, and realization deepens contemplation. This realization of God through prayer varies according to the spiritual capacity (*al-istiʿdād*) of the individual. This variation means that for each individual there is a particular notion of God and his own relationship with Him. The *Sharīʿah* insists on the limitation of that individual notion and stresses the transcendence of the essence of God. Whatever the individual realizes is true for him at that stage of his spiritual journey, but he must keep in mind that God transcends all such realizations. Therefore, the striving to realize God must be continuous until death. No one should be content with what he realizes through the *qalb*, because the *qalb* goes on changing and realization increases with greater perfection. As prayer is

15. "The Ka'bah surrounded by Muslims," Persian Miniature.

the means of progress toward God, it is also a means of making us obey God's orders and preventing us from doing that which God has prohibited and forbidden. The more complete the adorer's submission and concentration, the nearer is he to God and hence the more are his external character and conduct under the control of internal dictates. That is why the Quran says, "Prayer prevents transgressions of passions and the grave sin" (XXIX, 4). It is this nearness that made the Prophet say, "The freshness of my eyes is given to me in prayer."

This realization and complete submission may not be achieved by most people in prayer, but that does not completely destroy the possibility for human beings to draw closer to the Lord. The sincerity of man's motives and the submission of the body to the dictates of the *Sharīʿah,* insofar as the form of the prayer is concerned, are primary achievements. Even when the mind wavers, the will tries to control it and bring back concentration and complete submission. Thus, the benefits of realization are not lost. This itself is a step toward complete annihilation.

Fasting (*al-ṣawm*)

Fasting is both external and internal. External compulsory fasting is prescribed for all adult individuals during the lunar month of Ramaḍān. All such individuals must not eat, drink, smoke, or have sexual intercourse during daytime from dawn to sunset. Normal life is permitted from sunset to dawn. By internal fasting is meant the discipline imposed upon one's soul so that the self is restrained from indulging in passions and desires and prevented from engaging itself in evils, such as telling lies, backbiting, envy, jealousy, or pride. Another stage of internal fasting is had when the *muttaqī,* the God-fearing individual, abstains from even permitted things for fear of going beyond limits. The next and the highest stage of this kind of fasting is seen in those devoted adorers of God who see God and nothing else and fast from the presence of everything other than God.

It is to help an individual to proceed in the path of internal fasting that external fasting is prescribed. "Cultivate within yourself," says the Prophet, "the Attributes of God." Not to eat, drink, or engage in sex is to transcend the physical limitations of an individual and imitate the "habits" of God. Bodily passions and desires become thereby weakened. The spirit of man gains strength when he tries to obey God's orders and to restrain himself from those things that are prohibited by God. Unless he does so, physical abstentions alone cannot be counted as "fasting." Such restraint constitutes the minimum condition. Those who do not fulfill this minimum condition and indulge in morally evil acts, such as telling lies or backbiting, are the people about whom the Prophet has said, "There are many whose fasting is nothing beyond being hungry and thirsty." Both external and internal efforts are needed to fast properly. It is not an easy thing, for example, to control anger. In the month of fasting, this particular passion reaches almost beyond control because man becomes irritable. He must therefore keep constant watch over this and such other passions, so that not only are they properly controlled, but also they never gain the chance to control the individual. Otherwise our fasting will be soiled, and instead of acquiring benefits from external fasting we shall start committing sins.

The next stage of fasting is to abstain even from legally permitted things. Even when anger or revenge is justified, the individual restrains his anger and offers kindness instead; and instead of claiming justice, he invokes and showers mercy. Physically he limits his food and drink and sometimes abstains from those kinds of food that tempt him or energize physical passions, just to help his spirit have control over his temptations and passions. This kind of fasting gives man what in modern terminology is called "self-confidence," which in Sufi terminology will be called *taṭma'inn al-qulūb*, a peace that descends on the heart from above, giving the feeling that God has accepted this kind of fasting.

To reach that stage of complete peaceful confidence (*iṭmi'nān*) in which the self has surrendered wholly to God, the last type of fasting is necessary. It is a kind of fasting in which the individual abstains physically, mentally, and spiritually from anything that draws a veil between him and the Lord. God must become his only Beloved, his only goal, his only aim. If anything else absorbs his soul, this kind of fasting is immediately ruined and he has to start afresh to rouse within him the fullness of that craving and the freshness of that joy. It is with reference to this kind of fasting that God says in a *ḥadīth qudsī*, "Fasting is for Me and I shall grant reward for it Myself."

The two joys of fasting that, according to the Prophet, a person fasting is blessed with—*ifṭār* (breaking the fast) and the vision of the new moon (of *'īd* after the month of Ramaḍān)— refer to two other joys, the joy of seeing *jannah* (paradise) after death and the joy of having the vision of God after resurrection.

Pilgrimage (*ḥajj*)

Pilgrimage to Mecca is prescribed for all Muslims who can physically and financially perform it. God has prescribed certain rites that a pilgrim should observe properly. If he does not do so, his pilgrimage is not accepted. The most important and the essential obligatory rites are these: (1) to put on *iḥrām,* which consists of two pieces of unsewn cloth for men and covers all parts of the body except the face, hands, and feet for women; and to observe the rules of *iḥrām,* which are not to have sexual relationship, not to kill animals or insects, and not to remove any hair from the body; (2) to enter the city of Makkat al-Mukarramah (Mecca) and to perform the *ṭawāf al-qudūm,* that is, to circumambulate the Ka'bah, the house of God, seven times; (3) to be at 'Arafāt, which is a plain near Mecca, even if it is for a short while, on the ninth day of the lunar month of Dhu'l-ḥijjah; (4) to spend the night at a place near Mecca called Muzdalifah; (5) to throw stones at the three places where Satan tried to tempt the prophet Ismā'īl or Ishmael, the first son of Abraham; (6) to sacrifice an animal at Minā in commemoration of the sacrifice that Abraham decided to make of his son Ismā'īl; (7) to perform *ṭawāf* again; (8) to drink the water of Zamzam;[4] (9) to perform two *rak'ahs* of prayer at the place known as Maqām Ibrāhīm, the place where Abraham and his son stood and prayed after building the Ka'bah. If numbers (1), (2), (3), and (7) of these rites are performed, then the basic rites are said to have been observed. Even if the other rites are not performed properly, the pilgrimage is said to have been performed. But if the other rites are not observed, the pilgrim is expected to give compensation; otherwise his pilgrimage will remain defective.

Just as in the case of other rites, such as *ṣalāt* and *ṣawm,* in the case of *ḥajj* also the primary condition is purity of intention (*niyyah*). The pilgrim must intend to perform the pilgrimage only and not to indulge in any business transactions or something else. To perform the pilgrimage means to leave all worldly activities aside and proceed to meet the Lord. Purity of intention will be assessed by man himself. If his mind is invaded by worries about the life he has left in the hands of others, he has not been able to purify his intention. When a person puts on the pilgrim's garb (*iḥrām*), leaves his house, and proceeds toward the Ka'bah, he must behave as if he is a dead man having no control over his life and worldly activities. From that time until the *ḥajj* is over, he should concentrate fully on his pilgrimage to the Lord, pray for forgiveness and enlightenment, and devote himself to *dhikr,* which means nothing other than constant repetition of and concentration upon *Lā ilāha illa'Llāh* (There is no divinity but God). To enter Mecca and to perform *ṭawāf* means to enter the holy place where the first house of God on earth was established and to circumambulate the house that is the reflection of that Divine House in the Seventh Heaven, above and beyond which stands the glorified Throne of God, around which all angels and the entire creation are constantly rotating.

16. The faithful gathering at 'Arafat during the ceremony of the *hajj*.

17. Pilgrims drinking from the Zamzam.

Through the circumambulation (*ṭawāf*), the pilgrim participates with the angels and other creatures in their circumambulation of the Divine Throne. Going around the Ka'bah with the purity of intention to meet the Lord can become fully beneficial only if the heart continues to be purified of everything except God. The *qalb* must by now become engaged in the constant remembrance of *ism al-Dhāt,* which is nothing other than the Name *Allāh.* The *qalb* thus becomes purified of everything except God and enjoys both repeating with spiritual tongue and hearing with spiritual ears this *dhikr* in which, as God has said in the Quran, the entire creation is engaged. The next stage of the *ḥajj* is that of staying in the field of 'Arafāt. This is the stage of prayer (*munājāt*). It was in this field that Ādam (Adam) and Ḥawwā' (Eve) met after their expulsion from heaven, and it was on the Mount of Mercy (*Jabal al-raḥmān*) in this plain that their prayer for forgiveness was accepted. It was also in this field that at night God brought out from the back of Ādam all the souls that would come to earth until doomsday and asked them, "Am I not your Lord?" To which each of them answered, "Yes" (VII, 172). This exchange signifies the covenant between man and God to which God refers several times in the Quran—the covenant that man asks God to fulfill. God reminds man and then teaches him to say that his life and activities are all for Him alone and that he has been created only to worship God. To come to 'Arafāt is to become fully conscious of that covenant and to remember that "He" alone is all in all. All the pilgrims (*ḥujjāj*) are engaged in prayer. They must pray for forgiveness for every act and thought that separated them from their Lord. In other words, their consciousness of the duality of purpose and action, of the world and for the *ākhirah* (life after death), of society and God, of what made them commit the sin of polytheism (*shirk*) unknowingly must be realized to the full and cast aside, so that they can relive the time of the covenant. Those who can do so become truly purified. They alone know what pleasure is derived from the *dhikr* of *Hū* (He).[5] 'Arafāt is thus the place for reaching the pinnacle of the consciousness of God. From there the pilgrims proceed to Muzdalifah, where they spend the night in prayer and meditation establishing within themselves the realization achieved at 'Arafāt. That is why this is the place for the *dhikr* of the Divine Names *al-Ḥayy, al-Qayyūm* (the Living, the Self-Sustained). From Muzdalifah the pilgrims go to Minā to throw stones at Satan and to sacrifice some animal in the Name of God. Satan tried to deceive Abraham and Ishmael, but they realized who he was and threw stones at him. This external action of throwing pebbles at three stone blocks must be accompanied by an inner urge to kill or drive away the satan that is whispering within oneself. If the pilgrim is

18. The Ka'bah, Mecca.

19. The embroidery of the Kiswah, the cloth covering of the Ka'bah, woven by the members of the same guild over the centuries.

not conscious of this meaning, his throwing of stones remains an external act without any impact on his being.

The next action of the *ḥajj* is that of sacrifice. Abraham tried to sacrifice his own son Ishmael. The complete cooperation of his son in this act and the literal interpretation of the dream by Abraham, in which he was asked by God to sacrifice that which was dearest to him, are both acts that are not normal. That human sacrifice is neither desirable nor permissible in religion is proved by the way God ended this trial by substituting a ram in the place of Ishmael and by ordering Abraham to open his eyes and to realize that God had already accepted his sacrifice. Abraham could have interpreted his dream but he did not do so. The sacrifice of the dearest thing, such as one's life, for the cause of God is the final test of man's total surrender. Here both the father and the son were put to such a test. It was a severe test. Nor did either of them ever dream that God would intervene. Human sacrifice would have been seen as legal had this been allowed to happen. God's intervention legitimized the sacrifice of a life for a life—a ram for the son—but forbade human sacrifice. This act also symbolizes the sacrifice of man's *nafs* (self) before God, seen as the Name *al-Qahhār* (the Victorious), the Name that signifies the total annihilation (*fanā'*) of man. The sacrifice of the animal does not remain an external act, because the pilgrim is consciously or unconsciously involved in glorifying that *al-Qahhār* aspect of God's Attributes. Through this sacrifice a pilgrim is symbolically sacrificing himself and fulfilling the obligation of the covenant on the basis of which God has taught man this verse: "Say, Verily, my prayers, my sacrifice, my life and my death are for God, the Lord of the world who hath no peer." This sacrifice thus spiritually symbolizes the sacrifice of *al-nafs al-muṭma'innah* at the altar of God the *Qahhār*. In the spiritual journey to the Lord, the annihilation or *fanā'* thus achieved is accompanied by the removal of the veil of *kufr*, or unbelief, between the adorer and the well-beloved Lord.

The shaving of the head of the pilgrim or the cutting off of the hair of women symbolizes the next stage of man's spiritual progress—the removal of all stains of human attributes from the essential spirit breathed into the body by God. If one can attain to that stage, he can visualize the beauty of the Lord directly.

The Prophet has said that there are two stations behind the Throne of God—one of belief and the other of unbelief. The former creates a white veil and the other a dark veil between the slave and the Lord. The dark veil is removed when, along with the physical journey, a pilgrim succeeds in completing his spiritual journey. The other veil is removed when the final circumambulations of the Ka'bah are performed. If man's pilgrimage has been completed both externally and internally and his realizations are as depicted above, then he must once again go seven times around the Ka'bah, feeling this time as if he is going around the Throne of God. He is then entitled by God to enter into the station of nearness to the Almighty, Whose vision he achieves. It is to this achievement of direct vision of the Lord that God refers when He says, "And He made them drink the purest of drinks" (LXXVI, 21). This is symbolized externally by the drinking of the water of the holy well Zamzam after the completion of the circumambulation. When a person attains to this stage of consciousness, all veils are removed and he talks to the Lord without any veil between them.

The final stage of the *hajj* is the *ṭawāf al-wadā'* (circumambulation of farewell) or *ṭawāf al-ṣadr* (circumambulation of the breast) and return to one's homeland. The pilgrim's real homeland is, of course, the place of his spiritual origin, about which God has said that He made man in the best of forms and then cast him to the realm of the lowest of the low (XCV, 5). This *ṭawāf* symbolizes man's detachment from the lowest region and his journey to that region which is the highest of the high, his real homeland.

Shaykh 'Abd al-Qādir Jīlānī describes this aspect of pilgrimage as *Ḥajj al-ṭarīqah* (the pilgrimage in the spiritual path). This is the real significance of the various rites about which God says in the Quran, "Such is the pilgrimage. Whoever honors the sacred rites of God, for him it is good in the sight of his Lord" (XXII, 30).

Jihād

Islam is a religion of peace, but it prescribes war as the last resort to ward off the enemy, secure peace, and establish security so that God's prescribed way of life is maintained and not destroyed. That is why God says in the Quran, "And if God had not replied to one group of people by means of another, the earth would have been filled with chaos" (II, 25). God also has said that *jihād* is to repel all evil forces and destroy or control them. "Those who follow the way of Faith fight in the Way of God and those who follow the way of disbelief fight in the way of the devil. So fight against the helpers of Satan with this conviction. Satan's crafty schemes are in fact very weak and bound to fail" (IV, 76).

The primary meaning of *jihād* is exertion or use of effort, of which only a particular kind is identified with fighting. Even in this sense of the word, *jihād* means fighting in the Way of God against the forces of evil with life and wealth in order to make God's Way prevail on the earth and not fighting for any worldly cause. Sincerity and purity of motive and the condition of society must justify such an action. If anyone wants personal fame and glory, he is not a *mujāhid,* a fighter in the Way of God. Someone asked the Prophet, "One man fights for booty, one for the reputation of fighting and one for his quality (of bravery) to be witnessed; which of them is in God's Way?" The Prophet replied, "The one who fights that God's Word may have preeminence is following God's Way." The sincerity of this motive must also involve the degree of the fighter's love for God and the Prophet. A *mujāhid* must love God, His Messenger, and striving in His Way more than his wealth, relations, and his own life. God says in the Quran, "O Prophet, tell them plainly, 'If your fathers and your sons and your brothers and your wives, and your near and dear ones and the wealth you have acquired and the trade you fear may decline and the homes which delight you—if all these things are dearer to you than God and His Messenger and striving in His Way, then wait until God passes judgment on you for God does not guide the wicked people'" (IX, 24). All Muslims must be *mujāhids* because they must resist evil individually and collectively. When the condition of society is such that there is danger of elimination of the faithful, then the faithful must try to resist the spread of evil through fighting with their works or their pen. If that is also not possible, then internally they should resist the evil and not allow it to conquer their hearts. The last alternative is to leave the land of corruption and go to some place where fighting in the Way of God may be carried out. *Jihād,* therefore, is a compulsory function of a Muslim for both internal and external purification, purification of the individual and of society by resisting, fighting, and conquering the forces of evil. The test of this *jihād* lies in the sincerity with which the individual undertakes this task.

Jihād compels an individual to test himself through his sincerity and love for God and the Prophet. That love for God and the Prophet means love for the good, for selflessness, for all that God has prescribed and the Prophet has exemplified in order to lead man toward the final goal of mankind. That goal is to fulfill the function of vicegerency of God (*khalīfat Allāh*) on earth and hatred of all evil forces, including oppression, injustice, falsehood, cheating, backbiting, suppression of human freedom, and denial of basic human rights guaranteed in the Quran. Thus, although external *jihād* is necessary at different times for the purification of society, internal *jihād* is a constant action that must go on within man so that he may distinguish between truth and falsehood, justice and injustice, and right and wrong and kindle within himself the love for the good. Unless he tries to do so, he will probably falter or fail at the time of external *jihād* and be in the category of the "losers" (II, 27).

20. Woven miniature of the Ka'bah.

21. The faithful prostrating before the Ka'bah.

This internal *jihād* is more difficult and subtle than the external *jihād.* That is why when the companions returned from an early *jihād* the Prophet welcomed them and added that they had now come from the smaller *jihād* (*al-jihād al-aṣghar*) to the greater *jihād* (*al-jihād al-akbar*). The companions were surprised and inquired what that greater *jihād* could be. The Prophet replied, "*Jihād* with one's lower self (*nafs*)."

The *nafs* (self) is a difficult object to define. The Quran describes three different stages of *nafs* in man. The lowest and the most corrupt stage is that of *al-nafs al-ammārah* (the evil *nafs,* XII, 53), at which stage man is completely under the control of the evil forces within and outside himself. If man remains at this stage, he is defeated in *jihād.* He becomes himself a slave of evil forces and his self listens to the promptings of the evil jinn. Every individual, said the Prophet, has been given an angel by God to assist him in the right path, and an evil jinn by Satan to mislead him. Although the spirit (*rūḥ*) of man is always pure, it has become almost inactive because of these evil forces, including those forces within the self that are generated by the worldly elements that constitute his body and attract him toward this worldly life. In the case of many human beings, the self has become deaf to the suggestions of the angel, and it deliberately leads man toward the path of spiritual destruction. People of this kind struggle collectively at the social level to prevent the good from prevailing.

When the spirit of man tries to reassert itself and when with the help of God he becomes conscious of his condition, he begins to exert himself spiritually, to carry out *jihād* and to repent; but sometimes he wavers and falls and again recovers. This is the stage of internal *jihād* that is described in the Quran as a stage when the soul is called *al-nafs al-lawwāmah* (self-reproaching soul, LXXV, 2). This is the stage that may be described as "the pricking of man's conscience."

The next stage is attained by the self when, through remembrance of God and invocation (*dhikr Allāh*), man's spirit (*rūḥ*) starts dominating the soul and he is able to control the evil forces within himself thoroughly. Man achieves complete peace and satisfaction by submitting fully to the will of God. This is the stage of *al-nafs al-muṭma'innah* (LXXXIX, 27). Man is finally able to win real victory in his *jihād.* It is at this stage of victory that the soul is also described by the Quran as *rāḍiyatan-marḍiyyatan* (satisfied and satisfying), a stage in which God's Will and man's will act in unison. In a *ḥadīth qudsī* this stage has been described as that stage of consciousness when God acts through man's eyes, ears, hands, and feet and man does whatever God wills. Whatever man wills is also accepted by God because man cannot do anything but good at that stage (LXXIX, 28; XCVIII, 8).

Man must carry on *jihād* both internally and externally—the former to purify himself and control the evil forces and keep a watch over the frontiers of the soul and the latter to stop or prevent aggression and oppression or save the faithful and the Faith from being annihilated by the evil forces in society.

In both cases man's highest glory is achieved when he becomes a *shahīd* (martyr). In external *jihād*, if a *mujāhid* is killed, he becomes a martyr. In internal *jihād* also, a stage is reached when the spirit and the body become separated and the *nafs* is made to suffer the pangs of actual death. Man, therefore, becomes a *shahīd*, a martyr, although his state may remain unknown to others. It is about this death that the Prophet has said, "Die before you die."

Those who can kill their *nafs* in this manner as well as those who sacrifice the physical self for God reach the status of *shahīd*. These *shuhadā'* (martyrs) are, according to the Quran, forever alive: "Do not regard as dead those who have been slain in the Way of God; they are really alive and are well provided for by their Lord" (III, 169). Their rank is very high in the eyes of God, as is said in the Quran, "Those who believe and have left their homes and striven hard with their wealth and their lives in God's Way, have the highest rank in the sight of God" (IX, 20). That is why the Prophet said, "By God, Him in Whose Hand is my soul, I wish I could be killed in God's Way and brought to life, then be killed and brought to life, then be killed and brought to life, then be killed." This *ḥadīth* indicates that in the field of battle, provided it is a battle in the path of God, a person can become a martyr even if he has not undergone the hardships of an ascetic who kills his *nafs* by surrendering his body and soul to God and by becoming martyred inwardly. Therefore, the fact that through the lesser *jihād* one may achieve the benefits of the greater *jihād* indicates further that it is easy for a person who has won a victory in the greater *jihād* to participate in the lesser *jihād*, because he has already killed his *nafs*. He is already fully prepared to sacrifice his body over and over again for God, if that were possible, because by killing his *nafs*, such a person has, in a sense, already performed the sacrifice of his body. That is why such people and those who are killed on the battlefield for the preservation of the Faith are not dead but have already gained immortal life in paradise.

Notes

1. There are certain minor differences in various schools of Islamic Law concerning parts of the rite of purification, but the main elements are the same in all schools.

2. ʿAbd al-Qādir Jīlānī, *Sirr al-asrār* (Lahore, n.d.) 158.

3. As mentioned earlier, the *ḥadīth qudsī* is a Divine Word uttered by the Prophet but not a part of the Quran. In the *ḥadīth qudsī,* God speaks in the first person through the mouth of the Prophet.

4. Zamzam, the spring near the Kaʿbah whose water gushed forth, according to tradition, at the moment when Hagar, the mother of Ismāʿīl, was looking desperately for water to quench the thirst of her child, symbolizes for Muslims the water of paradise.

5. The supreme invocation referring to God's Essence and the final syllable of the Name *Allāh.*

7

The Spiritual Dimension of Prayer

Allahbakhsh K. Brohi

The Command to Pray

To begin with, it ought to be noticed by a student of Islam that prayer is a duty prescribed for the believer directly by the command of God. Thus, there is an order to pray and, what is more, to translate literally the commandment of the Quran, there is an order to establish prayer, *aqīmu'l-ṣalāh.* This commandment is absolutely binding. There are minor exceptions as when one is ill in a manner such that he cannot pray. One is ordered to pray even in war. This sense of obligation to pray is in reference to the formalized and institutionalized ritual prayer, which is to be performed five times a day. Although one can perform this prayer by oneself, the value of the prayer is enhanced if it is performed in congregation in a mosque. The ritual prayer, over and above its direct benefit to the individual, has a social aspect in that it brings one closer to his fellow men and promotes the life of the community by integrating its members into a fraternal feeling of oneness. The community prayer is led by an imam, who is the leader of the prayer. The rest stand in straight rows behind him and follow his commands and the prescribed course of movements necessary for completing the prayer.

The Canonical Prayers

The meaning of prayer in Islam and its link with the process of spiritualization of the being of man can be best understood if the very first chapter of the Quran, called *Sūrat al-fātiḥah* (literally, "The Opening Chapter"), is properly understood. This is so because that chapter (which has to be recited in every unit or *rak'ah* and which is a necessary component of the prayer process) sets forth the essence of the prayer, if not the soul of religion itself. The chapter consists of seven verses, which many scholars have treated as the quintessence of the whole of the Quran.

It has rightly been placed as a preface to the sacred Book because, in some sense, these seven oft-repeated verses are none other than what the Quran itself describes as *sab'an min al-mathānī* (seven of the oft-repeated verses) in the following verse: "We have given Thee [i.e. the Prophet] seven of the oft-repeated [verses], and the mighty Quran" (XV, 87). The Prophet is on record as saying that these seven oft-repeated verses are in reference to the *Sūrat al-fātiḥah,* which is as follows:

(1) Praise belongs to God, the Lord of all Being,
(2) the All-Merciful, the All-compassionate,
(3) the Master of the Day of Doom.
(4) Thee only we serve; to Thee alone we pray for succour.
(5) Guide us in the straight path,
(6) the path of those whom Thou hast blessed,
(7) not of those against whom Thou art wrathful,
nor of those who are astray.

It should be noticed that structurally the content of this opening chapter falls into three parts. The first is acknowledgment of the fact that praise and gratitude are due to Allah, Who is the Lord of the worlds (or universes) and Who is beneficent and compassionate: He is the Master of the Day that comes at the end of time, on which man will meet his Lord and give account of what he has done in his life. In the next phase, man makes a direct address to God and undertakes the commitment to serve Him alone and to ask help from Him alone. In the third and last phase, that help is elaborated in the form of a plea and invocation that the Lord guide the believers on the right path, this being the path (a) of those upon whom He has bestowed His favors and (b) not of those upon whom wrath is brought down nor (c) of those who go astray.

Thus, praise for the merciful Maker, Who is the Judge of man's deeds, and a commitment to serve only Him and to seek only His help finally and inevitably take the form of a supplication by the believer: to be guided to follow the right path so as to win God's favors and to be spared from having to suffer God's wrath, or to follow the path of those who go astray.

Since man's life is in the making, he cannot conceivably know in advance what destiny is in store for him and what his situation is in the scheme of things. He is not directly aware of the purpose for which life is given to him. Islam makes the believer conscious of the existence of God, Who is the sovereign Lord and Master of the universe and of man. God is worthy of man's praise. Furthermore, God is merciful, and with Him is the final judgment concerning what man has made of his life. The commitment he is called upon to make, in order to acquit himself creditably in the trials that confront him in this life, is to submit steadfastly to the Divine Law by serving God alone (thereby denying submission to any power apart from God) and to seek only His help. The help sought by man is that he be guided to follow the right path, which is a path of those for whom God has shown his favors and not of those on whom His wrath has descended or of those who have gone astray. When this prayer (*Fātiḥah*) is recited in any *rak'ah*, a portion of the Quran is read thereafter, and the belief is that that portion of the Quran which spontaneously wells forth from the interior depth of man's being is in response to the believer's invocation "show me the straight path." It contains God's answer to him and has reference to the guidance that he had asked for. Thus, the Islamic prayer is a means of communion of the human soul with its Creator, Who alone knows what destiny lies ahead for him and how it is to be realized by him in terms of the guidance he receives. Since "God does not directly speak to man except through the prophets" (XLII, 51), the portion of the Quran which is the Word of God recited by man is also God's response to man in the situation in which he finds himself placed in this life. Prayer thus helps man to perfect himself by traversing the path which leads to earning the pleasure of his Creator and avoiding His displeasure. To pray in this sense is inherent in the very nature of man. He needs to pray if only because, quite aside from this Divine Guidance that comes to man, there is no other intimation given to him about how best to conduct himself in life to be able to reach his appointed goal and to realize his prescribed destiny. The benefit of prayer is alluded to in the Quran, where the prophet Noah says,

> Seek pardon of your Lord. Lo! He is
> ever forgiving.
> He will let loose the sky for you
> in plenteous rain,
> and will help you with wealth and sons,
> and will assign unto you gardens and
> will assign unto you rivers.
> What aileth you that ye hope not toward
> Allāh for dignity
> When He created you by (diverse) stages?
> (LXXI, 10–14)

These last words undoubtedly speak of the development of man by stages and the various conditions through which he passes, beginning with his prenatal life in the womb of his mother on to his final end, viz., his death on earth. His prayer is linked with his supplication to this Lord to help him to realize these stages of his growth and orderly development consistent with that destiny which is prescribed for him to realize. Similarly, even the functional value of prayer has been set forth in clear-cut terms:

> [O Muḥammad] Recite that which hath been inspired in thee of the Scripture, and establish worship [prayer]. Lo! worship preserveth from lewdness and iniquity, but verily remembrance of Allah is more important. And Allah knoweth what ye do. (XXIX, 45)

The Remembrance of God

It should be noticed that recitation of the Quran and the keeping up of prayer or remembrance (*dhikr*) of the Blessed Name *Allāh* converge upon one and the same focal point, that is, the development of man's awareness, which is fostered by meditation upon the revealed Word of God and is fortified by obedience to what God wants him to do. For the believer, the revelation of the Quran is an act which is itself evidence of the Mercy of God, in that it was revealed to man for his benefit and to help him to cope with the problems of life. Continual and constant remembrance of God's Name or recitation of His revealed Word is one sure way of acquiring nearness (*qurb*) to Him. Prayer acts as a constraining influence upon the animal impulses of man and keeps him away from things that are foul, ugly, and unclean.

Prayer as Protection

It would appear that one of the important roles of Islamic prayer is to act as a protection against the defilement and contamination that affect man's life. When a man lives his life with consciousness of his link with the Lord, he acquires an inward disposition to absorb God's Attributes and obtains the capacity to resist evil. If a piece of iron has to be kept for long under water without rusting, the only way to achieve this difficult result is to take it out periodically, oil it, and then place it in the water again. So is it also the case with man. If five times a day he were to remove himself from the corrupting taint of worldly transactions in which he is apt to lose himself and were to make an effort consciously to identify himself with the pursuit of the supreme goal for which he has been created and were to seek persistently from his Creator the help he needs to steer clear of the possibility of deviating from the straight path, which is his appointed destiny to traverse if he is to be saved, then there can be no doubt that he would succeed in adhering to the path of righteousness.

Institutionalized Prayer

That prayer has been a perennial institution of all prophetic religions is attested to by the Quran over and over again, as, for instance, in relation to the prophet Moses:

> And We inspired Moses and his brother, (saying): appoint houses for your people in Egypt and make your houses oratories, and establish worship [prayer] and give good news to the believers. (X, 88)

The Israelites, it will be recalled, were obliged to pray in their houses since they did not enjoy full religious liberty in Egypt and did not have the freedom to establish public places of worship.

That prayer in Islam can also be petitionary is attested to by several verses in the Quran. There man is invited to ask his Lord for the satisfaction of his needs, with the implied assurance that his Lord would certainly accede to his request. More specifically, it has been said that the Prophet's acceptance of alms from those who offer it sincerely, after confessing their faults, would clean and purify them. The Prophet is asked to pray for them:

> Take alms of their wealth, wherewith thou mayst purify them and mayst make them grow, and pray for them. Lo! thy prayer is an assuagement for them.
> Allah is Hearer, Knower.
> Know they not that Allah is He Who accepteth repentance from His bondmen and taketh the alms, and that Allah is He Who is the Relenting, Merciful? (IX, 103–4)

It is further said:

> Pray unto Me, and I will hear you. (XL, 60)

And again:

> Is not He (best) Who answereth the wronged one when he crieth unto Him and removeth the evil, and hath made you viceroys of the earth? (XXVII, 62)

The ritual prayer in Islam must be performed at fixed times. This helps to build man's conscious dependence upon God. It helps him to so conduct his affairs in life that the possibility of his committing sins is minimized, if not eliminated. In this context it should be noticed that prayer is to be performed even when one is engaged in fighting a war:

> When ye have performed the act of worship [prayer], remember Allah, standing, sitting and reclining and when ye are in safety, observe proper worship [prayer]. (IV, 103)

Prayer indeed has been enjoined on the believers at fixed times as a duty, and it can be shortened when one is traveling (IV, 101).

Thus, Muslim prayer, or what has been called in this article the ritual prayer, is a disciplined activity regulated in meticulous detail by the law of Islam. And yet the Quran is quick to warn that prayer, when devoid of its real spirit, is not acceptable:

> So woe to those that pray and are heedless of their prayers, to those who make display and refuse charity. (CVII, 4–8)

Prayer as prescribed in Islam is a conscious act: the highest level of perfection in prayer is, as pointed out in a *ḥadīth:* "So pray as if you see God for if you do not see Him, He nevertheless sees you." In conformity with the demands of religious Law, one must pray in all conditions; but one enhances the efficaciousness of prayer if it is done in a spirit of detachment from the world and its ways. One must pray with serenity and calmness in one's heart and with singleness of devotion, thoroughness of concentration, and a sense of complete dedication to the Holy of the Holies.

Constant Prayer and Invocation

Apart from obligatory prayers, there are supererogatory prayers (*nawāfil*); indeed, in view of the total thrust of the message of the Quran it could be said that prayerful attitude is as large as life itself and that it is coextensive with its total range and activity. Through prayer we not only obey the Lord who is Lord of the worlds but also are privileged in being beneficiaries of the spiritual influence of His Divine Presence. We are transformed from darkness to illumination in Its light when we say repeatedly in the course of prayer, *Allāhu akbar* ("God is most great"). One must pray fervently, ceaselessly, and with full awareness of the Divine Presence. This is the most indispensable means for securing the fullest measure of realization of the spiritual potentialities of one's life and the surest method of fulfilling the commitment of the slave to serve his Lord and Master.

Jalāl al-Dīn Rūmī, the famous author of the *Mathnawī,* says that a piece of iron when kept for long in fire begins not only to look like fire but also to burn like fire. The soul of man in prayer soaks the substance of his being in the divine ocean of light and grace and draws nourishment from it. This helps him to obtain the purification of his *nafs* or lower self. Then he traverses the pathway to God. By engaging himself in the prayer of the heart, he lays himself open to the healing influences that emanate from the Holy Spirit. The Quran pertinently points out:

> Who have believed and whose hearts have rest in the remembrance of Allah. Verily in the remembrance of Allah do hearts find rest! (XIII, 28)

22. Prayer around the Ka'bah.

There are many references in the Quran that point out the value of invoking constantly God's Holy Name: "Say Allah: Then leave them alone, playing their game of plunging" (VI, 92). Constant invocation of the Supreme Name (*Allāh*) or one of His ninety-nine attributive Names brings about peace in the soul of man, a peace that surpasses all understanding. It deepens one's state of consciousness, enables one to have glimpses of eternal truths, and transforms human consciousness into a transparent medium through which God's light passes to illuminate the interior being of man.

One can refer to some of the relevant verses of the Quran that highlight the Islamic approach to prayer at the level of *iḥsān* (literally, beauty or virtue), which is the highest level where effective communion between the believer and his God takes place:

> Whosoever surrendereth his purpose to Allah while doing good, his reward is with his Lord: and there shall no fear come upon them nor shall they grieve. (II, 112; see also IV, 125; XXXI, 22)

In Islam, prayer is basically an attempt on the part of man to turn to God—that is, an attempt to transcend himself in the direction of the highest perfection and most majestic presence, which we attribute, on the authority of the Quran, to God, Who is the Lord and Master of the Universe. In the Quran, there is a reference also to the believers' meeting with the Lord. The highest reward of the believers is that, on the Day of Judgment, their faces will be bright while looking to their Lord. The actual verses are:

> That day will faces be resplendent,
> Looking toward their Lord;
> And that day will other faces be despondent,
> Thou wilt know that some great disaster is about to fall on them.
> (LXXV, 22–25)

Prayer and the Vision of God

The expression *ilā rabbihā nāẓiratun*, which means "looking toward or gazing upon their Lord," tends to underscore the highest reward for the believer, which is comprehensible only in visionary terms. Prayer at its highest level of perfection is an attempt on earth by the believer to behold the Face of the Lord and to derive, however indirect it be, the bliss and the joy that come from such a vision. The ultimate end for the believer is thus to earn the reward of beholding the vision of the Lord. According to the conception of prayer in Islam, the supreme opportunity that life provides is to turn to God consciously and purposively and to contemplate the beauty of His Face and His manifold Attributes. This helps man to secure the transformation of his being and to make it a fit vehicle upon which God's light and grace may descend. It is true that in the Quran it is said:

> The vision (of men) comprehendeth Him (God) not but He comprehendeth all vision. He is subtle, the Aware. (XVI, 104)

But this does not mean anything more than the fact that the limited powers of perception with which man is endowed cannot grasp in its fullness the beauty of the Face of God. Nor again does this mean that man is incapable of having even glimpses of the Face of the Lord. Indeed, there is an assurance in the Quran that wherever man turns, there is the Face of God. The reference to the Lord of the Throne, making the Spirit descend on whomsoever He pleases with His permission, is meant to emphasize the transcendence of God and the fact that the human being cannot, by himself, have access to the life of the Spirit. It points to God's grace, with which He condescends to favor His servants with intimation of His Presence (see XL, 15). God says: "They apprehend nothing of His knowledge except what He wills" (II, 255–56). On the last Day of Reckoning there will be faces which will be allowed to behold God's Face. His Messenger has proclaimed to his community that on that day they shall see the Lord as one sees the moon in full moonlight. Those radiant faces that will gaze upon the Lord will perhaps recall that in their earthly careers they were in some sense aware of the beauty of His Face and that when the veil will have been finally lifted, they will not be taken unaware; for of old, God had imparted His spirit to Adam.

The *rūḥ* (spirit) is the uncreated element lodged in man's being. This enables him to have knowledge of God (*ma'rifah*). Prayer is a process of preparation on earth to enable him to meet his Maker. The life to come is a continuation of this life, provided this life is lived by man earnestly and resolutely in an effort to fulfill the Law that the revealed Word of God has brought to his notice. Considering what has been said above as a preface, the meaning of the following verses becomes clear and gives full scope to the longing of those who pray, who serve and wait for the Lord's gifts to come to them:

> We shall show them Our portents on the horizons and within themselves until it will be manifest unto them that it is the Truth. Doth not thy Lord suffice, since He is Witness over all things? How are they still in doubt about the meeting with their Lord? Lo! Is not He surrounding all things? (XLI, 53–54)

Prayer as Communion

Enough has been said in the foregoing to emphasize the cardinal principle of Islamic prayer, namely, that it is man's communion with the Divine. From the time the believer hears the call to prayers coming from a mosque nearby, in response to this invitation to say the prayer and to achieve success (*falāḥ*), he proceeds to put on ritually clean dress and to perform the prescribed ablution to secure his physical cleanliness. He then declares his intention to pray by standing either by himself or in congregation behind an imam in the Divine Presence in all humility after he has pronounced the *takbīr* (God is most great). He recites the *Sūrat al-fātiḥah,* supplements it with a portion of the Quran, goes into *rukū*ʿ by kneeling down, and says, "Praise be to God the most exalted." Then he bows down and prostrates himself by putting his forehead on the ground and says, "Praise be to God the most high." Thereafter he sits in a reverential position to recite prescribed words called *tashahhud* and declares that God is one and Muḥammad is His slave and Messenger. He also invokes peace and prayers upon the Prophet of Islam and also upon the prophet Abraham. He finishes the prayer by saying *as-salāmu ʿalaykum wa raḥmat Allāh* (Peace be upon you and the mercy of God), turning his face to the right and then to the left. He thus ends his prayer by sending the salutation of peace and Mercy of God on all those who have been on either side of him engaged in prayer.

The invocation of God's prayer and peace upon the Prophet of Islam as also upon the prophet Abraham, who is the founder of monotheistic religion, is in the nature of the believer's affirmation of the continuity in the development of universal religion. It is an acknowledgment of man's indebtedness to God for the revelation that He has sent to His prophets, who are His chosen representatives. After all, it is through their intercession that the revealed Word of God has reached man and has enabled him to participate in the grand process of self-purification and self-transformation. Rightly regarded, prayer would appear to be the most important of all the prescribed rituals, if only because it makes concrete that which is subscribed in the abstract, namely, belief in the world of the unseen. Prayer helps man to realize the existence of the Divine, which in turn enables him to fulfill the Law. In keeping his faith with the Divine he becomes useful to his fellow men and is able to do his labor here below in his capacity as God's vicegerent on earth.

The congregational prayer provides additionally the opportunity to strengthen man's relations with his fellow men and to develop that sense of inner belonging to the community, or to the *ummah,* without which the unity of mankind and, therefore, peace on earth cannot be realized. The physical, psychological, and spiritual dimensions of prayer make possible the total absorption of man's being in the Divine and enable God's grace and light to descend in his soul. The moment he says the *takbīr*, *Allāhu akbar* (God is most great), he in effect detaches himself from the world and turns in humility to the Divine Being by acknowledging His Uniqueness, His Sovereignty and His Mercy. Muslim prayer is not a part-time activity; it is a continual act of dedication to the end that the Divine Purpose inherent in man's creation is fulfilled.

Prayer and the Challenges of Life

In the Quran there is a reference to the efficaciousness of seeking assistance through patience and prayer:

> Seek help in patience and prayer; and truly it is hard save for the humble-minded,
> Who know that they will have to meet their Lord, and that unto Him they are returning. (II, 45–46)

In this world, where man is called upon to live, for him to go through ordeals, face trials, or suffer tribulations is not easy. Indeed, it is the lot of all mankind to go through these tests. The Quran seems to point out that one way to cope with the challenge that life on earth poses is through patience and prayer. But patience and prayer are not easy in the face of hardships and troubles; man must be convinced that he is bound to meet his Lord and return to Him. This thought is the keynote of man's relation with his Maker: man has to render account to God of what he has done to keep the Law. He must therefore stay humble and obey the Law.

Prayer and Almsgiving

In addition to prayer, man is ordered also to give *zakāt*, the prescribed contribution to the poor. It is one of the mysteries of the Quran that it has imposed the duty to pray along with the duty to give *zakāt*. It would appear that the efficaciousness of the prayer is very much dependent on what man is freely able to give from his wealth in the Name of God. This is not merely a case of performing charity but of securing his purification, which is suggested by the use of the word *zakāt* (*zakā-yazkī* means "to purify"). It seems as if man is carrying a bone-breaking burden of wealth on his head as he is traveling on his way to God, and he is advised that by giving *zakāt* he would be able to jettison this burden. No wonder that prayer was likened by the Prophet of Islam to the flowing of a river that passes at one's doorstep. Abū Hurayrah quotes the Prophet:

> If one of you has a river at his door in which he washes himself five times a day, what do you think of him? Would it leave any dirt on him? The companion said it would not leave any dirt on him as he would be perfectly clean. The Prophet said, This is an example of five prayers with which Allah washes off all the evils of man.

Both prayer and the giving of *zakāt* are calculated to purify men: it will be recalled that the Prophet was explicitly enjoined to purify the believers (LXII, 2) (*yuzakkīhim*).

Inner Prayer

The holy Quran speaks of the faithful as those who remember Allah standing and sitting and lying on their sides (III, 19). This again shows that prayer is a continuous act; the life of a true believer is a long unending prostration. The ritual prayer is prescribed as an irreducible minimum, but constant remembrance of the Lord, ceaseless invocation of His Holy Name, and recitation of the revealed Word of God as it is contained in the Quran are recommended as man's sure means to reach a higher level of spiritual exaltation. There is no fixed day for rest in Islam, and even on Friday, when there is congregational prayer that is prescribed directly in the Quran, there are indications that after the prayer is over one is to go out of the mosque to seek the bounty of the Lord—that is to say, to do one's work. So there is no such rule as a fixed day for prayer and the rest of the week for business, when there is to be no prayer.

Prayer in Islam affords an opportunity for serene contemplation of the Divine Attributes for the purpose of realizing the Divine Attributes in one's being. Man in turn, as a result of this contemplation, experiences his own humility, his virtual nothingness. This helps him to transcend the mechanical processes involved in his biological life. Muslim prayer helps one to wake up—no wonder there is a significant addition to the text of the call to morning prayer: "Prayer is better than sleep"!

Cosmic Prayer

Islamic prayer, insofar as it consists in praising the Lord, is in tune with nature: according to the Quran even the seven heavens and the earth are constantly engaged in declaring the Glory of God:

> The seven heavens and the earth,
> And all beings therein,
> Declare His glory;
> There is not a thing
> But celebrates His praise;
> And yet ye understand not
> How they declare His glory!
> Verily He is Oft-Forbearing,
> Most Forgiving!
> (XVII, 44)

Not only the seven heavens and the earth but also the birds in their flight are engaged in His praise:

> Hast thou not seen that Allah, He it is Whom all who are in the heavens and the earth praise, and the birds in their flight? Of each He knoweth verily the worship and the praise; and Allah is aware of what they do. (XXIV, 41)

Thus, it would appear that the prayer of the believer in Islam is in step with what the world around him is constantly engaged in doing. One way to be in tune with the Infinite is to stay in a prolonged state of prayer and be receptive to the finer forces that descend from above to uplift man to a higher plane of existence.

Finally, and more decisively, there is a reference in the Quran where the prophet Moses received the following revelation:

> Lo! I, even I, am Allah. There is no God save Me. So serve Me and establish worship for My remembrance.
> Lo! the Hour is surely coming. But I will to keep it hidden, that every soul may be rewarded for that which it striveth (to achieve). (XX, 14, 15)

The Quranic concept of prayer is thus linked with man's struggle with his *nafs* (lower self) and is to be likened to an alchemical process, which transforms it into the angelic state of being and which is a sort of witnessing of a rebirth into the world of the Holy Spirit.

Part Two

ASPECTS OF THE ISLAMIC TRADITION

8

Sunnism

ABDUR-RAHMAN IBRAHIM DOI

The Meaning of Sunnism

OF ALL THE BRANCHES OF ISLAM, two are by far the largest: the *Shīʿah* or the Shīʿites, partisans of ʿAlī; and the *Ahl al-Sunnah wa'l-jamāʿah,* people who follow the prophetic practices and the majority, popularly known as the Sunnis. The Sunnis number about 80 percent of the total Muslim population of the world. The *Ahl al-Sunnah* emphasize the teachings of the Quran and the *Sunnah* (practices of the Prophet of Islam along with the collective judgment of the *ṣaḥābah,* or companions of the Prophet) as authoritative sources of Islamic legislation. The Sunnis stand fast by both the letter and the spirit of the Law emanating from these three sources.

Sunni means literally "one who is a traditionist." Actually, *Ahl al-Sunnah,* or "the people of the *Sunnah,*" are so called because they follow strictly the *Ḥadīth,* the traditions or sayings of Prophet, and the *Sunnah,* the practices of the Prophet. The most authentic collections of *Ḥadīth* are believed by the Sunnis to be the *Ṣiḥāḥ al-sittah* (the Six Authentic Works, that is, the six canonical collections of authentic *Ḥadīth*): the *Ṣaḥīḥ* of Muslim, the *Ṣaḥīḥ* of Bukhārī, the *Sunan* of Ibn Mājah, the *Sunan* of Abū Dā'ūd, the *Sunan* of Nasā'ī, and the *Ṣaḥīḥ* of Tirmidhī. The *Muwaṭṭa'* of Imam Mālik ibn Anas also is held in a very high esteem by the Sunnis, although it is not one of the six canonical works.[1] The inspiration for believing in the *Sunnah* of the Prophet is derived from his last sermon during the *ḥajj al-wadāʿ* (farewell pilgrimage), in which the Prophet emphasized the importance of his sayings and practices saying, "I leave for you two things. You will not go astray if you held fast unto them: the Book of God and the *Sunnah* of His Messenger."

Sunni Beliefs

The Sunnis believe that the words and deeds of the Prophet, who is, according to the Quran (XXX, 21), the *uswāh ḥasanah* (noble paradigm), must be followed in every walk of life, as they were followed by his *ṣaḥābah* (companions), *tābi'ūn* (followers of the companions), and *atbā' al-tābi'īn* (followers of the followers of the companions). "It is incumbent upon you," said the Prophet, "to follow my *Sunnah* and the *sunnah* of the righteous caliphs (*al-khulafā' al-rāshidūn*)."

The Sunnis are of the opinion that it was as a result of Divine Wisdom and Providence that all the male children of the Prophet died in his lifetime and that under Divine Inspiration he kept the question of his succession open, leaving it to the *ummah* (community of Islam) to decide the most competent person to become the leader of the *ummah.* As the Quran testifies: "The Prophet does not utter a word out of his caprice; it is but until a revelation that has come to him" (LIII, 3–4).

The Sunnis adhere to principles rather than personalities. They do not agree with the Ghadīr Khumm (Pool of Khumm) account accepted by the Shī'ites, according to which, while the Prophet was going on his journey from the *ḥajj al-wadā'* (farewell pilgrimage) to Mecca on the 18th Dhu'l-Ḥijjah in the eleventh year of *hijrah,* he made the following proclamation: "He for whom I am the *mawlā* (master) should henceforth have 'Alī as his *mawlā.*" Even if some of the Sunnis consider this *ḥadīth* to be authentic, they interpret *mawlā* to mean a "spiritual teacher" and to include all the pious and learned men of the community who are the successors of the Prophet. In fact, the Prophet did not confine himself to praising 'Alī; he had also praised Abū Bakr, 'Umar, and 'Uthmān at different times, paying them tributes as glowing as any recorded in the books of *Ḥadīth* and *Sīrah* (biography of the Prophet). Therefore, unlike Shī'ite Muslims, Sunni Muslims do not attribute a preemptive title of *khilāfah* (vicegerency or succession) to any particular individual; they insist that the right to choose the *khalīfah* (vicegerent or successor to the Prophet) belongs to the *ummah.* It was on this basis that, immediately after the death of the Prophet, the *Anṣār* (those who had embraced Islam in Medina) and the *Muhājirūn* (those who had migrated from Mecca to Medina) met at a place in Medina called Saqīfah Banū Sā'idah and, after some discussion, elected Abū Bakr as the first *khalīfah Rasūl Allāh* (successor or vicegerent of the Messenger of God).

According to the Sunni view, Abū Bakr merited this position. It was he who was chosen by the Prophet to accompany him on his *hijrah* (migration) from Mecca to Medina, and it was he who has been mentioned in the Quran: "God did indeed help him [the Prophet] when the unbelievers drove him out; he had no more than one companion [Abū Bakr]; the two were in the cave" (IX, 40).

The main features of the election of the *khalīfah* or caliph continued for the other three "rightly guided" (*rāshidūn*) caliphs, 'Umar, 'Uthmān, and 'Alī. They were elected through the process of *ijmā'* (consensus of opinion) of the *aṣḥāb ḥall wa'l-'aqd* (people who loosen and bind, that is, those who possess knowledge of religious injunctions and law). Once *ijmā'* was reached, people offered their *bay'ah* (oath of allegiance) to their elected caliph. The caliph in turn had to make a covenant (*'ahd*) with the *ummah* to rule and lead them according to the principles of the Divine Law as laid down by the Quran and the *Sunnah.* The *khalīfah* for the *ummah* was only a democratically elected spiritual and temporal leader (*imām*) possessing no *'iṣmah* (inerrancy). Thus, Abū Bakr al-Ṣiddīq, 'Umar al-Fārūq, 'Uthmān al-Ghaniy, and 'Alī al-Murtaḍā were elected as the consecutive successors of the Prophet and are called the *khulafā' al-rāshidūn* (rightly guided caliphs).

These four caliphs ruled the Islamic state for a total period of about thirty years, exactly in accordance with the teachings of the Quran and the *Sunnah* of the Prophet—hence their title, "rightly guided."

In spite of the fact that the Sunnis follow the noble example of the *ṣaḥābah* and particularly those of the four *rāshidūn* caliphs, they do not attribute *'iṣmah* to them, as is done by the Shī'ite in the case of their Imams. The Shī'ites believe that God prevents the prophets and the Imams from sin and that the Imams have the power of custodianship (*wilāyah*) over their followers.

The Sunnis believe that any sincere Muslim who strives to gain true knowledge of the Quran will be blessed by God, even if he comes from a very humble origin. They do not subscribe to the Shī'ite view that the true meaning of the Quran was available only to the *Ahl al-bayt* (members of the family of the Prophet) who were near and dear to him like 'Alī and 'Alī's eleven male lineal descendants, who are the Shī'ite Imams. The Sunnis, however, show great respect for the *Ahl al-bayt* and pray for them while uttering their names. All the *ṣaḥābah* are considered to be just (*'ādil*) by Sunni Muslims and by those who emphasize the truth of what has been reported in a prophetic *ḥadīth:* "My *ṣaḥābah* are like guiding stars; if you follow them, you follow the path of guidance." The role of some of the *ṣaḥābah* in the battles of Jamal and Ṣiffīh and some other lapses committed by them are considered to be mere errors of *ijtihād*, despite the best of intentions.

Sunni Caliphates and Sultanates

The next period of the Sunni caliphate after the *rāshidūn* caliphs was that of the Umayyad Dynasty, which ruled in Damascus, Syria. During this period, the religion of Islam was adopted by many of the conquered peoples, and a mode of coexistence was worked out with several other religious communities not converted to Islam. In the year 92/711, Umayyad forces crossed the Straits of Gibraltar into Spain (*Al-Andalus*), where Sunnism remained the dominating form of Islam. Much of Spain remained in Muslim hands until the Christian Reconquista in the eighth/fourteenth century. During the six centuries of Islamic rule in Spain, Sunni learning and piety characterized the life of the Islamic community, and culture in general flourished under the Spanish Muslims usually known as Moors. Spain served in fact as an important point of contact between Christianity and Islam, and some of the most important spiritual movements of Islam were associated with Andalusia.

In the year 132/750, the Umayyad caliphate in Damascus fell, to be replaced by another Sunni Arab dynasty, the Abbasids in the East; Umayyad rule in Spain was to survive for more than another two centuries. The Abbasid caliphs established their capital in Baghdad along the banks of the Tigris River in Mesopotamia. It was during the Abbasid caliphate that there emerged the four Sunni schools of Islamic jurisprudence: the Ḥanafī, Mālikī, Shāfiʿī, and Ḥanbalī schools, founded respectively by Imam Abū Ḥanīfah (d. 150/767), Imam Mālik ibn Anas (d. 179/795), Imam al-Shāfiʿī (d. 204/820) and Imam Aḥmad ibn Ḥanbal (d. 241/855).

The *Ṣiḥāḥ al-sittah,* the six most authentic collections of *Ḥadīth* of the Prophet, were also assembled during the Abbasid age. Instructions in traditional Islamic religious disciplines such as Islamic Law, Quranic studies, and studies of the prophetic traditions had previously gone on mainly in the schools maintained as parts of the mosques. It was during this period that the enlightened patrons of these disciplines established separate academies known as *madrasahs.*

With the invasion of the main Islamic lands by Mongols or Tartars, who had originated in eastern Siberia and had captured and sacked Baghdad in 656/1258, the Abbasid caliphate was destroyed. But, ironically, in just a few decades the Mongols who had conquered the Muslim lands were themselves conquered by Islam and became Muslims. Some embraced Shīʿism but many became Sunnis and supported Sunni schools of Law.

The Mamlūks, originally Turkish slaves, who were strict Sunni Muslims, ruled Egypt and Syria between 648/1250 and 922/1517. Great literary achievements in historical writing were made during the Mamlūk period. One scholar of the period, Jalāl al-Dīn al-Suyūṭī (849/1445–911/1505), wrote historical works on Islam and produced scholarly studies of the Quran from the Sunni perspective. These works became famous throughout the Muslim world.

23. Suleymaniye Cami, Istanbul.

The Mamlūks were succeeded by the Ottoman Turks, who in 816/1413 established, on the basis of their earlier sultanate, a Sunni Islamic empire that lasted until 1342/1924. Basing themselves mainly in Anatolia (modern Turkey), the Turks controlled Syria, Egypt, North Africa, and vast territory in Europe as far as Austria, and everywhere they spread the teachings of Sunnism.

The Sunni Mughals established their empire in India and ruled it between 933/1526 and 1274/1857. The Mughal rulers made Delhi their capital and built impressive royal palaces, mosques, and mausoleums, the best known of which is the Taj Mahal in Agra. However, the remarkable growth of Islam in India was due not so much to the efforts of the Sunni rulers as to the Sufis, whose piety influenced the Indian masses and brought a large number of people into the fold of Islam. From India, Muslim missionaries went to Malaysia and Indonesia, where Islam was accepted by the entire local population. Today, nearly all Muslims throughout Southeast Asia belong to the Sunni branch of Islam.

Sunni Islam has also seen a vital growth in Africa, south of the Sahara, where Islam had not penetrated in its initial spread across North Africa to Spain. The majority of the population of many West African and East African countries is Sunni Muslim.

Sunni Schools of Law

The four schools of Sunni Law derive their guidance from the Quran and the *Sunnah* as the primary sources, and *ijmā*ʿ (consensus of opinion) and *qiyās* (analogical deduction) as the secondary sources. *Qiyās*, which plays an important role in the Ḥanafī school, the largest of the four Sunni schools, is used to provide answers to new problems by drawing analogy between the accepted interpretations of the two primary sources in relation to the problems already solved by them and the reasons underlying the new problem at hand.

These sources represent God's Will for regulating the conduct of the community of Islam and are also known as the *Sharīʿah*. The *Sharīʿah* signifies a composite source of teachings and practices based upon the interrelation between divine and human activity. It is considered a duty of every Sunni Muslim to spend his life according to the dictates of the *Sharīʿah* as interpreted by the *ʿulamāʾ* (learned men) and the *fuqahāʾ* (jurists).

All Sunni schools provide for their adherents clear guidelines drawn from the light of the Quran and the *Sunnah* for all walks of life and every sphere of activity. For example, rules have been laid down for performing prayers, for formulating contracts of sale and purchase, for conduct of war, for dealing with non-Muslims, for marriage, divorce, inheritance, etc.

Certain minor differences of opinion and interpretation exist among the four Sunni schools, but a Sunni Muslim may conform his practice of Islam to any one of them. Usually a person born in one school conforms to the practice of that same school. This is called *taqlīd*, or imitation. But there are at present a number of Sunni Muslims who belong to the Salafiyyah movement, which claims that it is sufficient to follow the Quran and the *Sunnah* and that there is no need to follow any of the four Imams. The puritanical movement of Shaykh Muḥammad ibn ʿAbd al-Wahhāb, popularly known as the Wahhabī movement, rejects the *taqlīd* of any of the four Imams and their schools of thought. Another group, named *Ahl al-ḥadīth*, which is found in India and Pakistan, also follows the Quran and *Ḥadīth* and not the four Sunni schools of Islamic jurisprudence. It feels that the Quran and the *Sunnah* are sufficient to guide it upon the right path.

Sunni Beliefs and Practices

Like other Muslims, Sunnis offer five daily prayers, give *zakāt* (religious tax), fast in the month of Ramaḍān, and perform the *ḥajj*, or pilgrimage to Mecca, if they are able to do so.

Sunnis attach great importance to the *ṣalāt al-jumʿah* (Friday prayer), which is offered in congregation at *ẓuhr* time (after midday) on Fridays. The *ṣalāt al-jumʿah* is *wājib* (necessary) and must be performed by all male adults except those who are travelers or who have some handicaps which apply to other *farḍ* (obligatory) prayers. Women are not bound to offer this prayer in congregation, but they may join it if it does not upset their household duties.

Like other Muslims, Sunnis also believe in the seven articles of faith (*īmān*): belief in the Oneness of God, the angels, the Sacred Scriptures, the messengers of God, the Last Day, destiny coming from God–whether good or bad, and resurrection after death. Sunnis believe that God has created the universe and that He is its absolute Controller and Regulator; that everything in the universe has a predetermined set course (*al-qadar*) and nothing can happen without God's willing it and knowing it; that God knows the present, the past, and the future of every creature and that the destiny of every creature is already known to Him (XXV, 2–XXXIII, 38); that God has given free will to every human being by the exercise of which he can choose between right and wrong; and that God will judge every human being on the Day of Judgment on the basis of his actions in this world. The Sunnis also believe that on the Day of Judgment no one except the Prophet, with God's permission, will be able to intercede (*shafā'ah*) on behalf of anyone else. In other words, no Imam, no *khalīfah,* no *walī Allāh* (saint) will have any power of intercession.

After the assassination of the caliph 'Uthmān and the unsatisfactory arbitration between 'Alī and Mu'āwiyah in relation to their claims to the caliphate, there emerged three schools: the Khārijites, the Murji'ites, and the Shī'ites. Every school developed a different notion of its collective identity and began to view the boundaries of right belief differently.

The Khārijites

The Khārijites believed that faith was demonstrated in righteous acts and that without making faith explicit in public behavior, one could not claim to be a Muslim. They also thought that sinful acts committed by any Muslim, including the *khalīfah,* breached one's confession of faith and one's claim to be a Muslim. They based their conclusion on certain pronouncements in the Quran in which infidelity is related to some major acts of moral transgression through the use of such phrases as "there is no faith in him," "he does not belong to us," and "he has no place in Islam" to censure the conduct of the person who is guilty of such acts or to indicate the punishment of hell which is promised to him. The Khārijites argued that the caliph 'Uthmān had acted contrary to the mandate of the *Sharī'ah:* therefore, he and all those who committed grave sins should be expelled from the Islamic *ummah.* Initially they supported 'Alī in his struggle for the caliphate against Mu'āwiyah, but when 'Alī lost in the arbitration between him and Mu'āwiyah on the matter of the caliphate, the Khārijites withdrew from his forces to form a separate sect.

The Murji'ites

In contrast to the Khārijites, the Murji'ites believed that mere affirmation of faith by professing the *shahādah* was enough to ensure salvation for a person in the next life. In other words, even if a Muslim commits a number of sins in his life, he will still not go to hell; but his place in the hereafter will be somewhat inferior to that of a more virtuous Muslim. The Murji'ites held that outward acts of faith and sin could not be judged except insofar as they affected the common good. They believed that commission of sin did not imply that the sinner should be expelled from the community. Consequently, they thought that the decision regarding the caliph 'Uthmān's or any Muslim's status as a believer or sinner must be left to God. In other words, it must be postponed until the Day of Judgment.

The Murji'ites took their stand on the dictum in the Quran that bestows the glad tidings of heaven to everyone who possesses only the qualification of faith. With this moderate attitude, the Murji'ites found themselves largely in support of Mu'āwiyah and other Umayyad caliphs, although not without criticizing their alleged lack of piety.

The Khārijites were prone to thinking that the graver sins were fatal to faith and that committing them turned a Muslim into a *kāfir* (disbeliever). The Murji'ites, on the contrary, thought that to sin even in the extreme was not a matter of such importance as to destroy faith.

The Sunnis had all along emphasized the view held by the *ṣaḥābah* on this subject—the view that the commission of a major sin was neither the equivalent of *kufr* (disbelief), as the Khārijites thought, nor an insignificant matter, as the Murji'ites felt. In Sunni opinion, perpetration of a sin deserves divine reprobation and chastisement, and yet it is not unpardonable if God so wishes.

The Mu'tazilites

In the second/eighth century, Sunni Islam saw the emergence of a group called the Mu'tazilites. It was responsible for whetting the appetite of Muslims for speculative investigations. It adopted logic, philosophy, and rationalism to sharpen the tools of dialectical theology to defend Islam against Christianity, Manichaeism, and other forms of alien religious thought. The Mu'tazilites went into excesses in their beliefs, particularly in respect of *tawḥīd* (Oneness of God) and the creation of the Quran (*khalq al-Qur'ān*).

The beatific vision (seeing God in the hereafter) was another matter of controversy among them and other early Islamic schools of thought. The Quran says: "Some faces that Day will beam (in brightness and beauty) looking towards their Lord" (LXXV, 22–23). This verse implies that on the Last Day the faces of the loyal servants of God will be radiant with joy by looking at His Countenance. The same truth is emphasized by the *Ḥadīth,* many of which assert that one of the boundless blessings that the faithful (*mu'minūn*) will receive in the hereafter is that they will see God Most High and that this will be the source of the greatest bliss and happiness for them. But the Mu'tazilites denied the possibility of beatific vision on the ground that it was not logically possible because only a thing that exists in material form or has color or surface can be seen by the human eye. They argued that since God has neither form nor substance nor is He contained in space and time, the question of seeing Him does not arise. The possibility of seeing God was rejected by the Mu'tazilites on rationalistic grounds, even though such a rejection meant refuting the relevant verse of the Quran.

Although the Mu'tazilites were Sunnis, such views were not accepted by the majority of Sunnis, who believed that since the Prophet has asserted authoritatively the possibility of the beatific vision in his sayings, and that the *ṣaḥābah* too had drawn no other inference from these *aḥādīth* except that in the hereafter the faithful (*mu'minūn*) will be blessed with an unconcealed view of God, every Muslim must believe in the possibility of such vision.

Free Will and Determinism

Free will (*qadar*) and predestination (*jabr*) have constituted other areas of controversy among Sunnis. The Qadariyyah school regarded everything that comes to pass in this world including men's actions as entirely independent of fate. The Jabriyyah school, on the contrary, regarded every such event and action as having been determined by fate. Fatalists as they were, the Jabriyyah provided no possibility for man to act as a free being but rather turned him practically into an inanimate object.

The majority of Sunnis, however, take a middle-of-the-road course in this question. They believe that all happenings and all human actions are the results of both divine and human wills acting in a delicate balance. They insist that the general run of Muslims should place their full faith in the *ṣaḥābah* (companions) and follow implicitly the path marked out by them in this as in other matters, because in the appreciation and understanding of religion and its principles it is not possible to excel the *ṣaḥābah*.

The Significance of al-Ghazzālī

In the fourth/eleventh century, the world of Islam saw the emergence of three trends in the intellectual sphere: the Sunni theologians believed that the study of theology was causing more harm to common people than good; others felt that religious knowledge was incompatible with secular knowledge; and ordinary Muslims regarded the study of science as irrelevant to their spiritual life. A genius was needed to bring about an intellectual synthesis of these mutually repellent trends. The world of Islam found such a genius in the person of Imam Abū Ḥāmid al-Ghazzālī (450/1058–505/1111), who was one of the greatest Sunni scholars. After carefully considering the works of Muslim philosophers such as Abū 'Alī Sīnā (Avicenna) and al-Kindī as well as the works of Greek philosophers translated into Arabic, he came to the conclusion that they were not explaining, but were rather explaining *away*, Islamic beliefs. In criticizing them, al-Ghazzālī restricted the limits of human reason in apprehending Divine Truth. He strongly believed that Sufism alone could revive the religion through its emphasis upon spirituality.

Sunni Spirituality

Sunni spirituality aims at determining the limits of genuine spiritual experience in accordance with the perfect model (*uswāh ḥasanah*) of the Prophet as manifested in his *Ḥadīth* and *Sunnah*. The Sunnis judge the spiritual merits of the actions (*a'māl*) of Muslims on the basis of values and norms established by the Quran and the *Sunnah* of the Prophet. The most important of such values and norms is *taqwā*.

The Arabic word *taqwā* denotes a quality that is absolutely essential in the personality of every conscientious Muslim and comprises both the love and the fear of God. It can at best be loosely rendered in English as "God-consciousness" combined with reverential fear and purity. More exactly, *taqwā* refers to a constant awareness of a person that he stands always before God and that God knows everything concerning him, even his most secret thoughts deep down within the recesses of his heart. This awareness produces in a person an intense love for God combined with reverence, so that he wants to do only what is pleasing to God and tries to avoid what is displeasing to God. It creates such a keen consciousness of God in a person that he never for a single moment imagines that God is unaware of what he does or that he will not be held accountable for all his actions.

The lives of all notable *ṣaḥābah* were immersed in *taqwā* as defined in the *ḥadīth* narrated by 'Umar ibn al-Khaṭṭāb: "You should serve God in such a way that if you do not see Him, He sees you." It is this firm *īmān* (faith) that brings about and increases love for God (*ḥubb Allāh*), love for Muslim brotherhood (*al-ukhuwwat al-islāmiyyah*), and love for all of mankind, which in turn generates efficient moral power leading to peace between man and his Creator as well as between man and man.

Taqwā is used in a general sense to indicate a religious attitude of devotional feeling resulting from the fear of God. The faith of a *mu'min* (believer) lies between *khawf* (fear of God) and *rajā'* (hope in God). However, *taqwā* does not require a Muslim to practice austerity like a Christian monk. He has to curb his carnal desires, but not in any inhuman way. A Muslim with *taqwā* is expected to take up responsibilities in life, like contracting marriage and raising a family, with all that such responsibilities involve. Since Islam does not subscribe to the idea that intellectual knowledge (illumination), however correctly imparted, would rightly lead the human will by itself, it insists that a Muslim should strive to increase his *taqwā* or strengthen his *īmān*, by acquiring knowledge of the Quran and the *Sunnah*, by performing devotional acts (*'ibādah*) and by placing his reliance upon God alone (*tawakkul*).

The Quran indicates the qualities of men who possess *taqwā* in these words:

> Verily, the Believers are those whose hearts feel fear when God is mentioned, and when His signs (or revelations) are recited to them they increase their faith, and who put their trust in their Lord. (VIII, 2)
> Verily, those who live in awe and fear of their Lord, who believe in their Lord's signs (or revelations), who do not ascribe partners to their Lord, who give what they give in charity with their hearts full of fear because they are to return to their Lord: It is these who hasten in all good acts and they are foremost in them. (XXIII, 57–61)

The caliph 'Umar ibn al-Khaṭṭāb described graphically how a believer's *īmān* lies between fear of God and hope in Him. He said: "If God declared on the Day of Judgment that all people would go to paradise except one unfortunate person, out of His fear I would think that I am that person. And if God declared that all people would go to hell except one fortunate person, out of my hope in His Mercy I would think that I am that fortunate person."

Sufism in the Sunni World

Many Sunni Muslims happen to be the members of Sufi orders. Their notion of piety is to live in accordance with the dictates of the Sufi fraternity (*ṭarīqah*) to which they belong. The early Sufis were Sunni Muslims from Persia like Abū Yazīd of Basṭām (d. 261/874). The main Sufi fraternities that have sprung up throughout the world, such as the Qādiriyyah, the Shādhiliyyah, the 'Alawiyyah, the Tijāniyyah, the Chishtiyyah, the Naqshbandiyyah, etc., are of Sunni background. Numerous Sunni Muslims in the Indian subcontinent comprising India, Pakistan, and Bangladesh, in Southeast Asian countries, in North Africa, East Africa, and West Africa south of the Sahara happen to be *murīds* (spiritual disciples) under the spiritual guidance and surveillance of the shaykhs (spiritual masters) of the respective Sufi fraternities to which they belong. As a result, many shrines of the saints (*awliyā' Allāh*) throughout these countries are frequented by the devotees hoping to receive *barakah* (Divine Blessing), which is associated with the saints both when they are alive and when they are dead. Unfortunately, a number of Sufi disciples have at times shown disregard for the standard forms of expressing true faith through the performance of *ṣalāt* (prayer), *ṣawm* (fasting), or *ḥajj* (pilgrimage) and have thereby earned for themselves the wrath and hatred of the orthodox Sunni community, but the vast majority are orthodox Sunnis. Moreover, most of the Sufi shaykhs have been and remain authorities in the study of the *Sharīʿah*. For example, Shaykh Aḥmad Sirhindī of India popularly known as *Mujaddid al-alf al-thānī* preached fervently that "*ṭarīqah* is *Sharīʿah* and *Sharīʿah* is *ṭarīqah*." Sufi spirituality is, in fact, inseparable from that of Sunnism and constitutes its heart, from which it flows to the body and limbs of the Islamic community as a whole.

Note

1. Some of these collections have now been made available in European languages, such as the *Ṣaḥīḥ* of al-Bukhārī and *Mishkāt al-maṣābīḥ*. See *Mishkāt al-maṣābīh*, trans. J. Robson (4 vols.; Lahore: M. Ashraf, 1963–65); *Kitāb jāmiʿ al-ṣaḥīḥ*, trans. M. M. Khan (6 vols.; Lahore: M. Ashraf, 1978–80).

9

Twelve-Imam Shīʿism

Syed Husain M. Jafri

Twelve-Imam Shīʿism is the name of the second largest denomination of Muslims. They derive their religious code and spiritual inspiration, after the Prophet, from the twelve Imams who were among the descendants of the Prophet. The members of the denomination consider the Imams to be the only authoritative interpreters of the Quran and the *Sunnah.* Within the matrix of Islam and the totality of the Muslim Community, the term Shīʿah (party or followers—hence, the followers of the house of the Prophet) distinguishes them from the Sunni majority. The qualifying adjective twelve (in Arabic *ithnā ʿashar,* "twelve,"—hence, *ithnā ʿashariyyah,* "Twelver") differentiates them from the other smaller branches of Shīʿism such as the Zaydīs and the Ismāʿīlīs, who, although they believe that religious guidance is to be drawn only from the family of the Prophet, differ from the Twelvers concerning the number and the various members of his descendants whom they accept as the legitimate Imams.

The twelve Imams recognized in Twelver Shīʿism are as follows:

1. ʿAlī b. Abī Ṭālib (d. 40/661)
2. Al-Ḥasan b. ʿAlī (d. 49/669)
3. Al-Ḥusayn b. ʿAlī (d. 61/680)
4. ʿAlī b. al-Ḥusayn, Zayn al-ʿĀbidīn (d. 95/714)
5. Muḥammad al-Bāqir (d. 115/733)
6. Jaʿfar al-Ṣādiq (d. 148/765)
7. Mūsā al-Kāẓim (d. 183/799)
8. ʿAlī al-Riḍā (d. 203/818)
9. Muḥammad Jawād al-Taqī (d. 220/835)
10. ʿAlī al-Naqī (d. 254/868)
11. Al-Ḥasan al-ʿAskarī (d. 260/874)

12. Muḥammad al-Mahdī, al-Qāʾim al-Ḥujjah
(entered major occultation in 329/940).

Since the Prophet's sons died in infancy, these Imams sprang from his daughter Fāṭimah, whose husband ʿAlī ibn Abī Ṭālib, the cousin and ward of the Prophet, is the first Imam. Al-Ḥasan and al-Ḥusayn, the sons of ʿAlī and Fāṭimah, whom the Prophet brought up with ardent love and affection, are held as the second and third Imams respectively. After al-Ḥusayn, according to the Twelver Shīʿites, the Imamate remained in his descendants until it came to the twelfth Imam, Muḥammad al-Mahdī who, by the command of God, went into occultation to continue guiding the believers until the Day of Resurrection.

The Family of the Prophet and Divine Guidance

The belief that religious guidance must come from the descendants of the Prophet is taken in Shīʿism from the Quranic concept of the exalted and virtuous families of the prophets. In all ages, the prophets have been particularly concerned with ensuring that the special favor of God bestowed upon them for the guidance of man be maintained in their families and pass to their descendants. The Quran frequently speaks of the prophets praying to God for their progeny and asking Him to continue His guidance in their lineages. In answer to these prayers, the verses of the Quran bear testimony to the special favor of God granted to the direct descendants of the prophets, not only to become true examples of their fathers' righteousness but also to inherit their spiritual qualities and to continue their missions uninterrupted. The total number of such verses that mention special favor requested for and granted to the families of various prophets by God runs over one hundred in the Quran. A few of these verses, especially those relating to Abraham, the patriarch of the prophets, are quoted here to illustrate the point. Abraham's concern for his family is described, for example, when he is told by God: "Behold, I make you a leader [Imam] of the people." Whereupon Abraham pleads: "And of my seed [*dhurriyyatī*, meaning offspring]?" God replied: "My covenant shall not reach the evildoers" (II, 124), meaning that they will be virtuous people to continue the work of guidance. In a similar verse Abraham prays to God:

> Our Lord, I have made some of my "seed" to dwell in the valley where is no sown land by Thy Holy House; Our Lord, let them perform the Prayer, and make hearts of men yearn towards them, and provide them fruits; haply they will be thankful. (XIV, 37)

And the prayer was favorably answered when God declares:

> These are they whom God has blessed among the Prophets of the Seed of Adam, and of those We bore with Noah, and of the Seed of Abraham and Israel, And of those We guided and chose. (XIX, 58)

This special favor of God for the descendants of Abraham found even more emphatic expression in another verse when God says:

> Or, are they jealous of the people for the bounty that God has given them? Yet We gave the people of Abraham [*Āl Ibrāhīm*] the Book and the Wisdom, and We gave them a mighty kingdom. (IV, 54)

And again:

> God chose Adam and Noah and the House of Abraham, and the House of Imran above all beings. (III, 33).

Commentators of the Quran have maintained unanimously that Muḥammad belonged to the "family of Abraham" referred to in these verses. Abraham was not only recognized by the Arabs as their progenitor but was also acknowledged by them as the founder of the Kaʿbah to which four generations of Muḥammad's predecessors were so closely associated as custodians and were therefore the leaders of Mecca with priestly prerogatives.

It was in this family background that Muḥammad arose as the Last Prophet of God and the restorer of the true religion of Abraham and Ishmael, and so in him the sanctity of the house of Abraham, frequently referred to in the Quran, reached its highest perfection. It was this Quranic interpretation of the exalted position of the families of the prophets that made some of the Muslims believe that his successor could be only a man from his own family and endowed with the same personal qualities.

The history of Shīʿism or Shīʿite "sentiments" in Islam, taking into account this Quranic concept of religious leadership, can easily be found as early as the Medinan period of the prophetic mission of Muḥammad, when some of his companions started looking to his cousin and son-in-law, ʿAlī ibn Abī Ṭālib, as the nearest of kin and the closest disciple of the Prophet to lead the community after him. But it was soon after the death of the Prophet that this special regard for ʿAlī found an unequivocal expression when he was denied the leadership of the community, perhaps because of some political considerations. The question of succession to the Prophet became thus involved with the vision of the leadership of the Muslim community, with different approaches to and varying degrees of emphasis upon its political and religious aspects. To some it was more political than religious; to others it was more religious than political. Since Islam encompasses

24. Dome of Masjid-i-Shaykh Lutfallah, Isfahan.

all aspects of human life and destiny, this-worldly and otherworldly, the Prophet, along with his primary function as the Last Messenger of God sent by God to deliver His message to mankind, had also assumed the role of the temporal ruler and statesman when the newly born community in Medina needed his guidance in mundane affairs. It is in this sense that Islam, from its very birth, appeared in history to have been both a religious discipline and, so to speak, a sociopolitical movement.

The Prophet thus left behind a religious heritage and also a political legacy. When he died, the majority of his companions thought that the function of his successor was only to protect and preserve the community from disintegration, to safeguard its religiopolitical character, and to propagate the message of Islam beyond Arabia, but not to continue the divine and spiritual guidance that had come to an end with the death of the Prophet. To some others, however small in number, although the prophethood ended with Muḥammad and no one could be equal to him in status, yet the Divine Guidance had to continue through his successors, who should combine in themselves, like the Prophet, both the functions of Divine Guidance and leadership in mundane affairs. They should share the filial piety of the house of Abraham and the lineal sanctity of the "house of Hāshim," the head of the clan of Muḥammad and the chief custodian of the Kaʿbah. To them, thus, the question of succession to the Prophet was, first and foremost, of a great religious and spiritual significance; it was a question of continued Divine Guidance through the divinely inspired and appointed Imams hailing from the family of the Prophet, who could authoritatively interpret the Divine Revelation and the prophetic *Sunnah.*

Fundamental Beliefs

The basic principles of religion (*uṣūl al-dīn*), in Shīʿism as well as in the rest of Islam are (1) Unity of God (*tawḥīd*), (2) prophecy (*nubuwwah*), which ended with Muḥammad as the last of the prophets and the Quran as the last message of God to mankind, and (3) resurrection (*maʿād*) or the life hereafter. These three fundamental beliefs are common to Shīʿism and Sunnism and serve as the matrix of Islamic fraternity. The Shīʿah, however, add two more principles, considering them necessary for a comprehensive perspective of religious consciousness. These are (4) the Justice of God (*ʿadl*) and (5) the Imamate. As for the Justice of God, it is considered by the Shīʿah as an intrinsic quality of the Divinity rather than an extrinsic one, since the Shīʿite perspective is based more on intelligence than on will. In early Islam, however, it was not exclusively a Shīʿite doctrine, since it was also held by the Muʿtazilites, who belonged to Sunni Islam. Although the

Muʿtazilite school of thought died out in due course, this belief survived among the Shīʿah. What, however, separates Shīʿism from Sunnism is the cardinal belief of the Shīʿah in the Imamate of the descendants of the Prophet. According to the Shīʿah doctrine, the two aspects of the Imamate—its being restricted to the family of the Prophet, on the basis of what has been explained above, and its divine character—are not merely juxtaposed to one another but interpenetrate.

Doctrine of the Imamate

The word *imām* literally means "leader" or "guide," and in its specifically Shīʿite meaning it signifies him who is ordained by God to continue Divine Guidance after prophecy has come to an end. This is also called *wilāyah,* which has almost the same meaning as the Imamate, but *wilāyah* emphasizes more particularly that special quality of the Imam with which he is endowed by God to interpret the inner or esoteric meaning of Revelation. *Wilāyah* literally means to be friend or to be nearer to some one; hence, the *walī,* in Shīʿite terminology, is he who is nearest to God in love and devotion and therefore is entrusted by Him with the esoteric knowledge of religion. The Imams are thus the *awliyāʾ Allāh* par excellence.

The Imamate is based on two principles: *naṣṣ* and *ʿilm. Naṣṣ* means that the Imamate is a prerogative bestowed by God upon a chosen person from the family of the Prophet, who, before his death and with the guidance of God, transfers it to another by an explicit designation, *naṣṣ*. In order to continue the Divine Guidance necessary for mankind, the first *naṣṣ* was initiated by the Prophet himself who, before his death and under the Divine Command, designated ʿAlī ibn Abī Ṭālib as his successor. On the authority of *naṣṣ,* therefore, the Imamate is restricted, through all political circumstances, to a definite individual from among the descendants of ʿAlī and Fāṭimah, whether he claims temporal rule for himself or not.

The second principle embodied in the doctrine of the Imamate is that of *ʿilm.* This means that an Imam is a divinely inspired possessor of a special sum of knowledge of religion not possessed by anyone else, which can only be passed on before his death to the following Imam. In this way the Imam of the time becomes the exclusive, authoritative source of knowledge in religious matters, and without his guidance no one can keep to the right path. This special knowledge includes both the exoteric (*ẓāhir*) and the esoteric (*bāṭin*) meanings of the Quran. This esoteric knowledge of religion is *wilāyah,* which God entrusted to the Prophet, who, in turn, handed it over to ʿAlī; thus it became the inheritance of the Imams who followed him until it reached the twelfth Imam, Muḥammad al-Mahdī.

The doctrine of the Imamate in Twelver Shīʿism thus rotates around these two principles, *naṣṣ* and *ʿilm*, which are not merely conjoined or added to each other, but are so thoroughly fused into a unitary vision of religious leadership that it is impossible to separate the one from the other. Hence, *naṣṣ* in fact means transmission of that special knowledge of religion which had been exclusively and legitimately restricted to the divinely favored Imams of the house of the Prophet through ʿAlī and can only be transferred from one Imam to his successor as the legacy of the sacred family.

Function of the Imamate

The Imam has three functions: (1) to explain what has been revealed through the Quran and has been taught by the Prophet and to interpret the Divine Law, the *Sharīʿah;* (2) to be a spiritual guide to lead men to an understanding of inner meanings of things; and, because of these two qualities, (3) to rule over the Muslim community if the circumstances of the time allow him to do so.

According to Shīʿism, the Imamate is a covenant between God and mankind, and recognition of the Imam is the absolute duty of every believer. The Imams are the proof (*ḥujjah*) of God on earth; their words are the words of God and their commands are the commands of God, because in all their decisions they are inspired by God and they are in absolute authority. Obedience to them, therefore, is obedience to God, and disobedience to them is disobedience to God. They are possessed of the power of miracles and of irrefutable arguments (*dalāʾil*): "They may be likened, in this community, to the Ark of Noah: he who boards it obtains salvation and reaches the gate of repentance. . . . God delegated to the Imams spiritual rulership over the whole world, which must always have such a leader and guide."[1]

The Imam of the time is, according to the Shīʿite belief, the witness for the people, the gate to God (*bāb Allāh*), and the road (*sabīl)* and the guide (*dalīl*) to Him. He is the repository of God's Knowledge, the interpreter of His Revelations, and the pillar of His Unity. It is because of these functions of the Imam that he must be inerrant (*maʿṣūm*) and immune from sin and error. Inerrancy of the Imam guarantees the infallibility of his decisions in matters of law and religion and also preserves the purity and sanctity of the person responsible for such a task.

The function of the Imam can be better understood by comparing it with the caliph in Sunnism. The caliph is a servant of Law, the Imam is its authoritative interpreter and master. The caliph is elected by the people, the Imam is appointed by the previous Imam; that is, appointment of the caliph depends upon the wishes of the people, whereas that of the Imams is an "act of God," an ordinance promulgated by the previous Imam. The caliph can be removed for sinful acts; the Imam is sinless and infallible. Finally, there may or may not be a caliph in the world, but the Shīʿite Imam must always be in the world, whether present or hidden, as the Mahdī is now. The hidden Imam is for the Shīʿites the continuation of the personality and *barakah* of the Prophet and the means whereby the Quran is preserved. It is because of these functions of the Imam that he cannot possibly be elected by the people. A spiritual guide can only receive his authority from God.

The third function of the Imam, that of ruling over the community, is a logical corollary of the first two. An Imam is the best leader the people can have in their mundane affairs as well as in their spiritual affairs. If, however, historical circumstances do not allow the Imam of the time to exercise his temporal authority, according to Twelver Shīʿism, it is not at all incumbent upon him to rise in rebellion and to try to become a ruler. His place is above that of a ruler. Those in possession of temporal power should carry out what the Imam, as a supreme authority of religion, decides.

Obligatory Religious Duties

There are seven religious duties that have to be observed as obligatory acts of worship of God. These are (1) praying five times a day; (2) fasting during the whole month of Ramaḍān; (3) making the pilgrimage (*ḥajj*) to the Kaʿbah once in a lifetime if one is financially and physically able to do so; (4) giving alms (*zakāt*) amounting to one-tenth of certain commodities, to be paid at the end of the year for the general good of the community and the poor; (5) *khums* or one-fifth of one's yearly income to be paid as the prerogative of the Imam of the time; (6) *jihād*, commonly but not accurately translated as holy war; and (7) *al-amr biʾl-maʿrūf waʾl-nahy ʿan al-munkar*, exhorting others to do that which is good and forbidding them from doing what is evil.

Five of these obligatory religious rites, prayer, fasting, *ḥajj*, *zakāt*, and *jihād*, are common to Shīʿism and Sunnism with only minor variations in the performance of the first four, but there is some difference in the interpretation of the obligation of *jihād*. According to the Shīʿah when the Imam is not present and there is no special substitute for him, holy war cannot be launched. However, if an enemy attacks, placing an Islamic country or community in danger, it is everyone's duty to fight in defense of his country and its people.

Khums and "preaching good and forbidding evil" are particularly Shīʿite religious obligations. In addition to *zakāt,* the Shīʿah also pay *khums*—one-fifth of one's yearly income or any other profit earned—as the share of the Imam of the time. During the lifetime of the Prophet, it was paid to him, and since his death the Shīʿah have considered it incumbent upon themselves to pay it to the Imam and to the Prophet's descendants. Half of this religious tax as the share of the Imam goes now to the recognized religious authority, who, as deputy of the Imam in his absence and on his behalf, uses it in whatever way he thinks expedient. The other half is paid to the posterity of the Prophet, especially those in need, in order to protect their honor from the humiliation of financial hardship and also as an expression of love and regard for them. As for the duty of "preaching the good and forbidding the bad," it has been adopted by the Shīʿites as an obligation that keeps religious fervor active and effective. This was not an exclusively Shīʿite practice in the beginning but was also common to the Muʿtazilites. However, it is now only the Shīʿites who consider it an obligatory duty, together with others such as prayer and fasting.

Other Religious Observances

In addition to the obligatory duties mentioned above, there are two other religious practices observed by the Twelver Shīʿites with great dedication and zeal. These are the commemoration of the martyrdom of Ḥusayn ibn ʿAlī and the pilgrimage to the tombs of the Imams. Each of these observances is, in fact, a natural corollary and a practical expression of their belief in the Imams and love for the family of the Prophet. These observances, although not *Sharīʿah* obligations, are observed with utmost devotion and fervor, and they aid in understanding Shīʿite religious and spiritual ideals as well as Islamic concepts of love, justice, human values, and compassion for the oppressed and hatred for oppression and injustice.

Commemoration of the Martyrdom of Ḥusayn

Ḥusayn ibn ʿAlī, the most beloved grandson of the Prophet, the son of ʿAlī and Fāṭimah, and the third Imam of the Twelver Shīʿites, along with seventy-two of his relatives and companions, was brutally massacred at the plain of Karbalāʾ in Iraq on the 10th of Muḥarram 61/680 by the forces of Yazīd, the second Umayyad caliph of Islam. Yazīd inherited the office of the caliphate from his father Muʿāwiyah, who had appropriated it for himself through the use of force and deceit, and he represented tyranny, injustice, and oppression—all in the name of Islam. An embodiment of

25. *Nada 'alliyyan,* a common prayer used especially by Shi'ites at the time of calamity and danger.

all sorts of vices and despotic rule, Yazīd wanted Ḥusayn to pay him homage as the lawful caliph of Islam and to submit himself to his authority. The grandson of the Prophet refused to do so and, in order to save Islam and its value of the freedom and dignity of man, made one of the greatest sacrifices of human history. Eighteen male members of his family, including a six-month-old son, and forty-four of his companions were killed in front of him, and then he himself laid down his life at the altar of Truth and for the sake of humanity. Ḥusayn's body, already torn by numerous wounds, was trampled under the hoofs of the horses; his tents were burned and looted; and the helpless women and children were shamelessly paraded through the streets of Iraq and Syria and were treated to humiliation at the crowded courts of Ibn Ziyād in Kufa and Yazīd in Damascus as captives. This was the fate of the immediate family of the Prophet a mere fifty years after his death.

The martyrdom of Ḥusayn was of great religious and moral significance for the followers of the house of the Prophet and soon proved to be the most effective agent in the propagation and rapid spread of Shīʿite feelings. It ultimately played an immensely important role in the consolidation of Shīʿite identity in Islam. The tragic fate of the grandson of the Prophet henceforth added to Shīʿism an element of passion, which renders human psychology more receptive than do merely doctrinal arguments. The death of Ḥusayn thus set the seal of an official Shīʿism, and his name and memory became an inseparable part of its moral and religious fervor.

The commemoration of the tragedy has since been the most passionate and cherished religious observance of the Shīʿites all over the world. During the first ten days of Muḥarram, mourning assemblies (*majālis-i ʿazāʾ*) are held, in which the tragic events of Karbalāʾ and the atrocities inflicted on Ḥusayn and the people of the sacred house are described with touching eloquence and moving style. On the tenth day of Muḥarram, known as ʿĀshūrāʾ, the day of the massacre, mourning processions are carried out with frantic expressions of grief and sorrow, the participants beating their chests, reciting dirges and elegies, and raising the banner of Ḥusayn, who had so helplessly fallen in Karbalāʾ. Since the precise form of the Muḥarram observances has not been fixed like that of other religious duties, it is observed in different modes and forms in different parts of the world, according to the sociocultural traditions and genius of the people. In this way, the same theme and spirit find expression in heterogeneous cultural forms, representing a real unity of purpose in diversity of manifestations. Moreover, these observances, although focused on the martyrs of Karbalāʾ, concomitantly express Shīʿite feelings for human sufferings and their compassion for the downtrodden. Thus, the Arabs, the Persians, the Turks, the

Central Asians, the Shīʿites of the subcontinent of India and of the other parts of the world observe it with their own local coloring and ethno-cultural sentiments.

Another aspect of Karbalāʾ was that in the course of time it produced a tremendously rich and extensive volume of literature in almost all Islamic languages. Tragedy has been a most fertile soil for the finest literature man could produce, and the tragedy of Karbalāʾ had all the material to attract the attention of the poets and men of letters to express the eternal values and the noblest sentiments of man. Arabic was the first language in which short elegies were composed on Karbalāʾ, but soon the theme was taken over by the poets of other languages, who produced the finest pieces in all forms of poetry ranging from the most sophisticated to folk songs. Arabic, Persian, Turkish, Sindhi, Pashto, and Urdu abound in dirges, poems, and elegies on Karbalāʾ, but perhaps it is Urdu that enriched itself with the theme of Karbalāʾ more than any other Islamic language. Some of the great poetic geniuses of Urdu, such as Anīs and Dabīr, raised the form of elegy (*marthiyah*) to its zenith and made it the richest treasure not only of Urdu but of world literature. Karbalāʾ elegies have the same importance for students of Urdu literature that the plays of Shakespeare have for students of English literature.

Pilgrimage to the Tombs of the Imams

Besides the observance of Muḥarram, the pilgrimage to the tombs of the Imams is the second most popular practice among the Shīʿites in the expression of their religious consciousness. In Shīʿism, pilgrimage to the Kaʿbah is an obligatory duty, but the pilgrimage to the tombs of the Imams is a voluntary act of great piety and spiritual significance. Since the Shīʿites believe that Imams are divinely inspired religious and spiritual guides, the repositories of God's will and command, and the most beloved of God because of their devotion, love, and worship, their tombs have become the most venerated sanctuaries. It is, therefore, an ardent desire of every Shīʿite to visit these shrines at least once in his lifetime and, by paying homage to them, to evoke God's Mercy and blessings, which have been showered on these graves. These shrines in Najaf, Karbalāʾ, Mashhad, and Samarra and also the tombs of Imam Ḥusayn's sister Zaynab, in Syria, and that of Imam ʿAlī al-Riḍā's sister Fāṭimah, in Qumm, Iran, all embellished with gold and ornamented with splendid decoration, have been the centers of pilgrimage for a countless number of Shīʿite devotees. The practice of visiting and paying regards to the spiritually elevated souls is not, however, an exclusive practice of the Shīʿites. The majority of Sunni Muslims visit the tombs and shrines of the saints and the mystics. The only difference is that the Shīʿites concentrate mostly on the family of the Prophet, whereas the Sunni Muslims accord this honor to anyone who has attained mystical and spiritual excellence.

The Sources of Religious Law

The sources of the *Sharīʿah* (Law) in Shīʿism are almost the same as those in Sunnism, namely, the Quran, the *Ḥadīth* (traditions of the Prophet) and *ijmāʿ* (consensus) with some difference in their interpretation; the fourth source of Sunnism, *qiyās* (analogy), is replaced in Shīʿism by *ʿaql* (reason). In the case of the Quran, the fountainhead of the Divine Law, the Shīʿites accept only the interpretations given by one of their Imams. As for *Ḥadīth,* the Sunnis restrict it to the sayings of the Prophet, whereas the Shīʿites extend it to the traditions of the Imams as well. This gives the Shīʿites a unique advantage in that they follow a continuous and unbroken religious tradition which remained in one family, handed down from father to son, for a period of 261 years, beginning with ʿAlī, the first Imam, and continuing until the occultation of Muḥammad al-Mahdī, the twelfth, all in direct line of descent. The term *occultation* refers to the hidden state of the twelfth Imam after his disappearance from the visible world, without his having died or being totally absent from the visible world.

As for *ijmāʿ*, in Shīʿism it means consensus of religious scholars regarding the view of the Imam on a particular legal question. And finally *qiyās,* or analogical deduction, of Sunni Islam has been further expanded in Shīʿism by substituting reason (*ʿaql*) for it. The principle in adopting reason in place of analogy is that, the Shīʿah think, whatever reason favors religion agrees to; thereby the human intellect is given its due importance alongside Revelation.

Another distinctive feature of Shīʿism is seen in the question of *ijtihād,* or the personal endeavor of a religious scholar (*mujtahid*) to solve a given legal problem of his time by resorting to the original sources. In Sunnism the gate of *ijtihād* was closed after the death of the four great *mujtahids*—Abū Ḥanīfah, Mālik ibn Anas, Muḥammad ibn Idrīs al-Shāfiʿī, and Aḥmad ibn Ḥanbal—who lived in the second/eighth and third/ninth centuries of Islam. Whatever they had decided in their times became binding on the community, and no one was allowed to use the basic sources anymore. In contrast to this, in Shīʿism, the gate of *ijtihād* is always open, and in every generation there are *mujtahids* who can turn afresh to original sources to find an answer to a given question in accordance with the situation of his time. The *mujtahids* of each generation act as the representatives of the hidden Imam, the Mahdī, and every Shī'ah must follow them in *Sharī'ah* matters. The centers of learning and scholarship which produce such *mujtahids* have been the holy city of Najaf in Iraq, built around the shrine of 'Alī, and the city of Qumm in Iran, which has the shrine of Imam Riḍā's sister Fāṭimah.

However, in spite of these differences in the interpretation of and the approach to the original sources, the actual differences between Shī'ism and Sunnism in matters of *Sharī'ah* practices are not much more than those between the four rites of Sunni Islam. The Shī'ah, however, condone the hiding of one's faith if by its disclosure one's life is in danger. This is called *taqiyyah* and was allowed because of the adverse circumstances the community passed through during the political ascendancy of the Umayyads and the Abbasids, who considered people's adherence to the Imams a great threat to their power. Nor do the Shī'ites abrogate the provision of temporary marriage (*mut'ah*), allowed by the Prophet in his lifetime especially during the wars.

Shī'ite Literature

The Twelver Shī'ites developed their own collections of *Ḥadīth* and books of Law. Literary activity in Shī'ism started as early as the time of the first Imam, 'Alī ibn Abī Ṭālib; but it was developed extensively during the period of the sixth Imam, Ja'far al-Ṣādiq, when as many as four hundred of his disciples wrote down his discourses and traditions on doctrinal and legal matters. These treatises were known as the "Four Hundred Principles." Numerous disciples of the last six Imams after Ja'far al-Ṣādiq also preserved in writing whatever they heard from their Imams. Some of them were recognized as great authorities of their time on *Ḥadīth*, Law, and theology. This may be called the first and formative period of Shī'ite religious literature.

The period of consolidation and elaboration of the Shī'ite literature, however, began toward the end of the epoch of the Imams. A great Shī'ite divine, Muḥammad ibn Ya'qūb al-Kulaynī (d. 329/940, the year the twelfth Imam went into major occultation), compiled his monumental book of *Ḥadīth*, *Uṣūl al-kāfī*, in which he incorporated the famous "Four Hundred Principles" and most of the scattered treatises written during the period of the Imamate. It was followed by three other important works, namely, *Man lā yaḥḍuruhu'l-faqīh*, by Shaykh al-Ṣadūq ibn Bābawayh al-Qummī (d. 381/991), and *al-Istibṣār* and *Tahdhīb al-aḥkām* by Muḥammad ibn al-Ḥasan al-Ṭūsī (d. 460/1068). These four books established Shīʿism firmly and have since been the main source of the Shīʿites' *Ḥadīth,* jurisprudence, Law, and theology.

It is also this period in which Sayyid Sharīf al-Raḍī (d. 406/1015) compiled the sermons, orations, maxims, and letters of ʿAlī ibn Abī Ṭālib, which had until that time been scattered in bits and pieces throughout various early works of history, *Ḥadīth,* and biography. It is known as the *Nahj al-balāghah,* and for the Shīʿah it is the most venerated book after the Quran and the traditions of the Prophet. It is also held by the non-Shīʿite Muslims in great esteem and respect and has attracted a number of Sunni scholars to write commentaries on it, the most famous of which is by Ibn Abiʾl-Ḥadīd al-Muʿtazilī (d. 655/1257), who wrote a voluminous commentary which itself became a classic of Islamic literature.

ʿAlī, the first Imam of the Shīʿites and the fourth and the last of the rightly guided caliphs of the Sunnis, had embraced Islam at the early age of thirteen and, having been adopted by the Prophet during his childhood, grew up under the personal care and guardianship of the recipient of Divine Revelation, the founder of Islam. These circumstances gave him a unique authority to speak for Islam, its beliefs, its thoughts and fundamental concepts, its theories and practices, its principles and ideals, and to interpret the Quran and the *Sunnah* in all cases of conscience. Therefore, his expositions are held to be the most authoritative source of Islamic thought and practice, especially by those who follow him exclusively after the Prophet.

The material of the *Nahj al-balāghah* can be divided into three parts: historical, doctrinal, and ethical. As for the historical material, ʿAlī himself was an active and enthusiastic participant of all the events that took place from the time of Muḥammad's call to prophethood in A.D. 610 to that of his own death in 40/661. Thus, his discourses provide the most authentic contemporary account of the formative phase of Islam. As for doctrine, who could have more authority to speak on doctrinal teachings, which he received directly and intimately from the Prophet? Moreover, ʿAlī was himself an Imam and the *walī* and, therefore, divinely inspired as the source of doctrine. The following few lines on the concept of God from the very first sermon of the *Nahj al-balāghah* will give some idea of how ʿAlī's sagacious and philosophical mind was formed by Islamic teachings, which he expressed with unparalleled eloquence:

> Praise be to God whose praise cannot be attained by the (best of) orators, whose blessings cannot be counted by the enumerators and whose due cannot be paid by the strivers—He whom the utmost (human) ambitions cannot perceive and the deepest wisdom cannot reach; He for whose description there

26. "Firdowsi's parable on the Ship of Shi'ism," Persian, ca. 1530s.

> are no definable limits or available epithet, or countable time or stretchable duration.
>
> The first essential (i.e. beginning) of belief is His knowledge, the perfection of His knowledge is His verification, the perfection of verification is His unity, the perfection of His unity is to consider Him free (from human qualities) and the perfection of considering Him free (from anthropomorphic qualities) is the negation of (human) attributes from Him, as every attribute attests that it is other than the attributee and every attributee testifies that it is other than the attribute. So he who ascribes attributes to God, the Glorious, associates something with Him, and he who associates something with Him duplicates Him, and he who duplicates Him splits Him up, and he who splits Him up is ignorant of Him, and he who is ignorant of Him points towards Him, and he who points towards Him defines Him, and he who defines Him counts Him; and he who asks: "In what?" includes Him, and he who asks: "On what?" detracts from Him. He is a Being, not by creation or accident; existent not by being ever non-existent; with everything yet not by association, and other than everything but not by separation.

As for the importance of the *Nahj al-balāghah*, it may suffice to point out that all later works of the Shīʿites, whether in the field of Quranic commentaries, *Ḥadīth*, jurisprudence and Law, or in theology, philosophy, Sufism, and ethics, were immensely influenced by it. The impact of ʿAlī's thought is also clearly evident in Sunni works, especially those of ethics, philosophy, Sufism, and theosophy. Moreover, the *Nahj al-balāghah*'s effects on Arabic philology and literature have been most conspicuous.

Subsequent periods in the history of Shīʿite literature, spread over about eight hundred years, during the supremacy of the Mongols, the Safavids and the Qajars in Iran, and the Mughal Empire in India, are so rich both in quality and quantity in every branch of Islamic learning that even a brief reference to them is not possible in this article. However, the Safavid period of Iran is perhaps the most distinguished in that the convergence between the Sufism of Ibn ʿArabī, the philosophy of Avicenna, the illuminationist theosophy of Suhrawardī, and Shīʿite theology, which had started some time before, reached its zenith. This philosophical, mystical, theosophical, and theological blend, within the limits of Islamic principles, was perfected to its highest level at the hands of such great Shīʿite metaphysician-theologians as Mīr Bāqir Dāmād (d. 1041/1631) and Ṣadr al-Dīn Shīrāzī, better known as Mullā Ṣadrā (d. 1050/1640).

Devotional Prayers and Supplications

Recognizing God as the Merciful, the Forgiving, the sole Creator, and the sole Sustainer, a Muslim is concomitantly required to express these beliefs by making God the only object of his worship. This worship in its outward dimension expresses itself in prescribed prayers, fasting, etc.; but in its inward dimension it finds expression in touching supplications and moving devotional prayers. Supplications and devotional prayers are thus the most profound form of a Muslim's confession of his surrender to the will of the Almighty.

The Prophet of Islam and the twelve Imams from among his descendants, with their esoteric knowledge of the Godhead, their spirituality of the highest level, their purified souls, their ethical and moral ethos, their love and unceasing remembrance of God, and their self-denial and complete resignation to His will, left for us some of the most illuminating devotional prayers. These supplications reveal man's urgency of poverty, prostration of humility, the fervor of penitence, the firmness of trust. They are not just eloquence, but earnestness; not figures of speech, but compunction of soul and the cry of unshakable faith to the ear of mercy. These are thus the finest spiritual literature of Islam.

Some of the prayers composed by ʿAlī ibn Abī Ṭālib are not only the masterpieces of devotional literature but also the fountainhead of philosophical, mystical, metaphysical, ethical, and theological concepts of Islam. Such fundamental topics as those relating to God's Unity, Eternity, and Creativity, His Power and Majesty, His Mercy and Forgiveness, God in Himself and God in relation to mankind are dealt with in these prayers with devotional fervor and eloquence of exposition.

A few lines of the supplication that he wrote for one of his disciples, Kumayl ibn Ziyād, demonstrate these qualities:

Oh God, I ask Thee by Thy mercy,
which embraces all things;
by Thy strength,
through which Thou dominatest all things;
toward which all things are humble
and before which all things are lowly;
by Thy invincibility,
through which Thou overwhelmest all things;
by Thy might, which nothing can resist;
by Thy tremendousness, which has filled all things
by Thy force, which towers over all things;
by Thy face,
which subsists after the annihilation of all things;
by Thy Names;
which have filled the foundations of all things;
by Thy knowledge, which encompasses all things;
and by the light of Thy face,
through which all things are illumined!
. . . .

Oh God, forgive me every sin I have committed
and every mistake I have made![2]

A very important collection of supplications which must be given particular attention here is *al-Ṣaḥīfat al-sajjādiyyah* or *al-Ṣaḥīfat al-kāmilah* of the fourth Imam, Zayn al-ʿĀbidīn, also called al-Sayyid al-Sajjād, the leader of the worshipers. This collection is known also as the "Psalms of the Family of the Holy Prophet." The only surviving son of the martyr of Karbalāʾ, Zayn al-ʿĀbidīn witnessed the massacre of his father and eighteen male members of his family, which left a deep impression on his soul and made him cry throughout his life. These cries poured forth in the throbbing passion of devotional prayers seeking communion with God and entrusting the secrets of inner life to Him. In these prayers, one finds in the din and bustle of life, in the clash of emotions and interests, in the stress and strain of immediate urges, in the calamities and tensions of existence, and, above all, in the search for spiritual satisfaction, a man lonely and helpless, who stands before his Creator in direct communication with Him and calls Him from the very depths of his heart. Thus, the supplications of the *Ṣaḥīfah* are the best expression of the relationship between man and God, between the worshiper and the Worshiped, between the slave and the Master, between the lover and the Beloved, between the distressed and the Comforter, and, indeed, between the individual soul and the universal Soul. The following passage may give some idea of the beauties enshrined in his prayers:

> O Lord: Thou art the one through whose mercy the erring pray for redress; the one in the remembrance of whose grace the afflicted take refuge; the one in dread of whom the guilty bitterly weep! O solace of every sad straggler, and O delight of every brokenhearted sufferer, and O redresser of the forsaken and lonely, and O helper of the needy and far exiled, who hast surrounded everything with mercy and knowledge! It is Thou who hast allotted every creature a share in Thy blessings; and it is Thou whose forgiveness is superior to his chastisement; and it is Thou whose mercy walks in front of his wrath; and it is Thou whose generosity is more frequent than his refusal; and it is Thou whose power and prosperity embrace all creatures. . . . Here I am ready to obey Thee! Here I am at Thy call! Behold O Lord, here I am prostrate in Thy presence![3]

Notes

1. Quoted in S. M. Jafri, *The Origins and Early Development of Shiʾa Islam* (London: Longman, 1979) 294.

2. *Supplications (Duʿā) of Amīr al-mūʾminīn ʿAlī ibn Abī Ṭālib,* trans. W. C. Chittick (London: Muhammadi Trust: n.d.) 20.

3. *The Sahifat-ul-Kamilah,* trans. A. A. Mohani (Lucknow: Muayyed-ul-Uloom Association, 1969–70) Supplication No. 16, p. 61.

10

Ismāʿīlism

AZIM NANJI

ISMĀʿĪLISM IS A PART OF THE SHĪʿITE branch of Islam whose adherents constitute at present a small minority within the wider Muslim *ummah.* They live in over twenty-five different countries, including Afghanistan, East Africa, India, Iran, Pakistan, Syria, Yemen, the United Kingdom, North America, and also parts of China and the Soviet Union.

Historical Background

In common with Shīʿite Islam, Ismāʿīlism affirms that after the death of the Prophet Muḥammad his cousin and son-in-law, ʿAlī, became Imam, based on a specific designation made by the Prophet before his death. Such a leadership, it was believed, was to continue thereafter by heredity through ʿAlī and his wife Fāṭimah, the Prophet's daughter. Succession to the Imamate, according to Shīʿite doctrine and tradition, was to be based on *naṣṣ* (designation) by the Imam of the time.

In the course of Shīʿite history, differences arose over the issue of succession to the position of Imam. The most significant in terms of the subsequent emergence of Shīʿite Ismāʿīlism followed the death of Imam Jaʿfar al-Ṣādiq in 148/765. The body of Shīʿites who continued to give allegiance to the line of Imam Jaʿfar's descendants through his son Ismāʿīl came to be known as Ismāʿīliyyah; others who accepted a younger son Mūsā Kāẓim are known as Ithnā ʿasharīyyah.[1]

According to Ismāʿīlī sources, the next four Imams, while maintaining anonymity to avoid persecution, were engaged in organizing the Ismāʿīlī movement, so that when it finally emerged into the public limelight in the third/ninth century, there existed a sophisticated political and doctrinal structure by which Ismāʿīlism was able to gain widespread support and political success. The organization created by the Imams to undertake this work is known as the *daʿwā*—a term based on the Quran (LXI, 7), signifying a call or an invitation to Islam. Although not unique to the Ismāʿīlīs, the skillful organization and the highly effective network of communications, and the intellectual and diplomatic accomplishments of its representatives—each of whom was called a *dāʿī* in the organization—gave it a very special character within Ismāʿīlism.

During the period in which Ismāʿīlism was developing and spreading, the *daʿwā* was often beset with problems of organization and unity, which led to occasional defections over matters of policy and even doctrine. In spite of such setbacks and the adverse conditions under which the *daʿwā* often operated, great success was achieved in parts of Iran, Yemen, and North Africa, which led in 297/910 to the proclamation of the Imam of the time as the Amīr al-Muʾminīn (commander of the faithful) with the title of *al-Mahdī* (the guide). This marked the opening phase of the Ismāʿīlī attempt to give concrete shape to their vision of an Islamic society. The dynasty of the Imams, which ruled from North Africa and then Egypt for over two centuries, adopted the title al-Fāṭimiyyūn (Fāṭimids) after Fāṭimah, the Prophet's daughter who was married to ʿAlī.[2]

During the period of Fāṭimid rule, the influence and extent of Ismāʿīlism grew considerably. The Fāṭimid empire at its height exerted its influence far beyond Egypt to Palestine, Syria, the Hijaz, Yemen, Iran, Sind, and the Mediterranean. In 450/1058, the Fāṭimids also occupied Baghdad, the capital of their rivals the Abbasid dynasty, for a short period.

The Ismāʿīlī *daʿwā* played a very important role in maintaining ideological loyalty and support within this far-flung empire. It served also to create a unified doctrine and organization to offset the differences that had beset the movement during its earlier stages. Its efforts at preaching Islam extended its influence into India and to the remoter regions of Central Asia.

It was in the sphere of intellectual and cultural life that Fāṭimid Ismāʿīlī achievement seems most brilliant and outstanding. The Fāṭimid patronage of learning and its encouragement of scientific research and cultural activity made Cairo a renowned center, attracting mathematicians, physicians, astronomers, thinkers, and administrators of note from all over the Muslim world, particularly to its two great universities, al-Azhar and Dār al-Ḥikmah. These seats of learning also gave impetus to the development of legal, philosophical, and theological thinking among Ismāʿīlī scholars, which provided the basis for a comprehensive articulation of Ismāʿīlī thought and doctrine. The cultural and economic impact of Fāṭimid rule extended also into Europe, bridging the way for further development in the West of Muslim scientific achievements in fields such as optics, medicine, and astronomy.

The expansion of Fāṭimid influence and the efforts of the *daʿwā* brought the Fāṭimids into conflict with existing rulers such as the Abbasids and later the Seljuqs. In addition, during this later phase, the empire was adversely affected by famines and internal disputes among various sections of the army. After the death of Imam al-Ḥākim in 411/1021, a group of Ismāʿīlīs broke away from the *daʿwā,* preferring to remain faithful to the memory of al-Ḥākim. Thus, they gave birth to what later came to be known as the Druze movement.

A much more serious rift occurred following the death of Imam al-Mustanṣir in 487/1094. In Iran and parts of Syria, the Ismāʿīlīs supported his elder son and designated heir, Nizār, whereas in Egypt, Yemen, and Sind, Nizār's younger brother, al-Mustaʿlī, was believed to have been designated as the new Imam by al-Mustanṣir on his deathbed. These two Ismāʿīlī groups are called Nizārī and Mustʿalī Ismāʿīlīs respectively. Both groups shared a common Fāṭimid heritage, but their histories and development evolved in different directions. The division led to the subsequent dissolution of Fāṭimid rule in Egypt, but the continuing activity of the two groups was a vital factor in the survival and reemergence of Ismāʿīlʿ influence outside Egypt.

Mustaʿlī-Ṭayyibī Daʿwā

Yemen had been one of the strongholds of the Fāṭimid empire and a vigorous center of the Ismāʿīlī *daʿwā*.[3] After al-Mustanṣir's death, the *daʿwā* in Yemen supported al-Mustaʿlī and, after him, his son and successor, al-Āmir. With his death in 524/1130, there was a further division within the Mustaʿlī branch of Ismāʿīlism. In Yemen, the *daʿwā* supported the right of al-Āmir's infant son, al-Ṭayyib, to be Imam, rejecting the claims of the uncle-regent ʿAbd al-Majīd, who subsequently had himself proclaimed Imam. The latter's line did not last long, passing out of significance with the capture of Egypt by the Ayyūbids. The supporters of al-Ṭayyib, meanwhile, came to believe that he was in a state of concealment (*sitr*) and that the Imams who succeeded al-Ṭayyib would henceforth live in such a state until the time of manifestation. In their absence the *daʿwā*'s affairs were entrusted to a chief *dāʿī,* called *dāʿī muṭlaq.*

The center of this group remained in Yemen for several centuries, establishing a vigorous state for a while, but, faced with hostility, it moved eventually to India, where the new headquarters came to be established in 947/1567. The community in Yemen dwindled in time, although followers of this branch of Ismāʿīlism—particularly of a subsequent offshoot of the Ṭayyibī *daʿwā* known as the Sulaymānīs, who give allegiance to a chief *dāʿī* residing in Yemen—are still to be found in certain regions of that land.

In India, the Ṭayyibī Ismāʿīlīs continued to develop under a chief *dāʿī* and succeeded, sometimes under adverse conditions, in sustaining successfully their religious life and organization. The majority there are called Dāʾūdī, to distinguish them from the Sulaymānī line and both groups are referred to also as *Bohora,* which denotes their occupation as traders and merchants. The chief *dāʿī* of the Dāʾūdī group resides in Bombay; the community is concentrated in the provinces of Gujarat, Maharashtra, Rajasthan, in most major cities of India and Pakistan, in East Africa, and lately in smaller numbers in Europe and North America.

The Nizārī Ismāʿīlī Daʿwā

The history of the Nizārī branch of Ismāʿīlism is marked by their adherence to the goals set by the Fāṭimids as well as by the emergence of newer goals and policies in the context of a changing and increasingly hostile environment.[4] Particularly in Iran, where Ismāʿīlī influence had already been established under the Fāṭimids, the Nizārī *daʿwā* had to function in markedly changed circumstances, which were due not only to the severance of ties with Cairo but also to the presence of the powerful, militantly Sunni Turkish dynasty of the Seljuqs. In addition to the hostility prevailing in the political and military spheres, the *daʿwā,* like its predecessor under the Fāṭimids, became the object of theological and intellectual attacks that often sought to portray it in a deliberately negative and distorted fashion. This often led to quite fantastic and legendary notions about their history and thought. Pejorative terms like "assassins," etc. still persist in popular writings, although serious scholarly work has led to considerable revision of this distorted view and greater understanding of their history and aspirations.

The focal point of the Nizārī Ismāʿīlī movement was the fortress of Alamūt in the Alborz Mountains of northern Iran. This fortress, captured by the *dāʿī* Ḥasan-i Ṣabbāḥ in 483/1090, now became the center for a growing number of strongholds that were established through military and diplomatic means. In time, these centers became networks of Ismāʿīlī settlements in Iran as well as in Syria, where a similar pattern of establishing strongholds in mountainous regions took place. Ḥasan-i Ṣabbāḥ, according to Nizārī tradition, acted as the representative of the Imam, organizing the various settlements. This process of consolidation provided a basis for what was to become a Nizārī Ismā'īlī state that incorporated both Iranian and Syrian strongholds and was ruled from Alamūt by Ismā'īlī Imams, who assumed control after the initial period of establishment under representatives such as Ḥasan-i Ṣabbāḥ. Although under constant pressure from the Seljuqs, the state had a thriving existence for over 150 years. However, confrontation with the expanding Mongol power led to the downfall of the state, the demolition of its principal strongholds, and a general and widespread massacre of Ismā'īlīs.

The history of the Nizārī Ismā'īlīs following the destruction of their state and the dispersal of their leaders in Iran and elsewhere is little known. In Syria, as in Iran, they continued to survive despite persecution. Often in Iran their organization resembled that of the Sufi *ṭarīqahs* (orders), which by now had established themselves all over the Muslim world. The Nizārī sources speak of an uninterrupted succession of Imams in different parts of Iran and, in the ninth/fifteenth century, of an emergence of new activity on the part of the *da'wā* which led to a further growth of Nizārī Ismā'īlism in parts of India and Central Asia, to which the Imam in Iran remained linked through the activities of the *dā'īs*. In general, however, the various communities of Nizārī Ismā'īlīs in Iran, Syria, Central Asia, and India remained relatively isolated and self-protective for several centuries, mindful of the constant threat of persecution.

In the thirteenth/ninteenth century, the Imam of the time, Ḥasan 'Alī Shāh, called the Agha Khan, migrated to India from Iran. In the twentieth century, under the leadership of the last two Imams, Sir Sulṭān Muḥammad Shāh, Agha Khan III (1294/1877–1377/1957), and Shāh Karīm al-Ḥusaynī, Agha Khan IV (b. 1936), both of whom have played a major leadership role in Muslim as well as international affairs, the Nizārī Ismā'īlīs have effected a successful transition to the modern period in many parts of the world. This reorganization has encompassed developments in various spheres of education, health, economic and cultural life and has been linked wherever possible to national goals and in recent times on a more global scale to creating a greater self-consciousness among Ismā'īlīs as well as other Muslims of the role their Islamic heritage can play in modern life.

The Heritage and Its Themes

Ismā'īlīs have been designated by several names in the past. By those who were hostile to them and regarded their vision of Islam as heretical, they have been accused of heresy and extremism, of being exclusively *baṭīniyyah* (esotericists), and of having several legends fabricated about them and their teachings. Those heresiographers who sought significance in the sequence of Imams with its attendant numerology used the designation *sabʿiyyah*, "seveners," since the number seven was significant in the elaboration of Ismāʿīlī sacred history. Since early Western scholarship of Ismāʿīlism depended primarily on non-Ismāʿīlī sources, it inherited the biases already present in such accounts. Ismāʿīlī writers, for instance, used terms such as *al-daʿwat al-hādiyah* (the rightly-guided *daʿwā*) in referring to their movement, so that strictly speaking the term *Ismāʿīliyyah* and its variants originated with and were to be found primarily in the work of polemicists and heresiologists. Recent scholarship, based on a more judicious analysis of such sources and on Ismāʿīlī materials as they become more readily available, provides a considerably revised and more balanced picture.

Early Ismāʿīlī works are mostly in Arabic; Nāṣir-i Khusraw was the only Fāṭimid writer who wrote in Persian. The Arabic tradition was continued in Yemen and in India by the Mustaʿlīs, and in Syria by the Nizārīs. In Iran, the literature is in Persian, which for the Nizārī Ismāʿīlīs there, as in Central Asia, became the significant language. In India, the *dāʿīs* developed a traditional literature called *ginān* (knowledge) using the vernacular languages such as Sindhi and Gujarati. In the northern area of modern Pakistan, the Ismāʿīlīs of Hunza, Gilgit, and Chitral have also preserved and continue to evolve a literature based on what have been hitherto oral languages such as Burushaski, Shina, and Khowar, although the Arabic-Urdu script is being increasingly used at present.[5]

Thus, there is considerable diversity of thought and development represented in the literature, much of which still remains to be properly edited—let alone carefully studied. The following exposition of Ismāʿīlī doctrine and spirituality can be regarded as a heritage shared in general by all Ismāʿīlīs in the context of their effort to relate questions of authority and organization in the *ummah* to an understanding of the inner core of the Islamic message and the values contained in that message.

A very significant feature of Ismāʿīlī thought is the comprehensiveness of its scope and a specificity with regard to its method. It shares with other schools of Islam the ideal of understanding and implementing Islam in its totality in order that the *ummah* might be governed by Divine Will rather than human caprice. In common with the other Shīʿites, Ismāʿīlīs maintained that it was through the agency of a divinely guided Imam descended from ʿAlī that such an ideal could be realized. The doctrine of the Imam, therefore, occupied a central place in Shīʿism, and obedience and devotion to him were considered the principal indexes of acceptance of the Divine Message of Islam. This principle received a central and specific emphasis in Ismāʿīlism, because it was through the Imam that a true understanding of Islam was obtained, and in obeying him the duties of a true believer were fulfilled. Such a view did not rule out the use of the rational or intellectual faculty on the part of the believer. In fact, true understanding came to be defined as the ultimate unfolding of human reason (*ʿaql*) to its fullest potential under the guidance of the Imam. It is the working out of this process that provides the key to understanding the heart of Ismāʿīlī spirituality as exemplified in their literature and in their concepts of learning and knowledge.

The curriculum in Fāṭimid seats of learning led an individual through progressive and disciplined study of a wide variety of sciences. The student commenced study with the aim of mastering *al-ʿibādāt al-ʿamaliyyah* (practical worship), the sciences necessary to grasp and define the *Sharīʿah* in terms of the pillars of faith, a *Sharīʿah* which shared a number of essential characteristics with those of other Muslim legal schools. After mastering these subjects, the student then proceeded to a study of *al-ʿibādāt al-ʿilmiyyah* (intellectual worship), the sciences that expound and interpret the levels of meaning reflected in the pillars.

This methodology in Ismāʿīlī thought is best brought out by Nāṣir-i Khusraw's explanation of the nature of Revelation and, by inference, religion. There are two aspects of Revelation *tanzīl* (Revelation) and *ta'wīl* (hermeneutic interpretation), which are reflected in the *Ḥaqīqah* and the *Sharīʿah*, the latter being like a symbol of the *Ḥaqīqah* (truth).[6] *Tanzīl* thus defines the letter of the Revelation embodied in the coming down of the values of the *Sharīʿah*, and *ta'wīl* is the hermeneutical analysis of the letter leading to the original meaning. Jean Pépin, in analyzing the original Greek word *hermeneuein* states:

> As used generally the word has come to signify "interpretation" and that hermeneutics today commonly has as its synonym "exegesis." However, the original meaning of *hermeneuein* and of related words—or in any case their principal meaning—was not that at all, and was not far from being its exact contrary, if we grant that exegesis is a movement of penetration into the intention of a text or message.[7]

In context above, the Arabic sense of *ta'wīl*, to go back to the first or original meaning, can be said to designate a similar interpretive function. The goal of *ta'wīl* in Ismāʿīlī thought is to enable the believer to penetrate beyond the formal, literal meaning of the text and to create a sense of certitude regarding the ultimate relevance and meaning of a given passage in the Quran. All interpretation in Ismāʿīlī thought assumes such an exegetical basis, leading by way of levels of meaning to the ultimate truths expressed as the concept of *Ḥaqīqah*. The validity of the literal (*ẓāhir*) is not denied, but it is only one aspect of an overall meaning that also has an inner dimension (*bāṭin*). When applied to the study of the Quran, Islam, and religion, it led to the rise of two differing but complementary genres of literature among the Ismā'īlīs—*ḥaqā'iq* literature, which contains the esoteric tradition, and other forms of writing that are expository and whose subject matter related to Law, governance, and history.

The milieu within which Ismā'īlī thought flourished and developed had already been characterized by the steady integration of philosophical and analytical tools assimilated through translations from the Greek tradition, as well as influences transmitted through Persia and India. Ismā'īlī thought represents a self-conscious attempt to harmonize elements from these traditions that were considered compatible with its own understanding of Quranic wisdom. Nāṣir-i Khusraw calls this *jāmi' al-ḥikmatayn,* "synthesis of the two wisdoms,"[8] the title of one of his works, in which he seeks to harmonize the esoteric understanding of Islam with the wisdom of the ancients. In doing this he was following the fundamental Quranic notion of the universality of Revelation and the Islamic affirmation that God had vouchsafed the truth to others in the past. The synthesis, however, was not an indiscriminate one, and it has also been argued that in addition to Neoplatonism, early Ismā'īlī sources also reflect influences from Gnostic elements in the milieu.[9]

Unity and the Cosmos

Tawḥīd is the most fundamental concept of Islam. Its interpretation and exegesis by Ismā'īlī thinkers demonstrate the operation of the Ismā'īlī science of hermeneutics. One of the points of contention among early Muslim theologians had to do with an explanation of the Quranic verses concerning the Attributes of God, particularly where such Attributes reflected human associations such as sitting, hearing, speaking, etc. For the Ismā'īlī thinker, this controversy highlighted one of the problems he came to be concerned with in understanding and explicating through *ta'wīl* the seeming contradiction in these verses. Abū Ya'qūb al-Sijistānī (d. 360/971) and Ḥamīd al-Dīn al-Kirmānī (c. 411/1021), two well-known thinkers of the Fāṭimid period, established as their goal an interpretation that was free of the two errors they attributed to other theologians.[10] The first is *tashbīh* (anthropomorphism, i.e., trying to understand God by comparison or analogy); the second is *ta'ṭīl* (i.e., denying *tashbīh* and thereby deleting from the description of God all Attributes). Their concern was not to establish through rational means the existence of God, since rational proof of that which is beyond the capacity of rational understanding would represent a futile exercise in itself, but rather, according to Sijistānī, to understand God as He deserves to be understood, so as to accord Him the true worship that is due to Him alone. Kirmānī's exegesis occurs in his classic work *Rāḥat al-ʿaql* (*Balm for the Intellect*). The title of the work itself indicates the essentially spiritual goal of the intellectual exercise—a sense of contentment and satisfaction that comes to the human mind in its proper interaction with Revelation, rather than mere vindication of the power of the rational faculty as over against Revelation. It is this attitude that caused Ismāʿīlī writers to oppose the views of Rhazes (Abū Bakr Muḥammad Zakariyyā' Rāzī), particularly where the latter raises questions about the validity of the mission of the prophets and, by inference, the validity of a religious world view.

The *ta'wīl* applied to the Quranic verses regarding God leads in both writers to a process of dissociating all humanlike qualities from God. This is considered to be the first step; both writers recognize that such a position could, in fact, lead to an accusation that they too had committed *ta'ṭīl*, leaving them open to a charge of "hidden anthropomorphism." The step that must now be taken is that having denied that God cannot be described, located, defined, limited, etc., *one must negate the previous negation.* The absolute transcendence of God is established by the use of double negation, in which a negative and a negative of a negative are applied to the thing denied—the first freeing the idea of God from all association with the material and the second removing Him from any association with the nonmaterial. God is thus neither within the sensible world nor within the extrasensible. The process of *ta'wīl* here begins with an affirmation of what God is not, then a denial of that affirmation, thereby deleting both the affirmation and the denial. Such a process of double negation offers the only means whereby one can use the available language without fully accepting its premises. In the above discourse, the resources of language, that is, the letter of the Revelation, establish a starting point, and *ta'wīl* reveals how language itself is unable to express fully the reality inherent in the concept. Such a mode of defining the transcendence of God, in the Ismāʿīlī view, is an act of cognizance of God—indeed, an act of worship in itself.

This principle of unity is also reflected in Ismāʿīlī cosmological principles. In elaborating this cosmology, the writers adapted elements of the Neoplatonic schema of emanation, but not without establishing an Islamic context for the adaptation. At the heart of the cosmology is the principle of order, a harmonious totality. The various components of the cosmic structure were also regarded as constituting a hierarchical structure. The planets and the abstract principles that governed them were ranked one above the other, just as the prophets, the Imams, and the officials of the *daʿwā* and members of the community formed a hierarchy with clearly defined status.

God transcended the order and unlike in Neoplatonism, where the One brings forth by emanation the Universal Intellect, in Ismāʿīlī cosmology, Allāh creates by a timeless and transcendent command (*amr*). The process is defined as *ibdāʿ*, origination, which is an all-encompassing, timeless, creative act. Thus, all of creation is directly related to God in its origin, but manifested through a subsequent process of unfolding from the Universal Intellect, which is the First Originated Being. God is *badīʿ* (Originator), as described in the Quranic verse—the Originator of the heavens and the earth (II, 117). The Quranic terminology of *Qalam* (pen), *ʿArsh* (throne), and *qaḍāʾ* (decree) are also equated with the Universal Intellect as the prelude to a framework for what is called *ʿālam al-ibdāʾ* (the Universe of Origination) in a hierarchical series. This level is then made to correspond to the *ʿālam al-dīn* (the Universe of Religion), in order to provide a framework in religious life represented by a hierarchy of faith (*ḥudūd al-dīn*), which in turn corresponds to the various cosmic principles. The highest in this hierarchy constituting the first three intelligences were identified with the Prophet, his *waṣī* (heir), ʿAlī, and the succeeding Imams respectively. This order was expounded in systems first elaborated in detail by al-Nasafī (d. 331/943) and subsequently refined in the works of Sijistānī, Kirmānī, and Nāṣir-i Khusraw. The exact hierarchy of the various intellects and the terminology employed tend to differ in the various authors' works, but the fundamental principle of the absolute transcendence of God, the general order of the cosmic principles and underlying hierarchical notions are retained.

The architecture of the Ismāʿīlī cosmos, while affirming a strong sense of unity, is also the sacred canopy within which its religious conceptions unfold. Thus, cosmology, metaphysics, and religion are closely interlinked, where each element in the hierarchical universe mirrors the other, establishing a chain of being, making the cosmos intelligible and meaningful and at the same time rooting the religious life on earth to a dynamic cosmos, operating under divine command.

Sacred History and Human Destiny

In the view of the cosmos described above, history unfolds as a "sacred" series of events imbued with Divine Purpose. This unfolding is seen in cyclical terms based on the *ta'wīl* of creation in the following Quranic verse:

> God who created the heavens and the earth in six days (VII, 54).

Al-Mu'ayyad fi'l-dīn Shīrāzī (d. 470/1077) in his interpretation of the verse starts by demonstrating that the reference to days bears no relation to the conception of a day measured with the rising and setting of the sun.[11] Since there was no sun before creation, it would be absurd, he argues, to suppose such a measure of time in relation to God's creative power. He then refers to other Quranic references where God is said to create faster than the twinkling of an eye, and he concludes that the references to heaven and earth have in reality nothing to do with the heaven, earth, and days as conceived in terms of man's measure of space and time. The true *ta'wīl* of the verse reveals a sacred history, connoting the six cycles of prophecy, each an event of cosmic significance. The prophets and the time-cycles they represent are Adam, Noah, Abraham, Moses, Jesus, and the Prophet Muḥammad.

Each prophetic mission inaugurates a *Sharīʿah,* a revealed pattern of life to ensure that society accords with the Divine Will. Each prophet, however, is succeeded by the *waṣī,* who, while preserving and consolidating the *Sharīʿah,* also has the role of interpreting and communicating the inner meaning of the Revelation and the legal prescriptions. The completion of the sixth cycle also marks the onset of a seventh era, in which the Imam assumes his role and thereby completes a process referred to in the Quran's climactic verse:

> Today I have perfected your religion for you, and I have completed My blessing upon you, and I have approved Islam for your religion. (V, 4)

This fulfills the goals embodied in the missions of the six prophets, which like the "six days" do not originate to oppose one another, but rather to succeed one another. Such an interpretation of creation carries with it a sense of the sacredness of history, where the most significant occurrences turn on the prophetic missions and their fulfillment, which leads ultimately to the salvation of humankind. Time, in this sacred framework, returns to its source, and the whole "movement" finally culminates in the Quranic *qiyāmah,* the Great Resurrection, a resurrection of all souls to the esoteric garden of preeternal times.

This cyclical concept of history is in turn linked to the notion of human destiny and is best illustrated in the interpretation of the Quranic account of the fall of Adam. This drama in heaven, as explicated in the writing of al-Ḥāmidī (d. 595/1199) and others,[12] regards the story of Adam in the garden, his temptation by Satan and his subsequent fall, as having taken place on a cosmic plane, in the preexisting nonmaterial world of *ʿalam al-*

ibdāʿ. Adam, the human being, is called Adam *rūḥānī,* spiritual Adam. Using the cosmological system of the ten intellects already expounded by Kirmānī, this account represents Adam as having originally the status of the third intellect in rank. The good aspect of the "tree" in the "garden" which he was forbidden to approach is the status of the first universal intellect. Iblīs, who is Satan, is the representation of Adam's own desire not to accept the status accorded to him. This caused him to commit the sin of wrongful ambition, of desiring to attain equality of rank with those above. The subsequent punishment and expulsion from the garden mark the loss of both his rank and his preeminence over other intellects below him. He becomes the tenth intellect, but seeks through repentance to regain his original status. It is by returning through the intellects above him that Adam, now in the sense that he symbolizes humankind, reverts to his original status. It is also for this reason that the Universe of Intellects has as its counterpart on the earth the hierarchy of faith. Collectively this hierarchy represents the *daʿwā,* the call, returning the fallen to the true path and representing a step in the process of "ascent." The fall is not the prelude to the idea of "original sin," but rather the characterization of the cosmic process in which the cycles of prophecy and their subsequent consummation restore the true order of things. The role of the hierarchy is to designate for Adam, as for all humankind, the path that must be traversed, the steps they must ascend, in order to reach the Universal Intellect. Such a return represents the potential goal that each human being can attain and through which comes the proper recognition of God's Unity and the wisdom of the creative process. The return is to that state wherein Adam was endowed with knowledge that constituted an awareness of what the Quran calls "the names, all of them" (II, 31), which in Ismāʿīlī thought are no less than the *ḥaqāʾiq,* the universal truths.

Ritual Action, Cosmic Meaning

The *Daʿāʾim al-islām* of al-Qāḍī al-Nuʿmān preserves a definition of faith (*īmān*) given by Imam Jaʿfar al-Ṣādiq in response to a question regarding an issue of some significance among early Muslim theologians: "Tell me about faith," he is asked, "is it profession *with* action or profession *without* action?" The Imam answers:

> Faith consists entirely in action, and profession is part of action. Action is made obligatory by God, and is clear from His Book. . . . Faith possesses circumstances, stages, grades and stations. In faith, there can be total perfection; or else it may be imperfect. . . .[13]

This notion of faith, which establishes action as an integral part of spiritual development and perfection, is the basis for the hermeneutics of ritual in Ismā'īlism and for the interplay of the ideas of *ẓāhir* and *bāṭin*, which in this context can refer to ritual action and its inner universal meaning. These perfect the human capacity to act and to develop awareness of the meaning of that action on a cosmic scale. The *Dā'a'im* is a work defining the sphere of ritual action, the *Sharī'ah*, and al-Qāḍī al-Nu'mān also went on to write *Ta'wīl al-da'ā'im*, which defines the sphere of inner meaning related to ritual action. The discourse between the two spheres is best illustrated in the hermeneutics of the daily prayer (*ṣalāt*) in Islam.[14]

In defining the *ta'wīl* of *ṣalāt*, al-Nu'mān states that it symbolizes *da'wā*, not in the limited sense of the institution under the Fāṭimids, which carried on the tasks of studying and preaching Ismā'īlī doctrine, but in the wider sense of a call or summoning to the Prophet's message and its continuing affirmation by the Imam of the time. *Ṣalāt* then stands for Islam, to which the Prophet and the Imams after him call humankind.

Specifically, he begins with the *ta'wīl* of the times for ritual prayer, based on references to the Quran (II, 238; XVII, 78–79; etc.). The established prayers during each day signify the great epochs of the *Sharī'ah* initiated by the five great prophets who came after Adam—Noah, Abraham, Moses, Jesus, and Muḥammad.

Nāṣir-i Khusraw also attempts to elaborate the *ta'wīl* of the three stages of time he identifies within the ritual of prayer itself—the beginning, the middle, and the end. The beginning stage symbolizes the *nāṭiq*, the Ismā'īlī term for the Prophet as the promulgator of Revelation; the middle stage stands for *asās*, the interpreter of the inner meaning of Revelation; and the final stage stands for the *qā'im al-qiyāmah*, in which both the outer and the inner are fused and transcended. Such a cyclical view of history is an important aspect of Ismā'īlī thought and illustrates the dual dimension of time that Ismā'īlī writers saw reflected in the Quran. The first dimension provided a body of rituals and doctrines for a historical community; the second transposed these rituals and doctrines to a level of meaning beyond the historical constraints of time, where this *tanzīl* was metamorphosed by *ta'wīl* to provide the individual Muslim an opportunity to grasp the root cosmic meaning of the revealed Law.

Before discussing specifically the performance of the ritual prayer itself, al-Nu'mān makes an interesting reference to the *qiblah*, the point of orientation for prayer, taking as his reference the verse "so set thy face to *al-dīn* (the religion) *ḥanīfan* (as a primordial monotheist)" (XXX, 30). He points out that at one level this is the point of orientation to which *ḥunafā'* (primordial monotheists) like Ibrāhīm and Adam set themselves—the Kaʿbah (or even perhaps Jerusalem). In its esoteric sense, the verse refers to the *waṣī,* the Prophet's successor, through whom the Prophet turns his face to the community and through whom the *bāṭin* of religion is affirmed during the Prophet's own lifetime and the *ẓāhir* established to serve as a point of continuity after his death.

The discussion then proceeds to the steps incorporated within prayer itself. These according to Nāṣir-i Khusraw are seven: (1) *takbīr,* which symbolizes the taking of the covenant from a *mu'min.* During *takbīr,* the believers are required to be silent and to concentrate their attention fully on the performance of prayer—in the same way that a *mu'min* from whom the covenant has been taken should not manifest his quest for the *bāṭin* openly lest his intentions be misconstrued and his words misunderstood. (2) *Qiyām,* standing, which symbolizes the firm affirmation of the *mu'min* to stand by his covenant and not be swayed from it. (3) Recitation of the *Fāṭihah* and an additional sura, which symbolizes communication with the rest of the community, conveying to them the meaning of faith and elaborating it for them. (4) *Rukūʿ,* bowing, which symbolizes the recognition of the *asās* and during his absence the *ḥujjah,* who is the evidence for his existence. (5) *Sujūd,* prostration, which symbolizes the recognition of the *nāṭiq* as the heralder of a "great cycle" and the Imam of that cycle. (6) *Tashahhud,* which symbolizes the recognition of the *dāʿī.* (7) The offering of *salām* marks the giving of permission to manifest in conversation and action one's faith, just as after the offering of *salām* in ritual prayer one is permitted to converse.

When the worshiper completes the performance of *ṣalāt* in *ẓāhir,* he has correspondingly sought to fulfill his inner quest, which involves a recognition of the inner meaning of the steps. In essence, then, the *ta'wīl* of the steps within *ṣalāt* is that they are stages in the journey of the individual soul in its quest for the inner realities of the Faith.

The essence of such an interpretation of prayer is summed up thus by Nāṣir-i Khusraw:

> The exoteric (*zāhir*) of Prayer consists in adoring God with postures of the body, in directing the body towards the *qibla* of the body, which is the *Kaʿbah,* the Temple of the Most High God, situated at Mekka. To understand the esoteric of Prayer (*ta'wīl-e-bātin*) means adoring God with the thinking soul and turning towards the quest of the gnosis of the Book and the gnosis of positive religion, towards the *qibla* of the spirit which is the Temple of God, that Temple in which the divine gnosis is enclosed, I mean the Imam in Truth, salutations to him.[15]

One result of studying these examples of *ta'wīl* is a recognition of the dialectic that underlies the hermeneutics. As the *ta'wīl* unfolds, it moves always from the level of the specific and temporal to that of the cosmic and eternal. *Ta'wīl* is historically rooted in the community and in tradition; it builds and shapes itself until the individual experiences it as part of his intellectual and spiritual growth. In Islam, according to these writings, the performance of prayer ought to involve each Muslim in a constant dialogue with the meaning of life and the cosmos, an idea that is at the heart of Ismā'īlī doctrine. Another result of this study is the recognition that the *bāṭin* of *ṣalāt*, what Nāṣir-i Khusraw calls the "adoration with the thinking soul," complements the *ẓāhir*, so that in the outward performance of the act of prayer one is simultaneously involving the intellectual and spiritual faculties.

Quest and Transformation

Among the accounts of the activity of Ismā'īlī *dā'īs*, there occurs a type of narrative, a description almost "mythical" in form, which describes key moments in the birth and development of an inner consciousness, revealing at the level of personal and spiritual life the themes of quest and transformation. The idea of the quest is at the heart of the notion of *ta'wīl*, for by this tool of comprehension one begins the search for inner meaning. Simultaneously, as is evident in the analysis of prayer, the quest becomes the prelude for a transformation, which makes possible the acquisition of this knowledge of inner meaning as one ascends the steps of the hierarchy of faith. Besides an autobiographical *Ode* written by Nāṣir-i Khusraw, there are in Ismā'īlī literature works such as the *Kitāb al-'ālim wa'l-ghulām*,[16] and accounts preserved in the tradition of the *ginā̄ns* among the Nizārī Ismā'īlīs of the subcontinent,[17] which contain such narratives, symbolic of the two themes. The art of narratives lies in the way in which the motifs of seeking, initiation, and transformation are evoked and woven together so that the tapestry that emerges in each case reflects a common design and pattern, even though the "action" of the narrative is set in differing contexts.

The autobiographical account of Nāṣir-i Khusraw's conversion to Ismā'īlism refers to a dream that jars him from what has hitherto been a life of sloth, and he subsequently undertakes a pilgrimage to Mecca. On the way, he encounters and is converted to Ismā'īlism, and he is subsequently invested with the important role of preaching as a key member of the Fāṭimid *da'wā*. It is, however, in an ode celebrating this conversion that the pattern of *ta'wīl* woven into the narrative is made apparent. His sleep becomes the equivalent of the state of ignorance; the figure in the dream is the catalyst who causes the act of awakening leading to the quest; and the subsequent resolution is symbolized in the arrival at the *balad al-amīn* (Quran XCV, 31), the Cairo of the narrative, but in reality the secure abode of true understanding, which is the goal of the quest. The transformation is consummated through the act of commitment, the taking of the oath of allegiance to the Imam, the symbolism of which is evoked in the Quran (XLVIII, 18).[18]

In the *Kitāb al-ʿālim wa'l-ghulām*, the protagonist Abū Mālik is a type of spiritual exile who, as part of his mission, has left his home. He enters a town incognito and mingles with the crowd before encountering a disciple. The narrative then unfolds in a series of dialogues, so that the process of pedagogy in Ismāʿīlism becomes evident. This process is a threefold one. Initially, the disciple's sense of quest is aroused; he is sensitized to the meaning of symbols, the use of *ta'wīl*, which leads from the letter to the spirit. His desire for knowledge having now awakened, the disciple is eager to know more about the figure in whose hands are placed the keys to inner meaning and to the spiritual heaven, namely, the Imam. In a further stage, he acquires a new name, symbolizing his entry into a new pattern of understanding and way of life, and in a final stage, the act of transformation is marked in a ceremony. What transpires at this ceremony remains unrecorded. The text does not reveal the secret; it has only been communicated personally to the disciple.

In the narratives recorded in the *ginān* literature, the description of the activities of the Ismāʿīlī *dāʿīs*, also called *pīrs*, reflect a sequence of action with certain iterative features, such as the following: (1) the anonymous arrival at a well-known center of religious activity; (2) the performance of miracles and the winning over of a disciple or disciples; (3) a period of confrontation and even rejection; (4) eventual triumph and mass conversion; (5) departure.

The literal testimony of these narratives is, as in the last two cases, but a mirror of the original prototype in which the disciples pass through an initiatory process. A key set of images is that of the "raw" and the "cooked," where the disciple, a princess in one case, has taken a vow to daily taste cooked meat until the secret of who her bridegroom is to be is revealed to her. The day that the *pīr* is in the vicinity, her gamekeeper, unable to find a deer to hunt for her meat, encounters the animals of the jungle around the *pīr*, mesmerized by the playing of his song. Through a miracle, the *pīr* gives a piece of the deer's meat to the gamekeeper. When the princess cooks and tastes it, she, as if awakened, recognizes the nearness of her bridegroom's presence and seeks him out. In time a marriage takes place, bringing the metaphor of the bride and groom and their marriage, marking the transition from quest to transformation, to union.

Although all the narratives vary in context and in the setting of their action, they project identical themes, wherein the events lead through a quest to a transformation, at the heart of which lies the knowledge of universals. The image that best exemplifies this act of cognition and illumination is the Quranic symbol of divine radiant light, *nūr* (XXIV, 35).

H. Corbin has attempted to illustrate the image of the Imam as *nūr* (light) in the works of the Fāṭimid and post-Fāṭimid period to elucidate the essential elements of what he calls "the little known and scarcely studied form of Shīʿite Ismāʿīlian Gnosis,"[19] where reference is made to the complex image of the pillar of light (*haykal nurānī*), by whose power the members of the hierarchy of faith are raised upward until they are all gathered together in the *qiyāmah*.

The later period of Ismāʿīlism reflects features that are analogous in some respects to Sufi theosophy, this similarity being a result of common contexts and mutual influence. The language of devotion is one aspect where the influence is apparent—in particular, where the element of religious experience seeks to illuminate the apprehension by the intellect and the soul of the *Ḥaqīqah*. It is poetry rather than prose that captures best these moments of contemplation and acts of awakening. This mode of expression is already present in the *qaṣīdah* of Nāṣir-i Khusraw and is echoed also in the *ginān*s, as the examples below show. One is a description of Nāṣir's initiation and transformation, and the other evokes the moments of bliss and illumination in the *ginān*s, which can be described only in terms of a "spiritual concert."

> That sage set his hand upon his heart
> (a hundred blessings be on that hand and breast!)
> and said, "I offer you the remedy
> of proof and demonstration; but if you
> accept, I shall place a seal upon your lips
> which must never be broken." I gave my consent and he
> affixed the seal. Drop by drop and day
> by day he fed me the healing potion, till
> my ailment disappeared, my tongue became
> imbued with eloquent speech; my face, which had
> been pale as saffron now grew rosy with joy;
> I who had been as stone was now a ruby;
> I had been dust—now I was ambergris.
> He put my hand into the Prophet's hand,
> I spoke the Oath beneath the exalted Tree
> so heavy with fruit, so sweet with cooling shade.

> Have you ever heard of a sea which flows from fire?
> Have you ever seen a fox become a lion?
> The sun can transmute a pebble, which even the hand

of Nature can never change, into a gem.
I am that precious stone, my Sun is he
by whose rays this tenebrous world is filled with light.
In jealousy I cannot speak his name
in this poem, but can only say that for him
Plato himself would become a slave. He
is the teacher, healer of souls, favoured of God,
image of wisdom, fountain of knowledge and Truth.
Blessed the ship with him for its anchor, blessed
the city whose sacred gate he ever guards!

O Countenance of Knowledge, Virtue's Form,
Heart of Wisdom, Goal of Humankind,
O Pride of Pride; I stood before thee, pale
and skeletal, clad in a woolen cloak,
and kissed thine hand as if it were the grave
of the Prophet or Black Stone of the Kaaba.
Six years I served thee; and now, wherever I am
so long as I live I'll use my pen and ink,
my inkwell and my paper . . . in praise of thee![20]

When the unrecited name makes its abode in the interior
it becomes a lamp which illumines the heart;
the glories of true contemplation are felt within—
The world's tinsel can no longer dazzle.

The flame lit by recitation
swallows all remembrance and devotion.
Truth hovers on the Master's lip
because—as he says—"I am always on its side."

The world is dazed by brightness
and turns away from the blazing glare.
If you were to reveal the mystery of this radiance
the world would brand you a fool.

"In the heart, I make my seat" says the Master
"all seventy-two chambers ring with music,
the dark of night is dispelled
and the concert of *ginăns* begins."

The unrecited name plays on and on:
a symphony is heard within.
The seventy-two chambers fill with music, though
its essence is perceived by only a few.[21]

Cosmos and History

Ismā'īlī spirituality is ultimately rooted in two essentially Islamic themes—a cosmos-mirroring "Unity" and a sacred history reflecting the working out of Divine Will and human destiny. These themes as illustrated in the literature reveal a pattern in Ismāʿīlī thought where human life is an exalted destiny whose movement in its highest stage mirrors a return to its origin, as in the following Quranic verse: "From Him we are and to Him we return" (II, 156).

However, this goal has as its context the material world, where matter and spirit exist in a state of complementarity. The *ẓāhir* which defines the world of matter is the arena in which the context for a spiritual life is shaped. The essence of Ismāʿīlī thought shows no propensity for rejecting this material world; in fact, without action in it, the spiritual quest is regarded as unworthy. It is in this juxtaposition of *ẓāhir* with *bāṭin*, of the material with the spiritual, that the world of the believer comes to be invested with full meaning. Such is the continuing heritage that daily inspires Ismāʿīlī life and is summed up in its most universal aspect, in the words that conclude a memorable passage in the *Memoirs* of the forty-eighth Nizārī Ismāʿīlī Imam, Shāh Sulṭān Muḥammad Shāh, Agha Khan III:

> Life in the ultimate analysis has taught me one enduring lesson. The subject should always disappear in the object. In our ordinary affections one for another, in our daily work with hand and brain, we most of us discover soon enough that any lasting satisfaction, any contentment that we can achieve, is the result of forgetting self, of merging subject with object, in a harmony that is of body, mind and spirit. And in the highest realms of consciousness all who believe in a Higher Being are liberated from all the clogging and hampering bonds of the subjective self in prayer, in rapt meditation upon and in the face of the glorious radiance of eternity, in which all temporal and earthly consciousness is swallowed up and itself becomes the eternal.[22]

Notes

1. General summations of Ismāʿīlī history and more detailed references to specialized works will be found in the following: *Encyclopaedia of Islam*, s.v. "Ismāʿīliyya" (by W. Madelung); *Shorter Encyclopaedia of Islam*, s.v. "Ismāʿīliyya" (by W. Ivanow); Aziz Esmail and Azim Nanji, "The Ismāʿīlīs in History," in *Ismāʿīlī Contributions to Islamic Culture*, ed. S. H. Nasr (Tehran: Imperial Iranian Academy of Philosophy, 1977) 225–65; S. Stern, *Studies in Early Ismaʿilism* (Tel Aviv: Magnes Press, 1983).

2. For the Fāṭimids, see *Encyclopaedia of Islam*, s.v. "Fātimids" (by M. Canard); see also Abbas Hamdani, *The Fatimids* (Karachi: Pakistan Publishing House, 1962).

3. For an overview of the early period, see S. M. Stern, "The Succession to al-Āmir, the claims of the later Fatimids to the imamate and the rise of Ṭayyibī Ismāʿīlism," *Oriens* 4 (1951) 193–255; and *Encyclopaedia of Islam*, s.v. "Bohōras" (by A. A. Fyzee).

4. The most thoroughly researched study on the Nizārī Ismāʿīlī movement is M. G. S. Hodgson, *The Order of Assassins* (The Hague: Mouton, 1955). A summary of this work appears in Hodgson, "The Ismāʿīlī State" in *The Cambridge History of Iran*, vol. 5, ed. J. A. Boyle (Cambridge: University Press, 1968) 422–82.

5. The most comprehensive survey of Ismāʿīlī literature is I. K. Poonawala, *Biobibliography of Ismāʿīlī Literature* (Malibu, CA: Undena, 1977).

6. Translated from the quotation in H. Corbin, *Histoire de la philosophie islamique* (Paris: Gallimard, 1964) 17.

7. Quoted by Eugene Vance, "Pas de trois: Narrative, Hermeneutics and Structure in Medieval Poetics," in *Interpretation of Narrative,* ed. M. J. Valdes and Owen Miller (Toronto: University of Toronto Press, 1978) 122.

8. Nāṣir-i Khusraw, *Kitāb Jāmiʿ al-Ḥikmatayn,* edited with a preliminary study in French and Persian by H. Corbin and M. Moin (Paris: Adrien-Maisonneuve, 1953).

9. See Heinz Halm, *Kosmologie und Heilslehre der frühen Ismāʿīliya: Eine Studie zur islamischen Gnosis* (Wiesbaden: F. Steiner, 1978).

10. The analysis is drawn from Azim Nanji, "Shīʿī Ismāʿīlī Interpretation of the Qur'an," in *Selected Proceedings of the International Congress for the Study of the Qur'ān, Australian National University, 8–13 May 1980* (Canberra: Australian National University Press, 1982) 40–42. For the cosmology, see Halm, *Kosmologie;* and W. Madelung, "Aspects of Ismāʿīlī Theology: The Prophetic Chain and the God beyond Being," in *Ismāʿīlī Contributions,* 51–65.

11. A. Nanji, "Shīʿī Ismāʿīlī Interpretation," 42.

12. Reference to the account is made by W. Madelung, "Ismāʿīliyya," 204; see also B. Lewis, "An Ismaʿili Interpretation of the Fall of Adam," *Bulletin of the School of Oriental and African Studies* 9 (1938) 691–704.

13. *The Book of Faith from the Daʿā'im al-Islām of al-Qāḍī al-Nuʿmān,* trans. A. A. A. Fyzee (Bombay: Nachiketa Publications, 1974) 6. A complete translation is to be published soon by the Institute of Ismaʿili Studies in London.

14. See A. Nanji, "Shīʿī Ismāʿīlī Interpretation," 43–46.

15. Quoted by H. Corbin, "Nasir-i-Khusrau and Iranian Ismāʿīlism," in *The Cambridge History of Iran,* vol. 4, ed. R. N. Frye (Cambridge: University Press, 1975) 523.

16. For a description and analysis see H. Corbin, "Un roman initiatique du Xe siècle," in *Cahiers de civilisation médievale* 15 (April-June 1972) 1–25, 121–42.

17. For the literature and its background, see Azim Nanji, *The Nizārī Ismāʿīlī Tradition in the Indo-Pakistan Subcontinent* (New York: Caravan Books, 1978). The theme of transformation is dealt with on pp. 101–10.

18. For his "conversion" and contribution to Ismāʿīlī esoterics, see Corbin, "Nasir-i-Khusrau"; for his works, see Poonawala, *Ismāʿīlī Literature,* 111–24. The relevant portion of the *qaṣīdah* has been translated in *Nasir-i-Khusraw: Forty Poems from the Divan,* trans. P. L. Wilson and G. R. Aavani (Tehran: Imperial Iranian Academy of Philosophy, 1977) 4–9.

19. H. Corbin, "Divine Epiphany and Spiritual Birth in Ismāʿīlism Gnosis," in *Papers from Eranos Yearbooks* (Bollingen Series 30; New York: Pantheon Books, 1964) 5:71. Here, as elsewhere in this article, Corbin's contribution and influence in the interpretation of Ismāʿīlī spirituality will be very evident. Some of his articles are to be made available in English translation in the near future; also H. Corbin, *Cyclical Time and Ismāʿīlī Gnosis* (London: Kegan Paul International/Islamic Publications, 1983).

20. *Nasir-i-Khusraw, Forty Poems from the Divan,* 8–9.

21. The translation is part of a project on the *ginān*s supported by a grant from the National Endowment for the Humanities and is from a series of compositions entitled *Śloka.*

22. Sulṭān Muḥammad Shāh, Agha Khan, *The Memoirs of Agha Khan* (New York: Simon & Schuster, 1954) 335.

11

Female Spirituality in Islam

SAADIA KHAWAR KHAN CHISHTI

IN SPEAKING OF FEMALE SPIRITUALITY in the context of the Islamic tradition, one must turn not only to the possibilities of the spiritual life for Muslim women but also to those aspects of Islam which possess a feminine dimension. One must consider the spiritual life of the great female saints, from those who belonged to the household of the Prophet to saintly women who have adorned every century of Islamic history to this day. One must also study the spiritual aspect of those everyday roles of women, which are sacralized by virtue of being lived and practiced according to the *Sharīʿah* and, therefore, in conformity with God's Will. Likewise, one must delve into Sufi teachings and practices as they apply to women and as they provide concrete paths for spiritual realization. Finally, it is necessary to recall the feminine aspect of Islamic spirituality as such, as reflected in the doctrines concerning the nature of God, the wedding of the soul and the spirit, and the feminine symbolism employed in discussing the nature of the Divine Essence and the human being's quest of the Divine Beloved. Throughout all these discussions, one must also remember that female spirituality in Islam partakes of the immutability and continuity that characterize the Islamic tradition itself.

It is, in fact, miraculous that a period of fourteen centuries with all its trials and confrontations could not break the continuity in beliefs, thoughts, and actions between the women who were blessed with the company of the Prophet and led a spiritual life under his guidance (*ṣaḥābiyyāt*) in the beginning of the Islamic era, and those Muslim women who, in the succeeding centuries, followed in the spiritual footsteps of their predecessors even during those recent periods in Islamic history which have suffered from the gradual eclipse of spirituality and the desacralization of knowledge. Such women, adorned with spiritual virtues, live even now in the dawn of the fifteenth century of the *hijrah*. They are inspired by the illustrious lives of their spiritual models and lead truly spiritual lives in conformity with the tenets of Islam, despite the tendency of present-day society toward desecration and forgetfulness of God. Providentially, they in turn will inspire others to emulate them in the quest for the Divine and to embark on the path toward the One by identification with *al-ḥaqīqat al-muḥammadiyyah* (the Muḥammadan Reality), which is the fountainhead of Islamic spirituality. It is hoped that they will become a viable force for spiritual vitality and progress by combatting the opposing forces, which are on the increase in this materialistic age.

Quranic Impact

Realizing the intensity of the current of change that runs through the centuries, one wonders at this tangible continuity among spiritual women in their modes of belief, thinking, and behavior. Broadly speaking, this continuity is due—in this case, as in all that is Islamic—to the powerful effect of the teachings of the Quran and the *Sunnah* of the Prophet Muḥammad. In other words, Muslim women who follow a spiritual path continue to be alike for the definite reason that their lives are guided by their love of God, which they express according to the Quranic Revelation, with responses that are conditioned by the teachings of the Prophet. Although the crucial events recorded in the history of the world brought along patterns of thinking and styles of living that were not only radically different from those of Islam but even inimical to them, the women who followed the teachings of the Quran, like their Muslim counterparts, strove to model their behavior on the example set by the Prophet, his companions, and his household (*ahl al-bayt*). They thus continued to wear the dress of faith in the Unity and Oneness of God and to proclaim *Lā ilāha illa'Llāh* (There is no divinity but Allah). Their adornment consists in the remembrance of God, and through the travail of spiritual discipline they cultivate virtues such as patience, repentance, humility, charity, chastity, truthfulness, piety, and absolute dependence on God (*tawakkul*). In a spirit of love and devotion, they reach a *maqām* (state) wherein they experience submission to the Divine Will.[1] Consequently, through the grace of God, in this way they begin to partake of His Divine Attributes. In so doing they are following the Prophet's command to the faithful, "Acquire Attributes of Allah." "Know that the Named is One and the Names a hundred thousand, that Being is One but its aspects are a hundred thousand."[2] "Thy great and sacred Names are a proof of Thy bounty and beneficence and mercy. Each One of them is greater than heaven and earth and angel. They are a thousand and one and they are ninety-nine: each one of them is related to one of man's needs."[3]

Proximity to the Divine

Once the seeker is able to translate the acquired spiritual virtues into action, the door of spiritual realization opens wide and the seeker crosses the threshold of gnosis—spiritual realization or proximity to the Divine. The beautiful truth is that God (as mentioned in the Quran and *Ḥadīth*) is ever close to those (men and women) who seek Him. But those who fail to acknowledge that He is omnipresent, omnipotent, and omniscient, knowing and seeing all that they do, remain distant from Him. The very light of God is needed to perceive one's proximity to the Divine. Shabistarī's idea of proximity is expressed in the following way:

> In a moment this world passes away,
> None remains in the world save "The Truth,"
> At that moment you attain proximity
> You stripped of "self" are "united" to the Beloved.[4]

God's magnanimous response to those who seek His forgiveness and His majestic Presence is expressed in the following *ḥadīth:*

> He who approaches near to Me one span, I will approach to him one cubit: and he who approaches near to Me one cubit, I will approach near to him one fathom, and whoever approaches Me walking, I will come to him running, and he who meets Me with sins equivalent to the whole world, I will greet him with forgiveness equal to it.[5]

In this *ḥadīth* reference is to both men and women, and women share with men the magnanimous response of God to their spiritual effort.

God's Slaves

One of the features of spirituality in Islam is that, whereas the genuine lover is granted spiritual proximity to the Beloved, the man and woman as a human pair are created to function as the Creator's vicegerents on earth (II, 30); as seekers of the Divine, they always remain slaves (*al-ʿabd*). The Quran testifies to the primordial covenant between God and man (used here in the sense of both male and female) as mentioned in the verse "Am I not your Lord?" asked God of His slaves. They said, "Indeed Thou art" (VII, 172). The implication is that the bondage of the Master and the slave is not destined to be severed. As such, under all circumstances the seeker or the lover of God remains a slave. However, the slaves' spiritual progress, by way of attaining the Attributes of the Master, makes the slave worthy of the Master's choicest gifts. Once the slave reaches the spiritual *maqām* of having attained some of the Master's Attributes to a degree humanly possible, then the Master favors the slave with His friendship and *qurb,* or closeness. Nevertheless, the fact is that even those who attain the heights of spiritual realization always remain the Master's slaves. "There is none in the heavens and the earth but cometh unto the Beneficent as a slave" (XIX, 93), for "He is Allah the One! And there is none comparable to Him" (CXII, 1–4). However, the slaves of God are given the glad tidings in the verse or *āyah:* "Gardens of Eden which the Beneficent hath promised to His slaves, the gardens which are (at present) unseen; surely His promise must come to pass" (XIX, 61). Thus, God assigns to His slaves a high and true renown both in this world and in the hereafter. Gardens of Eden are promised by God to both men and women in return for recognizing His perfect Unity and following the straight path. A slave who passed through the hardships of the spiritual path and experienced the Master's Unity expressed it in the following words:

> He perfect is alone, and glorious for evermore,
> His Unity supreme above imagining,
> His wondrous work beyond analysis.
> I do not say, He is the soul's soul: whatso'er I
> say, that He transcends, for He is free of space,
> and may not be attained by swiftest thought or
> further sense.
>
> If thou wouldst serve the Friend, and win His
> grace, He is thine eye, thine ear, thy tongue, thy brain:
> And since through Him thou speakest, and through
> Him hearest, before His Being thou art naught;
> for so, when shines the sun's own radiance,
> the light of stars is darkened.[6]

The attainment of gnosis, or *ma'rifah,* is largely dependent upon the spiritual capability, effort upon the path, and the extent and intensity with which the male or female seeker is blessed with the *barakah*[7] that results from the absorption of the teachings of the Quranic Revelation as exemplified by the Prophet, his family, and his companions. In the words of Abū Sulaymān al-Dārānī, the celebrated Sufi, "If Gnosis (*ma'rifa*) were to take visible form, all that looked thereon would die at the sight of its beauty and loveliness and goodness and grace and every brightness would become dark beside the splendour thereof."[8] Now this gnosis is a possibility for women as well as for men, and the *barakah* that makes it possible is available even in a mode of life rooted in the social and family responsibilities which are those of women according to the *Sharī'ah.*

The exemplary lives of the noble women of the Prophet's household and of their physical and spiritual descendants echo the message contained in many verses (*āyāt*) of the Quran and corresponding *hadīths* to the effect that a Muslim woman's religious duties lie in keeping an orderly home which breathes tranquillity amid both the plenty and the scarcity of the necessities of life. If she is married, then she must aim to raise her family in accordance with the *Sharī'ah* of Islam. If she is unmarried, divorced, or a widow, as a member of her parents' family, she is expected to share the heavy burden of maintaining a household under the supervision of her parents or the elderly members of her family while seeking the pleasure of God, both in this world and in the hereafter. When a Muslim woman realizes that the sign of the lover of God is that she follows the "Beloved of Allah,"[9] she then follows the *Sharī'ah* in her daily life as a member of her family in particular and of the society in general. Her sincere attempt to follow the *Sharī'ah* in its exoteric aspects leads to the lifting of the veils and introduces her to the inner or the esoteric aspects of the Divine Law, the assiduous observance of which leads one to the path of *ma'rifah.*

Women and Family

There are those who have criticized the injunctions of the *Sharī'ah* concerning women and the role of women in general in Islam. Such people do not usually understand either the rights bestowed upon women in Islam or the situation of women in religious communities other than the Islamic. The discussion of women's rights, however, is not of concern to the present essay, which aims to discuss female spirituality. Suffice it to say that the Prophet conferred on women a dignified status commensurable with their feminine role and responsibilities. Most important of all, the vistas of spiritual growth and development were fully opened to the female sex. As a result, in the context of Islamic spirituality, once a woman strives in the spiritual life she is able to gain access to all the possibilities of the Islamic tradition and to become, like man, the vicegerent of God (*khalīfat Allāh*) on earth.

Although the Quran is addressed to all of humanity, it also addresses women specifically. In addition to *Sūrat al-nisā'* (women), there are numerous *āyāt* scattered throughout the various suras which refer to women's status, rights, and responsibilities. Thus, the first *āyah* in *Sūrat al-nisā':*

> O mankind! Be careful of your duty to your Lord Who created you from a single soul, created, of like nature, His mate and from them twain, scattered

> (like seeds) countless men and women. Reverence Allah, through Whom Ye demand your mutual (rights) and reverence the Wombs (that bore you) for Allah ever watches over you. (IV, 1)

It may be noted here that the male and the female in their relation with the metacosmic Reality are equal. But on the cosmic level, which means the biological, psychological, and social levels, their roles are complementary; in Islam, the roles of men and women are complementary rather than competitive. In any case, before God they stand as equals, but both men and women can approach the Divine only by remaining faithful to their respective forms created by the Creator and to the duties assigned to them by Him as their Master.[10]

The demand to be dutiful toward the Creator and toward women as mothers in the same *āyah* is an indicator of the honor bestowed on motherhood and Islam's recognition of the rights of a female in her spiritual role as a mother. There are several well-known *ḥadīths* that either state or imply that motherhood spent in accordance with the *Sharīʿah* is one of the expressions of the spiritual role of a female. The Quran and the *Sunnah* emphasize that the mother deserves reverence, service, and loving care; disobedience to her or deprivation of her needs or rights is severely condemned, and the children are counseled that "heaven lies at the feet of mothers."

In the context of Islamic spirituality, observance of the Divine Law enables the body as the abode of the soul to play a positive role in the very process of spiritual realization. The Creator's miracle of human creation takes place in the womb of the mother–hence the veneration and tenderness shown to an expectant mother. Esoterically, the very process of pregnancy and birth is a part of the Divine Command "Be! and it is" (III, 47). The Quranic description of the Virgin Mary, mother of Jesus, led the Muslims to hold Mary as the symbol of the spirit that receives the Divine Inspiration and becomes the model of purity and the spiritual characteristics of motherhood. The mother bears the "soul to come" in her womb from the moment of conceiving and passes through the succeeding stages, which are described in the Quran in these terms:

> Verily We created man from a product of wet earth; then placed him as a drop (of seed) in a safe lodging; then fashioned We the drop a clot, then fashioned We the clot a little lump, then fashioned We the little lump bones, then clothed the bones with flesh, and then produced it as another creation. So blessed be Allah, the Best of Creators! (XXIII, 12–14)

It is an instinctive part of a female's spiritual role to provide for the needs of her offspring, for the newborn's nourishment is a symbol of Divine Providence. It is a living testimony of God's Attributes as the Provider or

Sustainer that the nourishment for the baby comes from the mother's breasts in the form needed by the baby's digestive system for the normal growth and development of the body. In other words, the mother (human as well as the animal) functions as a means for Divine Provision for creatures of the Creator.

Moreover, a spiritual mother nurtures the soul of her child with the powerful effect of the recitation of the *Shahādah*, the oft-repeated prayer (*Sūrat al-fāṭiḥah*), and the beautiful Names or Attributes of God by singing them as a lullaby for putting the child to sleep or for comforting a wailing or a disturbed child. In doing so, the mother makes her contribution in permeating the very being of the child with the most powerful words of the Quran.

If the mother performs her spiritual role with a sincere intention to please God (to Whom she belongs and to Whom is her return according to the Quran), then the *raḥmah* of God descends on her and she herself attains proximity to the Divine.[11] Histories of the lives of spiritual adepts or saints frequently reveal that their mothers played a vital role in leading them toward the spiritual path. To cite an example: Sulṭān Bāhū, who is renowned for his spirituality, often mentioned his mother with the utmost reverence and firmly believed that his spiritual attainment was solely due to the efforts of his mother, who was a deeply spiritual person. It is interesting to note that he composed verses with a pun on his mother's name Rāstī, which means "truth." *Al-Ḥaqq* is one of the Names of God, meaning "the Truth." Sulṭān Bāhū said in Persian:

Raḥmat-i Ḥaqq bā rāwān-i rāstī
Rāstī az rāstī ārāstī

May the beneficence of the Truth flow on the being of truth
for I am bedecked by this truth through the Truth.[12]

In simple words, the spiritual master attributed his spirituality to his mother.

As for the role of the Muslim wife, it overlaps the role of the mother. In the Prophet's first wife, Khadījah, the Muslim wife finds her best example. Khadījah enjoys the unique honor of being the first person to accept the testimony of the faith of Islam and to witness the truth of the Oneness of God and the prophethood of Muḥammad, whom she married for his honesty, integrity, and acumen as a trader. She is known for her untold sacrifices in order to spread the message of Islam, while maintaining a household, serving her husband, and rearing her family in accordance with the tenets of Islam—as these were being received by her prophet-husband in the form of *āyāt* of the Holy Book. In this context, Ibn Hishām says, "So Khadījah believed and attested to the truth which came from Allah. Thus was Allah minded to lighten the burden of His Prophet: Whenever he heard something that grieved him, touching his rejection by the people, he had recourse unto her and she comforted, reassured and supported him."[13] Thus, the first *umm al-mu'minīn* (mother of the faithful) laid the foundations of Islamic spirituality and family life.[14]

The Mothers of the Faithful as Models

It befits a Muslim woman to take example from the mothers of the faithful, for each one of them excelled in one or another aspect of family life and contributed to the fulfillment of the Prophet's mission. The name of 'Ā'ishah is particularly important; it was in her arms that the Prophet died and in her company that he received revelations. She served her husband as his beloved wife. She entered the Prophet's household as a little girl with her toys but was destined to acquire that wisdom which serves as an instrument for attaining spiritual perfection and thereby delivers its possessor from human limitations.

'Ā'ishah, the learned mother of the believers, lived through the rules of the four rightly guided caliphs of Islam and wove the sapiential dimension into the fabric of their reigns. Her most intimate closeness with the Prophet as his wife makes her an inseparable part of him. She survived her prophet-husband for nearly half a century and guided the faithful with her Divine Knowledge. It is recorded that she narrated 2,210 *ḥadīths* of the Prophet, who is reported to have said, "Learn two thirds of religion from 'Ā'ishah." Her narrations about the Prophet have provided the Muslims with a vivid picture of the personality of the perfect man *par excellence.* The Prophet's sayings about the importance of spiritual practices, such as night vigils, and the constant remembrance of God in various forms have been transmitted to the Muslims through her. She served as an authentic source of information and knowledge of the Prophet's personal and private life. She seemed to have observed the Prophet with every breath of her life in a spirit of unflinching loyalty and oneness with his inner self; for she related, "when his eyes slept, his heart did not sleep."

A study of the Prophet's *ḥadīths* pertaining to family life reveals that Islam resolved the conflict between "spirit" and "flesh" by encouraging marriage. Sex finds an enjoyable expression in the bonds of lawful marriage for perpetuating the progeny of Adam and Eve, who were created for fulfilling the obligations and duties of the exalted office of the Creator's vicegerency

(II, 30–33). "On Earth the human pairs have affinity through their Vicegerency for God and they are complementary through being man and woman. The harmony of the Universe depends on analogous sameness and differences not only between individuals, but also between worlds."[15]

The Relationship of the Family to God

In Islam, life in general—and the family life in particular in all its aspects—is an indivisible unity in which the spiritual is not separate from the mundane. The religion of Islam is a definite and distinct way of life based on the *Sharīʿah* or laws as revealed to the Prophet. As such, religion is intended to find expression in family life in particular and in the affairs of Muslim people in general. Besides the relationships between husband and wife, children and parents, grandparents and other members of the larger family circle, on the one hand, and the relationship of one family to another as units of the Islamic *ummah,* on the other hand, the central feature of the family in Islam is its relationship with God. Raising one's family according to His commandments and preparing it to be of service to Islam with an awareness that "to God we belong and to Him is our return" (II, 156) is seen as a necessity. It is this relationship between the family and God that makes the family spiritual in its structure and functions. The family that corresponds to this description and serves as the best model for a truly spiritual life is the family of Sayyidah Fāṭimah, the epitome of Islamic spiritual life.

Fāṭimah, also called *Khayr nisāʾ al-ʿālamīn* (the best of women in all the worlds), was the blessed daughter of the Prophet of Islam who became the wife of ʿAlī. She was declared by the Prophet as one who served as the gate to the citadel of spiritual knowledge. She was the mother of Imam Ḥasan and Imam Ḥusayn, who both won the coveted crown of martyrdom. She was also the mother of Zaynab, who was the spiritual heroine of the battle of Karbalāʾ and who played the role of a veritable princess of female spirituality in Islam.

Although fourteen centuries have elapsed since her departure from this stage of life, Sayyidah Fāṭimah and her family are continually remembered both in the prose and in the poetry of Muslims throughout the world. The Muslims unanimously recognize her as the fountainhead of female spirituality in Islam, because she occupied herself with the purity of the Oneness and Unity of God and was confirmed in her absolute sincerity in the practice of the beliefs and tenets of Islam. She succeeded in attaining the state (*maqām*) in which the pristine purity of the spirit immersed in the Oneness of the Supreme Being enabled her to give up the body and reside in the world of Divine Beauty and Majesty. It was her destiny, however, to set the pattern for posterity by expressing her spirituality of the highest order through her role as a daughter, wife, and mother. While performing these roles, Fāṭimah lived in and through God. In her Prophet-father's blessed self and teachings, she saw God; in her saint-husband's personality, she saw God; and she brought up her children to serve God. They in turn sacrificed themselves at the altar of love for God and thereby revived His spiritual message.

Female Spirituality and the Styles of Life

Instead of citing extensively the lives of the women closest to the Prophet, an attempt is made here to exercise restraint in giving examples of models *par excellence* of Islamic spirituality, such as Fāṭimah. The rationale behind such caution is based on the fact that, despite deep reverence and love for such models of spirituality, one finds among the Westernized young women of the present generation a growing tendency to ignore the examples of these luminaries on the horizon of spirituality. They argue that these great personalities had the unparalleled advantage of being blessed by the company and the teachings of the Prophet. Therefore, care is taken to cite examples in the lives of those spiritually advanced women who could not be in the company of the Prophet and yet strove to know and follow his teachings with utmost devotion and who became well known for their spiritual attainment.

It is not a rare sight to find small huts presenting a contrast to the lofty and luxurious mansions found in the Islamic world. A particularly striking contrast in styles of living was presented by the hut of Rābi'ah al-'Adawiyyah, which stood near the Tigris, and the palace of Zubaydah, the queen of Hārūn al-Rashīd of the Abbasid Dynasty. Although Rābi'ah has always worn the spiritual crown of the servant of God and is well known as the queen of saintly women, Zubaydah, queen of Baghdad, was spiritually gifted in her own regal demeanor. The historians describe her as the most desirous of the good, the swiftest to perform pious deeds, and the readiest in benefactions. In discussing the piety and virtues of Zubaydah, on the one hand, and describing Rābi'ah's pure love for God and her complete absorption in Him, on the other hand, an attempt is made here to show that although spirituality may be expressed by individuals who are poles apart in their personal bearing and stations in life, the core of the concept of feminine spirituality in Islam, its mode of discipline, and its goal are always the same. However, the *maqām* of persons on the spiritual path differs from person to person, depending on the intensity of their efforts (*mujāhadah*) and the descent of God's grace upon them. In the case of Zubaydah it is clear that, while outwardly wearing the robes of a queen, she inwardly passed through many spiritual states and stations, which alone could give her the patience to be a loving wife of a king who was known for his attraction to women. She had the virtue to extend her motherly love to an infant whose deceased mother was a slave girl of her palace. This infant, Ma'mūn, became a claimant to the throne and thus a rival of Zubaydah's only son, Amīn. Later, when Ma'mūn was at war with Amīn for the throne, Zubaydah had the strength of heart to rise above her motherly love for her own son and to behave like a perfectly just queen-mother, as evidenced by the fact that she advised her general to remember while confronting Ma'mūn that he was a son and a brother and must be treated kindly. Although Ma'mūn was held responsible for the death of Zubaydah's only son, she refused to take revenge. In doing so she followed the patient statesmanship of the Prophet, who, after the conquest of Mecca, did away with blood feuds and later, in his sermon of the last pilgrimage, banished acts of revenge as an evil of the past. In the manner of a truly spiritually oriented person, Zubaydah said to Ma'mūn, "If I lost a son who was caliph, I now have a son who is caliph. No mother is bereft who holds you by the hand. There is a day when you two will meet again, and I pray God that He will forgive both of you." "Her magnanimity may have contributed to Baghdad's recovery and to the brilliance of the reign of al-Ma'mūn."[16]

Zubaydah's life was a shining example of female spirituality in Islam, for she was graceful in practicing the *Sunnah* of the Prophet in dealing with the affairs of her palace, amid melodious recitations of the Quran by one hundred girls who had memorized the Holy Book and recited three *sipārahs* daily. (A *sipārah* constitutes 1/30th of the Quran.) In addition, inspired by the love of God and His Messenger, she crossed the pilgrims' road to Mecca six times during her life, founding inns, wells, cisterns, and the like to make the journey comfortable for pilgrims. It is she who had the depth of the Zamzam, the sacred well in the sanctuary of the Ka'bah, increased. It is reckoned by the early historians that "the people of Mecca owe their very life to her, next to God." The echo of the slogan, "Allah bless Zubaydah" resounded for many centuries and testified to her spirituality.

Zubaydah's palace and its adornments would tend to blind the person unacquainted with spiritual states and stations to the jewel of spirituality and its light which shone within it. To the same person, Rābi'ah's hut would appear as a dwelling place of a poverty-stricken, illiterate, and perhaps eccentric individual. To the person whose eyes see the inner meaning of things, however, Rābi'ah's hut symbolized *faqr* or spiritual poverty, which served as a center of *barakah* (Divine Grace). The genuine *faqīrah* (woman who practices *faqr*) is a servant of God alone and desires to be possessionless in order to be possessed only by her love for God. In this voluntary state of material possessionlessness, the servant who is a genuine lover begins her life of service to the Beloved with the aim of reaching the final station on the spiritual path, known as *Ḥaqīqah* (the Truth). Her service is based on pursuing diligently the Master's Divine Commandments, both in their exoteric and esoteric aspects.

The servant's devoted service to the One, coupled with an intense longing for the Master's majestic presence, leads to the development of a close relationship between the two, whereby the servant begins to hear with the ears of the Master and to see with His eyes. It is at this juncture that the servant's hut becomes the treasure-house of spiritual wisdom, blessings, and the choicest gifts of the Master, wherein many seekers find the true meaning of *faqr* and start their journey on the spiritual path.

The perplexing question of how a hut that generally symbolizes poverty can serve as a treasure-house of spiritual wisdom and gifts can be answered by citing an episode from Rābi'ah's life. If the truth of this incident is doubted, the story is still able to serve as an allegory. Once a thief entered Rābi'ah's hut and found nothing save a pitcher of water. As he was about to leave, Rābi'ah called out to him, "If you are really a thief then do not leave without taking something." The thief replied sarcastically, "What is there to be taken?" Rābi'ah replied, "O needy one, perform the ablution with the water in the pitcher, enter this prayer room, and say two rakats of prayer. Then leave after receiving something." The thief obeyed and, when he stood for the prayer, Rābi'ah also raised her hands for prayer and said, "O Lord, this man found nothing here, I have brought him to Thy door, bless him by Thy bounty and grace." In response to Rābi'ah's appeal to the Hearer of prayers, the thief felt spiritual absorption and joy and thus continued his prayers throughout the night. Early in the morning when Rābi'ah entered the prayer room, she found him prostrate before the Almighty and heard him seeking repentance. This much of the incident should suffice to answer the question, How could a hut serve as a treasure-house of wisdom and God's Mercy.

Selfless service performed from the depths of love keeps the lover ready to lay down her life in order to earn the pleasure of the Beloved and develops in her an intense longing for that supreme moment when she will hear the Beloved's voice saying, "O soul at rest, return to thy Lord well-pleased, well-pleasing; so enter amongst My servants and enter My Garden" (LXXXIX, 27–30).

The biographers of Rābiʻah have recorded that the last words she spoke as she was closing her eyes in death showed her to be in a state of eternal bliss in the lap of her Beloved. Indeed Rābiʻah was one of those about whom the Quran says: "But those of Faith are overflowing in their love for God" (II, 165). Thus, Rābiʻah, the absolutely true lover, passed into the presence of her Beloved.

Rābiʻah, a model of selfless love, introduced the concept of love into the somewhat austere teachings of her ascetic predecessors. Rābiʻah dressed her yearnings of love in exquisitely beautiful verses. An example of her concept of Divine Love is the following stanza:

> I love Thee with two loves, a love that is passion
> And one which besides Thou hast earned as Thy due
> The passionate love is the thought which forgetting
> All else is of You, aye, for ever of You.
> Thou earnedst the other by rending asunder
> All veils and disclosing Thyself to my view.
> Not mine be the praise for the one or the other
> The praise and the thanks are all Thine for the two.[17]

Rābiʻah's life was a model of mutual love between the Creator and His creation—a state of perfect love in which the lover ceases to exist for her own person but lives for the Beloved, demonstrates invariable courtesy and efficient service in obeying the commandments of the Beloved, and finally becomes altogether His. Rābiʻah's life is a supreme example of the spiritual state in which lover, love, and Beloved become one.

Women and the Way of Sufism

Divine Union and the Sharīʻah

In Islam, union with the Divine is contingent upon love for the Prophet, who is the last of the spiritual monarchs ruling over the earth. In this respect, the Quranic mandate is as follows: "Say (O Muḥammad, to mankind) if ye love God, follow me: God will love you and forgive you your sins. God is forgiving, Merciful" (III, 31). It is noteworthy that this *āyah* addresses itself to the entirety of mankind, and its profound implication is that it applies to posterity till that Last Day in the existence of this world, when, according to the Quran, the heavens and the earth will be rolled up and God (*aḥkam al-ḥākimīn*, the justest of judges) will sit on the Throne of judgment for the announcement of the final reward or punishment to each male and female created by Him. The words "follow me" in the *āyah* refer to following the *Kitāb* and the *Sunnah*. Furthermore, these words are addressed as much to posterity as to the followers of the Prophet during his lifetime. The exemplification of the *Sharī'ah* by the Prophet, his household (*ahl al-bayt*), and companions for attaining the love of God have made it mandatory for the seekers of the Divine to follow the *Sunnah*.

Since, in their union with the Divine, distinctions are not made among the lovers of God, it follows that no distinction can be made between Muslim men and women in their capacity and longing to reach the Divine. It must be pointed out that the Quran admonishes the seekers of the Divine, both male and female, to love the Prophet as a prerequisite for loving God. No one can claim to love the Prophet unless he or she recognizes that the *Sharī'ah*, in its exoteric reality as well as its esoteric aspects, furnishes a perfect code of life and that it has been given to humanity in order for us to strive to live a perfect life in this world with the aim of passing into the presence of the perfect Being. Perfection, however, can be achieved only when one remains faithful to the innate nature of the form, male or female, in which the perfect Being has placed the soul. It may be emphasized here that, whenever individuals rebel against forms and their corresponding roles, they fall from the pedestal of perfection and the possibility of attaining the spiritual realm.

Although both the male and the female are assigned different roles by nature, in Islam the roles of men and women are seen as complementary rather than competitive. As human souls, both the male and the female are absolutely equal in their relationship with their Creator; and as Muslims both the male and the female need to cultivate the same virtues and perform the same Islamic rites, and before God they bear the same accountability for their actions.

Islamic rites and rituals are basically the same for both men and women. Performance of the rites may differ in minor details for women because of their different role; for example, the woman may not join the congregational Friday prayers held in the mosque but can perform the prayer at home. She may not join the funeral procession, and she is not supposed to take part in the burial rites. She is also exempted from saying the five prayers during menstruation and childbirth. The reasons for her exemptions are obvious. Islam is known as *Dīn al-fiṭrah* (a way of life according to the nature of the male and female) and *Dīn al-sahl* (a way of life in which there is ease). As such, the performance of the religious rites and ceremonies is based on the consideration of offering ease to the performer, which enables women to perform their own role efficiently.

The undeniable additional evidence of the spiritual equality of the Muslim male and female is furnished by the Quranic mode of addressing both men and women as follows:

Men who surrender unto Allah,
  And women who surrender,
And men who believe,
  And women who believe,
And men who speak the truth
  And women who speak the truth,
And men who persevere in righteousness,
  And women who persevere,
And men who are humble,
  And women who are humble,
And men who give alms,
  And women who give alms,
And men who fast,
  And women who fast,
And men who guard their modesty,
  And women who guard their modesty,
And men who remember Allah much,
  And women who remember Allah much,
Allah hath prepared for them forgiveness
  and a vast reward.
(XXXIII, 33–35)

About the men and the women mentioned in the above *āyah,* the Quran provides further knowledge in these words:

> The Believers, men and women are protecting friends of one another; they enjoin the right and forbid the wrong, and they observe regular prayers, and they pay the poor due and they obey God and His messenger. (IX, 71)

These verses not only bring out the spiritual equality of the believers, men and women, but also describe most exquisitely those spiritual virtues whose cultivation is necessary for attaining the greatest spiritual reward.

Keeping in mind the various verses concerning the believers, both men and women, and their obligation to observe the Divine Law, Taqī al-Dīn al-Ḥasanī presented the ideas expressed in those verses as follows:

> Praise be to God, who created the earth and the heavens . . .and gathered together the believers, men and women, and established the sacred law. . . . And the people of happiness obeyed Him and did His work, from among the dutiful men and women. . . . And when He exhorted the creatures to be obedient, He did not single out the men, but spoke of the Muslims, men and women, and the believers of both sexes and those who observed the law, men and women, and the verses dealing with this are many and are not secret.[18]

Ḥasanī's views emphasize the fact that Islam has once and for all made a declaration of the spiritual equality of the male and the female before their Creator, who exhorts them "to be obedient to Him and His Messenger"

(V, 92). Furthermore, the Quran proclaims: "Say, obey Allah and the Messenger. But if they turn back, Allah loves not those who reject Faith" (III, 32). This *āyah* is also clearly addressed to all of the human race and brings out characteristics of human nature common to both the sexes. Hence, it is implied that both the male and the female as human beings share the same basic traits of human nature—the tendency both to do good and to indulge in evil. As such, on the one hand, they are given the choice of choosing the right path (*al-ṣirāṭ al-mustaqīm*) and thereby nurturing and developing their souls. On the other hand, if they choose the path of evil, their souls are starved and ultimately perish. These two categories of the males and the females are perfectly contrasted in the following verses.

Concerning those who incur God's wrath:

> The hypocrites, men and women, (have an understanding) with each other:
> They enjoin evil, and forbid what is just, and are close with their hands.
> They have forgotten Allah; so He hath disregarded them.
> Verily the hypocrites are rebellious and perverse. (IX, 67)

Concerning those who incur God's mercy:

> The believers, men and women are protectors, one of another:
> They enjoin what is just, and forbid what is evil: they observe regular prayers, practice regular charity,
> and obey Allah and His Apostle.
> On them will Allah pour His mercy; for Allah
> is exalted in power, wise. (IX, 71)

Since in Islam there is no clergy or ecclesiastical system, every man and woman is recognized as having the potential to practice Islam directly as the perfect religion chosen to complete God's blessing on mankind. "This day have I perfected your religion for you and completed My favour upon you, and chosen for you Islam as your religion" (V, 3). Therefore, the first step for either the male or the female belonging to the category that incurs God's wrath is to repent and to seek God's forgiveness and thereby take the initial step toward following the exoteric aspects of *Sharī'ah.*

If a woman regularly follows the beliefs and the five pillars of Islam in her daily life and if their practice becomes second nature to her, then the *barakah* inherent in practicing the *Sharī'ah* will enable her to enter into the esoteric or the inner dimensions of the Divine Laws. Such a woman is already at the starting point of the spiritual path, whether she lives in a hut, in an average house, or in a palace—or, if need arises, moves in and out of these during her lifetime. In any case, such a woman follows the dictate in these verses:

> Guard strictly your (habit of) prayers and stand before God in a devout (frame of mind). (II, 238)
>
> Celebrate the praises of the Lord ere the rising of the sun and ere the going down thereof. And glorify Him some hours of the night and at the two ends of the day, that thou mayest find acceptance. (XX, 130)

The first verse alludes to the five canonical prayers and the second to the *dhikr*, remembrance of God along with prayers. It is noteworthy that a sincere obedience to the commandments contained in the verses eventually raises the follower from the level of obedience to that of pure love for the Divine and whispers to her the spiritual message of *taṣawwuf*, confirming to her that love (*ʿishq-i ilāhī*) is the instrument for taking the lover (*ʿāshiq*) into the close proximity of the Beloved (*Maʿshūq*). It thereby enables her to attain *maʿrifah* (Divine Knowledge).

Sharīʿah, Ṭarīqah, Ḥaqīqah

Islam as a religion consists of an essential outward, an irreplaceable exoteric, dimension known as the *Sharīʿah*. More often than not, those persons who are assiduous in following the *Sharīʿah* are seen as being led to the *ṭarīqah* (the path of *taṣawwuf* or Sufism). For the few successful travelers on the path, the grace of God terminates their journey at the exalted station of *Ḥaqīqah* (Divine Truth). An unshakable belief in Divine Unity (*tawḥīd*) is the cornerstone of the structure of spirituality in Islam. Therefore, those persons who devoted themselves to the spiritual life came to be called *ahl-i tawḥīd* (people of Unity) or *ahl-i ḥaqq* (people of Truth, i.e., of God).

Taṣawwuf (Islamic mysticism) is appropriately called the "science of purity" of the human soul, and those who adhere to it live a purely virtuous life based on the *Sharīʿah*. The *Sharīʿah* and *ṭarīqah* are both expressions of *taṣawwuf*, like the reverse sides of a coin. These two aspects of *taṣawwuf* as a discipline are aimed at providing the means of union with the Divine. Both the male and the female go through the special discipline provided by *taṣawwuf* and delineated by the renowned masters of the Islamic spiritual orders, who have provided guidance ever since the physical departure of the embodiment of Islamic spirituality, namely, the Prophet of Islam and his companions.[19]

The Ṭarīqah and Its Discipline

The female seeker of the Divine, like her male counterpart, begins her spiritual training by receiving initiation from a living spiritual master (male or female). Then, under the vigilant eye of her spiritual teacher, she goes through the process of self-purification (*tazkiyat al-nafs*). The Quran mentions that one of the functions of the Prophet consisted in purifying his followers and teaching them the scriptures and the wisdom contained in God's Revelation (III, 164; LXII, 2).

One of the individual and group practices that plays a crucial role in bringing about an inner transformation by way of linking the heart with the Divine is *dhikr,* or remembrance of God. This practice is as available to women as it is to men. The Quran mentions the significance of *dhikr* both directly and indirectly in verses scattered throughout the Book, one of which is the following: "Verily in the remembrance of Allah do hearts find rest" (XIII, 28).

The significance of *dhikr* is also described in many *ḥadīths.* According to one of these, the best *dhikr* is *Lā ilāha illa'Llāh* (there is no divinity but Allah), and the best prayer is the *Sūrat al-fātiḥah,* the opening chapter of the Quran. Another *ḥadīth* suggesting the momentous practice of *dhikr* may be translated as follows: "When My slave remembers Me quietly in isolation, I too remember him quietly in My own Being. But when he remembers Me in a group, then I remember him in a better group."

In describing the essence of *dhikr,* we must state that through *dhikr* both the male and female seekers of the Divine sow the seed of Truth (*ḥaqq*) in their minds, of perfection (*kamāl*) in their hearts, of vision (*kashf*) in their eyes, and in their very selves an unshakable belief in the Unity and Oneness of their Lord, through which they reap the fruits of everlasting life and proximity to the Divine. In fact, success in this life and in the hereafter is dependent on realizing the Truth and attaining perfection. The Quran gives glad tidings to those who remember God: "And men and women who remember Allah much—Allah has prepared for them forgiveness and a vast reward" (XXXIII, 35).[20]

This spiritual discipline is aimed at changing the insinuating self (*al-nafs al-ammārah*) to the state of self at peace (*al-nafs al-muṭma'innah*) (LXXXIX, 27). The characteristic of the self at peace is that it merges into the Divine Will and attains *ma'rifah* or reaches the station of *Ḥaqīqah,* where the lover experiences the unveiling of the vision of the Beloved. In that sublime moment, the lover experiences the passing away of the personal self (*fanā'*) and entrance into eternal life (*baqā'*), into the Unity of the One Being.

The Position of the Woman Saint

A study of the history of Sufism reveals that the dignity of sainthood is conferred on Muslim women as well as on men. "As far as rank among the 'friends of God' was concerned, there was complete equality between the sexes."[21] The goal of the spiritual quest being union with the Divine, it leaves no room for the distinctions of sex.

> So the title of saint was bestowed upon women equally with men, and since Islam has no order of priesthood and no priestly caste, there was nothing to prevent a woman from reaching the highest religious rank in the hierarchy of Muslim saints. Some theologians even name the Lady Fāṭimah, daughter of the Prophet, as the first "*quṭb*" or spiritual head of the Sufi fellowship. Below the *quṭb* were four "*awtād*," from whose ranks his successor was chosen, and below them, in the next rank of the hierarchy, were forty "*abdāl*" or substitutes, who are described as being the pivot of the world and the foundation and support of the affairs of men. Jāmī relates how someone was asked, "How many are the '*abdāl*'?" and he answered, "Forty souls." And when asked why he did not say "Forty men," his reply was, "There have been women among them."[22]

Several works on women in Islamic history mention distinguished women saints outstanding in their spiritual character–sapiential knowledge, perfection, wisdom, graciousness, and magnanimity–but the light of the hidden jewel of the inner personality of hundreds of women saints whose shrines are found all over the Islamic world has not shone on the pages of Islamic history, and the memorial to their truly spiritual way of life has not as yet been built.

One of the recent voluminous works entitled *A'lām al-nisā' fī 'ālam al-'arab wa'l-islām* by 'Umar Riḍā Khalāh lists 2,556 distinguished women and gives their life sketches. These women adorned themselves with spiritual virtues and equipped themselves with various branches of Islamic knowledge and learnings and engaged themselves in spiritual activity. However, the list is far from being an exhaustive one, for the writer knows of several women saints who are not mentioned but whose shrines are spread throughout the Indo-Pakistani subcontinent. It would not be out of place to mention here that the writer had the good fortune of being in the company of Rābi'ah Baṣrī (a namesake of Rābi'ah al-'Adawīyyah), a truly great saint of Pakistan who passed away a few years ago leaving behind her a valuable spiritual work entitled *Fazān-i murshid*, which is a living testimony of her sainthood.

In conclusion, it is maintained that not only a male but also a female who succeeds in realizing her spiritual potential earns the coveted title of "friend of God" (*ḥabīb Allāh*) and fulfills her destiny as the servant of God (*'abd Allāh*). It should be recalled that to be *'abd Allāh* is the proudest rank a Muslim can claim, for the bondage to God implies liberation from all other servitudes. The chosen ones, and especially devoted men and women, are called slaves of God in the Quran. It is noteworthy that one of the epithets of the Prophet is ʿAbd. So a Muslim saint—male or female—is a servant worshiping and fulfilling duties of servantship (*ʿubūdiyyah*). Saintly persons are engrossed in the practices of Aḥmad[23] and are absorbed in the love of *Aḥad.*[24] They occupy their time with all kinds of meritorious work (*qurābāt*) truthfully and righteously. It is about such servants that the Quran says:

> Those who believe and do right:
> joy is for them and bliss their
> journey's end.
> (XIII, 29)

Notes

1. *Maqām* is a term used for denoting a well-established station on the spiritual path. It is differentiated from the term *ḥāl,* which means a temporary stage experienced during one's spiritual journey.
2. Saying of Shāh Niʿmat Allāh Walī quoted in E. G. Browne, *A Literary History of Persia* (London: T. F. Unwin, 1928–29) 3:472.
3. Abu'l-Majd Sanā'ī, *Ḥadīqatu'l-Ḥaqīqat,* trans. J. Stevenson (Calcutta: Baptist Mission Press, 1910) 1.
4. Maḥmūd Shabistarī, *Gulshan-i-Rāz,* trans. E. H. Whinfield (London: Trubner, 1880) 52.
5. This *ḥadīth,* from the collection *Mishkāt al-maṣābīḥ,* is quoted here from S. G. Campion, *The Eleven Religions* (London: G. Routledge & Sons, 1944) 188.
6. Fakhr al-Dīn ʿIrāqī, *The Song of Lovers,* trans. A. J. Arberry (London and New York: Oxford University Press, 1939) 22–23.
7. This is a term that is more comprehensive in meaning than the word grace, by which it is usually translated. *Barakah* stands for spiritual blessing issuing from the Sacred and having the power of leading to the Sacred.
8. M. Smith, *The Sufi Path of Love* (London: Luzac, 1954) 118.
9. *Maḥbūb Allāh* is one of the titles of the Prophet Muḥammad. It means literally "the Beloved of Allah."
10. See S. H. Nasr, *Islamic Life and Thought* (Albany, NY: State University of New York Press, 1981) 212–13.
11. *Raḥmah,* which is related to the Divine Names *al-Raḥmān* and *al-Raḥīm,* implies God's Loving-kindness, Forgiveness, and Mercy, which create harmony and put things in order.
12. Sulṭān Bāhū's shrine is located in the eastern part of Pakistan in a village named after him. Several of his biographers have mentioned the verse about his mother in their books. The above is translated from a book entitled *Abyā-te Sulṭān Bāhū,* written in a local dialect.
13. Hishām, son of ʿUrwah, was one of the Prophet's biographers. He was honored in receiving the traditions from ʿĀ'ishah, the "Mother of the Believers," who is among the most authentic transmitters of accounts of the Prophet's family life.

14. *Umm al-mu'minīn* is the title given to the wives of the Prophet. "The Prophet is closer to the faithful than their selves and his wives are (as) their mothers" (XXXIII, 6).

15. M. Lings, *What is Sufism?* (Berkeley and Los Angeles: University of California Press, 1981) 53.

16. C. Waddy, *Women in Muslim History* (London: Longman, 1980) 45.

17. M. Smith, *The Sufi Path,* 118.

18. From Taqī al-Dīn al-Ḥasanī's *Lives of Good Women.* The author was from Damascus and died ca. 824/1420.

19. The Sufi disciplines apply to women as well as men. On female spirituality in Sufism, see L. Bakhtiar, *Sufi: Expressions of the Mystic Quest* (London: Thames & Hudson, 1979); and A. M. Schimmel, *Mystical Dimensions of Islam* (Chapel Hill: University of North Carolina Press, 1975) 426–35.

20. The word reward in this verse refers to proximity to the Divine in this world and to the attainment of the royal rank of spiritual beings in the hereafter.

21. M. Smith, *Rabia the Mystic and Her Fellow Saints in Islam* (Cambridge: University Press, 1928) 1.

22. Ibid., 3.

23. Aḥmad is one of the names of the Holy Prophet Muḥammad referring to his inner or spiritual nature.

24. The One God, Allah.

Part Three

SUFISM:

The Inner Dimension of Islam

12

The Nature and Origin of Sufism

ABU BAKR SIRAJ ED-DIN

If We had sent down this Quran upon a mountain thou wouldst have seen it humbled, split asunder out of the fear of God. (LIX, 21)

IN THE LIGHT OF THIS VERSE it was indeed to be expected, with regard to the Revelation on which Islam is based, that such an overwhelming approach from God to man should have awakened, in the opposite direction, a response from man to God which infinitely transcended the mediocrity of exoterism. "Without doubt. But when?" is perhaps an obvious comment. There is no reason to suppose that the revelation of the Torah was any less overwhelming, and in that case the esoterism seems to have taken some time to develop, though it would be difficult to be certain about this point. However that may be, the Quran is the herald of "the Hour," and one of Islam's most striking features is precipitance. The answer to "when" is likely to be "now," and this urgency is implicit in the following verse, which occurs in two of the very earliest suras: "Surely this [the Revelation] is a Reminder; so let him who will, take unto his Lord a way" (LXXIII, 19; LXXVI, 29). Islam is spoken of in general throughout the Quran as "the Way of God," that is, the path ordained by God, which may be said to include both esoterism and exoterism. But "the Way to God," mentioned only in these two suras, is clearly the esoteric path, and the causality here is strengthened by the word "Reminder"—that which produces remembrance (*dhikr*), which is itself the essence of Sufism.

All that these verses suggest is fully confirmed elsewhere, likewise at the outset of the Revelation. In another of the earliest suras (LVI), the Islamic community is spoken of as comprising two groups, "the Foremost" and "those on the right." This second group is the generality of believers, in contradistinction to "those on the left," who are the damned. As to "the Foremost," they are said to be "many among the first (generations) and few among the last," whereas "those on the right" are "many among the first and many among the last." "The Foremost," who are to be eventually the esoteric minority, are further described as "brought nigh (to God)" (*muqarrabūn*), a term used to distinguish the archangels from the angels. This nearness, we are told in another sura, means the privilege of having direct access to the fountain of *Tasnīm.*

A third group also is spoken of in the earlier Revelations, namely, "the Righteous" (*al-abrār*). This does not alter the main twofold division of the community, for the Righteous are given to drink a draft that has been flavored at *Tasnīm* (LXXXIII, 27–28), the same fount at which "the Nigh" drink directly. This suggests that the Righteous are following in the footsteps of the Foremost and that their aspirations are set toward the station of nearness. In a parallel way, they are not yet fully realized; nonetheless, esoteric status is confirmed in another very early sura where they are said to drink a draft that has been flavored at the fountain of *Kāfūr* (LXXVI, 5–6). Those who are privileged to drink directly from this other supreme fountain are named "the slaves of God" (*'ibād Allāh*), a designation that has two distinct meanings in the Quran, one inclusive of all beings—even Satan is a slave of God—and the other, as in the present context, exclusive of all who have not realized the essence of slavehood, which is extinction in God. The slaves of God not only drink directly from *Kāfūr* but they cause it to flow at will, "making it gush forth abundantly." This suggests a spontaneous and inevitable cause–effect connection between the "irresistible" emptiness of the slaves, in themselves the personification of spiritual poverty (*faqr*), and the extreme plentitude of Divine Riches symbolized by the fountain. "Seek to draw nigh unto Me by that which I have not." By making nearness the result of poverty, these words of God to the Sufi Abū Yazīd Basṭāmī, often quoted by Ibn 'Arabī, imply that "the slaves" are, in fact, "the brought nigh."[1] The same identity, which is in the nature of things, is also implicit in one of the first commands addressed to the Prophet: "Prostrate thyself and draw nigh" (XCVI, 19), and in his commentary, "The slave is nearest his Lord when he prostrateth himself," prostration being the posture of *faqr.*[2] Moreover, nearness to God has a double significance analogous to that of slavehood. Metaphysically speaking, nearness, like slavehood, is an inescapable fact that concerns everybody. This truth, already in the Divine Name *al-Qarīb*, the All-Near, is affirmed by the Quran: "We are nearer to him (the dying man about whom ye are gathered) than ye are but ye see not" (LVI, 85). Mystically speaking, however, "He is Near to us; we are far from Him"[3] Only those who directly perceive the truth of nearness can be called near.

With regard to slavehood and nearness in their higher and exclusive sense, a distinction has further to be made between the relative and the Absolute. When the Quran speaks of "the brought nigh" and "the slaves of God," the plurals show that the reference is to what might be called the highest degree of relative nearness and relative slavehood, a degree that brings the souls of saints as near as possible to the Divine Presence without totally extinguishing their separate existence. This is the summit of the hierarchy of the celestial gardens in the ordinary sense of the word paradise. Beyond it is the Absolute Nearness of the Supreme Identity, which the Sufis name "the Paradise of the Essence" and which excludes all duality. "We are nearer to him (man) than his jugular vein" (L, 16), and "God cometh in between a man and his own heart" (VIII, 24), says the Quran; and the possibility of realizing this identity was made explicit toward the end of the Prophet's mission, if not before, in the following holy tradition: "My slave ceaseth not to seek to draw nigh unto Me with devotions of his free will until I love him; and when I love him, I am the hearing with which he heareth and the sight with which he seeth and the hand with which he graspeth and the foot on which he walketh."[4]

It follows that sainthood has two aspects: one of relative nearness and one of Absolute Nearness–Identity. In other words, the highest goal for man's aspiration is a dual one. Thus, in an early Revelation, the believer is promised two paradises (LV, 46), and this duality had already been affirmed in a Quranic address to the perfected soul: "O thou soul which art at peace return unto thy Lord, pleased thou and whelmed in His good pleasure. Enter thou among My slaves. Enter thou My Paradise" (LXXXIX, 27–30). If the following utterance of the Prophet is not a commentary on these verses, it may nonetheless be used as such: "God will say to the people of Paradise: 'Are ye well pleased?' and they will say: 'How should we not be well pleased, O Lord, inasmuch as Thou has given us that which Thou hast not given unto any of Thy creatures else?' Then will He say: 'Shall I not give you better than that?' and they will say: 'What thing, O Lord, is better?' and He will say: 'I will let down upon you My *Riḍwān.*'"[5]

The ultimate beatitude of *Riḍwān* is interpreted to mean God's taking of a soul to Himself and His eternal good pleasure therein. In the above passage from the Quran, the words "pleased thou" express the soul's own pleasure at the blessings of a relative nearness ("Enter thou among My slaves") and of Absolute Nearness ("Enter thou my Paradise"). In other words, God's own paradise is the paradise of *Riḍwān,* and it is "better than that"—better than paradise in the ordinary sense. The same duality is mentioned and the same precedence reaffirmed in one of the later Revelations:

> God hath promised the believers, the men and the women, gardens that are watered by flowing rivers wherein they shall dwell immortal, abodes of excellence in the Paradise of Eden. And *Riḍwān* from God is greater. That is the immense attainment. (IX, 72)

It is also significant that when a choice was offered by God to the Prophet regarding his future, the end he chose is expressed in dual terms, "the meeting with my Lord and Paradise."[6]

What has been said in these opening paragraphs has been given pride of place in order to make it clear from the outset that, with regard to the supreme spiritual possibility offered to man for his aspiration, the companions of the Prophet were doctrinally well informed. To pass now to the question of method, the following Quranic verses, by general consent among the earliest to be revealed, are particularly significant:

> Keep vigil the night long save a little—a half thereof, or abate a little thereof or add (a little) thereto—and chant the Quran in measure . . . and invoke in remembrance the name of thy Lord and devote Thyself to Him with an utter devotion. (LXXIII, 2–4, 8)

This Revelation enjoins upon the Prophet—and therefore indirectly upon his closest followers—an intensity of worship that goes far beyond anything that could be imposed as a legal obligation upon a whole community. It is to be noticed, moreover, that what has always been the essence of Sufi practice, the invocation of the Divine Name, is prescribed already here, at the outset of the religion, possibly even before the ritual prayer had been shown to the Prophet and certainly well before the five daily prayers had been established as the central aspect of the exoteric path. The other most essential aspects of Sufi method, if not all as early as this, are nonetheless of apostolic origin. Some were established in Mecca, others in Medina. One of them, the spiritual retreat (*i'tikāf* or *khalwah*), is in fact pre-Islamic and may be said to mark a continuity between Abrahamic esoterism and Islamic esoterism. As to its complement, the spiritual gathering for the performance of communal voluntary rites (which may include one or more of the obligatory prayers if they should happen to be due), it takes its name, "session of remembrance" (*majlis al-dhikr*), from the many traditions in which the Prophet mentioned it with praise. The Sufis have kept these two practices alive throughout the centuries, and, generally speaking, they are the only Muslims who still practice them today. The same applies to certain other aspects of Sufi method which have been inherited from the Prophet and his companions.

If the term *dhikr,* "remembrance" or "invocation," is used above all in the sense of the already quoted verse—"Invoke in remembrance the name of thy Lord"—it has always been used by extension to include other practices, such as the reading or chanting of the Quran as well as the recitation, usually a specific number of times, of certain Quranic verses or other formulas recommended by the Revelation or by the Prophet. Needless to say, the recitation of the Quran is by no means confined to the Sufis, and the recommended formulas are likewise at the disposition of all Muslims. What distinguishes esoterism here is the methodic regularity of the recitations, that is, their quantity (the Quran enjoins "much *dhikr*"), and the mystical intent that bestows on them their quality. In many Sufi orders three of these formulas are woven into one litany, which expresses a triple aspiration toward purity, perfection, and truth. They are, respectively, the prayer for God's forgiveness, the invocation of blessings and peace upon the Prophet, and the affirmation of the Divine Oneness. We have no reason to suppose that such composite litanies were recited at the time of the Prophet, but the separate formulas themselves with their respective intentions were unquestionably bequeathed by the first generation of Islam to future seekers of nearness. The prototype of the rosary of beads used by the Sufis is said to have been the knotted cord which the companion Abū Hurayrah devised for himself.

By the time that Islam had become firmly established in Medina, the esoterists were already a minority. This is clear from a Revelation that came not long after the *hijrah,* which speaks of "a group of those that are with these" (LXXIII, 20) in reference to those of the companions who followed most closely the practices of the Prophet and who may therefore be considered to form a spiritual elect. The purpose of the verse in question was to modify somewhat the long night vigils, which, as we have seen, had been imposed by one of the earliest Revelations. But this modification is not to be considered merely as a concession to exoterism. It should rather be taken together with another verse revealed about the same time, "We have appointed you a middle nation" (II, 143), as evidence of the providential leaning of the new religion as a whole, including its esoteric aspect, toward moderation and normality—that is, conformity to the nature of things. Significant also in this respect is a conversation between the Prophet and one of his companions which likewise took place in the early years at Medina. ʿUthmān ibn Maẓʿūn was, according to his brother-in-law ʿUmar, "the severest of us all in abstaining from the things of this world." It was to him that the Prophet said: "Hast thou not in me an example?" And when ʿUthmān fervently assented, the Prophet told him to cease his practice of fasting every day and keeping vigil every night. "Verily thine eyes have their rights over thee, and thy body hath its rights, and thy family have their rights. So pray, and sleep, and fast, and break fast."[7] Natural pleasures consecrated by praise and thanks were the *dhikr* of primordial man, and it was as a mode of remembrance of God that the Prophet mentioned them together with worship in his well-known utterance: "It hath been given me to love perfume and women, and coolness hath been brought to mine eyes in the prayer."[8] Although not denying the exemplary nature of the Prophet, the more ascetic Sufis of subsequent generations would no doubt have justified the lengths to which they went on the grounds that they themselves were in greater need of purification than the companions had been. But the golden mean of the Prophet, the balance between abstentions for the sake of God and natural pleasures spiritualized by gratitude to God and by intellectual perception of their Divine Archetypes, has always had a powerful strain of representatives among the Sufis—not the least illustrious.

Thus far, with regard to the origins of Sufi method, we have considered only voluntary devotions and not those which the Law of Islam makes obligatory and which are therefore practiced by all Muslims. As far as they concern the majority, they may be called exoteric. In virtue of their simplicity and transparency, however, they could be described as exoterized esoterism; and as practiced by the spiritual minority they are re-esoterized. "The esoterism of these practices resides not only in their obvious initiatic symbolism, it resides also in the fact that our practices are esoteric to the extent that we ourselves are esoteric."[9] Moreover, the obligatory rites of Islam revert all the more easily to their basic inward significance by reason of the performer's independence of any intermediary—inasmuch as every Muslim is his own priest. Nor can there be any doubt that the origin of this interiorization of the outward is to be traced back to the Prophet himself. A great and far-reaching precedent that he established in this respect is in his well-known utterance on returning from one of his last campaigns: "We have returned from the Lesser Holy War to the Greater Holy War,"[10] and in his subsequent definition of the Greater Holy War as "the war against the soul" (*jihād al-nafs*). Since he said also that the *jihād* of women was the pilgrimage, it is therefore possible—and indeed necessary for those who have the vocation—to differentiate between an outer and an inner pilgrimage. The same applies to the fast and to almsgiving, which symbolize respectively abstention from the world and giving oneself to God. As to the ritual prayer, we have already seen the innermost significance of the prostration which marks its climax. The difference between exoterism and esoterism depends here, as also for the ritual ablution which precedes the prayer, on "the extent to which we ourselves are esoteric," that is, in these

27. "Sufis in Ecstasy," attributed to Muhammad Nadir al-Samarqandi, Mughal, ca. 1650–1655, Johnson Album 7, No. 5.

two cases, the depth and scope of our conceptions—and therefore our intentions—of humility and purity.

The first pillar of Islam, which sums up the whole religion, exoterically as well as esoterically, consists of the two testimonies "There is no divinity but God" and "Muḥammad is the Messenger of God." Here again, it is a question of the extent of understanding and aspiration. For one who has a sense of the Absolute, that is, an adequate sense of Divinity, the first testimony allows only a fleeting ephemerality to other than God. When the esoterist says there is no divinity but God, included in his meaning is the truth that there is no reality save the one Reality. In the face of objection, he can quote the saying of the Prophet with regard to what preceded creation: "God was, and there was nothing with Him" and the appended comment, anonymous but in itself irrefutable, "He is now even as He was."[11] The exoterist can make nothing of this, but he cannot deny it, for to do so would be to incur the blasphemy of ascribing mutation to the Immutable. The Quran, moreover, upholds the rights of the Absolute:

> There is no god save Him. Everything will perish save His Face. His is the command, and unto Him ye will be brought back. (XXVIII, 88)

Also relevant is the verse from which are derived the Sufi terms *fanā*' (extinction) and *baqā*' (subsistence, remaining, survival, eternity):

> All that is thereon suffereth extinction: and there remaineth the Face of Thy Lord in Its Majesty and Bounty. (LV, 26–27)

This is the level of *Riḍwān,* the beatific reintegration of manifested spirits into the Infinite Oneness of the "Hidden Treasure." This designation of the Divine Essence is taken from the holy tradition: "I was a Hidden treasure, and I loved to be known, and so I created the world."

As to the second testimony, it establishes a communion between the relative and its Origin-End, the Absolute, inasmuch as a messenger not only proceeds from his sender but also returns to him. If Muḥammad is an ideal and therefore a model, the first thing to be imitated is his most essential characteristic, namely, this communion, and with it as intense a consciousness as possible of the whence of Origin and the whither of End.

It does not appear to be on record that the Prophet was ever asked in so many words to define his own most essential characteristic. But when a person whose function it is to be the personification of excellence is asked to define excellence, the chief point of the question is that the answer should be subjective. What is in fact hoped for is the answer to that other question. When asked "What is excellence?" by the archangel, the Prophet might have replied, "Muḥammad is the Messenger of God," except that it would have been too elliptical. His answer was nonetheless parallel to the second testimony of Islam in that it traces out a line of connection between the Absolute and the relative: "Excellence is that thou shouldst worship God as if thou sawest Him. And if thou seest Him not, yet He seeth Thee."[12]

In the case of the Prophet himself—and by extension the saint—that line is operative in both directions. "As if thou sawest him," which has a more negative implication than the Arabic original, could almost be translated, "as one that seeth Him"; it could, moreover, be paraphrased "as one whose heart is awake," and the Prophet said on another occasion, "My heart is awake." Also relevant are the words of the already quoted holy tradition "and when I love him . . . I am the eye wherewith he seeth." For those whom God loves, the Absolute "lends" its sight to the relative so that the primordial line of vision from earth to heaven, disconnected by the fall, may be reestablished. The essential function of man is mediation, which means that human excellence depends precisely on access to the Transcendent. As to "worship," it includes faith and practice, both of which the archangel had asked the Prophet to define before asking him about excellence (*iḥsān*). "To worship God as if thou sawest Him" thus means excellence of faith (*īmān*) and excellence of conformity (*islām*) to the Divine Will, expressed by the Law.

This amounts to the addition of a third dimension to faith and practice, that of height and depth, the axis of man's mediation between heaven and earth. Nor are the Sufis alone among Muslims in holding that *iḥsān* is the domain of mysticism or esoterism, that is, of Sufism.

Since Sufism is based, as we have seen, on a revelation that is not for esoterists only, it is necessarily linked with an exoterism together with which it forms a religion. That religion, like Buddhism and Christianity and unlike Hinduism and Judaism, is a world religion. But unlike the other two world religions, Islam is based, like Judaism, on a revealed message rather than on the messenger himself. That message is, moreover, the last revelation of this cycle of time, which means that its inner aspect, in addition to the universality that every esoterism possesses by its very nature, will also be universal in the way that any final summing up is bound to be. Significant in this respect is the Islamic *credo*, which affirms belief "in God and His Angels and His Books and His Messengers" (II, 285). Moreover, man is the representative (*khalīfah*) of God, and a representative must conform to the nature of Him Whom he represents, in Whose image he is made. The stage is, as it were, set for universality in the following verse:

Unto God are the East and the West, and whithersoever ye turn, there is the Face of God. Verily God is Infinitely Vast, Infinitely Knowing." (II, 115)

Three times the Quran complains: "They esteem not God as He hath the right to be esteemed" (VI, 91; XXII, 74; XXXIX, 67), nor does it tolerate, in particular, such narrownesses of perspective, which tends, without being conscious of the fact, to sacrifice the Glory of God to the glory of one particular religion. More than one exoteric outlook is based on assumptions which, if pushed to their logical conclusions, would seem to imply that God has left large parts of the globe in spiritual darkness for long periods of time. The Quran sweeps all such illusions aside: "For every nation there is a Messenger" (X, 47), and "Verily We have sent Messengers before thee, about some We have told thee, and about some We have not told thee" (XL, 78). We may quote also, in this connection the following: "Verily the Faithful [Muslims] and the Jews and the Christians and the Sabaeans—whoso hath faith in God and the Last Day and doeth deeds of piety—their meed is kept for them with their Lord, and no fear shall come upon them, neither shall they grieve" (II, 62). Finally, lest it be imagined that such declarations refer only to the past and that all other revelations have been superseded by itself, the Quran expressly states: "For each We have appointed a law and a path; and if God had wished He would have made you one people. . . . So vie one with another in good works. Unto God is your return, all of you together, and He will then inform you of that wherein ye were at variance" (V, 48).[13]

Side by side with universality, there is another characteristic, which belongs to every esoterism as such but which Sufism possesses in a double sense—namely, primordiality. The end of a cycle rejoins, in a sense, its starting point, and Islam is defined as the primordial religion, "God's original upon which he originated mankind" (XXX, 30). This mysterious affinity between the end and the beginning is marked by the Quran's insistence on the miracle of creation. The created universe is set before man as a stuff that is woven with "the signs (or symbols) of God" (*āyāt Allāh*). "The seven heavens and the earth and all therein glorify Him. Nothing is, but glorifieth Him with Praise" (XVII, 44). The praise in question is the fact of manifesting an aspect of the Divinity, and there is absolutely nothing that does not owe its existence to the overflow of the Divine Nature in Its Will to manifest Itself. The holy tradition quoted above, "I was a Hidden Treasure, and I loved to be known, and so I created the world," may be said to sum up the cosmogonic doctrine of all mysticism. For the esoterist, creation means nothing other than God's manifestation of Himself. There could be no possible divergence between the Christian mystic, for example, and the

Sufi in this respect. But it cannot be said that the New Testament is haunted by the idea of creation, whereas in the Quran the theme of God's creation of the world is like a continually repeated refrain. The Sufi, formed by the Quran, has the obligation to be primordial not only in his aspiration to regain the original perfection of man—the preliminary goal of every mysticism—but also in what might be called "creation-consciousness." It is reasonable to suppose that our first ancestors were of all men the least in need of being reminded how they and the world came into existence. If religion was not yet necessary, that was because the "ligament," after which religion is named and which it seeks to *re*novate, was still vibrant. To use the traditional symbol of the tree as an image of the cosmos—both of macrocosm and microcosm—the first men were profoundly and directly aware of being attached to their Divine Root, and they extended this subjective certainty to all that surrounded them. Everything was an object of wonder, in virtue of the Transcendent Reality which it manifested, the Hidden Treasure which it had to make known. The failure to live up to that attitude—the failure to maintain the consciousness of the symbolic nature of each object, the choice of something for its own sake regardless of its archetype—was the cause of the fall. Typical of the Quran and of the perspective it has generated is its dismissal of any need for miracles in the ordinary sense. The following passage is primordial also in virtue of its extreme simplicity: "Will they not behold the camels, how they are created? And the firmament, how it is raised aloft? And the mountains, how they are established? And the earth, how it is spread?" (LXXXVIII, 17–20).

Primordiality and universality—the one implies the other. At the beginning of a cycle, prejudices, partialities, and other factors of limitation have not yet come into existence to blur and distort man's conception of the nature of things. Both universality and primordiality are reflected, to a certain extent, in the outer aspects of Islam. But both are by definition esoteric, and there is a limit to what the exoteric Muslim can draw from them. It falls upon the Sufi alone to do justice to the universal and primordial aspects of the Quranic message. Nor can there be any adequate definition of the nature of Sufism which fails to take into account this burden and this privilege. However, few members of the Sufi orders are in fact able to escape sufficiently from the contagious limitations of the exoterism that surrounds them.

In virtue of its claim to be *al-Furqān* (the Criterion, the Distinguisher), the Quran demands extreme discrimination, which likewise dominates the Sufi perspective as complement to universality. The structure of the universe calls for a sense of hierarchy. Although everything reflects a Divine Aspect and "nothing is, but glorifieth Him with praise," the praise is loud or faint, the reflection clear or dim, in proportion to the nearness or farness of the world of the praiser and according to the praiser's own relatively central or peripheric status in that world. The Quran insists continually on differences and precedences, often in asides addressed to the esoteric minority and prefixed with vocatives such as "O ye who have insight" or "O ye who have hearts." The Sufi has no choice but to be vigilant, observant, and discerning, to put everything in its rightful place, and to give everything its due.

Vastness and precision—these two intellectual demands made of the Sufi—are complementary aspects of the perspective of Truth which characterizes Islam as a whole and which its esoterism has the responsibility of carrying to the widest and deepest conclusions. It is in virtue of this perspective that Sufism is a way of knowledge rather than a way of love. As such it tends to repudiate partialities which the perspective of love necessarily condones and even encourages. Fidelity to a person means looking neither to the right nor to the left, and the New Testament, which tells of a way of love, is, as it were, wrapped round the person after whom this way is named. Fidelity to truth, on the other hand, means looking as far as possible—and as clearly as possible—in all directions, and that is the outlook which the Quran imposes. Two of the great Sufis have nonetheless been called "the Lover" (Sumnūn ibn Ḥamzah al-Baṣrī [d. 303/915]) and "the Sultan of those who long" ('Umar ibn al-Fāriḍ [d. 632/1235]). This second title has its implication for Sufism as a whole, since "the longers" are the Sufis. But the love in question is rather the result than the starting point of metaphysical penetration: in other words, it is based on Oneness which transcends all duality. As such its presupposes the extinction (*fanā'*) of the relative in the Absolute, the finite in the Infinite.

The Sufi doctrine of *al-baqā' ba'd al-fanā'* (survival after extinction) or *fanā' al-fanā'* (the extinction of extinction) is implicit in the verse quoted above: "All that is thereon suffereth extinction, and there remaineth the Face of Thy Lord in Its Majesty and Bounty." Of particular significance is the final word. If it be asked how there can be any question of bounty when all its possible recipients have been extinguished, the answer is that a mother's bounty to an unborn child in her womb is a symbol of the bounty of the Divine Essence to the archetypes of all beings which are mysteriously one with It. But by inverse analogy the state of the embryo in the womb is the state of least development, whereas in the Essence the archetypes are the Supreme Plenitudes from which all manifested beings derive and into which they are ultimately reabsorbed. These archetypes are what Muḥyī al-Dīn ibn 'Arabī terms "the immutable essences" (*al-a'yān al-thābitah*),[14] and they are the themes of his lines: "We were letters, exalted, not yet altered,

Held aloft in the Keep of the Highest of Summits. I therein am Thou, and We are Thou, and Thou art He, and all is in He is He—ask of any that so far hath reached."[15]

To approach the same truth from another angle, one of the "signs" most frequently held out to man by the Quran for his meditation is "the difference between day and night." This difference is richly symbolic at more than one level. But above all, transcending all differentiation yet retaining all that is positive in differentiation, day and night have, as their Divine Prototypes, the Majesty and Beauty (or Bounty) of God, that is, the Absolute and the Infinite respectively. But since day may be said to come forth from night, day represents, below its highest significance of Majesty, the whole of manifestation that proceeds from the Infinite Night of the Essence. As the Supreme Object of aspiration, the Essence is thus personified as *Laylā,* a woman's name meaning "Night"; and from the fourth/tenth century to the present day, many Sufi love poems have been addressed to her. In this context the stars are immutable essences. Hidden in the day of illusion, they come into their own in the Night of Reality. In his poem to Laylā, the Shaykh al-ʿAlawī thus affirms his own spiritual realization in these words: "My star resplendeth in her firmament."[16] A thousand years previously "the Lover" had expressed the same reality, addressing himself directly to God, and using the symbolism of the ocean, which is parallel to that of night: "Thou hast thrown me to swim in the ocean of Thy holiness, And inexistent, without trace, I desire Thee from within Thee."[17] Both formulations are typical of Sufism inasmuch as they are expressions of love within the framework of gnosis, and both are related to the mystery of *Riḍwān.*

Another question that needs to be considered in connection with the nature of Sufism is that of development. If the esoterism of every religion is a prolongation of the presence of its founder, it must also be something of a compensation for his absence. And if Sufism has its roots in the apostolic age and draws in fact its substance from that age, it has also been enriched directly and "vertically," in various domains, by the inspirations with which the great spiritual masters have been blessed throughout the centuries.

It has already been said that all essential aspects of Sufi method are of apostolic origin. That is what the Sufis claim. And, if occasion arises, in justification of the rhythmic bodily movement performed in many of the orders at their sessions of remembrance, they quote the saying of the Prophet: "Ungenerous is he who shaketh not at the remembrance of the Beloved." Moreover, it is in the nature of things to sway from side to side or to make some other comparable movement as an aid to concentration.

It is scarcely possible, however, to account in this way for a formal dance such as is performed by the Mawlawīs, who are known to the West as "the whirling dervishes." The essential feature of the dance is the whirling motion upon the axis of the perfectly upright body with arms stretched out to the full on either side, the right palm upward to receive the graces of heaven and the left palm downward to transmit them to earth. This bodily enactment of universality and primordiality is altogether Quranic in spirit, but it was destined to remain latent for more than six centuries until it dropped, as a gift from heaven, upon Jalāl al-Dīn Rūmī, the great seventh/thirteenth-century Persian Sufi who lived in Anatolia. Earlier and later Sufi masters have also been inspired with movements which, if less spectacular than the Mawlawī dance, can be no less operative as aids to concentration. In one sense such "postapostolic" practices are not "essential aspects of Sufi method," since they are not practiced in all the orders. But in themselves they are of undeniably essential spiritual importance, and as such they must be counted as an exception—one might say the only exception—to the general rule of apostolic origin for all that is essential in Sufi method.

The exoterism which, in Islam, surrounds esoterism is in general suspicious of any practice or theory that has no warrant from the apostolic age. Rightly so, since there is no heresy that does not claim to be based on a special Divine Inspiration. For the Sufis these considerations impose a discretion and even a secrecy which are not unfavorable to esoterism and which have their roots in Medina, from the last years of the Prophet's life. Abū Hurayrah said: "I have treasured in my memory two stores of knowledge which I had from the Messenger of God. One of them I have divulged; but if I divulged the other, ye would cut this throat," and he pointed to his own neck.[18]

It is no doubt in the domain of doctrine that most of the Sufi acquisitions since the outset of Islam are to be found—not with regard to the principles themselves but by way of analytical formulations—and we have already seen the striking example of Ibn 'Arabī's theory of "the immutable essences." The whole work in which this occurs is manifestly at a very high degree of inspiration, and the same may be said of other Sufi treatises, by him and by others. Likewise relevant to this context are utterances that lie at the opposite pole from analysis, flashes of poetic light, and also ejaculated aphorisms, typical of Sufism, such as "the Sufi is not created" and "thine existence is a sin wherewith no other sin may be compared." These are purely esoteric; but mention must be made, in addition, of more general blessings, likewise held in reserve by Providence for nonapostolic and therefore more needy generations—modes of development which, though initially dependant on Sufism, concern the whole of Islam. The Prophet promised: "The earth shall never be found lacking in forty men of the like of the Friend [Abraham] of the All-Merciful. Through them shall ye be given to drink, and through them shall ye be given to eat." The forty men are clearly the esoteric nucleus which constitutes the heart of the religion. Just as the heart of the breast receives the mysterious gift of life from above and then transmits it to the rest of the body, so Sufism—"the heart of Islam," as it is often called—is obliged to transmit a sufficiency of what it receives to the arteries of the religion in its entirety. In connection with the closing words of the above promise, it must be remembered that every religion, during the first few centuries of its existence, has to develop its own particular civilization and make it as perfect as possible a setting for its spirituality. One of the dominating elements of every such setting, that is, of every theocratic civilization, is sacred art, which, far from being a mere human invention, must always come initially as a gift from heaven. The history of sacred art shows it to be inextricably bound up with esoterism in every age and clime, and Sufism had an untold influence on the development of the sacred arts of Islam, of which the most important are no doubt architecture and calligraphy.[19]

These last paragraphs must not, however, be allowed to give the impression that Sufism is pervaded by what is sometimes called "the spirit of development." Aside from the question of providential acquisitions which are part of the normal growth of a traditional civilization, the Sufis are the most implacably conservative element in the Islamic community. In other words, if they necessarily yield to pressure from above, they have shown themselves to be, like the representatives of all other esoterisms, adamantine in resisting pressures from below, like those which demand "conformity to the age in which we live." Such slogans are parried by Sufism, in virtue of the "*furqānic*" discrimination that it stands for, by the question: "Does the age deserve conformity to it?" The same sense of values includes both the consciousness of all that is most essential to the spiritual heritage of Islam and the will to protect it. For three generations and more, the Sufis have been blamed throughout the Near and Middle East for "centuries of stagnation in the Muslim world," and they have incurred hostility from many sides as the last outposts of resistance to modernization in every Islamic country. Only now is there a gleam of recognition, perhaps increasing, that the Sufis were right.

Notes

1. Ibn 'Arabī, *al-Futūhāt al makkiyyah* (Beirut: Dār Ṣādir, n.d.) 2: 16, 214, 263, 561.

2. Ibn Ḥanbal, II, 421.
3. This saying in various forms is mentioned by Farīd al-Dīn ʿAṭṭar, in his *Manṭiq al-ṭayr* and in many other classical works of Sufism.
4. Bukhārī, LXXXI, 37.
5. Muslim, LI, 2.
6. Ibn Isḥāq, 1000.
7. Ibn Saʿd, III/1, 289–90.
8. Ibn Saʿd, I/2, 112.
9. F. Schuon, *Sufism: Veil and Quintessence,* trans. W. Stoddart (Bloomington, IN: World Wisdom, 1981) 147.
10. Aḥmad al-Bayhaqī, *al-Sunan al-kubrā* (*Kitāb al-zuhd*).
11. Bukhārī, LIX, 1.
12. Muslim, I, 1.
13. The Quran speaks with the voice of Divinity not only in the first person (both singular and plural) but also in the third person, sometimes changing from one to the other in two consecutive sentences as here.
14. *Fuṣūṣ al-ḥikam,* chapter on Seth.
15. Quoted in a seventh-eighth/thirteenth-fourteenth century Sufi treatise of uncertain authorship, *Laṭāʾif al-iʿlām* from Ibn ʿArabī's *al-Manāzil al-insāniyyah* (a presumably lost work). I am indebted to M. Chodkiewicz for this reference.
16. Cf. M. Lings, *A Sufi Saint of the Twentieth Century* (London: Allen & Unwin, 1971) 225.
17. Abū Naṣr al-Sarrāj, *Kitāb al-lumaʿ*, ed. R. A. Nicholson (London: Luzac, 1914) 250.
18. Bukhārī, III, 42.
19. See T. Burckhardt, *Art of Islam* (London: Festival of the World of Islam, 1976) 9; M. Lings, *The Quranic Art of Calligraphy and Illumination* (London: Festival of the World of Islam, 1976) 13–41, 100–101.

13

The Early Development of Sufism

VICTOR DANNER

The Period of Revelation

SUFISM TRACES ITS ORIGINS back to the Quranic revelation and the *Sunnah* (norm) of the Prophet. If we examine a typical *silsilah,* or chain of transmission of a Sufi order, we note that the Divine Name *Allāh* comes first, followed by the name of the archangel Gabriel (or *Jibra'īl,* in Arabic), after which comes that of Muḥammad, and then the name of one or another of his companions, and so on through a series of different names until we reach the latest teacher of Sufism in our days. The *silsilah* really indicates that the ultimate origin and root of the path (*ṭarīqah*) is to be found in the Divinity, who revealed it to the Messenger through the archangel of Revelation, Gabriel, the personification of the revelatory function of the Spirit. Because the path traced out by the Prophet has a transcendent spiritual inception, it cannot but manifest itself in the Quran and in the *Sunnah,* the two foundations of the Islamic religion. These two are also the foundations for the Law (*Sharī'ah*) of Islam, which has to do with the domain of action, whereas the path is concerned with the life of contemplation. That both the Law and the path should repose on the same Quran and *Sunnah* simply shows that we can look at the Islamic message from two different but complementary perspectives, the exoteric and the esoteric. The latter is the spiritual or mystical content of the doctrine of Divine Unity (*tawḥīd*), and the former is the literal or even the purely dogmatic affirmation that God is One. Both dimensions are to be found in the Quran and in the *Sunnah.* In other words, there is an esoteric spiritual interpretation of the revealed Book and of the *Sunnah* of the Prophet that is addressed to a small mystical minority of contemplatives. And there is an exoteric interpretation that reaches out to the vast majority of believers, who are not preoccupied with contemplation for many reasons, but who are attentive to the commandments and prohibitions contained in the Law of Islam.[1]

Since exoteric Islam embraces the overwhelming mass of believers, it is not surprising that the Quran and the *Sunnah* seem exclusively addressed to them, with apparently no provisions for the contemplatives of the community. This is not a historical accident that could have been otherwise; both the Book and the Prophet of Islam do seem, at first glance, quite ordinary when compared, for example, with the mystical message of the Gospels or the mysterious and even dazzling spiritual nature of the Christ, who divulged the mystical truths in the marketplace, so to speak. It is only after immersion into the inner depths of the Quranic revelation and the *Sunnah* of the Prophet that we discover a spiritual world previously unnoticed on the exoteric surface of the religion. What this means is that it is the contemplative mind that can perceive the deeper layers of the Revelation or that can sense the inner being of the Prophet. The exoteric mind does not fathom the mystical facets of the Islamic Faith and tends even to reject them. Yet to understand the spiritual teachings of Islam, one must first grasp the conventional or exoteric message. It is all a question of degree: *tawḥīd,* therefore, can be simple and rather literal in meaning, or it can be deep and metaphysical. Between those two extremes there are innumerable stratifications of meaning. This is as much as to say that the *Shahādah* (testimony of faith), which is the sacred formulation of *tawḥīd* in Islam, can be interpreted in exoteric and esoteric terms: *Lā ilāha illa'Llāh, Muḥammadun rasūl Allāh* ("There is no divinity but God, Muḥammad is the Messenger of God") is the most concise expression of *tawḥīid,* not only from the exoteric viewpoint of the Law but also and, above all, from the spiritual outlook of Sufi esoterism.

Although neither the Quran nor the Messenger of Islam seems mystical to the outsider, whether Muslim or non-Muslim, this is not because there are no esoteric truths objectively present in them. Rather, it is because of the subjective veiling of the outsider. For Sufism, that veiling, which is equivalent to the blindness of the inner eye of the Spirit within man, "the eye of the heart" (*'ayn al-qalb*), is either temporary and curable or permanent and incurable. The path, when all is said and done, is really the progressive unveiling of the inner eye, which then begins to see what it had not perceived before. But until then, its subjective state is one of blindness. That being so, the mystical or esoteric truths embedded in the verses of the Quran or in the statements and deeds of the Prophet's *Sunnah* will not be intuited save by a person of contemplative intelligence. However, given that Sufi esoterism is not of uniform outlook, it stands to reason that one will discover different and even conflicting attitudes within the ranks of the Sufis themselves on the contents of the Islamic message, even though all would agree that theirs is an esoteric as opposed to an exoteric interpretation.[2]

The *ṭarīqah* that the Messenger of Islam brought to this community was a spiritual path based on the realization of the love and knowledge of Allah. The *Sharī'ah* that he established furnished the prescriptive framework of actions that served as the foundation, so to speak, upon which the aspirant could build his devotional and sapiential life. The norm left behind by the Prophet—his all-embracing *Sunnah*—is addressed to all aspirations in his community and contains directives for both the contemplative and the noncontemplative life, the latter covering warfare, commerce, marriage, liturgy, morality, government, and a host of commandments and prohibitions addressed to the individual and society in general. It is obvious that the mystical and nonmystical facets of his *Sunnah* are not always in harmonious balance or that they cannot be pursued simultaneously to the limit without sooner or later extinguishing the inner life altogether ("For the letter killeth, but the Spirit giveth life," according to the Gospel). To be an example for all in his community, however, the Prophet had to balance the contemplative and the active life in such a way that even the most modest spiritual aspirations among the believers could be integrated into the Faith without any hesitation.

The Nature of the *Ṭarīqah*

According to the *Bhagavad-Gita* of the Hindu tradition, the ways of approaching God can be subsumed under the headings of action, love, and knowledge, individuals being vocationally drawn to God through one or another of those paths. The founders of religion—the great Avataras, as the Hindus would say—are themselves a synthesis of the three approaches because they are examples to their respective communities. It is true that Muḥammad would not be considered an Avatara within the Islamic world because that presupposes the divinization of the Messenger and, therefore, associationism (*shirk*), which is opposed to *tawḥīd.* But as Messenger he nevertheless represents in his mission the three approaches. The *Sharī'ah* that he brought is a good example of the path of action, which has in view the paradisal states within which there is no more suffering or death. The path of love is exemplified in his devotional attitudes toward the personal nature of Allah, as Lord of the Universe, and as described in the anthropomorphic Names of the Divinity contained in the Quran. The path of knowledge of the Messenger is best seen in those statements of his having to do with the nonanthropomorphic Names of the Divinity, those that refer to the impersonal Divine Essence, the One in the absolute sense. In short, the ninety-nine Names of Allah that we find in the Quran, "the Most Beautiful Names," as the scripture says, can be viewed in accordance with the ways of action, love, or knowledge—or all of these approaches simultaneously. Indeed, the Divine Names play a role in the metaphysical, spiritual, and cosmological esoterism of the Sufis that is of capital importance.

The religion that Muḥammad left behind was based on three principles, *islām* (submission), *īmān* (faith), and *iḥsān* (virtue or morality), which were described in a famous *ḥadīth* wherein the archangel Gabriel, in the form of a man, interrogated the Prophet. The principle of *islām* refers to the five pillars of the religion, namely, the testimony of faith (*Shahādah*), the five daily ritual prayers (*ṣalāt*), the fast of Ramaḍān (*ṣawm Ramaḍān*), the legal alms (*zakāt*), and the pilgrimage to Mecca (*ḥajj*). The principle of *īmān* is the elementary creed of the religion: faith in Allah, His angels, His Books, His messengers, the Day of Judgment, and the predestination of good and evil. Finally, the principle of *iḥsān* is summed up in the famous sentence: "It is that thou shouldst adore God as if thou were to see Him; for if thou seest Him not, He in any case seeth thee." All three of these principles describe likewise the condition of the Muslim or of Islam: they are descriptive, and even normative, and the individual as well as the community at large rises or falls in accordance with their presence or absence in him or in society as a whole. But at the same time they are interrelated: the more *iḥsān* in the believer, the more *īmān* and *islām*, in the deeper sense, he will have. The opposite is also true: the less *iḥsān*, the less *īmān* and *islām* in him. It is not for nothing that the Sufis have made the art or science of *iḥsān* the key to the spiritual path. In this connection it is well to remember that the three principles can be seen from an exoteric point of view as well as from the esoteric. Likewise, they can be interpreted from the perspectives of action, love, or knowledge, or all together. All of this has to be borne in mind when assessing the nature of the Prophet. His *islām*, *īmān*, and *iḥsān* were simple enough in formulation and deed to capture the imagination of the generality of believers; yet they contain the esoteric premises of a deeply contemplative life, when seen in conjunction with the mystical aspects of his *Sunnah* and the Quran.

In spite of all that has just been said about the mystical elements in the Quran and the *Sunnah*, most Western scholars see nothing particularly spiritual about either one. This means that the development of Sufism must have come about from extraneous, non-Islamic sources, not from the revealed message of Islam itself. As previously stated, however, Sufism bases itself on the Quran and the *Sunnah*, mystically interpreted. This leads to the conclusion that the Quran is really the first and foremost mystical text of Islam and that the Prophet is the first and the greatest of the Sufi sages and saints, even though the term *ṣūfī,* in reality, is of later origin. Both modernist Muslims, who are antitraditional and get their ideas from Western sources anyway, and diehard fundamentalists, who are opposed to the mystical or contemplative life, reject such conclusions out of hand. Although some Westerners accept the possibility that there is something spiritual in either the Quran or the Prophet, or even in both together, the general tendency is to strip both of their transcendent nature and to account for the presence of a mystical tradition in Islam by reference to non-Islamic doctrines such as Neoplatonism, Hinduism, Buddhism, Christianity, and the like.[3] But there is a confusion here between the spiritual reality of Sufism and its verbal expressions. The latter can easily incorporate foreign formulations drawn from Neoplatonism, for example, if they correspond more exactly to the inspirations of the Sufi teachers. There is nothing unusual in that process, especially in view of the fact that Neoplatonism is simply a Greek intellectual mysticism that could not but square, in a somewhat more analytical fashion, with the Semitic expressions of the Sufi esoterists of early Islam.

Mysticism is a teaching about the Divine Reality and a method of realization that permits the seeker to reach It in one way or another. In Islam, that teaching revolves around *tawḥīd,* which is the central doctrine of both the Quran and the *Sunnah.* The method of realization has always been "the remembrance of God" (*dhikr Allāh*), which has no doubt many general meanings, going from the simple recitation of Quranic verses to the permanent invocation of a Divine Name, particularly *Allāh.* The essence of the Islamic Faith is to be found in *tawḥīd* and *dhikr:* the former dissolves the associationism (*shirk*) that is characteristic of fallen human nature, and the latter removes the tendency toward forgetfulness (*ghaflah*) that is part and parcel of the fall. The mystic's *tawḥīd* and *dhikr* are not different in kind from those of the ordinary Muslim throughout the ages; but they are different in degree and quality, and that is precisely what constitutes the distinction between the exoteric and the esoteric view of things. For the Sufis, the Prophet's *tawḥīd* and *dhikr* embraced both the nonmystical and mystical levels of Islam, and could not but do so, given that he was to be a model for his entire community and not just simply for the mystics or the nonmystics.

In addition to the doctrine and the method of concentration, the Messenger also bequeathed to the contemplatives of his community the initiatic pact (*bayʿah*), which is the Muḥammadan grace (*barakah muḥammadiyyah*) transmitted from master to master throughout the centuries and from them to their disciples. This is said to be the "second birth," which is purely spiritual. It is referred to in Islam as "the pact of Divine Contentment" (*bay'at al-riḍwān;* cf. Quran XLVIII, 10). One of the significations of the *silsilah* in the Sufi orders has been to show the unbroken transmission of that initiatic grace throughout the long centuries from the Messenger's day to those masters of our times who confer the *bay'ah.*

Finally, mention must also be made of the aesthetic legacy left by the Prophet as an important aspect of the *ṭarīqah.*[4] This has to do not only with the protocol of conduct (*ādāb*) between the Prophet and his companions but also the actual aesthetic ambience he left behind as an integral part of his *Sunnah:* the fact of his sitting on the ground surrounded by circles of his companions; the clothing worn by him; the spiritual retreats he performed and the character of his pious life; and the general aesthetic atmosphere found in his home and in the places of worship. All of that became a kind of prototypal form that would be developed into more sophisticated and even more ornate structures later on in the history of Sufism. The aesthetic *Sunnah* of the Prophet especially has played a considerable role in the contemplative life of Islam.

Those four elements—the spiritual doctrine on *tawḥīd,* the method of concentration known as the *dhikr,* the initiatic *bay'ah,* and the aesthetic *Sunnah* of the Prophet—also have their exoteric applications in the conventional forms of Islam. The *Sharī'ah* has its own version of *tawḥīd,* its own "remembrance" in the daily ritual prayers, its own pact in commercial and political agreements, and its own aesthetic forms in the mosques and other religious edifices, not to mention the traditional garments. Here it is important to remember that, in talking about the *ṭarīqah* as a mystical way, one is talking not simply about abstract teachings unrelated to daily existence but about a whole way of life that is imbedded in the Islamic religion and that is the actual heart of the tradition.

The Companions of the Prophet

When the Prophet died (in 11/632), the religion he had founded was transmitted to posterity through his Companions, who occupy a rank all unto themselves in the eyes of the Muslims because of their proximity to him. The tradition has never fixed once and for all the actual number of his Companions. When the number is quite large, it is easy to see that not all of them could have been mystics, to say the least. For example, the first Umayyad caliph, Mu'āwiyah (d. 60/680), is sometimes considered to be a Companion, but it would be difficult indeed to attribute any contemplative traits to him. When, on the other hand, the number of Companions is quite small, including the first four caliphs of Islam ("the orthodox caliphs," who reigned from 11–40/632–661), then it is possible to discern a more mystical mentality among them. Sufism also points to some of the Prophet's wives as having an esoteric cast of mind, such as Khadījah, 'Ā'ishah, and Zaynab, not to mention his daughter Fāṭimah. Among his Companions, Abū Bakr, 'Umar, 'Uthmān, 'Alī, Abū Hurayrah, Salmān al-Fārsī, and others are seen as mystical sages.

From all of these individuals the tradition has preserved sayings, proverbs, deeds, poems, or sermons, according to case. Some of these words belonged to "the People of the Veranda" (*ahl al-ṣuffah*), who led a contemplative and saintly existence in the Prophet's mosque in Medina. But in no case do we find extensive works on the spiritual life emanating from the Companions. We have to await the caliphate of the Imam 'Alī ibn Abī Ṭālib (d. 40/661) before numerous sermons, long letters, poems, and proverbs containing mystical nuggets can be found. Tradition would have it that in the first century of Islam some individuals had many works in their libraries that were compilations of the Imam 'Alī's sermons and letters. All of that has been lost, and what remains is scattered in the early anthologies of Arabic literature or partially collected in the *Nahj al-balāghah* (*The Way of Eloquence*), a famous late Shī'ite compilation by the Sharīf al-Raḍī (d. 406/1015). For the Shī'ites, the *Nahj al-balāghah* is a venerable work because it contains the sermons, letters, and proverbs of the Imam 'Alī, "the third of the three" (the Quran, the Prophet, 'Alī) in his Arabic eloquence. Even if all of its contents could be attributed to the Imam 'Alī, the fact remains that the mystical element is not always present. Nevertheless, the Arabic style of the Imam 'Alī, especially in his sermons and letters, already reveals a much more analytical structure than one finds in the *ḥadīths* or sermons of the Prophet, and this testifies to the development that Arab culture underwent in its contacts with the Persians in Iraq. A number of technical expressions in the *Nahj al-balāghah,* bordering on the philosophical, distinguish the Imam 'Alī's words from those of other Companions. There is a synthetic mysticism in his thinking, with strong intrusions of gnosis (the *'irfān* of the Shī'ite Imams of the first century or so of Islam) here and there. Yet, for all that, the works attributed to the Imam, like the *ḥadīths* of the Prophet, are far from being exclusively mystical—or esoteric, if one will. Instead, one finds in them the three "ways" (action, love, and knowledge) previously mentioned as embodied in the person of the Prophet. His Companions, after all, played the vital role of transmitters who were anxious to ensure that both the Law and the path reached the next generation intact. The Imam 'Alī, therefore, in spite of his being renowned in Islam for his esoteric authority, was also one of the pillars of the exoteric *Sharī'ah.*

If we examine the numerous *silsilahs* of the Sufi orders that go back to the Messenger through one or another of his Companions, the Imam ʿAlī's name crops up more often than that of any other companion.[5] He seems to have had a radiant, charismatic personality already in the days of the Prophet, and he drew around him a party (*shīʿah*) of admiring followers. In contrast, the other Companions, such as Abū Bakr (d. 13/634) or ʿUmar (d. 23/644), the first and second caliphs, seem rather muted in their spirituality, at least in their outward manifestations of it. But the fact of the matter is that the initiatic chain of transmission emanating from the Prophet is not monopolized by the Imam ʿAlī; the names of other Companions, such as Abū Bakr and Abū Hurayrah, just to mention these, are also to be found as transmitters of the Prophet's mystical teachings and practices pertaining to the *ṭarīqah.*

The *silsilah* of the Sufi orders should be understood as a transmission of the four elements previously mentioned as integral parts of the path inaugurated by the Messenger—the doctrine of *tawḥīd,* the *dhikr,* the *bayʿah,* and the aesthetic forms. Although it is seen as a transmission, it must not be construed as devoid of spiritual spontaneity that can, and even must, arrange those fundamental elements in ways that suit the changing circumstances of the times. The Imam ʿAlī's words at Kufa, where he no doubt had numerous contacts with Persian sages and culture, already reflect a certain readaptation of the spiritual life to the novel conditions brought about by the lightning-like expansions of Islam in the reign of the caliph ʿUmar. The Buddhist teachings on the nature of the celestial tactic or strategy (*upaya*) that brings about a fresh new school of Buddhism without distorting the original message of the founder should be applied to the long series of names in the *silsilah* of a typical Sufi order. Each name represents a saintly sage who has readapted the original message of the Prophet to different circumstances, without violating the spirit of the Quranic revelation or of the *Sunnah* in their essential nature. In this respect, it is possible that the Imam ʿAlī played a very crucial role in the first readjustments of Islam, both esoteric and exoteric, when it emerged outside of its Arabian homeland and came into contact with the non-Arab world, especially the Persians in Iraq, whom the Imam knew at first hand. Other Companions, such as Salmān al-Fārsī (Salmān the Persian), who are known for their mystical sapience, no doubt also had similar functions. But the Imam ʿAlī, by virtue of his being part of the *ahl al-bayt* (people of the household) of the Prophet—a designation that included his wife Fāṭimah, who was the Prophet's daughter, and their two sons, Ḥasan and Ḥusayn—had obviously a central authority. We have only to recall that the early Shīʿite Imams of the first century or so of Islam were also authorities in Sunnism and in

Sufism precisely because they were the most prestigious of the Prophet's descendants, the ʿAlids. The later Sufis constantly refer to these early Imams as sages of the path. Since three of them, the Imam ʿAlī (d. 40/661), the Imam Ḥasan (d. ca. 50/670), and the Imam Ḥusayn (d. 61/680), were members of the *ahl al-bayt* and intimately bound up with the Prophet's life and mission, it is only normal that we should find their names in the *silsilahs* of many orders. The descendants of the Prophet through his daughter Fāṭimah and her husband ʿAlī were therefore graced in a twofold fashion: they were the actual descendants of Muḥammad and the transmitters of his eso-exoteric message. That seems to have been their function in the first century of Islam. But they were not the only authorities on the scene, especially with respect to the spiritual path. There were others; their time had not yet come. In the days of the Companions, the integral message of Islam was no doubt transmitted by a number of them, but the Imam ʿAlī was in the forefront, if only because of his charismatic brilliance.

The Followers of the Companions

Within the Islamic tradition, the rank of Companion carries with it the attributes associated with the apostles in the time of Jesus. Thus, the epoch of the Companions is really the apostolic generation in Islam. When the last of the Companions died, the burden of transmission fell on the shoulders of the next rank, the Followers (*al-tābiʿūn*) of the Companions. They did not see the Prophet but were taught by those who did, the Companions. The Followers have a prestige of their own that puts them in a light similar to that of the fathers of the church. In other words, they have a lofty and authoritative spiritual function within the tradition as a whole: they not only transmit what they themselves received from the Companions, but they also exercise a kind of magisterial role of their own. If the exact number of the Companions has always varied according to the different authorities, there is likewise no unanimity regarding the number of the Followers. In the case of the Followers, however, there can be no hesitation in saying that the esoterists or mystics among them were in the minority, for there were simply too many of them to permit of our saying that they were all equally bent on treading the path.

The mystical tradition of Islam attributes esoteric teachings to a number of the Followers, but two of them are outstanding: the Sunni, Ḥasan al-Baṣrī (d. 110/728), and the fourth Imam of the Shīʿites, ʿAlī Zayn al-ʿĀbidīn (d. 95/714). Of the two, Ḥasan al-Baṣrī looms as the great patriarch of the ascetico-mystical life, whose long career was decisive for the Islamic tradition. Zayn al-ʿĀbidīn led a rather secluded existence in Medina with only a handful of Followers around him. The sermons of Ḥasan al-Baṣrī are prototypal for Islam; his constant preoccupation with the terrible events of Judgment lead one to surmise that the general tenor of his outward life revolved around the fear of God (*makhāfah* or *khawf*). That is a conclusion that emerges from the fragments of his works that have come down to us in later anthologies. Since his sermons were addressed to the public of his time, we do not sense what might have been his more sapiential positions in his private oral instruction.

The case is different for the fourth Shīʿite Imam, ʿAlī Zayn al-ʿĀbidīn. Shīʿism has preserved for us a collection of his prayers, *al-Ṣaḥīfat al-sajjādiyyah* (*The Scripture of the Worshiper,* the Imam being called al-Sajjād, "the worshiper"), that are radiantly beautiful and yet tinged with a certain melancholic serenity that is very touching. Apart from these prayers, the tradition has transmitted a number of luminous statements (*ḥadīths*) that reveal his gnostic and devotional dispositions. Like Ḥasan al-Baṣrī, he was a great patriarchal figure of early Islam and seems to have had the same twofold function of transmitting the Law and the path to his generation.

Care must be taken here to distinguish between the Imam, as seen within the Shīʿite tradition, and the same Imam as viewed by the Sufis and Sunnism in general. There is considerable difference between the two, especially if we take into account the later Shīʿite speculations on the role of their Imams in relation to the Prophet and to the community in general. No such role is attributed to them within esoteric or exoteric Sunnism. Even though the Sufis and Sunni religious authorities refer to them as Imams, this in no wise means that they attribute to the Imams the same infallible religio-political functions given to them by Shīʿite theologians, such as the moderate Twelvers. That the early Shīʿite Imams were conscious of their special role in those days because of their descent from the Prophet and their religious and mystical authority is something easily perceived by anyone who studies the lives and activities of the first six Imams. Their missions spanned the days of the Umayyad Dynasty and reached into the beginning of the Abbasids in the second/eighth century of Islam, or well over a century. But they were not the sole eso-exoteric authorities of Islam. In some of the Sufi initiatic lines, one finds the name of the fourth Imam, Zayn al-ʿĀbidīn. His name is not there because of his function as a Shīʿite Imam; it is there because he is considered to be one of the eminent gnostic teachers of early Islam, an authority on the path and a transmitter of the initiation. In other Sufi chains of transmission, the name of the great Sunni teacher, Ḥasan al-Baṣrī, is to be found, which is but another way of saying that the *ṭarīqah* was transmitted through different sages in the epoch of the Followers and was not in the least dependent on the unique lineage of the Imams.

The Spiritual Elect after the Followers

By the time the last Followers left the historical scene, Islam was split up into different sects, from the Khārijites to the Murji'ites to the Shī'ites to the Sunnis to the Mu'tazilites, and so on, each claiming to represent authentic Islam. The different sects all pointed to the elect (*al-khāṣṣah*) in their midst, who generally formed part of the swelling ranks of ascetics found everywhere in Umayyad days. Asceticism (*zuhd*) was a characteristic of the spiritual elite in that epoch. Perhaps this was a reaction against the increasing worldliness that the expansive Islamic civilization was generating in the cities and towns as new wealth and new lands and populations rallied to the Faith. Perhaps it was an attempt to maintain, for as long as possible, the desert simplicity of primordial Islam. Whatever the reason, we find a rather intense asceticism among all those who led a spiritual life, and this includes those whom the Sufi tradition claims for itself, such as Dāwūd al-Ṭā'ī (d. 162/777), Fuḍayl ibn 'Iyāḍ (d. 187/803), Shaqīq al-Balkhī (d. 194/810), Ḥabīb al-'Ajamī (d. ca. 156/772), Ibrāhīm ibn Adham (d. ca. 165/782), Ma'rūf al-Karkhī (d. ca. 199/815), the Imam Ja'far al-Ṣādiq (d. 148/765), and the great woman saint, Rābi'at al-'Adawiyyah (d. 185/801). Their asceticism, however, was not an end in itself and was accordingly subordinated to their devotional and sapiential aspirations. It was a discipline in view of the love and knowledge of God. Although it seemed to go against the *Sunnah* of the Prophet, this was so only if we take into account his social *Sunnah* and leave out of consideration the mystical or spiritual *Sunnah* he left behind. At times the latter can clash with the exoteric *Sunnah*—and even must clash with it—in view of the priority of its transcendent goal, which is the Divinity, Allah, who is beyond all limitations.

Most of the above-mentioned saintly figures have left only concise and suggestive remarks or allusions that we can find in later Sufi works. Some of them composed books, but these are mostly lost. In Shī'ite literature, the observations and statements of the sixth Imam, Ja'far al-Ṣādiq, are quite numerous, touching on all aspects of the Islamic tradition, from Quranic commentary to eschatology to gnostic teachings. Indeed, the Imam Ja'far is one of the great names in the early Sufi tradition. Living at a time when the Umayyad Dynasty had collapsed and the Abbasid Dynasty had begun, he was relatively free, at least for a while, to preach openly. A master of the gnostic way, he was a teacher of the famous Jābir ibn Hayyān, the alchemist, one of the first to be called a Sufi. Although we can discern a gnostic element in the Imam's teachings, he belonged to the formative period of Islam and was therefore an authority both in the *ṭarīqah* and *Sharīʿah.* It is this role as a member of the *salaf,* "the pious ancestral authorities" of Islam, that accounts for his exoteric teachings. The Sufis consider him primarily as an esoteric teacher, but this function is not in the least evident in a goodly number of statements attributed to him that have a purely exoteric or legalistic nature.

The opposite is the case with the celebrated woman sage, Rābiʿat al-ʿAdawiyyah of Basra, who incarnated the mystical way of love in all its radiance, and who was in no wise limited by the exoteric formulations of Islam.[6] The ways of action, love, and knowledge, which we find in synthetic fashion in the Messenger of Islam, are to be found in varying mixtures in the early authorities of Islam, as was said. But in the second/eighth century, we begin to see intensifications of these different approaches to God. Perhaps the extraordinary manifestations of love found in Rābiʿah are to be accounted for as spiritual compensations for the growing exoteric legalism that led to the calculated amassing of good deeds in exchange for posthumous rewards—the fear of punishment, and not the love of the Lord, being the motivation behind such deeds. Moreover, the example of Rābiʿah occurs at a time when the *salaf* were laying down the classic contours of the religion. She herself, and therefore the way of love, are prototypal in the spiritual tradition of the community, and this means that she is one of the *salaf* herself, in a mystical sense. This no doubt explains her subsequent renown and presence in later Sufi literature, as if she had been a kind of avataric manifestation of pure love untrammeled by the legal codes of the religious authorities.

Rābiʿah left this world at the very beginning of the third/ninth century. Her life unfolded in the midst of great cyclical changes in the history of the Islamic religion. When she came into the world, the word *ṣūfī* was practically nonexistent. However, at her death some eighty years later, in 185/801, it was synonymous with the adept of the path, and *taṣawwuf* (esoterism) meant the integral spiritual path, the *ṭarīqah.* Throughout her long life all sorts of movements and historical forces in Islam contrived to make that identification of Sufism and the path an absolute necessity and not simply an accidental occurrence. What took place?

Sufism Emerges as the Integral Path

In his *Kitāb al-lumaʿ*, Abū Naṣr al-Sarrāj (d. 378/988) says that the word *ṣūfī* was already known in the days of Ḥasan al-Baṣrī (d. 110/728). Born in

28. "Khwajah Khidr," ca. 1775–1780, Johnson Album 55, No. 3.

21/643, Ḥasan lived to be around ninety years of age. At what point in that long period of time the term *ṣūfī* was used cannot be determined with exactitude. But what is certain is that already in the middle of the second/eighth century we hear of the word in conjunction with certain individuals, such as the aforementioned Jābir ibn Ḥayyān, a disciple of the sixth Imam, Ja'far al-Ṣādiq (d. 148/765), or Abū Hāshim al-Kūfī al-Ṣūfī (d. ca. 160/776). As the second/eighth century wore on, the term and its cognates (such as *taṣawwuf*, "esoterism") became more widespread in usage. To account for the eventual identification of Sufism and *ṭarīqah*, which we see taking place in the third/ninth century, we have to examine what was happening within the Islamic tradition that would make Sufism as such emerge. When we look into the matter, we see that a number of historical events were taking place at that time, all of which had a hand in the surfacing of Sufism: (1) the tendency to confuse asceticism with the path; (2) the establishment of the exoteric schools of jurisprudence; (3) the Shī'ite claims about the Imams; (4) the rise of Islamic philosophy; (5) the increasing formalism of the doctors of the Law; and (6) the need to make sure that the integral message of the Revelation was associated from then on with Sufism. If we examine these six points, we can see how pertinent they were to the emergence of Sufism as an Islamic institution.

The second/eighth and third/ninth centuries constitute a period of time best described as the first major watershed in the history of Islam. The original synthetic vision of things, which we see in the early days of the religion, had given way gradually to the increasing separation between the esoteric and exoteric domains. The incredible expansion of Islam through its conquests of vast regions of the known world had brought millions into the community. This in turn created a need for the codification of everything necessary to preserve the integrity of the Faith: *ḥadīth*-literature, grammar, pre-Islamic poetry, history, biography, jurisprudence, and a host of other disciplines were all set down in written works for the benefit of the newcomers to the Faith and for the old-timers who needed to be reminded of its articles of belief. Moreover, numerous sects had arisen in the bosom of the religion, disputing its articles of belief. Each one of them claimed to possess the ascetical elect of the community. Asceticism itself had gotten out of hand and had become a kind of art for art's sake. Under such circumstances, the path was confused with exaggerated asceticism, and in the process its gnostic goal was threatened with extinction.

Like the others among the ascetics of those early days, the actual Sufis, whose view of the *ṭarīqah* was gnostic or sapiential, wore plain garments made of wool (*ṣūf*), in imitation of the Prophet. As time went by and asceticism (*zuhd*) began to draw armies of partisans into its ranks, the sages of the integral path began to call themselves Sufis and their discipline *taṣawwuf,* in order to distinguish themselves and their Way from the purely ascetic seekers and their asceticism. The name *ṣūfī* was confined to those who preached the total spiritual path, with its aspects of action, love, and knowledge, but especially knowledge. They thus set themselves apart from those who practiced asceticism exclusively, which was really a kind of "way of action" and represented a truncated path. At the same time, because of its gnostic teachings (its *ma'rifah,* "gnosis," as the later Sufis would say), Sufism also distinguished itself from those mystical ways that were devotional and nonintellective, the "way of love" of the devotees (*'ubbād,* pl. of *'ābid*) of early Islam. At the risk of imposing an artificial scheme on the mystical wayfarers of the first century or so of Islam, one might say that the strictly ascetic types (the *zuhhād,* pl. of *zāhid*) were those who followed the way of action; the *'ubbād* followed the way of love; and the gnostics (*'ārifūn,* pl. of *'ārif,* "gnostic") followed the way of knowledge. In reality, things were not quite so clear, but the main point to stress is that the Sufi of those times, by emerging into the full light of day, proclaimed that the complete path was not only one of action and love but, above all, of knowledge. Once that point had been made, the name *ṣūfī* and its cognates stuck with the followers of the sapiential way, whether they wore wool or not.

The second reason for the rise of Sufism lies in the establishment of the great Sunni schools of jurisprudence (*madhāhib,* pl. of *madhhab*), such as the Ḥanafī, the Mālikī, the Shāfi'ī, and the Ḥanbalī. None of these existed in primitive Islam—any more than the term *ṣūfī.* The schools are really crystallizations of the *Sharī'ah* of Islam, its exoteric domain. The doctors of the Law, the *'ulamā',* now come into their own with the backing of the Abbasid state. This showed that exoteric Islam had taken on its characteristic features. That led inevitably to the exteriorization of the complementary esoteric spiritual dimension of the religion, which resulted in the surfacing of Sufism, with its own teachers (the shaykhs, or masters of the path), its own terminology, doctrines, institutions, methods of realization, and contemplative goals. Exoterism, in other words, provoked the rise of esoterism, since the two always go together in the different religions. That is yet another explanation for the appearance of Sufism in the community.

There is a third reason for the appearance of Sufism, and this has to do with what was happening within Shī'ism. At this period, which had already seen a century of Islam's existence pass by, six or seven Imams had come and gone. Shī'ism claimed for its Imams not only a certain infallibility in political and religious matters but also a kind of exclusive guardianship over the integral message of the Faith, which, of course, reduced everyone else of authority to a peripheral function, including even the masters of the *ṭarīqah.* To ensure that no one confused the path with such Shīʿite conceptions about their Imams, and to make certain that the existence of the *ṭarīqah* was in no way dependent on the Imams alone, Sufism manifested itself, proclaiming thereby that it contained the complete spiritual message of Revelation and that its teachers stood in no need of the continued existence of the Shīʿite Imams. Indeed, after the seventh and eighth Imams, Mūsā al-Kāẓim (d. 183/799) and ʿAlī al-Riḍā (d. 203/818), it is rare to find much interaction between the remaining Imams of the Twelver school of Shīʿism and the Sufi sages. The reason is simple enough: the remaining Imams do not have the authoritative roles that the early Imams—at least up to the sixth Imam—exercised over all of Islam. On the contrary, they are of importance in a restricted Shīʿite sense that no longer has spiritual repercussions in the Sunni world. The sixth Imam, Jaʿfar al-Ṣādiq (d. 148/765), had a kind of cosmic function in the community as a whole which the remaining Imams could not possibly have. It is not by accident that Sufism comes into the picture with increasing frequency after his days.

The rise of Islamic philosophical schools also had a role in bringing Sufism to the fore. The translation of Greek philosophical texts into Arabic generated a lively interest in Greek wisdom and this in turn encouraged a kind of rational enquiry into the tenets of the Faith, which we see in the Muʿtazilite theologians of early Abbasid times. As a way having gnostic realization for its goal, Sufism also had to distinguish itself from the rationalistic schools of the day, whether Muʿtazilite or purely philosophical, like the Neoplatonism of the Arab philosopher al-Kindī in the third/ninth century. Consider that Neoplatonism is a mystical philosophy calling for intellective identity with the One through spiritual purification, and it is easy to see how a purely rational approach to its teachings, without regard to its gnostic goals, can lead to the cult of rationalism, even though al-Kindī himself was interested in Sufism. Nevertheless, the presence of philosophical thinking in Islam, with its reduction of knowledge to abstract, mental categories, bereft of direct, spiritual vision of the Real (*al-Ḥaqq*), no doubt had a hand in forcing Sufism to present itself as the embodiment of gnostic realization. This is one reason why, in the third/ninth century, the term *maʿrifah* (gnosis) begins to replace the term *ʿilm* (knowledge) as the goal of the path; the former means experiential, direct knowledge, whereas the latter had gradually lost such meanings and been reduced simply to mental knowledge, abstract and theoretical.

The increasing formalism of the *ʿulamāʾ* provided a fifth reason for Sufism to emerge publicly as the path. That formalism led to the creation of the schools of jurisprudence, on the one hand, and to the abusive conclusion that the doctors of the Law were the unique interpreters of the revealed message, on the other. We see the gradual reduction of the Islamic message to its exoteric aspects taking place in the second/eighth century without any overt or violent opposition on the part of the newly created schools of Sufism. In truth, that century reveals only a quiet manifestation of Sufism here and there. We have only to recall that the Umayyad Dynasty came to an end in the middle of the century. The religious leaders of Islam had never been integrated into the Umayyad state for many reasons, but with the rise of the Abbasid regime things changed completely. Now the *'ulamā'* were brought right into the administrative, juridical, and even executive functions of the state, wielding a measure of power they had not previously exercised. With that power came the feeling that they had a kind of exclusive monopoly on the contents of the Islamic revelation. Had they been allowed to go along in such a fashion, with no opposition to their claims, Islam would have seen something similar to what took place in early Christianity, when the official church stamped out all spiritual esoterism that claimed an independent existence for itself. An awareness of the gradually intensifying formalism of the *'ulamā'* can be sensed in the words and deeds of the early Sufis and is one of the reasons why the Sufi path had to assert itself and claim that it represented the contemplative message of Islam, exoterism having only a dogmatic-legalistic version of the Faith.

Finally, if the total spiritual teaching of Islam were not to disappear altogether, Sufism had to come forward as its authoritative representative. Exoteric Islam, with its *Sharī'ah* and dogmatic-theological positions, was at best only a limited version of the "way of action," having entrance into paradise at death as its goal. Even so, this was not even the ascetical kind of "way of action" we find in the first century or so of Islam. Rather, it is simply salvation through works out of fear of damnation. Nor could the early "way of love" of Islam be the whole story, for it left out of consideration the possibility of union or identity with God through the Spirit, the fruit of the "way of knowledge." In other words, as time went by, the originally synthetic message of action, love, and knowledge, such as we find in the Quran and the *Sunnah* of the Prophet, was being progressively reduced by the limitations of men either to simple devotionalism or to salvation through observance of the commandments and prohibitions of the Law. Not only that, but all attempts to go beyond such confines were sensed by the *'ulamā'* as innovations, if not as heresies. Since the majority of the believers were noncontemplative and not in the least interested in treading the spiritual path, the law of numbers was on the side of the *'ulamā'*, so to speak, who thus had their illusions of being the sole authorities in Islam reinforced all the more.

Conflicts in the Third/Ninth Century

In the second/eighth century, the relatively peaceful relations that existed between the religious authorities of the Law (the *'ulamā'*) and the spiritual authorities of the path (the shaykhs) were of such a nature that they could not possibly last forever, precisely because of the pretensions of the doctors of the Law. Thus, throughout the third/ninth century, a gradually increasing tension between the two camps becomes evident. This is not something that could have been averted by the Sufis, if only because of the mounting resentment of the exoteric religious authorities, who were themselves looking for a scrap and for some means to bring about a resolution of the conflict in their own favor. The hostility that the doctors of the Law felt toward the Sufis was exacerbated by those mystics who deliberately provoked the religious chiefs. In the third/ninth century we find two types of Sufism: there is the kind that is "sober" and the kind that is "drunk," to use Sufi terms. From the sober Sufis, the *'ulamā'* had little to fear; they could be counted on to act cooperatively in society and to align themselves with the general prescriptions of the Law. It was the Sufi drunks, as it were, who were the bulls in the china closet and who inspired both repulsion and fear in the hearts of the religious leaders.

The sober-minded Sufis were the intellectual leaders of the path. Unlike the previous century, the third/ninth century witnessed the appearance of a number of important Sufi works that have lasted down to our times. Among the many compositions left behind by the Sufi al-Muḥāsibī (d. 243/857), the *Ri'āyah li-ḥuqūqi 'Llāh* (*The Observance of God's Rights*) has been a popular spiritual treatise revolving around self-examination (the name al-Muḥāsibī means "the one who examines himself").[7] His is a mitigated devotionalism based on a dialectic that drew fire from the Ḥanbalīs of his day, who felt that all discursive thinking was somehow related to Mu'tazilite rationalism.

The most intellectual sage of the epoch was al-Ḥakīm al-Tirmidhī (d. 285/898), the author of a number of works seeking to explain the esoteric aspects of Islam, including such realities as sanctity and prophethood, the "seal of sanctity," and the like. His all-important work, *Kitāb khatm al-awliyā'* (*The Seal of the Saints*), established important distinctions within the domain of sanctity and had a great influence on later schools of Sufism. In his works, we see a more analytical approach to Sufi doctrine, reflecting the gradual loss of the synthetic view of things characteristic of earlier times.

Only brief statements or meager works on the inner life have come down to us from the other Sufis of the day, such as Sarī al-Saqaṭī (d. 255/871), Bishr al-Ḥāfī (d. 227/842), Ibn Karrām (d. 257/869), and Dhu'l-Nūn al-Miṣrī (d. 245/860), to mention only a few of the more important names. Around these and other masters, circles of adepts would form, such as the Karrāmiyyah around Ibn Karrām. The Sufi meetinghouse, the *khānaqāh* (in Persian; *zāwiyah* in Arabic), which can already be found in the second/eighth century, now is more frequently encountered. However, the general style of life of the Sufi teachers and their disciples remains on the whole faithful to the more ascetic *Sunnah* of the Prophet. Still, one can sense an institutionalized life coming over Sufism just as one can perceive that the entire Islamic tradition was now entering into official molds with the establishment of the schools of jurisprudence and the rise of the great Islamic civilization in Baghdad and the provincial capitals. Likewise, there is a tendency in the Sufis of the day to spell out things in more detail, as we saw in the case of Tirmidhī. Thus, Dhu'l-Nūn al-Miṣrī takes pains to associate the path with gnosis (*ma'rifah*) in order to bring out more clearly the mystical experience involved in Sufi knowledge, which the word *'ilm* (knowledge), as was said previously, could not adequately convey any longer. He also gave a more orderly presentation of the different "stations" (*maqāmāt*) of the virtues, which would influence later Sufis.

The other category of Sufis found at that time, the ones described as "drunk" with spiritual fervor, are best exemplified by the renowned Abū Yazīd al-Basṭāmī (d. 261/874). Whereas in Islam one says *Subḥāna-'Llāh* ("Glory be to God!"), Abū Yazīd is said to have cried out *Subḥānī* ("Glory be to me!"). This is known as an ecstatic expression (*shaṭḥ*), and although it is supposedly the less sober-minded Sufis who give vent to them, in reality one finds even the sober Sufis at times uttering such expressions, which are always characterized by their boldness and even scandalous nature. Throughout the third/ninth century, different Sufis would utter ecstatic expressions that created powerful reactions among the *'ulamā'*, who already were searching for a showdown with Sufism, which came to them in the person of al-Ḥallāj.

The Case of al-Ḥallāj

There were different reasons why many of the Sufis of the third/ninth century engaged in seemingly wild actions or spoke in scandalous fashion. The Islamic tradition had become increasingly formalistic, as mentioned previously, and could have become even more so if allowed to follow its natural course under the direction of the excessively exoteric *'ulamā'*. The latter were concerned merely with the exoteric message of the religion, which corresponded to their actual capacity to understand, for the purely spiritual contents of the Revelation were not part of that understanding. Although the intensification of formalism had not yet reached the degree one finds among the rabbinical authorities in the days of Jesus, there were similarities. Just as Jesus had to preach in a bold and even scandalous manner to break through the rigid legalism of the Jews with his message of love, so similarly the Sufis of the third/ninth century had to break through the hardening shell of exoterism that was more and more in evidence as time went by if they wanted to draw attention to the mystical message of Islam. These were intrusions of the Spirit into the increasingly opaque substance of the community with a view to illuminating the gathering darkness. In later ages the same thing would happen again and again. This first crisis for Islam was of immense importance, cyclically speaking, because of the attempt by the exoteric authorities to lay hands on the entire tradition, including the path. Had they succeeded, the purely exoteric *'ulamā'* would have emerged as religious tyrants with no limits whatsoever to their authority. The resolution of the crisis came in the execution of the great Sufi al-Ḥallāj by the *'ulamā'* of Baghdad in the year 309/922.[8]

Al-Ḥallāj ("the wool-carder" in Arabic) was a great Persian Sufi raised in the Arab world of Wāsiṭ, where he perfected his religious education. When he was still young, his spiritual tendencies found their home in *taṣawwuf* and he became the disciple of a number of masters. He married the daughter of one of them, and she bore him several children and remained his sole wife throughout his years. From Basra, where he established his family, he began his wandering life as a preacher of Sufism. He performed the pilgrimage to Mecca three times, traveled all the way to India and Turkestan, teaching people union with God through love and knowledge. Eventually he made Baghdad his home, taught in the streets and markets of the city, and incurred the hostility of the religious authorities in the process. He was arrested and imprisoned for some nine years. Finally, after an irregular trial, he was sentenced to death on charges of heresy. Subjected to a terrible scourging, the amputation of his limbs, and exposure on a gibbet, he was finally beheaded, his body burned and his ashes strewn over the Tigris. His mystical poetry remains his only literary legacy of importance.

Unlike Rābi'at al-'Adawiyyah, in the second/eighth century, whose "way of love" (*maḥabbah*) was serene and lucid, the "way of love" of al-Ḥallāj, which was also combined with gnosis, was dramatic and stormy in its outward manifestations. His life is a kind of recapitulation, within the framework of Sunni Islam, of the life of Jesus. Both were aware of their sacrificial mission; both knew what awaited them as a result of divulging the mysteries of the path; and both were subjected to public humiliation, beating, and execution. The role of the founder of Christianity is obviously greater, for cosmic reasons, than that of al-Ḥallāj; yet the two figures are similar in that their lives unfolded in the midst of communities heavily weighed down by religious legalism. The only difference is that the mystical side of Judaism was moribund when Jesus preached, while *taṣawwuf* in Islam was alive in the days of al-Ḥallāj. But if Sufism was then alive, it was nevertheless extremely prudent, as we see in the case of al-Junayd (d. 298/910),[9] not to mention other eminent Sufis of the day, who joined in the condemnation of al-Ḥallāj. They condemned him because he preached the inner secrets of *taṣawwuf* to the people at large. The famous ecstatic phrase of al-Ḥallāj, *ana'l-Ḥaqq* ("I am the Truth"; *al-Ḥaqq* meaning also "God" or "the Real"), was an example, in their eyes, of his immoderate fervor.

The life and death of al-Ḥallāj resulted in the clarification of the spiritual atmosphere of the community, more or less as a bolt of lightning purifies the air. With al-Ḥallāj, the downward, heavy tendencies of the religious formalism of his day were temporarily arrested, which allowed everyone to see that there was more to Islam than the prescriptions of the *'ulamā'*. It is true that al-Ḥallāj does not represent normative Sufism, while his great teacher al-Junayd, with his sober esoterism, embodies the harmonious, discreet, and prudent Sufism of the perennial sort. But it is also true that, at that particular juncture in the history of Islam, normative Sufism could not by itself have brought about the spiritual reorientation engendered by the public martyrdom of al-Ḥallāj. His *ana'l-Ḥaqq* was a divulgation of the supreme mystery embedded in *tawḥīd*, and his entire life as a Sufi was a direct celestial unveiling of the priority of the Spirit over the Law and its guardians. Nothing less than this—including the sacrificial immolation of al-Ḥallāj—could have arrested the powerful sanhedrinism of the times.

Reconciliation between the Law and the Path

By the beginning of the fourth/tenth century, Sufism was evident everywhere in the Muslim world and was synonymous with the *ṭarīqah*. The head-on collision between the doctors of the Law and Sufism, which resulted in the execution of al-Ḥallāj, had served to show just how limited Islamic exoterism was and just how perfidious its representatives could be when left to their own devices. In other words, exoterism as such could not stand on its own two feet independently of all spiritual influences coming from *taṣawwuf* without this leading in the end to the impoverishment of the religion and even to its eventual demise.

It was therefore necessary to point that out to the community with a kind of reconciliation between the Law and the path, which we see in the Sufi manual, *Qūt al-qulūb* (*The Nourishment of Hearts*), written by Abū Ṭālib al-Makkī (d. 380/990). This work has since become a well-known treatise circulating not only in Sufi milieus but also among the non-Sufi pious elements of Islam. Al-Makkī belonged to the developed Sālimiyyah school of *taṣawwuf* founded by one of the masters of al-Ḥallāj, Sahl al-Tustarī (d. 283/896),[10] but named after his disciple Muḥammad ibn Sālim (d. 297/909). In the *Qūt*, al-Makkī sought to do what al-Ghazzālī (d. 505/1111) would attempt later on in his *Iḥyā' 'ulūm al-dīn* (*The Revival of the Religious Sciences*), namely, to put down in writing what characterized the Law and the path. That al-Makkī's reconciliation between the two was not definitive is clear from the later reconciliation written by al-Ghazzālī. There would even be much later reconciliations, such as that of 'Abd al-Qādir al-Jīlānī (d. 561/1166), in his *al-Ghunyah* (*The Self-Sufficient*); but all of this is understandable, given the natural tendency of exoterism to become embroiled in the world of forms and prescriptions and to shut out, as a result, the light of the Spirit.

By the fourth/tenth century, likewise, we notice the end of the primordial epoch of Islam. The rise of theological schools, especially that of Ash'arism and Māturīdism, the integration of Greek philosophy into the intellectual life of the community in the form of *falsafah*, as we see in the *Rasā'il* (*Treatises*) of the Brethren of Purity (Ikhwan al-ṣafā'), and the development of all sorts of cosmological and scientific disciplines in the midst of the great Islamic civilization of the times meant that the primordial style of Sufism and its simple Quranic atmosphere could no longer be maintained. Neoplatonic thinking, now Islamicized, circulated everywhere among the cultivated classes.[11] The masters of Sufism had to take this into account when expounding the doctrines of the path. Although this would not change the essence of Sufism, it would change some of its formulations, in the sense that now they would become much more scholastic in expression.

One last example of the archaic Sufi style is to be found in the works of al-Niffarī (fl. in the middle of the fourth/tenth century), from Niffar, in Iraq. His works, the *Mawāqif* (*Stoppings*) and *Mukhāṭabāt* (Addresses), written down as inspirations that came to him, are unique in the history of Sufism and even of Islam in general. They are written in a style that has no precedent in Arabic and that resembles more the prophetic biblical style of the Hebrew Bible than Quranic eloquence. In content, they are almost exclusively conversations of Divine Origin addressed to al-Niffarī during his itinerant life. They are, in effect, direct "revelations," although Sufism eschews using the word "revelation" in such a context for fear of reducing the prestige of the Quranic Revelation, and prefers instead to use the term "inspirations" (*ilhāmāt*). The content of these "divine utterances" is pure gnosis (*ma'rifah*); very little is said of the *Sharī'ah,* the emphasis being on the contemplative nature of the path. This is the "way of knowledge" in its most rigorous aspect, and it is easy to see why Niffarī, even in the Sufi tradition, has not been widely known. His fame has been confined mostly to the strictly gnostic circles of the path; the less gnostic types, who are in the majority, tend to ignore him precisely because of his rather impersonal spirituality.

Once the developing conflict between the doctors of the Law and the Sufi adepts had been brought to a head with the martyrdom of al-Ḥallāj, it was necessary not only to reconcile the *Sharī'ah* and the *ṭarīqah* but also to record the names and sayings of the Sufi saints instrumental in transmitting *taṣawwuf.* This would allow the intelligent and pious Muslims to see for themselves who were the actual authorities in the esoteric tradition of Islam. The first work to do this was the book entitled *Kitāb al-ta'arruf li-madhhab ahl al-taṣawwuf* (*The Presentation of the Doctrine of the Sufis*) by Muḥammad al-Kalābādhī (d. 385/995), which listed the important Sufis of earlier times and gave their statements on different aspects of the path.[12] Its brevity and comprehensiveness won for it wide acceptance in the Muslim world. Although it did not have the fullness of the *Kitāb al-luma'* (*Book of Flashes*) of Abū Naṣr al-Ṣarrāj (d. 378/988) nor the elegant Arabic of the more technical *Qūt al-qulūb* of al-Makkī, the *Ta'arruf* did have the virtues of simplicity and aptness. Its definitions of key terms in Sufism would continue a practice that is found in the works of third/ninth century Sufis. Later on, the famous Sufi work, the *Risālah* (*Treatise*) of al-Qushayrī (d. 465/1072), would carry on this important task of defining the corpus of technical terms common to the esoteric Sufi way.[13] Others, likewise, would refer back to the sayings of the earlier Sufi authorities, as we see in the *Ṭabaqāt al-ṣūfiyyah* (*The Classes of the Sufis*) by 'Abd al-Raḥmān al-Sulamī (d. 412/1021), in order to establish the historical identity of the path across the centuries.

It remained, however, for al-Ghazzālī (d. 505/1111), in the fifth/eleventh century, to put all of these different Sufi currents together in a definitive fashion.[14] Plagued by doubts and uncertainties after he had reached eminence as a theologian and religious authority in Baghdad, he sought to still his heart in Sufism, as he explains in his spiritual autobiography, *Al-Munqidh min al-dalāl* (*The Redeemer from Error*).[15] After his enlightenment in the Sufi path, he wrote his famous *Iḥyā' 'ulūm al-dīn* (*The Revival of the Religious Sciences*), in which he presented the integrality of the Islamic religion as being both the *Sharī'ah* and the *ṭarīqah.* In lucid Arabic with Quranic verses, *ḥadīths,* and colorful anecdotes drawn from the lives of the Sufi saints and other pious figures, and in a masterfully well-organized fashion, al-Ghazzālī describes the illuminative knowledge of the path, which confers immediate certitude and graces, as the very summit of the believer's life. In brief, the *Sharī'ah* did not suffice unto itself, nor did the religious authorities have any competence in the affairs of the *ṭarīqah,* which was the domain of the Sufi shaykhs. After his day, it would not be easy for any knowledgeable religious scholar to reject the *ṭarīqah* without exposing his ignorance about the spiritual contents of the Islamic message. All that the future critics of Sufism, like the Ḥanbalī theologian Ibn al-Jawzī (d. 597/1200), could do was to criticize particular Sufis or some of their teachings, but not the path itself. That was due largely to the extremely effective critique of the *'ulumā'* of Islam made by al-Ghazzālī in his *Iḥyā'*, which remains to this day an extraordinarily clear account of the complete teaching of the Islamic revelation by a saintly sage who knew how to write for the intelligent and pious circles of the Islamic world in a way that would become a model for later generations. Summing up the Islam of the first four centuries, he also set down its general contours for the traditional Muslim of medieval and later times. With al-Ghazzālī the early Sufi tradition comes to a close, as it were, and a door is opened unto a new epoch, that of the great Sufi orders (*ṭuruq,* pl. of *ṭarīqah,* which means both the general "spiritual path" and a specific "Sufi order," like the Qādiriyyah or Shādhiliyyah). Not long after al-Ghazzālī died (505/1111), the renowned Sufi 'Abd al-Qādir al-Jīlānī (d. 561/1166), founder of the Qādiriyyah, would be preaching in Baghdad, but that would be a new age in the history of *taṣawwuf.*

Conclusions on the Early Period of Sufism

Enough of the Sufi doctrines and practices are revealed in the early mystical works to permit the reader to discern in them a tendency toward greater and greater precision and detail as time went by. From the simple remarks of the second/eighth-century Sufis to the *Iḥyā'* of al-Ghazzālī, there is an inclination in the Sufi tradition to divulge more and more of the actual teachings of the way. This corresponds to an increasing need for more explanation on the part of the seekers of the way. In the collections of the words of the early Sufis, we find only suggestive spiritual statements (*ishārāt*), rather concise and allusive; perhaps their private instruction was more developed. Later, however, the statements become more analytical. We can only assume that the masters found it expedient to reveal more and more of the oral instruction of Sufism because only in this way could a convincing case be made to those who were full of the questions raised by the urban culture of early Islam as it absorbed Greek and other forms of wisdom. By the fifth/eleventh century, Sufism had long been an institutional part of the Islamic world and had its own societal structures, its own authorities, and its own hierarchies. Nothing would be further from the truth than to imagine that the Sufis were more or less exotic or isolated figures; all of the eminent Sufis were often surrounded by great numbers of disciples.

A striking aspect of Sufism as it develops on the historical scene from its appearance in the second/eighth century on is the amazing richness and variety of its teachings and practices. This is quite evident in the innumerable and often contradictory definitions the early and later Sufis gave to simple technical terms of the path, like trust (*tawakkul*), patience (*ṣabr*), remembrance (*dhikr*), and the like.[16] The underlying spiritual reality of a term is always sensed as one, but its expressions in language can be diverse and even contradictory. Thus, the basic elements of the path that we find already in the Quran and the *Sunnah,* namely, the doctrine of the Divine Unity (*tawḥīd*), the remembrance of God (*dhikr Allāh*), the initiatic pact (*bay'ah*), and the aesthetic *Sunnah* of the Prophet, remain essentially the same throughout the history of early—and even later—Sufism. Some of these elements undergo elaboration from the simple to the complex or from the synthetic to the more analytical. *Tawḥīd,* for instance, is capable of extraordinary diversity and complexity of formulation without, for all that, losing its essential oneness of nature. Similarly, the *dhikr* can be manifested in a variety of forms derived from the Quranic Revelation, these forms depending on the perspectives of the different Sufi schools, the inspirations of particular masters, and other conditions; but this variegated manifestation in no way detracts from the fundamental character of the *dhikr.* Consequently, the elements of the *ṭarīqah* remain the same after the days of the Prophet, to be sure, but their combinations and expressions can vary from master to master—and even within the lifetime of one master. Indeed, it would seem that one of the important functions of Sufism has been to furnish these elements of the path to its seekers in the right proportions and in accordance with the needs of each generation.

In the final analysis, what is called the development of Sufism is really the history of the formal expressions of the above-mentioned elements by the teachers of the path. This is but another way of saying that the transcendent Reality (*al-Ḥaqīqah*), although It is transhistorical and even nontemporal in Its nature, is forever intruding Itself, through the intermediary of the eminent Sufi masters, into this world of time and space—this world of history—in order to keep alive the spiritual message of *tawḥīd.*

Notes

1. A contemporary spiritual view of the Sufi path that reveals the perennial value of Sufism is to be found in M. Lings, *What is Sufism?* (Berkeley and Los Angeles: University of California Press, 1981).

2. A summary of these early teachings of Sufism is found in the classic Persian work by ʿAlī al-Hujwīrī, *Kashf al-Mahjūb,* trans. R. A. Nicholson (London: Luzac, 1911).

3. L. Massignon situates Sufism in its Quranic roots, ascribing indirectly to the Islamic Revelation an esoteric dimension not previously recognized in the West (*Essai sur les origines du lexique technique de la mystique musulmane* [rev. ed.; Paris: J. Vrin, 1968]).

4. The relations between the spiritual life of Islam and its art have been convincingly displayed in T. Burckhardt, *The Art of Islam* (London: Festival of the World of Islam, 1976).

5. Some *silsilahs* can be found in O. Depont and X. Coppolani, *Les Confréries religieuses musulmanes* (Algiers: A. Jourdan, 1897).

6. See Margaret Smith, *Rābiʿah the Mystic and Her Fellow-Saints in Islam* (Cambridge: University Press, 1928).

7. In his *Kitāb al-tawahhum fī waṣf aḥwāl al-ākhirah* (trans. A. Roman as *Une vision humaine des fins dernières* [Paris: Klincksieck, 1978]), al-Muḥāsibī reveals how the fear of the hereafter can be integrated into the way.

8. The life of this great sage has been written by L. Massignon in *The Passion of al-Hallāj: Mystic and Martyr of Islam,* trans. H. Mason (4 vols.; Princeton, NJ: Princeton University Press, 1982).

9. His views on al-Ḥallāj are to be found in *The Passion of al-Hallāj,* vol. 1, pp. 125–27.

10. See G. Böwering, *The Mystical Vision of Existence in Classical Islam: The Qur'anic Hermeneutics of the Ṣūfī Sahl Al-Tustarī* (Berlin and New York: de Gruyter, 1980).

11. Sufism had by now affected even the profane literature of the epoch, as we can see in the fifth/eleventh-century prose work by Abū Ḥayyān al-Tawḥīdī, *al-Ishārāt al-ilāhiyyah* (Beirut: Dār al-Thaqāfah, 1973), a series of prayers and supplications done with literary grace but without the real depth of the Sufis.

12. Al-Kalābādhī, Muḥammad, *Kitāb al-taʿarruf li-madhhab ahl al-taṣawwuf,* trans. A. J. Arberry as *The Doctrine of the Sufis* (Cambridge: University Press, 1935).

13. The *Manāzil al-sāʾirīn* of Khwājah ʿAbdallāh al-Anṣārī (d. 481/1089), trans. S. de Beaurecueil as *Les étapes des itinérants vers Dieu* (Cairo: Imprimerie de l'Institut français d'archéologie orientale, 1962), is an important Sufi technical work with a Ḥanbalī coloration.

14. See W. Montgomery Watt, *The Faith and Practice of al-Ghazālī* (London: Allen & Unwin, 1953).

15. Al-Ghazzālī, Abū Ḥāmid, *al-Munqidh min al-ḍalāl,* trans. R. J. McCarthy as *Freedom and Fulfillment* (Boston: Twayne, 1980).

16. B. Reinart examines one of these virtues, trust (*tawakkul*), in *Die Lehre vom tawakkul in der klassischen Sufik* (Berlin: de Gruyter, 1968), which shows the richness of meaning that apparently simple words in Sufism can have.

14

The Spiritual Practices of Sufism

Jean-Louis Michon

The Mystical Quest in Islam: Scriptural and Historical Roots

It has already been shown how Islam has as its first pillar of faith the affirmation of Divine Unity and how this is expressed through the profession of faith, the *Shahādah,* which makes up the dominant theme of the Quranic Revelation. The Quran repeats unceasingly that God is One without equal, All-Powerful, that He created the world, that He is the Lord of the worlds, the Lord of the Last Judgment, that to Him all things return, that nothing occurs without His Will and that everything except Him is doomed to disappear. Between this all-powerful, transcendent, infinite God and the ephemeral, imperfect, and limited creature is there a possible connection? All religions have provided an answer to this fundamental question, and it is affirmative, seeing, as the word religion itself implies, the existence of a bond between the creature and the Creator, religion being that which "binds" (*religat*) man to God. From one religion to another that which varies is not, therefore, the existence of a liaison between heaven and earth, which is universally recognized, but the modalities through which this bond is realized, actualized. This realization can never, obviously, be man's doing. God alone, Who created the human being according to certain modalities, with the limitations that make him what he is, can deliver him and efface his individual and separate nature. What man can do, however, is to collaborate with Divine Action through his intelligence and his will to efface himself, to make room in his heart for the descent of grace, of spiritual intuitions.

In a famous teaching, the Prophet Muḥammad defined very precisely the type of relationship that is set up between the effort of man and Divine

Action.[1] On that day the Prophet was surrounded by numerous companions and in this assembly a young man dressed in white appeared whom the Prophet recognized as the archangel Gabriel. This young man posed three consecutive questions to the Prophet corresponding to the various stages of penetrating into the meaning of religion (*al-dīn*). By the answers he gave to the archangel, the Prophet defined these three stages: (1) *al-islām,* voluntary submission; (2) *al-īmān,* faith; and (3) *al-iḥsān,* perfect virtue, excellence. In defining *islām* the Prophet explained that it consisted of respecting the five pillars which constitute the Muslim religion, that is, witnessing to Divine Unity and the authenticity of Muḥammad's mission, prayer, the fast of Ramaḍān, legal tithing, and pilgrimage. Therefore, it is the stage of exterior religion, of submission and obedience, that which asks one to know the prescriptions of the Sacred Law and to conform to them. The second stage, that of faith, marks a more advanced step in religious experience. It is no loner a question of a simple act of obedience but rather of a grace which enters the heart and makes one recognize the foundations of the revealed prescriptions and adhere inwardly to them with fervor and clarity. As for the third stage, it implies a total commitment of the body, the soul, and the spirit. It entails not only respect for outer prescriptions, not only inner faith, but in addition to these a total disengagement from worldly concerns at all times and an openness to that which God wills. The man who has come to the stage of *iḥsān* is, in a way, no longer in possession of himself. In fact, according to the words of the Prophet to the archangel Gabriel, this stage of perfect virtue consists "of adoring Allah as though thou didst see Him, and if thou dost not see him He nonetheless seeth thee." The man who is in a state of *iḥsān,* the *muḥsin,* is truly the *khalīfah,* the vicegerent of God on earth. He rediscovers "the most beautiful form" in which he was created (according to the Quran XCV, 4), because his heart is like a pure, well-polished mirror in which the Divine can be reflected. Leading man back to this station is the goal of Sufi practices.[2]

Another Quranic idea that plays a fundamental role in the mystical quest is that of being completely at God's disposal, the equivalent of the *vacare Deo* of Christian mystics, an idea that is translated by the Arabic word *faqr,* meaning literally "poverty." From *faqr* comes the word *faqīr,* a term that, like its Persian equivalent, *darwīsh,* means "poor" and serves to designate the Muslim mystic. A verse of the Quran says, "O men, you are the poor (*al-fuqarā'*, plural of *faqīr*) before God; He is the Rich!" (XXXV, 15). This saying has an obvious literal meaning; that is, it affirms the infinity of Divine Plenitude and, in the light of this richness, the state of man's dependence and his utter indigence. But this verse also contains an exhortation and a promise, because it is, in fact, in becoming aware of his impoverished condition and in drawing all the conclusions that this implies that man realizes the virtue of humility, that he empties himself of all pretentions including that of existing "at the side" of God or, in the words of the Christian evangelists, that he passes through that narrow gate through which the rich cannot pass and which leads to the kingdom of God (Matthew 7:13ff.; Luke 13:23ff.). Such is truly the stripping away to which the mystics, the *fuqarā'*, aspire, and it is no different in this regard from that of the Christian anchorites of the desert or of the *poverello,* that is, Saint Francis of Assisi. This same diminutive, moreover, exists in Arabic, where the name *al-fuqayr* (the little poor one), was used for centuries by several Sufis.

According to generally accepted etymology, the word *ṣūfī* itself is derived from *ṣūf,* meaning "white wool," because the clothing made of white wool, which was particularly liked by the Prophet and by the early disciples who wished to follow his example, very soon became a symbol of ascetic renunciation and orientation toward the contemplative life. A mystic from Baghdad, Sumnūn (d. 303/915), defined Sufi in this way: "The Sufi is he who possesses nothing and is possessed by nothing." This definition alludes to two kinds of poverty. The first, "to possess nothing," designates material poverty; it is never considered an absolute condition for coming to God but is a means, often very useful and even necessary, of achieving inner purification. The second kind of poverty, "to be possessed by nothing," is imperative, because it implies the detachment from passions, from desires in which the soul is engrossed and which prevent God from penetrating man's innermost heart.

This observation concerning the wool clothing worn by the Sufis, from which they take their name, provides the opportunity to underline how inherent mysticism is in the Muslim religion and how it has been since the beginnings of Islam. Sufism is not, as some would like to have it believed, something that superimposed itself onto primitive Islam and conferred on it, as a later addition, a dimension that was lacking in the original. In fact, as seen in chapter 13 of this volume, this profound dimension is present in all the pages of the Quran in innumerable verses which teach, for example, that God is near to man, "nearer to him than his jugular vein" (L, 16); that "He is the best and the most beautiful recompense" (LXXIII, 20); that He illuminates the hearts of those who invoke Him morning and night with humility, veneration, and love; that He shelters His friends from fear and sadness. In other words, God loves to communicate directly through His Word and to provide the means for drawing nearer to Him. And that which He does not state explicitly in the Quran He makes known through His Messenger, whose words and deeds make up the commentary and the illustration of the revealed message.

By his personality, by his teaching, by the virtues he exemplified, the Prophet Muḥammad was the first Sufi, the model that would inspire mystics for all the generations to come. It is from the prophetic tradition, the *Sunnah,* that the Sufis draw much of the directives and counsels which, at all times and in all circumstances, aid the seeker of God in realizing the ideal of *faqr,* spiritual poverty. Even before receiving the Quranic message, Muḥammad had made numerous retreats in the mountains around Mecca, especially in the cave on Mount Ḥirā' where the angel of Revelation came to him for the first time, and it is certainly because his soul was already a clear mirror capable of reflecting the truths of heaven that God chose this man in particular to entrust with the prophetic mission.

The history of the beginnings of Islam teaches us also that among the first companions were found several individuals of great spiritual scope, in particular Abū Bakr and ʿAlī and the group of ascetics called "the People of the Bench" (*ahl al-ṣuffah*). These people were among the very first emigrants to abandon everything in Mecca in order to follow the Prophet to Medina. They occupied a kind of bench at the entrance to the mosque of the Prophet in Medina, where they spent the greater part of the day and the night, having no other home and preferring to live in this place where they could be near the Prophet and benefit from his teaching as often as possible. To this group in particular belonged the celebrated traditionist Abū Hurayrah, "the father of the little she-cat," whose prodigious memory recorded several thousands of the sayings of the Prophet, and also Bilāl, the black African, who, after having been tortured in Mecca for converting to Islam, was saved in the nick of time by Abū Bakr, who ransomed him from his torturers. Bilāl was later to become the first muezzin of Islam.

If, over the course of the centuries, Muslim mysticism showed itself capable of integrating the doctrinal perspectives and the elements of spiritual techniques belonging to other cultures—for example, to Neoplatonic Hellenism, to Byzantine Christianity, to the Mazdeism of ancient Iran, indeed, to Hinduism and Buddhism—such a capacity for assimilation, far from showing a lack of originality or deficiency, proves rather the vitality of the way of the Sufis. Moreover, it proves the universality of the mystical quest, that which Frithjof Schuon has so justly named "the transcendent unity of religions."[3]

Human Effort and Divine Effusion

The Muslim mystic, the *ṣūfī,* does not passively wait for grace to come to illumine him, even if the coming of this light is always regarded as a spontaneous gift from God. Among the innumerable definitions that have been given to Sufism (*al-taṣawwuf*), many put in perspective its operative aspects—the fact that it is a path requiring a strong adhesion of the intelligence and a strong exertion of the will.[4] Thus, Maʿrūf al-Karkhī (d. 200/813), who was probably the first to define Sufism, said, "Sufism means seizing realities and renouncing that which is between the hands of the created beings."[5] It is an opening, therefore, of the spirit and the heart which leads to gnosis and makes man "one who knows through God" (*al-ʿārif bi'Llāh*) and is a purification of the soul which renders it free for the manifestation of its Lord by emptying it of futile preoccupations, worldly passions, and selfish desires. Often, the order of the terms is inverted, and one speaks of first emptying the human "recipient" (*al-āniyyah*), the individual "mold" (*al-qālib*), so that the Divine Presence—the elixir of life, the wine of knowledge—can penetrate within.

It is also in this way that the celebrated theosopher Abū Ḥāmid al-Ghazzālī (Algazel, d. 505/1111) described the journey of the Sufis:

> They begin by combatting their unworthy qualities, cutting their ties to the world, directing all of their thoughts towards God; this is the good method. If someone succeeds at it, Divine Mercy is shed on him, the mystery of the Divine Kingdom is revealed and Reality is shown to him. The only effort on the part of the mystic consists in preparing himself by purification and concentration, while maintaining a sincere will, from absorbing desire and then awaiting the hoped-for mercy on the part of God. . . . "Whoever belongs to God, God belongs to him."[6]

This last formula, in its conciseness, reaffirms the whole doctrine of *ittiḥād*, the union between the creature and the Creator, which is, for the Sufi, a concrete possibility, because he knows that nothing, in reality, is separate from God and exists outside of Him. In addition, it sums up the two complementary and inseparable fundamental aspects of the journey of the mystic: (1) to realize that he belongs to God, that he is completely dependent in relation to Him, the Powerful, who subsists in Himself; and (2) to welcome in his purified substratum the theophanies of the Names and Attributes of the Divinity, the ineffable Presence of the Generous, the Dispenser of every grace (*al-Karīm, al-Wahhāb*). The first action includes a voluntary element, the gift of self, the battle of the believer for God's cause "with his possessions and his soul," according to an oft-repeated Quranic injunction (IV, 94; IX 21, 42, 82; XXI, 11, etc.). As for the second move—that of God giving Himself to man—it can only be the result of a supernatural blessing, a spontaneous unveiling, illuminating the innermost heart with a light which is not of this world and in which man recognizes his true nature.

The desire to achieve the state of ideal poverty and inner detachment, which is the prelude to union with God and its necessary condition, is not for everyone. More often such an aspiration is manifested after years of assiduous practice of religion in its ordinary sense; but it can also occur as a sudden and irresistible event. That is why, if the religious Law, the *Sharīʿah,* is obligatory for all people without exception—or at least for all the members of the Islamic community—the spiritual path, the *ṭarīqah,* does not make the same claim. That is to say, it is only for those who are predisposed and called to set out on the great adventure which is the quest for the Divine.

The Way of Poverty (*al-ṭarīqah*)

The way that traverses the infinite distance separating man from God is called the *ṭarīqah,* a term that means two things. On the one hand, it means the mystical journey in general—that is to say, the sum of the teachings and the practical rules that have been drawn from the Quran, the prophetic *Sunnah,* and the experience of spiritual masters. On the other hand, in a more limited sense, the word *ṭarīqah* (pl. *ṭuruq*) signifies a brotherhood or a particular order of Sufis and usually bears a name derived from that of the founder of this order: for example, *ṭarīqah qādiriyyah,* founded by ʿAbd al-Qādir al-Jīlānī; *ṭarīqah mawlawiyyah,* founded by Mawlānā ("our master") Jalāl al-Dīn Rūmī; or *ṭarīqah shādhiliyyah,* founded by Imam Abu'l-Ḥasan al-Shādhilī. In a certain sense, these *ṭuruq* can be compared with what in Christianity are called the "third orders," those that do not require vows of celibacy or conventional reclusion but aim at an ideal that is akin to that of the monastic orders.

Initiation

The Persian Sufi Hujwīrī (fifth/eleventh century) explained that in order to know if one possesses a true mystical predisposition it is necessary that one feel ready to do three things: (1) to serve people, that is, to know how to place oneself at the rank of a servant and to consider each person a master; (2) to serve God, that is, to cut one's ties with everything that concerns one's present life and even one's future life, because whoever hopes to gain something by serving God is, in reality, serving his own ego; and (3) to know how to guard his own heart, to maintain it in a state of fervent concentration, in a communion through which the servant proves his desire to devote himself exclusively to the Lord.[7]

When these conditions are realized, the aspirant to the mystical path, the *ṭālib,* can ask to be admitted into a Sufi order by performing an act of obedience to a spiritual master, the *shaykh* (literally "the old one"), *murshid* (guide) or *pīr* (Persian equivalent of *shaykh*). That which the master confers is, first, the initiatic link, the affiliation with the lineage of masters who have succeeded uninterruptedly since the Prophet Muḥammad, transmitting both the influence of blessings (*barakah, sakīnah*) necessary for the "greater battle" (*al-jihād al-akbar*) against the inner enemies and the spiritual means appropriate for this battle.

The ritual of affiliation can vary according to initiatic lineage. Most often, it reenacts the handshakes (*muṣāfaḥah*) given by the Prophet to the companions when they sealed the covenant of Ḥudaybiyyah with him under the tree, promising to remain faithful to their commitment to serve God and His Prophet under all circumstances. While renewing this solemn promise (*ʿahd, bayʿah*), the shaykh, holding in his hand the hand of the neophyte, recites the tenth verse of the sura of victory: "Those who swear fealty to thee swear fealty in truth to God; God's hand is over their hands. Then whosoever breaks his oath breaks it but to his own hurt; and whoso fulfils his covenant made with God, God will give him a mighty wage" (XLVIII, 10). Frequently at this moment the disciple receives a name that is added to the name that he already bears, and this becomes the symbol of his second birth into the world of the Spirit.

In certain *ṭuruq*, the initiatic charge is transmitted by means of a cloak (*khirqah*) with which the shaykh covers the shoulders of the disciple.[8] This cloak might be a patched tunic (*muraqqaʿah*), as among the Darqāwā of Morocco, who thus display their disdain of exterior riches. Other ritual objects, such as prayer beads or pages on which litanies (*awrād*) particular to the *ṭarīqah* have been transcribed, are often given to the new *faqīr* at the time of his initiation.

Upon completing the rite of aggregation, which generally takes place during a collective prayer gathering, the *fuqarāʾ* greet their new fellow disciple one by one and recite in unison the *Fātiḥah,* the sura that opens the Quran, so as to commend him for divine solicitude. Sometimes the gathering closes with a communal meal, which seals the entry of the new member into the family in which the shaykh is the father and all the *fuqarāʾ* are brothers, *ikhwān* (sg. *akh*).

The Spiritual Master

Connection to a master is considered a condition *sine qua non* for spiritual success. Without a master, without a guide, all illusions and all distractions are to be feared. This is what is meant by the well-known Sufi adage "He who does not have a shaykh has Satan for his shaykh." The true master is, of course, one who has himself already traversed the path, who knows its route, its pitfalls, and its dangers, so that he can guide others. When a disciple has been accepted by a master, he must place himself entirely in his hands and become, according to the saying, "like a corpse in the hands of the body-washer." The goal of this submission is the total effacement of the ego, the psychic death, which signals the true birth into the spiritual life.

To illustrate what the relationship between a disciple and his master is, one can refer to the disclosures made by the "very great master" (*al-shaykh al-akbar*) Ibn 'Arabī, who was born in 560/1165 in Murcia and died in Damascus in 638/1240 and who left in his *Risālat al-quds* (*Epistle on Sanctity*) animated descriptions of the spiritual masters whom he had visited in Andalusia during the first part of his life.[9] Ibn 'Arabī speaks, for example, of his master Abū Ya'qūb al-Qūmī and says of him:

> He was much given to private devotions and always gave alms in secret. He honoured the poor and humbled the rich, ministering in person to the needs of the destitute. . . . He was seldom seen without a frown on his face, but when he saw a poor man his face would light up with joy; I have even seen him take one of the poor into his lap. . . . When I would sit before him or before others of my Shaykhs, I would tremble like a leaf in the wind, my voice would become weak and my limbs would shake.

Another famous and convincing example of the fruits born by submission to a master is that of Jalāl al-Dīn Rūmī, founder of the order of whirling dervishes and one of the greatest spiritual masters the world has ever known. He abandoned his position as professor and the honors he had received in Konya to follow the spiritual teaching of the mysterious Shams al-Dīn Tabrīzī and reached, through love of this master and annihilation in him (*al-fanā' fi'l-shaykh*), the highest peaks of Divine Love and contemplative vision.

Seyyed Hossein Nasr has recently defined the function of the spiritual master as follows:

> The role of the spiritual master, the *shaykh*, *murshid*, or *pīr*, as he is known in Arabic, Persian and other Muslim languages, is to make this spiritual rebirth and transformation possible. Being himself connected through the chain of initiation (*silsilah*) to the Prophet and to the function of initiation (*wilāyah*) inherent in the prophetic mission itself, the Sufi master is able to deliver man from the narrow confines of the material world into the illimitable luminous space of the spiritual life. . . . To behold the perfect master is to regain the ecstasy and joy of the spring of life and to be separated from the master is to experience the sorrow of old age. . . . To become initiated into a Sufi order and to accept the discipleship of a master is to enter into a bond that is permanent, surviving even death.[10]

Nasr says further:

> Man may seek the fountain of life by himself. He may seek to discover the principles of spiritual regeneration through his own efforts. But this endeavor is in vain and will never bear fruit unless the master is present together with the discipline which only he can impart. Without the philosopher's stone no alchemical transformation is possible. Only the power of the *shaykh* can deliver man from himself—from his carnal soul—so as to enable him to behold the Universe as it really is and to rejoin the sea of Universal Existence.[11]

Good Company (*al-ṣuḥbah*)

When he joins a brotherhood, the *murīd*, the disciple, finds—apart from a master—companions, brothers who, like him, walk on the path of God. The companionship of these brothers gives numerous opportunities for mutual encouragement in the devout life and the practice of the virtues—that is, humility, generosity, and equanimity, which lift from the heart the burdens weighing on it and, at the same time, embellish it, because they are the reflection of the Divine Qualities and are, according to the honored saying, "the tongues which glorify the Lord."

In a treatise on Sufism in which he devotes a chapter to the company of the master and to brotherhood with the fellow disciples, Shaykh Shihāb al-dīn ʿUmar al-Suhrawardī (d. Baghdad 632/1234–35), founder of the Suhrawardiyyah order, which is widespread in the Orient and reaches as far as India, teaches:

> [The *faqīr* must] abandon any idea of ownership, live in good understanding with his brothers . . . love them . . . show himself to be generous and mindful of the words of the Prophet: "Give to whomever asks, even if he is mounted on a horse," be affable, kind of an equal temperament . . . ; show a smiling face . . . , not be underhanded and permit no one other than the *shaykh* to elicit confidences; observe the greatest justice towards one's brothers . . . ; maintain a correct balance between excessive austerity and penitence and a too easy life.[12]

Good company thus becomes the very token of spiritual success. Aḥmad ibn ʿAjībah, master of the Shādhiliyyah-Darqāwiyyah *ṭarīqah* (d. A.D. 1809), stated in a letter to a disciple:

> The fruit borne through companionship with men of God is the realization of the station of attainment (*taḥqīq maqām al-wiṣāl*); and the attainment is that of extinction in the Essence (*al-fanāʾ fiʾ l-dhāt*), the station of perfect accomplishment (*iḥsān*), the station of contemplative vision wherein the existant is extinguished and only the source of all Existence remains. . . . If,

> while living in company with men of God, someone does not succeed in reaching this station, it is because of a deficiency in him, either his aspiration (*himmah*) is weak, or his zeal (*qarīḥah*) has grown cold, or he has committed an error which causes him to be content with his present state.[13]

In another letter the same master writes:

> It is necessary either that the disciple find the time to get together with his brothers where he is or that he go live near them, or that he visit them frequently in order to know the sweetness of the path and to drink at the springs of realization. Then he will free himself, in God, from all that is not He![14]

Spiritual Meetings

The advice given to the *faqīr* to make himself free to invoke the name of God communally underlines the importance that Sufism attaches to collective practices. Once initiated, each member can, and even in principle must, attend meetings of the *ṭarīqah* (*majālis;* sg. *majlis*), which are held at least once a week at locations and times specified in advance. These are held sometimes on Friday following noon prayers, in the same mosque where the canonical prayer is held; more often they are held in the evening, between *maghrib* and *'ishā'*, in the oratory, mosque, *zāwiyah, takiyyah, khānaqāh,* or *samā'khānah* (literally, "auditorium"), which serves as the seat of the *ṭarīqah,* or even in the home of the shaykh or that of one of the *fuqarā'*.

Although there are considerable differences among brotherhoods in terms of the rules of the meetings, the choice of the texts that are recited and sung, and the techniques of concentration practiced, the same format is found everywhere. It is made up of two parts: the first part is introductory and prepares those attending to participate in the incantory rite that forms the final and essential part of the meeting. The liturgical elements used in the course of the preparatory phase are mainly songs and cadenced recitations performed in an order that forms the "stages" (*marātib*) destined to lead the participants from an ordinary state of consciousness to a level of receptivity and fervor favorable to the mystical experience. As for the principal spiritual exercise, that which has the virtue of opening the doors of the "states" and "stations" of the contemplative way for the participants, it can be clothed in different modalities, which are distinguished by the respective usage they make of three technical elements: music, corporeal movement, and breathing. Given the important place they occupied or still do occupy in the spiritual life of the Muslim community, two major types of incantory rites will be brought out here. The first, which is the most widespread among the *ṭuruq* such as the Qādiriyyah and Shādhiliyyah, is based on the rhythmic repetition of the Divine Name, *Allāh;* the second is the "spiritual concert" (*samā'*), the most justly celebrated example of which is found in the Mawlawiyyah (Mevlevis in Turkey) or "whirling dervishes," characterized by the use of music and the technique of a turning dance.

Before beginning a description of the various components of the mystical gathering, it is necessary to pause for a moment upon the thread that connects them and forms the woof of the gathering as it weaves together all the instants of the life of each true *faqīr.* This guiding thread is the remembrance, the invocation of God.

Invocation (*al-dhikr*)

Wa ladhikru'Llāhi akbar, "the *dhikr*—remembrance, recollection, mindfulness, naming, or invocation—of Allah is greater" or "the greatest thing."[15] With these words the Quran (XXIX, 45) states the primacy of the *dhikr* both in terms of relative value in relation to other ritual prescriptions, such as the canonical prayer mentioned in the preceding verse, and in terms of absolute value, the invocation being affirmed as the path of salvation *par excellence.* Doctrinally speaking, the *dhikr* is the becoming aware by the creature of the connection that unites him for all eternity to the Creator. Seen in this way, the *dhikr* constitutes the very essence of religion, as much in its exoteric dimension (where man remembers God as his Master and transcendent and omnipotent Judge) as in the esoteric order (where the Divine Presence reveals itself as the inner dimension of the human being). From an operative and theurgical point of view, each of the means that the Revelation has placed at the disposal of believers in order to help them to attain this awareness is *dhikr.* There are, on the one hand, ritual practices that are obligatory for all of the faithful, those who are connected to the five pillars of Islam and whose powers of recollection (*quwwāt al-dhikr*) have often been commented upon by the mystics.[16] Next come the supererogatory deeds that the most devout Muslims, Sufis or non-Sufis, are able to carry out *ad libitum* to get nearer to their Lord, such as the reading of the Quran, preferably during the night, the voluntary fasting and almsgiving and the numerous prayers and rogations (*du'āt*) recommended by the *Sunnah.* There are, finally, in the Sufi cadre, spiritual exercises based on the repetition and contemplative penetration of certain Quranic formulas, especially those that contain the Names of the Divinity.

Numerous verses of the sacred Book recommend multiple performances of *dhikr,* invoking God morning and night, in fear and humility, until the soul is appeased. The following are some of these injunctions:

> Call upon God, or call upon the Merciful; whichsoever you call upon, to Him belong the Names Most Beautiful. (XVII, 110)
>
> Remember Me, and I will remember you (or Mention Me, and I will mention you). (II, 152)
>
> O believers, remember God oft, and give Him glory at the dawn and in the evening. It is He who blesses you, and His angels, to bring you from the shadows into the light. . . . (XXXIII, 41–43)
>
> In temples God has allowed to be raised up, and His Name to be commemorated therein; therein glorifying Him, in the mornings and the evenings, are men whom neither commerce nor trafficking diverts from the remembrance of God and to perform the prayer, and to pay the alms. (XXIV, 36–37)
>
> God guides to Him . . . those who believe and whose hearts are at rest in God's remembrance because surely, in God's remembrance are hearts at rest. (XIII, 27–28)

Some sayings of the Prophet as recorded by his disciples have the same import:

> Men never assemble to invoke Allah without being surrounded by angels and covered by Divine Blessings, without peace (*sakīnah*) descending on them and Allah remembering them.
>
> There is a way of polishing everything and removing rust and that which polishes the heart is the invocation of God.
>
> "Shall I tell you the best of your deeds? The purest in the eyes of your King, He Whom you hold to be at the highest level, Whose proximity is more beneficial than the act of giving (in the guise of alms) gold and silver or of meeting your enemy and striking him down or being struck?" The companions said, "Tell us." The Prophet answered, "It is the invocation of God the Most High." (Al-Tirmidhī, as told by Abu'l-Dardā')

Among the numerous formulas employed in invocation, certain ones have always found favor among the Sufis, such as "the most beautiful Names" mentioned in the Quran, from which a list of ninety-nine, corresponding to the number of beads on the rosary, are recited individually or collectively.

The majority of the Divine Names taken individually can also be made the object of a *dhikr,* just as several Names possessing special affinities in common can be associated in the formulas of invocation. Some of these groupings are *yā Ḥayy, yā Qayyūm!* (O Living, O Immutable!), *yā Raḥmān, yā Raḥīm!* (O Merciful, O Forgiving), and similarly the *basmalah,* the formula for consecration in the Name of God, which contains the latter two Names. The repetition of the first part of the profession of faith, *Lā ilāha illa'Llāh,* is universally practiced in mystical circles, in conformity with the teaching of the Prophet, "the best invocation is 'There is no divinity but God,'" (Al-Tirmidhī, as told by Jābir). Its particular effectiveness comes from evoking the two phrases of spiritual realization, negation (*nafy*) of all divinity, that is, of all secondary reality that has not sufficient meaning in itself, and affirmation (*ithbāt*) of the sole Reality of the Absolute Being, effacement of the creature and return to the Creator, annihilation of the separate self (*farq*) and reunification with God (*jam'*).

However, the invocation *par excellence* is that of the Name *Allāh*, the unparalleled name of the Divinity, the Supreme Name (*al-ism al-a'ẓam*), the Unique Name (*al-ism al-mufrad*), the Name of Majesty (*ism al-jalālah*). With its symbolic two syllables and four letters, this Name concentrates all the redemptive efficacy of the Divine Word.[17] "God is present in His Name," say the Sufis. To the degree that, through the conjunction of this Presence and a serious concentration on the part of the invoker, he finds himself effaced, absorbed in the One invoked, the *dhikr* becomes God's *dhikr* alone, in which the invocation, the invoked, and the invoker are one with the One without second.[18]

Given its incomparable grandeur, the invocation of the Supreme Name can only be practiced under certain conditions, with the authorization of the *murshid* and under his control. Thus, the authorization to practice invocation outside of collective gatherings is not generally granted to the *murīd* at the time of his entry into the *ṭarīqah* but at a later stage, when the shaykh has sufficiently tested the disciple's qualifications and has recognized in him the quality of "traveler" (*sālik*) on the mystical path and not only that of being "affiliated with the blessings" (*mutabarrak*) that surround the *ṭarīqah*.

The right to invocation thus constitutes for the *faqīr*, according to the saying of Abū 'Alī al-Daqqāq, master and father-in-law of Qushayrī (d. 465/1072), the "symbol of initiation" (*manshūr al-wilāyah*), so that "he who receives the *dhikr* is enthroned, while he who loses it is dismissed."

If such precautions are necessary to avoid the dangers to which novices could expose themselves by wrongly performing *dhikr*, they are not needed at collective sessions, where the presence of the older and experienced shaykh and *fuqarā'* provides a guarantee and a security against excesses and other undesirable psychic manifestations to which the beginners on the Sufi path could be subjected.[20]

The Wird (Access)

The spiritual meeting opens with a collective recitation, in a loud and rhythmic voice, of the *wird*, sometimes called *ḥizb* or *waẓīfah*, which is the litany proper to the brotherhood. Made up essentially of a series of formulas taken from the Quran which individually are repeated a certain number of times—3, 7, 10, 29, 33, 100, or 1000 times—the *wird* represents a symbol for the *fuqarā'* of their connection with the initiatic chain (*silsilah*) going back to the Prophet, with the master who brought them into the *ṭarīqah* being the most recent link. To recite the *wird* is, in a sense, to renew the pact made with the shaykh, with the Prophet, and with God Himself. And it is also, symbolically at least, to traverse the entire distance of the spiritual path, the order in which the formulas are arranged having been conceived to retrace the principal steps to the approach toward God.

Thus, the *wird* of the Qādiriyyah, the first to be recorded from the great Sufi orders, founded in the sixth/twelfth century by 'Abd al-Qādīr al-Jīlānī, like that of the Shādhiliyyah (seventh/thirteenth century), always includes at least one hundred repetitions of the following formulas: (1) the plea for forgiveness (*istighfār*), (2) the prayer upon the Prophet (*ṣalāt 'ala'l-nabī*), (3) the testimony of faith (*Shahādah* or *haylalah*).[21] These formulas correspond to fundamental spiritual attitudes which each aspirant to the mystical life must assimilate: (1) the station of fear of God (*makhāfah*), which implies repentance (*tawbah*) and renunciation of worldly pleasures (*zuhd*); (2) the station of love (*maḥabbah*) which implies patience (*ṣabr*) and generosity (*karam*), qualities that were united in an exemplary fashion in the person of Muḥammad; and (3) the station of gnosis (*ma'rifah*), that is, of discernment (*furqān*) and of concentration on the Divine Presence (*muḥāḍarah*).

The Sufis also establish a concordance among these three formulas and the three stages of religion (*al-dīn*) mentioned in the *ḥadīth* called "from Gabriel": the stage of *islām*, which engages the external faculties (*jawāriḥ*) and consists in carrying out the prescriptions of the religious Law (*Sharī'ah*) and in abstaining from that which it forbids; the stage of *īmān*, which gives access to the internal faculties (*bawāṭin*), which asks for progress along the mystical path (*ṭarīqah*) and the total giving of oneself; and, finally, the stage of *iḥsān*, wherein the Divine Light penetrates and illuminates the innermost souls of beings (*sarā'ir*), becoming the place where total Reality (*Ḥaqīqah*) is unveiled. The first stage is that of the common people, the second that of the elite, the third that of the elect among the elite, the gnostics who have "attained" God (*wāṣilūn*).

The Hymns (anāshīd)

The recitation of the *wird*, which lasts about a half hour, is sometimes followed by a brief period of spiritual exhortation (*mudhākarah*) during which the shaykh reads and comments upon some passage of a treatise on

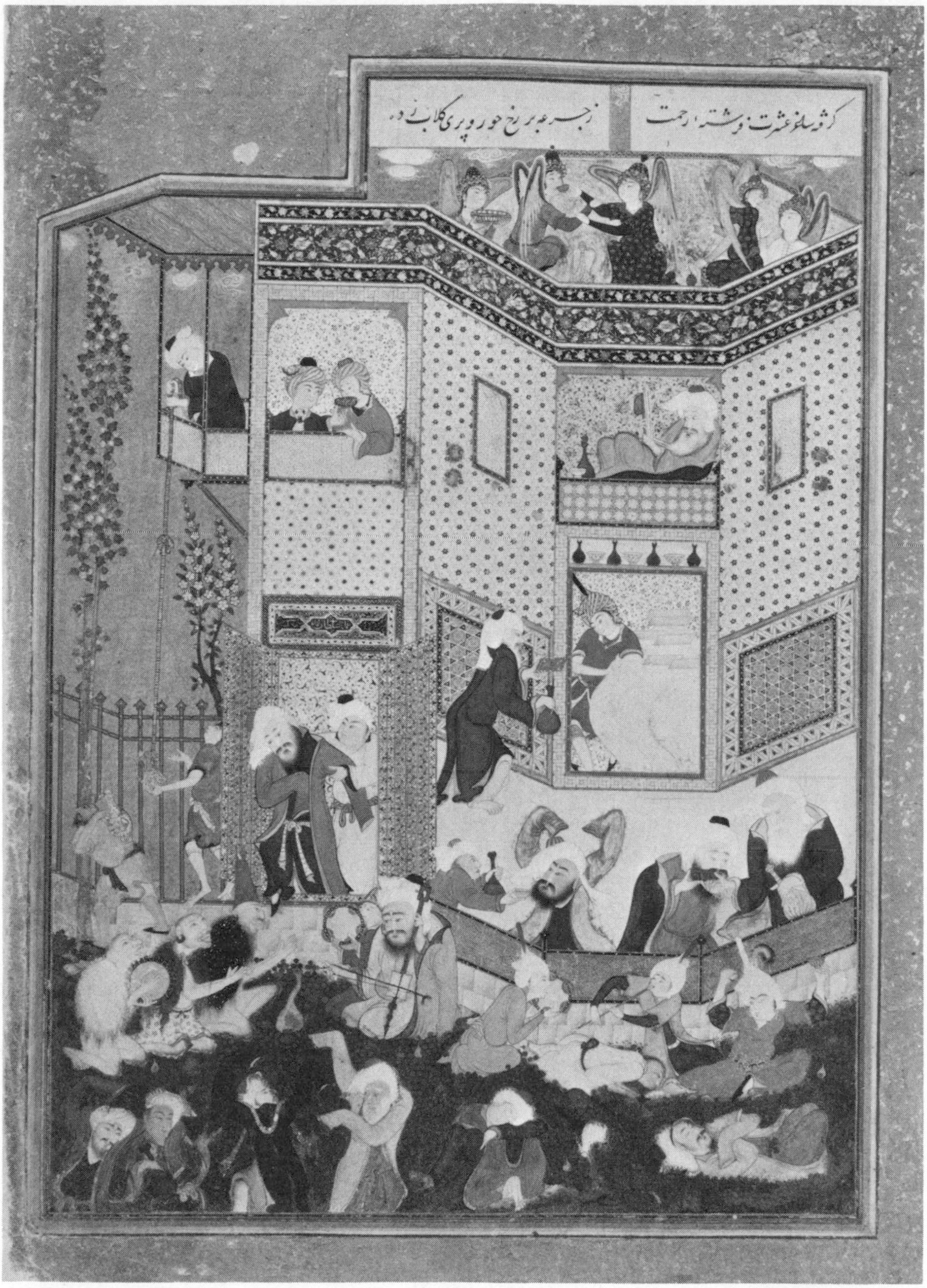

29. "Worldly and Otherworldly Drunkenness," signed Sultan Muhammad, ca. 1626–1627.

Sufism or exposes an aspect of the mystical path and then answers disciples' questions concerning the subject discussed.

After this comes the part called the spiritual concert (*al-samāʿ*), which includes first the performance of several sacred songs taken from the vast repertoire of Sufi poetry, odes, and quatrains from Arab, Persian, or Turkish poets, or poems in the local dialect often composed by anonymous bards. One very popular category of hymns is made up of praises (*amdāḥ, mawlidāt*) which traditionally celebrate the anniversary of the birth of the Prophet (*mawlid al-nabī*) the 12th of Rabīʿ I of each lunar year but which, for the past century, have slowly been introduced into the ordinary meetings of the *ṭuruq*.

At their gatherings, the Shādhilī dervishes of Syria, whose order is representative of a large number of initiatic circles, sing, among others, hymns drawn from the collection of poems (*Dīwān*) of the Sufi ʿAbd al-Ghanī al-Nābulusī (from Naplus, in Palestine) who lived from A.D. 1641 to 1731. Here are some of the verses that a young *munshid* with a beautiful voice sang recently (1964) in a *zāwiyah* in Hama. Unfortunately, only the meaning of the words can be given, translation being unable to convey the harmony and the rhythm of this psalmody:

> O thou who appearest at the rising of the spheres
> of the Invisible,
> O thou who stoppest in the tent of the men of the heart!
> Do not blame me, O censor, for loving the beautiful
> ones with supple bodies.
> Since I have no other attachment but towards the
> One who is present behind the veils.
> The perfume of secrets is exhaled in the garden of
> the meeting,
> And its emanation has made us drunk.

This piece is typical of the symbolic images used by the Sufi poets, be they Arab or Persian. Thus, "he who stops in the tent of the men of the heart" is the intellect, the First Intellect (*al-ʿaql al-awwal*), which the Sufis consider to be the first created thing and, consequently, like a ray of light that unites all the worlds. "The beautiful ones with supple bodies" are the incorruptible beauties of the subtle world, the houris, who are, for the mystic emanations, rays from the Absolute Essence. "The perfume of secrets" is the tangible manifestations of the Divine Presence, each of which intoxicates because it brings to the heart the light and warmth of this Presence, itself often associated with wine[22] or with Layla, the Beloved.

As for the evocation of the Prophet, which is also made in the form of sung poems, it possesses the same virtue as the *ṣalāt* (prayer) contained in the second formula of the *wird:* Muḥammad, "the best of created beings," "the evident prototype" is the channel through which Divine Benediction descends to earth and spreads among men; he is the intermediary (*al-wāsiṭah*) for anyone wishing to return to the very source of benedictions, the prayer to him leading to the Lord by a path of love and beauty.

Thus, in their weekly gatherings of recollection, the *fuqarā'* of the Shādhilī order from Morocco to Iraq sing in unison passages from the *Burdah* ("the Coat"), a poem of the Egyptian shaykh al-Būṣīrī (d. 694/1296) which came to him in a vision. Such verses as, "When you see him, to him alone is demanded respect equal to that for an escort, or for an army"; or again, some extracts from the *Hamziyyah* (poem rhyming with *hamzah*), in which the same author, after having described the virtues of the Prophet, concludes: "The image that men can give of thy qualities is none other than that of the stars reflected in water."[23]

The hymns dedicated to the Prophet never fail to create a climate of intense fervor in which the listeners commune with the beloved and, through contact with him, are stripped of their egotistical pretensions and prepared to enter into the rite that is the heart of the Sufi meeting—the ecstatic dance.

The Sacred Dance

The majority of the *ṭuruq* possess a mode of collective invocation that lends itself to corporeal movement. The Mawlawīs, the whirling dervishes, call it *samā'*, spiritual concert, because it pertains to a rite in which dance is sustained by a complete musical ensemble—vocal, instrumental, and rhythmic. The music itself is considered a form of invocation.

Many other *ṭuruq* such as the Qādiriyyah and the Shādhiliyyah speak rather of *ḥaḍrat al-dhikr,* meaning literally "presence of invocation," because the Name that is pronounced in the meetings is the Name of God Himself, *Allāh,* the Name in which God is present and through which He makes Himself present. Pronouncing the Divine Name, on which the rhythm of the *ḥaḍrah* is based, is thus a sacrament in the strictest sense of the term—that is, a supernatural act that allows man to leave his nature and to be transformed, absorbed in a dimension that surpasses him. In the Maghreb, where there are numerous branches of the Shādhilī order, such as the 'Īsawiyyah, the Zarrūqiyyah, the Nāṣiriyyah, the Darqāwiyyah, etc., this form of sacred dance is also called '*imārah,* or plenitude, because the name of the Divine Essence, *Allāh* (or simply *huwa,* He), in penetrating the human receptacle, fills it beyond measure.

There are numerous ways of invoking the name *Allāh.* The invocation can be silent, scarcely audible, or it can be spoken aloud. The Name can be pronounced slowly or quickly and rhythmically. The most widely used method of invocation, that of the Shādhilī or Qādirī, is rhythmic, called "the invocation from the chest" (*dhikr al-ṣadr*), because, after having begun by pronouncing the name *Allāh* in its entirety with all its letters, the participants finish by pronouncing only the final *hā'*, in a breath that no longer uses the vibration of the vocal chords but only alternating contraction and expansion of the chest.

At the start of this rhythmic invocation, all the participants stand side by side and join hands, forming one or more either concentric circles or rows facing one another. In the center stands the shaykh or one of his assistants. This arrangement, which is also found among the whirling dervishes, evokes the symbolism of the circle of angels or the rows of angels that surround the Divine Throne. The session begins with a slow rhythm. The dancers pronounce the Divine Name in unison, bowing the trunk of the body rapidly and fully at the moment of exhaling the second syllable, *lāh.* When they inhale, they stand erect again. The rhythm increases in tempo little by little, and the movements of the body always accompany the two phases of the breath. The name *Allāh* is soon no longer clear and only the last letter *hā'* remains, which all the chests exhale in an immense burst of air. Each of these exhalations symbolizes the last breath of man, the moment when the individual soul is reintegrated into the cosmic breath, that is to say, into the Divine Spirit, which was blown into man at the time of creation and through which man always remains in communication with the Absolute. Keeping with the movements of the chest, the body is alternately lowered and raised as if at each instant it were being pulled toward the sky and then sent back toward the earth. All the eyes are closed; the faces express a kind of painful rapture. One need not fear pointing out that, if breathing of this *dhikr* evokes that of a rapture of a more sensual order, it is not an accident. There are precise correspondences between the higher order and that here below. That is why, for example, earthly love is able to serve as the point of departure for the realization of Divine Love, and it is also why the houris of paradise symbolize the delights of heaven.

The Mawlawī session, the *samā'*, is also entirely woven from symbolic elements, which all concur on the same goal, the *dhikr,* the call to the Divine. The very costume of the dancers is charged with significance. Their headgear, a large tarboosh of brown felt, represents the vertical dimension, the axis that escapes the tribulations of desire and passion; it represents also the tombstone and reminds the wearer of the unavoidable door of death, the ephemeral nature of this lower world, and the necessity for seeking in this life the Truth which does not die. At the beginning of the session, the dervish wears a black robe which he removes at the time of the dance; this means that he is abandoning his gross individuality in order to appear purified before the master of the dance and before his brothers. The white robe in which he then dresses signifies the shroud in which his corpse will one day be wrapped, and at the same time it prefigures the resurrection and the joyous meeting with the Divine Beloved. During the session the dervish sings:

> The frock is my tomb, the hat my tombstone . . .
> Why wouldn't a corpse dance in this world
> when the sound of the trumpets of death
> raise him to dance?[24]

In their orchestra the Mawlawīs use the small violin with three strings, the lute, the drum, and the reed flute (*nay*) as their principal instruments. The reed flute is their favorite instrument and their most eloquent means of expression. The reed from which it is made is the symbol of human existence—fragile, fragmentary, since it is cut off from its origin just as the reed was pulled from the reedbed. However, this existence can be regenerated when it is traversed and transformed by the Divine Breath and is lent Its strength, Its energy, Its voice.[25] Jalāl al-Dīn Rūmī, in the prologue to the *Mathnawī* (*Mesnevī*), his mystical epic in 26,000 couplets, likens the song of the flute to the call of the soul that longs to return to his Lord:

> Listen to the song of the reed and listen to its story.
> Weeping from the pain of separation
> It cries: "Since I was severed from my native land,
> Men and women have longed to hear my songs
> And the agony of separation has broken my heart. . . ."

One of the dominant themes of Mawlawī spirituality is that earthly music is an echo of celestial music. Harmonious vibration of strings, the repeated striking of the drum, and the voice of the flute are reminders of our Divine Origin, and they awaken in us the desire to find once again our distant homeland. The Quran teaches that in the beginning God made a solemn pact, the *mīthāq,* with souls before creation, asking them, "Am I not your Lord?" "Yea!" they responded, accepting perpetual obedience (VII, 172). Nevertheless, souls were unfaithful to the pact; they desired to live a separate existence, which is the cause of all their miseries. To find again the original purity is therefore the most profound, the most normal aspiration of the human being. As a Mawlawī friend, a professor of French at the high school of Konya who had just cited in the text the first verses of the "Lake" by Lamartine, told me, "Each beautiful thing—a flower, the song of a bird—awakens in our soul the memory of our origin. Let us learn how to listen to the voice of beautiful things; it will make us understand the voice of our soul."

The dance itself, in the form that was realized by Rūmī, which he transmitted to his disciples, draws its efficacy from a rich and eloquent symbolism at the same time that its action concentrates and focuses on the human faculties. Gathered into an octagonal enclosure, the dervishes arrange themselves to dance in several concentric orbits, creating an image of the planets in the heavens. One dervish, usually the oldest, occupies the center of the room, where he represents the "pole." He turns slowly in place, while the others, arranged in a crown shape, spin around and at the same time turn around in the orbits in which they were placed. The dance is accompanied by several gestures of the arms. At the beginning, the hands are crossed over the chest in a gesture of humility and contraction of the soul (*qabḍ*). Then the arms spread apart in a sign of expansion (*basṭ*); the right hand opens toward the sky and the left hand turns toward the ground. By this gesture the dervish indicates that he is opening himself to the grace of heaven in a gesture of confidence and that he leads the grace thus received toward the terrestrial world and all the beings who inhabit it. Having become like a rotating cross, he moves about smoothly, his head slightly bowed, his shoulders held constantly at the same level. His white robe, swollen like a corolla, is the image of the fullness (*'arḍ*) of the universe penetrated by Divine Wisdom (*al-ḥikmah*). The vertical axis of his body, elongated by the high tarboosh, is the sign of the exaltation (*ṭūl*) to which the creature can accede only after his extinction in the All-Powerful (*al-qudrah*).

Reproducing on earth the movements of the stars, themselves symbols of angelic powers and hierarchies, the dervish is conscious of participating in the universal harmony and of contributing to making the order that is in the skies reign here below. Giving himself up to the rhythm of celestial harmonies, he becomes an instrument through which Divine Love communicates with creatures suffering from separation and from the cosmic illusion. Through his rotation, he affirms the unique presence of God in all directions in space, "Wherever you turn, there is the Face of God" (II, 115), and he identifies himself with this Center and omnipresent Principle.

Spiritual Progress

Whatever their operative strength, the collective rites alone could not assure arrival at the final steps of the journey toward God. Spiritual realization can only be an affair of each instant, as is well put in the expression "son of the moment" (*ibn al-waqt*), by which the Sufi is defined. For each moment of the life of the *faqīr* there is a corresponding *adab*, a convention, which can be a ritual practice, a correct behavior, or, better still, an inner attitude in conformity with that which God expects from His servant. In fact, according to a teaching of Abu'l-'Abbās al-Mursī (d. 686/1287), who was the master of Ibn 'Aṭā' Allāh of Alexandria:

> For the servant four moments exist, not one more: the blessing and the test of which he is the object on the part of God, the obedience and the disobedience with which he himself tests. And at each of these moments, the servant has a duty to God: in blessing, this duty is gratitude; in the test, constancy; in obedience, the awareness of grace; and in disobedience, repentance and contrition.[26]

In order to reach such a "presence of spirit" (*muḥāḍarah*), which allows, according to a *ḥadīth* frequently encountered in treatises on Sufism, "to render to each one and to each thing his due," the *faqīr* must follow, under the direction of his master, a discipline that includes two inseparable aspects: a sustained effort toward self-knowledge and daily spiritual exercises based essentially on invocation.

"Know Thyself"

That self-knowledge is not only the condition but also the very goal of the mystical quest is affirmed by the *ḥadīth* of the Prophet, "He who knows himself knows his Lord" (*man 'arafa nafsahu faqad 'arafa rabbah*).[27] Such a knowledge obviously would not stop at the simply psychological level, since the human soul, the psyche, always makes up a fragmentary entity that veils the vision of the total Reality, of the Divine Self. However, the very existence of this veil allows, on its own level, for a seizure of the source of existence, and the concern of the *faqīr* must be to render the veil transparent so that the lights of heaven can illumine it and pass through it unhindered. This means first to recognize our shortcomings, which are displeasing to God and prevent Him from shining in us, and to work toward their elimination through ascetic discipline (*al-mujāhadah*). This is the purgative aspect of inner knowledge, the aspect that often predominates during the initial portion of the path. As for the positive aspect of this same knowledge, it consists in recognizing in oneself the reflection of the qualities and beauties of the Creator and of attributing to Him all glory; this increases the intimacy between the praiser and the Praised.

The practices recommended by the masters for better self-knowledge include notably the "setting of conditions" (*mushāraṭah*), which takes place in the morning upon awakening and consists in admonishing oneself and in reaffirming one's intention to consecrate oneself entirely to God. One then tells oneself, "Here is a new day which will be a test for you, so force yourself, oh my soul, to fill each instant with that which draws you nearer to God. . . ."[28] The same evening, the *faqīr* must examine his conscience (*muḥāsabah,* literally, an accounting), the object of which is not only the measurement of how the morning's resolutions were followed, but a "gathering up of time" (*ittiḥād al-waqt*) by evoking simultaneously a vision of the acts and the thoughts of the day in imitation of the man on the threshold of death who sees his entire life pass before him.[29]

The two techniques are, in fact, only particular methods for maintaining a constant vigilance, which the *faqīr* must have in order not to waste time, not to be distracted by "that which does not concern him" (*mā lā yughnīh*) and in order to keep himself constantly attentive to the desire of the Beloved. This vigilance is called *murāqabah,* a word derived from the Divine Name *al-Raqīb,* the All-Seeing, and it is synonymous with "the guardian of the heart" (*al-'assa 'ala 'l-qalb*). It is this same disposition of the soul that the Hesychasts, the recluses of the Eastern Orthodox Church, described as "the way of all the virtues and all the commandments of God, which consist of tranquillity of the heart and of a mind perfectly free from all imagination."[30] Its importance has been stressed by such eminent masters as Muḥāsibī, Qushayrī, and Ibn 'Aṭā' Allāh al-Iskandarī,[31] for reasons identical to those of the Christian mystics who were adepts in the "prayer of the heart." The reason is that only an innermost heart free from distractions and random thoughts can be illuminated by perpetual prayer.

The acquisition of *murāqabah* is the highest level of self-mastery, the victory on three fronts of the interior battle waged by the *faqīr:* that of the external faculties, which implies scrupulous respect to the legal prescriptions and abstentions; that of the internal faculties, where the battle consists of dispelling evil thoughts and of remaining fixed on the Divine Presence; and that of the depths of the heart, in which no other concern must enter except that of the Adored. "Vigilance," wrote Ibn 'Ajībah, "is the source of all goodness and contemplation (*mushāhadah*) is in proportion to it; he whose vigilance is great will attain great contemplation."[32]

"Invoke Often"

Whereas the exercises of introspection aim at purifying the human recipient and at making *faqr,* the blessed destitution, reign therein, the *dhikr,* the pronouncing of the Divine Word, is made to communicate to the *faqīr* His inexhaustible Richness.

In accordance with the Quranic injunction to multiply the acts of invocation, each *ṭarīqah* suggests to its members, according to their level of preparation and their individual zeal, a large range of ejaculatory prayers (*adhkār*, pl. of *dhikr*). First comes the *wird* particular to the order, the same one that is sung in the collective sessions mentioned earlier, which each *faqīr* must recite twice a day, morning and night, using his rosary (*sibḥah*). The shaykh can, in addition, propose that the *murīd* regularly read certain litanies composed by the inspired masters, often by the founder of the *ṭarīqah*. These are, for example, among the Qādiriyyah the *qunūt*, made up entirely of Quranic verses; among the Shādhiliyyah the *Ḥizb al-baḥr* and the *Ḥizb al-barr* ("Incantations of the Sea and the Land") of Imam Shādhilī, or the *Ṣalāt mashīshiyyah* by the "Pole" ʿAbd al-Salām ibn Mashīsh (d. 625/1228), master of the former; among the Khalwatiyyah the *Wird al-sattār;* among the Tijāniyyah the *Jawharat al-kamāl,* etc.[33]

Strictly speaking, however, the invocatory practices are those that are based on the systematic repetition of short formulas containing one or more Divine Names and, more particularly, of the *Shahādah,* of the sole name *Allāh* or of its substitute, the pronoun *huwa,* "He." Being acts of pure devotion performed in order to bring the *faqīr* face to face with himself, to test his ability to offer the sacrifice of his thoughts and his feelings, and to aid him in abandoning himself (*tafrīd*) in God, these exercises require recollection and solitude. Moreover, the invocation performed in retreat (*khalwah*) is the most often recommended mode of *dhikr,* the same one that the Prophet taught to ʿAlī ibn Abī Ṭālib, his cousin and son-in-law. When ʿAlī once asked the Prophet the shortest way to God, the Prophet answered, "ʿAlī, always repeat the Name of God in solitary places . . . ." After this, with eyes closed, he said out loud three times, "*Lā ilāha illa' Llāh,*" making ʿAlī repeat this formula with the same intonation.[34] ʿAlī later initiated Ḥasan al-Baṣrī to this *dhikr,* which has been perpetuated in numerous *ṭuruq,* such as the Khalwatiyyah, founded by the Persian anchorite ʿUmar al-Khalwatī (d. in Caesarea, Syria, in 800/1397). It should be noted that this *ṭarīqah,* still active in North Africa and the Near East, added to the invocation of the *Shahādah* and the name *Allāh* the pronoun *huwa* and the four Divine Names *Ḥaqq* (Truth), *Ḥayy* (Living), *Qayyūm* (Eternal), and *Qahhār* (Dominant). These seven names correspond to the celestial spheres, to the colors emanated by the fundamental light, and to the stages of the soul on the path to perfection. The soul is first "prone to evil," then "blameworthy," "inspired," "appeased," "satisfied," "satisfying," before being rendered "perfect."[35]

A very similar teaching is found in the Suhrawardiyyah order, whose founder, Shihāb al-Dīn ʿUmar, already mentioned concerning his advice on good companions, also figures among the ancestors of the initiatic chain of the Khalwatīs. The Suhrawardī *dhikr* also includes seven names, of which only the last two—*al-Raḥmān* (the Merciful) and *al-Raḥīm* (the Forgiving)—differ from the preceding list. It is also practiced during retreats, whose normal duration is forty days, and is accompanied by the visualization of the seven symbolic colors—blue, yellow, red, white, green, black, and undifferentiated—which correspond to the various levels or worlds of universal manifestation.[36]

Of all the formulas of invocation, it is the name *Allāh* which, even among the *ṭuruq* with a multiform *dhikr*, has always been considered the most complete and the most efficacious way to grace. Thus it is, for example, that when the celebrated Sufi and theologian Abū Ḥāmid al-Ghazzālī, after having exhausted the possibilities of speculative reasoning, had the desire to follow the path of direct experience and revealed this to a Sufi, he was given the following advice:

> The best method consists of breaking totally your ties with the world, in such a way that your heart is occupied with neither family nor . . . money. . . . In addition you must be alone in a retreat to carry out, from among your acts of worship, only the prescribed *salāt* . . . and, being seated, concentrate your thoughts on God, without other interior preoccupation. You will do this, first by saying the Name of God with your tongue, repeating without ceasing *Allāh, Allāh,* without relaxing your attention. The result will be a state in which you will effortlessly feel this Name in the spontaneous movement of your tongue.[37]

This is found as the first step in a process of inner penetration in three stages as suggested bv the same Ghazzālī in his celebrated *Revival of the Sciences of Religion.*

> After seating himself in solitude, he (the *ṣūfī*) does not cease to say with his mouth "*Allāh, Allāh,*" continually and with presence of heart. And he continues thus until he reaches a state wherein he abandons the movement of the tongue, and sees the word as if flowing upon the tongue. Then he arrives at the point of effacing any trace of the word upon his tongue, and he finds his heart continually applied to the *dhikr;* he perseveres assiduously, until he effaces from his heart the image of speaking the letters and the shape of the word, and the meaning of the word alone remains in his heart, present in him, as if joined to him and not leaving him.[38]

Integral religion (*al-dīn*) includes three stations capable of sanctifying the entire man—body, soul, and spirit—through submission (*islām*) to the prescriptions and prohibitions of the Law (*Sharīʿah*), through the faith (*īmān*) that blooms on the spiritual path (*ṭarīqah*) and through the conformity (*iḥsān*) of the individual to the Divine Reality (*Ḥaqīqah*). In the same way, the practice of the *dhikr,* which is the central method of this sanctification, takes place on three levels—that of acts, that of qualities, and that of the Essence—and in each of these achieves sanctifying union. In effect, what occurs is the following: (1) The invocation of the tongue (*dhikr al-lisān*) unites all the separate moments of the man in the single act of the *dhikr* and thus restores primacy to the only real Agent, Which is God (*tawḥīd al-af'āl*). (2) The invocation of the heart (*dhikr al-qalb*) causes the appearance of all the qualities of the universe in a single place, a blessed center, while attributing them to the only One Who is worthy to be qualified by the most beautiful Names (*tawḥīd al-ṣifāt*). (3) The invocation of the depths of the heart, of the "secret" (*dhikr al-sirr*), has neither point of departure nor end, nor distinct subjects and objects. Because of a clear vision, it affirms that nothing exists except the One Who is the Name, the Named, and the Namer, in His Absolute and Unconditional Essence (*tawḥīd al-dhāt*).

Mastery of the first stage of the *dhikr,* which corresponds to the acquisition of the "science of certainty" (*'ilm al-yaqīn*), is largely attributable to the clarity of the mind, thus to the aptitude of the *faqīr* to meditate on himself (according to the Quran XXX, 8) as well as on "the creation of the heavens and the earth" (III, 191) and, in general, on all the signs of God (X, 24). Not only does meditation (*tafakkur*) aid in eliminating distractions and in maintaining a fixed attention on the *dhikr,* but it causes doubt and existential worry to cease and confirms the *murīd* in his vocation of seeking God.

The second stage, that of the heart, is also that of "the eye" or the "source of certainty" (*'ayn al-yaqīn*). It implies an unfailing adherence of the will, a confidence that the *dhikr* fills all needs and that it leads to salvation. It is the stage of love of God, that of the man who resides in the "inward dimension, . . . the domain of unity, synthesis and permanence."[39]

As for the third stage of the *dhikr,* that of the "truth of certainty" (*ḥaqq al-yaqīn*), it is a gift from heaven, incommensurate with the effort of the thought and will that preceded it. The individual abandons himself to it. He is said to have "disappeared" (*ghā'ib*), to be absorbed by the One invoked and "made one" with Him. He becomes, then, through a direct vision (*shuhūd*) a perfect witness (*shahīd*) to the Truth. According to the testimony of one of those who arrived at this final stage, the "master of the circle" (*shaykh al-ṭā'ifah*) of the Sufis of Baghdad, Abu'l-Qāsim al-Junayd (d. 298/910), "It is the supreme reality of *tawḥīd* professed by one who attests to the One after having been himself effaced."[40]

Epilogue

Over fifty years ago, in 1931, a great scholar of Muslim mysticism, Emile Dermenghem, published, along with the French translation of the famous poem of Ibn al-Fāriḍ on the mystical wine, a letter which a young Moroccan had written him.[41] This young man described gatherings of *dhikr,* of invocation, which he had attended several years earlier in a small mosque in Fez. The dervishes who participated in these gatherings belonged to the Shādhiliyyah order and the correspondent concluded his letter with these words: "All that, alas, is only a memory.... Where are the fakirs of yesteryear? The old ones have passed away or become infirm. The young ones have become modernized and prefer to spend their time drinking aperitifs in cafes or strolling through the new city. The Orient, unfortunately, is losing its essence along with its charm. The divine Breath which exhaled the verses of Ibn al-Fāriḍ no longer fills chests. Where will this lead?"

No doubt these observations are true; this sadness is legitimate. Inexorably, all people are adopting, with varying degrees of enthusiasm, a mode of life as well as of thought—since one does not engage the body without engaging the soul—diametrically opposed to the course of religion and, *a fortiori,* to the mystical path. The Prophet Muḥammad, or perhaps his son-in-law 'Alī, once said, "Act for this present world as if you were going to live forever, and act for the other world as if you were going to die tomorrow." More and more, modern man, whether of the West or the East, has the tendency to retain only the first part of this advice; he devotes all his energy to organizing his well-being here on earth, as if this world would last forever. By doing this he loses sight of the fact that the passage on earth is, in reality, only one step. He forgets that according to the teaching of Jesus, Sayyidnā 'Īsā, "Man does not live by bread alone, but by all the words which come from the mouth of God" (Matthew 4:4); or that, according to the teaching of the Quran (XCIII, 4), "The other life, certainly, is better for you than this one."

However, let us not be totally pessimistic. Behind the picture we are currently given of the Orient divided and prey to the agony of difficult economic, social, and political organization remain stable values and an authentic civilization. Men remain, again according to a Quranic saying, whose "business dealings do not turn them from the remembrance of God" (XXIV, 37). If certain spiritual centers have disappeared, others, even beyond the classical borders of the *dār al-islām,* have taken up the refrain which has lasted more than thirteen centuries. Thus, the Muslim Orient has not failed in its traditional mission, that which generations of dervishes and

Sufis have fulfilled: to pass from century to century the good news that there exists a path that leads to God, and to guide along this path the souls enraptured by a Truth that never dies.

Translated by Katherine O'Brien

Notes

1. It concerns the *ḥadīth* called "of Gabriel" or "or ʿUmar," in the name of the companion who reported it. It figures in the collection of Muslim, *Īmān*, I.

2. By "Sufi" (adjective and noun) and "Sufism," we mean here that which relates to the interior, mystical, esoteric dimension of Sunni Islam. Although it has certain close relationships with Sufism, Shīʿite mysticism, which includes Ismāʿīlī gnosis and Imāmī gnosis, is distinguished by specific traits which form a subject of other chapters in this volume.

3. F. Schuon, *The Transcendent Unity of Religions*, trans. P. Townsend (London: Theosophical Publishing House, 1984). No student of Sufism can dispense with consulting the other works of the same author, namely, *Understanding Islam*, trans. D. M. Matheson (London: Allen & Unwin, 1963); *Sufism: Veil and Quintessence*, trans. W. Stoddart (Bloomington, IN: World Wisdom, 1981); and *Dimensions of Islam*, trans. P. Townsend (London: Allen & Unwin, 1970).

4. The English orientalist R. A. Nicholson collected seventy-eight of them ("A Historical Enquiry Concerning the Origin and Development of Sufism with a List of Definitions of the Terms '*ṣūfī*' and '*taṣawwuf*' arranged chronologically," *Journal of the Royal Asiatic Society* [1906] 303–48), but ʿAbd al-Qādir Baghdādī had in the fifth/eleventh century already collected a thousand, according to L. Massignon, *Essai sur les origines du lexique technique de la mystique musulmane* (Paris: J. Vrin, 1954) 156.

5. Cited by E. Dermenghem, *L'Eloge du Vin (Al-Khamriya): Poème mystique de ʿOmar Ibn al-Fâridh* (Paris: Les Éditions Véga, 1931) 37.

6. *Mīzān al-ʿamal*, cited by A. J. Wensinck, *La Pensée de Ghazzālī* (Paris: Adrien-Maisonneuve, 1940) 143–44.

7. See al-Hujwīrī, *Kashf al-Maḥjūb*, trans. R. A. Nicholson (London: Luzac, 1911).

8. See the article "Khirḳa" in *Encyclopaedia of Islam* (2nd ed.) (by J.-L. Michon); see also J. Spencer Trimingham, *The Sufi Orders in Islam* (London and New York: Oxford University Press, 1971) 181–93. The latter work, based on extensive documentation, gives a good survey of the whole of Sufism, considered in the light of its historical development, its doctrinal variations, its ritual practices, and the organization of the brotherhoods.

9. Translated by R. W. J. Austin as *Sufis of Andalusia* (London: Allen & Unwin, 1971). The passages reproduced here are from pp. 69–70.

10. S. H. Nasr, *Sufi Essays* (Albany, NY: SUNY, 1972) 57–59.

11. Ibid., 58.

12. Al-Suhrawardī, *Kitāb ʿawārif al-maʿārif* (*The Blessings of Knowledge*), chap. 55. Extracts have been translated by E. Blochet in *Etudes sur l'ésotérisme musulman* (Louvain: Isras, 1910).

13. J.-L. Michon, *L'Autobiographie (Fahrasa) du Soufi marocain Aḥmad Ibn ʿAjība (1747–1809) et son miʿrāj* (Leiden: Brill, 1969) 163.

14. Ibid., 160.

15. The immense body of literature treating the *dhikr* cannot be summarized here.

One could consult the article "*Dhikr*" in *Encyclopaedia of Islam* (2nd ed.) (by L. Gardet) and, especially, the few pages that T. Burckhardt dedicates to this topic in *An Introduction to Sufi Doctrine*, trans. D. M. Matheson (Wellingborough: Thorsons, 1976) 99ff. See also M. Lings, *What is Sufism?* (Berkeley and Los Angeles: University of California Press, 1981) chap. 7, "The Method"; and W. Stoddart, *Sufism: The Mystical Doctrines and Methods* (Wellingborough: Thorsons, 1976) 64–70).

16. Especially by Abū Ḥamīd al-Ghazzālī, who made of this one of the major themes of *The Revival of the Sciences of Religion (Iḥyā' 'ulūm al-dīn)* (Cairo: al-Maktabat al-Tijāriyyat al-Kubrā, 1352 A.H.) III. Likewise, in the contemporary period, the Algerian Sufi Aḥmad al-'Alawī (d. 1934) explained all the religious prescriptions of Islam in terms of their value for *dhikr*. See *al-Minaḥ al quddūsiyyah fī sharḥ al-murshid al-mu'īn bi ṭarīq al-ṣūfiyyah* (Tunis, 1324 A.H.) extracts of which have been translated by M. Lings in *A Sufi Saint of the Twentieth Century, Shaykh Aḥmad al-'Alawī* (London: Allen & Unwin, 1971) chaps. 10 and 11.

17. See especially F. Schuon, *Understanding Islam*, 122–28.

18. This doctrine is developed with great clarity by Ibn 'Aṭā' Allāh of Alexandria, the third great master of the Shādhilī order (d. 709/1309), in his treatise entitled *Kitāb miftāḥ al-falāḥ wa misbāḥ al-arwāḥ* (*The Key of Felicity and the Lamp of Souls*) (Cairo: Muṣṭafā al-Bābī al-Ḥalabī, 1381/1961) 143 pp. The introduction to this treatise was translated into French by M. Gloton, *Traité sur le nom Allāh* (Paris: Les Deux Océans, 1981) 209–20.

19. Cited by Ibn 'Ajībah in *Mi'rāj al-tashawwuf ilā ḥaqā'iq al-taṣawwuf;* French translation in J.-L. Michon's *Le Soufi marocain Aḥmad Ibn 'Ajība (1746–1908) et son mi'rāj, glossaire de la mystique musulmane* (Paris: J. Vrin, 1973) 215.

20. For a description of the modalities and techniques applied in the two "traditions" of the solitary *dhikr* and the collective *dhikr*, see L. Gardet, "La mention du Nom divin, *dhikr*, dans la mystique musulmane," *Revue Thomiste* 52 (1952) 648–62.

21. The repetition of these formulas has its foundations in the prophetic tradition. Thus, the Prophet said, "There is not a server or a servant who has said seventy times each day, 'I ask forgiveness from God' without God having pardoned him of seven hundred sins; the loser is the server or servant who would commit in one day and one night more than seven hundred sins" (al-Bayhaqī in *Shu'ab al-īmān*, according to Anas).

Anas heard the Prophet say, "whoever prays to me one hundred prayers, God inscribes between his two eyes innocence from hypocrisy and safeguards him from hell; on the Day of Judgment, He places him with the martyrs" (Ṭabarānī).

"Never has a servant said, 'There is no divinity but God, Unique, without equal, to Him the Kingdom, to Him the praise, and He is All-Powerful above every thing,' with pure adherence of spirit, sincerity of heart and pronunciation of tongue without God opening wide the heavens to look down upon the one who speaks thus from the earth; or the one whom God looks down upon seeing his prayers granted" (Nasā'ī, according to *Majmū' al-awrād*, compiled by 'Uddah ibn Tūnis [2nd ed.; Damascus: Matba'a at-tawfīq, 1350/1932]).

22. As in the famous *Khamriyyah* of the Egyptian Sufi 'Umar ibn al-Fāriḍ (d. 632/1235), a poem for which, in fact, Nābulusī wrote a commentary. See Dermenghem, *L'Eloge du vin*.

23. Another example of *madḥ nabawī*, taken from the Mawlawī meeting, appears in the section entitled "Praises on the Prophet" of my chapter on "Sacred Music and Dance" to appear in volume 20 of this Encyclopedia. The same chapter, for the most part, completes the descriptions of the sacred dance given here while analyzing in particular the controversial question of the licentiousness of *samā'* and of the seeking out of ecstasy, as well as the various elements of the spiritual concert—the human voice,

the musical instruments, the melody, and the rhythms.

24. Paraphrased from the *Traité sur la séance mawlawie* of Dîvâne Mehmed Tchelebi (16ème s.), cited in M. Molé, *Les Danses sacrées* (Paris: Seuil, 1963) 248–49.

25.This can be compared with a letter in which a dervish likens the *nay* to the "perfect man," cited in E. Meyerovitch, *Mystique et poésie en Islam—Rūmī et l'ordre des derviches tourneurs* (Brussels: Desclée de Brouwer, 1972) 89.

26. Cited by Ibn 'Ajībah in *Īqāẓ al-himam fī sharḥ al-Ḥikam* (Cairo: Muṣṭafā al-Bābī al-Ḥalabī, 1381/1961) 357.

27. See the commentary on this *ḥadīth* attributed to Ibn 'Arabī but actually by Awḥad Al-Dīn Balyānī, *"Whoso Knoweth Himself. . .,"* trans. T. H. Weir (London: Beshara, 1976).

28. Ibn 'Ajībah, *Mi'rāj, al-muḥāsabah wa'l-mushāraṭah* (rubrics 14–15), trans. J.-L. Michon, *L'Autobiographie,* 190–91.

29. The *muḥāsabah* found a famous exponent in the person of the Sufi Ḥārith ibn Asad al-Muḥāsibī (d. 243/857 in Kufa), who took his surname from it; see M. Smith, *An Early Mystic of Baghdād* (London: Sheldon Press, 1935); Mahmoud Abdel-Ḥalīm, *Al-Mohasibi* (Paris: Geuthner, 1940); and J. Van Ess, *Die Gedankenwelt des Ḥārith al-Muḥāsibī* (Bonn: Selbstverlag des orientalischen Seminars der Universität Bonn, 1961).

30. According to Hésychius de Batos, cited in *La Philocalie,* trans. J. Gouillard (Paris: Éditions des Cahiers du Sud, 1953) 202.

31. See P. Nwyia, *Ibn 'Aṭā' Allāh (m. 709/1309) et la naissance de la confrérie shādhilite* (Beirut: Dār al-Mashriq, 1972); *Ḥikma* nos. 22, 96 and pp. 242–43 note.

32. Ibn 'Ajībah, *Mi'rāj, al-murāqabah* (rubric 13), trans. J.-L. Michon, *L'Autobiographie,* 189–90.

33. Many of these litanies, although composed originally by Sufis, later fell into the public domain and nourished popular piety, such as the *Dalā'il al-khayrāt* of the Moroccan Imam ibn Sulaymān al-Jazūlī (d. 870/1465), the *Ḥiṣn al-ḥaṣīn* of ibn al-Jazarī (d. 833/1429), and many others, a fairly complete repertory of which was compiled by C. E. Padwick, *Muslim Devotions* (London: S.P.C.K., 1961).

34. This tradition is reported by Sidi Yūsuf al-'Ajamī in his work *Riḥān al-qulūb,* cited by O. Depont and X. Coppolani, *Les Confréries religieuses musulmanes* (Algiers: A. Jourdan, 1897) 370–72.

35. The Khalwatī teaching is recorded, particularly, in the *Fahrasah* (*Book of Succor*) of Sī Muḥammad ibn 'Alī ibn Sanūsī (d. 1276/1869), founder of the Sanūsiyyah *ṭarīqah,* whose politico-religious authority rapidly spread to Tripolitania, Cyrenaica, and the Sudan. See L. Rinn, *Marabouts et Khouans* (Algiers: A. Jourdan, 1884) 295–99, and the table of the seven degrees leading to perfection, pp. 300–301.

36. See *Kitāb 'awārif al-ma'ārif* (Cairo: Dār al-Kutub al-Ḥadīthah, 1358/1939), especially chaps. 26–28, which treat the merits and the modalities of this retreat called "*arba'īniyyah*" (the "quarantine").

37. *Mīzān al-'amal,* cited by A. J. Wensinck, *La Pensée de Ghazzālī,* 144.

38. *Iḥyā' 'ulūm al-dīn,* chap. III, 16–17, cited by G. C. Anawati and L. Gardet, *La Mystique musulmane* (Paris: J. Vrin, 1961) 277.

39. F. Schuon, *Dimensions of Islam,* chap. 9, "Earthly Concomitances of the Love of God." "The man who 'loves God' . . . is one who dwells in . . . the 'inward dimension' . . . the domain of unity, synthesis and permanence."

40. Ali Hassan Abdel-Kader, *The Life, Personality and Writings of Al-Junayd,* Gibb Memorial Series 22 (London: Luzac, 1962) 57 (Arabic text), 178 (English translation): "This, then, is the highest stage of the True realization of the Unity of God in which the worshipper who maintains this unity loses his individuality (*dhahab huwa*)."

41. Dermenghem, *L'Eloge du vin.*

15

Sufi Science of the Soul

MOHAMMAD AJMAL

Science of the Soul and Metaphysics

WHEN WE TALK ABOUT PSYCHOTHERAPY TODAY, we generally mean a mode of nonmedical treatment of mentally disturbed people that employs psychological methods. The mode of treatment may not be based upon a comprehensive theory of personality and may isolate a segment of human experience, concentrate upon it, and thus produce a "cure." "Cure" itself is a word that has a plenitude of meanings, with the result that no sensible or rational discussion of it can take place about it—unless one defines it as the removal of a symptom or the disappearance of a syndrome. Syndrome is another expression that psychiatrists use frequently but with their own personalized meaning.

Another aspect of modern psychotherapies is that they are not related to any metaphysical principles. Any reference to metaphysics, psychotherapists think, would vitiate the scientific character of their theories and would certainly create disorder in their practice—if it is not already in a state of confusion. By metaphysics, I do not mean the modern metaphysics which creates an endless chain of arguments and only sets up more puzzles rather than solving genuine problems. By metaphysics, I mean what René Guénon asserts, "In all true metaphysical conceptions it is necessary to take into account the inexpressible."[1]

The Sufi science of the soul and the cure of its maladies, or psychotherapy, are, however, a mode of psychological treatment based on a metaphysics that embodies the principles of the Islamic tradition in the sense that tradition is used by such writers as Guénon and F. Schuon.[2] The Islamic tradition points out that the origin of every soul is paradise. This archetypal reality is a "primordial idea" that is veiled in every soul. It can, however, manifest itself through spiritual practice based upon sustained invocation (*dhikr*), or repeated remembrance of the Supreme Name of God. In this way, the forgotten "trust" center of the personality becomes activated—a center that is both immanent and transcendent.[3]

Traditional View of Personality

Traditional metaphysics has a clear theory of personality. Human personality, according to the Islamic tradition, has three aspects: spirit (*rūḥ*), heart (*qalb*), and soul (*nafs*). A distinction must be made among the following: (1) *al-nafs al-ḥayawāniyyah*—the animal soul, the soul as passively obedient to natural impulsions; (2) *al-nafs al-ammārah*—"the soul which commands," the passionate, egoistic soul; (3) *al-nafs al-lawwāmah*—"the soul which blames," the soul aware of its own imperfections; and (4) *al-nafs al-muṭma'innah*—"the soul at peace," the soul reintegrated in the Spirit and at rest in certainty. The last three of these expressions are from the Quran.

This view of the personality has been elaborated by various Sufi authorities. For example, M. Ashraf 'Alī Thanvi, in his *Bawādil al-nawādir,* has given a very clear account of human thought process and its stages.[4] Thought passes through five stages before it becomes a decision. The first stage (*hājis*) is the stage of a passing thought. The second stage (*khāṭir*) is the stage at which the thought persists for some time. The third stage is *ḥadīth al-nafs*, the inner dialogue that the ego has with its "soul" (*nafs*). The fourth stage (*hamm*) is reached when there is a readiness for decision, and the fifth stage (*'azm*) is the level of decision making itself. From the point of view of mental disease, the third stage is the most crucial one. It is the stage of inner verbalization or possibly subvocalization, and if one continues to talk to oneself mental disturbance is created. These inner stages have been described by a great Darqāwī Sufi, Shaykh Ḥabīb of Tetuan, as "thought-impulses." He says, "Beware of the deception of thought-impulses; they weaken good counsel and they are lies."[5]

According to a tradition of the Prophet, "Allah has forgiven for my *ummah* those thoughts about which they talk to themselves, provided they do not express them."[6] M. Thanvi has commented on this saying and provided an analysis of man's thought process. He thinks that if one enters into a state of *murāqabah,* or meditation on thought, he will find that thought is circular. It can, in fact, be regarded as a vicious circle. This vicious circle of thoughts can be broken only by entering into a higher circle. Therefore, he says, "Take a sincere brother as your intimate. He will discriminate between the thought-impulses and dispel the source of doubt in you."

All subvocal verbalization implies a philosophical proposition and is an indication of a particular attitude to life. Such a verbalization may appear to be sheer nonsense, but if you analyze it, it turns out to be a serious expression of a latent attitude. It is really a statement of a philosophical proposition that expresses fear and anxiety.

From another perspective, the picture of human personality according to the Sufi point of view is this:

> The spirit (*al-rūḥ*) and the soul (*al-nafs*) engage in the battle for the possession of their common son, the heart (*al-qalb*). This is a symbolical way of expressing the nature of the spirit, which is masculine and the nature of soul, which is feminine. By (*al-rūḥ*) we mean the intellectual principle which transcends the individual nature and *al-nafs* is the self-centered compulsive tendencies which are responsible for the diffuse and changeable nature of the "I". *Al-qalb* is the point of intersection of the "vertical" ray, which is *al-rūḥ*, with the horizontal plane, which is *al-nafs*.[7]

The two contraries *al-rūḥ* and *al-nafs* try to capture the *qalb*. If the *nafs* wins the battle, the heart is "veiled" by her. The *nafs* is also interested in the nimble transitions of the conditions of the world. She passively clings to form which dissipates. There is a tradition of the Prophet according to which, "it should be known that there is a lump of flesh in the body of a man on which depends his being good or bad. When this piece of flesh is healthy, man remains (spiritually) healthy. When it is not healthy, man goes astray—and that lump of flesh is man's heart."[8] Heart in this context should not be confused with either the physical heart, the human emotions, or the mind. It would be relevant here to quote F. Schuon, who has given an excellent account of the functions of the heart which are related to the intellect and intellectual intuition. He says: "Intellectual genius must not be confused with the mental acuteness of logicians. Intellectual intuition comprises essentially a contemplativity which in no way enters into the rational capacity, the latter being logical rather than contemplative. It is contemplative power, receptivity in respect of the light which distinguishes transcendent intelligence from reason."[9] To understand the continuous temptation brought about by the *nafs*, it is necessary to delve further into the meaning of the heart and its nature.

The heart is the abode of Divine Light. Divine Knowledge can be attained through its activity. In the mortal human body, it is the only organ that is the locus of the energies one receives from the spiritual realm. It opens up ways for spiritual development. God has called it His own abode. The Prophet has said that heart is the house of God.

All hearts are only potentially the houses of God. Most hearts can never lift the veil of mundane passions and desire which cover the heart. Some Sufis describe it as being covered by the "rust" of earthly passions, which settles on the heart. This rust can be removed only by ardent and persistent invocation (*dhikr*). The *nafs* creates unbreakable bonds—passive habits and ambitions—while the Spirit unites, because it is above form. With a rapier-like thrust it separates reality from appearance. If the Spirit wins the battle, the heart will be transformed into spirit and at the same time transmute its soul, suffusing her with spiritual light. Then the heart reveals itself; it becomes the tabernacle (*mishkāt*) of the Divine Mystery (*sirr*) in man.[10]

The heart can be quickened only by invocation and contemplation, by the attainment of virtues, and by realizing their relationship to metaphysics. Emotional conflicts, anxieties, worries, and almost all forms of neurosis can be outgrown by a change in cognitive reorientation and a shift in perspective. Whenever there is an anxiety, a free-floating state of fear expecting a disaster at every turn of the corner, and a sense of doom on waking up to a new dawn, there is a need for a deliberate and willful redirection of attention to the Absolute, to God. Very soon the invocation will capture the heart, and the invocation will become spontaneous. Energy will begin to flow to the spirit, and once the spirit is awakened and sharpened the temptations to worry will die out.

There is another function of the heart. There is, of course, the physical heart with its physiological functions, but the heart the Sufis talk about is the seat of Divine Knowledge and Love. In fact, the intellectual intuition that Schuon speaks about is equivalent to love as understood by the Sufis, the love that, according to Rūmī in the prelude to his *Mathnawī*, is "the physician of all our maladies." This love is primarily the love of God. "The Eye of the Heart" begins to see the Eternal Essence. Only subsequently is it love for human beings and for existence in general. It is also love for nature, virgin nature in both its aspects—the aspect of beauty (*jamāl*) and the aspect of rigor (*jalāl*). This love does not exclude the "wisdom of fear," which is an aspect of love for the awesome grandeur of the eternal Substance.

Sufi Practices and the Cure of the Soul

Strictly speaking, there can be no cure for the maladies of the soul unless the sick man enters into *bay'at* with a master (receives spiritual initiation from him). Some Sufis say: "One who has no master, Satan is his master." Relationship with the master gives the novice a new sense of being, which gradually develops into a new consciousness and finally reaches beatitude. This relationship draws the novice from the turmoil of the world into the refuge provided by the master's spiritual presence and protection. This result demands, however, that two conditions be fulfilled: (1) confession and (2) compliance with the master's guidance. Confession consists in the statement of what the novice (*murīd*) experiences, his fears, his anxieties, and his problems. The master responds to the confession by guidance and provides directions with which the novice has to comply if he wants to emerge from his agony and suffering.

Prayer by itself cannot eliminate the imperfections and compulsive tendencies of the novice. Prayer awakens the "heart" but needs spiritual will (*himmah*), effort (*mujāhadah*), and meditation (*murāqabah*) on one's tendencies to heal one's sick soul. Meditation can be of two kinds: (1) *takhliyah*, that is, self-analysis with a view to obviating one's moral weaknesses; (2) *taḥliyah*, that is, self-analysis with a view to strengthening one's virtues so that vices become weak and ultimately die out. Schuon has spoken of the six stations of wisdom, which are forms of meditation aiming at the spiritual development of the novice and complementing invocation.[11] M. Ashraf ʿAlī Thanvi takes up each imperfection of the novice separately and guides him toward its cure. He expects the novice to meditate on both his imperfection and the suggested cure. These and other methods employed by the Sufis have proved effective in bringing relief from suffering and inducing in the novices a sense of the sacred. But, as already mentioned, all these methods require a master, and the Sufi master has to be chosen with care and caution. Not everyone who claims to be a master is really so. Jalāl al-Dīn Rūmī has, in fact, called some of these self-proclaimed masters "devils." The seeker has to realize that all genuine Sufi masters derive their authority from the Prophet Muḥammad. The Quran refers to the Last Messenger in these words: "Verily in the messenger of Allah ye have a good example for him who looketh unto Allah and the Last Day, and remembereth Allah much" (XXXIII, 21).

On the *Laylat al-miʿrāj* (Night of Ascension) Muḥammad ascended all the scales of being. His body was reabsorbed into the soul, soul into spirit, and spirit into Divine Presence. This reabsorption traces the stages of the Sufi path.[12] The Prophet is the fount from which all orders of Sufism flow. The Sufi master is thus a representative of the Prophet, and allegiance (*bayʿat*) to him is indirectly *bayʿat* with the Prophet and finally with God. One who becomes a pilgrim on this path has to give his whole self to it. Piecemeal devotion is poor devotion. "Knowledge only saves us on condition that it enlists all that we are, only when it is a way which works and transforms and wounds our nature even as the plough wounds the soil—metaphysical knowledge is sacred. It is the right of the sacred things to require of man all that he is."[13]

Within the context of the master–novice relationship, the novice turns a new leaf and begins a new life in order to have the ailments of his soul cured. He begins with repentance. The sura *al-Qiyāmah* (LXXV) begins with the following words:

> Nay, I swear by the Day of Resurrection.
> Nay, I swear by the accusing soul.

The accusing or reproachful soul (*al-nafs al-lawwāmah*) is the soul that blames and is aware of its imperfections. It is the conscience, the inner voice, which persuades man to repent for his sins. Some Sufis have given a detailed account of the diverse aspects of this force.

Repentance

Sufis of the Chishtiyyah order have described three kinds of repentance (*tawbah*): (1) Repentance of the present—which means that man should be penitent about his sins. (2) Repentance of the past—which reminds man of the need to give other people's rights to them. If one has reprimanded someone unduly, he should ask for forgiveness from the victim of his hostility. If one has committed adultery, he should seek forgiveness from God. (3) Repentance of the future—which means that one should decide not to commit any sin again. Sufis, however, do not ask their followers to dwell on their sins because dwelling on one's sins gives them a secret pleasure. It fulfills the neurotic need for self-persecution or masochism. The more one wallows in repentance on sins, the more one tends to repeat them. It is one instance of the general principle of *enantiodromia* enunciated by Heraclitus. The principle simply states that if you try to reach the extreme of anything, you will achieve the opposite. Quite a few people get involved in the vicious circle of creating self-defeating situations. It is, therefore, desirable that after a solemn resolve one may try to direct one's attention to the image of the shaykh and begin the invocation of the Supreme Name.

The main point of repentance is that it does not mean wallowing in penitence or self-pity or self-devaluation. As Rūmī points out, wallowing in penitence is itself a form of self-indulgence. The best time to start the process of spiritual transformation is the present—here and now. One who dwells on the past is driven to the past through regression. He who has the *himmah* (spiritual will) to transcend himself can alone be himself. It is quite probable that the novice may lapse into an old habit, but he can always return to the domain of the Spirit. As Abū Sa'īd Abi'l-Khayr says: "If you have broken your vow of penitence a hundred times, return to the spiritual fold."

Time and again Sufis have emphasized that there is no need to despair even when one has broken one's vows of repentance a thousand times. One can begin again afresh, but sincerity and wholeheartedness are the principal conditions. "Believe that sins of a hundred worlds can be removed from the (Right) Path by one sigh of repentance." "Again if you come to the Right Path with sincerity for a moment, you will attain a hundred stations (of spiritually) every moment."[14]

Sufis have always regarded repentance as a positive turning away from sin and directing one's vision toward God. The relative significance of repentance varies from one religion to another. Sufis, by and large, attach a great deal of importance to repentance, but they strongly discourage "wallowing in repentance" or enjoying repentance. When one is penitent, the Sufi way is to redirect one's will to invocation, persistent and ardent invocation.

Disease

The Quran refers to "disease" in various contexts. In the sura *al-Baqarah* (The Cow) there is a verse about the "sickness in the heart":

> And of mankind are some who say: We believe in Allah and the Last Day, when they believe not. They think to beguile Allah and those who believe, and they beguile none save themselves; but they perceive not. In their hearts is a disease, and Allah increases their disease. (II, 8–10)

Khwājah 'Abdallāh Anṣārī in his voluminous commentary on the Quran has defined "disease" in various ways. In discussing the above verse, he defines it as follows:

> It is a sickness which has no limit, and it is a pain which has no remedy. It is a night which has no dawn. What could be a more miserable state than the state of the hypocrite? That is a state of alienation from the beginning to the end. Today he is in an inward agony and tomorrow he will be in external despair.[15]

In another place, Khwājah Anṣārī explains disease as "doubt" and dissociation (*nifāq*), a condition from which modern man is suffering so grievously.

The first symptom of this "sickness" is alienation—from self, from society, from one's own history, and from one's cultural roots. Modern man is seeking a balm for his psychological wounds, but in all respects his solutions to problems themselves become problems. This is true of all fields today, be they economic, administrative, or psychological. Modern psychologists have called this phenomenon self-healing. Psychoanalysis has been facetiously defined as a disease of which it is supposed to be the cure.[16]

The second symptom is "desacralization." Desacralization is not necessarily a deliberate and willful phenomenon. It can be subliminal in the sense that a person, on account of the barrage of glamorous and exciting stimuli that impinge on his senses, has no opportunity to expose himself to sacred objects and associate himself with people who possess a sacred presence. He, therefore, cannot perceive and experience the sacred. This desacralization has led to the spiritual impoverishment of the youth. A large number of young men and women throughout the world are seriously interested in the "return of the sacred."

The third symptom, which is derived from the first two, is what Guénon has called "dispersion into multiplicity." The attractive objects around him lure modern man in diverse and contrary directions, and each direction exercises such a fascination for him that he feels imprisoned in them. He would like to lead a single-directed and wholehearted life but fails to find a center.

A related symptom is the crisis of identity. Mass migration has accentuated this crisis. Immigrants in a new country, however affluent, feel empty within. Their inner conflicts generated by the process of adjustment to the new environment create in them a sense of meaninglessness of life. The "void" they feel within because of the nostalgia for the past and the environmental pressures goading them to move forward with the times are so acute that they affect their belief system, their morality, and their attitude toward life.

Cure

Sufis believe that these symptoms can be removed by a sustained effort (*mujāhadah*) to subordinate one's "thought-impulses" to the moral will and thus bring oneself closer to God. The Supreme Being is reflected in the Supreme Name, and invocation of the Supreme Name alone can bring relief to suffering. "Orison (*dhikr*) is a space into which no evil enters," says Schuon.[17]

There are some other methods of helping the novice to overcome his or her diseases of the soul and emotional diffculties. They are, roughly speaking, the following:

(1) *Therapy through Opposites.* Some Sufis have advocated this mode especially for the cure of emotional disturbances caused by jealously and envy. A novice suffering from jealousy may be advised to talk affectionately and lovingly to the person toward whom he is jealous and say good things about him in public. In case he is not present in the vicinity, the novice should write to him an affectionate letter. Deliberate opposition to a negative conscious attitude has to be cultivated. The assumption is that the desire to love and to understand others is latent in all human beings; it has only to be brought into consciousness.

(2) *Therapy through Similars.* This form of therapy consists in pointing out to the novice that his experiences are not unique, especially when they are accompanied by a negative effect. A novice suffering from depression or anxiety may be given examples of other people suffering from similar maladies. This form of therapy induces in the novice a feeling of sharing and helps to alleviate the yoke of his isolation.

The first essential element of the Sufi science of the soul or psychotherapy is confession or admission of one's problems. Verbalization of one's thoughts and feelings, disturbing questions and problems need to be communicated to the master (*murshid*). As Ḥāfiẓ Shīrāzī has said, "He told the friend our spiritual condition. It is not possible to conceal one's pain from our real friends." After communication has been made to the master, it is imperative for the novice to comply with his instructions. These instructions or interventions are not authoritative commands, but they are based upon acceptance by the disciple. The master also accepts the condition of the novice. This mode of therapy is the most effective method for eliminating vices like pride, arrogance, and egotism. The worst form of pride is subliminal pride (*kibr-i ʿaẓīm*). A man who is very proud is likely to assume an air of humility and self-abnegation. If he declares in false humility, "I am an ignorant man," the best therapy for him is to confirm his statement by saying, "Yes, you are an ignorant man." If he is genuinely humble, he will not be disturbed by this response. If his humility is only a pretense, however, he is likely to become furious. The motive for such a humble statement is to evoke a denial by others. Once this expectation is frustrated, the proud person is likely to be shaken out of his fake attitude. This mode is very much like Viktor Frankl's "paradoxical intention." But it is not a twentieth century invention. It was known to the Sufi masters who were fully aware that long morbid cogitations in turn breed more conflicts. These conflicts are relevant only to the passional level of existence. Once one abandons that level and rises up to the higher level, the inner chatter and the corresponding conflicts are gradually diminished both in frequency and in intensity.

Some Sufis have advocated a dialogue with God every night before going to sleep. The novice has to confess all to God, verbalizing his main weaknesses. The confession has to be accompanied by a true statement that the novice will not persist in his sins. The point is that the novice should not make any *false* promises to God. If the novice feels helpless in the clutches of a bad habit, he should not make a promise to God that he will abandon the habit. By persisting in his dialogue, he will become more aware of the

Divine Presence in his heart, and he is likely to muster inner strength to outgrow the disturbing habit. It has been observed by some Sufis, especially M. Ashraf ʿAlī Thanvi, that quite a few novices have experienced an inner conversion by persisting in the dialogue with God and have thus abandoned unwholesome tendencies. But he also advises the novice to accept his states. It is only by acceptance that one can change.

The concept of acceptance as employed by Sufis is based upon the distinction between voluntary and involuntary thoughts. Strong and distracting thoughts impede concentration. *Ḥadīth al-nafs* (or "inner chatter") generally obstructs free flow of invocation or meditation. But this obstruction is generally involuntary. The best way to outgrow it is to accept it, that is, neither to attempt to force it out of one's consciousness nor to pay heed to it. In other words, it is only by consciously *ignoring* it, that one can outgrow it. Shaykh al-ʿArabī al-Darqāwī says:

> The sickness afflicting your heart, *faqīr,* comes from the passions which pass through you; if you were to abandon them and concern yourself with what God orders for you, your heart would not suffer as it suffers now. . . . Each time your soul attacks you, if you were to be quick to do what God orders and abandon your will entirely to Him, you will be saved from psychic and satanic suggestions and from all your trials. But if you begin to reflect in these moments when your soul attacks you, to weigh the factors for or against, and sink into inner chatter, then psychic and satanic suggestions will flow back towards you in waves until you are overwhelmed and drowned, and no good will be left in you, but only evil.[18]

The last and by far the most humanistic method is to imagine what the other man is feeling by saying to oneself, "Suppose I am this man, why should I be ranting and raging against something unimportant?" By this imaginative reversal one can empathically imagine the other man's emotional problems. As a result, one is likely to feel less concerned about how his behavior affects us. This is the essence of empathy, of putting oneself in another man's position. In personal relations, malice or hostility develops on account of misunderstanding. Such a reversal helps to remove the misunderstanding and thus eliminates the feeling of hostility. It may be mentioned that the gestalt psychologists employ this method for making a client aware of his repressed feelings.

Another aspect of Sufi treatment of the soul or psychotherapy is that it discourages statements of generalizations by the disciples. Generalizations are instances of thinking in connotation which keep the disciple in a state of vagueness and sometimes ambiguity. A Sufi master always requires denotation of specific instances and symptoms. If a novice writes to him,

"I am depressed," the Sufi master wants to know the specific reason for depression and the context in which it occurs. It is only then that he gives guidance. Sufis also emphasize the value of prayer—prayers which are uttered in an attitude of humility, surrender, and helplessness before God. They also insist that special prayers should not be expressed in generalities but should be addressed to God in the form of specific requests.

Sufis realized that thinking in connotation is itself a sickness. It encourages ambiguous cogitations and is a rich source of exaggerations, overstatements, and understatements. It makes disciples confused and leads to other sicknesses like self-pity and seeking care and attention from others.

In modern times, Alfred Korzybski (in his *Science and Sanity*) and Samuel Hayakawa and others have built up a system of psychotherapy based upon the principle of reducing all connotations to denotations. The basis of their therapy, however, is materialistic and profane. It reduces all mental and spiritual processes to brain functions.

The question-and-answer method, which has been hallowed by its association with Socrates, is venerated by philosophers. This method has dominated European thought for centuries, but it is only in the present times that its limitations and the nature of its fascination have been determined. Psychoanalysts have explained children's questions as revealing their repressed impulses, and any literal understanding of these questions is regarded as self-defeating. Today psychologists, especially gestalt psychologists like Frederick Perls, regard the question-and-answer method as a torture game. They think that quite a few questions are disguised commands and that several others are ways of escaping an unpleasant situation.

During the spiritual guidance of his followers (*murīdīn*), M. Ashraf 'Alī Thanvi always scrutinized the questions his novices asked him. If the question was rooted in the novice's experience, only then would he reply. If the question was general and not relevant to the novice's stage of spiritual development, M. Thanvi would dismiss the question as emanating from a "confused mind" or a mind that finds it irksome to meditate over the real problems. He admonished them to refrain from asking such questions. He thus teaches them the virtue of relevance. He thinks "irrelevance" is an expression of frustrated spirituality. When the great Muslim scholar Syed Suleiman Nadvi requested M. Thanvi to admit him into his fold, M. Thanvi acceded to the request on condition that M. Nadvi would never ask him an academic question. In the case of scholars and "intellectuals," M. Thanvi demanded a sacrifice of their superior functions, because he knew that they would not grow spiritually if their minds remained cluttered with "empty words."

Dream Interpretation

One of the methods that Sufi masters employ in helping novices to emerge from their suffering is interpreting their dreams. Such interpretations are never reductive but always teleological. In these interpretations, dream fragments are generally symbolically treated. For example, one disciple of M. Ashraf 'Alī Thanvi described a dream to him in a letter. In the letter he said: "I was very depressed. Last night I had a dream that a woman clad in a white dress appeared in the form of my mother. She kept on repeating an Urdu verse very vigorously which means that Allah is not obliged to please everybody. If you want such a God, try to find another God. When I heard this verse, I was very upset and I woke up crying." M. Thanvi replied that this is divine guidance. Sarmad (an Indian Sufi poet) has made a similar point in his quatrain: "Sarmad, one should make one's plaint brief. One should resort to one of the two alternatives. Either you surrender yourself to the Will of the Friend, or abandon the Friend." "Sometimes guidance comes through sternness, and at other times through love. This guidance was through love. That is why the form of the mother appeared."[19]

This was a symbolic interpretation of the dream and anagogic in character. There is no reductionism, no profanation in the interpretation. Such interpretations are to be found throughout Sufi literature, and some of the most illuminating examples of symbolic interpretation are those described in the *Kitāb al-ibrīz* concerning an unlettered Sufi saint of the Shādhiliyyah order, 'Abd al-'Azīz al-Dabbāghī.

The Goal of the Sufi Science of the Soul

"Sufi psychology does not separate the soul either from the metaphysical or from the cosmic order."[20] Metaphysics provides the basis and qualitative criteria for psychology and cannot form a part of empirical psychology. Empirical psychology studies aspects of phenomena, psychic and behavioral, and seeks their immediate causes. This hunt for "causes" and "explanations" has produced a plethora of hypotheses and theories that are a source of confusion and bewilderment for the modern student. Sufi psychology, on the contrary, presents an adequate account of symbols and does not reduce them to the thought-impulses of a repressed mind and gives a living meaning to them by creating an attitude of reverence toward them.

The final aim of the Sufi science of the soul or psychotherapy is to create in the novice a sense of detachment from and noninvolvement in the world. The Sufi has to renounce his attachment to the world but not to abandon living fully. In fact, he has to reach that station wherein he finds himself in the presence of God. He begins to perceive reality in a new light, the light of God. In the process of the gradual unfolding of his spirit, he begins to be moved by symbols and integrates them into his life. Without an appreciation of symbols, no one can attain mental health. Without developing a capacity of discernment between truth and illusion, the sacred and the profane, beauty and ugliness, no one can claim to be normal. The spirit becomes open to the Infinite once the impediments of the psyche are removed.

The spiritual life is equivalent to symbolic life, regulated by the perception of different aspects of the Spirit. Different forms express different facets of reality. Man is the central expression of the Spirit on the earth. One aspect is revealed in the form of a tree of which the trunk symbolizes the axis of the Spirit passing through the whole hierarchy of the world while its branches and leaves correspond to the differentiation of the Spirit in the many states of existence. Similarly, some birds like the peacock and the dove reveal other aspects of the reality of the Spirit, and some Sufis have said that the most luminous of all symbols are "the shining stars, and the brilliant precious stones."

The norm of the human state is the saint, and only his soul can be said to be completely healthy, as it has become wed to the Spirit. Sufism sees the ordinary soul as being in a state of sickness resulting from separation from God and in turn causing the forgetfulness of God. There has, as a result, developed a vast Sufi science of the soul, whose aim is to reinstate man in his original perfection and to rid him of the often-neglected diseases that weigh upon his soul. Ultimately, only a science such as the Sufi science of the soul can succeed in curing the soul's diseases and in being an effective psychotherapy. Only the Spirit can cure the soul of its ills. Only the soul that is united with the Spirit possesses health; for it alone is the soul of man as God created him in his primordial perfection.

Notes

1. See J. Needleman, *The Sword of Gnosis* (Baltimore, MD: Penguin Books, 1974) 44.
2. "Tradition" is "truths or principles of a divine origin, revealed or unveiled to mankind . . . through various figures envisaged as messengers, prophets, avataras, the Logos or other transmitting agencies, along with all the ramifications and applications of these principles in different realms, including law and social structure, art, symbolism, the sciences, and embracing of course Supreme Knowledge along with the means of its attainment" (S. H. Nasr, *Knowledge and the Sacred* [New York: Crossroad, 1981] 68).
3. The Quran states, "Lo! We offered the trust (*amānah*) unto the heavens and the earth and the hills, but they shrank from bearing it and were afraid of it and man assumed it. Lo! He hath proven a tyrant and a fool" (XXXIII, 72).

4. Born 1280/1863, M. Ashraf 'Alī Thanvi was easily the greatest Sufi saint and scholar of the Indo-Pakistan subcontinent in the twentieth century. His great influence over a large number of people earned him the title *Ḥakīm al-ummah,* the Wise Man of the *Ummah.* He wrote about six hundred books, which include a detailed commentary on the Quran, a commentary on the *Mathnawī* of Rūmī, a classical exposition of the basic concepts of Sufism, and books on various aspects of Islam. One of his books, *Islam and Modern Sciences,* has been translated into English by the late M. Hasan Askari. Thanvi died in 1943 in Thana Bhawan in India, which was also his birth place.

5. See his *Diwan* (London: Diwan Press, 1982) 31.

6. Quoted in Thanvi's, *al-Ṣiḥḥat ḥukm al-waswasah* (Deoband, 1365 A.H.).

7. Ibid.

8. Ibid., 255.

9. F. Schuon, *Gnosis: Divine Wisdom,* trans. G. E. H. Palmer (London: John Murray, 1959) 49.

10. See T. Burckhardt, *An Introduction to Sufi Doctrine,* trans. D. M. Matheson (Lahore: M. Ashraf, 1983) 27.

11. See Schuon, *Stations of Wisdom,* trans. G. E. H. Palmer (London: John Murray, 1961).

12. See M. Lings, *What is Sufism?* (Berkeley and Los Angeles: University of California Press, 1975) 35.

13. F. Schuon, *Spiritual Perspectives and Human Facts,* trans. D. M. Matheson (London: Faber & Faber, 1953) 138.

14. 'Abd al-Majīd Daryābādī, *Taṣawwuf-i islām* (Azamgarh, 1947) 177.

15. See Anṣārī, *Kashf al-asrār,* ed. 'A. A. Ḥikmat (Tehran: Dānishgāh, 1952–60) 1: 75.

16. J. Haley, *Changing Families* (New York: Grune & Stratton, 1970) 70.

17. Personal communication 1979.

18. See *Letters of a Sufi Master,* trans. T. Burckhardt (Bedfont, Middlesex: Perennial Books, 1969) 9.

19. Thanvi, *Tarbiyat al-sālik* (Thana Bhawan: University Press, 1964).

20. Burckhardt, *Introduction to Sufi Doctrine,* 37.

Part Four

KNOWLEDGE OF REALITY

16

God

Seyyed Hossein Nasr

The Divine Nature

The Quranic verse "He is the First and the Last, the Outward and the Inward" (LVII, 3) refers not only to the Divine Nature but also to God's role and function in Islamic spirituality, for God is the alpha and omega of Islamic spirituality and both its inner and outer reality. He is at the center of the arena of Islamic life, and all facets and dimensions of spirituality revolve around Him, seek Him, and are concerned with Him as the goal of human existence. The *raison d'être* of the Quranic Revelation and the religion of Islam is the unveiling of the doctrine of the Divine Nature in its fullness, of the knowledge of God as He is in Himself, not as He has manifested Himself in a particular message or form. At the heart of the Quranic message lies the full and plenary doctrine of God as both transcendent and immanent, as both majesty and beauty, as both the One and the Source of the manifold, as both Origin of Mercy and Judge of all human actions, as the Originator and Sustainer of the cosmos and the goal to which all beings journey, as the suprapersonal Essence beyond all creation, and as the personal Deity Whose Will rules over all things, Whose love for knowledge of Himself is the cause of creation, and Whose Mercy is the very substance of which the threads of His creation are woven. The Quranic doctrine of God reveals Him as being at once Absolute, Infinite, and Perfect, as the Source of all reality and all positive qualities manifested in the cosmic order. Islamic spirituality is nothing other than knowing, loving, and obeying God through the means revealed in the Quran and promulgated and exemplified by the Prophet on the basis of the full doctrine of the Divine Nature contained in the Quran and *Ḥadīth*. This doctrine is made explicit and unfolded in the sapiential commentaries upon these sources and also in other traditional works of wisdom written over the ages by Muslim gnostics, philosophers, and theologians.

Each school of Islamic thought has revealed some aspect of the Divine Nature: the jurists the concrete embodiment of His Will in the *Sharīʻah;* the Muʻtazilite theologians His transcendence; the Ashʻarites the power of His Will as it orders all things; and the philosophers the necessity of His Being, which also necessitates the manifestation of existence. It remained for the people of the inner path, the Sufis and gnostics, to reveal the doctrine of the Divine Nature in its fullness, for only through access to the inner center of man's being, which the Sufis, following the Quran, identify with the heart, can man gain the full knowledge of the Divine Nature. Furthermore, it is this "knowledge of the heart" concerning God that is the goal of all spiritual striving in Islam, whose spirituality is essentially of a gnostic nature.[1]

The Names and Qualities

God is referred to by many names (*asmā'*) in the Quran, for according to this sacred text, "To Him belong the beautiful Names" (LIX, 24), but the Supreme Name (*al-ism al-aʻẓam*) by which He is known is *Allāh.* This is the Name of God's Essence (*al-Dhāt*) as well as of all the Divine Names (*asmā'*) and Qualities (*ṣifāt*) as related to and "contained" in the Divine Nature. All that can be said of the Divine Nature as being both transcendent and immanent, Creator and beyond creation, personal and suprapersonal, Being and Beyond-Being pertains to Allah, Who is the Divine as such and not one of the aspects of the Divinity to which other Quranic Names of God refer.

Divine Oneness

Allah is first and before everything else One, and it is the Oneness of God that lies at the center of both the Quranic doctrine of God and Islamic spirituality. The first Islamic testimony (*Shahādah*), which contains all metaphysics and which also possesses the power to operate the transformation of the human soul in the direction of its primordial perfection is *Lā ilāha illa'Llāh* (there is no divinity but God, but Allah). This supreme synthesis of Islamic doctrine is, first of all, a statement about the Divine Nature as being One, beyond all duality and otherness and, second, as being the Source of all reality, beauty, and goodness, of all that is positive in the universe. The testimony means also that "there is no reality but the Divine Reality," "there is no beauty but the Divine Beauty," etc. Finally, the testimony is the means of integration of the human being in the light of the Oneness which belongs to God alone. All Islamic spirituality may be said to issue from the awareness of the Oneness of God and the realization in one's life of unity, which is the fruit of *al-tawḥīd*[2]—that is, at once oneness and integration. To be a Muslim is to accept this Divine Oneness not only as a theological assertion but also as metaphysical truth and a living spiritual Reality which can operate a transformation in the human soul in the direction of perfection. All the levels of Islamic spirituality are related to degrees of realization of this *tawḥīd*. As the eighth/fourteenth-century Sufi poet Shaykh Maḥmūd Shabistarī sang centuries ago,

> See one, say one, know one;
> With this are sealed the trunk and branches
> of the tree of faith.

Islamic mystical treatises as well as theological ones based on the text of the Quran and *Ḥadīth* are essentially one long commentary on the Divine Oneness and its meaning, ranging from the famous sermon of ʿAlī ibn Abī Ṭālib on *al-tawḥīd*,[3] to the short *Treatise on Unity* of Awḥad al-Dīn al-Balyānī concerned with the purely gnostic understanding of *tawḥīd*, to the elaborate treatises of al-Ghazzālī and Fakhr al-Dīn al-Rāzī on the Divine Names.[4] The knowledge of this Oneness is the highest science, and its realization the supreme goal of human life. According to the traditional teachings of Islam, in fact, the greatest sin that man can commit is the denial of this Divine Oneness or of accepting a partner (*sharīk*) for God—hence the odium which surrounds every form of "polytheism" (*shirk*), which implies exoterically the formal acceptance of another divinity besides God and esoterically the acceptance of any force or power, whether it be within the soul of man or in the outside world, as being independent of God. At the heart of all Islamic spirituality stands the doctrine of God's Oneness and its implications for and ramifications within the human soul.

The Quran is like one long melody whose refrain is the Divine Oneness, for God is at once One in Himself (*al-aḥad*) and One with respect to His creation (*al-wāḥid*).[5] According to the verse "Verily I am God. There is no god but I: therefore serve Me, and perform the prayer of My remembrance" (XX, 14), the very necessity of worship issues from the Divine Oneness. Likewise, the mercy associated so closely in the Muslim mind with the Divine Being issues from His Oneness, for again according to the Divine Word, "To me it has been revealed that your God is One God; so go straight with Him, and ask for His forgiveness" (XLI, 6). Moreover, He is Lord of the worlds (*Rabb al-ʿālamīn*) as a consequence of His being One, for "surely your God is One, Lord of the heavens and the earth, and of what between them is, Lord of the Easts" (XXXVII, 4).

The Quranic doctrine of Divine Unity is summarized in the Quranic chapter bearing this title (and also the title *al-Ikhlāṣ*) (CXII):

> In the Name of God, the Most Merciful, the Most Compassionate
> Say: "He, God is One (*aḥad*);
> God, the Self-sufficient Besought of all (*ṣamad*);
> He begetteth not, nor is He begotten,
> And none is like unto Him."

In this short sura, often recited in the daily prayers and forming a cornerstone of Muslim piety, God's Oneness is stated in the most majestic terms in combination with His being the source of all that is, the everlasting and eternal Reality which in its fullness contains the source of all that exists and which is also the refuge against the withering effect of temporality, which causes all save the "Face of God" to perish.

The Divine Oneness implies not only transcendence but also immanence. The Quran asserts over and over again the transcendence of God above and beyond all categories of human thought and imagination, for He is "beyond all that they describe [of Him]" (VI, 100) and "All things perish save His Face" (XXVIII, 88). The first *Shahādah* itself is the most powerful way of pointing to God's transcendence, and the well-known Islamic motto *Allāhu akbar,* usually translated "God is great," means in reality that God is greater than whatever is asserted and affirmed about Him. Islamic spirituality is based on the constant awareness of this transcendence, of the impotence of all things before His Power and the perishable nature of all existence in contrast to His ever-living and eternal Nature.

Yet God is also immanent in the light of His transcendence, for not only is He beyond all things and all levels of human and cosmic existence, but, as He Himself asserts in the Quran, "We are nearer to him [to man] than the jugular vein" (L, 16). Moreover, "God stands between a man and his heart" (VIII, 24). Spirituality implies not only the awareness of transcendence but also the experience of immanence in the very light of this transcendence. It is not only to experience God as beyond all things but also to see His "signs" in all things, to see God everywhere. That is why the Prophet taught that the highest form of *tawḥīd* is to see God before, in, and after all things. No full understanding of Islamic spirituality is possible without taking into consideration the Quranic doctrine of Divine Immanence in the light of Divine Transcendence and its effect upon the spiritual life, for the same sacred text that asserts, "There is nothing like unto Him" (XLII, 11) also states, "Whithersoever ye turn, there is the Face of God" (II, 115). Quite naturally, however, the exoteric dimension of Islam emphasizes more the dimension of transcendence, and the esoteric immanence. But this must be understood in the light of the fundamental truth that the esoteric already assumes the acceptance and the practice of the exoteric. Therefore, although most Sufis have emphasized the Divine Immanence and Proximity, some of the most sublime pages concerning Divine Transcendence also have come from their pens. At the same time, the reverential attitude toward the transcendent One Who is victorious over all that is and before Whom all that is is reduced to nothingness (*Huwa' l-Wāḥid al-Qahhār*) is basic to all authentic Sufi spirituality and a necessity for the realization of Union.

The Divine Reality

If vis-à-vis His creation God is both transcendent and immanent, in Himself He is at once Absolute, Infinite, and Perfect, these "hypostases of Unity"[6] providing a metaphysical knowledge of the Divine Nature and pointing to the different aspects of the Divine Reality, which remains One while possessing these hypostases. In the language of the Quran, the absoluteness of God refers to His majesty (*jalāl*), His infinitude to beauty (*jamāl*), and His perfection to *kamāl*, which in Arabic means both perfection and totality. God is the Absolute which reduces all otherness (*mā siwa' Llāh*) to nothingness and which manifests Itself as all that is majestic, the supreme quality of majesty belonging to God alone. God is also the Infinite, containing the "possibility" of all things in Himself; for "unto God belong the treasures (*khazā' in*) of the heavens and of the earth" (LXIII, 7–8). The root of all things (the *malakūt* of the Quran) is contained in the Divine Nature by virtue of this infinitude, which is also the cause of that irradiation and creativity that is the origin of the universe. The world exists not only because God is absolute but also because He is infinite—"rich" (*al-ghanī*), in Quranic language, that is, containing all possibilities within Himself. The Divine Infinitude is at once the Divine Possibilities, which the Sufis were later to identify as the source of the immutable archetypes (*al-a'yān al-thābitah*) of all things, and the Divine Compassion (*al-Raḥmah*) by virtue of which both the cosmos and revelation were manifested.

God is also the Perfect, possessing every possible perfection in Himself. He is the Source of all positive qualities manifested in the universe and all that is of beauty and goodness. All that radiates the love and grace (*barakah*) that run through the arteries and veins of the universe originate in the Divine Perfection. As the Absolute, God is the Source of all being; He bestows miraculously the gift of existence upon nonexistence and brings about the distinction between the real and the unreal. As the Infinite, He is the Source of the archetypal reality of all things and the expansive and creative "compassion" which is the metaphysical cause of creation. As the Perfect, God is the Source and Origin of all perfection and all quality in creation. Man realizes God by realizing the Source of all quality, by breathing in the vivifying rays of the Divine Compassion, and by remaining aware of the wonder of existence and reality, of the incredible chasm that separates the existent from the nonexistent. The metaphysical doctrine of the Divine Nature thereby permeates the whole of Islamic spirituality, even if it is understood in its fullness only by the few gnostics in whom theoretical comprehension and spiritual realization are combined in perfect union.

Precisely because God is at once absolute and infinite, the Divine Nature, although usually referred to in the masculine, also possesses a feminine "aspect," which is, in fact, the principle of all femininity. If God in His absoluteness and majesty is the Origin of the masculine principle, in His Infinitude and beauty God is the Origin of femininity. Moreover, if as Creator and Judge God is seen in Islam as He, the Sufis point out that as Mercy and Forgiveness God can be envisaged and symbolized as the Beloved or the female who is the object of the spiritual quest. The Divine Compassion, *al-Raḥmah,* is grammatically feminine in Arabic, as is the Divine Essence (*al-Dhāt*) Itself, so that femininity symbolizes the aspect of inwardness, beauty, and mercy of the Divine. The Islamic conception of God, while emphasizing His Majesty, is certainly not oblivious to His Beauty, and this truth is reflected not only in female spirituality in Islam but in the female dimension of all Islamic spirituality—not to speak of the interiorizing role of the female even in the external context of traditional Islamic society.

God and Creation

If in Himself God is the Absolute, the Infinite, and the Source of all perfection, He is the Source of all positive quality that is to be found in the created order. Not only is He the Creator (*al-Khāliq*) and Lord (*al-Rabb*) of the universe, but He is also the Living (*al-Ḥayy*) and the Giver of Life (*al-Muḥyī*), without whom there would be no life in the world. He possesses speech, and it is He who speaks or produces the word (*al-Kalimah*) and without whom there would be no human speech. Likewise, He is the Knower of all things (*al-'Alīm*) without whom there would be no knowledge and no intelligence of any kind. The first *Shahādah, Lā ilāha illa' Llāh,* in fact not only asserts the Unity of God in the most universal and metaphysical manner possible but also returns all positive cosmic qualities back to their Divine Origin. It also means that "there is no life but the Divine

Life," "there is no goodness but the Divine Goodness," etc. Through His Names and Qualities God manifests the universe, and the goal of Islamic spirituality is to rediscover through these manifestations their unique Source and to recognize God's sovereignty over all that is contained in the bosom of time and space.

The opening chapter of the Quran, the *Sūrat al-fātiḥah,* which according to the Prophet is the synopsis of the whole Sacred Text and which is repeated throughout the days and years of a Muslim's life on earth as the heart of the daily prayers, recapitulates this doctrine of God's sovereignty and man's relation to Him.

> In the Name of God, the most Merciful, the most Compassionate.
> Praise be to God, the Lord of the worlds,
> The Infinitely Good, the All-Merciful,
> Master of the day of judgement,
> Thee we worship, and in thee we seek help.
> Guide us upon the straight path,
> The path of those on whom thy grace is,
> not those on whom thine anger is,
> nor those who are astray.

The Divine Mercy

As indicated in the formula of consecration (*Bismi'Llāh al-Raḥmān al-Raḥīm*), God is at once Mercy and Compassion, and it is by virtue of this Mercy that the whole universe is brought into being and all religions are revealed. God is Lord of the worlds, the Master of all that is contained in "space"—the space not only of this visible world which surrounds us but also of all the worlds above. He is also Master of the Day of Judgment, which comes at the end of the historical cycle. Hence, He is Master of time and all that takes place within its fold. Between this lordship of space and of time there is repeated His Qualities of Goodness and Mercy, which thereby "fill" these containers of the created order and which manifest His Names and Qualities everywhere. It is this Divinity Whom man, in his normal state as created "in God's own image" (*'alā ṣūratihi*), worships, and Who provides shelter for man in the storm of terrestrial existence. Before this supreme Divinity man can have but three attitudes: to remain on the path of His Grace, which is none other than the straight path (*al-ṣirāt al-mustaqīm*), the path that may be said to be the very definition of the way of Islam as such; to go astray in the forgetfulness of God in a life of passionate dispersion; and, finally, to oppose God actively and to incur His wrath. Islamic spirituality may be said to be nothing other than marching upon the straight path that leads every man by virtue of being born in the human state to that Divinity Who is the Sovereign and Master of the universe and Whose Mercy and Goodness are the very root of existence and the means whereby the Divine Qualities and Names are reflected upon the mirror of cosmic existence. This latter in turn is nonexistence parading in the guise of existence, for ultimately all existence and reality belong to God alone.

The Divine Essence and the Names

The Quranic doctrine of the Divinity is based on the distinction between God in His Essence and His Names and Qualities which are at once the same as the Essence and distinct from It and also from each other. This doctrine, which has been elaborated by theologians, philosophers, and Sufis in numerous works, is also the cornerstone of Islamic spirituality inasmuch as the invocation (*dhikr*) of the Names of God not only permeates all Islamic life but also, in its technical and esoteric sense, constitutes the very heart of all Islamic spiritual practice.[7] The Divine Essence (*al-Dhāt*) is beyond all description and definition. It is the Ipseity which is usually referred to by the final letter of the Supreme Name Allah—hence, *huwa*, "He"—which some Sufis have also interpreted in feminine rather than masculine terms. But God also possesses Names (*asmā'*) that represent determinations and aspects of the Divine Nature, such Names as the Supremely Merciful (*al-Raḥmān*) and the Forgiver (*al-Ghafūr*) but also the Giver of Death (*al-Mumīt*) and the Just (*al-'Ādil*). God's Names, on the basis of the Quran and *Ḥadīth*, are usually considered to number ninety-nine.[8] The Prophet instructed Muslims to meditate on the ninety-nine Names rather than on the Divine Essence. The Names are usually divided into Names of Majesty (*al-jalāl*) and Names of Beauty (*al-jamāl*). Both the qualities of rigor and mercy come from God, and He is at once the stern King who judges human actions and punishes evil while recompensing the good and the merciful Being who forgives those who seek His forgiveness, the Being whose compassion knows no bound. The life of the Muslim moves like a winding road toward a mountain top, vacillating from one side to another between rigor and mercy, fear of God's retribution and trust in His forgiveness.

In some mysterious fashion God's Name as revealed in the Quran and made known to the Prophet is inseparable from Him and leads to Him. God hears the voice of him who calls upon His hallowed Name and remembers him who remembers God, for, according to the Quran, "Remember Me and I shall remember you" (II, 235). But this remembrance is also the invocation of His Name, for the Arabic word *dhikr* means at once invocation, remembrance, and calling upon God. In revealing His sacred Names, God has not only provided the doctrine whereby He can be known metaphysically and theologically but has also provided the means whereby He can be known experientially and realized inwardly. The whole life of the Muslim is punctuated by constant remembrance of His Name as contained in such formulas as *inshā' Allāh* (if God wills) or *al-ḥamdu li'Llāh* (praise be to God), which are repeated throughout everyday life. As for Islamic spirituality at its highest level, it is nothing other than being transmuted by the invocation of the Divine Name until one lives in constant remembrance of God, until man ceases to be separative consciousness and becomes nothing other than the reverberation and echo of His Name whose power transforms the creature in such a way that finally the invoker (*dhākir*) becomes the invocation (*dhikr*) and the invocation the invoked (*madhkūr*). There abides only the "Face of thy Lord, the possessor of Majesty and Splendor" (LV, 27). The Names of God both reveal His Nature to man and lead man back to God, Who alone is the Source of all reality.

The Experience of God

During the earthly journey of man, God is experienced first of all as the Creator and Sustainer of the universe. Man begins his journey to God in this world, which displays, in its existence, forms, harmony, and laws, the Creator Who bestowed existence upon it. As the Quran says, "God is the Creator of everything, and He is the One, the Omnipotent" (XIII, 16). Therefore, "To God bow all who are in the heavens and the earth, willingly or unwillingly" (XIII, 15). The Muslim sees total obedience to God as the natural consequence of God's being the Creator of the world as well as the Being Who rules over the universe and Whose Will governs all things, for "to God belongs all that is in the heavens and the earth. Whether you publish what is in your hearts or hide it, God shall make reckoning with you for it. He will forgive whom He will, and chastise whom He will; God is powerful over everything" (II, 284). Islamic spirituality is involved with this awareness of God's rule over the world, the necessity of submission to His Will—hence, *islām*—and the judgment God makes upon all human action, which He knows and in which He is present. "Surely God is powerful over everything. Whatsoever mercy God opens to men, none can withhold and whatsoever He withholds, none can loose after Him. He is the All-mighty, the All-wise" (XXXV, 2).

God's omnipotence is, of course, combined with His omniscience, for He is the Knower of all that is and all that takes place in this world. For, "with

Him are the keys of the Unseen; He knows what is in land and sea; not a leaf falls, but He knows it. Not a grain in the earth's shadows, not a thing, fresh or withered, but it is in a Book Manifest" (VI, 59). This Book Manifest (*al-kitāb al-mubīn*) is none other than Divine Knowledge, which is the root and origin of the reality of all that exists, for God's Will reigns supreme in a universe in which His Power dominates over all things and all human actions and where His Knowledge encompasses all orders of reality from the angelic substances to the pebbles on a beach.

Yet in such a world man is mysteriously endowed with the gift of freedom of action, which holds him responsible before God for whatever action he commits. Without this freedom, the role of God as Judge, His Justice and even His Mercy would lose their ultimate significance, for how could God judge human action if man were not responsible for that action? The Quranic description of the Divinity, therefore, emphasizes the omnipotence and omniscience of God and His Justice, in the light of which man is judged, while also reminding man over and over again of his responsibility before his Lord, Who is the final Judge of all his actions.

The aspect of God as the Just and Judge of human affairs is complemented by the description of Him as the Merciful and the Forgiving. It is true that man must surrender himself to God's Will and thereby gain protection, for God alone is the ultimate protector (*al-Wakīl*). It is true also that man must try to follow the concrete embodiment of the Divine Will as contained in the Sacred Law (*al-Sharī'ah*) and the ethical principles enunciated in the Quran and *Ḥadīth* and that he will be judged accordingly by God on the Day of Judgment. Nevertheless, it is true that God forgives, that His Mercy knows no bounds, and that often He acts in imponderable ways. In fact, according to a well-known *ḥadīth*, upon the Divine Throne (*al-'arsh*) is written, "Verily My Mercy precedes My Wrath" (*inna raḥmatī sabaqat ghaḍabī*). Moreover, in the Quran it is the Names of Divine Mercy, such as *al-Raḥmān, al-Raḥīm,* and *al-Ghafūr,* that are repeated more than others—not to speak of the fact that every chapter of the Quran but one begins with the name of *Allāh* followed by *Raḥmān* and *Raḥīm* and not the Names of Majesty or Justice. The Quran itself, in fact, identifies the name *al-Raḥmān,* which signifies the supreme form of Mercy, with the Divine Essence Itself, with the very Nature of God, for it asserts, "Call upon God, or call upon the Most Merciful (*al-Raḥmān*)" (XVII, 110).

God also penetrates His creation through His "signs" (*āyāt*), which are manifested both in the world of nature and within the soul of man, for the Quran asserts, "We shall display to them our signs (*āyāt*) upon the horizons (*āfāq*) and within themselves (*anfus*) until it becomes manifest to them that it is the truth (*al-ḥaqq*)" (XLI, 53). God is at once Truth and Reality; the word *Ḥaqīqah*, which is related to the Divine Name *al-Ḥaqq*, means both truth and reality. This *Ḥaqīqah* manifests itself everywhere in the macrocosmic as well as the microcosmic world. Moreover, the verses of the Quran are also called *āyāt*, so that it can be said that the Muslim breathes in a universe in which the *vestigia Dei* (literally, *āyāt Allāh*) are manifested everywhere. God has left His "signature" upon all things in a language whose key is provided by Revelation.

God as Love and Light

As far as Islamic spirituality is concerned, the aspect of God as Love and also as Light are particularly significant and have led to distinct modes of spirituality. As far as love is concerned, it is asserted in the Quran that, there are "a people He loves and who love Him" (V, 54). The well-known sacred *ḥadīth* "I was a hidden treasure; I wanted to be known. Hence I created the world so that I would be known" places the very cause of creation in God's "wanting" or "loving" (*ḥubb*) to be known. In both cases the word *ḥubb* or love is used to relate God to man as well as God to His own creation. Moreover, one of God's Names is *al-Wadūd*, He Who loves, and Sufis usually refer to the Divine as the object of love. It is true that the technical term used for love by later Sufis is *ʿishq*, a non-Quranic term implying intense love, but the emphasis on the love that God has for man and the creation and that man should have for God is to be found in the very sources of the Islamic Revelation. It must never be forgotten that one of the Prophet's names is *Ḥabīb Allāh*, literally, friend or beloved of God, and that Muslim saints over the centuries have seen in the love of God for the Prophet and in his love for God the prototype of all love between man and his Creator. God loved the Prophet so much that He addressed him in these words: "If thou wert not, I would not have created the heavens." No understanding of Islamic spirituality is possible without comprehension of the element of love for God which marks all authentic expressions of this spirituality, although in the case of Islam this love (*al-maḥabbah*) is always combined with sapience or gnosis (*al-maʿrifah*).

As for the Name of God as Light (*al-Nūr*), it is directly connected to those spiritual paths which emphasize the way of knowledge, for, according to the Prophet, "al-*ʿilm*^{u} *nūr*^{un}," knowledge is light. The Quran states that "God is the Light (*nūr*) of the heavens and the earth" (XXIV, 35). Therefore, all light issues from His Light, from the physical light of the candle to the light of the sun and even beyond to the angelic and archangelic lights which illuminate the soul. The reality of God as Light has left its impact upon

Islamic spirituality not only through the distinct School of Illumination (*ishrāq*), founded by the sixth/twelfth-century Sufi and philosopher Shihāb al-Dīn Suhrawardī, but also in a more general illuminationist strand that is to be found far and wide in many different forms and schools of Sufism and Islamic philosophy.

The Face of God

The Quran speaks in several places of the Face of God (*wajh Allāh*). The Face of God is that aspect of the Divinity which He has turned toward the world or, on another level, a particular world determined by a distinct religion or revelation. His Face refers to His Names and Qualities not in themselves but inasmuch as they are reflected upon the myriads of mirrors of existence. This Face is also none other than the face which the spiritual man turns toward God. Man returns to God by turning his face toward God's Face and by finally realizing that he is himself the mirror in which God contemplates His Holy Face. Moreover, all the worlds and the countless creatures in them perish save this Face, for, as the Quran asserts, "All things perish, except His Face" (XXVIII, 88) and "All that dwells upon the earth is perishing, yet still abides the Face of thy Lord, majestic, splendid" (LV, 26–27). The goal of human life is to realize this Face while man resides in the human state as the being whom God created in "His image" (*'alā ṣūratihi*).

On the highest level, the realization of this Face through "self-effacement" —or annihilation (*fanā'*), as the Sufis have called it—means to be already resurrected in God while in this life and to see God "wherever one turns." Those who have died to their ego have gained thereby the right to assert with such saints as Ḥallāj and Basṭāmī their "union" with the Divine and to express through their ecstatic utterances such sayings as "I am the Truth" or "Glory be unto me." In such cases, it was not the individual Sufi but God in them who uttered such ecstatic sayings. Through this self-effacement or annihilation, which represents the highest possibility of the human state, the spiritual masters of Islam came to realize the ultimate meaning of the *Shahādah*, which is not only that God is One but also that He is the only Reality in the absolute sense. Whether called the "transcendent unity of being" (*waḥdat al-wujūd*) or "unity of consciousness" (*waḥdat al-shuhūd*) and despite varying metaphysical expositions and interpretations given to these terms over the centuries by mystics and gnostics, this doctrine represents the highest fruit of spiritual realization, which is to know God and to see Him as He is. The fruit of the spiritual path of Islam is the plenary knowledge of the Divine. He who has gained such a knowledge through the means made available in the Islamic tradition and by virtue of the grace issuing from His Names experiences God as at once transcendent and immanent, as before all things and after all things, as both the Inward and the Outward. He sees God everywhere, and wherever he turns he sees His Face; for did not the Quran assert "Whithersoever ye turn, there is Face of God"? Such a person is already dead to the world even if he continues to live actively in it. His gaze is fixed upon God, and his tongue and heart never cease repeating His Name. Before the profane world, which understands him not, he simply repeats the Quranic injunction "Say Allah, then leave them to plunge themselves in vain and trifle discourse" (VI, 92). He already lives in Allah's Sacred Name, having died to his passionate self. Through this death he has gained access to the world of the spirit and has come to know His Lord, thereby fulfilling the goal of creation and the purpose of the Quranic Revelation, which is none other than to enable man to know and love God and to obey His Will during this earthly journey.

Notes

1. Even within Islamic esoterism there is a "quintessential Sufism" wherein the full and complete doctrine of the Divine Nature is to be found, formulated usually in a symbolic language, but also sometimes in an explicitly metaphysical language. See F. Schuon, *Sufism: Veil and Quintessence*, trans. W. Stoddart (Bloomington, IN: World Wisdom, 1981).

2. This word implies at once the state of oneness and the action of making into one or integration. It is, therefore, not possible to translate it into a single term in English.

3. *A Shi'ite Anthology*, ed. and trans. W. Chittick (London: Muhammadi Trust, 1981) 27–29.

4. See Balyānī, *Épître sur l'Unicité Absolve*, trans. M. Chodkiewicz (Paris: Les Deux Océans, 1982); al-Ghazzālī, *Maqsad al-asnā fī sharḥ ma'ānī asmā' Allāh al-ḥusnā*, partly trans. J. McCarthy in his *Freedom and Fulfillment* (Boston: Twayne, 1980) 333–61; and Fakhr al-Dīn al-Rāzī, *Traité sur les noms divins*, trans. M. Gloton (Paris: Les Deux Océans, 1983).

5. *Tawḥīd*, technically speaking, embraces at once *aḥad* and *wāḥid* as well as the act of integration in the light of the Divine Oneness.

6. This terminology belongs to F. Schuon; see *Sufism: Veil and Quintessence*, chap. 7.

7. Such treatises as the *Miftāḥ al-falāḥ* of Ibn 'Aṭā' Allāh al-Iskandarī and *Allāh, al-qawl al-mutamad* of Shaykh al-'Alawī contain explicit teachings about Sufi doctrine of *dhikr*, and many other Sufi texts allude to this central practice indirectly. See Ibn 'Aṭā' Allāh, *Traité sur le nom Allah* (Paris: Les Deux Océans).

8. Actually God's Names are infinite, but they are summarized and recapitulated in the set of ninety-nine Names in the specifically Islamic form of revelation. There are, in fact, several sets of ninety-nine Names all based on the Quran and *Hadīth*, and all Muslim rosaries possess ninety-nine beads corresponding to this traditionally determined number of Divine Names.

17

The Angels

SACHIKO MURATA

ANGELS ARE UNSEEN BEINGS of a luminous and spiritual substance that act as intermediaries between God and the visible world. Belief in their existence enters into the definition of faith itself: "The Messenger believes in what was sent down to him from his Lord, and the believers: Each one believes in God, His angels, His Books, and His Messengers" (II, 285; cf. II, 177, IV, 136). The word for angel, *malak* (pl. *malā'ikah*), whose root meaning is "messenger," occurs more than eighty times in the Quran and repeatedly in the *Ḥadīth.* The Islamic concepts of creation, revelation, prophecy, the events that occur in the world, worship, the spiritual life, death, resurrection, and the central position of man in the cosmos cannot be understood without reference to the angels. In philosophical and Sufi texts, angelology is often an essential component of both cosmology and spiritual psychology, since the angels enter into the definition of both the macrocosm and the microcosm.

Angels in the Quran and Ḥadīth

The angels belong to the "world of the unseen" (*'ālam al-ghayb*). When the unbelievers asked why an angel had not been sent down with the Prophet Muḥammad, God replied, "Had We made him an angel, yet assuredly We would have made him a man" (VI, 9). Even if the angels were to be seen by the outward eye, they would appear in forms suitable for the visible world (*al-shahādah*). Moreover, if God had sent down an angel, then "the matter would be judged, and no respite would be given [to mankind]" (VI, 8). For, "upon the day when they see the angels—no good tidings that day for the sinners. . . . On the day when the heavens and the clouds are split asunder and the angels are sent down in a grand descent, the dominion that day will belong truly to the All-Merciful; it will be a harsh day for the unbelievers" (XXV, 25–26).

The Quran often refers to the angels' eschatological function not only at the resurrection, but also at death and in heaven and hell: "The angel of death, who has been charged with you, will gather you; then to your Lord you will be returned" (XXXII, 11). "If you could only see when the evil-doers are in the agonies of death and the angels are stretching out their hands: 'Give up your souls!'" (VI, 93). "Believers, guard yourselves and your families against a Fire whose fuel is men and stones, and over which are harsh, terrible angels" (LXVI, 6). "Gardens of Eden which they shall enter . . . and the angels shall enter unto them from every gate" (XIII, 23). Several of these angels are mentioned by name. Riḍwān ("Good-pleasure," IX, 21; LVII, 20) is taken to be the proper name of the angel given charge of paradise, whereas Mālik ("Master," XLIII, 77) rules over hell. Nakīr and Munkar, the two angels who question the dead in their graves, are mentioned in many *ḥadīths;* traditions also speak of Rūmān, who subjects the dead to various trials.

The sacred history of the Prophet's mission provides many examples of explicit angelic activity in key events. As an infant, the Prophet was visited by "two men clothed in white, carrying a gold basin full of snow." In the Prophet's own words, these angelic beings "split open my breast and brought forth my heart. This also they split open, taking from it a black clot which they cast away. Then they washed my breast with the snow." God revealed the Quran to the Prophet by means of the angel Gabriel, who also acted as his guide on the Night of Ascension (*Laylat al-mi'rāj*). Many witnesses reported the participation of angels in battles fought by the nascent community. Concerning the battle of Badr, the Quran itself says: "When thy Lord revealed to the angels, 'I am with you, so confirm the believers. I shall cast terror into the unbelievers' hearts, so strike off their heads and smite their every finger'" (VIII, 12).

In this world, before death the angels record the deeds of men: "There are over you watchers, noble writers, who know whatever you do" (LXXXII, 10–12). "Over every soul there is a watcher" (LXXXVI, 4). The Prophet added, "They mind your works: when a work is good, they praise God, and when one is evil, they ask Him to forgive you." The Prophet also reported that angels take turns watching over men and assemble together at the afternoon and dawn prayers. "Those who spent the night among you then ascend, and their Lord asks them—though He is best informed about you—how they left His servants. They reply, 'We left them while they were praying, and we came to them while they were praying.'" In the same way, when people gather together to remember (*dhikr*) God, "the angels surround them, mercy covers them, peace descends on them, and God remembers them among those who are with Him." Among the important pious acts

Muslims perform—in imitation of God and the angels—is the invocation of blessings (*ṣalāt*) upon the Prophet: "God and His angels bless the Prophet. Oh believers, you also bless him, and pray him peace" (XXXIII, 56). Here the angels also perform a second function; in the words of the Prophet, "God has angels who travel about in the earth and convey to me greetings from my people." As for the evildoers, they call down upon themselves the angels' curses. According to a *ḥadīth,* "If anyone sells a defective article without calling attention to the defect, he will be the object of God's anger and the angels will curse him continually." The angels are worthy of special veneration; when the name of a major angel is mentioned in Islamic texts, it is usually followed by the same formula (*'alayhi's-salām,* "upon him be peace") that follows the name of a prophet. In his *Ṣaḥīfat al-sajjādiyyah,* the fourth Shī'ite Imam, Zayn al-'Ābidīn 'Alī ibn al-Ḥusayn (d. 95/714), has left a remarkable prayer, often recited by the pious, asking God to bestow blessings upon the various angels.

The Quran provides many keys to the nature and ontological status of the angels. A verse constantly quoted in later discussions represents the words of the angels themselves: "None of us there is but has a known station" (XXXVII, 164). God also says, "They are honored servants who precede Him not in speech and act as He commands" (XXI, 27). Basing themselves on these and other verses, the Quran commentators were able to discern a hierarchy of different kinds of angels, each performing a specified task. The Sufi 'Izz al-Dīn Kāshānī (d. 735/1334–35), author of the well-known Persian paraphrase of Abū Hafṣ Suhrawardī's *'Awārif al-ma'ārif,* summarizes these discussions as follows:

> All believers have faith in the existence of the angels, who dwell in the monasteries of holiness and the communities of divine intimacy. . . . Some of them are more excellent, others lower in degree. Their stations are various and their ranks multiple, as is explained by the verse, "By the rangers in their ranks" (XXXVII, 1). Some have been brought nigh to the Presence of Majesty and cling to the Threshold of Perfection; these are alluded to in the words, "Then those who are foremost in going ahead" (LXXIX, 4). Others govern the affairs of creation: "Then those who govern the Command" (LXXIX, 5). Another group guards the doorway to the Court of Magnificence: "By the drivers driving (XXXVII, 2). Others sing the praises of the Presence of Kingship and the Divine Books: "By the reciters of a Remembrance" (XXXVII, 3). Others carry news and relay reminders: "By those who deliver a reminder" (LXXVII, 5). Many are their levels and ranks; each busies himself with a specific command and possesses a known station: "None of us there is but has a known station" (XXXVII, 164).[1]

In his *'Ajā'ib al-makhlūqāt* (*Marvels of Creation*) the famous cosmographer al-Qazwīnī (d. 682/1283) utilizes the Quran, the *Hadīth,* and the later tradition to provide a detailed description of fourteen kinds of angels:[2]

1. The Bearers of the Throne. Mentioned in the Quran (XL, 7), these are four angels in the form of an eagle, a bull, a lion, and a man; they are also called "Those brought nigh" (IV, 172). According to Ibn 'Abbās, God will add four more to their number on the Day of Resurrection; hence, the Quran says, "On that day the Terror shall come to pass and heaven shall be split . . . ; the angels shall stand upon its borders, and on that day eight shall carry above them the Throne of thy Lord" (LXIX, 15–17).

2. The Spirit. He occupies one rank, and the remaining angels together occupy another rank, a fact alluded to in the verse, "On the day the Spirit and the angels stand in ranks . . ." (LXXVIII, 38). He is charged with governing the spheres, the planets, and everything beneath the moon–in other words, all the affairs of heaven and earth. Certain traditions place all the angels under his control, making him correspond to the Creative Principle itself.[3]

3. Isrāfīl. He delivers commands, places spirits within bodies, and will blow the trumpet on the Last Day. With one of his four wings he fills the west, with the second he fills the east, with the third he descends from heaven to earth, and with the fourth he keeps himself veiled. His two feet are below the seventh earth, and his head reaches the pillars of the Throne. When God wants something to happen in creation, He causes the Pen to write upon the Tablet, which is situated between Isrāfīl's eyes, and then Isrāfīl relays the command to Michael.

4. Gabriel. According to 'Ā'ishah and others, the Prophet saw him in his true form only twice, as is indicated by the Quran: "This is naught but a revelation revealed, taught him by one terrible in power, very strong [i.e., Gabriel]; he stood poised, being on the higher horizon. . . . He saw him another time by the Lote Tree of the Far Boundary" (LIII, 4–14). The first vision took place at the cave of Ḥirā', during the revelation of the first verses of the Quran, the second during the *mi'rāj*.. According to another account, having seen Gabriel in his true form, the Prophet fainted. Regaining consciousness, he said, "Glory be to God! I did not know that any of the creatures were like this!" Gabriel replied, "What if you had seen Isrāfīl? He has twelve wings, one of which is in the east and the other in the west. The Throne rests upon his shoulders, yet he shrinks because of God's Tremendousness until he becomes like a suckling child."

5. Michael. Mentioned by name once in the Quran (II, 98), he is charged with providing nourishment for bodies and knowledge for souls. He stands above the "Swarming Sea" (LII, 6) in the seventh heaven, and if he were to open his mouth, the heavens would fit within it like a mustard seed in the

ocean. According to a *ḥadīth,* "Every prophet has two viziers from the inhabitants of heaven and two from the inhabitants of earth; my two from heaven are Gabriel and Michael." When Isrāfīl blows the trumpet, Gabriel will stand at his right hand and Michael at his left.

6. 'Izrā'īl. He is mentioned by the Quran as the "angel of death"; his name is supplied by the commentators.

7. The cherubim (*al-karrūbiyyūn*). They have withdrawn into the precinct of Holiness and turned their attention away from all but God; drowned in the contemplation of His Beauty, they "glorify Him by night and day, never failing" (XXI, 20).

8. The angels of the seven heavens. Ibn 'Abbās mentions the form of these angels and the name of the angel in charge of each heaven as follows (beginning with the sphere of the moon): cattle, Ismā'īl; eagles, Mīkhā'īl; vultures, Ṣā'idyā'īl; horses, Ṣalṣā'īl; houris, Kalkā'īl; heavenly youths (*ghilmān*), Samkhā'īl; mankind, Rūfā'īl.

9. The guardian angels. They are also called the "honored writers" (LXXXII, 11); two of them are charged with each human being.

10. The attendant angels (XIII, 11). They descend upon mankind with blessings and ascend with news of their works.

11. Nakīr and Munkar. They question the dead in their graves.

12. The journeyers (*sayyāḥūn*). They visit assemblies where men remember the Name of God.

13. Hārūt and Mārūt (II, 102). See below, p. 341.

14. The angels charged with each existent thing. They keep things in good order and ward off corruption. The number of them charged with each thing is known only to God.

Cosmology: The Angels and the Macrocosm

Systematic analyses of the ontological function of the angels are found in the writings of certain philosophers and Sufis. Ibn Sīnā (Avicenna) (d. 428/1037), the greatest of the Peripatetics, wrote a separate *Treatise on the Angels,* in which he shows that the angelic hierarchy affirmed by Islam corresponds to the gradation of intelligences discerned by the philosophers. He identifies the ten Intellects that form the hierarchy of intelligible existence with ten angels, the lowest of whom is Gabriel, that is, the Active Intellect (*al-'aql al-fa''āl*). Just as Gabriel is the celestial intermediary who conveys knowledge to the prophets, so also he and the angels under his command are the immediate source of every intelligible form that enters the human mind. In other words, nothing can be known without the intervention of the angels. The Sage attains to supreme knowledge by purifying himself of the dark clouds of the lower world and establishing contact with the Active Intellect at the center of his own being. As H. Corbin has shown so forcefully, the loss of this dimension of Ibn Sīnā's teaching in the West helped prepare the ground for the secularization of knowledge and the eclipse of religion.[4]

Though Ibn Sīnā's philosophy became more and more "occidentalized" at the hands of Christian thinkers, it was increasingly "orientalized" by the Muslims, who placed ever-greater emphasis upon the Orient, the source of the intelligible lights known as angels. Here Shihāb al-Dīn Suhrawardī (d. 587/1191), the founder of the Illuminationist School (*ishrāq*), plays a key role. Combining the rational scheme of Ibn Sīnā with a suprarational vision of the pleroma of lights, he made full use of the Zoroastrian angelology of pre-Islamic Iran, recognizing within it a powerful tool with which to explain the nature of the unseen world. For example, in his treatise called *The Song of Gabriel's Wing*, Suhrawardī explains that all of creation manifests the luminous Words of God, which radiate from His noble countenance. The first Word of God is the supreme light, referred to in the Prophet's words, "If the sun's face were to become manifest, it would be worshiped in place of God." The last of these "greatest words" or archangels is Gabriel, from whom the spirits of all mankind come into existence, each as a word of God. From him an infinite number of "smaller words" also enter into manifestation; alluding to them the Quran says, "Though all the trees in the earth were pens, and the sea [were ink]—seven seas after it to replenish it—yet would the words of God not be exhausted" (XXXI, 27). Between the greatest words and the smaller words dwell the "intermediate words," the hosts of angels.

Gabriel, Suhrawardī continues, has two wings. The right wing is made of pure light and is totally disengaged (*mujarrad*) from creation and connected to God, who is Absolute Being. But the left wing displays a trace of darkness, like the spots on the face of the full moon. It represents Gabriel's own personal existence, which has one side turned away from God and toward nonexistence. When a shadow falls down from Gabriel's mottled left wing, this lower world of falsehood and deception comes into existence. Hence the Prophet said, "God created the creatures in darkness," thereby alluding to the dark stains on the left wing, "then He sprinkled them with some of His light," alluding to the ray of light that shines down from the right wing. The Quran says, "He made the darkness and the light" (VI, 1). In the present context, the darkness that God made is this world of deception, and the light that follows it is a ray from the right wing, the source of every light that falls into the lower world. Hence, concludes Suhrawardī:

> The World of Deception is the song and shadow of Gabriel's wing, that is, his left wing, while enlightened souls derive from his right wing. The realities that God deposits in the minds of human beings all derive from the right wing, as, for example, "He has written faith upon their hearts, and He has confirmed them with a spirit from Himself" (Quran 58:22). . . . But Wrath, the Cry (cf. Quran 11:67), and mishaps derive from the left wing.[5]

The Sufis developed a number of cosmological schemes making use of the Quran, the *Ḥadīth* literature, the insights of the philosophers (especially those who were more mystically inclined), and their own vision of the unseen world. One of the clearest schemes is found in the Persian writings of Ṣadr al-Dīn al-Qūnawī (d. 673/1274), Ibn 'Arabī's chief disciple. Having discussed the Divine Essence and Attributes, he turns to God's Acts (*af'āl*) or creatures, which are of two kinds—those that belong to the world of the spirits (*arwāḥ*) and those that belong to the world of corporeal bodies (*ajsām*). The Quran refers to these two as the command and the creation (e.g., VII, 54). The creation, also called the lower world, the world of the visible (*shahādat*), and the dominion (*mulk*), is the world to which our sensory faculties have access. The command, also referred to as the higher world, the world of the unseen (*ghayb*), and the kingdom (*malakūt*), is inaccessible to sense perception. In the Quran, "No! I swear by what you see" refers to the world of corporeal bodies, while the rest of the passage, "and by what you do not see" (LIX, 38–39), alludes to the world of the spirits.

After briefly describing the structure of the cosmos, al-Qūnawī turns to explaining the nature of the creatures that dwell in its various levels. The world of the spirits is inhabited by two kinds of angels:

(1) The cherubim pay no attention to the world of corporeal bodies and are divided into two classes: (a) The "enraptured ones" (*muhayyamūn*) have no news of the world and its inhabitants since, in the words of the *ḥadīth,* "They have been enraptured by the Majesty and Beauty of God ever since their creation." The Prophet described them by saying, "God has a white earth in which the sun takes thirty days to cross the sky, and each of these days is thirty times longer than the days of the lower world. That earth is filled with creatures who do not know that God has been disobeyed in the earth or that He has created Adam and Iblis." (b) The "Inhabitants of the Invincibility" (*ahl-i jabarūt*) are enthralled by the vision of God and act as chamberlains for the court of Divinity and intermediaries for the effusion of Lordship. Their Lord and Master, called the Greatest Spirit, is the highest of the archangels and chief of the supreme council (*al-mala' al-a'lā*). In one respect he is known as the "Supreme Pen," for, according to the Prophet, "The first thing created by God was the Pen." In another respect he is called the First Intellect, for, again in the Prophet's words: "The first

30. "Alexander and Khidr in quest of the Foundation of Life of Nizami," Supplement Persian 1956, Folio 245.

thing created by God was the Intellect. He said to it, 'Come forward,' so it came forward. He said to it, 'Go backward,' so it went backward. Then He said, 'By My Majesty and Might, I have created no creature more honored in My eyes than thee. Through thee I shall give, through thee I shall take, through thee I shall reward, and through thee I shall punish.'" The Greatest Spirit stands in the first row of this group, while the Holy Spirit, also known as Gabriel, stands in the last. "None of us there is but has a known station" (XXXVII, 164).

(2) Angels of the second kind govern and control the world of corporeal bodies. Called the Spirituals (*rūḥāniyyūn* [read by some authorities as *rawḥāniyyūn*, the Reposeful]), they also are of two classes: (a) The inhabitants of the upper kingdom control the heavenly spheres. (b) The inhabitants of the lower kingdom govern earthly things. At least one of them is charged with everything found in the corporeal universe. A pre-Islamic prophet said, "Everything has an angel," while the Prophet Muḥammad reported that an angel descends with every drop of rain. Those who are endowed with mystical vision say that seven angels are needed for a single leaf to be created on a tree. The *Ḥadīth* literature mentions angels of mountains, wind, thunder, and lightning. But, says al-Qūnawī, unless the beauty of "So glory be to Him, in whose hand is the kingdom (*malakūt*) of each thing" (XXXVI, 83) throws off its veil, you will not be able to grasp the inward meaning of these sayings.

Al-Qūnawī then turns to the human being, whom he calls the "subtle essence of Lordship" (*laṭīfa-yi rubūbiyyat*). Man is the quintessential mystery of the world of the kingdom. Compounded of both worlds, spiritual and corporeal, he is the most perfect existent thing. No intermediary stands between him and God, while he acts as intermediary between God and all other creatures. Only the supreme council is exempt from his control.

There are also other worlds, situated on intermediary levels. The fiery spirits, known as the jinn and the satans, can be classified as part of the lower kingdom. But between the world of the spirits and the world of the corporeal bodies stands another group of worlds, often referred to collectively as the world of image exemplars (*mithāl*) or the world of imagination (*khayāl*). Everyone is able to perceive a trace of this world in dreams, and it is here that the events described in the eschatological literature take place.

> Embodiment of spirits, spiritualization of corporeal bodies, personification of moral qualities and works, manifestation of meanings in appropriate forms, and contemplation of disengaged realities in corporeal forms and semblances all take place in this world. In it the Prophet saw Gabriel in the form of [his contemporary] Diḥyah Kalbī. The spirits of past prophets and

saints that are contemplated in forms and semblances by shaykhs and Masters of the Way dwell in this world. Khiḍr is also seen in this world.[6]

In its entirety the above passage classifies all existents into five broad categories, called elsewhere by al-Qūnawī the Five Divine Presences: God, the spiritual world, the intermediate world of imagination, the sensory world, and the perfect man, who embraces all these Presences within himself. In his Arabic works, al-Qūnawī follows Ibn 'Arabī by pointing out that the angels correspond to the spiritual faculties of the perfect man, who is the prototype of both mankind and the universe:

> Animal men [i.e., those human beings who have not attained to spiritual perfection] are forms manifesting the properties of the totality of the Human-Divine Reality [elsewhere called the Perfect Man] in respect of that Reality's outward manifestation. The angels with all their various degrees are forms that manifest the properties of Its inward states and faculties. Thus the Supreme Angels and the Bearers of the Throne are related [to the Perfect Man] as the major organs are related to the faculties deposited in each of the limbs [of the human body]. The planets correspond to the limbs. The angels who dwell below the Bearers of the Throne pertain to the remaining faculties and to the specific characteristics of each faculty.[7]

In Ibn 'Arabī's voluminous writings, especially the *Futūḥāt al-makkiyyah,* there are many references to and discussions of the angels and the role they play in the cosmos. One of his followers, Sa'īd al-Dīn Farghānī (d. ca. 700/1300), clarifies some of his master's teachings by connecting the archangels to four fundamental attributes of God: Life, Knowledge, Will, and Power, which are often called the Four Pillars of Divinity. He begins by referring to the Quranic "Guarded Tablet," upon which the Pen is said to write out God's knowledge of creation and which the cosmologists call the Universal Soul, the receptive complement of the First or Universal Intellect. Each of the Four Pillars of Divinity is reflected in a specific form within the tablet without excluding the properties of the other three pillars. Isrāfīl is the locus of manifestation for Life, the fundamental root from which all other perfections derive. Isrāfīl's connection with Life is illustrated by the fact that his first blast on the trumpet (*al-ṣūr*) brings all life in this world to an end and his second blast begins the everlasting life of the next world. Gabriel represents the pillar of Knowledge, which explains why he is the angel of revelation, conveying all sorts of knowledge in various degrees. The Quran refers to him as a teacher in the verses, "This is naught but a revelation revealed, taught to him by one terrible in power, very strong . . ." (LIII, 4–5). Michael manifests Will, since he is put in charge of handing out the formal and supraformal sustenance upon which the continued existence of the creatures depends. This includes spiritual food like knowledge and understanding, imaginary food like position and honor, and sensory food like property and the bounty of the earth. ʿIzrāʾīl is the locus of manifestation for Power, since he overwhelms all things through death and annihilation.

Just as all the Divine Names and all the creatures are subordinate to these Four Pillars, so also all spirits and angels are subordinate to and faculties of the four archangels, with the exception of the Supreme Pen and the enraptured angels, since they are the "exalted ones" who were not included in God's command when He ordered the angels to bow down before Adam. This is mentioned in God's words to Iblis: "What prevented thee to bow down before what I created with My own two hands? Hast thou waxed proud? Or art thou one of the Exalted Ones?" (XXXVIII, 76).

Farghānī then classifies all the angels, whether "exalted" or encompassed by the tablet, in a scheme reminiscent of what we have seen elsewhere but fresh enough to warrant a summary. There are three basic kinds of angels: The first kind cannot take a locus of manifestation, whether imaginal, elementary, or sensory. The second kind must have a locus of manifestation on at least one of these levels. The third kind is free and nondelimited, since it may or may not manifest itself. The first kind includes the enraptured angels. The second kind is divided into two classes, depending upon the relationship to the locus in which the angel manifests itself. Loci of manifestation are ascribed to the first class, whereas the angels of the second class are ascribed to the loci. (1) The first class of the second kind includes the angels of the heavens and the earth, to whom are attributed all sorts of affairs and effects that play the role of their faculties. They are alluded to in such Quranic verses as, "then those who govern the Command" (LXXIX, 5), "by those who scatter far and wide" (LI, 1), "by those that distribute by command" (LI, 4), "then those who are foremost in going ahead" (LXXIX, 4). (2) The second class includes human spirits, which are attached to bodily forms and constitutions, as well as the spirituality (*rūḥāniyyah*) of every individual of any kind, including inanimate things, animals, and the jinn.

The third kind of angels is limited neither by possessing a locus of manifestation nor by a lack of one. Such angels manifest themselves in whatever form they desire, or without any form. They are the messengers and emissaries between God and His creatures referred to in the verse, "Messengers having wings—two, three, and four; He adds to creation as He will" (XXXV, 1). Here "wings" refers to the varous faculties possessed by the angels. Each of them must have two "wings" to fly in the proximity of God, one being the faculty of knowledge, the other the faculty of action through which it acts according to its knowledge. If God adds a third wing, that is the ability to teach others, as for example in the verse concerning Gabriel, where the Prophet is said to have been "taught by one terrible in power, very strong" (LIII, 5). The fourth wing is action for the sake of others, as in the verse concerning some of the angels, "They proclaim the praise of their Lord, and have faith in Him, and they ask forgiveness for those who have faith" (XL, 7). The four wings represent the fundamental kinds of angelic faculties, and other faculties branch off from these four. But there is no limit to the number of wings or faculties that an angel may have, and this is why the verse about wings ends with the words, "He adds to creation as He will." The well-known *ḥadīth* in which the Prophet reported that Gabriel appeared to him with six hundred wings refers to the faculties that God adds to His creatures as He will.[8]

Psychology: The Angels and the Microcosm

Just as the angels fill the macrocosm, so also they populate the microcosm. As Farghānī has pointed out, from a certain point of view the human spirit is itself an angel; all of the faculties of the soul are then lesser angels subordinate to it. In commenting on al-Qūnawī's statement quoted above that "seven angels are needed for a single leaf to be created on a tree," Jāmī (d. 898/1492) remarks, following the teachings of the natural philosophers, that these are the faculties of the vegetative soul: the nutritive, augmentative, generative, attractive, digestive, retentive, and expulsive.[9] Al-Ghazzālī (d. 505/1111) had already shown that this type of interpretation was in accord with the mainstream of Islamic thought. In the *Iḥyā'* he explains that the smallest morsel of food cannot become part of him who eats it without the intervention of a number of angels. His terminology in explaining the angelic functions follows the standard terms used by the philosophers for the natural faculties: "There must be an angel to *attract* the food toward flesh and bones, for food does not move by itself. A second is necessary to *retain* the food . . ." etc.[10]

Sufi writings emphasize that the angels are created of an intelligible light that corresponds to the intellect within man. In Rūmī's words, "The intellect is the same kind as the angel, even though the angel—in contrast to the intellect—has assumed a form and possesses wings and feathers; but in reality they are one thing and perform the same activity."[11] The specific angel to whom the intellect corresponds is Gabriel, whom Rūmī seems to identify with the First Intellect. Ultimate spiritual perfection, attained by the Prophet and certain of his followers, involves union with the One, who lies far beyond any of His creatures. Rūmī praises the intellect but holds that love is a higher reality, since it alone can bring about union. Once intellect takes you to the door of the king, "then divorce the intellect, for now it will bring you only loss."[12] "Like Gabriel the intellect says, 'O Aḥmad, if I take one more step I will be consumed.'"[13] If the intellect corresponds to man's angelic substance, his lower soul or ego (*nafs*) represents his satanic side: "The ego and satan were a single individual, but they have shown themselves in two different forms."[14]

Other Sufis make similar use of the traditional data. 'Azīz Nasafī (d. before 700/1300) writes: "When the intellect assumed the vicegerency in the microcosm, all the microcosmic angels prostrated themselves to it except fancy (*wahm*), who refused. . . . When the intellect assumed the vicegerency, a call came to it, 'O intellect! Know thyself and know thy attributes and acts, so that thou mayest know My Attributes and Acts.'"[15] Nasafī draws correspondences among all the parts of the macrocosm and microcosm:

> The sperm drop that falls into the womb represents (*numūdār*) the primary substance [of the universe]. When [the embryo] becomes fourfold, it represents the four elements and the four natures. Once the parts of the body appear, the outward parts—the head, hands, stomach, pudendum, and feet—represent the seven climes, while the inward parts—the lungs, brain, kidneys, heart, gall-bladder, liver, and spleen—represent the seven heavens.

Next Nasafī declares that each organ corresponds to one of the heavens and to the angels that inhabit it. His remarks can be summarized in the following table:

Heaven	Planet	Organ	Name of Chief Angel	Chief Angel Given Charge Over
1.	moon	lungs	–	temperate weather
2.	Mercury	brain	Gabriel	acquisition of knowledge and management of livelihoods
3.	Venus	kidneys	–	joy, happiness, sensuality
4.	sun	heart	Isrāfīl	life
5.	Mars	gall-bladder	–	severity, anger, striking, killing
6.	Jupiter	liver	Michael	sustenance
7.	Saturn	spleen	'Izrā'īl	taking of spirits

Nasafī concludes by saying that the animal spirit corresponds to the eighth heaven (the footstool or sphere of the fixed stars), the psyche (*rūḥ-i nafsānī*) represents the ninth heaven (the Throne or the sphere of spheres), and the intellect is God's vicegerent ruling over all.[16]

One of the most penetrating analyses of the role of the angels in the microcosm is found in the writings of the philosopher Bābā Afḍal Kāshānī (d. ca. 610/1213–14), a follower of Avicenna deeply influenced by the Hermetic currents of Greco-Islamic thought. He brings out with clarity in liquid Persian prose the ascending movement of all creatures in the universe on the path of the "return" (*ma'ād*) to God. Each level of creation from the mineral up to the human represents a fuller actualization of Being, whose fundamental characteristic is pure consciousness. Bābā Afḍal calls the world a tree whose fruit is mankind, mankind a tree whose fruit is the soul, the soul a tree whose fruit is Intellect, and Intellect a tree whose fruit is the meeting with God.

In this cosmos dominated by the movement toward the self-consciousness of the self (*dhāt*), the four archangels represent the specific powers of the human soul, as contrasted with the powers of the mineral, vegetal, and animal souls. Isrāfīl, who breathes spirits into bodies, corresponds to thought; Michael, who gives creatures their sustenance, to memory; Gabriel, who delivers God's messages to creatures, to speech; and 'Izrā'īl, who takes away souls or spirits, to writing.

On the macrocosmic level, 'Izrā'īl is the human soul, which relates to other spiritual powers in the same way that the hand relates to the body, since its function is to bring unseen meanings into the corporeal world. Just as a writer takes ideas from the unseen world of thought and causes them to fall into the world of the hand and paper, so the soul manifests the realities of its own world on the bodily level. The human being is God's vicegerent in the creation's return to God (just as the First Intellect is His vicegerent in the journey away from God). In this process the soul is like 'Izrā'īl (and unlike Isrāfīl) in that it "takes" spirits (it does not "give" them), since its specific characteristic is to know things, and to know a thing is to separate out its spirit or "meaning" (*ma'nā*). The soul rules over every transformation man undergoes during the return, appearing at each level in an appropriate guise. Each time the individual passes on to a new level of existence during his own development, from the period in the womb through the mineral, vegetal, animal, and human stages until the meeting with God, he meets the angel of death—his own true soul—and experiences the "taking" of the soul with which he mistakenly identifies himself. At the same time, he also meets with God's forgiveness (*āmurzish*), since he moves on to a higher level of being and consciousness. Bābā Afḍal summarizes this process in the following terms:

> The angel of death—the taker of the mineral soul—is the vegetal soul, which delivers the mineral soul over to God's forgiveness by removing it from its

> mineral form and displaying it in a nobler form. The taker of the vegetal soul is the animal soul, which delivers the plant's soul out from vegetal clothing into God's forgiveness by dressing it in an animal robe. The taker of the animal soul is the human soul, which separates the animal soul from the animal's form and body through the act of knowing and which displays it in a more lasting form. At every station the soul passes through during these transformations, it never desires to return to the previous state, since no mature person wants to go back to childhood, nor does a man who has knowledge desire to return to ignorance. . . . Hence you should know that the angel of death brings good news.[17]

Mankind and the Angels

A series of ever more luminous beings fills the hierarchy between man and God, whether this hierarchy is viewed as an inward or an outward reality, or as both at once. The angels are so all-pervasive that man cannot perform a single task or conceive a single idea without their aid. Innumerable Quranic verses and prophetic sayings praise their excellence. It was only natural for certain Muslim thinkers to conclude that the angels are the best of God's creatures. But other traditional data support the view that mankind is superior, and in the long theological debate that has ensued, this position has been confirmed almost universally. For mankind is made directly in the image of God and reflects Him in a total fashion, whereas the angels, though more excellent in substance, do not possess the same centrality in the Divine Scheme.

Perhaps the Quranic passage most often cited to prove mankind's superiority is the following: "When We said to the angels, 'Prostrate yourselves to Adam,' they prostrated themselves, except Iblis" (II, 34, etc.). As for Iblis, in one of the five instances where this verse occurs the Quran adds, "He was one of the jinn" (XVIII, 50). The position taken by al-Bayḍāwī (d. ca. 685/1286) and others that Iblis was an angel is rejected by most authorities. In another passage Iblis tells God why he refused to obey His command: "I am better than he; Thou createdst me of fire, and him Thou createdst of clay" (VII, 12). Elsewhere the Quran alludes to the creation of jinn from fire (XV, 27; LV, 15), and, according to the universally accepted *ḥadīth* related by 'Ā'ishah, the angels were created from light, the jinn from fire, and mankind from clay.

Most authorities have held that the angels' prostration indicates the superiority of the prophets and believers. As Rūmī remarks, "How could God's Justice and Gentleness allow a rose to prostrate itself before a thorn?"[18]

An early Quran commentator, Rashīd al-Dīn Maybudī (d. 530/1135–36),

31. “Angels ministering to Ibrahim ibn Adham,” MS Pers. B.1, Folio 33r.

summarizes some of the arguments for the superiority of human beings as follows: Everyone recognizes that the prophets and the believers are more excellent than the angels, since God showed the former various favors and kindnesses that He did not show to the latter. Though the angels are nearer to the Divine Presence, they are blinded by the veils of Awesomeness and the fiery splendor of Majesty, while the prophets and believers have been singled out for the light of contemplation, the breeze of intimacy, the radiance of unveiling, and the favor of love. Among the proofs of the superiority of human beings are Quranic verses such as the following: God affirms His love for the prophets and the faithful with His words, "He loves them and they love Him" (V, 54). Concerning Abraham in particular He says, "God has taken Abraham as a friend" (IV, 125). Concerning some of the prophets He says, "We purified them with a quality most pure . . . and in Our sight they are of the chosen, the excellent" (XXXVIII, 46). About the believers God declares, "Those who believe and do righteous deeds are the best of creatures" (XCVIII, 7). Among the *ḥadīths* that confirm the superiority of human beings, the following can be cited: "The angels said to God, 'Our Lord, Thou hast created the children of Adam and appointed them for the world, so appoint for us the next world.' God replied, 'I will not make My righteous servant—him whom I created with My own two hands [cf. Quran XXXVIII, 75]—like him to whom I said "Be!" and he was.'" Or again, "The Prophet said, 'On the Day of Resurrection, nothing will be greater than the children of Adam.' Someone said, 'Oh Messenger of God! Not even the angels?' He replied, 'Not even the angels. They are compelled like the sun and the moon.'" The sun and the moon have no choice but to rise and to set, and in the same way the angels have no choice but to obey God. Unlike human beings, they have no "soul commanding to evil" (XII, 53), no sensuality pulling them this way and that, no Satan whispering to them and distorting their vision, and no lower world to fill them with fancies. Their obedience is part of their very nature, like the breathing of an animal.[19]

The nature of man in relation to the angels is summarized in an oft-quoted *ḥadīth:* "God created the angels from intellect without sensuality (*shahwah*), the beasts from sensuality without intellect, and mankind from both intellect and sensuality. So when a person's intellect overcomes his sensuality, he is better than the angels; but when his sensuality overcomes his intellect, he is worse than the beasts." Nasafī comments, "The angels are luminous existence, while the beasts are tenebrous existence. Neither the angels nor the beasts have more than one of the two worlds, but man has both."[20] Rūmī often comments on this *ḥadīth.* In one instance he remarks in his inimitable style: "Man's situation is comparable to an angel's wing that has been attached to a donkey's tail so that perhaps, through the angel's radiance and companionship, the donkey may itself become an angel."[21]

A similar lesson can be understood from the story of the two angels Hārūt and Mārūt, alluded to in the Quran (II, 102) and amplified by the commentators—though certain authorities, such as Ibn Ḥazm (d. 456/1064), deny that these two were angels. When the sons of Adam were given the earth, the angels marveled at their iniquities and protested to God: "Our Lord, Thou hast favored these dust-creatures of the earth, but they disobey Thee." God replied, "If that sensuality that is within them were within you, your state would be the same." The angels said, "We would not rebel against Thee and disobey Thy command." At God's request they chose two of their number to be sent to the earth possessing sensuality and the other attributes of man. Hārūt and Mārūt were the most worshipful and humble of the angels; sending them down to the earth, God commanded them to avoid idolatry, fornication, wine, and the unjust spilling of blood. Eventually they committed all these sins and God gave news of their state to the angels in heaven. From that day on, the angels have continued to "ask forgiveness for everyone on earth" (XLIII, 5), for they realize that man's sensuality is a tremendous burden, and those able to overcome it are truly the best of creatures.[22]

The superiority of human beings over the angels has not been affirmed categorically by all who maintain it. In the passages quoted above, al-Qūnawī refers to the superiority of the "supreme council" while his disciple Farghānī speaks of the "exalted ones" who were not required to prostrate themselves before Adam. In a similar manner Ibn 'Arabī writes as follows:

> Once in a vision I asked the Messenger of God about the drawn-out debate over the excellence of mankind and the angels. He replied, "The angels are superior." I asked what I should say if asked the reason. He answered, "You know that I am the best of mankind. This has been established among you, and it is correct. Now I related from God that He said, 'When someone remembers Me in himself, I remember him in Myself; and when someone remembers Me in an assembly, I remember him in an assembly better than it.' How many there were who remembered God in an assembly when I was among them! Yet God remembered them in an assembly better than the assembly in which I was.[23]

In other passages, Ibn 'Arabī looks at the matter from a different point of view. In the first chapter of the *Fuṣūṣ* he writes:

> The angels do not grasp that which is supplied by the ontological plane of the vicegerent [i.e., man], nor do they grasp the worship of the Essence that is demanded by the ontological level of God. For no one can know God except in keeping with what his own essence provides, and the angels do not

> possess Adam's all-comprehensiveness [since only mankind manifests the Name "*Allāh*," which comprehends all other Names]. They do not grasp the Divine Names pertaining only to Adam's all-comprehensive level. They glorify God and call Him holy (Quran II, 30), but they do not know that He has Names which their knowledge does not embrace. Thus they do not glorify Him by these Names, nor do they call Him holy in the same way that Adam does.[24]

Inspired by the above passage, Farghānī enumerates eighteen blameworthy qualities of the angels that were only corrected by mankind's vicegerency.[25]

The contradiction between the two positions taken by Ibn 'Arabī and his followers may perhaps be resolved by saying that in the first case they consider mankind as the microcosm, whereas in the second they look upon him as the perfect man, the intermediary between the Divine Essence and all creatures, including the Greatest Spirit and the angels. However this may be, the position set down in the *Fuṣūṣ* has dominated Sufi teaching up to the present. One of its more eloquent spokesman was the poet and metaphysician Jāmī:

> At the time of Adam's creation, the angels spoke in pride and pretension:
> "O God, we hymn Thy Praise, we are Thy righteous glorifiers, so why
> Dost Thou stir up a form out of water and clay?
> He will work corruption and spill blood. . . . [cf. Quran II, 30]
> We are roses—what good are thorns and twigs? What use is a fly in face of a phoenix?"
> Then "God taught Adam all the Names" (II, 31), i.e., the realities of things.
> In the eyes of the gnostic, the Names of God are naught but the realities of the existent entities.
> God taught him all the Names, thus making him understand the Attributes of His Essence.
> Then He said to the angels, "Tell Me those Names" (cf. Quran II, 31).
> All the angels had gone astray through pride, but all admitted their incapacity:
> "We do not know beyond what Thou hast taught us; we understand nothing but what we understand" (cf. II, 31). . . .
> Then God's call reached Adam a second time: "Tell them the Names through which thou hast become manifest, for thou hast knowledge of their mysteries" (cf. II, 33).
> Adam began to speak at God's command, explaining each and every one of the Names,
> For man is the whole, while others are parts.
> The whole contains everything in the parts, but the parts cannot attain to the whole.
> No part knows the whole perfectly, but all parts exist within it.
> When the whole comes to know its own essence, then it knows all the parts.
> But if the part comes to perceive itself, it cannot step beyond this knowledge.
> Even if it gains knowledge of itself, it remains ignorant of the other parts.

What is man? An all-comprehensive isthmus, within which is placed the form of both Creator and creation.
He is a summary transcription of the Essence of God and His ineffable Attributes.
Joined to the details of the Invincible Realm, he comprises the realities of the Kingdom.
His inward nature is drowned in the Ocean of Oneness, while his outward substance stays dry-lipped on the shore of separation.
Every single Attribute of God is to be found in his essence. . . .
In the same way, every reality of the world is placed within him,
Whether the spheres or the four elements, the minerals, plants, or animals.
Written within him is the form of good and evil, kneaded into him is the character of devil and beast.
If he is not the mirror of God's Countenance, then why did the angels prostrate themselves to him?
He is the mirror that reflects the Beauty of the Immaculate Presence.
If Iblis cannot fathom this, what does it matter?[26]

Islamic spirituality can only be envisaged in connection with the angels, who are intertwined with all dimensions of human life as seen by Islam. The key events of sacred history, such as the Revelation itself, the Prophet's Nocturnal Ascent, and the battle of Badr, are explicit instances of angelic intervention. The angels record the deeds of each individual from birth to death. They are the constant companions of the faithful, participating with them especially in their prayers, and play a soteriological and illuminative function for those who follow the path of spiritual realization. By God's leave they govern all macrocosmic and microcosmic forces, and they accompany man to the next abode on his departure from the earthly plane. To speak of Islamic spirituality from its most popular to its most esoteric level is to call attention to the role of the angelic hierarchy.

Notes

1. Kāshānī, *Miṣbāḥ al-hidāyah,* ed. J. Humā'ī (Tehran: Chāpkhāna-yi Majlis, 1325/1946) 42.
2. Al-Qazwīnī, *'Ajā'ib al-makhlūqāt,* on the margin of al-Damīrī, *Ḥayāt al-ḥayawān* (Cairo: Maṭba'at al-Istiqāmah, 1374/1954) 1:94–107.
3. For a far more detailed account of the nature and kinds of angels according to both Shī'ite and Sunni sources, see Majlisī, *Biḥār al-anwār* (2nd ed.; Beirut: Mu'assasat al-Wafā', 1983) 56, esp. pp. 202–16.
4. H. Corbin, *Avicenna and the Visionary Recital,* trans. W. Trask (London: Routledge & Kegan Paul, 1960) 62, 77, 101–10.
5. Suhrawardī, *Oeuvres philosophiques et mystiques 3,* ed. S. H. Nasr (Tehran: Imperial Iranian Academy of Philosophy, 1977) 217–22.

6. Al-Qūnawī, *Tabṣirat al-mubtadī wa tadhkirat al-muntahī,* ed. N. 'A. Ḥabībī *Ma'ārif* 2nd. ser. 1 (Tehran) (1364/1985) 87–88, 89–90, 93, 94.
7. Al-Qūnawī, *Al-Nafaḥāt al-ilāhiyyah* (Tehran: Aḥmad Shīrāzī, 1316/1898–99) 85.
8. Farghānī, *Muntaha'l-madārik* (Cairo: 'Abd al-Raḥīm al-Bukhārī, 1293/1876) 1:51–52.
9. Jāmī, *Naqd al-nuṣūṣ,* ed. W. C. Chittick (Tehran: Imperial Iranian Academy of Philosophy, 1977) 32.
10. Quoted in F. Jadaane, "La place des anges dans la théologie cosmique musulmane," *Studia Islamica* 41 (1975) 52.
11. Rūmī, *Fīhi mā fīhi,* ed. B. Furūzānfar (Tehran: University of Tehran, 1330/1951) 106; cf. Rūmī, *Mathnawī,* ed. R. A. Nicholson (London: Luzac, 1925–45) book 3, vv. 3193, 4054.
12. Rūmī, *Fīhi mā fīhi,* 112.
13. Rūmī, *Mathnawī,* book 1, v. 1066.
14. Ibid., book 3, v. 4053.
15. Nasafī, *Insān-i kāmil,* ed. M. Molé (Tehran: Bibliothèque Iranienne, 1962) 143.
16. Ibid., 147–48.
17. Bābā Afḍal Kāshānī, *Jāwidān-nāmah,* in *Muṣannafāt-i Afḍal al-Dīn Muḥammad ibn Maraqī Kāshānī,* ed. M. Mīnuwī and Y. Mahdawī (Tehran: Dānishgāh, 1331–37/1952–58) 291–92, 315, 319–20.
18. Rūmī, *Mathnawī,* book 2, v. 3332.
19. Maybudī, *Kashf al-asrār,* ed. 'A. A. Ḥikmat (Tehran: University of Tehran, 1331–39/1952–60) 2:783–84. For a thorough presentation of the arguments, Quranic and otherwise, for man's superiority over the angels, see Majlisī, *Biḥār al-anwār,* 57:268–317.
20. Nasafī, *Insān-i kāmil,* 323.
21. Rūmī, *Fīhi mā fīhi,* 107.
22. Maybudī, *Kashf al-asrār,* 1:295–98.
23. Ibn 'Arabī, *Al-Futūḥāt al-makkiyyah* (Beirut: Dār Ṣādir, n.d.) 2:61.
24. Ibn 'Arabī, *Fuṣūṣ al-ḥikam,* ed. A. 'Afīfī (Beirut: Dār al-Kitāb al-'Arabī, 1966) 50–51.
25. Farghānī, *Muntaha'l-madārik,* 1:67–71.
26. Jāmī, *Haft awrang,* ed. M. Mudarrisī-Gīlānī (Tehran: Kitābfurūshī-yi Sa'dī, 1337/1958) 77–79.

18

The Cosmos and the Natural Order

Seyyed Hossein Nasr

> We have not revealed unto thee this Quran that thou shouldst be distressed,
> But as a reminder unto him who feareth,
> A revelation from Him Who created the earth and the high heavens,
> The All-Compassionate, who is established on the Throne.
> Unto Him belongeth whatsoever is in the heavens and whatsoever is in the earth, and whatsoever is between them, and whatsoever is beneath the sod. (XX, 2–6).

The Cosmos and Revelation

The Revelation that comes from Him to Whom belong the heavens and the earth and all that is between them and below the earth also addresses itself to all these realms of the cosmic hierarchy as well as to man. The Quran is, in a sense, a Revelation unto the whole of creation, and one of its primary functions is to awaken in man an awareness of the Divine Presence in that other primordial revelation which is the created order itself. Primordial man saw the phenomena of nature *in divinis,* as the story of Adam in paradise reveals. Islam, in bestowing upon man access to this primordial nature and in addressing itself to the primordial man within every man, unveils once again the spiritual significance of nature and the ultimately theophanic character of the phenomena of the created order. It enables man to read once again the eternal message of Divine Wisdom written upon the pages of the cosmic text.

Islamic spirituality is therefore based not only upon the reading of the written Quran (*al-Qur'ān al-tadwīnī*) but also upon deciphering the text of the cosmic Quran (*al-Qur'ān al-takwīnī*) which is its complement.[1] Nature in Islamic spirituality is, consequently, not the adversary but the friend of the traveler upon the spiritual path and an aid to the person of spiritual vision[2] in his journey through her forms to the world of the Spirit, which is the origin of both man and the cosmos. The Quranic Revelation created not only a community of Muslims but also an Islamic cosmic ambience in which the signs of God (*āyāt Allāh*) adorn at once the souls of men and women and the expanses of the skies and the seas, the birds and the fish, the stars and the creatures living in the bosom of the earth. As the text of the Quran is woven of verses (*āyāt*), which are the words of God, so are the events in the souls of men and the phenomena of nature so many *āyāt* of the Supreme Author, Who caused the reality of all things to be written upon the Guarded Tablet (*al-Lawḥ al-Maḥfūẓ*) by the pen (*al-Qalam*). As the Quran itself bears witness, "We shall show them our portents [*āyāt*] upon the horizons and within themselves, until it becomes manifest unto them that it is the Truth" (XLI, 53), and also, "And in the earth are portents for those whose faith is sure. And (also) in yourselves. Can ye not see?" (LI, 20–21).[3] The inner relation between man, the cosmos, and Revelation is clearly demonstrated in the use of the same term (*āyah*, pl. *āyāt*) to designate the verses of the sacred Book, the inner reality of man, and the verses written upon the pages of the cosmic book.

But not everyone is able to read the message of the cosmic text. The profane man, no matter how lettered in some human language, is illiterate as far as the reading of the cosmic text is concerned. For the Muslim, only the message brought by the unlettered Prophet can teach man to read the Divine Message upon the face of creation.[4] Even within the fold of those who have accepted this message, only the spiritually inclined men and women who can penetrate into the inner meaning of the message and of themselves can hope to see in the phenomena of nature the signature of the noumenal world, to see in them not facts but the *vestigia Dei.*[5] To the extent that man turns to the spiritual world within, nature unveils her inner message to him and acts as both support and companion in his spiritual journey.

Since all levels of cosmic existence belong to God, all creatures also praise Him with their very existence. The Quran says, "The seven heavens and the earth and all that they contain praise Him, nor is there anything that does not celebrate His praise, though ye understand not their praise. Behold, He is clement, forgiving" (XVII, 44). Also, "Hast thou not seen that unto God prostrate themselves whatsoever is in the heavens and whatsoever is in the earth—the sun and the moon and the stars and the hills and the trees and the beast and many of mankind?" (XXII, 18).[6]

The Breath of the Compassionate

According to a Sufi doctrine expounded especially by Ibn ʿArabī, the very substance of the universe consists of the Breath of the Compassionate (*nafas al-Raḥmān*) breathed upon the archetypal realities (*al-aʿyān al-thābitah*).[7] The very substance of things is, therefore, the breath that issues from the Divine Compassion (*al-Raḥmah*) while every creature praises the Lord through its very existence. The sage hears in the existence of every creature of nature the invocation (*dhikr*) of His Name and in the qualities of the created order reflections of His Attributes. He sees upon the face of all things the sign of His Oneness, according to the well-known Arabic poem: "In every creature there exists a sign (*āyah*) from Him, Bearing witness that He is Unique."[8] The Quran emphasizes the Divine Origin of all the order that is observed in the universe. "He it is who appointed the sun a splendour and the moon a light, and measured for her stages, that ye might know the number of the years and the reckoning. God created not (all) that save in truth (*bi'l-ḥaqq*). He detaileth the portents (*āyāt*) for people who have knowledge" (X, 6). The Muslim mind is, in fact, much more impressed by the order and regularity of the natural order than by those extraordinary events that break that order, that is, miracles. It is just as miraculous that the sun does rise every morning from the east as it would be if it were to rise suddenly from the west. Islam does, however, accept the existence of miracles and believes that a day will come when, according to a *ḥadīth*, the sun will rise from the west.

Moreover, the world is created in truth and by the truth (*bi'l-ḥaqq*) and not in vain. "We created not the heaven and the earth and all that is between them in play" (XXI, 16). The study of nature can therefore reveal an aspect of Divine Wisdom provided that study does not divorce the world from its Divine Principle. The Islamic view of nature permitted and encouraged the cultivation of the sciences of nature but never as profane knowledge.[9] Even particular branches of the Islamic sciences such as physics and botany possessed a spiritual aspect as well as a rational one. Being created in truth, nature reflects the Truth on its own level of reality and this Truth can be contemplated by the sage gazing upon a flower as well as by a student of the traditional sciences studying the works of the Muslim scientists, who carried out their study of the natural order always in the light of discovering the vestiges of the Hand of the Divine Artisan.

The Fragility of the World

While it emphasizes that God has created the world by the truth, the Quran also asserts over and over again, especially in the last chapters, the fragility of the created order. A day will come when all the earth, from the mightiest mountain to the lowliest rock will be rendered unto dust before the Majesty of God. "And thou seest the mountains, which thou deemest so firm, pass away as clouds pass away" (XXVII, 88). The spiritual significance of nature resides not only in conveying the message of the One through its beauty, harmony, order, and the symbolism of its forms, but also in being witness to the grandeur of the One Who alone abides while all else passes away. To stand before a mighty mountain and to meditate upon its passing away before the Divine Majesty are to gain a glimpse of that Divine Face which alone subsists while all else dies and perishes, according to the verse, "Everything perishes save His Face" (XXVIII, 88). But this fragility of the natural order is not as immediate as that of the world of man, and Islamic spirituality emphasizes over and over again that in the span of the ordinary life of humanity the works of man perish while the order of nature abides. Islam has always inculcated the importance of man's being the custodian of nature and has instructed man not to struggle to destroy it but rather to live with it in peace, aware that if man seeks to annihilate and subdue nature he will inevitably fail and that it is always nature that will have the final word.

> We must tread carefully upon the earth, treating it with the same respect that we show to the Book of Allah, for although "He hath made the earth humbled to you," and although we are free "to walk in its tracts and eat of His providing," yet: "Are ye assured of Him that is in heaven that He might not cause the earth to swallow you? For behold! The earth is quaking." (LXVII, 15–16)[10]

Nothing is farther removed from traditional Islamic spirituality than the raping of the earth in the name of man's earthly welfare and without consideration of the welfare of the whole of creation.

Nature as Support in the Spiritual Life

Virgin nature is a source of grace in that in its bosom the Muslim contemplative senses the presence of God and the resonance of the world of the Spirit. He hears the prayer of creatures and sees reflected in their complete surrender to the Divine Will the perfection of the state of *islām,* which itself is complete surrender to the Will of God. The saint is the person whose will is perfectly integrated into and in harmony with the Divine Will and is therefore, in a sense, the counterpart of the creatures of nature whose very life is in accordance with His Will. The prayer of the saint is in fact the prayer on behalf of all creation and for all creation in the same way that the Muslim canonical prayer addresses God using the plural form of the subject to emphasize that man prays as representative of the whole of creation.[11]

Nature, moreover, is the sanctuary in which the supreme Muslim rite of *ṣalāt* takes place. These canonical prayers can be performed anywhere in nature, for the whole earth was sanctified by God to allow Muslims to pray on it.[12] The mosque does not in fact seek to create a "supernatural" space but to recreate within the man-made ambience of the urban environment, the harmony, tranquillity, peace, and equilibrium that characterize virgin nature. Being the creation of the Divine Artisan, virgin nature is the supreme work of art, a source of inexhaustible beauty, and the ally of man in quest of God. She remains an ever present witness to the cosmic and metacosmic reality of the truth of Islam, and although man may waver in his faith and religious practice, she abides in her perfect surrender to the One in her perpetual state of being *muslim.*

Nature is also a source for gaining knowledge of God's Wisdom as reflected in His creation. The laws, activities, energies, forms, forces, and rhythms of nature reveal a knowledge that possesses a spiritual significance lying beyond the domain of nature itself. In fact, nature is also the source of metaphysical knowledge in the sense that there exists a symbolic science of nature that is of a metaphysical character. There is, moreover, an immediate knowledge of a purely spiritual character imparted by nature to those qualified to receive such a knowledge. For the contemplative, nature provides not only such a knowledge but also an aid for the spiritual life. In her embrace man is already freed from the pettiness of the human world and savors the foretaste of paradise. The grandeur of nature—the incredible beauty of her forms and harmony of rhythms and cycles—can help to melt the hardened heart and untie the knots in the soul so that man comes to see nature as the counterpart of that primordial revelation of which the Arabic Quran is the final crystallization in the life of present humanity.

Islamic Cosmological Sciences

The spiritual significance of nature in Islam cannot be understood fully without considering the Islamic cosmological sciences which reveal the imprint of the One upon the manifold and relate the world of multiplicity to its Unique Origin. Islamic cosmology acts as a bridge between the metaphysical teachings of the Quranic Revelation and the particular sciences and provides the framework whereby particular branches of knowledge can be sacralized and integrated into the supreme knowledge of the *Shahādah.* It might be said that if all metaphysical knowledge is contained in the first *Shahādah, Lā ilāha illa'Llāh,* all cosmological knowledge is, in a sense, contained in the second *Shahādah, Muḥammadun rasūl Allāh.* Inasmuch as Muḥammad also means all that is positive in the cosmos, the second

Shahādah means esoterically that all that is positive in the universe comes from—that is, is *rasūl* of—God, and that is precisely the ultimate function of Islamic cosmology.[13]

The root of all Islamic cosmology is to be found in the Quran, and the earliest Islamic cosmological studies must be sought in the works of the Quranic commentators of the first few generations of Islamic history. There are, however, many cosmological schemes developed by Muslims on the basis of Quranic teachings but using languages as diverse as letter symbolism and the hierarchy of light.[14] The Quran itself contains the principles of several cosmological schemes as found in such verses as the Throne Verse (*āyat al-kursī*) and the Light Verse (*āyat al-nūr*).[15] These verses have been the subject of numerous commentaries by nearly all classes of Quranic commentators ranging from theologians to philosophers to Sufis. Some of the most important works of Quranic cosmology, such as the *Mishkāt al-anwār* of al-Ghazzālī and *Tafsīr āyat al-nūr* of Ṣadr al-Dīn Shīrāzī, are in fact commentaries upon the Light Verse and certain *ḥadīths* that complement this verse.[16] The Throne (*al-ʿarsh*), the Pedestal (*al-kursī*), the Supreme Spirit (*al-Rūḥ*), the four archangels, the eight angels holding the Throne, and other aspects of the cosmic and angelic realities described in the Quran and *Ḥadīth* literature comprise the foundation of Islamic cosmology providing spiritual significance for the universe in which the Muslim lives and breathes.

The goal of Islamic cosmology is to provide a science that displays the interrelation of all things and the relation of the levels of the cosmic hierarchy to each other and finally to the Supreme Principle. Thereby it provides a knowledge that permits the integration of multiplicity into Unity, a goal which is no more than a commentary upon the Quranic verse, "Verily we belong to God and to Him is our return" (II, 156). By virtue of the integrating and synthesizing power inherent in the Islamic tradition, various schools of Islamic thought developed different cosmologies over the centuries, drawing from many diverse sources. These cosmologies differ in their language and form but not in content, which is always the assertion of the Unity of the Divine Principle, which is the origin of the cosmos, the reality of the hierarchy of cosmic and universal existence, and the interdependence and interrelation of all orders of cosmic reality and various realms of nature. These cosmologies may in fact be described as so many versions of what one might call a *cosmologia perennis.*[17]

Some of the earliest cosmological schemes in Islam are to be found in circles that were involved in the study of Pythagorean and Hermetic texts being translated into Arabic from the second/eighth century on. A cosmology based on the symbolism of numbers and the language of alchemy

32. Traditional Islamic Cosmos.

and astrology is already to be found in the writings of the first major Islamic alchemist, Jābir ibn Ḥayyān, who lived in the second/eighth century.[18] This type of cosmology was often combined with the symbolism of letters related to the science of *jafr*, which is of purely Islamic origin inextricably related to the Arabic language and the structure of the Quran itself.[19] In such cosmological schemes, each letter or number signifies a grade of being, a particular existent within the cosmic or metacosmic hierarchy, while the cosmic dimensions of the alchemical natures and qualities are brought out.

Ismāʿīlī Cosmology

Early Ismāʿīlī cosmologies were closely related to the world of the Jābirean corpus, while the *Epistles* of the Brethren of Purity, which have a strong Pythagorean flavor,[20] were also related to the Shīʿite and, more particularly, Ismāʿīlī circles. Early Ismāʿīlī writings as well as those of the Fāṭimid period—such works as the *Umm al-kitāb*, the treatises of Abū Ḥātim al-Rāzī, Ḥamīd al-Dīn Kirmānī and Nāṣir-i Khusraw—contain elaborate cosmological discussions. In such works, the number seven, which dominates over Ismāʿīlī cosmological thought, is the basis of schemes that relate the cycles of prophecy and Imamate, the cycles of cosmic existence and the levels of the cosmos.[21] A special feature of these Ismāʿīlī cosmologies is their insistence upon the transcendence of the Divine Principle not only beyond the cosmos but also beyond Being Itself. The source of cosmic existence in these works is not Pure Being but the Beyond-Being whose first act is then identified with Being.[22]

Peripatetic Cosmology

Islamic Peripatetic (*mashshāʾī*) philosophy, developed by al-Kindī and al-Fārābī and reaching its peak with Ibn Sīnā (Avicenna), is based on ontology to the extent that Ibn Sīnā has been called by some of his Western students the "philosopher of being." The cosmological schemes of this school, elaborated most fully in Ibn Sīnā's *Kitāb al-shifāʾ (Sufficientia)*, relate the levels of existence to the hierarchic Ptolemaic cosmos and correlate each planetary orb with a particular state of being in an ascending hierarchy. This hierarchy passes beyond the visible cosmos to the *Premium mobile* and the Divine Presence,[23] much like medieval European cosmologies, which often derived their schemes from Islamic sources but which Christianized them.[24] In the case of Ibn Sīnā, angelology is inseparable from cosmology, and angels play a central role in the cosmos described by Ibn Sīnā. It is they who preserve the order of the cosmos as well as act as agents through which knowledge is imparted to man.[25]

Ibn Sīnā was also interested in the symbolism of letters and numbers, and the more esoteric cosmology associated with such esoteric sciences as *al-jafr* as can be seen in his *Risālat al-nayrūziyyah.* Moreover, toward the end of his life, he turned toward what he called "the Oriental philosophy" (*al-ḥikmat al-mashriqiyyah*), in which cosmology became not a theoretical scheme but a plan to enable the traveler upon the path of spiritual perfection to journey through the cosmic crypt, to be liberated from all limitation, and thereby to gain spiritual freedom.[26] This later cosmology of Ibn Sīnā is a prelude to the cosmology that was to be expanded a century and a half after Ibn Sīnā by Suhrawardī, the founder of the School of Illumination (*ishrāq*).[27] *Ishrāqī* cosmology is based on the symbolism of light. The Supreme Principle is called by Suhrawardī the "Light of lights" (*nūr al-anwār*), and there issues from this transcendent source the longitudinal and latitudinal hierarchies of light which govern every aspect of cosmic existence. The cosmos itself consists, in fact, of grades of light, and matter is nothing more than the absence of light. Every light is but a faint glimmer of that Light which as the Quran asserts is neither of the east nor the west and which is the Light of the heavens and the earth according to the Quranic verse, "God is the Light of the heavens and the earth" (XXIV, 35).

Sufi Cosmology

Later Sufis also dealt extensively with cosmology, especially Muḥyī al-Dīn ibn ʿArabī, who integrated Hermetic, Pythagorean, Neoplatonic, and Empedoclean elements into doctrines drawn from the inner meaning of the Quran.[28] In his writings, the science of Divine Names and Qualities (*al-asmāʾ waʾl-ṣifāt*) serves as the basis for an elaborate science of the cosmos which reveals how all cosmic qualities are reverberations of various Divine Names and Qualities and how each level of cosmic existence is itself nothing but a Divine Presence. There are essentially five Divine Presences (*al-ḥaḍarāt al-ilāhiyyat al-khams*), ranging from the Divine Essence (*al-hāhūt*), through the world of Names and Qualities (*al-lāhūt*), the archangelic world (*al-jabarūt*), the lower angelic and subtle worlds (*al-malakūt*), and the corporeal world (*al-mulk*).[29] Ibn ʿArabī depicts the levels of cosmic reality in the light of the well-known doctrine of the "transcendent unity of being" (*waḥdat al-wujūd*), according to which there is ultimately but one Being, one Reality, all else consisting of reflections of the Divine Names and Qualities upon the mirror of nonexistence.

Many of the followers of the school of Ibn 'Arabī, such as Ṣadr al-Dīn al-Qūnawī, 'Abd al-Karīm al-Jīlī, and Sayyid Ḥaydar Āmulī, have expanded further the cosmological doctrines found in the numerous works of Ibn 'Arabī. Among these followers Āmulī adds a new dimension to Ibn 'Arabī's cosmological teachings by integrating them into Shī'ite gnosis. In the writings of Āmulī, who held special interest in geometric schemes depicting levels of the cosmic reality,[30] the Twelve Shī'ite Imams play an important cosmic role as links between the Divine and the human order both microcosmically and macrocosmically. In fact, in Shī'ite cosmology of a gnostic and esoteric nature, not only is cosmology inseparable from angelology but it is also inseparable from imamology. The knowledge of the Imam in both its soteriological and cosmological aspects is found in its most developed and elaborate form in the writings of Ṣadr al-Dīn Shīrāzī (Mullā Ṣadrā).[31]

The Spiritual Significance of Cosmology and Nature

The spiritual significance of all Islamic cosmologies is to provide a knowledge of the cosmos so as to transform the cosmic reality from opacity to transparancy, from a veil to the means of unveiling the Divine Reality, which the cosmos veils and unveils by its very nature. The goal is to provide a map of the cosmic labyrinth so as to enable man to escape from the prison of all limitative existence. The goal is to reveal Unity (*al-tawḥīd*) as reflected in the world of multiplicity and hence to aid man to realize Unity. In order to realize God, some men may be able to fly directly to the Divine Empyrean without concern for the cosmic reality that surrounds them. But Islamic spirituality provides the means for those human beings whose inner nature is such that they must read the pages of the cosmic book before being able to put this book away and experience the moment described in the Quran as follows: "On the day when We shall roll up heaven as a scroll is rolled for the writings" (XXI, 104).

The role of the natural order and the sciences related to it are, however, not limited to the intellectual significance of the cosmological sciences. Nature is also the foretaste of the beatitude of the Islamic paradise. The Quranic description of paradise includes animals and plants, and there are those Muslim sages such as Mullā Ṣadrā who have spoken of the resurrection of all of creation at the Day of Judgment. The Muslim contemplative experiences in the bosom of nature something of the delights of paradise and sees in the beauty of nature, in the majestic mountains that uphold the earth, in the stars that adorn the heavens, and in the seas that hide the treasures of creation in their infinite expanse, reflections of the Face of the Beloved. The experience of virgin nature is related to that beatific vision whose subject transcends all that is created. Islamic spirituality brings into being that "creation-consciousness" which enables man to see in nature the theophany of the Divine Names and Qualities and to hear in the flight of the bird soaring toward heaven the prayer of creation to the Divine Throne, for, as the Quran asserts, "Seest thou not that it is God whom all things in the heavens and earth praise—and the birds in flight outstretched? Each knoweth its [mode of] prayer and praise to Him, and God is aware of all that they do" (XXIV, 41).

Notes

1. Traditional Islamic commentaries refer to the Quran revealed in Arabic as *tadwīnī,* that is, put together as a book, and to the cosmos as *takwīnī,* that is, as the book of existence itself. The eighth/fourteenth-century Sufi 'Azīz al-Dīn Nasafī writes concerning the book of nature, "Each day destiny and the passage of time set this book before you, *sūrah* for *sūrah,* verse for verse, letter for letter, and read it to you . . . like one who sets a real book before you and reads it to you line for line, letter for letter, that you may learn the content of these lines and letters"; see his *Kashf al-ḥaqā'iq,* trans. F. Meier in "The Problem of Nature in the Esoteric Monism of Islam," in *Spirit and Nature: Papers from the Eranos Yearbooks,* trans. R. Manheim (Princeton, NJ: Princeton University Press, 1954) 203.

2. These are the people to whom the Quran refers as *ūlu' l-abṣār,* the "possessors of vision."

3. "The Quran and the great phenomena of nature are twin manifestations of the divine act of Self-revelation. For Islam, the natural world in its totality is a vast fabric into which the 'signs' of the Creator are woven. It is significant that the word meaning 'signs' or 'symbols', *āyāt,* is the same word that is used for the 'verses' of the Quran. Earth and sky, mountains and stars, oceans and forests and the creatures they contain are, as it were, 'verses' of a sacred book. 'Indeed Allah disdaineth not to coin the similitude of a gnat or of something even smaller than that' (Q.2.26). Creation is one, and He who created the Quran is also He who created all the visible phenomena of nature. Both are the communications from God to man" (G. Eaton, *Islam and the Destiny of Man* [Albany, NY: State University of New York Press, 1985] 87.

4. One of the titles of the Prophet of Islam is *al-nabī al-ummī,* the unlettered Prophet, since the Prophet was unlettered in the sense that his soul remained pure and untainted with human knowledge so as to be worthy of being the recipient of the Divine Word. We do not mean that only the Islamic Revelation makes possible the reading of the cosmic text, but Revelation in general, of which Islam is the last and final synthesis.

5. We have dealt extensively with this theme in several writings, including *An Introduction to Islamic Cosmological Doctrines* (London: Thames & Hudson, 1978); *Science and Civilization in Islam* (Cambridge, MA: Harvard University Press, 1964); *Islamic Life and Thought* (Albany, NY: State University of New York Press, 1981) chap. 19; and *Man and Nature* (London: Allen & Unwin, 1975).

6. See Eaton, *Islam and the Destiny of Man,* 91.

7. On this doctrine, see T. Burckhardt, *An Introduction to Sufi Doctrine,* trans. D. M. Matheson (Lahore: M. Ashraf, 1959) chap. 9.

8. *Wa fī kulli shay' in lahū āyatun tadullu 'alā annahu wāḥidun.*

9. See the introduction of Nasr, *Science and Civilization;* also idem, *Islamic Science: An Illustrated Study* (London: World of Islam Festival Trust, 1976) part 1.

10. See Eaton, *Islam and the Destiny of Man,* 91.

11. As already mentioned, at the heart of the canonical prayers stands the *Sūrat al-fātiḥah,* in which man addresses God in these terms: *iyyāka na'budu wa iyyāka nasta'īn* ("Thee only *we* serve; to Thee alone *we* pray for succour").

12. See S. H. Nasr, *Islamic Art and Spirituality* (Albany, NY: State University of New York Press, 1987) chap. 3.

13. See T. Burckhardt, *The Mirror of the Intellect,* ed. W. Stoddart (Cambridge: Quintessential Books, 1987).

14. On Islamic cosmology, see S. H. Nasr, *Islamic Cosmological Doctrines;* idem, "Philosophy and Cosmology," in *The Cambridge History of Iran,* vol.4, ed. R. N. Frye (Cambridge: University Press, 1975) 419–41.

15. The *āyat al-kursī* is as follows: "God—there is no god but He, the Living, the Everlasting. Slumber seizes Him not, neither sleep; to Him belongs all that is in the heavens and the earth. Who is there that shall intercede with Him save by His leave? He knows what lies before them and what is after them, and they comprehend not anything of His knowledge save such as He wills. His Throne comprises the heavens and earth; the preserving of them oppresses Him not; He is the All-high, the All-glorious" (II, 255). As for the *āyat al-nūr,* it asserts, "God is the Light of the heavens and the earth; the like of His Light is as a niche wherein is a lamp (the lamp in a glass, the glass as it were a glittering star) kindled from a Blessed Tree, an olive that is neither of the East nor of the West whose oil well nigh would shine, even if no fire touched it; Light upon Light; God guides to His Light whom He will. And God strikes similitudes for men, and God has knowledge of everything" (XXIV, 35).

16. Of special significance is the series of *ḥadīths* dealing with the veils of light and darkness and the hierarchy of angels. See F. Schuon, *Dimensions of Islam,* trans. P. Townsend (London: Allen & Unwin, 1970) chap. 8, "*An-Nūr,*" and chapter 17 in this volume.

17. The goal of Islamic cosmology was shared by other traditional cosmologies and sciences, without which Islam would not have integrated some of these cosmologies and cosmological sciences into its intellectual world. That is why one can speak of a *cosmologia perennis* as one can speak of a *philosophia perennis.* See T. Burckhardt, "Cosmology and Modern Science," in *The Sword of Gnosis,* ed. J. Needleman (Boston, MA: Arkana Paperbacks, 1986) 102ff.; and Nasr, "The Role of the Traditional Sciences in the Encounter of Religion and Science—An Oriental Perspective," *Religious Studies* 20 (1984) 519–41.

18. There are numerous cosmological treatises in the Jābirean corpus, and whether they are all by him or his school is not of consequence here. On the name of these treatises, see P. Kraus, *Jābir ibn Ḥayyān, Contribution à l'historie des idées scientifiques dans l'Islam* (2 vols.; Cairo: Institut français d'archéologie orientale, 1942–43); and H. Corbin "Le Livre du Glorieux de Jābir ibn Ḥayyān," *Eranos Jahrbuch* (Ascona) 18 (1950) 47–114.

19. See the study of J. Canteins, "The Significance of the Hidden Sciences" in volume 20 this Encyclopedia.

20. On their emphasis upon numerical symbolism and Pythagorean number, see

Nasr, *Islamic Cosmological Doctrines,* 47ff., 209–11.

21. On Ismāʿīlī cosmology, see H. Corbin (with the collaboration of S. H. Nasr and O. Yahya), *Histoire de la philosophie islamique* (Paris: Gallimard, 1964); Corbin, *Cyclical Time and Ismāʿīlī Gnosis* (London: Kegan Paul International, 1983) and chap. 10 of this volume.

22. See W. Madelung, "Aspects of Ismāʿīlī Theology: The Prophetic Chain and the God Beyond Being," in *Ismāʿīlī Contributions to Islamic Culture,* ed. S. H. Nasr (Tehran: Imperial Iranian Academy of Philosophy, 1977) 51–65.

23. See Nasr, *Islamic Cosmological Doctrines,* chap. 12.

24. Perhaps the foremost example is the *Divine Comedy,* which uses a cosmological scheme and the idea of journeying through the cosmos, drawn from Islamic sources, but integrates it into a completely Christian perspective. See M. Asín Palacios, *La escatologia musulmana en la Divina Comedia* (Madrid: Hiperion, 1984); and E. Cerulli, *Il 'Libro della Scala' e la questione delle fonte arabo-spagnole della Divina Commedia* (Vatican City: Biblioteca apostolica vaticana, 1949).

25. On this angelology in relation to cosmology, see H. Corbin, *Avicenna and the Visionary Recital,* trans. W. Trask (New York: Pantheon Books, 1960).

26. See Nasr, *Islamic Cosmological Doctrines,* chap. 15.

27. On Suhrawardī and his cosmology, see S. H. Nasr, *Three Muslim Sages: Avicenna, Suhrawardī, Ibn 'Arabī* (Cambridge, MA: Harvard University Press, 1964) chap. 2; H. Corbin, *En Islam iranien* (4 vols.; Paris: Gallimard, 1970) vol. 2.

28. On Ibn 'Arabī and his cosmological teachings, see T. Burckhardt, *Mystical Astrology according to Ibn 'Arabī* (London: Beshara Publications, 1982); Ibn 'Arabī, *Shajarat al-kawn,* trans. with notes by A. Jeffery, *Studia Islamica,* 10 (1959) 43–77; and 11 (1960) 113–60; *Ibn 'Arabi, L'Alchimie du bonheur,* trans. S. Ruspoli (Paris: Berg International, 1981); and W. Chittick, "Ibn 'Arabī and His School," chapter 4 of volume 20 of this Encyclopedia.

29. On the five Divine Presences, see F. Schuon, *Dimensions of Islam,* chap. 11.

30. The *malakūt* mentioned by Ibn 'Arabī also corresponds to the imaginal world—the world of "hanging forms" (*al-ṣuwar al-muʿallaqah*), where forms exist without matter, in the Aristotelian sense of the term. This intermediate imaginal world, not to be confused with imagination as understood in the ordinary sense, plays an important role in not only cosmology but also epistemology, eschatology, and the Islamic theory of art. See H. Corbin, *Creative Imagination in the Sufism of Ibn 'Arabī,* trans. R. Manheim (Princeton, NJ: Princeton University Press, 1969); and Sayyid Ḥaydar Āmulī, *La Philosophie shiʿite* (Tehran and Paris: Andrien-Maisonneuve, 1969).

31. Such as his *Asfār* and *Asrār al-āyāt.* On Mullā Ṣadrā, see H. Corbin, *En Islam iranien,* vol. 4, chap. 2; S. H. Nasr, *Ṣadr al-Dīn Shīrāzī and His Transcendent Theosophy* (Tehran: Imperial Iranian Academy of Philosophy, 1978); Nasr, "Ṣadr al-Dīn Shīrāzi," in M. M. Sharif, *A History of Muslim Philosophy,* vol. 2 (Wiesbaden: Harrassowitz, 1966) 932–61; and F. Rahman, *The Philosophy of Mullā Ṣadrā* (Albany, NY: State University of New York Press, 1976).

19

Man

CHARLES LE GAI EATON

THE CONTEMPORARY MIND LOOKS for consistency both in ideologies and in any general system of concepts. Consistency may well be seen as the test of their validity. We may not agree with the Marxist view of man or the Freudian view, but we acknowledge that each system has its own internal logic even though we may not accept the assumptions upon which the system is constructed. This expectation must be put aside when we approach the Islamic view of man. Here we are dealing not with a consistent pattern of concepts devised by the human mind functioning within its own limitations but with the paradoxes and ambiguities inherent in the created world and in the shattered reflections, perceived here and now, of what lies beyond creation and infinitely transcends it. We can no longer insist that man must be either this *or* that. We are obliged to admit that he may be both this *and* that.

Man as God's Vicegerent and Slave

Islam sees man as the vicegerency of God on earth and the projection, as it were, of the vertical dimension onto the horizontal plane. Gifted with intelligence in the true sense of the term, he alone of all creatures is capable of knowing the Reality of which he himself is a manifestation and, in the light of this knowledge, of rising above his own earthly and contingent selfhood. Gifted with the power of speech, he alone stands before God as His valid interlocutor. Through Revelation as also through inspiration God speaks to His creation; through prayer as also through an awareness which is a silent form of communication man speaks to God and does so on behalf of the inarticulate creation that surrounds him. He is, potentially if not actually, higher than the angels, for his nature reflects totality and can be satisfied with nothing less than the Total. It is a synthesis from which no element, from the highest to the lowest, is excluded, and it is a mirror in which are reflected the Names and Attributes of the God before Whom he stands upright, now and forever.

This is one side of the human coin. A simple change of perspective shows the other, and Islam sees man as a creature of dust or clay, a nothingness before the overwhelming splendor of the Real–impotent before Omnipotence, a little thing (brother to the ant) who walks briefly upon the earth from which he was molded, vulnerable to a pinprick and destined soon to be seized upon and taken to Judgment. He is a slave whose highest achievement is to obey without question his Master's Will or (in more esoteric terms) to rid himself of everything that might appear to be "his," so that the Divine Will may operate through him without impediment. Any good that he may do comes from elsewhere. He can take no credit for it since it did not originate with him. Only the evil that he does is his to claim and possess as his own. Knowledge and virtue, if they are reflected in his being, are a loan from his Creator. So too are the senses, through which he perceives the theater of his experience but which may be taken from him at any moment.

We have here the positive and negative poles of human existence or human identity according to the Islamic view of our situation. They might appear irreconcilable, but, for the Muslim, they represent the concrete reality of this situation and they interpenetrate each other much as do the positive and the negative, the light and the dark, in the Chinese *yin-yang* figure. Mastery–that is to say, the quality of vicegerency–is intimately linked to "slavehood," and "slavehood" as such is neither more nor less than the excellence of a clear mirror that reflects the higher realities and could not reflect them if it were less than clear. According to the mystic and theologian al-Ghazzālī (d. 505/1111), everything including the human creature has "a face of its own and a face of its Lord; in respect of its own face it is nothingness, and in respect of the face of its Lord it is Being." This image suggests a further dimension: the creature who in this fashion faces two different ways is, in consequence, a meeting-point, a bridge. The human heart, which Islam identifies as the seat of knowledge rather than the seat of emotion,[1] is sometimes described as the *barzakh* ("isthmus"), which both separates and unites the "two seas," the divine and the earthly. It is precisely on account of this function that man can be defined as *khalīfat Allāh fi' l-arḍ*, the vicegerent of God on earth.

Adam and Eve, the Prototypes of Humanity

The prototype of this identity as vicegerent is man as he first issued from the hand of God–Adam, primordial man. The Quran states:

> God spoke to the angels in that time (the time beyond time), saying: Indeed I shall place on earth a vicegerent. They asked: Wilt Thou place upon it one who will make mischief therein and shed blood? While, as for us, we celebrate Thy glory and extol Thy holiness. Their Lord answered: Truly I know what ye know not! Thereupon He taught Adam the names of all things, then placed them before the angels, saying: Tell me the names of these if ye are truthful. They said: Glorified art Thou! No knowledge have we save that which Thou hast taught us. Thou indeed art the Omniscient, the Wise. He said: O Adam! Inform them of the names of these things. And when (Adam) had informed them of the names, He said: Did I not tell you that I know the secrets of the heavens and the earth, and I know what you show and what you hide? (II, 30–33)

The angels were then commanded to prostrate themselves before this new creation, man, and they did so, all save Iblis, the satanic power or spirit of rebellion, who refused out of blind pride to humble himself before a creature whose glory is masked by dust.

The chroniclers, relying sometimes upon what the Prophet himself said concerning these matters and sometimes upon inspired imagination, have filled out this brief narrative in rich detail. According to the fourth/eleventh century commentator al-Kisā'ī, the archangel Gabriel was commanded to assemble the angel ranks before Adam, who then spoke to all the inhabitants of the heavens, who stood in twenty thousand rows around him. A pulpit was set up for him and he was clad in robes of honor with a golden crown on his head, jewel-encrusted and having four corner points each set with a pearl whose brightness would have put out the light of sun and moon (being transparent to the Divine Light, which eclipses all other lights). When he held up before them the rod of light which God had given him, the angelic hosts stood in awe of him, saying of him: "O our Lord, hast Thou created any creature superior to this?" Then he addressed the celestial assembly with the authority that his Creator had delegated to him, and when he came down from the pulpit his radiance was even greater than it had been before.

His radiance, so al-Kisā'ī tells us, was not unique, for God created for him a mate, equal "in splendour and in beauty," *Ḥawwā'* (Eve), so called because she was created out of Life (*ḥayy*) itself. She was of the same form as Adam except that her skin was more tender, her coloring lighter, her voice sweeter, her eyes wider and darker, and her teeth whiter. "O Lord, for whom has Thou created her?" asked Adam. "For him who will take her in faithfulness and be joined with her in thankfulness!" And their Lord, Who Himself performed the marriage ceremony between them, added: "This is My handmaiden, and thou art My servant, O Adam! Nothing is dearer to Me in all My creation than ye twain, so long as ye obey Me." "Glory to Him who created the pair" says the Quran (XXXVI, 36), and Muḥammad told his companions that "marriage is half the religion."

Then, according to the same author, a magnificent steed, saddled with a saddle of emerald and chrysolite and bridled with a bridle of jacinth, was brought to Adam, a winged steed which, when its rider had praised God, told him, "You have spoken well, Adam, for none may ride me save one who is thankful." For Eve, there was a superb she-camel as mount. The incomparable pair then made their way to the garden created for them, with angels to the right and to the left, before and behind, and others of the angelic host lining the route. God addressed Adam, saying: "Now remember My favors to you, for I have made you the masterpiece of My creation, fashioned you a man according to My will, breathed into you of My spirit, made My angels do obeisance to you and carry you on their shoulders, made you a preacher to them, loosened your tongue to all languages. . . . All this I have done for you as glory and honor, so beware of Iblis whom I have made to despair. . . ."[2] But this warning was ignored or forgotten when Iblis, the agent of division and separation, tempted the celestial pair with the glamor and glitter of relativity and a spurious independence. So began a process that leads from that time to the present day. It must be noted, however, that they "fell" together, equal in guilt as they had been equal in glory. Eve was no temptress so far as the Islamic tradition is concerned. And although they were exiled, as are all who live upon this earth, yet they were promised by Him Who is named the Ever-Forgiving, the All-Forgiving, the Effacer of sins, that their posterity would never be left without guidance through the dark alleyways of the lower world. This "guidance," according to Islam, culminated and was completed in the coming of Muḥammad, who, as it were, closes the circle.

The Prophet as the Perfect Human Model

Although such myths and legends as that of al-Kisā'ī are rich in meaning and symbolism and cannot be regarded merely as human inventions, the fact remains that "Adam," in whatever manner we may understand this name, is remote from the practical life in which men and women need to find their direction and orientation. There is, however, a prototype of human perfection (in small matters as in great) very close to the pious Muslim, closer to him—so the Quran tells us—than his own selfhood. Since Muḥammad is also, by definition, close to God, it follows that he provides not only guidance but also a human—viceregal—link between the Divine and the earthly. A man or a woman qualifies as a Muslim when he or she makes, in good faith, the dual profession or witnessing, first to the Divine

Unity and then to the messengerhood of Muḥammad. If this second truth were not joined to the first, there would be an impassible barrier between what is above (Divine Reality) and what is below (the creature of earthly dust). For the ordinary believer, the entirely exoteric Muslim, this suffices. It is enough that the Creator should have commissioned His chosen messenger Muḥammad (having commissioned many others before him) to bring mankind guidance and the Law, together with the promise of paradise and the threat of hellfire. For the esoterists—that is to say, for the Sufis—the function of providing a link between God and man, heaven and earth, is reflected—at least as a virtuality—in every human creature, provided he models himself, inwardly as well as outwardly, upon the model provided. "In the messenger of God," says the Quran, "you have a good example (*uswatun ḥasanatun*)" (XXXIII, 21). Addressing His messenger directly in the chapter of The Pen, God says: "Thou art truly of a tremendous nature" (LXVIII, 4). Questioned concerning her husband, 'Ā'ishah said: "His nature is the nature of the Quran"; in other words, he was not only the messenger but also the embodiment of the message.

It follows that the key to the Muslim view of man is to be found in the person of the Prophet of Islam. He has many titles of glory, but the first, which even precedes the designation "messenger" in the confession of faith, is "slave" or "servant" (*'abd*). For the Muslim, this attribute of "slavehood" always comes first, whatever else may follow, for reasons that will be clear from what was said earlier. Thus, the adherent of Islam is a Muslim ("one who submits") rather than a *mu'min* ("one who believes"). Just as the quality of obedient passivity is a precondition of the Messenger's activity in the world, so this quality determines the ordinary human creature's fitness to fulfill the function for which he was created. It is the starting point or springboard without which there can be no journeying and certainly no viceregality. The human will is perfected only when it reflects the Divine Will. Closely related to this is the title *al-nabī al-ummī,* the "unlettered Prophet," and it is precisely this title that guarantees the authenticity of the Scripture, the Quran, since a divine messenger can only convey the message accurately if he adds nothing to it in terms of human knowledge. The Muslim as such receives the message at second hand, but he too is required to receive it—through the Quran—without permitting his receptivity to be distorted by any trace of profane knowledge or by his personal likes and dislikes.

But the perfect scribe, who misses no syllable of what is dictated to him and who is, so to speak, all ear, is also *ḥabīb Allāh* (the beloved of God), just as Adam was "most dear to God." With this image the whole picture changes, and the relationship between Creator and creation is seen from a different perspective. It is said that the Arabic word for man, *insān*, is derived from the root *uns*, which has the meaning "intimacy," and the poets and mystics of Islam moved swiftly from the Master/slave image to that of Lover/beloved, a relationship of mutuality. According to a holy tradition (*ḥadīth qudsī*), "I was a Hidden Treasure and I desired to be known; therefore I created Man" (or, according to a different version, "the worlds"). Many exoteric Muslims question the authenticity of this saying because they take it to imply that God "needs" something outside Himself, and to ascribe "needs" to God is, in Muslim terms, close to blasphemy. It is true that the Andalusian mystic Ibn 'Arabī, whose influence upon the metaphysical doctrines of Sufism can hardly be exaggerated, did at times write as though there were, at the very heart of the Divine, a yearning for a relationship of mutuality. H. Corbin has analyzed this perspective with great subtlety, but to interpret "need" in human terms is to miss the point.[3] Reality, which is also by definition absolute Perfection, can have only one obligation, the obligation to be Itself. This implies a plenitude which, by its very nature, "radiates" or "overflows" outward or—to use a more human image—desires to give Itself. This does not imply any lack in the Divine Perfection but, on the contrary, refers to a particular dimension of this Perfection, except for which the existence of anything outside or—though only in appearance—separated from the Absolute would be incomprehensible.

This doctrine, whatever suspicions it may arouse in the minds of certain Muslims jealous to preserve the utter transcendence of a God in relation to Whom blind obedience is the only possible human response, assists us nonetheless in defining the Islamic view of man's role and therefore in understanding the concept of "slavehood." The predestined receptacle of the "overflowing" of the Divine Plenitude is necessarily passive and necessarily empty of all other contents. In this context humility is no longer a moral or sentimental concept, but neither more nor less than the most favorable existential attitude for anyone who wishes to receive what is given.

In the Islamic view the role of the Messenger of God—the role of Muḥammad—is both to be the perfect receptacle and to provide a model of perfect receptivity. But the imitation of the Prophet in Islam has a very different character from the purely spiritual "imitation of Christ" to which the pious Christian aspires. The fact that Muḥammad, unlike Jesus, was destined to live through all the major experiences to which a human being may be exposed in the course of his life gives the practice of the religion its specific character and lends to this "imitation" a remarkable precision, even in the simplest acts of daily life. Faced with some common human problem, the Christian will seek in his own heart to discover what Jesus might have done; the Muslim, more often than not, knows what Muḥammad did.

During his formative years, he had run through the gamut of youthful experience; orphaned very early in life yet sheltered by the love and care first of his grandfather and then of an uncle, born a townsman yet passing a part of his childhood with a Bedouin family in the desert, traveling in adolescence with the great trading caravan to Syria, rubbing shoulders with the extraordinary variety of people drawn to Mecca by its wealth. He had been a merchant, with all that this implies in the way of practical experience and of assessing the honesty of those with whom one must deal; he had married a widow considerably older than himself and had given an example of faithful and devoted monogamous marriage, later (after her death) to give a complementary example of justice and kindness as the husband of a number of wives; he had experienced the joy of fatherhood and the sadness of seeing all but one of his children die before him; he had suffered bitter persecution, which he faced with exemplary patience; and he had suffered, above all, the shattering impact of the encounter with Divine Reality.

Fully formed and now a master of men, he completed his mission during the Medina years as the ruler of a sacred community—a city-state dedicated to the worship of the One God—and as the guide, counselor, and friend of that community. During those final ten years he organized no fewer than seventy-four campaigns, leading twenty-four of them himself. Yet the record of those years in the *ḥadīth* literature pays less attention to such public events than to his relationship to the people around him, people who turned to him for counsel and comfort in every conceivable human situation while observing his every action and recording for posterity the details, great and small, which have provided the Muslims throughout the ages with the concrete model for their living and their dying. In all this they have been made aware of a particular element in the human situation, which is decisive in determining this situation as Islam understands it. Passivity toward what is above us—"slavehood" in other words—has its complement in activity and initiative here where we find ourselves, in this world and in that part of ourselves that belongs to this world. This is *jihād*, a word that means "effort" or "struggle," but is commonly translated as "holy war." The viceroy of God on earth cannot be idle; it is his function to rectify what is amiss both in the world around him and within himself. This obligation is in proportion to his receptivity.

The imitation of the Prophet, however, can take different forms, as can the "holy war," which may, on occasion, be directed against the enemies of the Faith and of the Good, but which may equally be directed against those elements within ourselves which are the root of all the evils that appear outwardly in the theater of this world. It is in the nature of religion, since it engages the whole personality, to run to certain excesses when enthusiasm destroys the sense of proportion and zeal overcomes judgment. There are Muslims whose desire to imitate every action and every gesture of the Prophet exceeds the bounds of what is universally applicable, so that the sheer weight of outward observance smothers inwardness and leads almost inevitably to hypocrisy. Meticulous outward imitation is one vocation among others and is justified as a spiritual method insofar as—and only insofar as—it engenders corresponding inward attitudes, attitudes that might simply be defined as "virtues" in the deepest sense of the term. Through playing a part—in this case, the "part" played by the Prophet in his outward behavior—the ultimate intention is that the personality as such should enter into the mold provided by his personality.

Others whose aim it is to follow the "perfect example" may—particularly under the conditions of modern life, which make it, to say the least, difficult to live exactly as though one were a member of Muḥammad's community in Medina in the seventh century of the Christian era—seek their exemplar in his inward nature, going to the source of his actions and striving to imitate the virtues that found expression in all that he did and said. If we bear in mind that his nature was "the nature of the Qurān," it can be seen that to enter into the mold of the Prophet's personality is, in effect, to enter into the mold of the Quran. It might, indeed, be permissible to describe the Prophet of Islam as "the Quran in action or in application," and, by derivation, the same might be said of the Muslim who is all that he should be and who, as such, incorporates in his own person the Islamic concept of man.

The Muslim who aspires to such excellence is greatly assisted by the wealth and extent of the *Ḥadīth* record and by the fact that this record includes so much that might be considered "trivial" but for the fact that it relates to a manifestation of the Sacred and conceals beneath a seemingly commonplace surface indications of momentous significance. It is not only in grave matters or in promulgating the ordinances of the community that Muḥammad demonstrated his innermost nature but also in his dealings with his family, with his friends, and with those who sought his advice on the minor aspects of everyday life. This relates to what may be described as the totality of his mission, which was destined and required to penetrate every level of human experience and to bring the light of an all-encompassing guidance even into the darkest corner, the smallest crevice, of life in this world. The Muslim does not only learn his religion, his duties, and his rules of conduct from the *Ḥadīth* literature; he learns from it what it is to be human as Islam understands the human role, and he drinks from it, as though from a great pool, the water of perfection, the perfection of vicegerency.

Adam, Muḥammad, and the View of Man

The Islamic view of man may best be defined and exemplified in relation to these two poles, Adam and Muḥammad, the first prophet and the last, the beginning of the story and the end of it. To lay stress upon the "closing of the circle" represented by Muḥammad's mission is to stress also the primordial nature of this mission. History had unfolded and humanity had pursued its predestined course. There had to be—and there was—a return to the origin, insofar as such a return might be possible at so late a stage in the cycle. Islam justifies itself as the *dīn al-fiṭrah,* which might be translated as "the religion of primordiality" or even as "the original religion."[4] The perfect Muslim is not a man of his time or indeed of any other specific historic time. He is man as he issued from the hand of God. "You are all the children of Adam" (or "the tribe of Adam") as Muḥammad told his people.

In relation to man as such, the word *fiṭrah* may be taken to refer to the human norm from which, according to the Quran, humanity has fallen away.[5] But the word is derived from a verb meaning "he created" or "he cleft asunder" (the act of creation being described as a cleaving asunder of the heavens and the earth)—hence, its reference back to the origins. It follows that the image of human perfection (or, quite simply, of human normality) lies in the past, not in the future, and the way to its attainment lies not in an aspiration focused on a distant goal or in any miraculous redemption from inherent sinfulness but rather through the removal of accretions and distortions that have both corroded and twisted a perfection that is, in essence, natural to mankind. It is a question not of leaping over the world or of being rescued from it but of retracing, in an upward direction, the downward slope of time.

We have here a sharp contrast to the Christian view, which posits a primordial corruption of the innermost core of the human creature. For Islam this core remains sound and cannot be otherwise. Neither time nor circumstance can totally destroy what God has made, but time and circumstance can cover it with layer upon layer of darkness. This offers a clue to the deeper meaning of the term *kāfir,* usually translated as "infidel," "unbeliever," or "denier of the truth." The word *kafara* means "he covered," in the way that the farmer covers seed he has sown. In fallen man—man at the bottom of the slope—there has taken place a covering of the Divine "spark" within and, as a direct result of this, he himself covers (and so ignores or denies) the Truth, which has been revealed with dazzling clarity and which is, at the same time, inherent in the hidden "spark." Islam envisages this man as imprisoned in a cell the walls of which he reinforces by his own

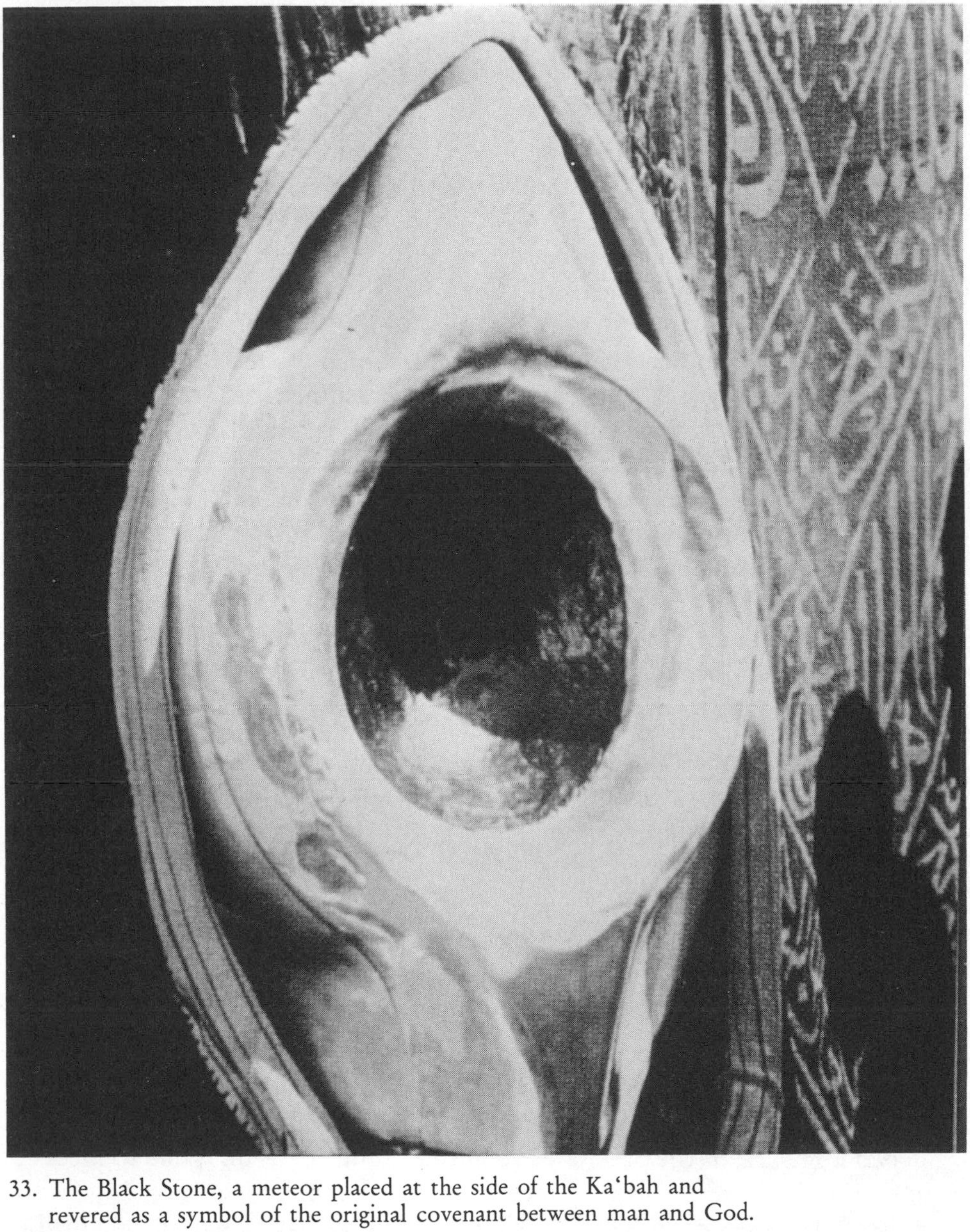

33. The Black Stone, a meteor placed at the side of the Ka‘bah and revered as a symbol of the original covenant between man and God.

misguided efforts, the cell of the ego, which sets itself up as a little god and isolates itself from the stream of Divine Mercy which flows at its doorstep. The guidance provided by the Messenger of God offers him the opportunity, if he will take it, to come out into the open, the sunlight, which is his natural environment. The command inherent in this message is: *Be* what in truth you are! From this point of view it may be said—and has often been said although seldom with full understanding—that the Islamic concept of man is "static." All is here and now, neither distant nor in another time.

In referring to a return to the origins and a remounting of the stream of time, we are brought back to the Quranic story of the creation of Adam and to the legends that surround it. The Quran cannot be said to take a flattering view of human nature, and the first man wasted little time in giving way to temptation. One may reasonably assume that God knew better than did the angels what mischief this creature would do, and it does not seem fanciful to read into the text the implication that his stature, his vicegerency, was not unconnected with his capacity for mischief making. In the realm of relativity (which is, of necessity, foreign to the angels), light and darkness, good and evil, are inextricably mixed together. The angels cannot deviate from their Creator's Will, and yet they were commanded to bow down before this creature so prone to rebellion. One is led inevitably to ask what could be the secret of his manifest superiority. The answer relates, in the first place, to the concept of totality, which is in itself ambiguous.

Man as a Central Being

The concept of totality is ambiguous because, when it disintegrates as it does in the nature of fallen man, we find, in place of unity and good order, a chaos of mutually conflicting forces and characteristics. If, as Islam asserts, the human heart reflects the Names and Attributes of God, then this little vessel of clay must break into many pieces unless held together by Him Who has chosen it as His mirror. This is why the *kāfir* is, by definition, a shattered creature, at war with himself even as he is at war with his God, his Origin and his Source. He has severed, at least in the context of relativity, his link with the Reality upon which his own being and his function depend. He has, in the precise sense of this common term, "gone to pieces"; and as a direct consequence—since man is its linchpin—the world "goes to pieces." To understand why this should be so we have to grasp one of the most fundamental and universal concepts known to humankind, shared by the Chinese tradition and by African tribal religion as also by Islam and other major traditions—the concept of man's centrality. If, for convenience, we envisage the earth as a flat disk, then the thread that holds it in place and connects it with all that is above and beyond passes through its center. In terms of this image, this doctrine, man is the aperture at the center. He alone of all created beings and things is situated directly beneath the Divine Axis. It is for this reason and only for this reason that he can be said to reflect Totality in the mirror of his innermost heart, and it is for this reason and only for this reason that he qualifies as the viceroy of God on earth and, according to a *ḥadīth,* "Allah and His angels, together with the inhabitants of the heavens and the earth—even the ant in its hole, even the fish—invoke blessings upon whomsoever teaches what is good."

For "aperture" we might substitute the word "window." "The house without a window," says Rūmī, "is hell," and he adds that "the function of religion is to make a window."[6] According to Abu Bakr Siraj Ed-Din, "If the earth be likened to a windowless house, then man is the watch-tower in the house, and the Eye of the Heart is as a single window in that watch-tower to which all the dwellers in the house look up for their light. Without this Eye man ceases to fulfil his essential function, having fallen from his true nature; but with this Eye he is the sole earthly receptacle of the spiritual light of which he is the dispenser among his fellow creatures. . . ."[7] From this point of view the *kāfir* (who "covers" the Truth, the Light, even from himself) might be defined as one who pulls down a curtain over the window and plunges the whole house into darkness.

The notion of man's centrality does not refer only to his existential situation; it refers also to the knowledge that is contained, at least in virtuality, in his heart. "He [God] taught Adam the names," so the Quran tells us. This might be defined as universal or all-encompassing knowledge, for the name of anything defines its identity and is intimately linked to the creative act of God. By "naming" it He brings it out of "nonexistence" into the light of day; He causes it to be knowable. The gift of knowledge, the privilege—precisely—which gave Adam his superiority over the angels, may be said to follow logically from the assertion that man's heart reflects Totality. But it follows also that the knower of the "names" knows also the "Namer" of all things or is capable of knowing Him. In the Islamic view, and particularly in the view of the Sufis, the human creature is capable of knowing the Creator, capable of hearkening to God's words and speaking to Him. The being who stands at the center point of relativity is potentially able to know the Absolute. Islam is "the religion of Law." It is also "the religion of knowledge," and the duty to acquire knowledge is a recurrent theme in the sayings of Muḥammad, as it is in the Quran. Since the summit of knowledge is the knowledge of God, the Quran identifies man's highest duty in terms of "seeking the Face of his Lord."

Islam, however, does not demand of mankind that they should observe a duty to which they have not assented, and this assent is identified with what is known as the Day of "*Alast.*" "And when thy Lord brought forth from the children of Adam, from their loins, their posterity [He] caused them to testify concerning themselves [saying]: Am I not your Lord (*alastu bi-rabbikum*)? They said: Yea, truly, we testify!" (VII, 172). The passage concludes by explaining that we are told this "lest you should claim on the Day of Resurrection that you were unaware of it. . . ." We have, in other words, assented to this commitment and this acknowledgement before ever our conscious life began. The same implication is apparent in another Quranic passage, which may be said to emphasize man's viceregal function. "We offered the Trust (*amānah*) to the heavens and the earth and the mountains, but they drew back from bearing it and feared to do so. It is Man who bore it . . ." (XXXIII, 72). The reference to "the mountains" is illuminated by the following: "Had We caused this Quran to descend upon a mountain, thou wouldst indeed have seen it humbled and cleft asunder from fear. . ." (LIX, 21). Revelation, knowledge, vicegerency, centrality: all these are aspects of the burden that the human creature freely bears, and it is in terms of this burden that he is defined as truly "human." It is also in terms of this burden that the *kāfir* is seen by Islam as less than human.[8] The supreme Trust was given to the open-eyed creature, capable of choice and, for that very reason, capable of betraying the Trust. If he does so, what then is left of him but the dust from which he was made?

Islam and the Primordial Religion

The term *dīn al-fiṭrah* ("primordial religion") mentioned earlier has an alternative translation more familiar to those in the modern world who seek a universal faith beyond all confessional divergencies. The *dīn al-fiṭrah,* since it refers back to a time before the different "religions" were revealed or crystallized, is the "perennial philosophy" which is to be found behind the veil of every authentic religion (and is itself the guarantee of authenticity) and also in the background of the mythological religions of so-called primitive peoples. Islam, however, claims by implication a particularly direct relationship to this "perennial philosophy," since it defines itself as the final revelation of a timeless message of which mankind has been "reminded" again and again by countless "messengers of God." The Quran acknowledges without ambiguity that the laws and practices of the different crystallizations of the *dīn al-fiṭrah* have differed according to time and place,[9] but the truth of the Divine Unity and the decisive principles that are derived from this do not change, have not changed, and can never change. "The doctrine of Unity is unique" (*al-tawḥīd^u wāḥid*), so it is said. All else is illusion.

The connection between the "primordial religion" and the final one is underlined by the absence of any priesthood in Islam. The '*ulamā'*—that is to say, the men learned in religious matters (and particularly in the minutiae of the Law)—may at times appear to occupy the role of "clergy" in other faiths, but such authority as they may possess depends upon the respect of the community, a respect that must be earned. They have an advisory function but cannot act as intermediaries between the worshiper and the Object of his worship. It follows that each Muslim is, from this point of view, his own "priest," as is already apparent from the fact that any Muslim may lead his fellows in prayer, provided he knows a few verses of the Quran. By the very fact of having made the attestation of faith, affirming his adherence to the religion and to the community, the Muslim speaks directly to his Creator with nothing to soften this tremendous encounter, and his situation would be no different were he to find himself the last man left on earth. Many Western observers visiting the lands of Islam before modern manners infiltrated the community and before modern dress, with all that it implies in the way of vulgarization of the human form, was widely adopted have remarked upon the "priestly bearing" of ordinary Muslims going about their everyday business.

This air of dignity, control, and self-containment—as of one who walks always in the presence of the Sacred—relates directly to the concept of "vicegerency," for it goes without saying that the representative of God on earth must of necessity comport himself with dignity. The bearer of the burden—the "Trust"—is not free to live carelessly or to slip into the ways of vulgarity. This would be to live beneath himself and, in the pejorative sense of the term, to forget himself. Moreover, there is no area of life and no corner of the world, however humble or however hidden, in which he might cast aside his priestly role. The unitarian perspective of Islam does not admit the existence of a secular realm in which man might act purely as a creature of this earth, a "human animal," and it does not recognize the division between the worldly and the Sacred, which appears self-evident to the Christian. To do so would seem to the Muslim dangerously close to the sin of *shirk* ("idolatry" or, to be more precise, the belief that there are realities independent of The Reality). It would suggest to him that the world or some particular aspect of the world could be treated as though it possessed an existence outside the Divine Pattern. Islam, by its own inner logic, embraces every possible facet of existence, for God has named Himself *al-Muḥīṭ*, the All-Embracing.

If every Muslim is a "priest," then there can be no laity in Islam. The *ummah* ("community") is, in essence, a sacred community—hence, the importance of the "consensus of the believers," by which many matters are decided, and also the Quranic principle of *shūrā* ("consultation"), which should determine matters of government however often this principle may be ignored in the actual practice of politics. The integrated life of the community—or of "the city"—is made possible by the fact that the Prophet was, for the final ten years of his life, the ruler and spiritual director of a self-governing city-state, which crystallized, as it were, in the mold of the revelation which had "descended" upon him. It is not the laws of man that determine the structure of family life, the business of trade, bartering in the market, or the craftsman's work, but the Law of God.

Man and the Crafts

It is perhaps in the work of the craftsman that we may identify with particular clarity one of the functions of God's viceroy on earth. To make out of raw materials, by means of human skill and effort (an effort that might aptly qualify as a type of *jihād*), objects that are both pleasing to God—since, according to a *ḥadīth*, "God is beautiful and He loves beauty"—and useful to man is a labor worthy of the "children of Adam" and entirely compatible with their delegated splendor. To fulfill its function, however, the object that has been made, humble as it may be—a table, a pot, even a comb for the hair—must have a dual aspect; it must be useful for entirely practical purposes, and it must "remind" its user of the Creator of all things. The craft as such cannot, therefore, be a merely human invention—and here we are drawn back to the "perennial philosophy"—for it is axiomatic among those peoples who, in small corners of the world, have survived with their most ancient traditions intact, that the crafts were taught to their ancestors through revelation (by "the gods" or "spirits"). Islamic tradition echoes this belief by attributing the revelation of craft techniques to different messengers of God.

Each craft may be said to have a "secret"—as, indeed, has often been stated by Muslim craftsmen—just as every human being has a "secret" which is also his point of contact with the Divine. This view of the crafts shatters all glorification of modern technology, for this technology, on the one hand, produces objects that are exclusively utilitarian and entirely divorced from the Sacred and, on the other, makes the craftsman obsolete. Such objects are no longer a "reminder" for those who handle them and no longer a form of prayer for those who produce them. The viceroy is thereby deprived of one of his essential functions—that of imitating (on however humble a scale) the creative act, which itself produces in the visible universe the natural phenomena that are both useful to mankind and, at the same time, "signs (of God) for people who understand," as is stated repeatedly in the Quran.

It is in understanding these natural "signs," which are an aspect of God's eternal message to mankind, that the viceroy acquires that knowledge which is his most characteristic gift. It is in treating these signs with respect—that is to say, in respecting his environment as a whole—that he demonstrates another aspect of his God-given function. The Muslim is commanded to "walk softly upon the earth"[10] and, although he is permitted to make use of its products to sustain his life, there is not a single text either in the Quran or the *ḥadīth* literature that could be taken to justify the exploitation of its riches in a destructive manner.

Man and the Social Order

The Islamic concept of man, however, although it gives absolute precedence to the individual's direct and unmediated relationship with God, always places him firmly in his social context, and it is in his relationship with his fellows that he is most severely tested. "Manners" (*ādāb*) are a part of the religion, and Western observers have made frequent reference to the "Muslim cult of manners." All this follows directly from the principle of vicegerency and from the "priestly" identity of the believer. The individual "representative of God on earth" lives and works among others of his own kind; they are as he is and must be treated as such. This involves a certain formalism in human relationships, which contemporary Westerners sometimes find "unnatural" but which is entirely appropriate for the Muslim, who sees the human creature as something more than a child of nature. It has however another aspect, no less important, and this relates not to man's glory but to his wretchedness.

The Muslim is required to treat others with a respect due not to what—in most cases—they are but to what they might be. This presents a sharp contrast to the modern tendency to detect feet of clay in every hero and to interpret "realism" in terms of unmasking the vices and weaknesses of men and women from an unspoken assumption that evil is in some way more "real" than good and ugliness more significant than beauty. This leads all too easily to the assumption that, in discovering some minor flaw in an otherwise virtuous man, we have succeeded in exposing falsehood and bringing truth to light. By the same token, we condemn the "hypocrisy" of the imperfect man who still attempts to set a good example to others, and we praise the "honesty" of one who confesses his shortcomings to the world. From the Muslim point of view it is difficult to perceive what purpose this "honesty" serves, beyond setting a bad example to the community.

In this matter Islam starts from first principles. Beauty and goodness relate to God, Who is the supreme Reality, and have their source in Him; ugliness and evil relate to nothingness and have the insubstantiality of shadows. Positive qualities are, in the proper sense of the term, more *real* than negative ones. The pious Muslim, therefore, averts his eyes with a decent courtesy (which is also a kind of courtesy toward the Divine Image) from the sores on an otherwise healthy body and from the flaws which may spoil but cannot annihilate the potential nobility of those around him, or he will do so as long as the person concerned desires to be better than he is. It is the direction that a man or woman tries to follow rather than the stumbling on the way that is significant.

Muḥammad promised his people that those who "cover" the sins of their fellows in this world will have their own sins "covered" by God when they come to judgment, and he warned them that those who go out of their way to expose the sins of their fellows in this world will have their own sins mercilessly exposed on Judgment Day. He told them also that one sin in the sight of men may be worse than a hundred in the sight of God. Social stability and the maintenance of "ties of relationship" are among the highest priorities in the Islamic scale of values, and, while a private sin may be readily forgiven, the setting of a bad example is an offense against the sacred community, which is the vehicle of the Faith.[11] The Quran itself rigorously condemns all malicious gossip and backbiting, and it compares the seeking out of a man's past sins to "eating the dead flesh of your brother."

There is, moreover, in all gossip and in every effort to draw attention to the weaknesses of our fellows an unspoken assumption that we "know all about them." In the Islamic view God alone knows all about anyone. He knows every thought and hears the secret whisperings of which the soul itself may be less than fully aware, for He is the sole Owner of our souls, our minds, and our senses. Above all, He knows the *sirr,* the "secret" or innermost nucleus of each being, and no man can know another's "secret."[12] In its deepest sense, therefore, respect for others derives from the hiddenness of each being's true identity; and since this identity is intimately linked to its Source, its Creator and Owner, we dare not presume that it is worthless. However misshapen the outer husk may appear, we know that the kernel is present within it; the husk is corruptible but the kernel is inviolable.

To Become What One Is

For the individual Muslim who aspires to become what he should be—what in essence he *is*—the intention to set a good example to his community does not preclude an unflinching awareness of his own shortcomings and of his own inadequacy to fulfill the Trust which he accepted while still in the "loins of Adam." Indeed, this awareness is the precondition for any betterment in his condition. Except in very rare cases his vicegerency is no more than a virtuality yet to be realized. Neither the Quran nor the *aḥādīth* of the Prophet present a flattering picture of human nature as it exists; quite the contrary. The principal motive for following the example of Muḥammad is that in him the Muslim sees the perfect example of one who did fulfill his function.[13] The Muslim feels privileged if he can at least stumble in these footsteps. He believes that in doing so he has done all that he can do. To climb from where he is to the high peak that is the fulfillment of his human role is clearly an impossible task, but he does not despair since he knows with certainty that *lā ḥawl*[a] *wa lā quwwat*[a] *illā bi'Llāh,* "there is no strength and no force save with God."

Man's role in the "impossible ascent" may be summed up in two words: intention and *jihād* (understood in this context simply as "effort"). According to a *ḥadīth qudsī* recorded by the most reliable authorities, the taking of one step toward his Lord brings man the Divine Help he needs: "And if he draws near to Me by a hand's span, I draw near to him an arm's length; and if he draws near to Me an arm's length, I draw near to him a fathom's length; and if he comes to Me walking, I race to him." In other words, God requires very little of this creature of dust who was nonetheless glorified at the beginning of time, but He requires that little absolutely. First, the Muslim must know—knowledge being a duty laid upon him—what his role is in the created universe and in the theater of his brief experience of worldly life. Second, he must wish to fulfill this role and intend to do so with God's help. Third, he must put his little strength and his little talents at the service of this intention.[14] The rest is in other hands.

The ambiguities in the Islamic concept of man and in the human situation as such are therefore resolved in the effort that the children of Adam, made from dust, exert in the direction of the viceregal ideal and in the Divine Help that is offered in response to this effort. And yet the fulfillment of the viceregal role is but a by-product of man's primary function, which is to worship God and to open himself to the Light. "All that is in the heavens and the earth glorifies God," according to the Quran, animals by following their God-given instincts, inanimate objects by obeying the God-given laws of the material world. But the child of Adam (to whom God taught the "names" of all things) stands above this vast current of universal worship; he does from choice what the rest of creation does willy-nilly, and he knows what he is doing.

This it is that makes him the spokesman of creation, doubly representative; for, if he "represents" God in the province of the world, he also "represents" the world before God. This is what it means to be the *khalīfat Allāh fi'l-arḍ*, composed of earthly dust and yet borne aloft by the angels, knower of the "names," bearer of the Trust, and yea-sayer in response to the Divine Question, "Am I not thy Lord?"

Notes

1. "When we speak of the Heart-Intellect we mean the universal faculty which has the human heart for its symbolical seat but which, while being 'crystallised' according to different planes of reflection, is none the less 'divine' in its single essence" (F. Schuon, *Gnosis: Divine Wisdom*, trans. G. E. H. Palmer [London: John Murray, 1959] 95).

2. See al-Kisā'ī, *Qiṣāṣ al-Anbiyā'* (English translation published in *A Reader on Islam*, ed. A. Jeffery [The Hague: Mouton, 1962] 187).

3. H. Corbin, *Creative Imagination in the Sufism of Ibn 'Arabī*, trans. R. Manheim (Princeton, NJ: Princeton University Press, 1969).

4. "So set thy face towards the religion as one by nature upright—the *fiṭrah* of God in which He created (*faṭara*) man—there is no altering the creation of God. That is the eternal religion" (XXX, 30).

5. "By the declining day! Verily man is in a state of loss, save for those who believe and do good and exhort one another to Truth and exhort one another to patience" (CIII).

6. Jalāl al-Dīn Rūmī, *Mathnawī*, book 3, v. 2404.

7. Abu Bakr Siraj Ed-Din, *The Book of Certainty* (New York: Samuel Weiser, 1970) 30–31.

8. "To the Muslims a real atheist is not deemed to be a romantic rebel or a superior philosophical free-thinker, but a sub-human of limited intellect . . . degraded to the level of bestiality, if not below" (A. Bennigsen and M. Broxup, *The Islamic Threat to the Soviet State* [London: Croom Helm, 1983] 62).

9. "For each of you have We appointed a Divine Law and a way of life. Had God so willed, He could have made you one people; but so that He might try you by that which He hath bestowed upon you (He willed otherwise); so compete in doing good. Unto God ye will all return, and He will inform you concerning that wherein ye differ" (V, 48).

10. "And the (faithful) servants of the All-Merciful are those who walk softly upon the earth, and when the foolish ones address them answer: Peace!" (XXV, 63).

11. "Who is the truly good-mannered Muslim?" asks François Bonjean, and he answers: the one "who is judged least unworthy of serving as a model for his children, for his relatives, for his neighbours, for the inhabitants of his quarter, for his city or for simple passers-by and for travellers—for the whole of humanity" ("Culture occidentale et culture musalmane," *Les Cahiers du Sud*, 1947, p. 185).

12. The *sirr* may also be said to contain the seeds of the future, which is concealed from mankind but known to God, and none can foresee what a man may become in the course of time. The Christian might ask himself whether those who were acquainted with the rhetorician Augustine in the whorehouses of Carthage could have guessed that

this dissolute man would grow into Saint Augustine, the greatest of all the fathers of the church.

13. "The Prophet as Norm is not only the Whole Man (*al-insān al-kāmil*) but also the Ancient Man (*al-insān al-qadīm*). Here there is a sort of combination of a spatial with a temporal symbolism; to realize the 'Whole' or 'Universal' man means to come out from oneself, to project one's will into the absolutely 'Other', to extend oneself into the universal life which is that of all things; while to realize the 'Ancient' or 'Primordial' man means to return to the origin which we bear within us; it means to return to eternal childhood, to rest in our archetype, in our primordial and normative form, or in our theomorphic substance" (F. Schuon, *Understanding Islam,* trans. D. M. Matheson [London: Allen & Unwin, 1979] 102).

14. The Quran emphasizes that God does not "change a people" until they change themselves, and this is a double-edged sword. On the one hand, man is helped when he attempts to change himself for the better; on the other, his first tentative steps on a downward slope soon gather momentum.

20

Eschatology

WILLIAM C. CHITTICK

THE "LAST DAY" IS A BASIC ARTICLE of Islamic faith, along with "God, His angels, His Books, and His Messengers" (Quran IV, 136; cf. II, 177). The Quran discusses what occurs after death in a detail unparalleled by other scriptures, and the *Ḥadīth* literature on the subject is voluminous. Hence, scholastic theologians, philosophers, and Sufis—not to speak of Quran commentators—all made eschatology one of their principal concerns.

The term *maʿād* ("return" or "place of return"), used generically for discussions of eschatological realities and events, is derived from such Quranic verses as "They say, 'What, when we are bones and broken bits. . . . Who will cause us to *return*?' Say: 'He who created you the first time'" (XVII, 49–51). Systematic discussions of *maʿād* are often paired with studies of a second concept, *al-mabdaʾ* ("origin" or "place of origin"), for, as the Quran affirms, "As He originated you, so you will return" (VII, 29; cf. XXI, 104). Works on "the Origin and the Return" deal with such questions as the nature of the human being and his relationship with God, the reason for man's creation, his ultimate good and the manner in which he can achieve it, the various types of individuals that make up the human race and their respective lodging places in the next world, the ontological distinctions between this world and the next, and the interpretation of the data found in the Quran and the *Ḥadīth* concerning death, resurrection, and heaven and hell. In a wider context, the topic of "the Origin and the Return" covers everything that touches upon the manner in which man can achieve his proper place in creation or attain to human perfection, whether moral, spiritual, or intellectual. In this sense, jurisprudence (*fiqh*) can be considered a branch of eschatology, since the *Sharīʿah* is the *sine qua non* in the path of human perfection. In the domain of *falsafah* or philosophy, ethics (*akhlāq*) describes the human qualities that bring about the "practical"

ʿ*amalī*—as opposed to the "theoretical," ʿ*ilmī*) perfections of the soul, while in Sufism lengthy discussions of the spiritual stations (*maqāmāt*) play a similar role. Even politics, which describes the ideal human society and the means to achieve it, can be considered a branch of eschatology, since man's temporal good can be understood only in terms of his eternal good. In short, the ramifications of eschatological teachings are so broad that it is difficult to study anything Islamic without touching upon them. Here we can only allude to certain wider implications while dealing in some small detail with the science of the "last things" as such.

Eschatology in the Quran and the *Ḥadīth*

A number of studies on the eschatological teachings of the Quran and the *Ḥadīth* exist in English, and two of the standard *Ḥadīth* collections devoted to the subject have been translated. Here there is room only for a brief outline. A standard statement of Sunni Muslim faith, the "Creed" of Najm al-Dīn Nasafī (d. 537/1142–43), is quoted below. In the commentary that follows, a few relevant Quranic verses and *Ḥadīth* are cited; most of the *Ḥadīth* are from Shīʿite sources, which are not well known in English.

> The chastisement of the grave for the infidels and some of the disobedient faithful and the bliss in the grave for the People of Obedience, as known and willed by God, and the questioning of Munkar and Nakīr are established by proofs [i.e., explicit revealed texts]. The Upraising is true, the Weighing is true, the Book is true, the Questioning is true, the Pool is true, the Path is true, the Garden is true, and the Fire is true. These last two are created and exist now; they will subsist, and neither they nor their inhabitants will pass away. . . . The signs of the Hour, such as the appearance of al-Dajjāl [the Antichrist], the Beast of the Earth, and Gog and Magog, the descent of Jesus from heaven, and the rising of the sun in the west, are true.[1]

The Prophet called death "the only preacher you need," and its remembrance colors all of of Islamic spirituality. One might say that a Muslim is not sincere until he takes to heart such Quranic verses as "What is with you is perishing, but what is with God abides" (XVI, 96); "God is better, and more abiding" (XX, 73); "Everything is perishing but His Face" (XXVIII, 88); "Every soul will taste death" (III, 185); "Oh man! Thou art laboring unto thy Lord laboriously, and thou shalt encounter Him!" (LXXXIV, 6); "Surely the death from which you are fleeing will meet you: then you will be returned to the Knower of the Unseen and the Visible, and He will tell you what you were doing" (LXII, 8). Probably the most common epitaph in the Islamic world is this verse: "Surely we belong to God, and to Him we return" (II, 156).

The Grave. Death is brought about by the intervention of the "angel of death," called 'Izrā'īl; giving up the soul to him is a difficult process, but it is made easy for the faithful. The dead person is aware of his body after death and observes the process of burial. On the first night in the grave, he is questioned by two angels, Munkar and Nakīr, concerning his faith. According to Imam Ja'far al-Ṣādiq (d. 148/765), "The spirits of the faithful are in rooms of the Garden: they eat its food, drink its drinks, and visit one another. They say, 'Our Lord, bring the Hour to accomplish what Thou hast promised.' . . . The spirits of the infidels are in rooms of the Fire: they eat its food, drink its drinks, and visit one another. They say, 'Our Lord, bring not the Hour to accomplish what Thou hast promised!'" According to the Prophet, "The grave is one of the plots of the Garden or one of the pits of the Fire." The period between death and the Day of Resurrection is known as the *barzakh* or "isthmus"; it is alluded to by this name in the Quranic verse, "Behind them is a *barzakh* until the day they are raised up" (XXIII, 100). The term *barzakh* gradually assumes major importance in discussion of eschatology, especially in Sufism and philosophy.

The Upraising. The dead remain in their graves until the Day of Resurrection, which corresponds to the end of this world. "And the Trumpet shall be blown; then behold, they are hastening from their tombs unto their Lord" (XXXVI, 51). Al-Ghazzālī lists over one hundred names for this event, derived from Quranic verses and *ḥadīths;* among them are the Day of Regret (XIX, 39), the Day of Reckoning (XXXVIII, 16), the Day of the Earthquake (XXII, 1), the Day of the Terror (LVI, 1), the Day of the Clatterer (CI, 1), the Day of the Indubitable (LXIX, 1), the Day of the Encounter (XL, 15), the Day of the Gathering (XLII, 7), the Day wherein is no doubt (III, 9), the Day when no soul will avail another in aught (II, 48), the Day when eyes will stare (XIV, 42), the Day a man will flee his brother, his mother, and his father (LXXX, 34), and the Day they shall not speak (LXXVII, 35).[2]

The Weighing. Once the resurrection takes place, the works of people will be evaluated: "We will set up the just balance for the Resurrection Day, so that no soul will be wronged anything: even if it be the weight of a grain of mustard seed, We will produce it" (XXI, 48). According to 'Alī, "The creatures will be seized by the Balance of Justice on the Day of Resurrection: God will requite them on behalf of each other through the Balance."

The Book. "On that day you will be exposed, not one secret of yours concealed. Then as for him who is given his book in his right hand, he will be in a pleasing life, in a lofty Garden. . . . But as for him who is given his book in his left hand, he will say, 'Would that I had not been given my book and had not known my reckoning!' . . ." (LXIX, 18–26). Concerning the verse, "Read thy book! Thy soul suffices thee this day as a reckoner against thee" (XVII, 14), Imam Ja'far says, "The servant will remember everything he has done and is written against him, exactly as if he had done it in that hour. This is the meaning of God's words, 'And the book shall be set in place; and thou wilt see the sinners fearful of what is in it and saying, "Alas for us! How is it with this book, that it leaves nothing behind, small or great, but has counted it?"'" (XVIII, 50).

The Questioning. "We shall surely question them, every one, about what they were doing" (XV, 92–93). According to Ibn 'Abbās, the questioning will not take the form, "Did you do such and such?" but rather, "Why did you do such and such?" Asked about predestination, Imam Ja'far replied, "When God gathers His servants on the Day of Resurrection, He will ask them concerning that which he entrusted to them (*'ahada 'alayhim*), not that which He predestined for them."

The Pond. The Prophet often spoke of the Pond which God had bestowed upon him, as mentioned in Quran CVIII, 1: "Verily We have given thee 'al-Kawthar' [the pond]." For example, "My Pond is one month's journey wide, its water whiter than milk, its fragrance sweeter than musk, and its jugs like the stars of heaven; whosoever drinks from it will never thirst." According to 'Alī, the Prophet said, "He who does not have faith in my Pond will not be given entrance to it by God."

The Path. This is a bridge that stretches over hell; for the faithful it is wide, for infidels narrow and sharper than a sword. Of the thirty-eight occurrences of the word *ṣirāṭ* in the Quran, most refer to the "straight path" of Islam, and only one or two are said to refer to the bridge (cf. XXXVII, 23–24). Ibn 'Abbās reports that the verse "Verily thy Lord is at the Watch" (LXXXIX, 14) refers to the Path's seven stations, at each of which God questions men: at the first concerning the testimony of faith, at the second concerning the ritual prayer, etc. According to Imam Ja'far, "People will cross the Path, which is thinner than a hair and sharper than a sword, in groups: some will cross it like lightning, some like galloping horses, some crawling, some walking, and some while dangling from it."

The Garden. Numerous Quranic verses promise the faithful the everlasting enjoyment of paradise. Among its delights will be "gardens underneath which rivers flow" (II, 25 etc.), "purified spouses" (II, 25 etc.), "God's good pleasure" (III, 15 etc.), "a shelter of plenteous shade" (IV, 57), "forgiveness and a generous provision" (VIII, 4 etc.), "palaces" (XXV, 10), "goodly dwelling places" (IX, 27 etc.), "couches set face to face" (XV, 47 etc.), "abundant fruits" (XXXVIII, 51 etc.), "maidens restraining their glances" (XXXVII, 48 etc.), "wide-eyed houris" (XLIV, 54 etc.), "immortal youths, going round about them with goblets, ewers, and a cup from a spring" (LVI,

17–18), "platters of gold" (XLIII, 71), and "all that your souls desire" (XLI, 31 etc.).

The Fire. The infidels' share of the next world is "the Fire, whose fuel is men and stones" (II, 24 etc.). Its chastisement is "tremendous" (II, 7 etc.), "painful" (II, 10 etc.), "the most terrible" (II, 85 etc.), "humbling" (II, 90 etc.), "lasting" (V, 37 etc.), "evil" (VI, 157 etc.), and "harsh" (XXIV, 17 etc.). The infidels will encounter "the curse of God, the angels, and men, altogether" (II, 206 etc.), "an evil cradling" (II, 206 etc.), "an evil homecoming" (II, 126 etc.), drinks of "boiling water" (VI, 79 etc.) and "oozing pus" (XIV, 16), "garments of fire" (XXII, 19), "hooked iron rods" (XXII, 21), "fetters and chains on their necks" (XL, 71), "burning winds and boiling water and the shadow of a smoking blaze" (LVI, 42–43), "fetters, and a furnace, and food that chokes" (LXXIII, 12–13), and "a threefold shadow, unshading and giving no relief against the flames" (LXXVII, 30–32). "When they are cast, coupled in fetters, into a narrow place of the Fire, they will call out there for destruction. 'Call not out today for one destruction—call for many!'" (XXV, 13–14).

The Hour. Many verses and a number of short chapters of the Quran (e.g., LXXXI, LXXXII, LXXXIV, XCIX, CI) are dedicated to describing the end of this world, which takes place immediately preceding the Resurrection: "the Day of Doom . . . when the command shall belong only to God" (LXXXII, 17). God alone knows the time of its arrival (VII, 187; XXXIII, 63), but the preparatory signs are described in detail. Gog and Magog and the Beast of the Earth are mentioned in the Quran: "When Gog and Magog are unloosed, and they slide down out of every slope, and nigh has drawn the true promise . . ." (XXI, 96); "When the Word falls on them, We shall bring forth for them out of the earth a beast that shall speak unto them" (XXVII, 82). According to 'Alī, when the beast appears, "he will carry Solomon's seal and Moses' staff. He will place the seal on the face of every believer, leaving the words, 'This is a believer in truth'; and on the face of every infidel, leaving the words, 'This is an infidel in truth.' . . . Then the Beast will raise its head, and everyone from east to west will see it, after the sun has risen from the west. When it lifts its head, repentance will no longer be accepted." Before the world's end al-Dajjāl will rule for a period, and then be killed by Jesus. The Mahdī, a descendant of the Prophet who "resembles me more than anyone else" and is identified in Shī'ite sources with the twelfth Imam, will also appear at the end of time, and Jesus will pray behind him. According to some *ḥadīths,* Jesus will establish a reign of justice; according to others, the Mahdī "will fill the earth with justice and equity as it had been filled with injustice and oppression." As the final end approaches, "God will send a cold wind from the direction of Syria, and no one who has in his heart as much as a single grain of good shall remain in the earth without being taken." Then the trumpet will be blown, and everyone will perish.

The eschatological teachings outlined above have often been taken at face value; this was especially the case among theologians, traditionists, and Sufis before al-Ghazzālī, though the philosophers from the beginning offered interpretative views. Even in the eighth/fourteenth century, 250 years after al-Ghazzālī and 100 years after Ibn ʿArabī, a Sufi of the stature of ʿIzz al-Dīn Kāshānī (d. 735/1334–35) could write as follows in his classic *Miṣbāḥ al-hidāyah* (*Lamp of Guidance*):

> It is incumbent upon everyone to have faith in the World of the Unseen and the states of the next world just as they are described in the Quran and the *Hadīth*. . . . He must not begin to interpret and explain these for himself with his weak intellect and feeble understanding, nor try to understand how and in what manner they occur, for the human intellect cannot encompass the sciences of faith.[3]

But al-Ghazzālī had already answered such objections in a manner that the community as a whole had to accept:

> You may say that these explanations and details are opposed to what the men of knowledge have discussed in their books, for they have said, "These affairs can only be known through imitation (*taqlīd*) and tradition (*samāʿ*); human insight cannot reach them." . . . But my words are not opposed to theirs, and everything they have said in explaining the next world is correct. However, it has not gone beyond the explanation of what will be perceived there. Either they have not known the spiritual realities, or they have not explained them, since most people cannot understand them. Whatever [in the next world] is of a corporeal nature can only be known through tradition and imitating the Prophet, but these other things are a branch of the knowledge of the spirit's reality, and there is a way to know that: spiritual insight and inward contemplation.[4]

Elsewhere al-Ghazzālī points out that the reality of death cannot be known without understanding the reality of life, and this in turn depends upon knowledge of the spirit (*rūḥ*), "which is your own self" (or "soul," *nafs*).[5] The terms *rūḥ* and *nafs* are often used interchangeably to designate the ultimate human substance, though many authorities distinguish between them; in general theologians and Sufis prefer *rūḥ*, philosophers *nafs*. Thus, in what follows, "spirit" and "soul" are essentially synonymous.

The Origin and the Return

Islamic teachings about the nature of man revolve around the fact that, according to the Prophet, God created man "upon His own Form" or "upon the Form of the All-Merciful." In the Quranic account God made Adam His vicegerent (*khalīfah*), knowing "all the names" (II, 30–31), gave him the Trust (XXXIII, 72), "honored" his children (XVII, 70), and subjected to him "everything in the heavens and the earth" (XXXI, 20). These and many other passages are interpreted to refer to the unique position of man among the creatures.

Ibn ʿArabī and his followers provide a clear commentary on such verses in harmony with Islamic teachings in general. The Divine Names mentioned in the Quran are the archetypes of all creatures; the heavens and the earth and all they contain, often referred to in the Quran as the "signs" of God, are the outward manifestations of the ontological perfections referred to by the Names. In their multiplicity the individual creatures of the cosmos reflect the multiple Names of God, and the cosmos as a whole reflects the "all-comprehensive" Name *Allāh* or its near synonym the "All-Merciful" (*al-Raḥmān*). "Call upon Allah, or call upon the All-Merciful: whichever you call upon, to Him belong the Names Most Beautiful" (XVII, 110). At the same time each human being, made upon God's Form, also reflects the Name *Allāh:* microcosm and macrocosm are mirror images, and each in turn reflects God. Man's uniqueness lies in the fact that he brings together all the realities of the universe in a summarized and all-comprehensive unity; he embraces within himself—at least potentially—the ontological perfections of all things.

Existence in its total deployment can be pictured as a circle. Beginning as a single point that represents the Creative Principle, the various existents become deployed in a clockwise descent that includes spiritual entities such as angels, intermediate entities connecting the spiritual and corporeal worlds, and then the whole range of corporeal entities, from the simple (the four elements) to the complex (minerals, plants, and animals). The human embryo then represents the lowest point in the circle and the beginning of the "arc of ascent," which extends back through the corporeal, intermediate, and spiritual worlds to the Divine Presence. The full circle represents the outward manifestation of all archetypes or Divine Names, i.e., the whole cosmos, in both its unseen (or spiritual) and visible (or corporeal) dimensions. The perfect man, who traverses the circle of being and actualizes each point, then becomes the point at the center of the circle, standing equidistant from all points on the circumference. As the actualized Form of the Name *Allāh,* the perfect man manifests all other Names equally; were one of them to dominate over him, he would fall into disequilibrium and imperfection, since he would no longer be an "all-comprehensive" creature but would manifest certain realities more than others.

When a human being is born into this world, he is, as a child of Adam, created upon the form of *Allāh,* but the infinite ontological perfections alluded to by this Name remain potentialities hidden within him. As he grows, he begins to actualize his potential perfections. Philosophical, theological, and Sufi texts on the soul often point out that man first gains the perfections of the vegetative soul, then those of the animal soul, and only then does he begin to become a true human being. But his entry into the human world around the time of puberty—when the practice of Islam becomes incumbent upon him—marks only the first step on an infinite ascent. Man, made in God's image, knows no limits.

In a formulation somewhat different from that found in Ibn 'Arabī's school, Najm al-Dīn Rāzī (d. 654/1256) speaks of five stages of man referred to in the Quran: (1) nonexistence in God's knowledge, (2) existence in the world of the spirits, (3) attachment of the spirit to the body, (4) separation from the bodily frame, (5) return to the frame. Each stage is necessary for the actualization of the perfections required by certain Divine Names. Through the first stage man perceives God as Creator; through the second he comes to know Him by such Attributes as Will, Life, Speech, Sight, and Power; through the third he knows Him as the Provider, the Forgiver, the Munificent, etc.; through the fourth he comes to know Him as the Slayer, and through the fifth as the Reviver.[6]

The goal of the passage through the worlds is the "acquisition of knowledge" or the realization of every concomitant and every concrete manifestation of the Names taught to Adam. For, in the words of the Sufi poet and philosopher Jāmī (d. 898/1492), "Man in his primordial nature (*fiṭrah*) is plain, a receptacle for all attributes."[7] In the more philosophical language of Mullā Ṣadrā (d. 1050/1640), "Every human soul, because of its primordial nature given by God, is worthy to know the realities of all things."[8] This conception of the human reality is often expressed by affirming an innate knowledge of universal realities that cannot be actualized until the soul learns the particular things. In Najm al-Dīn Rāzī's words,

> In the beginning the spirit had knowledge of universals and not of particulars; it had knowledge of the World of the Unseen but not of the visible world. When it was joined to this world and duly trained and nurtured, it acquired knowledge of both universals and particulars, and became "knower of the Unseen and the visible" as God's vicegerent. In the world of the spirits, it had not the strength or instruments required for the tasks of the Lord's vicegerency; it was in this (lower) world that it acquired the necessary strength and instruments, and thus attained the perfection of the degree of vicegerency.[9]

Another well-known Sufi, 'Azīz al-Dīn Nasafī (d. before 700/1300), describes man's ascent to perfection in terms of spiritual light:

> Every individual existent possesses in itself and of itself what it must have. The spirit does not come from anywhere nor go anywhere. The spirit is light, and the cosmos is overflowing with light, for light is its spirit, moving it toward perfection. . . . At one level this light is called "nature," at another level "spirit," at another "intellect," and at still another "Nondelimited Light." . . .
>
> At the first level, life, knowledge, will, and power [the fundamental divine Attributes] do not exist in actuality. But as the existents move up through the levels, gradually life, knowledge, will, power, hearing, sight, and speech come to exist in actuality. . . . In other words, that light which is the spirit of the cosmos and with which the cosmos is overflowing does not possess at that level knowledge, will, and power in actuality, but as the light gradually moves up the levels, life, knowledge, will, and power come to exist in actualized mode.[10]

Man's Infinite Potentiality

Ibn Sīnā (d. 428/1037), the "chief shaykh" of the Peripatetic philosophers, provides a clear formulation of the fundamental human nature in the language of *falsafah:*

> The perfection peculiar to the rational soul is for it to become an intellective world within which is inscribed the form of the whole, the intelligible order of the whole, and the good that is effused into the whole; it begins with [knowledge of God, i.e.] the Origin of the whole, moves on to [knowledge of] nondelimited, spiritual, noble substances; then to spiritual substances having a kind of attachment to bodies; and then to the celestial corporeal bodies with all their dispositions and faculties. The soul continues in this manner until it realizes fully within itself the disposition peculiar to existence as a whole. Hence it is transformed into an intelligible world parallel to the entire existent cosmos; it contemplates that which is Absolute Comeliness, Absolute Good, and True Beauty, and it becomes united with it.[11]

As the form of all the Names—all the ontological possibilities—the human substance is able to achieve a total correspondence with the entire cosmos. But there is no guarantee that a person will reach such a station, and in fact the vast majority of human beings stop short before realizing their full perfection. In effect, they actualize only some of the ontological potentialities embraced by their all-comprehensive primordial nature; they cease to reflect all the Divine Names and become loci of manifestation for only some of them. They become mirrors for part of the universe instead of the whole. They leave the centrality of the human state, and, instead of being all creatures and all creation, they become this creature or that. Particularly in Sufi texts, the infinite potentiality of the human state is perceived as a kind of unlimited malleability that allows man to become anything at all.

34. "Satan in the form of a dragon," Add. 18576 (11a).

Thus 'Azīz al-Dīn Nasafī explains that the earth cannot play the role of water, nor the grape vine that of the almond tree, nor the eye that of the ear.

> Have you not recognized that each thing fulfills its fixed function, but that man can necessarily fulfill the function of all? . . . Thus man is defined in the sense that he can assume the qualities of every other creature. . . . According to whether he assumes the qualities of this or that creature, it is this or that creature that he becomes, even though outwardly he may have the form of a man.[12]

Long before Nasafī, the poet Sanā'ī (d. 525/1130–31) had described man as compounded of all the worlds—material, psychic, and spiritual—and hence "molded of heart and clay." Each existent other than man assumes a single aspect, according to its fixed place in the hierarchy of existence, but man cannot be reduced to "one color."[13] Rūmī (d. 672/1273) often refers to man's infinite potentiality: "God will give you what you seek. Wherever your aspiration lies, that you will become."[14] His son Sulṭān Walad (d. 712/1312) makes an explicit connection between this teaching and eschatology:

> Man is compounded of form and meaning, of satanic and divine; every instant the houris of paradise and the devils of hell show their faces from his inward reality so that it may be seen which vein and which attribute dominate over him. His desire takes him to that form with which he has a greater affinity (*munāsabah*); it becomes his *qiblah* and beloved. Necessarily in the end he will become identical to it and be resurrected with it.[15]

Again in Rūmī's words,

> Whatever makes you tremble—know that you are worth just that! That is why the heart of God's lover is greater than His Throne.[16]

According to the *ḥadīth qudsī*, "My heavens and My earth encompass Me not, but the heart of My gentle, faithful, and meek servant does encompass Me." The servant whose heart encompasses God has become the perfect man by actualizing the Divine Form upon which he was created; having comprehended all the Divine Names, he contains within himself the form of every creature. This is the meaning of Ibn 'Arabī's famous verse, "My heart has become a receptacle for every form, a pasture for gazelles and a cloister for Christian monks."[17] In a similar vein Ibn 'Arabī alludes to a *ḥadīth* found in Muslim's authoritative collection: God will appear at the Resurrection in a multitude of forms, but His creatures will deny Him until He appears in a form that corresponds to their own belief. It is only the perfect men, whose hearts encompass all the Divine Names in perfect equilibrium, who will recognize God in whatever form He displays.

> He who delimits God [according to his own belief] denies Him in everything

> other than his own delimitation, acknowledging Him only when He reveals Himself within that delimitation. But he who frees Him from all delimitation never denies Him, acknowledging Him in every form in which He appears.[18]

Mullā Ṣadrā summarizes this discussion in philosophical terms:

> The soul is the "junction of the two seas" (XVIII, 59) of corporeal and spiritual things. . . . If you consider its substance in this world, you will find it the principle of all the bodily powers, employing all the animal and vegetal forms in its service. But if you consider its substance in the world of the Intellect, you will find that at the beginning of its fundamental nature it is pure potential without any form in that world. . . . Its initial relation to the form of that world is that of the seed to the fruit, or of the embryo to the animal: just as the embryo is in actuality an embryo, and an animal only potentially, so (at first) the soul is in actuality a mere mortal man, but potentially (realized) Intellect.[19]

Through life in this world the soul's potentialities become actualized; death is in no way an imperfection, since, as stated in the commonly quoted *ḥadīth,* it is merely "transferal from one abode to another." In Mullā Ṣadrā's terms, death occurs once the soul has actualized all its potentialities. Having no more need for the material body, it discards it in order to move on to the next stage of its existence.

> The reason for physical death is that the soul reaches perfection and independence in existence, so it turns through its ingrained activity and effort toward another world. Thus, as its essence gains strength, little by little, until it attains a new kind of existence, it cuts off its connection [with the body] by strengthening its connection to another body, which is acquired in accordance with its moral qualities and psychic dispositions. Hence, first and in essence it takes on a second life; but as an accidental corollary, its physical life comes to an end. . . .
>
> Attaining the degree of substantiality, actuality, and independence is shared by faithful and infidel . . . and by many animals that have an actualized imaginal faculty. There is no contradiction between this ontological perfection and substantial independence on the one hand and wretchedness and suffering torment through the fire of hell . . . on the other; on the contrary, these things merely confirm our conclusion. For the fact that the existence [of the individual] is strengthened and accentuated and that it departs from material coverings and veils results in an increased intensity in the perception of pains.[20]

The Role of the Body

In the above passage, Mullā Ṣadrā speaks of the soul's discarding its body through its connection to "another body." He, Ibn 'Arabī, and others maintain that a body is indispensable to the soul at all stages of its existence; in fact, they are following Quranic usage, where *nafs* most often refers to the whole human reality, not just to the spiritual side of man's existence.[21] In Ibn 'Arabī's words, "When God created the human spirit, He created it governing a natural (*ṭabīʿī*) sensory form, whether in this world, in the *barzakh,* or wherever."[22] Like Rūmī, Ibn 'Arabī compares the individual souls of men to patches of light thrown down into separate courtyards by the "sun," that is, the "single soul" (Quran VII, 189) from which the souls were created. The individual existence of a soul thus depends upon the locus within which it becomes manifested. After death, "God desires the subsistence of these lights in keeping with the disparity they have assumed," so He creates bodies for them in the *barzakh,* through which they remain distinct from other souls.[23] Mullā Ṣadrā explains that the total potentiality of the human primordial nature cannot be actualized without bodies, since man is in need of the physical senses to actualize his imaginal faculty. "Then, on the basis of correct images, the soul is able to extract disengaged meanings, and from these it can come to understand its own world, its Origin, and its Return."[24]

The all-comprehensive human reality has to be a potential locus of manifestation for every Divine Name, including those, like the "Outward" (*al-ẓāhir*), which demand a mode of existence at the outermost limit of manifestation. Otherwise, man would not encompass "all the worlds" and would cease to be man. Hence, for Mullā Ṣadrā, the resurrection of the body follows from the very definition of the human being, and he marshals his formidable powers of reasoning to prove its reality. It is impossible here even to allude to his various complicated proofs; it need be mentioned only that he maintains vehemently the fundamental identity of the resurrection body and the body man possesses in this world, in spite of certain differences. This is because bodily nature is determined solely by "form" (in the Aristotelian sense) and not by "matter," which is nonmanifest without form. Therefore the body is the same body, even though the ontological conditions of the *barzakh* and the resurrection differ in certain respects from those in this world.[25]

A *barzakh* is an intermediate reality that both separates and comprehends what lies on either side. It is a name given to the "world of suspended images" (Suhrawardī) or the "world of imagination" (Ibn 'Arabī), the intermediate ontological realms that separate the ocean of the spirits from that of the corporeal bodies: "He let forth the two seas that meet together, between them a *barzakh* they do not overpass" (Quran LV, 20). Like the world of the spirits, the *barzakh* is immaterial, but like that of the corporeal bodies, it possesses shape, form, and number. Without it, the spiritual beings, which are luminous and disengaged (*mujarrad*) from matter, could have no contact with beings of the corporeal world, which are material and tenebrous. Ibn 'Arabī states:

> The *barzakh* is the junction of the two seas: the sea of spiritual meanings and the sea of sensory objects. The sensory things cannot be meaning (*ma'nā*), nor can the meanings be sensory. But the World of Imagination, which we have called "the junction of the two seas," gives meanings corporeal shape and makes sensory objects into subtle realities.[26]

In the same way, without the animal soul, which is the locus of imagination in man, the human spirit or "rational soul" could not govern his body.

Ibn 'Arabī distinguishes between the *barzakh* located on the descending arc of the circle of being and that on the ascending arc. The first of these *barzakhs* acts as the ontological nexus between spiritual and corporeal realities, while the second—called the "grave" in many *ḥadīths*—grows up from human acts and moral qualities as a fruit grows on a tree.[27]

In the human microcosm, the world of imagination is directly reflected in the faculty of imagination, which is experienced most clearly in dreams, when we see, hear, smell, taste, and feel without any corresponding objects outside of the mind. In the view of Mullā Ṣadrā, the imagination is a faculty that creates images in our mind, whether or not these correspond to objects in the outside world. Hence, even during wakefulness, the imagination creates in the mind the image of the object that the eye has "perceived." The imagination has an infinite power of conjuration, since it can picture all that exists and all that does not exist. The ultimate source of this ability is the fact that man is the microcosm containing all things in himself, while his imagination is a locus of manifestation (*maẓhar*) for the Divine Name "He who gives form" (*al-Muṣawwir*).

The conclusion reached by Mullā Ṣadrā is that after death man exists in the *barzakh* in an imaginal body whose very substance is produced by himself. This does not mean that the *barzakh* is "imaginary"; in fact, it is far more real than this world, since it lies at a higher point on the circle of being. In the words of the Prophet, "People are asleep, but when they die, they wake up." None of what man witnesses in the next stage of existence is outside his own soul, but the reality of the soul, as the Form of God, is ultimately without limits. So it should not be surprising when Mullā Ṣadrā calls the "imaginal" experiences of the next world "more strongly substantial, more firmly established, and more permanent in reality than material forms."[28]

Equilibrium and Deviation: Mercy and Wrath

The goal of Islam is to guide mankind to ultimate felicity by establishing equilibrium on the individual level and on the social level. This means that the human substance, made upon the form of the all-comprehensive Names *Allāh* and All-Merciful, must be shown the way to actualize all the concomitants of the individual Divine Names. Mullā Ṣadrā summarizes the destiny and felicity of the soul in the following terms:

> In respect to its intellective essence, the felicity of the soul lies in its attaining to pure intellectual realities and becoming the locus for divine forms, for the order of existence, and for the disposition of the Whole, from God Himself down to the lowest levels of existence. As for the soul's perfection and felicity in respect to its companionship with the body . . . this lies in the attainment of "justice." . . . This means that it must achieve perfect balance among opposing moral qualities.[29]

By employing the term "justice" (*ʿadālah*), derived from the same root as the word "equilibrium" (*iʿtidāl*), Mullā Ṣadrā is alluding to the point of contact between the ultimate perfection of the human soul—sometimes called the station of the perfect man, who stands at the point at the center of the circle—and the science of ethics, whether considered as a branch of philosophy, Sufism, or the *Sharīʿah.* In the words of perhaps the greatest Muslim authority on the philosophical study of ethics, Naṣīr al-Dīn al-Ṭūsī (d. 672/1274), "Among virtues, none is more perfect than the virtue of Justice, as is obvious in the discipline of Ethics, for the true mid-point is Justice, all else being peripheral to it and taking its reference therefrom."[30]

Already al-Ghazzālī had identified justice with the straight path of Islam, "the true mean among the opposite moral qualities."[31] He summarizes Islamic ethics in his *Iḥyāʾ* when speaking of the four basic kinds of human attributes: beastly (*bahīmī*), predatory (*sabʿī*), satanic (*shayṭānī*), and lordly or seigneurial (*rabbānī*). It is as if "the total in man's skin is a pig, a dog, a devil, and a wise man." The first three kinds of attributes must be put under the domination of the fourth, which is manifested most clearly in man's intellect (*ʿaql*). If the latter dominates, "the matter is in equilibrium, and justice appears in the kingdom of the body and all proceeds on the Straight Path."[32] Otherwise man will be in the service of the pig, dog, or devil, and he will fail to achieve human status. This is in fact the state of most men, and it explains their lot in the next world.

The *Sharīʿah* and the *ṭarīqah* provide the framework in which the "true mean" among the moral qualities can be achieved; they allow man to follow the advice of the oft-quoted *ḥadīth:* "Assume the moral traits of Allah (*takhallaqū bi-akhlāq Allāh*)"; in other words, "Actualize all the Divine

Names upon the form of which you were created." Al-Ghazzālī refers to the actualization of these Names as the station of *ta'alluh* (a word derived from the same root as the Name *Allāh*), i.e., "being like unto *Allāh*" or "theomorphism."[33] Later philosophers adopted this term as a definition of human perfection; thus Mullā Ṣadrā is often referred to as the "theomorphic sage" (*al-ḥakīm al-muta'allih*).

Al-Farghānī (d. ca. 700/1300), a follower of Ibn 'Arabī, explains that man must follow the *Sharī'ah*, because only it can open the way toward the actualization of his theomorphic nature; only the Law can protect him from being overcome by the multiplicity and disequilibrium of the sensory world. In our present state, nature veils the spiritual world and its properties of oneness, equilibrium, and simplicity. By following the *Sharī'ah*, a person gains an actualized connection (*ta'alluq*) to certain Divine Names closely related to Unity that formerly had only been latent within himself. Thus, God is the Guide (*al-Hādī*), the Right-Guider (*al-Rashīd*), the All-Compassionate (*al-Raḥīm*), the Forgiver (*al-Ghafūr*), and the Pardoner (*al-'Afū*), but to benefit from these Names a person must accept the Divine Guidance and Compassion that are offered—that is, he must submit to the message from heaven.[34]

In this discussion it is essential to recognize the distinction between the Names of Mercy and Gentleness, such as those mentioned above, and those of Wrath and Severity, such as the Vengeful, the Terrible, the Abaser, and the Almighty. According to the *ḥadīth qudsī*, "My Mercy precedes My Wrath"; so the Names of Mercy take precedence over those of Wrath. The reason for this is simply that Mercy is the very nature of God, whereas Wrath comes into play in connection with certain of His creatures. In the words of 'Abd al-Karīm al-Jīlī (d. ca. 832/1428), "God said, 'My Mercy embraces all things' (Quran VII, 156), but He did not say, 'My Wrath embraces all things,' for He created all things as a mercy from Him. . . . The secret in this is that Mercy is the Attribute of His Essence, but Wrath is not."[35] Moreover, since man is created upon the "Form of the All-Merciful," the equilibrium attained by the perfect men relates directly to the Attributes of the Essence, such as Unity. But disequilibrium, deviation, and multiplicity relate to those Names—the Names of Wrath—which are in one respect opposed to the Names of Mercy.

This is why theologians and jurists such as Abū Ḥanīfah (d. 150/767) often point out that evil deeds are debarred from any connection with such merciful Attributes as Good-Pleasure (*al-riḍā*) and Guidance.[36] In expanding on such teachings, Ibn 'Arabī draws a clear distinction between the paths of Mercy and Wrath: though all things return to God, their returns are conditioned by the particular Names to which they are connected. Hence God calls us to follow the path of justice and equilibrium, which will lead us to the Names of Mercy: "God calls us to worship Him according to the path which connects us to our own particular felicity." As his commentator points out, all paths lead to God but each takes us to a different name.

> Names are different in respect of their realities and effects. How is "He who harms" comparable to "He who benefits," or "the Bestower" comparable to "the Preventer"? How is "the Avenger" comparable to "the Forgiver," or "the Benign Benefactor" to "the Vanquisher"?[37]

God is the Just (*al-ʿadl*), and thus He "puts everything in its proper place" (*al-ʿadl huwa waḍʿ al-shayʾ fī mawḍiʿihi*). This means that those creatures who have actualized the Form of the All-Merciful upon which they were created enjoy Mercy, while those who have not actualized the human potential suffer Wrath, since they remain in multiplicity and disequilibrium. The Quran makes a clear connection between Wrath and the chastisement of hell (e.g., IV, 93; VIII, 16; XLII, 16; XLVIII, 6). The early Sufi al-Niffarī (d. 360/971) points out the relationship between the Names of Wrath and the fire on the one hand and the Names of Mercy and the garden on the other; he declares that the fire derives from "otherness," that is, being veiled from God and from one's own primordial nature by separation and plurality. "Unveiling is the Garden of the Garden, veiling the Fire of the Fire."[38] In short, "to enter the garden" is to actualize the form upon which one was created and to attain to Mercy, whereas "entering the fire" means to be separated from one's theomorphic selfhood. In the words of F. Schuon:

> The good reason for the sanctions beyond death is apparent once we are aware of human imperfection; being a disequilibrium that imperfection ineluctably calls forth its own repercussion. . . . The fire beyond the grave is definitely nothing but our own intellect actualized in opposition to our own falsehood. . . . Man therefore condemns himself; according to the Quran [XXIV, 24, XXVI, 64, XLI, 20–22] it is his members themselves which accuse him; once beyond the realm of lies his violations are transformed into flames.[39]

Certain Sufis maintain that after death—as before death—God reveals Himself to man primarily in the mode of Mercy, but the infidel's corrupted nature perceives that Mercy as Wrath. In Niffarī's words, "That through which He blesses in the Garden is the same as that through which He chastises in the Fire." Ibn ʿArabī is more explicit: "Chastisement occurs through the very things that causes bliss . . . , just as a man of cold temperament enjoys the heat of the sun, while a man of hot temperament is tortured by it. In the last analysis, the very thing that causes bliss causes pain."[40]

In discussing the torments of hell, Muslim thinkers eventually come back to the precedence of God's Mercy over His Wrath. The Names of Mercy in the Quran outnumber the Names of Wrath by at least five to one; the Name Vengeful does not occur as such, but only once in verbal form, whereas its opposite, the Forgiving, occurs about one hundred times. Considerations such as these explain why the view that hell cannot be everlasting has prevailed, even among exoteric theologians. For Ibn 'Arabī and his followers, the precedence of God's Mercy means that the chastisement (*'adhāb*) of the infidels will one day turn sweet (*'adhb*), even if they remain in hell forever.[41]

Death and the *Barzakh*

Long before Muslims began writing about an independent "world of imagination" identified with the *barzakh*, the community was well aware that "sleep is the brother of death" (a saying normally cited as a *ḥadīth*). The Quran states, "God takes their souls at the time of death, and that which has not died in its sleep" (XXXIX, 42), and authorities such as the Quran commentator al-Zamakhsharī (d. 538/1143–44) could argue that sleep and death were the same reality.[42] The science of dream interpretation is mentioned in the Quran (e.g., XII, 44, 100) and was practiced by the Prophet. The vast literature that developed on the subject shows that it has been popular throughout Islamic history. Since the close connection between sleep and death was affirmed from the first, it is not surprising that the eschatological data came to be "interpreted" following much the same principles that were employed for dreams.

In dreams the imaginal faculty displays ideas in forms that possess a "correspondence" or "affinity" (*munāsabah*) with the underlying meaning or content. The task of the interpreter is to understand the original meaning behind the form. His task is made easier, of course, if the dream is "true" (*ṣādiq*) and derives therefore not only from the dreaming subject but also from the objective world of imagination outside and beyond him. The Prophet himself said that a true dream is "one-forty-sixth part of prophecy."

Al-Ghazzālī points out that since sleep is the twin brother of death, through it "we have gained an aptitude for understanding certain states which we could not understand through wakefulness." He explains that the works of men have "spirits" (*arwāḥ*) and "realities" (*ḥaqā'iq*) that cannot be perceived in this world but that appear after death, for in the next world "Forms are subordinate to spirits and realities, so everything seen there will be seen in a form appropriate to its reality."[43] In the same way, the forms we see in dreams correspond closely to their meanings, as can be understood from an account of the famous dream interpreter Ibn Sīrīn (d. early second/eighth century). When asked about a man who had dreamed he was sealing the mouths and private parts of people with a seal ring, he explained, correctly, that the man must be a muezzin who calls people to prayer in the early morning of Ramaḍān (thus announcing to them that they must commence the fast). Al-Ghazzālī explains:

> When this man became separated somewhat from the world of corporeal sensation, the spirit of his work was unveiled to him. But since he was still in the world of imagination (*'ālam al-takhayyul*)—for a dreamer never ceases to imagine things—his imaginal faculty veiled the spirit [of his work] in an imaginal likeness (*mithāl mutakhayyal*), i.e., the seal-ring and the sealing. This likeness reveals the spirit of his work more clearly than the call to prayer itself, since the World of Dreams is nearer than this lower world to the next world.[44]

"What is really strange," remarks al-Ghazzālī, "is that you have been shown so many examples of the Resurrection in sleep, yet you remain totally oblivious of its reality."[45] So dreams provide a key to understanding the Islamic teachings concerning the next world. For example, the Prophet describes the reality of the present world by saying that on the Day of Resurrection it will be brought in the form of an ugly old woman, and everyone who sees her will say: "We seek refuge from you in God." Then they will be told, "This is the world that you spent so much effort in trying to acquire."[46] Again, the Prophet speaks of the infidel in his grave being tormented by ninety-nine *tinnīn,* each of which is ninety-nine serpents with nine heads. These represent the infidel's evil qualities, such as pride, hypocrisy, envy, and greed, while the exact numbers refer to the fact that such qualities can be divided into a limited number of general principles possessing subdivisions (as can be observed, for example, in the science of ethics). "It is these qualities which are the mortal sins; they themselves are transformed into scorpions and serpents."[47]

Al-Ghazzālī's conclusion is clear, especially since it is repeated in numerous texts on eschatology over the centuries: In death, man finds nothing but his own attributes, no longer veiled by the corporeal body but revealing themselves to him in forms appropriate to his new abode. "The soul's connection to the body veils it from the perception of the realities of things, while death removes the veil: 'We have now removed from thee thy covering, so thy sight today is piercing' (Quran L, 22)."[48] Man awakens to the realities of his own words, acts, and moral qualities; his moral substance, whether good or evil, assumes corporeal shape. Everything that had been hidden in the lower world becomes outwardly manifest. This is why, in the words of al-Ṭūsī, "Whoever is afraid of natural death is afraid of the concomitant of his own essence and the completion of his own quiddity."[49] Rūmī makes the same point:

> If you fear and flee from death, you fear yourself, Oh friend. Take heed!
> It is your own ugly face, not the face of death. Your spirit is like a tree, and death its leaves.[50]

According to al-Qūnawī (d. 673/1274), the *barzakh* is a world where the outward becomes inward and the inward outward. It is referred to as follows:

> "The day every soul shall find what it has done of good brought forward, and what it has done of evil; it will wish there were a far space between it and that day" (III, 30). Every attribute that dominated over man in this world will manifest itself to him in the *barzakh* in an appropriate form. . . . This is the meaning of the Prophet's words, "Men will be mustered on the Day of Resurrection in keeping with their intentions."[51]

The Persian poet Sanā'ī expresses these ideas as follows:

> When they lift the veil of sensory perception from your eyes, if you are an infidel you will find scorching hell,
> if a man of faith the Garden.
> Your heaven and hell are within yourself: Look inside!
> See furnaces in your liver, gardens in your heart.[52]

Rūmī asks:

> How many children of your thoughts will you see in the grave,
> all surrounding your soul crying, "Papa!"?
> Your good thoughts give birth to youths and houris;
> your ugly thoughts give birth to great demons.[53]

Such ideas explain the eschatological significance of these famous lines of Rūmī:

> You are your thought, brother, the rest of you is bones and fiber.
> If you think of roses, you are a rosegarden; if you think of thorns, you are fuel for the furnace.[54]

'Ayn al-Quḍāt Hamadānī (d. 525/1131) explains that all vision of the spiritual world or of the next world is based on *tamaththul*, "the display of images (*mithāl*)." Thus, according to the Quran, Gabriel appeared to Mary as "a man without fault" through *tamaththul* (XIX, 17). On this basis we can understand the questioning of the dead by the angels Munkar and Nakīr:

> It takes place within yourself. Those of our contemporaries who are veiled from the truth have come up with this problem: How can two angels, in one instant, visit a thousand different individuals? [They conclude that] one must accept this as an article of faith [since it contradicts reason]. But in this

connection Ibn Sīnā—God have mercy on him—provided a world of explanation in two sentences: "Munkar is his evil deeds, and Nakīr his good deeds." . . . The ego is the mirror of blameworthy qualities, and the intellect and heart are the mirror of praiseworthy qualities. When a man looks, he sees his own attributes revealing themselves in images (*tamaththul-garī kunad*). His own existence is his torment, though he thinks someone else is tormenting him. . . . If you want to hear the Prophet himself say this, listen when he speaks of the chastisements of the grave: "They are only your works given back to you."[55]

The Lesser Resurrection

The experience of death for the microcosm corresponds to the coming of the Hour for the macrocosm. Hence the Quranic accounts of the end of the world can also be understood as referring to the death of the individual. Many Quranic commentators, such as 'Abd al-Razzāq Kāshānī (d. 730/1330) in his famous *ta'wīl,* or "esoteric interpretation," understand verses referring to the resurrection in such terms. Al-Ghazzālī had already brought this type of commentary under the protective wing of mainstream Islam in his *Iḥyā'*: "I mean by 'Lesser Resurrection' the state of death, for the Prophet—God bless him and give him peace—said, 'He who has died has undergone his resurrection.'" He explains that all the terms that refer to the Greater Resurrection have their equal (*naẓīr*) in the Lesser Resurrection. Thus, the earth corresponds to the body, mountains to bones, the sky to the head, the sun to the heart, the stars to the senses, grass to hair, trees to limbs, etc.

> So when the elements of your body are destroyed through death, "The earth will be shaken with a mighty shaking" (XCIX, 1); when the bones are separated from the flesh, "The earth and the mountains will be lifted up and crushed with a single blow" (LXIX, 14); when the bones decay, "The mountains will be scattered like ashes" (LXXVII, 10); when your heart is darkened through death, "The sun will be darkened" (LXXXI, 1); when your hearing, sight, and other senses cease to work, "The stars will be thrown down" (LXXXI, 2); when your brain is split, "The sky will be split asunder" (LV, 37). . . . . The instant you die, the Lesser Resurrection will take place for you; nevertheless, you will not miss anything of the Greater Resurrection.[56]

Bābā Ṭāhir of Hamadān (fifth/eleventh century) employs a similar method of interpretation to explain the events that follow the resurrection:

> People are now standing on the Path though they are unaware, for in the eyes of the Sufis, this world is the next world. In the hereafter there will be a Path, a Balance, a Garden, and a Fire. The Path of the Sufis in this world is their way, which is "sharper than a sword." Their Balances are their hearts,

35. "The Mirāj of the Prophet," *Khamsah Nizami.*

which are the best of all balances; their Garden is the turning of their hearts [toward God], and their Fire is the turning of their hearts away [from Him].[57]

In discussing the Lesser and Greater Resurrections, al-Qūnawī adds the Greatest Resurrection (*qiyāmat-i ʿuzmā*), which he defines as "the Arrival (*wuṣūl*) achieved by the gnostic, the moment when the two created worlds are erased and obliterated by the light of Unity, so that nothing remains but the Living, the Self-Subsistent."[58] ʿAzīz al-Dīn Nasafī speaks of lesser, intermediate, greater, and greatest resurrections and identifies them with four stages of human life: birth, the acquisition of faith, perfection in knowledge, and perfection in sanctity.[59] Sayyid Ḥaydar Āmulī (d. after 787/1385), a follower of Ibn ʿArabī who is careful to support his views with the sayings of the Shīʿite Imams, details several kinds of resurrection, as indicated in the accompanying table.[60]

KINDS OF RESURRECTION
according to Sayyid Ḥaydar Āmulī

			lesser	intermediate	greater
microcosmic	formal (*ṣūrī*)		physical death	the period in the grave (the *barzakh*)	the gathering on the Day of Resurrection
microcosmic	supraformal (*maʿnawī*)		"voluntary death" or spiritual awakening	transmutation of moral qualities	annihilation of self and subsistence in God
macrocosmic	formal	one view	destruction of the world through the return of compound things to the domain of simple elemental bodies	return of simple things to the *materia prima*	return of the souls and spirits to the First Substance
macrocosmic	formal	another view	the appearance of the Mahdī	transformation of the sensory world into the *barzakh*	the bodily resurrection
macrocosmic	supraformal		return of particular souls to the Universal Soul	return of particular spirits to the Greatest Spirit	return of intellects to the First Intellect

Al-Jīlī interprets the events that take place at the end of time in terms of the voluntary death or Greatest Resurrection experienced by the spiritual traveler. According to a *ḥadīth,* Gog and Magog will appear on the earth, eating its fruits and drinking its seas; once they are slain, the earth will revive. In the same way, the ego's agitation and corrupt thoughts take possession of the earth of man's heart, eat its fruits, and drink its seas, so that no trace of spiritual knowledge can appear. Then God's angels annihilate these satanic whisperings with sciences from God: the earth is revived and it gives abundant harvest. This is a mark of man's gaining proximity to God. As for the beast of the earth, it will come to tell the earth's inhabitants about the truth of the promises concerning the resurrection. In the same way, the traveler reaches a stage of unveiling where he comes to understand the inward mysteries of religion; this is a favor from God, so that "the troops of his faith will not retreat before the armies of the continuing veil." Just as the people will not be convinced of the coming of the Hour until the appearance of the beast, so the gnostic will not understand all the requisites of Divinity until the spirit appears from out of the earth of his bodily nature. The conflict between al-Dajjāl and Jesus refers to the battle between the ego and the spirit, while the appearance of the Mahdī alludes to man's becoming "the Possessor of Equilibrium at the pinnacle of every perfection." Finally, the rising of the sun from the west marks the realization of the ultimate human perfection.[61]

The Greater Resurrection

In discussing Quran L, 22, the commentator Rashīd al-Dīn Maybudī (early sixth/twelfth century) points out that the world of the *barzakh* has been compared to the womb. Ibn 'Arabī expands on this idea, explaining that after death man begins to reap the fruit of his life in this world; "having undergone various stages of development, he is born on the Day of Resurrection."[62] The imaginal bodies that men possess in the *barzakh* are like lamps within which the spirit is lit. Then "the Trumpet shall be blown, and whosoever is in the heavens and whosoever is in the earth shall swoon, save whom God wills" (XXXIX, 68). At this first blast on the trumpet, the lamps will be extinguished and transferred into resurrection bodies. "Then it shall be blown again, and lo, they shall stand beholding" (XXXIX, 68); that is, once again the lamps will be lit. Some of those newly awakened will ask, "Who roused us out of our sleeping place?" (XXXVI, 52). People will gradually forget their situation in the *barzakh* and imagine that it had been a dream, even though, when they first entered the *barzakh,* that had been an awakening compared with their life in the world.[63] The resurrection is far more real and intense than the *barzakh,* just as the latter is more real than the world. This is why, after death, the people of Pharaoh are "exposed morning and evening" to the fire (XL, 45), but they do not enter into it, since they are still in the *barzakh.* But "on the day when the Hour is come: 'Admit the people of Pharaoh into the more intense chastisement'" (XL, 46).[64]

Although most theologians maintained that the resurrection body would be the same body as that which existed in the world, al-Ghazzālī among others points out that even this earthly body does not stay the same, since it constantly changes throughout life. The truth of the matter is that "the body is only a mount; though the horse should change, the rider stays the same."[65] Najm al-Dīn Rāzī suggests that the difference between the earthly body and the resurrection body lies in its degree of "subtlety" (*laṭāfah*). In both cases the body belongs to the realm of nature and is therefore compounded of the four elements; but in this world earth and water predominate, whereas in the next world fire and air predominate. Then, "when the form is subtle and luminous, it no longer interferes with the spirit." So on that day people will display outwardly the realities that are today latent in their hearts.[66]

As already indicated, Mullā Ṣadrā holds that the resurrection body is identical with the earthly body in "form." Ibn 'Arabī and his followers speak of a "sensory" resurrection at the level of "nature," that is, within the domain of the four elements, but the ontological level of hell will correspond to that of this lower world, with its multiplicity and disequilibrium. Al-Qūnawī explains that the people of wretchedness will meet all their thoughts, knowledge, states, and works in forms appropriate to their debased ontological level, while the spiritual dimensions of these things will depart from them. In contrast, the thoughts, states, and works of the people of felicity will be transformed into spiritual entities, while their resurrection bodies will subsist inside themselves. In this world, a person's inward reality is infinitely malleable and "nondelimited" (*muṭlaq*), whereas his outward form and acts are defined and determined. In paradise, "the property of nondelimitation will pertain to the outward dimension, while the property of delimitation will belong to the inward."[67]

If it is true that the inward state of man is revealed at the Lesser Resurrection, this is even more true at the Greater Resurrection, the day when "that which is in the breasts is brought out" (C, 10) and "secrets are divulged" (LXXXVI, 9). In the words of Sanā'ī,

> If you die with an ugly character, you will be resurrected in the form of a beast. . . .
> When meaning comes out of the house into the street, your face will be impressed with what is in your heart.

For the sake of display, the Originator of Qualities will put potentiality
on the inside and actuality on the outside.[68]

The result of not having realized "justice" and "equilibrium" in this world becomes manifest in the very form in which the resurrection body appears. Al-Ghazzālī had spoken of the "pig" and the "dog" within man, that is, the faculties of beastliness or "concupiscence" (*shahwah*) and predatoriness or "irascibility" (*ghaḍab*), which must be overcome by the intellect. Al-Qūnawī among others states that man will assume corporeal shape in the *barzakh* according to the character that dominated over him in this world. Thus, "if concupiscence dominated, he will appear in the form of a pig, and if irascibility dominated, he will appear as a dog."[69]

According to Rūmī,

There are thousands of wolves and pigs in our existence, good and evil, fair and foul.
Man's properties are determined by the trait that predominates:
If gold is more than copper, then he is gold.
Of necessity you will be given form at the Resurrection in accordance with the character that predominates in your existence.[70]

Among the philosophers, al-Fārābī (d. 339/950) had interpreted certain teachings of Plato in similar terms, and Shī'ite thinkers like Ibn Abī Jumhūr (d. 901/1494) and especially Mullā Ṣadrā develop this mode of interpretation in detail, citing many Quranic verses and *ḥadīths* in support of their arguments. Mullā Ṣadrā holds that the very essences of human souls will diverge in the hereafter and that they will become many species, falling into four main genera (corresponding to al-Ghazzālī's pig, dog, devil, and wise man). This is not transmigration (*tanāsukh*), say our authors, since it does not take place in this world, but on another plane of existence.[71]

Though the theologians and most Sufis did not question the reality of the bodily resurrection, the early philosophers were inclined to be skeptical, since they could find no rational proofs outside revelation to support it. Nonetheless, they considered the survival of the soul a foregone conclusion, since it belongs by nature to the domain of disengaged and incorruptible spiritual substances; then its bliss is for it to contemplate the highest realities and God Himself. According to Ibn Sīnā, if the soul attains to perfection, after death it will become connected to the Divine and be plunged into true pleasure. Imperfect souls experience various degrees of pleasure or pain, according to the degree to which they have become detached from the body or remained immersed in the world. Concerning bodily resurrection, Ibn Sīnā anticipates later developments in Islamic thought by suggesting that certain souls may experience the events described in the Quran and the *Ḥadīth* because these descriptions had shaped their imaginal faculties; they will then perceive what they had believed they would perceive. After all, he says, imaginal forms are stronger than sensory forms, as can be observed in dreams. But the images contemplated in the next world are more stable than those seen in dreams because the body no longer interferes with perception.[72]

Ibn Sīnā also suggests that the Islamic teachings about bodily resurrection should be interpreted allegorically. Islam is addressed to all men, not just philosophers and sages, so it has to speak a language understood by everyone, that of corporeal realities. "Our Prophet–God bless him and give him peace–perfected this mode of explanation such that nothing can be added to it." Ibn Sīnā then turns the tables on those Christian missionaries who were later to criticize Islam for its "sensual" descriptions of paradise. He says that the Christians accept the bodily resurrection but fail to describe the various forms of corporeal ease and punishment; instead they suggest that men will be like angels. But "most people think–though they do not dare say so because of their fear [of the religious law]–that angels are miserable creatures who have no ease or joy. They do not eat, drink, or have sexual intercourse, and they occupy themselves constantly with unrequited worship. The common people think this way since they cannot begin to understand the nature of true felicity and spiritual joy."[73]

Many Sufis agreed that the Quranic data need not be taken literally. Sulṭān Walad writes:

> The true nature of meanings (*ma'ānī*) cannot be expressed in words; they do not resemble anything, nor are they opposed to anything. But something has to be said in keeping with the understandings of people so that they will strive to reach those meanings. In the same way, one explains to a child the pleasure of kissing by comparing a woman's lips to sugar. . . . But in fact, what is the relationship between lips and sugar? There is no resemblance at all. Likewise God explains the Garden in terms of houris, castles, trees, and rivers in order that it may be understood in these terms. But in fact, how should the Garden resemble such things? For they are transitory, while it is eternal. What relation is there between the transitory and the eternal?[74]

Al-Ghazzālī displays the concern of the theologian to affirm the bodily nature of the resurrection, but he reminds us that the soul will also be resurrected, so spiritual delights and torments must also be taken into account. The Quran refers to them in such verses as, "What shall teach you about the Crusher? The kindled Fire of God, roaring over the hearts" (CIV, 5–7). Al-Ghazzālī divides this spiritual fire into three kinds: (1) the fire of separation from worldly desires, which is particularly strong at death and in the *barzakh;* (2) the fire of shame and disgrace, which overcomes man at the resurrection when all his deeds are displayed; (3) the fire of regret over being deprived of the vision of God, which is the lasting torment of hell.[75]

All the inhabitants of the garden will possess "bodies," but their spirits will dwell in different degrees of proximity to God. Already at the time of the Prophet, there are references to eight levels and one hundred degrees of paradise; many authorities rank the levels in accordance with different names employed in the Quran.[76] The Quran distinguishes between the companions of the right (as opposed to the companions of the left in hell) and the Foremost or "Those Brought Nigh" (LVI, 8–10). In al-Qūnawī's words, "The Garden, houris, castles, fowl, and sweetmeats belong to the Companions of the Right; theophany (*tajallī*), true knowledge, and Encounter belong to Those Brought Nigh."[77] According to some accounts, the vision of God guaranteed to the faithful in several *ḥadīths* and alluded to in the Quran (e.g., LXXV, 23) will take place at the Dune of White Musk; Ibn 'Arabī states that all of the people of the garden will take stations there, "in keeping with their degrees of knowledge of God, not the degree of their works; for works pertain to the bliss of the Garden, not to the contemplation of the All-Merciful."[78] In this context many authorities cite the *ḥadīth* "I have prepared for My righteous servants what eye has not seen, nor ear has heard, nor has entered the heart of any man . . . 'No soul knows what is laid up for them secretly' (Quran XXXII, 17)"; or again, "God has a Garden in which are no houris, castles, milk, or honey; our Lord shows Himself in theophany, laughing (*ḍāḥik*)."

According to Bāyazīd Basṭāmī (d. ca. 261/874), all the faithful will see God once in the garden, but after that only the elect will continue to see Him. For, according to the well-known *ḥadīth,* "in the Garden is a market where there is no buying or selling, only the forms of men and women; when a man desires a form, he enters into it." Those who enter a form, says Bāyazīd, will never again go to visit God: "God misleads you in this life as to the market, and also in the next; you will always be enslaved to the market."[79] Ibn 'Arabī and his followers explain the market of the garden as a branch of the world of nondelimited imagination: from it the forms of the felicitous will be constantly renewed.[80]

The various realities that will be observed after the resurrection, such as the balance, the path, the Book, and the pool, are interpreted in many ways. Imam Ja'far had already explained that the balance is in fact the prophets and their appointed heirs (i.e., the Imams). Al-Ghazzālī points out that a "balance" is "that which distinguishes more from less"; even in this world balances take many forms, so there is no reason to suppose that the balance in the next world will necessarily resemble anything we know here. 'Ayn al-Quḍāt says that the balance is the human intellect; al-Qūnawī that it is the personification in imaginal form of the Divine Attribute of Justice; and 'Azīz al-Dīn Nasafī that it is man's very existence, the two pans being his receptivity toward good and evil.[81] Analogous explanations of other eschatological realities can be found in the works of these and many other figures. In his *Wisdom of the Throne* Mullā Ṣadrā makes use of the whole tradition of Islamic eschatology in offering several interpretations for each symbol.[82]

To sum up the Islamic teachings, one can recall that man, through the very fact that he was created upon the Form of the All-Merciful, has been given God's Trust: "We offered the Trust to the heavens and the earth and the mountains, but they refused to carry it and were afraid of it; and man carried it" (XXXIII, 72). The role of Islam is to guide man on the straight path of justice and equilibrium, so that he can carry the Trust and fulfill his rightful function as God's vicegerent. But, the above verse continues, man is "sinful, very foolish" to the extent that he fails to live up to his Divine Form. Hence, through the very majesty of his freedom and responsibility, he is able to cut himself off from the effusion of Mercy and Light that fills the universe. Whether he experiences God's Mercy or Wrath, the next stages of his existence depend upon his own choice.

Notes

1. Sa'ad al-Dīn Taftāzānī, *Sharḥ al-'aqā'id al-nasafiyyah* (Delhi: Kutubkhāna-yi Rashīdiyyah, n.d.) 76–82, 123; see the translation in E. E. Elder, *A Commentary on the Creed of Islam* (New York: Columbia University Press, 1950) 99, 165.
2. Al-Ghazzālī, *Iḥyā' 'ulūm al-dīn* IV.8.2 (Cairo: Maṭba'at al-'Āmirat al-Sharafiyyah, 1326/1908) 4:370.
3. Kāshānī , *Miṣbāḥ al-hidāyah*, ed. J. Humā'ī (Tehran: Chāpkhāna-yi Majlis, 1325/1946) 49.
4. Al-Ghazzālī, *Kīmiyā-yi sa'ādat*, ed. A. Ārām (Tehran: Markazī, 1319/1940) 98.
5. Al-Ghazzālī, *Al-Arba'īn*, ed. M. M. Abu'l-'Alā' (Cairo: Maktabat al-Jundī, 1970) 275.
6. Rāzī, *Mirṣād ad-'ibād*, trans. H. Algar, *The Path of God's Bondsmen from Origin to Return* (Delmar, NY: Caravan Books, 1982) 387–93.
7. Jāmī, *Haft awrang*, ed. M. Mudarrisī Gīlānī (Tehran: Kitābfurūshī-yi Sa'dī, 1337/1958) 109.
8. Mullā Ṣadrā, *Al-Asfār* (Tehran, 1282/1865–66) 857.13.
9. Rāzī, *Path*, p. 363, with minor changes.
10. Nasafī, *Zubdat al-ḥaqā'iq*, appended to Jāmī, *Ashi''at al-lama'āt*, ed. H. Rabbānī (Tehran: Kitābkhāna-yi 'Ilmiyya-yi Ḥāmidī, 1352/1973) 325–27.
11. Ibn Sīnā, *Al-Najāh* (Cairo: Maṭba'at al-Sa'ādah, 1938) 293; cf. A. J. Arberry's translation of this passage in Avicenna, *On Theology* (London: John Murray, 1951) 67.

12. F. Meier, "The Problem of Nature in the Esoteric Monism of Islam," in *Spirit and Nature: Papers from the Eranos Yearbooks,* trans. R. Manheim (Bollingen Series 30.1; Princeton, NJ: Princeton University Press, 1954) 195.

13. Sanā'ī, *Ḥadīqat al-ḥaqīqah,* ed. Mudarris Raḍawī (Tehran: Sipihr, 1329/1950) 382.

14. Rūmī, *Fīhi mā fīhi,* ed. B. Furūzānfar (Tehran: Amīr Kabīr, 1348/1969) 79; cf. A. J. Arberry, trans., *Discourses of Rumi* (London: John Murray, 1961) 89; see also W. C. Chittick, *The Sufi Path of Love: The Spiritual Teachings of Rumi* (Albany, NY: State University of New York Press, 1983) 206–12.

15. Sulṭān Walad, *Walad-nāmah,* ed. J. Humā'ī (Tehran: Iqbāl, 1316/1937) 261.

16. Rūmī, *Kulliyyāt-i Shams yā dīwān-i kabīr,* ed. B. Furūzānfar (Tehran: University of Tehran, 1336–46/1957–67) verse 6400.

17. Ibn ʿArabī, *Tarjumān al-ashwāq,* trans. R. A. Nicholson (London: Oriental Translation Fund, 1911) 67.

18. Ibn ʿArabī, *Fuṣūṣ al ḥikam,* ed. A. ʿAfīfī (Beirut: Dār al-Kitāb al-ʿArabī, 1946) 121; cf. *The Bezels of Wisdom,* trans. R. W. J. Austin (Ramsey, NJ: Paulist Press, 1980) 149.

19. Mullā Ṣadrā, *The Wisdom of the Throne,* trans. J. W. Morris (Princeton, NJ: Princeton University Press, 1981) 148–49.

20. S. J. Āshtiyānī, *Sharḥ bar zād al-musāfir-i Mullā Ṣadrā: Maʿād-i jismānī* (2nd ed.; Tehran: Imperial Iranian Academy of Philosophy, 1359/1980) 218, 244.

21. F. Rahman, *Major Themes of the Qur'ān* (Minneapolis and Chicago: Bibliotheca Islamica, 1980) 17, 112.

22. Ibn ʿArabī, *Al-Futūḥāt al-makkiyyah* (Beirut: Dār Ṣādir, n.d.) vol. 2, 627.27.

23. Ibid., vol. 3, 187–88; cf. Chittick, *Sufi Path,* 71–72.

24. *Al-Asfār,* 853.15.

25. See Mullā Ṣadrā, *Wisdom of the Throne,* 161ff.

26. Ibn ʿArabī, *Al-Futūḥāt,* vol. 3, 361.5.

27. Cf. Jāmī, *Naqd al-nuṣūṣ,* ed. W. C. Chittick (Tehran: Imperial Iranian Academy of Philosophy, 1977) 56–57.

28. Mullā Ṣadrā, *Wisdom of the Throne,* 163.

29. Mullā Ṣadrā, *Al-Asfār,* 853.23.

30. Al-Ṭūsī, *The Nasirean Ethics,* trans. G. M. Wickens (London: Allen & Unwin, 1964) 95; cf. Avicenna, *On Theology,* 72; al-Ghazzālī, *Iḥyā'* III.2.2, 3,39–40.

31. Al-Ghazzālī, *Al-Madnūn bihi ʿalā ghayr ahlihi,* in *Al-Quṣūr al-ʿawālī min rasā'il al-Imām al-Ghazzālī* (Cairo: Maktabat al-Jundī, 1970) 2:160.

32. R. J. McCarthy, *Freedom and Fulfillment: An Annotated Translation of al-Ghazālī's al-Munqidh min al-Dalāl and other Relevant Works of al-Ghazālī* (Boston: Twayne, 1980) 377; cf. Mullā Ṣadrā, *Wisdom of the Throne,* 146.

33. McCarthy, *Freedom,* 349; *Ninety-nine Names of God,* trans. R. Stade (Ibadan: Daystar Press, 1970) 12.

34. Al-Farghānī, *Muntaha'l-madārik* (Cairo: ʿAbd al-Raḥīm al-Bukhārī, 1293/1876) 2:82; idem, *Mashāriq al-darārī,* ed. S. J. Āshtiyānī (Tehran: Imperial Iranian Academy of Philosophy, 1357/1978) 467–68. Concerning the name *al-Raḥīm,* note the Quranic distinction, pointed out by Ibn ʿArabī, between the "mercy of gratuitous gift," given to all creatures, and the "mercy of prescription," given to the faithful; see W. C. Chittick, "Ibn ʿArabī's Own Summary of the *Fuṣūṣ,*" *Journal of the Muhyiddin Ibn ʿArabi Society* 1 (1982) 62.

35. Al-Jīlī, *Al-Insān al-kāmil,* chap. 58 (Cairo: Muḥammad ʿAlī Ṣabīḥ, 1963) 2:30.

36. Abū Ḥanīfah, *Wasiyyah,* article 7; cf. A. J. Wensinck, *The Muslim Creed* (London: Frank Cass, 1932) 126, 142ff.

37. Chittick, "Ibn ʿArabī's Own Summary," 61.

38. Al-Niffarī, *The Mawāqif and Mukhāṭabāt,* ed. A. J. Arberry (London: Luzac, 1935): *Mukhāṭabāt* 27.10; *Mawāqif,* 67.65–70, 17.6.

39. F. Schuon, *Understanding Islam,* trans. D. M. Matheson (London: Allen & Unwin, 1979) 71, 73.

40. Al-Niffarī, *Mawāqif* 1.21; Ibn 'Arabī, *Al-Futūḥāt al-makkiyyah,* ed. ʿU. Yaḥyā (Cairo: al-Hay'at al-Miṣriyyat al-ʿĀmmat li'l-Kitāb, 1975) 4:389.

41. J. I. Smith and Y. Y. Haddad, *The Islamic Understanding of Death and Resurrection* (Albany, NY: State University of New York Press, 1981) 95; Ibn 'Arabī, *Fuṣūṣ al-ḥikam,* chap. 7; *Al-Futūḥāt,* ed. Yaḥyā, 3:67; Beirut ed., vol. 3, 315.-3, 328.-9, 389.-14.

42. J. I. Smith, "The Understanding of *Nafs* and *Rūḥ* in Contemporary Muslim Considerations of the Nature of Sleep and Death," *The Muslim World* 69 (1979) 153–54.

43. Al-Ghazzālī, *Al-Madnūn,* 166 (cf. Ibn 'Arabī, *Al-Futūḥāt,* Beirut ed., vol. 3, 198.23); idem, *Kīmiyā,* 93 (cf. *Al-Arbaʿīn,* 291).

44. Al-Ghazzālī, *Al-Arbaʿīn,* 290; cf. *Kīmiyā,* 93–94; *Iḥyā'* IV.10.8, 4, 362.

45. Al-Ghazzālī, *Kīmiyā,* 94.

46. Ibid., 94; *Al-Arbaʿīn,* 291.

47. Al-Ghazzālī, *Iḥyā'* IV.10.7, 4, 358–59; *Kīmiyā,* 85; *Al-Arbaʿīn,* 282.

48. Al-Ghazzālī, *Al-Madnūn,* 158.

49. Al-Ṭūsī, *Nasirean Ethics,* 138.

50. Rūmī, *Mathnawī,* ed. R. A. Nicholson (London: Luzac, 1925–40) book 3, vv. 3441–42.

51. Al-Qūnawī, *Tabṣirat al-mubtadī,* 3.3, trans. W. C. Chittick, forthcoming.

52. Sanā'ī, *Dīwān,* ed. Mudarris Raḍawī (Tehran: Ibn Sīnā, 1341/1962) 708.

53. Rūmī, *Kulliyyāt,* vv. 20435–36; cf. W. C. Chittick, *Sufi Path,* 101–7.

54. Rūmī, *Mathnawī,* book 2, vv. 277–78.

55. 'Ayn al-Quḍāt, *Tamhīdāt,* ed. 'A. ʿUsayrān in *Muṣannafāt-i 'Ayn al-Quḍāt Hamadānī* (Tehran: Tehran University, 1341/1962) 287, 289. For a good summary of this whole discussion, see Lāhījī (d. 912/1506–7), *Sharḥ-i Gulshan-i rāz,* ed. K. Samīʿī (Tehran: Kitābfurūshī-yi Maḥmūdī, 1337/1958) 521–27.

56. Al-Ghazzālī, *Iḥyā'* IV.2.1, 4, 46–47.

57. J. Maqṣūd, *Sharḥ-i aḥwāl wa āthār wa du-baytīhā-yi Bābā Ṭāhir ʿUryān* (Tehran: Anjuman-i Āthār-i Millī, 1354/1975) 403.

58. Al-Qūnawī, *Tabṣirat al-mubtadī,* 3.3.

59. Nasafī, *Kashf al-ḥaqā'iq,* ed. A. Mahdawī Dāmghānī (Tehran: Bungāh-i Tarjamah wa Nashr-i Kitāb, 1344/1965) 211.

60. Āmulī, *Asrār al-sharīʿah wa aṭwār al-ṭarīqah wa anwār al-ḥaqīqah,* ed. M. Khwājawī (Tehran: Mu'assasa-yi Muṭālaʿāt wa Taḥqīqāt-i Farhangī, 1362/1983) 104–36.

61. Al-Jīlī, *Al-Insān al-kāmil,* chap. 61; 2:49–52.

62. Ibn 'Arabī, *Al-Futūḥāt,* Beirut ed., vol. 3, 250.19.

63. Ibn 'Arabī, *Al-Futūḥāt,* ed. Yaḥyā, 4:456–67.

64. Ibid., 4:424.

65. Al-Ghazzālī, *Kīmiyā,* 80.

66. Rāzī, *Path,* 391–92.

67. Al-Qūnawī, *Al-Nafaḥāt al-ilāhiyyah* (Tehran: Aḥmad Shīrāzī, 1316/1898–99) 115.

68. Sanā'ī, *Ḥadīqah,* 380.

69. Al-Qūnawī, *Tabṣirat al-mubtadī,* 3.3.

70. Rūmī, *Mathnawī,* book 2, vv. 277–78.

71. M. Mahdi, *Alfarabi's Philosophy of Plato and Aristotle* (New York: Free Press of

Glencoe, 1962) 64; Ibn Abī Jumhūr, *Al-Mujlī* (Tehran: Aḥmad Shīrāzī, 1329/1911) 506–7; Mullā Ṣadrā, *Wisdom of the Throne,* 145–47; al-Qūnawī, *Al-Nafaḥāt,* 116; Āshtiyānī, *Sharḥ bar zād al-musāfir,* 56, 122–23, 128.

72. Ibn Sīnā, *On Theology,* 69ff.; quotations from 75; cf. Suhrawardī, *Ḥikmat al-ishrāq,* in *Oeuvres philosophiques et mystiques,* ed. H. Corbin (Tehran and Paris: Institut Franco-Iranien, 1952) 229ff.

73. Ibn Sīnā, *Risālah aḍḥawiyyah fī amr al-ma'ād,* ed. S. Dunyā (Cairo: Dār al-Fikr al-'Arabī, 1949) 60–62; cf. *Averroes' Tahāfut al-tahāfut,* trans. S. van den Bergh (London: Luzac, 1969) 1:361.

74. Sulṭān Walad, *Walad-nāmah,* 298.

75. Al-Ghazzālī, *Kīmiyā,* 98, 91–96; *al-Arba'īn,* 288–97.

76. See the *ḥadīths* in *Mishkāt al-maṣābīḥ,* trans. J. Robson (Lahore: M. Ashraf, 1963–65) 1197, 1200; cf. Al-Kisā'ī's account in *A Reader on Islam,* ed. A. Jeffery (The Hague: Mouton, 1962) 172.

77. Al-Qūnawī, *Tabṣirat al-mubtadī,* 3.3.

78. Ibn 'Arabī, *Al-Futūḥāt,* ed. Yaḥyā, 5:77.

79. L. Massignon, *The Passion of al-Ḥallāj: Mystic and Martyr of Islam,* trans. H. Mason (Princeton, NJ: Princeton University Press, 1982) 3:166–67.

80. Ibn 'Arabī, *Al-Futūḥāt,* Beirut ed., vol. 2, 628.3; al-Qūnawī, *Al-Nuṣūṣ,* appended to al-Kāshānī, *Sharḥ manāzil al-sā'irīn* (Tehran: Ebrāhīm Lārījānī, 1315/1897–98) 292.

81. Majlisī, *Biḥār al-anwār* (2nd ed.; Beirut: Mu'assasat al-Wafā', 1983) 7:249; al-Ghazzālī, *Al-Madnūn,* 159; 'Ayn al-Quḍāt, *Tamhīdāt,* 290; al-Qūnawī, letter to a disciple, MS 1633 in the Konya Mevlana Müzesi, fol. 115; Nasafī, *Kashf al-ḥaqā'iq,* 184; cf. Mullā Ṣadrā, *Wisdom of the Throne,* 212–14.

82. Mullā Ṣadrā, *Wisdom of the Throne,* 180ff.

Glossary

ʿabd. Slave, servant, the state in which man should be before God, according to Islam.

ʿabd Allāh. The servant of God, also one of the names of the Prophet.

adab. Courtesy, culture, correct comportment.

ʿadālah. Justice.

ādam-i rūḥānī. Spiritual Adam, man's archetype, according to Ismāʿīlī teachings.

ʿadhāb. Suffering and pain usually associated with the posthumous states of those who have committed sin.

ʿādil. Just, fair, a Divine Name, God being the Just, *al-ʿĀdil.*

al-ʿAfū. The Forgiver, a Divine Name.

al-Aḥad. The One, a Divine Name.

aḥadiyyah. Oneness, the state in which all of God's Names and Qualities are one with His Essence.

ʿahd. Covenant, agreement, promise.

ahl al-bayt. "People of the household," a term used in Shīʿism to refer to the family of the Prophet such as Fāṭimah, ʿAlī, their sons Ḥasan and Ḥusayn and their descendants.

ahl al-sunnah. The people who follow the traditions of the Prophet, constituting the majority who are usually referred to as Sunnis.

ākhirah. The next world, the world of resurrection and eschatological realities.

akhlāq. Ethics and also character.

ʿālam al-ghayb. The invisible world, the spiritual world.

ʿālam al-ibdāʿ. The world of origination used in Ismāʿīlī cosmology to refer to the highest level of the cosmos.

ʿālam al-mithāl. The world of similitude, usually identified with the imaginal world.

ʿālam al-takhayyul. The imaginal world, standing between the physical and the purely intelligible worlds.

al-ʿAlīm. The Knower, a Divine Name.

Allāhᵘ akbar. "God is the greatest," the "motto" of Islam.

ʿamal (pl. *aʿmāl*). Act, understood both in the ordinary and in the religious sense.

amānah. The trust that God has placed upon man's shoulders by creating him in His image and giving him the freedom to accept His Lordship through faith or to reject it.

amīr al-muʾminīn. Commander of the faithful, a title given in Sunnism to the caliphs and in Shīʿism only to ʿAlī ibn Abī Ṭālib.

amr. Command, order.

al-amr biʾl-maʿrūf waʾl-nahy ʿan al-munkar. To order the good and exhort against that which is forbidden, one of the important precepts of nearly every school within Islam.

anṣār. Helpers, those in Medina who helped the Prophet in establishing the first Islamic community after his migration from Mecca to that city.

ʿaql. The intellect, also reason, at once metacosmic, cosmic, and within the human microcosm.

al-ʿaql al-awwal. The First Intellect.

al-ʿaql al-faʿʿāl. The Active Intellect.

ʿArafāt. The plain near Mecca where the pilgrims assemble before the end of the rite of pilgrimage.

al-ʿārif biʾLlāh. The gnostic, he who knows by God

ʿArsh. The Divine Empyrean and Throne.

asās. The "foundation," the interpreter of the inner meaning of Revelation; a title given by the Ismaʿīlis to ʿAlī.

aṣḥāb ḥall waʾl-ʿaqd. People of loosening and binding, a title given to the religious scholars (*ʿulamāʾ*) who have the authority to interpret the Divine Law.

ʿāshūrāʾ. The tenth day of Muḥarram, when Ḥusayn was martyred.

al-asmāʾ waʾl-ṣifāt. The Names and Qualities or Attributes of God.

ʿaṣr. Afternoon, the third time specified for the performance of the daily prayers, between midday and sunset.

al-aʿyān al-thābitah. The "immutable archetypes" or fixed "entities"; the essences of all things as they possess reality in Divine Knowledge and before becoming existentiated.

āyah (pl. *āyāt*). Sign, symbol, or portent. The phenomena of the created order both macrocosmic and microcosmic are identified as "signs" of God. The verses of the Quran are also called *āyah.*

āyat Allāh (pl. *āyāt Allāh*). Sign or portent of God. In Shīʿism since the late thirteenth/nineteenth century the term has become an honorary title for the highest religious dignitaries.

ʿayn al-yaqīn. Eye of certainty.

ʿazm. Determination.

balad al-amīn. The city or abode of peace and protection.

baqāʾ. Subsistence, the highest station in Sufism, in which the soul subsists in God after experiencing annihilation (*fanāʾ*).

barakah. Grace or Divine Presence, which permeates the universe and draws man back to God.

barzakh. Intermediate state, isthmus, the period between death and resurrection.

basṭ. Expansion.

bāṭin. The inward, esoteric, or hidden aspect of a being, doctrine, or religion.

bayʿah. Pact made between the head of the Islamic community and leaders within the community, as well as the initiatic pact made between the spiritual master and the disciple. Both of these practices go back to the Prophet.

al-Dajjāl. The Antichrist.

dāʿī. Ismāʿīlī missionary.

dalīl (pl. *dalāʾil*). Argument, proof, guide.

dār al-islām. The land or abode of Islam.

daʿwā. Invitation to accept a religion or a particular school within a religion; missionary activity associated in the classical period especially with Ismāʿīlism.

dhākir. Invoker.

al-Dhāt. The Divine Essence or Ipseity.

dhawq. Taste, tasted knowledge, intuition.

dhikr Allāh. The invocation, remembrance, and mentioning of the Name of Allah.

dhikr al-lisān. Invocation of the tongue.

dhikr al-qalb. Invocation of the heart.

dhikr al-ṣadr. Invocation of the chest in which the Divine Name is invoked in a rhythmic and audible manner, often accompanied by bodily movements.

dhikr al-sirr. Invocation of man's secret and innermost self.

dīn. Religion, tradition.

dīn al-fiṭrah. The primordial religion which man carries at the depth of his nature and with which Islam identifies itself.

al-dīn al-ḥanīf. The primal or primordial religion of monotheism.

fajr. Dawn, daybreak, associated with the first time set for the performance of the daily prayers.

falāḥ. Salvation, deliverance.

falak. Heavenly sphere, heaven, sky.

falsafah. Philosophy.

fanā'. Annihilation or extinction, a state in Sufism in which the soul becomes annihilated before God.

al-fanā' fi'l-Dhāt. Annihilation in the Divine Essence.

al-fanā' fi'l-shaykh. Annihilation in the spiritual master.

faqīh (pl. *fuqahā'*). Jurisprudent, doctor of the Sacred Law (*Sharī'ah*).

faqīr. A male Sufi disciple.

faqīrah. A female Sufi disciple.

faqr. Poverty, used in the religious context as spiritual poverty and identified with the practice of Sufism.

farḍ. That which is obligatory upon a person according to the dicta of the *Sharī'ah.*

farq. Separation from God.

fawātiḥ al-suwar. Letters that begin various chapters of the Quran.

fi'l (pl. *af'āl*). Act.

fiṭrah. Primordial nature, original perfection.

al-Furqān. "Discernment," "Criterion," one of the names of the Quran.

Ghadīr Khumm. A pool of water near Mecca where the Prophet stopped after the last pilgrimage and, according to the Shī'ites, chose 'Alī as his successor.

al-Ghafūr. The Forgiver, a Divine Name.

al-Ghālib. The Victorious, a Name of God.

al-Ghanī. The Rich, a Divine Name.

ghulām (pl. *ghilmān*). Lad, servant.

ginān. Ismā'īlī religious literature, often in the form of poetry and of a popular nature making use of local languages of India and often mixing Hindu mythology with Islamic teachings.

ḥabīb. Friend, one of the titles of the Prophet, who was called "the Friend of God," Ḥabīb Allāh.

al-ḥaḍarāt al-ilāhiyyat al-khams. The five Divine Presences which Ibn 'Arabī and certain members of his school consider to constitute reality as such.

al-Hādī. The Guide, one of the Names of God.

ḥadīth (pl. *aḥādīth*). Saying of the Prophet of Islam. In Shīʿism the term is used also for the sayings of one of the twelve Imams, but a clear distinction is made between the sayings of the Prophet and those of the Imams.

ḥadīth qudsī. "Sacred" *ḥadīth*, a saying of the Prophet in which God speaks in the first person.

ḥaḍrat al-dhikr. Audible invocation of the Names of God in a Sufi gathering usually accompanied by the rhythmic movement of the body.

al-hāhūt. The Divine Essence or Ipseity.

ḥajj. Pilgrimage to the house of God in Mecca.

ḥakīm (pl. *ḥukamāʾ*). Sage, wise man, theosopher, philosopher, physician.

al-ḥakīm al-mutaʾallih. Theosopher, theomorphic sage.

ḥāl (pl. *aḥwāl*). State, usually used in Sufism as spiritual state or condition which the disciple experiences upon the path. It is also used as state of ecstasy induced by music, poetry, or any other form of beauty.

ḥaqīqah (pl. *ḥaqāʾiq*). Truth, essential reality, spiritual reality.

al-ḥaqīqat al-muḥammadiyyah. "The Muḥammadan Reality," identified with the inner nature of the Prophet as Logos.

al-Ḥaqq. The Truth, the Real, a Name of God.

ḥaqq al-yaqīn. Truth of certainty.

al-Ḥayy. A Divine Name: the Living.

hijrah. The migration of the Prophet from Mecca to Medina, which marks the beginning of the Islamic calendar.

ḥikmah. Wisdom; philosophy.

al-ḥikmat al-mashriqiyyah. "Oriental philosophy" or that philosophy inclined more toward illumination and intuition than ratiocination, which Ibn Sīnā tried to develop in the later years of his life and which was completed by Suhrawardī in his School of *ishrāq* or Illumination.

himmah. Spiritual will.

ḥizb. A litany chanted in a Sufi order.

ḥubb Allāh. The love of God.

al-Hudā. "Guidance," one of the names of the Quran.

ḥujjah. Proof; in Shıʿism, the Imam.

Huwa. "He," referring to the Essence of God; also the final syllable of the Divine Name *Allāh*.

ʿibādah. Worship.

al-ʿibādāt al-ʿamaliyyah. Worship based on action.

al-ʿibādāt al-ʿilmiyyah. Worship based on knowledge.

ibdāʿ. Creation *ex nihilo,* or "origination."

Iblis. The devil.

ibn al-waqt. The "son of the moment," a title that is often given to the Sufis because they seek to live in the present, in the eternal now.

ʿīd. A day of celebration and festivity, the most important in the Islamic calendar being that at the end of Ramaḍān and the termination of the rites of *ḥajj* to Mecca.

ifṭār. The meal taken at sunset at the end of a day of fasting.

iḥrām. The special two-piece white cloth worn by pilgrims when they perform the *ḥajj* at Mecca.

iḥsān. Virtue and beauty, identified with the inner dimension of Islam.

ijmāʿ. Consensus or agreement, a principle of certain schools of Islamic Law, where it is usually used in reference to the agreement of the religious scholars (*ʿulamāʾ*) about a legal question not determined explicitly by the Quran and *Ḥadīth.*

ijtihād. Expressing an independent legal opinion based on both intellectual and moral qualifications.

ikhlāṣ. Sincerity.

ikhwān. Brothers or brethren, usually used by members of a Sufi order when referring to other members.

ʿilm. Knowledge, science.

ʿilm al-yaqīn. Knowledge of certainty.

imām, Imam. Literally, "he who stands before," leader of prayer, authority in religious sciences, caliph. In Shīʿism the term is used in a special sense and refers to those descendants of the Prophet who bear within themselves the "Prophetic Light."

īmān. Faith.

ʿimārah. Literally, "plenitude," a form of Sufi dance in which the Divine Name fills the human receptable completely.

insān. Human, implying the state of the human being with the possibility of its full perfection rather than its earthly and imperfect condition.

al-insān al-kāmil. The universal or perfect man, the human being who has attained the fullness of the human state and has become the perfect mirror, in which are reflected God's Names and Qualities.

inshād (pl. *anāshīd*). Recitation of poems and litanies in Sufi gatherings.

inshirāḥ. Expansion, which the Quran identifies with the gaining of faith and spiritual realization especially in reference of the "expansion of the breast" (*inshirāḥ al-ṣadr*).

'ishā'. Night, the fifth time specified for the performance of the daily prayers and set from a certain period after sunset to midnight or later.

ishārah (pl. *ishārāt*). Indication, allusion, directive.

'ishq-i ilāhī. Divine Love.

ishrāq. Illumination.

islām. Surrender to the will of God.

'iṣmah. Inerrancy, a quality associated with prophets in certain schools of Islamic theology and also with both the prophets and the Imams in Shī'ism.

al-ism al-a'ẓam. The Supreme Name of God.

ism al-Dhāt. Name of the Essence, referring to those Divine Names that pertain to the Essence of God and not His Attributes or Actions.

al-ism al-jalālah. The "Name of Majesty," i.e., *Allāh*.

al-ism al-mufrad. The "Unique Name," i.e., *Allāh*.

isti'dād. Capability, preparedness, potentiality.

istighfār. Seeking pardon.

ithbāt. Affirmation.

ithnā 'ashariyyah. The Twelvers, referring to the most numerous school in Shī'ism, which believes that there are only Twelve Imams after the Prophet.

i'tikāf. Seclusion, removing oneself from the crowd to devote oneself to worship and spiritual practice.

ittiḥād. Union.

ittiḥād al-waqt. Bringing together all the moments of the day simultaneously in order to examine and evaluate them.

'Izrā'īl. The angel of death.

al-jabarūt. The archangelic world.

jabr. Coercion, predestination.

jafr. The science of the symbolic, numerical significance of the letters of the Quran. This science is said traditionally to have been first taught by 'Alī ibn Abī Ṭālib and is used widely in many traditional sciences especially in the commentary on the Quran.

jalāl. Majesty; also *al-Jalīl*, the Majestic, one of the Names of God encompassing His aspect of Rigor.

jam'. Collectedness, reunification with God.

jamāl. Beauty; also the Beautiful (*al-Jamīl*), one of the Names of God encompassing His aspect of Mercy.

jannah. Paradise, the "Garden."

jihād. Literally, "effort" or "exertion," but usually translated as "holy war." *Jihād* in the widest sense means all action performed to establish equilibrium in life according to the norms of Islam.

al-jihād al-akbar. The greater *jihād*, referring to the battle within man to overcome his passions and subdue his lower nature.

al-jihād al-aṣghar. The "smaller holy war," referring to any external effort in the path of God and for the preservation of religion.

jihād al-nafs. The battle against one's passions.

jism (pl. *ajsām*). Body.

Ka'bah. The house of God in Mecca, built, according to Islamic belief, first by Adam, then by Abraham. It determines the direction toward which Muslims pray and is also the site to which Muslims make the pilgrimage (*al-ḥajj*).

kāfir. Infidel, the person who, having covered the truth, stands against religion.

Kalām. Literally, "word." One of the names of the Quran. Later it became the name for theology or that discipline which sought to defend the tenets of the faith through the use of rational arguments.

al-Kalimah. The Word of God, also used in reference to the Quran.

kamāl. Perfection.

karam. Generosity.

al-Karīm. The Generous, a Name of God.

kashf. Unveiling, intellectual intuition, discovery.

khalīfah rasūl Allāh. Vicegerent of the Messenger of God, the title given to the caliphs who became heads of the Islamic community after the death of the Prophet.

khalīfat Allāh. The vicegerent of God on earth, the title given to Adam and his progeny in the Quran.

al-Khāliq. The Creator, a Divine Name.

khalwah. Spiritual retreat, which constitutes a central part of the practice of Sufism.

khānaqāh. A Sufi center.

khawf. Fear, understood both in the ordinary sense and as the fear of God.

khazīnah (pl. *khazā'in*). Treasury, used in a religious context in reference to the treasury of the invisible world wherein the essential reality of things is to be found.

al-Khiḍr. The mysterious prophet mentioned in the Quran, who is always alive and who is identified with the esoteric dimension of religion. He has been compared to the Jewish prophet Elijah.

khirqah. The cloak worn by the Sufis.

al-khulafā' al-rāshidūn. The "rightly guided caliphs," consisting of Abū Bakr, 'Umar, 'Uthmān, and 'Alī.

khums. One-fifth, a religious tax levied in Shī'ism and paid to the religious authorities as representatives of the Imam.

kitāb. Book, usually used in the sense of sacred scripture and especially the Quran, but also other revealed books such as the Torah and the Gospels.

kufr. Infidelity, unbelief.

al-Kursī. The pedestal of the Throne (*al-'Arsh*) of God according to Quranic symbolism. Also the Throne itself.

al-lāhūt. The world of Divine Names and Qualities.

al-Lawḥ. The Guarded Tablet, upon which God has "written" the archetypical realities with the Pen. See also *al-Lawḥ al-Maḥfūẓ.*

al-Lawḥ al-Maḥfūẓ. The "Guarded Tablet," upon which the reality of all things was written before God created them externally and bestowed upon them objective existence.

Laylat al-mi'rāj. The "Night of Ascent," when, according to the Quran, the Prophet was taken by the archangel Gabriel from Mecca to Jerusalem and from there ascended to the highest heaven and drew nigh to the Divine Presence Itself.

Laylat al-qadr. The "Night of Power" or "Night of Descent," one of the odd nights of the last ten nights of Ramaḍān, when the Quran was first revealed.

ma'ād. The "return" to God; i.e., eschatology and also resurrection, in reference to both the individual and the cosmic order.

mabda'. Source, origin, often used as a Name for God.

madhkūr. The invoked.

madrasah. The traditional Islamic school of a more advanced nature than the Quranic schools where the earliest instruction was imparted.

maghrib. Evening or sunset, the fourth time specified for the performance of the daily prayers.

maḥabbah. Love, used especially in Sufism as the love of God.

al-Mahdī. The "rightly guided one" who is expected to save humanity from oppression and injustice and to establish a reign of peace as part of the eschatological events connected with the second coming of Christ and the end of the world.

majālis-i 'azā'. Sessions devoted to mourning, especially of Ḥusayn. These religious gatherings are popular in Shī'ism and are held mostly during the month of Muḥarram.

majlis (pl. *majālis*). Gathering, used in Sufism in a technical sense as the gathering of the Sufis.

majlis al-dhikr. Gathering of the Sufis in which God's Names and various litanies are invoked.

makhāfah. Fear, used usually in Sufism as the fear of God and the first stage of spiritual perfection.

malak (pl. *malā'ikah*). Angel.

al-malakūt. The angelic and psychic worlds.

ma'nā. Meaning or inward aspect as opposed to form or external aspect of things.

ma'nawiyyah. Spirituality, that which is related to the world of meaning (*ma'nā*).

maqām (pl. *maqāmāt*). Used as a technical term in Sufism to denote a spiritual station attained permanently as a result of traveling upon the spiritual path.

ma'rifah. Knowledge, gnosis.

martabah (pl. *marātib*). Stage, level.

marthiyah. Elegy, popular especially in Shī'ism in connection with the death of the Imams.

mashshā'ī. Peripatetic, referring to that school of Islamic philosophy founded by al-Kindī, developed by al-Fārābī and reaching its peak with Ibn Sīnā, in which Aristotelian philosophy in its Neoplatonic interpretation was combined with tenets of Islam into one of the major Islamic philosophical schools.

ma'shūq. The beloved.

mā siwa'Llāh. All that is other than God.

ma'ṣūm. Inerrant, the person who possesses the quality of *'iṣmah* or inerrancy.

mathnawī. Rhyming couplet of poetry. This has also become the name of Rūmī's most famous poetical work, written in rhyming couplets.

mawlā. Master, lord, patron, also client.

mawlid (pl. *mawlidāt*). Birthday of the Prophet or a saint, often marked by celebrations.

mawlid al-nabī. Birthday of the Prophet.

maẓhar. The locus of theophany, place of appearance of a Divine Quality.

mishkāt. Niche.

mithāl. Symbol, image, similitude, parable.

mīthāq. Covenant, especially the covenant made between God and man before the creation of the world.

miḥrāb. The niche in the mosque in the direction of Mecca before which the faithful stand when praying.

mi'rāj. See *Laylat al-mi'rāj*.

mudhākarah. Spiritual exhortations and deliberations of a Sufi master usually given during Sufi gatherings.

muhājirūn. The immigrants who migrated with the Prophet from Mecca to Medina.

Muḥarram. The first month of the Islamic lunar year during which Ḥusayn was martyred in Karbalā'.

muḥāsabah. Examination of one's conscience by rendering an account of all of one's acts.

muḥsin. The person who possesses virtue or *iḥsān*.

al-Muḥyī. The Giver of Life, a Divine Name.

mujāhadah. Ascetic discipline and spiritual struggle upon the Sufi path; synonymous with *al-jihād al-akbar*.

mujāhid. The person who exerts himself in the path of God.

mujarrad. Disengaged or divorced from matter, potentiality, and imperfection.

mujtahid. An authority who can give independent opinion in the *Sharī'ah*, that is, practice *ijtihād*. Nowadays this term is used almost exclusively in Twelve-Imam Shī'ism, where such authorities constitute a distinct class and wield great power.

al-mulk. The corporeal or visible world consisting of the three kingdoms.

mu'min. The person of faith, the Muslim who not only has surrendered his will to God and followed the injunction of Islam but also has ardent faith in God in his heart.

al-Mumīt. The Slayer or Giver of death, a Divine Name.

munājāt. Supplications, prayers.

murāqabah. Vigilance upon the spiritual path; meditation and self-reflection.

muraqqa'ah. Patched cloak worn by the Sufis.

murīd. The disciple in a Sufi order. In the sense of one who wills, it is also a Divine Name, God being *al-Murīd*, He Who wills.

murshid. The spiritual master or guide.

muṣāfaḥah. Shaking of hands especially as practiced in a special manner by the Sufis.

al-Muṣawwir. The "producer of form," one of the Names of God.

mushāraṭah. "Putting conditions" to have the intention to devote oneself completely to God.

mutabarrak. Blessed—one who has received the blessing of a Sufi order without journeying actively upon the Sufi path.

mut'ah. Temporary marriage allowed in Shī'ism but not in Sunnism.

muttaqī. The person who possesses reverential fear of God and piety.

muwaḥḥid. "Unitarian," one who confesses to God's Unity and lives accordingly.

nabī. Prophet, he who is appointed by God to bring some kind of message from Him to men. If this message is a book or new dispensation from heaven, then the *nabī* is called *rasūl.*

al-nabī al-ummī. The "unlettered Prophet," one of the titles of the Prophet, since his soul was pure from all human knowledge and "virgin" before the Divine Word which descended upon it.

nafas al-Raḥmān. The "breath of the Compassionate," by which God as the Compassionate has brought the world into being.

nāfilah (pl. *nawāfil*). Supererogatory rites and performances.

nafs. The self, the soul.

al-nafs al-ammārah. The passionate soul which incites man to evil.

al-nafs al-ḥayawāniyyah. The animal soul.

al-nafs al-lawwāmah. The blaming soul, the stage in the development of the soul where the soul begins to understand its own faults and blame itself for its shortcomings.

al-nafs al-muṭma'innah. The soul at peace and resting in certitude.

nafy. Negation.

naṣṣ. Text, writ, designation from the Imam or Divine Realm.

nāṭiq. He who speaks. Used by Ismā'īlīs in reference to those prophets and Imams whose function it was to teach openly what was revealed or transmitted to them.

nifāq. Hypocrisy, dissemblance

niyyah. The intention that lies behind an act.

nubuwwah. Prophecy, the power and function by virtue of whose possession a person becomes a prophet.

nūr. Light.

nūr al-anwār. The "Light of lights," the Name given by Suhrawardī to God as the Supreme Light, Who is the source of all the lights that constitute the universe.

al-nūr al-muḥammadī. "Muḥammadan Light," the inner reality of the Prophet, which is identified by Sufis and also Shīʿites with his spiritual function and nature and which is reflected in one degree or another in the Imams and saints.

pīr. Spiritual master, shaykh; in Ismāʿīlism, a *dāʿī.*

qabḍ. Contraction.

qaḍā'. The Divine Judgment or Decree; what has been willed for man.

al-qadar. That which is man's lot or portion in life, predestination, destiny.

al-Qahhār. A Name of God: the Subduer, the Almighty, the Dominant.

al-Qalam. The Pen, usually used as a symbol of the Divine Intellect and the instrument of God's creative act.

qalb. Heart, identified in the Quran with the seat of intelligence and the center of the microcosm.

al-Qarīb. He Who is near; a Divine Name by virtue of which God is nearer to man than man is to himself.

al-Qayyūm. A Name of God: the Self-Subsistent.

qiblah. The direction determined by the location of the Kaʿbah which Muslims must face while offering their prayers.

qiyām. Uprising, also used to signify a religious movement connected in Shīʿism with the Imam or his representatives.

qiyāmah. Resurrection.

qiyās. Analogical reasoning used in certain schools of Islamic Law. In logic and philosophy, it means syllogism.

qudrah. Power, might.

al-Qur'ān al-tadwīnī. The written and recorded Quran, which is known to man as the book in Arabic containing the Revelation of God.

al-Qur'ān al-takwīnī. The cosmic Quran, or the cosmos seen as God's primordial Revelation, upon whose "pages" are inscribed God's message.

qurb. Proximity, nearness; usually used in Sufism in reference to man's nearness to God.

al-Rabb. A Divine Name meaning Lord or Master.

Rabb al-ʿālamīn. Lord of the Worlds, a Divine Name.

rabbānī. Lordly, godly.

al-Raḥīm. A Name of God, the Divine Compassion which touches beings directly.

al-Raḥmān. A Name of God, the all-encompassing Divine Mercy.

*raḥmat*un *li'l-ʿālamīn.* Mercy unto the worlds, a title of the Prophet.

rajā'. Hope in God's mercy and benevolence.

Ramaḍān. The holy lunar month of the Islamic calendar during which all Muslims who have the capability are obliged to fast from dawn to sunset.

al-Rashīd. The One Who guides upon the straight path, a Name of God.

al-Rāqib. A Name of God: the Vigilant.

rasūl. Messenger, he who has been chosen by God to bring His message to mankind.

riḍā'. Satisfaction, contentment with what God has given to man.

riḍwān. The highest paradise.

rūḥ. The Spirit, including both the Supreme Spirit and the spirit within man.

rūḥāniyyah. Spirituality, that which is related to the Spirit (*rūḥ*).

rukū'. Bowing in the daily prayers.

sabīl. Path, way.

sab'iyyah. The Seveners, often used erroneously as a name for the Ismā'īlīs.

ṣabr. Patience.

ṣaḥābah. Companions of the Prophet.

ṣāḥib al-tanzīl. He who has the knowledge and authority to interpret the outer meaning of the Quran.

ṣāḥib al-ta'wīl. He who has the knowledge and authority to interpret the inner meaning of the Quran.

ṣaḥīḥ (pl. *ṣiḥāḥ*). Literally, "the correct book," the title given to the canonical collections of *Ḥadīth* accepted by the Sunni community as being authentic.

sakīnah. Divine Peace that descends upon the heart of the faithful.

al-Salām. Peace, a Divine Name, and also the greeting used by all Muslims, who, upon the instruction of the Prophet, greet each other by saying "Peace be upon you."

ṣalāt (namāz in Persian). The canonical daily prayers which are obligatory for all Muslims to perform five times a day.

ṣalāt 'ala'l-nabī. Benediction or blessing upon the Prophet.

ṣalāt al-jum'ah. The congregational prayers of Friday performed at midday.

ṣalāt al-ṭarīqah. The canonical prayers interiorized and understood according to their inner meaning.

sālik. One who journeys upon the spiritual path in an active manner; hence, another name for the disciple upon the Sufi path who actually travels upon the path and is not simply passive.

samā'. Heaven, sky.

samā'. Spiritual concert of the Sufis.

samā' khānah. A place where the Sufi music and dance takes place.

al-Ṣamad. A Divine Name, the everlasting Reality which is not in need of anything and which is rich in Itself.

ṣawm. Fast, identified especially with the obligatory fast of the month of Ramaḍān.

shafā'ah. Intercession both in this world and in the hereafter.

shahādah. Literally, "bearing witness." It refers to the two testimonies of faith in Islam: "There is no divinity but God" and "Muḥammad is the messenger of God," called the first and second *Shahādah* respectively.

shāhid. Witness.

shahīd (pl. *shuhadā'*). Martyred, one who has lost his or her life for God.

shahwah. Passion, inclinations of the lower soul toward lust and concupiscence.

sha'n al-nuzūl. The conditions under which a particular verse of the Quran was revealed.

Sharī'ah. The Divine Law, which is rooted in the Quran and *Ḥadīth.* Muslims also refer to the sacred laws of other religions as their *sharī'ah.*

sharīk. Partner.

shaykh. Elder, a revered person, a learned man or teacher—more specifically, a spiritual master.

shayṭān. Satan.

shirk. "Associationism," or the cardinal sin of taking a partner unto God and associating another divinity with Him; believing that there are realities independent of God.

shuhūd. Vision, contemplation.

shūrā. Consultation, a principle mentioned in the Quran, according to which Muslims should conduct their affairs.

sibḥah. The rosary used during litanies and invocation.

ṣifah (pl. *ṣifāt*). Quality, attribute.

silsilah. Chain, used in the religious sciences as the chain of authorities linking a particular saying or idea to its origin, usually the Prophet in the case of *ḥadīth* or the founder of a particular school; in Sufism it is the initiatic chain which links a particular master through generations of masters before him to the Prophet and finally God.

sīrah. Biography or history, used especially in reference to the life of the Prophet.

al-ṣirāṭ al-mustaqīm. The "straight path," which defines the life of Islam in general and the spiritual life in particular.

sirr. Secret, depth of the heart, inmost consciousness.

sitr. The state of being hidden from view in reference to Ismāʿīlī beliefs about certain of their imams.

ṣuḥbah. "Good company," or being in the company of the Sufis; the relationship of the disciples to one another.

sujūd. The position of prostration during the canonical prayers when the forehead touches the ground.

sunnah. The tradition of the Prophet embracing his manner and ways of doing and acting in different circumstances in life.

sūrah. A chapter of the Quran.

ṣūrah (pl. *ṣuwar*). Form, in the Aristotelian sense and as the outward aspect of a being.

Sūrat al-fātiḥah. The opening chapter of the Quran, which is repeated during the daily canonical prayers.

ṭabīʿah. Nature, both in the philosophical sense of the nature of something and in the ordinary sense of the world of creation.

tābiʿūn. Followers of the companions, the generation which followed the companions.

tafakkur. Meditation.

tafsīr. Commentary, usually associated with the Quran but also used in other instances.

ṭahārah. Ritual purification required before performance of certain Islamic rites.

taḥliyah. Embellishment of the soul with virtues.

tajallī. Theophany, reflection of a Divine Name upon the mirror of cosmic existence.

takbīr. Invoking the formula *Allāhu akbar.*

takhliyah. Emptying the soul of all imperfection.

takiyyah. A center of religious gatherings; a Sufi center.

ṭālib. The seeker after knowledge or the spiritual path.

tanāsukh. Transmigration.

tanzīl. Descent, referring to the Revelation of the Quran to the Prophet, as it "descended" upon him.

taqiyyah. Dissimulation, hiding of one's religious beliefs in the face of danger.

taqlīd. Imitation or emulation of a religious model, authority, or pattern of thought.

taqwā. Fear of God, piety.

ṭarīqah. The spiritual way or path identified with Sufism; also a Sufi order.

taṣawwuf. Sufism, Islamic esoterism and mysticism.

tashbīh. Comparing a Divine Quality to a cosmic or human one in order to make it comprehensible; immanence; symbolic interpretation; anthropomorphism.

ta'ṭīl. Refusing to the human intellect the power to understand the meaning of God's Names and Qualities for fear of anthropomorphizing the Divinity.

ṭawāf. Circumambulation around the Ka'bah.

tawakkul. Reliance upon God.

tawbah. Repentance before God for one's sins.

tawḥīd. Unity, oneness, and also the act of bringing about oneness or integration.

tawḥīd al-ṣifāt. Unity of Divine Qualities.

ta'wīl. Inner, esoteric commentary or hermeneutics of the Sacred Text but also of the "cosmic text" as well as inspired writings.

ta'wīl-i bāṭin. Hermeneutic or esoteric interpretation of the inward.

tazkiyat al-nafs. Purification of the soul.

'ubūdiyyah. The state of servitude before God.

ufuq (pl. *āfāq*). Horizon.

ukhuwwat al-islāmiyyah. Islamic brotherhood.

'ulamā' (sg. *'ālim*). Class of learned men in Islamic society usually but not completely identified with those learned in the religious sciences, particularly Law.

ummah. The community, usually identified with the Islamic people but also applied to the followers of other prophets and therefore other religious communities.

Umm al-kitāb. The "mother of Books," one of the names of the Quran, referring to its nature as the source of all knowledge.

umm al-mu'minīn. Mother of the faithful, a title used in reference to the wives of the Prophet, especially Khadījah.

uṣūl al-dīn. The principles of religion.

uswah ḥasanah. The good or perfect model to follow, a description given in the Quran to the Prophet.

al-Wadūd. He who loves, one of the Names of God.

waḥdāniyyah. The state of unity in multiplicity but before the manifestation of existence, the state in which the Divine Names have become distinct one from another but have not as yet become manifested.

waḥdat al-wujūd. The "transcendent unity of being," the doctrine held by many Sufis according to which only God possesses Being, all that exists deriving its existence from the One Being Who alone is.

al-Wahhāb. The Bestower, a Name of God.

al-Wāḥid. A Divine Name: the One.

wajh (pl. *wujūh*). Face, used in the singular for God, as in the expression *wajh Allāh* (Face of God), which means that aspect of the Divinity turned to the created order.

wājib. That act which is obligatory for a Muslim according to the injunctions of the religion. The term is used mostly but not exclusively in the domain of Law.

al-Wakīl. A Divine Name: the Trustee.

walī Allāh (pl. *awliyā' Allāh*). Literally, "friend of God," a term usually used to designate a saint.

waṣī. Inheritor, used in Shī'ism in the specific sense of 'Alī's inheriting the non-prophetic functions of the Prophet.

wāṣil. One who has reached the end of the spiritual path and experienced union.

wāsiṭah. Link, connection, intermediary.

wilāyah. Domination, rule; also the inner and esoteric function of the Prophet, which, according to Shī'ism, was transmitted to the Imams. In Sufism it is associated with esoterism as such.

wird. The litany recited usually twice a day in Sufi orders.

wiṣāl. Union, usually understood mystically.

wuḍū'. Ablution required before the daily prayers and usually made before entry into a holy place.

wuṣūl. Arriving or reaching the end, usually used mystically in association with the final goal of the spiritual path.

al-Ẓāhir. The outward or manifest; also a Name of God, Who is the Manifest, the Outward.

zakāt. Religious tax which is obligatory and constitutes one of the pillars of Islam.

Zamzam. The spring of water near the Ka'bah, which, according to tradition, gushed forth when Hagar sought water in the precinct of the Ka'bah.

zāwiyah. A Sufi center.

zuhd. Asceticism.

ẓuhr. Noon, the second time specified for the performance of the daily prayers and set at midday.

Bibliography

[Since most works on Islam treat it from the Sunni point of view, a separate bibliography will not be given for Sunnism. The bibliography is limited to works in European languages. Full publication information is given only at the first citation of a work.]

Reference Works

Encyclopaedia of Islam. Old and new editions. Leiden: Brill.

Pearson, J. D. *Index Islamicus.* Cambridge: Heffer, 1958–. [Continues to this day and includes a thorough list of articles and, since 1976, also books on all aspects of Islam, including spirituality.]

Sauvaget, J. *Introduction to the History of the Muslim East: A Bibliographical Guide.* Berkeley and Los Angeles: University of California Press, 1965.

Part One: The Roots of the Islamic Tradition and Spirituality

Abul Quasem, M. *The Recitation and Interpretation of the Quran: al-Ghazzālī's Theory.* London and Boston: Kegan Paul International, 1982.

Ali, Muhammad. *A Manual of Ḥadīth.* Lahore: Ahmidiyya Anjuman, 1951.

Andrae, T. *Mohammad: The Man and His Faith.* Translated by T. Menzel. New York: Harper Torchbook, 1960.

Arberry, A. J. *The Koran Interpreted.* London: Allen & Unwin, 1955.

Archer, J. C. *Mystical Elements in Mohammad.* Yale Oriental Series 11.1. New Haven, CT: Yale University Press, 1980.

Baljon, J. *A Mystical Interpretation of Prophetic Tales by an Indian Muslim: Shah Wali Allah's Ta'wil al-ahadith.* Leiden: Brill, 1973.

Brohi, A. K. *Islam in the Modern World.* Karachi: Islamic Research Academy, 1968.

Bukhārī, Abū 'Abd Allāh. *Kitāb jāmi' al-ṣaḥīḥ.* Translated by M. M. Khan. 6 vols. Lahore: M. Ashraf, 1978–80.

Burckhardt, T. *An Introduction to Sufi Doctrine.* Translated by D. M. Matheson. Lahore: M. Ashraf, 1959.

Corbin, H. *En Islam iranien.* 4 vols. Paris: Gallimard, 1971–72.

——. *Face de Dieu, Face de l'homme.* Paris: Flammarion, 1983.

—— (with S. H. Nasr and O. Yahya). *Histoire de la philosophie islamique.* Part I. Paris: Gallimard, 1964.

——. "L'intériorisation du sens en herméneutique soufie iranienne." *Eranos Jahrbuch* 26 (1957) 57–187.

Cragg, K. *The Mind of the Quran: Chapters in Reflection.* London: Allen & Unwin, 1973.

Danner, V. *The Islamic Tradition.* Warwick, NY: Amity House, 1987.

Dermenghem, E. *Muhammad and the Islamic Tradition.* Translated by J. M. Watt. New York: Harper, 1958.

——. *The Life of Mahomet.* London: Routledge, 1930.

Denny, F. M. *An Introduction to Islam.* New York: Macmillan, 1985.

Eaton, C. G. *Islam and the Destiny of Man.* Albany, NY: State University of New York Press, 1985.

Esin, E. *Mecca the Blessed, Medina the Radiant.* London: Paul Elek, 1963.

Garaudy, R. *Promesses de l'Islam.* Paris: Seuil, 1981.

Gardet, L. *Mohammedanism.* Translated by W. Burridge. New York: Hawthorn Books, 1961.

——. *La Cité musulmane, vie sociale et politique.* Paris: J. Vrin, 1961.

Al-Ghazzālī, Abū Ḥāmid. *The Jewels of the Quran.* Translated by M. Abul Quasem. London and Boston: Kegan Paul International, 1983.

——. *Mishkāt al-anwār.* Translated by W. H. T. Gairdner. Lahore: M. Ashraf, 1952.

Gheorghiu, G. *La Vie de Mahomet.* Paris: Gallimard, 1964.

Gibb, H. A. R. *Mohammedanism.* New York: Oxford University Press, 1982.

Gilis, C. *Le Coran et la fonction d'Hermes.* Paris: Les Editions de l'Oeuvre, 1984.

Graham, W. *Divine Word and Prophetic Word in Early Islam.* The Hague: Mouton, 1977.

Guillaume, A., trans. *The Life of Muhammad: A Translation of Ishaq's Sirat Rasul Allah.* London: Oxford University Press. 1955.

Hamidullah, M. *Le Prophète de l'Islam.* 2 vols. Paris: J. Vrin, 1959.

Izutsu, T. *God and Man in the Koran.* Tokyo: The Keio Institute of Cultural and Linguistic Studies, 1964.

——. *Ethico-Religious Concepts in the Quran.* Montreal: McGill University Press, 1966.

Jeffery, A., ed. *A Reader on Islam.* The Hague: Mouton, 1962.

Lings, M. "The Quranic Symbolism of Water." *Studies in Comparative Religion* 2 (Summer 1968).

——. *What is Sufism?* Berkeley and Los Angeles: University of California Press, 1975.

——. *Muhammad.* London: Allen & Unwin, 1984.

Lory, P. *Les Commentaires ésotériques du Coran d'après 'Abd ar-Razzāq al-Qāshānī.* Paris: Les Deux Océans, 1980.

McClain, E. *Meditations through the Quran: Tonal Images in an Oral Culture.* York Beach, ME: Nicolas Hays, 1981.

Mahmud, Abdel Haleem. *The Creed of Islam.* London: World of Islam Festival Trust, 1978.

Malik, C. *God and Man in Contemporary Islamic Thought.* Beirut: American University of Beirut Centennial Publications, 1972.

Muslim, ibn Ḥajjāj. *Ṣaḥīḥ.* Translated by A. H. Siddiqi. 4 vols. New Delhi: Kitab Bhavan, 1982.

Nasr, S. H. *Muhammad, the Man of Allah.* London: Muhammadi Trust, 1982.

——. *Ideals and Realities of Islam.* London: Allen & Unwin, 1985.

——. *Islamic Life and Thought.* Albany, NY: State University of New York Press, 1981.

Nurbakhsh, J. *Traditions of the Prophet.* 2 vols. New York: Khaniqahi Nimatullahi Publications, 1981–83.

Nwyia, P. "Le tafsir mystique attribué à Ga'far Ṣādiq." *Mélanges de l'Université Saint-Joseph* 43 (1967) 179–230.

Padwick, C. *Muslim Devotions.* London: SPCK, 1961.

Paret, R. *Mohammad und der Koran Geschichte und Verkündigung des arabischen Propheten.* Stuttgart: Kohlhammer, 1980.

Pickthall, M. M. *The Meaning of the Glorious Koran.* New York: New American Library, 1963.

Rahman, Fazlur. *Major Themes of the Qur'ān.* Minneapolis and Chicago: Bibliotheca Islamica, 1980.

Schimmel, A. M. *And Muhammad is His Messenger.* Chapel Hill: University of North Carolina Press, 1985.

Schuon, F. *Understanding Islam.* Translated by D. M. Matheson. London: Allen & Unwin, 1976.

——. *Islam and the Perennial Philosophy.* Translated by J. P. Hobson. London: World of Islam, 1976.

——. *Dimensions of Islam.* Translated by P. N. Townsend. London: Allen & Unwin, 1970.

——. *Christianity/Islam: Essays on Esoteric Ecumenism.* Translated by G. Polit. Bloomington, IN: World Wisdom, 1985.

Ṣiddīqī, M. Z. *Ḥadīth Literature.* Calcutta: Calcutta University Press, 1961.

Siraj Ed-Din, Abu Bakr. *The Book of Certainty.* New York: Samuel Weiser, 1974.

Suhrawardy, A. *The Sayings of Muhammad.* London: John Murray, 1941.

Al-Tabrīzī. *Mishkāt al-maṣābīḥ.* Translated by J. Robson. 4 vols. Lahore: M. Ashraf, 1963–65.

Valiuddin, Mir. *The Essential Features of Islam.* Hyderabad, Daccan: Da'iratu'l-Ma'arif Press Osmania University, n.d.

Widengren, G. *Muhammad: The Apostle and His Ascension.* Uppsala: Lundquist, 1955.

Yusuf 'Ali, A. *The Personality of Muhammad the Prophet*. Lahore: M. Ashraf, 1931.
Yusuf, S. M. *An Essay on the Sunnah*. Karachi: Institute of Islamic Culture, 1966.

Inner Meaning of Rites (including Prayer)

Arnold, E. *Pearls of the Faith or Islam's Rosary*. Boston: Roberts Brothers, 1883.
Corbin, H. *Creative Imagination in the Sufism of Ibn 'Arabī*. Translated by R. Manheim. Princeton, NJ: Princeton University Press, 1981. Part 2, "Creative Imagination and Creative Prayer."
——. *Temple et contemplation*. Paris: Flammarion, 1980. Pp. 197–283, "La configuration du temple de la Ka'ba comme secret de la vie spirituelle."
Cragg, K. *The Dome of the Rock*. London: SPCK, 1964.
——., trans. *Dalā'il al-khayrāt*. Cairo, n.d.
Al-Ghazzālī, Abū Ḥāmīd. *Al-Ghazālī–Inner Dimensions of Islamic Worship*. Translated by M. Holland. Leicester: Islamic Foundation, 1983.
——. *Ghazali on Prayer*. Translated by K. Nakamura. Tokyo: The Institute of Oriental Culture, 1973.
Gilis, C. *La Doctrine initiatique du pelerinage à la maison d'Allah*. Paris: Les Editions de l'Oeuvre, 1982.
Massignon, L. *Opera Minora*. Edited by Y. Moubarac. 3 vols. Beirut: Librairie Orientale, 1963.
Nasr, S. H. *Islamic Life and Thought*. Pp. 191–99, "The Interior Life in Islam."
Padwick, *Muslim Devotions*.
Valiuddin, Mir. *Contemplative Disciplines in Sufism*. London: East-West Publications, 1980.

Part Two: Aspects of the Islamic Tradition

Twelve-Imam Shī'ism

Ayoub, M. *Redemptive Suffering in Islam: A Study of the Devotional Aspects of 'Āshūrā in Twelver Shī'ism*. Hawthorne, NY: Mouton, 1978.
Chelkowski, P., ed. *Ta'ziyeh: Ritual and Drama in Iran*. New York: New York University Press, 1979.
Chittick, W. C., trans. *Supplications (Du'ā) Amīr al-Mu'minīn 'Alī b. Abī Ṭalib*. London: Muhammadi Trust, n.d.
Donaldson, D. M. *The Shi'ite Religion*. London: Luzac, 1933.
Al-Ḥillī, Ḥasan b. Yūsuf. *Al-Bāb al-ḥādī 'ashar*. Translated by W. M. Miller [*A Treatise on the Principles of Shī'ite Theology*]. London: Royal Asiatic Society, 1928.
Hollister, J. N. *The Shi'a of India*. London: Luzac, 1953.
Ibn Bābawayh al-Qummī. *Risālat al-I'tiqādat*. Translated by A. A. A. Fyzee [*A Shī'ite Creed*]. London: Oxford University Press, 1942.

Jafri, H. M. *Origins and Early Development of Shī'a Islam.* 2nd ed. London: Longman, 1981.

——. "Morality and Conduct of Life in Islam" [Eng. trans. of *Nahj al-Balaghah's* letter No. 31]. *Hamdard Islamicus* [Karachi] 2 (1979) 3–29.

——. "An Interpretation of the Fundamental Beliefs and Some of the Institutions of Islam" [Eng. trans., with an introduction, of *Nahj al-Balaghah's* first sermon]. *Arabica* [Paris] 30 (1984) 290–302.

Kattānī, Sulaymān. *Imām 'Alī: Source of Light, Wisdom and Might.* Translated by I. K. A. Howard. London: Muhammadi Trust, 1983.

Nasr, S. H. *Ideals and Realities of Islam.* Pp. 147–78, "Shī'ism and Sunnism: Twelve Imām Shī'sm and Ismā'īlism."

——. *An Introduction to Islamic Cosmological Doctrines.* Cambridge, MA: Harvard University Press, 1964. Section on the relation of Shī'ism to the arts and sciences in Islam.

——. "The spiritual significance of *Jihād.*" *Alserāt* 6 (1980) 4–10.

——. "Ithnā 'Ashariyya." *Encyclopaedia of Islam,* new ed., 277–79.

Sachedina, A. A. *Islamic Messianism: The Idea of the Mahdī in Twelver Shī'ism.* Albany, NY: State University of New York Press, 1980.

Shaykh al-Mufīd. *Kitāb al-irshād.* Translated by I. K. A. Howard. [*The Book of Guidance*]. London: Muhammadi Trust, 1981.

Ṭabāṭabā'ī 'Allamāh Sayyid Muḥammad Ḥusayn. *Shī'ah dar Islām.* Translated by S. H. Nasr [*Shī'ite Islam*]. London: Allen & Unwin; Albany, NY: State University of New York Press, 1975.

——. *A Shī'ite Anthology.* Translated by W. C. Chittick. Introduction by S. H. Nasr. London: Muhammadi Trust, 1980.

Ismā'īlism

The Cambridge History of Iran. Vol. 4. Edited by R. N. Frye. Cambridge: University Press, 1975.

The Cambridge History of Iran. Vol. 5. Edited by J. A. Boyle. Cambridge: University Press, 1968.

Corbin, H. *Cyclical Time and Ismā'īlī Gnosis.* London: Kegan Paul International, 1983.

——. *Histoire de la philosophie islamique.*

Halm, Heinz. *Kosmologie und Heilslehre der frühen Ismā'īlīya: Eine Studie zur Ismailischen Gnosis.* Wiesbaden: F. Steiner, 1978.

Hamdani, A. *The Fāṭimids.* Karachi: Pakistan Publishing House, 1962.

Hodgson, M. G. S. *The Order of Assassins.* The Hague: Mouton, 1955.

Ivanow, W. *Brief Survey of the Evolution of Ismā'īlism.* Leiden: Brill, 1952.

——. "Ismā'īliyya." *Shorter Encyclopedia of Islam.*

Lewis, B. *Origins of Ismā'īlism.* Cambridge: W. Heffer and Sons, 1940.

Madelung, W. "Das Imamat in der frühen ismailitischen Lehre." *Der Islam* 37 (1961) 43–135.
——. "Ismāʿīliyya." *Encyclopaedia of Islam,* 2nd ed.
Nanji, Azim. *The Nizārī Ismāʿīlī Tradition in the Indo-Pakistan Subcontinent.* New York: Caravan Books, 1978.
Nasr, S. H., ed. *Ismāʿīlī Contributions to Islamic Culture.* Tehran: Imperial Iranian Academy of Philosophy, 1977.
Poonawala, I. K. *Biobibliography of Ismāʿīlī Literature.* Malibu, CA: Undena, 1977.
al-Qāḍī al-Nuʿmān. *Daʿāʾim al-Islām.* Translated by A. A. A. Fyzee. London: Institute of Ismāʿīlī Studies, forthcoming.
Stern, S. M. *Studies in Early Ismaʿilism.* Leiden: Brill, 1983.
Walker, Paul. "Cosmic Hierarchies in Early Ismāʿīlī Thought." *Muslim World* 66 (1976) 14–28.

Female Spirituality in Islam

Austin, R. W. J. "Islam and the Feminine." In *Islam in the Modern World,* 36–48. Edited by D. MacEoin and A. al-Shahi. London: Croom Helm, 1983.
Bakhtiar, L. *Sufi—Expressions of the Mystic Quest.* London: Thames & Hudson, 1979.
Nurbakhsh, J. *Sufi Women.* New York: Khaniqahi-Nimatullahi Publications, 1983.
Schimmel, A. M. *Mystical Dimensions of Islam.* Chapel Hill: University of North Carolina Press, 1975. Appendix 2, pp. 426–35, "The Feminine Element in Sufism."
Smith, M. *Rabiʿa the Mystic and Her Fellow-Saints in Islam.* Cambridge: University Press, 1928.
Waddy, C. *Women in Muslim History.* London: Longman, 1980.
Yashruṭiyyah, al-Sayyidah Fāṭimah. "Contemplation and Action: The Sufi Way." In *Contemplation and Action in World Religions,* 212–17. Edited by Y. Ibish and I. Marculescu. Seattle: University of Washington Press, 1978.

Part Three: Sufism: The Inner Dimension of Islam

The Nature and Origin of Sufism

Austin, R. W. "Some Observations on the Study of Sufi Origins." In *Actas IV Congresso de Estudios Arabes & Islamicos,* 1968 (1971), 101–7.
Burckhardt, T. *An Introduction to Sufi Doctrines.* 1:3–11, "At-Taṣawwuf."
Danner, V. "The Necessity for the Rise of the Term Sufi." *Studies in Comparative Religion* 6 (1972) 71–77.
Lings, M. *What is Sufism?*
——. *A Sufi Saint of the Twentieth Century.* Berkeley and Los Angeles: University of California Press, 1971. Chapter 2, pp. 34–47, "The Origins of Sufism."

Massignon, L. "La meditation coranique et les origines du lexique soufi." *Actes Congres International Histoire des Religions* 2 (1923) 412–14.
Nasr, S. H. *Ideals and Realities of Islam.* Chapter 5, pp. 121–46, "The *Ṭarīqah*–The Spiritual Path and its Quranic Roots."
——. *Sufi Essays.* Albany, NY: State University of New York Press, 1985.
Nicholson, R. A. "A Historical Enquiry Concerning the Origin and Development of Sufism with a List of Definitions of the Terms '*ṣūfī*' and '*taṣawwuf*' arranged chronologically." *Journal of the Royal Asiatic Society* (1906) 303–48.
Schimmel, A. M. "The Origin and Early Development of Sufism." *Journal of the Pakistan Historical Society* 7 (1959) 55–67.
Schuon, F. *Understanding Islam.* Chapter 4, pp. 106–59, "The Way."
Stoddart, W. *Sufism: The Mystical Doctrines and Methods.* Wellingborough: Thorsons, 1976.

The Early Development of Sufism

Al-Anṣārī al-Harawī. *Les Étapes des itinérants vers Dieu.* Edited and translated by S. de Laugier de Beaurecueil. Cairo: Imprimerie de l'Institut français d'archéologie orientale, 1962.
'Aṭṭār, Farīd al-Dīn. *Tadhkirat al-Awliyā'*. Translated by A. J. Arberry [*Muslim Saints and Mystics*]. London: Routledge and Kegan Paul, 1966.
Böwering, G. *The Mystical Vision of Existence in Classical Islam: The Quranic Hermeneutics of the Ṣūfī Sahl At-Tustarī* (d. 283/896). Berlin and New York: de Gruyter, 1980.
Burckhardt, T. *An Introduction to Sufi Doctrines.*
——. *The Art of Islam.* London: Festival of the World of Islam, 1976.
Depont, O., and X. Coppolani. *Les Confréries religieuses musulmanes.* Algiers: A. Jourdan, 1897.
Al-Ghazālī, Abū Ḥāmid. *Al Munqidh min al-Ḍalāl.* Translated and annotated by R. J. McCarthy [*Freedom and Fulfillment: An Annotated Translation of al-Ghazālī's al-Munqidh min al-Ḍalāl and other Relevant Works of al-Ghazālī*]. Boston: Twayne, 1980.
Al-Hujwīrī, 'Alī. *Kashf al-Maḥjūb.* Translated by R. A. Nicholson. London: Luzac, 1911.
Al-Kalābādhī, Muḥammad. *Kitāb al-Ta'arruf li-Madhhab Ahl al-Taṣawwuf.* Translated by A. J. Arberry [*The Doctrine of the Sufis*]. Cambridge: University Press, 1935.
Laugier de Beaurecueil, S. de. *Khwādja 'Abdullāh Anṣārī (396–481/1006–1089): mystique ḥanbalite.* Beirut: Imprimerie catholique, 1965.
Lings, M. *What is Sufism?*
Massignon, L. *Essai sur les origines du lexique technique de la mystique musulmane.* Rev. ed. Paris: J. Vrin, 1968.
——. *The Passion of al-Hallāj: Mystic and Martyr of Islam.* Translated by H. Mason. 4 vols. Princeton, NJ: Princeton University Press, 1982.

Molé, M. *Les Mystiques musulmans.* Paris: Presses universitaires de France, 1965.
Nasr, S. H. *Sufi Essays.*
Nwyia, P. *Exégèse coranique et langage mystique.* Beirut: Librairie Orientale, 1970.
Reinart, B. *Die Lehre vom tawakkul in der klassischen Sufik.* Berlin: de Gruyter, 1968.
Schimmel, A. M. *Mystical Dimensions of Islam.*
Schuon, F. *Islam and the Perennial Philosophy.*
Siraj Ed-Din, Abu Bakr. *The Book of Certainty.*
Smith, M. *Rabiʿa the Mystic and Her Fellow-Saints in Islam.*
Watt, W. M. *The Faith and Practice of al-Ghazālī.* London: Allen & Unwin, 1953.

Spiritual Practices of Sufism

Anawati, G. C., and L. Gardet. *La Mystique musulmane.* Paris: J. Vrin, 1961.
Ibn ʿAbbād of Ronda. *Letters on the Sufi Path.* Translated by J. Renard. New York: Paulist Press, 1986.
Ibn ʿAṭāʾ Allāh. *Traité sur le nom Allāh.* Translated by M. Gloton. Paris: Les Deux Océans, 1981.
Bannerth, E. "*Dhikr* et *Khalwa* d'après Ibn ʿAṭāʾ Allāh." MIDEO (1974) 65–90.
Burckhardt, T. *An Introduction to Sufi Doctrines.* Pp. 99–105, "Rites."
Canteins, J. *La Voie des lettres.* Paris: Albin Michel, 1981.
Ad-Darqāwī, al-ʿArabī. *Letters of a Sufi Master.* Translated by T. Burckhardt. Bedfont, England: Perennial Books, 1961.
Gardet, L. "La mention du Nom divin, *dhikr,* dans la mystique musulmane." *Revue Thomiste* 52 (1952) 542–676; 53 (1953) 197–216.
Lings, M. *What is Sufism?* Pp. 74–91, "The Method."
Michon, J. L. *Le Soufi marocain Aḥmad Ibn ʿAjība (1746–1809) et son Miʿrāj.* Paris: J. Vrin, 1973. Pp. 122–31, "L'invocation du nom divin."
Valiuddin, Mir. *Contemplative Disciplines in Sufism.*

Sufi Science of the Soul

Arasteh, R. "Psychology of the Sufi Way to Individuation." In *Sufi Studies: East and West,* 89–113. Edited by L. F. Rushbrook Williams. London: Octagon Press, 1973.
Asín Palacios, M. "La Psicologia segun Mohidin Abenarabi." *Actes du XIV Congres Inter. des Orient. Alger, 1905,* vol. 3, Paris, 1907.
Burckhardt, T. *An Introduction to Sufi Doctrine.*
Al-Darqāwī, al-ʿArabī. *Letters of a Sufi Master.*
Heer, N. "A Sufi Psychological Treatise." *Muslim World* 5 (1961) 25–36, 83–91, 163–72, 244–58.
Ibn ʿArabī, Muḥyī al-Dīn. *L'Alchimie du bonheur parfait.* Translated by S. Ruspoli. Paris: Berg International, 1981.

Nasr, S. H. *Sufi Essays.* Chapter 2, pp. 43–51, "Sufism and the Integration of Man."
Nurbakhsh, J. *What the Sufis Say.* New York: Khaniqahi-Nimatullahi Publications, 1980. Part 1, "Sufism and Psychoanalysis."
Schimmel, A. M. *Mystical Dimensions of Islam.* Pp. 187–92, "Some Notes on Sufi Psychology."
Shafii, M. *Freedom from the Self.* New York: Human Sciences Press, 1985.
Valiuddin, Mir. *Contemplative Disciplines in Sufism.*

Part Four: Knowledge of Reality

God

Balyānī, Awḥad al-Dīn. *Épître sur l'Unicité absolue.* Translated by M. Chodkiewicz. Paris: Les Deux Océans, 1982.
Corbin, H. *Creative Imagination in the Sufism of Ibn 'Arabī.* Part 1, "Sympathy and Theopathy."
Chittick, W. C. "Ṣadr al-Dīn Qunawī on the Oneness of Being." *International Philosophical Quarterly* 21 (1981) 171–84.
———. *The Sufi Path of Love: The Spiritual Teachings of Rumi.* Albany, NY: State University of New York Press, 1983. Part 1-C, pp. 42–58, "God and the World."
McCarthy, R. J. *Freedom and Fulfillment: An Annotated Translation of al-Ghazālī's al-Munqidh min al-Ḍalāl and other Relevant Works of al-Ghazālī.*
Al-Rāzī, Fakhr al-Dīn. *Traité sur les Noms divins.* Translated by M. Gloton. Paris: Les Deux Océans, 1983.
Schuon, F. *From the Divine to the Human.* Translated by G. Polit and D. Lambert. Bloomington, IN: World Wisdom Books, 1982. Part 2, "Divine and Universal Order."
———. *Sufism: Veil and Quintessence.* Translated by W. Stoddart. Bloomington, IN: World Wisdom Books, 1981. Pp. 157–63, "Hypostatic Dimensions of Unity."
Zia Ullah, Mohammad. *Islamic Concept of God.* Boston: Kegan Paul International, 1984.

Angels

Calverly, E. E. "Nafs." *Encyclopaedia of Islam,* old ed., 3:827–30.
Chittick, W. C. *The Sufi Path of Love.*
Corbin, H. *Avicenna and the Visionary Recital.* Translated by W. Trask. London: Routledge and Kegan Paul, 1960. Chapter 2, "Avicennism and Angelology."
———. *En Islam iranien.*
———. "Notes pour une étude d'angelologie islamique." In *Anges, démons et êtres intermédiaires,* 49–59. Paris: Labergerie, 1969.

Gardet, L. "Les anges en Islam." *Studia missionalia* 21 (1972) 207–27.
Jadaane, F. "La place des anges dans la théologie cosmique musulmane." *Studia Islamica* 41 (1975) 23–61.
MacDonald, D. M. "Djinn." *Encyclopaedia of Islam,* new ed., 2:546–48.
———. "Malā'ika." *Encyclopaedia of Islam,* old ed., 3:189–92.
Mokri, M. "L'ange dans l'Islam et en Iran." In *Anges, démons et êtres intermédiaires,* 66–87.
Nasr, S. H. *Three Muslim Sages: Avicenna, Suhrawardī, Ibn 'Arabī.* Cambridge, MA: Harvard University Press, 1964.
———. *An Introduction to Islamic Cosmological Doctrines.*
Pedersen, J. "Djabrā'īl." *Encyclopaedia of Islam,* new ed., 2:362–64.
Rāzī, Najm al-Dīn. *Mirṣād al-'ibād.* Translated by H. Algar [*The Path of God's Bondsmen from Origin to Return*]. Delmar, NY: Caravan Books, 1982. Pp. 80–93 et passim.
Schuon, F. *Dimensions of Islam.* Chapter 8, "An-Nūr."
Suhrawardī. *The Mystical and Visionary Treatises of Shihabuddin Yahya Suhrawardi.* Translated by W. H. Thackston. London: Octagon Press, 1982.
Vajda, G. "Hārūt wa-Mārūt." *Encyclopaedia of Islam,* new ed., 3:236–37.
Wensinck, A. J. "Isrāfīl." *Encyclopaedia of Islam,* new ed., 4:211.
———. "'Izrā'īl." *Encyclopaedia of Islam,* new ed., 4:292–93.

The Cosmos and the Natural Order

Burckhardt, T. *Alchemy.* Translated by W. Stoddart. Baltimore, MD: Penguin Books, 1971.
Corbin, H. (with S. H. Nasr and O. Yahya). *Histoire de la philosophie islamique.* Pp. 179–214, "Philosophie et science de la nature."
Meier, F. "The Problem of Nature in the Esoteric Monism of Islam." In *Spirit and Nature: Papers from the Eranos Yearbooks,* 149–203. Translated by R. Manheim. Princeton, NJ: Princeton University Press, 1954.
Nasr, S. H. *Islamic Life and Thought.* Pp. 200–206, "Contemplation and Nature in Sufism."
———. *Islamic Science: An Illustrated Study.* London: World of Islam Festival Trust, 1976.
———. *Science and Civilization in Islam.* Cambridge, MA: Harvard University Press, 1968.
———. *An Introduction to Islamic Cosmological Doctrines.*

Man

Corbin, H. *The Man of Light in Iranian Sufism.* Translated by N. Pearson. Boulder, CO: Shambala, 1978.
Durand, G. *Science de l'homme et tradition.* Paris: Berg International, 1979. Chapter 3, "*Homo proximi orientis:* science de l'homme et Islam spiritual."

Eaton, C. G. *King of the Castle: Choice and Responsibility in the Modern World.* London: Bodley Head, 1977. Chapter 5, "Man as Viceroy."

Jīlī, 'Abd al-Karīm. *Universal Man.* Translated by T. Burckhardt. London: Beshara Publications, 1983.

Nasafī, 'Azīz al-Dīn. *Le Livre de l'homme parfait.* Translated by I. de Gastines. Paris: Fayard, 1984.

Nasr, S. H. "Who is Man: The Perennial Answer of Islam." *Studies in Comparative Religion* 2 (1968) 45–56.

Eschatology

Works dealing primarily with the Quran and the Ḥadīth

'Abd al-Raḥīm ibn Aḥmad. *Islamic Book of the Dead: Hadith Concerning the Fire and the Garden.* Translated by A. 'Abd al Rahman at-Tarjumana. Wood Dalling, England: Diwan Press, 1977. Essentially the same work, attributed to Abu'l-Layth al-Samarqandī, was translated by J. Macdonald, *Islamic Studies* 3 (1964) 285–308, 485–519; 4 (1965) 55–102, 137–79; 5 (1966) 129–97, 331–83.

Eklund, R. *Life Between Death and Resurrection According to Islam.* Uppsala: Almqvist & Wiksell, 1941.

Gardet, L. "Ḥisāb." *Encyclopaedia of Islam,* new ed., 3:465–66.

——. "Ḳiyāma." *Encyclopaedia of Islam,* new ed., 5:235–38.

al-Ghazzālī. *The Precious Pearl (al-Durra al-Fakhira).* Translated by J. I. Smith. Missoula, MT: Scholars Press, 1981.

Meier, F. "The Ultimate Origin and Hereafter in Islam." In *Islam and its Cultural Divergence,* 96–112. Edited by G. L. Tikku. Urbana: University of Illinois Press, 1971.

O'Shaughnessy, T. *Muhammad's Thoughts on Death: A Thematic Study of the Qur'anic Data.* Leiden: Brill, 1969.

Rahman, F. *Major Themes of the Qur'ān.*

Sachedina, A. A. *Islamic Messianism.*

Smith, J. I., and Y. Y. Haddad. *The Islamic Understanding of Death and Resurrection.* Albany, NY: State University of New York Press, 1981.

Al-Tabrīzī. *Mishkāt al-maṣābīḥ.* Pp. 34–38, 320–70, 1120–1218.

Works dealing primarily with the developed eschatological teachings

Avicenna. *On Theology.* Translated by A. J. Arberry. London: John Murray, 1951. Pp. 64–76.

Chittick, W. C. "Death and the World of Imagination: Ibn al-'Arabī's Eschatology." *Muslim World,* forthcoming.

——. *The Sufi Path of Love.* Pp. 61–107, 173ff.

——. "A Sufi View of Islamic Eschatology: Rūmī on Death." *Alserāt* forthcoming.

Corbin, H. *Spiritual Body and Celestial Earth.* Translated by N. Pearson. Princeton, NJ: Princeton University Press, 1977.

De Bruijn, J. T. P. *Of Piety and Poetry: The Interaction of Religion and Literature in the Life and Works of Ḥakīm Sanā'ī of Ghazna.* Leiden: Brill, 1983. Pp. 200–218.

Lory, P. *Les Commentaires ésotériques du Coran d'après 'Abd ar-Razzāq al-Qāshānī.* Pp. 107–21.

Mensia, M. "La Mort chez les Soufis." *IBLA* 43 (1980) 205–44.

Mullā Ṣadrā. *The Wisdom of the Throne.* Translated by J. W. Morris. Princeton, NJ: Princeton University Press, 1981.

Rahman, F. *The Philosophy of Mullā Ṣadrā.* Albany, NY: State University of New York Press, 1975. Pp. 247–65.

Rāzī, Najm al-Dīn. *Mirṣād al-'ibād.*

Schimmel, A. M. "Creation and Judgment in the Koran and in Mystico-Poetical Interpretation." In *We Believe in One God,* 149–80. Edited by A. M. Schimmel and A. Falaturi. New York: Seabury, 1979.

Schuon, F. *Dimensions of Islam.* Pp. 136–41.

Taylor, J. B. "Some Aspects of Islamic Eschatology." *Religious Studies* 4 (1968) 57–76.

Contributors

SEYYED HOSSEIN NASR is University Professor of Islamic Studies at George Washington University and a former professor at Tehran University and Temple University and president of the Iranian Academy of Philosophy. He is the author of *Ideals and Realities of Islam, Sufi Essays,* and *Knowledge and the Sacred* (the 1981 Gifford Lectures).

MOHAMMAD AJMAL is former professor and chairman of the Department of Psychology of the University of the Punjab in Lahore. He has served in many different capacities as an educator and has devoted a lifetime of study to Sufi psychology in relation to and in comparison with Western psychology. He is the author of several works on this subject.

SYED ALI ASHRAF is a specialist from Bangladesh on Islamic education. For many years professor in Dacca and later in Saudi Arabia, he is now director of the Islamic Academy in Cambridge (U.K.), editor of the Islamic Education Series and *The Muslim Education Quarterly,* and author of *New Horizons in Muslim Education* and *Literary Education and Religious Values.*

ALLAHBAKHSH K. BROHI is one of Pakistan's leading thinkers, public figures, and philosophers. Brohi practices law and has played a major role in the formulation of constitutional laws in Pakistan, acting twice as federal minister of law and religious affairs. He has lectured widely throughout the Islamic world on the philosophy and spirituality of Islam; his works include *Islam in the Modern World, A Testament of Faith,* and *A Faith to Live By.*

SAADIA KHAWAR KHAN CHISHTI is professor at the College of Education for Women in Lahore and the only woman member of the Council of Islamic Ideology of Pakistan. She has written several articles on education and Sufism.

WILLIAM C. CHITTICK has been assistant professor of religious studies at the State University of New York at Stony Brook and is a former assistant professor at Aryamehr University in Tehran. He is a specialist in Sufism, and his works include *The Sufi Path of Love: The Spiritual Teachings of Rumi* and a translation of Fakhr al-Dīn 'Irāqī's *Divine Flashes.*

VICTOR DANNER is professor of religion and Islamic studies at Indiana University. An authority on Sufism, he is the translator of the *Aphorisms* of Ibn 'Aṭā' Allāh al-Iskandarī and the author of *The Islamic Tradition.*

ABDUR-RAHMAN IBRAHIM DOI is professor in Islamics and director of the Centre for Islamic Legal Studies at the Ahmadu Bello University in Nigeria. A specialist in

Islamic Law, he is the author of *Introduction to the Qur'an, The Cardinal Principles of Islam, Islam in Nigeria,* and numerous other books and articles on Islam, especially in its African context.

CHARLES LE GAI EATON is the deputy director of the Islamic Centre in London and the deputy editor of the *Islamic Quarterly.* He has had long experience in the study of the Islamic world, and his books include *The King of the Castle* and *Islam and the Destiny of Man.*

ABDURRAHMAN HABIL is a Libyan scholar currently writing a doctoral thesis on esoteric commentaries on the Quran. Habil has been concerned for years with the study of Quranic commentaries that have tried to bring out the inner and spiritual significance of the Sacred Text.

SYED HUSAIN M. JAFRI is director of the Pakistan Study Centre in the University of Karachi, coeditor of *Hamdard Islamicus,* and a former professor of Islamic studies at the Australian National University and the American University of Beirut. His articles and books include *The Origin and Early Development of Shi'a Islam.*

JEAN-LOUIS MICHON is a French scholar who specializes in Islam in North Africa, Islamic art, and Sufism. He has participated in several UNESCO projects on Islamic art and is the author of many works on Sufism and art, including *Le Soufi marocain Aḥmad Ibn 'Ajiba* and *L'Autobiographie (Fahrasa) du Soufi marocain Aḥmad Ibn 'Ajiba (1747–1809).*

SACHIKO MURATA has been assistant professor of religious studies at the State University of New York at Stony Brook and was formerly assistant director of the Japanese Institute for West Asian Studies in Tehran. She is a specialist in Islamic thought and jurisprudence and is the author of several works in Japanese on Islam as well as a treatise in Persian on Shī'ite laws of marriage.

Azim Nanji is associate professor of Islamic studies at Oklahoma State University and a specialist in Ismā'īlī thought and history. He has published several works on Ismā'īlism, devoting himself especially to Ismā'īlī writings in India.

JA'FAR QASIMI is a Pakistani scholar of Islam and Sufism who has spent years in the study of Sufism in the subcontinent of India, especially in the Punjab, as well as in the study of Sufi psychology. He is the author of several monographs and articles on Islam and Sufism, including one on Bābā Farīd Ganj-i Shikar, and has translated some Sufi works into Urdu.

FRITHJOF SCHUON is the leading authority on the perennial philosophy today. Schuon was born of German parents in Switzerland and traveled widely in the Middle East and North Africa, where he met the celebrated Algerian Sufi Shaykh al-'Alawī. Schuon has written extensively on questions of spirituality in general; his works dealing with Islam include *Understanding Islam, Dimensions of Islam, Sufism: Veil and Quintessence,* and *Islam and the Perennial Philosophy.*

ABU BAKR SIRAJ ED-DIN is a well-known contemporary authority on Sufism and the author of the classic work on Sufism, *The Book of Certainty.* He has also contributed to *Studies in Comparative Religion* and *The Sword of Gnosis* (ed. J. Needleman).

Photographic Credits

The editor and the publisher wish to thank the custodians of the works of art for supplying photographs and granting permission to use them.

1. Topkapi Saray Museum.
2. By permission of The British Library.
3. By permission of The British Library.
4. Photography by Hans C. Seherr-Thoss.
5. Le Bibliothèque Nationale, Paris.
6. Giraudon/Art Resource, New York.
7. Le Bibliothèque Nationale, Paris.
8. The American Institute for Islamic Affairs, Washington, D.C.
9. The American Institute for Islamic Affairs, Washington, D.C.
10. The American Institute for Islamic Affairs, Washington, D.C.
11. Le Bibliothèque Nationale, Paris.
12. ARAMCO.
13. Editions Atelier 74—Le Paccard, Annecy.
14. Photograph by K. O'Brien.
15. Giraudon/Art Resource, New York.
16. The American Institute for Islamic Affairs, Washington, D.C.
17. ARAMCO.
18. From "Islam: An Introduction," courtesy of The American Institute for Islamic Affairs, Washington, D.C.
19. The American Institute for Islamic Affairs, Washington, D.C.
20. From "Islam: An Introduction," courtesy of The American Institute for Islamic Affairs, Washington, D.C.
21. The American Institute for Islamic Affairs, Washington, D.C.
22. The American Institute for Islamic Affairs, Washington, D.C.
23. Photograph by Ulku Bates.
24. Islamic Art Archive, Asian Photographic Distribution, University of Michigan, Ann Arbor.
25. Reproduced by courtesy of The Trustees of The British Museum.
26. The Metropolitan Museum of Art, Gift of Arthur A. Houghton, Jr., 1970.
27. By permission of The British Library.
28. By permission of The British Library.
29. Private collection.
30. Le Bibliothèque Nationale, Paris.
31. Bodleian Library, Oxford.
32. Photograph by Roland Michaud.
33. The American Institute for Islamic Affairs, Washington, D.C.
34. By permission of The British Library.
35. By permission of The British Library.

Indexes

Subjects

ablutions, 79, 111, 140
academies and schools, 15, 253, 254, 257, 260
afterlife, 18, 122, 139, 155, 156. *See also* death; eschatology; resurrection
Age of Ignorance, 89
angels, 3, 4, 14, 22, 56; Bābā Afḍal on, 337–38; bodily organs and, 336; cherubim among, 330, 332; cosmological role of, 324–25, 327–28; Farghānī on, 333–35, 342; as a guide against evil, 128, 328; Hagar and, 65; Iblis (Satan) as an, 14–15, 330, 338, 360; Ibn 'Arabī on, 333, 341–42; intellect, microcosm and, 335-36; Jāmī on, 342–43; mankind and, 14–15, 338, 340–43; Muḥammad and, 3, 4, 76, 78, 239, 266, 325–27; al-Qūnawī on, 330, 332-33, 335; Quranic references to, 324–26; Suhrawardī on, 329–30
Arabic, 3, 4, 26, 28, 31, 171
art, 8–9, 57–58, 237, 349
ascension, 3, 14, 60, 61, 78–80, 190
ascesis, 49, 59
asceticism, 249, 252–53, 285
awareness, 11, 12, 22, 88, 134; and Adam's return to grace, 190; between man and God, 157, 275

barzakh, 390–91, 395, 397, 401–2
beauty, 54, 56, 59, 61, 98–100, 138
being, states of, 56, 61, 62, 78, 100, 138; perfection and, 212; soul and, 298

caliphs, 3, 59, 95, 148–50, 154
calligraphy, 4, 5, 58
caves, 3, 60, 82
certitude, 53, 54, 56, 57
charity (*zakāt*), 83, 91, 100, 101, 141–42, 168
Christianity, 4, 52, 73, 76, 150, 286; and Islamic motherhood, 204; Jesus, death of al-Ḥallāj and, 258–59; and mankind's status, 363, 366
circumambulation of the Ka'bah, 66, 120, 122, 125
companions of the Prophet, 3, 29, 30, 82, 85
constitution of Medina, 83
converts, 85, 86, 88, 193
cosmos, 5, 9, 41, 42, 50; angelic role in the, 324–25, 327–28; Farghānī's angelology and the, 333–35; God as the originator of the, 188, 232; *Ḥadīth* on the nature of the, 106, 107; Ibn 'Arabī's doctrines of the, 333, 346–47, 353–54; and Ibn Sīnā's doctrines, 329, 352–53; Muḥammad's journey through the, 78–80; al-Qūnawī on the, 330, 332–33; Quran and the revelation of the, 345–46
cultured behavior (*adab*) 101–2, 373–74

Day of Judgment, 138, 139, 153, 154, 211, 279–80. *See also barzakh;* death, eschatology; hell; paradise; resurrection
death, 3, 5, 42, 92–93, 104, 129; angelic questioning after, 380, 397–98; and the angel of death ('Izrā'īl), 328, 380; awareness of one's body after, 380; *barzakh* and, 390–91, 395, 397; dreams, sleep and, 395–96; of Ḥusayn ibn 'Alī, 168, 170; and knowledge of God, 323; occultation of Muḥammad al-Mahdī and, 172, 173; resurrection of the body and soul after, 380, 389–91, 402–5; stations of the soul after, 337–38
degrees of the excellences (*darajāt*), 79
Descent, the, 3, 60, 61
determinism, 8, 106, 128, 153, 156, 320
devotional literature, 177–78
dhikr (remembrance of God), 134, 215, 216, 223, 227, 228; Divine names and, 318-19; Islamic mysticism, Sufism and, 243, 263, 275–77, 290; liturgical invocations and, 275–77, 286–89
Divine Law (*Sharī'ah*), 8, 15, 18, 19, 22, 39. *See also* law, Islamic; conflict with Sufis and doctors of, 256–59, 261; *Ḥadīth* and codification of, 106; Ismā'īlī doctrines of, 185; as the matrix of Islamic life, 97; Shī'ite interpretations of, 172–73; transcendence of God in; 116; women as followers of, 203, 213–15

Names

Colophon

Islamic Spirituality: Foundations,
Volume 19 of World Spirituality: An Encyclopedic History of the Religious Quest, was designed by Maurya P. Horgan and Paul J. Kobelski.
The type is 11-point Garamond Antiqua and was set by
The Scriptorium, Denver, Colorado.